CHALLENGING MYTHS ON SEXUAL & GENDER-BASED VIOLENCE IN ASYLUM PROCEDURES

CHALLENGING MYTHS ON SEXUAL & GENDER-BASED VIOLENCE IN ASYLUM PROCEDURES

Lore Roels

INTERSENTIA
LEFEBVRE GROUP

Intersentia
Lefebvre Belgium SA
Avenue Jean Monnet 4
1348 Louvain-la-Neuve
Belgium
Email: contact@larcier-intersentia.com

Distribution for the UK, Ireland and
Rest of the World (excl. France, Belgium and Luxembourg)
Ingram Publisher Services UK
1 Deltic Avenue, Rooksley
Milton Keynes MK13 8LD
United Kingdom
Tel: +44 1752 202 301 | Fax: +44 1752 202 331
Email: ipsuk.customercare@ingramcontent.com

Distribution for France and Rest of the World (excl. Ireland and the UK)
Interforum Editis
Avenue de France 92
75013 Paris
France

Distribution for Belgium and Luxembourg
Larcier-Intersentia
Avenue Jean Monnet 4
1348 Louvain-la-Neuve
Belgium

Artwork on cover: Stop! – Doaa Eladl / The Cartoon Movement

ISBN 978-1-83970-624-0
D/2026/06040/0060
NUR 820

GPRC
Guaranteed
Peer Reviewed
Content
www.gprc.be

British Library Cataloguing in Publication Data. A catalogue record for this book is available from the British Library.

This research was funded by the Flemish Fund for Scientific Research (FWO) under grant number 11I9722N

TRIGGER WARNING | This research contains descriptions of sexual and gender-based violence and suicidal thinking. This may trigger disturbing memories and/or thoughts in some readers. If you, or someone close to you, had similar experiences and wish(es) to talk, you/they can contact the Sexual Assault Care Centres (SACC) at https://sac.belgium.be or the Suicide Line at www.zelfmoord1813.be/+32800 32 123 (in Belgium) or find a helpline at https://findahelpline.com.

'[W]here the words of women are crying to be heard, we must each of us recognize our responsibility to seek those words out, to read them and share them and examine them in their pertinence to our lives. That we not hide behind the mockeries of separations that have been imposed upon us [...] [a]nd all the other endless ways in which we rob ourselves of ourselves and each other.'[1]

Audre Lorde, *Sister Outsider* (1984)

1 Audre Lorde, 'The Transformation of Silence into Language and Action', *Sister outsider: essays and speeches* (Crossing Press 1984) 32.

SUMMARY

'[You] have been working since you were 17 [...], are financially independent, [...] [sell] goods on credit [...], [are a member of a] religious community [...], the choir [...], the majorettes [...], [you participate] in multi-day retreats [...], and [...] financed part of your trip yourself [...]. These elements demonstrate an [...] independence, which is difficult to reconcile with your [...] status as a young woman alone and without resources, at the mercy of a [sexually] abusive stepfather.' | CASE OF AMANI

With this argument in the decision to refuse Amani international protection, the Belgian first instance asylum authority seems to suggest that individuals who are able-bodied, financially independent, professionally experienced, and socially connected are unlikely to risk sexual and gender-based violence (SGBV). This reasoning shows strong parallels with rape myths identified in the criminal justice context. These incorrect beliefs about rape risk excluding those who do not fit the stereotypical 'ideal victim' image from protection. While rape myth acceptance has been extensively studied in the criminal justice system, its role in asylum procedures remains largely unexplored.

Against this background, the UN Refugee Agency (UNHCR) already raised the concern that asylum authorities might base their decisions on stereotypical and/or erroneous gender perceptions. For over 50 years, refugee advocates have worked towards centralising SGBV in refugee law. While 'gender-sensitive refugee status determination' is now an obligation under international law (such as the Istanbul Convention), scholars argue that its meaning remains unclear and its implementation incomplete. The fact that the Istanbul Convention's monitoring body (GREVIO) has labelled the Belgian asylum procedure as insufficiently gender-sensitive, despite the authorities' initiatives towards more gender-sensitive decision making, makes it a fascinating case study to examine the role of rape myth acceptance in SGBV-related asylum procedures.

Therefore, this research analyses how SGBV myths permeate asylum procedures and decisions, using Belgium as a case study. In order to do so, it translates 'rape myths' in the criminal justice context to 'SGBV myths' in the asylum context, identifies SGBV myths relevant to asylum procedures, and analyses to what extent these SGBV myths are accepted/rebutted in Belgian asylum decisions, as well as how the procedural and institutional frameworks impact these. In doing so, the research relies on method triangulation, consisting of: a law, literature, and case law (n=202) analysis, interviews with asylum applicants (n=19) and officials (n=22), and a survey with asylum officials (n=209).

The research identifies six specific SGBV myths, namely the: 1) resourcefulness, 2) disclosure, 3) survival, 4) non-state protection, 5) state protection, and 6) private issue myth. It concludes that 76% of the analysed decisions/judgments (n=202) relied on at least one of these myths and 20% on four or more cumulatively. This acceptance occurs across all types of SGBV and all regions of origin, regardless of applicants' age or gender identity. SGBV myth acceptance is no marginal phenomenon, as it widely occurs both in first instance (at the Office of the Commissioner General for Refugees and Stateless Persons/ CGRS) and in appeal (at the Council for Alien Law Litigation/CALL), as well as across both procedural languages (Dutch and French).

Although 'gender-sensitive refugee status determination' remains legally undefined, this research argues that it cannot allow for asylum officials to accept SGBV myths. Asylum decisions that do rely on such myths, especially those where the conclusion does not hold ground when stripped of SGBV myth-based arguments, must be considered gender-insensitive. Such decisions would not only violate the legal obligation on gender sensitivity, but also other (inter) national refugee and human rights law obligations. The research concludes by offering both conclusions and practical recommendations on the role of SGBV mythology in obstructing survivors'/victims' path from survival to (refugee) recognition.

SAMENVATTING

'[U] werkt sinds uw zeventiende [...], u bent financieel onafhankelijk [...], [lid van] een religieuze gemeenschap [...], het koor [...], [en] de majorettes [...], [en] u heeft een deel van uw reis zelf gefinancierd[...]. Al deze elementen getuigen van uw niveau van onafhankelijkheid en zelfredzaamheid [...], waardoor het moeilijk is te geloven in uw profiel als jonge vrouw [...] ten prooi van een gewelddadige stiefvader.' | ZAAK VAN AMANI

Met dit argument in de beslissing om Amani internationale bescherming te weigeren, lijkt de Belgische asielinstantie in eerste aanleg te suggereren dat personen die fysiek gezond, financieel onafhankelijk, professioneel ervaren en sociaal omringd zijn weinig risico lopen op seksueel en gendergerelateerd geweld (SGG). Deze redenering vertoont sterke parallellen met verkrachtingsmythes zoals geïdentificeerd in de strafrechtscontext. Deze onjuiste opvattingen over verkrachting kunnen ertoe leiden dat personen die niet aan het stereotype beeld van het 'ideale slachtoffer' voldoen, van bescherming worden uitgesloten. Hoewel de acceptatie van verkrachtingsmythes al uitgebreid is onderzocht in het strafrecht, is de rol ervan in asielprocedures nog grotendeels onbekend.

In dit licht heeft het VN Vluchtelingenagentschap (UNHCR) reeds bezorgdheid geuit over het feit dat asielautoriteiten hun beslissingen zouden baseren op stereotiepe en/of onjuiste genderpercepties. Al meer dan 50 jaar zetten pleitbezorgers zich in om SGG te centraliseren in het vluchtelingenrecht. Hoewel de 'gendersensitieve bepaling van de vluchtelingenstatus' nu een verplichting is volgens het internationaal recht (zoals het Verdrag van Istanbul), stelt rechtsleer dat de betekenis ervan onduidelijk en de implementatie ervan onvolledig blijft. Het feit dat het toezichthoudende orgaan van het Verdrag van Istanbul (GREVIO) de Belgische asielprocedure als onvoldoende gendersensitief heeft bestempeld, ondanks de asielinstanties' inspanningen tot meer gendersensitieve besluitvorming, maakt het een fascinerende casestudy om de rol van de acceptatie van verkrachtingsmythes in SGG-gerelateerde asielprocedures te onderzoeken.

Daarom analyseert dit onderzoek hoe SGG-mythes doordringen in asielprocedures en -beslissingen, met België als casestudy. Daartoe vertaalt het 'verkrachtingsmythes' in de strafrechtscontext naar 'SGG-mythes' in de asielcontext, identificeert het SGG-mythes die relevant zijn voor asielprocedures en analyseert het in hoeverre deze SGG-mythes worden geaccepteerd/weerlegd in de Belgische asielbesluitvorming, alsook hoe de procedurele en institutionele context hierop van invloed zijn. Het onderzoek maakt daarbij gebruik van methodetriangulatie, bestaande uit: een wetgeving-, literatuur- en rechtspraakanalyse (n=202), interviews met verzoekers (n=19) en asielinstanties (n=22), en een enquête met asielinstanties (n=209).

Het onderzoek identificeert zes specifieke SGG-mythes, namelijk de: 1) zelfredzaamheids-, 2) onthullings-, 3) overlevings-, 4) niet-statelijke beschermings-, 5) statelijke beschermings- en 6) privéprobleemmythe. Het concludeert dat 76% van de geanalyseerde beslissingen/arresten (n=202) op ten minste één van deze mythes berustte en 20% op vier of meer cumulatief. Deze acceptatie komt voor bij alle soorten SGG en alle regio's van herkomst, ongeacht de leeftijd of genderidentiteit van verzoekers. De acceptatie van SGG-mythes is geen marginaal fenomeen, gezien het zowel grootschalig in eerste aanleg (bij het Commissariaat-Generaal voor de Vluchtelingen en de Staatlozen/CGVS) als in beroep (bij de Raad voor Vreemdelingenbetwistingen/RvV) en in beide proceduretalen (Frans en Nederlands) voorkomt.

Hoewel een 'gendersensitieve bepaling van de vluchtelingenstatus' juridisch ongedefinieerd blijft, kan het volgens dit onderzoek geen acceptatie van SGG-mythes door asielinstanties tolereren. Beslissingen die wel steunen op SGG-mythes, vooral wanneer de conclusie niet standhoudt als dergelijke argumenten wegvallen, moeten als gender-<u>in</u>sensitief worden beschouwd. Deze beslissingen zouden niet alleen de wettelijke verplichting tot gendersensitiviteit schenden, maar ook andere (inter)nationaal vluchtelingen- en mensenrechtelijke bepalingen. Het onderzoek sluit af met conclusies en aanbevelingen over de rol van SGG-mythologie bij het belemmeren van de weg van SGG-overlevenden/slachtoffers van overleven naar erkenning (als vluchteling).

CONTENTS

LIST OF ABBREVIATIONS

CALL	Council for Alien Law Litigation
CEDAW	Convention or Committee on the Elimination of All Forms of Discrimination Against Women
CGRS	(Office of the) Commissioner General for Refugees and Stateless Persons
CJEU	Court of Justice of the European Union
COI	Country of origin information
ECHR	European Convention on Human Rights
ECtHR	European Court of Human Rights
EU	European Union
EUAA	European Union Asylum Agency
GMC	Genital mutilation/cutting
GREVIO	Group of Experts on Action against Violence against Women and Domestic Violence
IFA	Internal flight alternative
IO	Immigration Office
MA	Myth acceptance
MR	Myth rebuttal
PO	Protection Officer
PTSD	Post-traumatic stress disorder
SGBV	Sexual and gender-based violence
SOGI	Sexual orientation and gender identity
UN	United Nations
UNHCR	United Nations High Commissioner for Refugees (the UN Refugee Agency)

LIST OF FIGURES

PART I

INTRODUCTION

1. THE BURDENSOME ROAD FROM SURVIVAL TO RECOGNITION

Gender (In)Sensitivity in Asylum Procedures & Decisions

> *'[You] have been **working** since you were **17** [...], are **financially independent**, [...] **[sell]** goods on credit [...], [are a member of a] **religious community** [...], the **choir** [...], the **majorettes** [...], [you participate] in **multi-day retreats** [...], and [...] **financed** part of **your trip** yourself [...]. These elements demonstrate an [...] independence, which is **difficult to reconcile** with your [...] status as a young woman alone and without resources, at the **mercy of a [sexually] abusive stepfather**.'*[2] | CASE OF AMANI

With these words (among other arguments), the Belgian first instance asylum authority in 2021 assessed the fear of Amani, a Congolese applicant for international protection (see Chapter 1 of Part III), of sexual abuse by her stepfather as non-credible and therefore refused her refugee status. The Commissioner General for Refugees and Stateless Persons (CGRS) seems to suggest here that able-bodied, adult, financially independent, and professionally experienced persons with a social network are unlikely to be subjected to SGBV.

This type of reasoning shows strong characteristics of what is termed a rape myth in the criminal justice context. More specifically, it can be categorised as a 'victim precipitation myth': the idea that SGBV only happens to certain types of persons.[3] This belief is grounded in an image of the ideal survivor/victim of sexual violence[4] as vulnerable and dependent. It excludes applicants who do not fit this stereotype (for example because they appear too resourceful) from international protection and appropriates their stories in a way that undermines their self-understanding.[5]

---

2 NC004_CGRS 1 (refusal)_1991_F_DRC_RSA_DV_21/12/2021_FR_NANSEN_p. 4.

3 Sarah Ben-David and Ofra Schneider, 'Rape Perceptions, Gender Role Attitudes, and Victim-Perpetrator Acquaintance' (2005) 53 Sex Roles 385, 386.

4 Nils Christie, 'The Ideal Victim' in Ezzat A Fattah (ed), *From Crime Policy to Victim Policy: Reorienting the Justice System* (Palgrave Macmillan UK 1986); Melanie Randall, 'Sexual Assault Law, Credibility, and "Ideal Victims": Consent, Resistance, and Victim Blaming' (2010) 22 Canadian Journal of Women and the Law/Revue Femmes et Droit 397.

5 Susan Kneebone, 'Women within the Refugee Construct: Exclusionary Inclusion in Policy and Practice – the Australian Experience' (2005) 17 International Journal of Refugee Law 7, 37–39.

As Baillot, Cowan and Munro suggest, there are few, if any, reasons to believe that asylum authorities' refugee status determination would not risk to be influenced by gender stereotyping like rape mythology.[6] This is all the more plausible in the 'culture of disbelief' already identified in asylum procedures generally,[7] knowing that the key reason for refusal of gender-related refugee status is non-credibility.[8] Rape myth acceptance occurs across all social and institutional contexts[9] and has been widely studied in the criminal justice context,[10] but to my knowledge, never in the asylum context. Therefore, the question arises as to what other parallels (and differences) exist between rape mythology in the criminal justice system and assessments of SGBV-related applications for international protection in the asylum system.

Refugee advocates have worked towards centralising SGBV in (inter) national refugee law and scholarship since the 1970s.[11] Has gender since then moved 'from the margins to the centre' and can the debate on this centralisation thus be wrapped up? Not according to Arbel, Dauvergne and Millbank[12] or Querton,[13] who firmly call the work of interpreting the refugee definition in a

---

6 Helen Baillot, Sharon Cowan and Vanessa E Munro, 'Reason to Disbelieve: Evaluating the Rape Claims of Women Seeking Asylum in the UK' (2014) 10 International Journal of Law in Context 105, 106.

7 Cécile Rousseau and others, 'The Complexity of Determining Refugeehood: A Multidisciplinary Analysis of the Decision-Making Process of the Canadian Immigration and Refugee Board' (2002) 15 Journal of Refugee Studies 43, 50; Jenni Millbank, '"The Ring of Truth": A Case Study of Credibility Assessment in Particular Social Group Refugee Determinations' (2009) 21 International Journal of Refugee Law 1, 16; Olga Jubany, 'Constructing Truths in a Culture of Disbelief: Understanding Asylum Screening from Within' (2011) 26 International Sociology 74, 74.

8 Baillot, Cowan and Munro, 'Reason to Disbelieve' (n 6) 105–106; Hana Cheikh Ali, Christel Querton and Elodie Soulard, 'Gender Related Asylum Claims in Europe: A Comparative Analysis of Law Policies and Practice Focusing on Women in Nine EU Member States' (EU Directorate-General for International Policies 2012) 77; Annemarie Middelburg and Alina Balta, 'Female Genital Mutilation/Cutting as a Ground for Asylum in Europe' (2016) 3 International Journal of Refugee Law 416, 452; Debora Singer, 'Falling at Each Hurdle: Assessing the Credibility of Women's Asylum Claims in Europe' in Efrat Arbel, Catherine Dauvergne and Jenni Millbank (eds), *Gender in Refugee Law: From the Margins to the Centre* (Routledge 2014) 98.

9 Katie M Edwards and others, 'Rape Myths: History, Individual and Institutional-Level Presence, and Implications for Change' (2011) 65 Sex Roles 761, 761.

10 Helen Baillot, Sharon Cowan and Vanessa E Munro, 'Seen but Not Heard? Parallels and Dissonances in the Treatment of Rape Narratives across the Asylum and Criminal Justice Contexts' (2009) 36 Journal of Law and Society 195, 195.

11 Connie Oxford, 'Where Are the Women?' in Efrat Arbel, Catherine Dauvergne and Jenni Millbank, *Gender in Refugee Law: From the Margins to the Centre* (Routledge 2014) 157–158.

12 Efrat Arbel, Catherine Dauvergne and Jenni Millbank, 'Introduction: Gender in Refugee Law: From the Margins to the Centre' in Efrat Arbel, Catherine Dauvergne and Jenni Millbank (eds), *Gender in Refugee Law: From the Margins to the Centre* (Routledge 2014) 14.

13 Christel Querton, 'Gender and the Boundaries of International Refugee Law: Beyond the Category of "Gender-Related Asylum Claims"' (2019) 37 Netherlands Quarterly of Human Rights 379, 379–381.

gender-sensitive manner incomplete, still. When reading argumentation like the CGRS' in Amani's case above, I agree. I came to the same realisation concerning the European Court of Human Rights' (ECtHR) non-refoulement[14] case law. This Court for example judged an application for protection from being forcibly returned to Afghanistan as inadmissible, similarly arguing: 'As an adult single male, healthy and capable of work, the applicant cannot be considered particularly vulnerable [to further sexual exploitation], even in the absence of any support network.'[15]

This Court rules on human rights violations by state parties to the European Convention on Human Rights (ECHR), setting the human rights standards for and operating within the framework of the Council of Europe. This is the same international organisation that called into life the Istanbul Convention on Preventing and Combating Violence against Women and Domestic Violence. The Istanbul Convention obliges its parties to ensure gender-sensitive determination of refugee and non-refoulement protection.[16] However, how this 'gender sensitivity' should be understood and implemented was never defined in the Convention and still remains unclear.[17] Therefore, the question remains: did the *de jure* recognition of SGBV as refugee status-worthy lead to *de facto* protection for applicants with gender-based applications for international protection?

Against this background, the United Nations High Commissioner for Refugees (UNHCR) (and other international organisations indirectly)[18] has already raised the concern that: 'asylum authorities [...] [risk] reach[ing] conclusions based on stereotypical, superficial, erroneous, or inappropriate perceptions of gender.'[19] Beyond refugee law, on gender stereotyping in legal decision making in general, the UN Committee on the Elimination of All Forms of Discrimination Against Women (CEDAW) voiced that states have an obligation to address gender stereotypes, both in individual acts and in legal and societal structures.[20] The UN

14 The prohibition to return any person to a country where they would risk their life or torture, inhuman or degrading treatment/punishment. Art 3 Convention for the Protection of Human Rights and Fundamental Freedoms (ECHR) 1950 (CETS, no 005); *Soering v The United Kingdom* [1989] ECtHR 14038/88.

15 *MH v Finland* [2020] ECtHR 42255/18 [57–58].

16 Art. 60 *jo.* 61 Council of Europe Convention on Preventing and Combating Violence against Women and Domestic Violence (Istanbul Convention) 2011 (CETS, no 210).

17 Adrienne Anderson and Michelle Foster, 'A Feminist Appraisal of International Refugee Law' in Cathryn Costello, Michelle Foster and Jane McAdam (eds), *The Oxford Handbook of International Refugee Law* (Oxford University Press 2021) 60.

18 British Red Cross and the VOICES Network, 'We Want to Be Strong, but We Don't Have the Chance: Women's Experiences of Seeking Asylum in the UK' (2022) 6; Human Rights Watch, 'Fast-Tracked Unfairness: Detention and Denial of Women Asylum Seekers in the UK' (2010) 61; Helen Muggeridge and Chen Maman, 'Unsustainable: The Quality of Initial Decision-Making in Women's Asylum Claims' (Asylum Aid 2011) 4.

19 UNHCR, 'Beyond Proof. Credibility Assessment in EU Asylum Systems (Full Report)' (2013) 70.

20 CEDAW, 'General Recommendation No. 25, on Article 4, Paragraph 1, of the Convention on the Elimination of All Forms of Discrimination against Women, on Temporary Special Measures' (2004) para 7.

Special Rapporteur on the independence of judges and lawyers added: 'Judges must be in a position to challenge gender stereotyping and discrimination when they encounter it.'[21]

Specifically for the Belgian context, the Council of Europe's Expert Group monitoring the implementation of the Istanbul Convention (Group of Experts on Action against Violence against Women and Domestic Violence or GREVIO), in a report of 2020, labelled the Belgian asylum procedure insufficiently gender-sensitive.[22] Already ten years earlier, Mahieu et al. had signalled the lack of a systematic study analysing the SGBV-related case law of the Belgian asylum authorities.[23] The Belgian Women's Council also flagged the research gap on gender sensitivity in Belgian asylum procedures, based on lawyers' testimonies.[24] Building on Baillot, Cowan and Munro's suggestion above, this research will provide an in-depth contribution to fill this gap, by using rape mythology as an analytical framework to examine the gender sensitivity of Belgian asylum procedures and decisions on persons in need of international protection against SGBV.

The structure of this research is built up as follows: in this Part I, I will discuss the legal and theoretical framework shaping the research. I will then provide an overview of the research questions, the methods used to answer them, and the ethical safeguards and reflections that guided the process. In Part II, I analyse the institutional setting of the Belgian asylum procedure and how it may influence SGBV-related asylum decision making. The following parts then each address the specific SGBV myths I identified at the micro or personal level (Part III), meso/exo or interpersonal/institutional level (Part IV), and macro or societal level (Part V) in the Belgian asylum procedure and how these play a role in refugee status determination by decision makers. Finally, in Part VI, I draw: theoretical conclusions on the application of rape mythology in the criminal justice to the asylum context; legal conclusions on the gender sensitivity of the Belgian asylum procedure and its decisions; and practical conclusions on how to challenge the acceptance and support the rebuttal of SGBV myths in this asylum context.

---

21 UN Special Rapporteur on the independence of judges and lawyers, 'Report of the Special Rapporteur on the Independence of Judges and Lawyers (UN Doc. A/66/289)' (2011) 20.

22 Group of Experts on Action against Violence against Women and Domestic Violence (GREVIO), 'GREVIO's (Baseline) Evaluation Report on Legislative and Other Measures Giving Effect to the Provisions of the Council of Europe Convention on Preventing and Combating Violence against Women and Domestic Violence (Istanbul Convention) Belgium' (2020) 62–63.

23 Rilke Mahieu, Dirk Vanheule and Christiane Timmerman, 'De genderdimensie in het Belgische en Europese asiel- en migratiebeleid' (Instituut voor de gelijkheid van vrouwen en mannen 2010) 52 & 81.

24 Belgian Women's Council, 'Vrouwenraad-Memorandum Gendergerelateerd Geweld: Aanbevelingen Voor de Vlaamse En Federale Regering' (2019) 138.

1.1. SGBV IN INTERNATIONAL AND EUROPEAN REFUGEE LAW

The 1951 UN Refugee Convention has long been criticised as a gender-blind instrument.[25] According to its definition, a refugee is any person who 'owing to well-founded fear of being persecuted for reasons of race, religion, nationality, membership of a particular social group or political opinion, is outside the country of his nationality and is unable or [...] unwilling to avail himself of the protection of that country.'[26] The exclusive use of the male pronoun symbolises how, following feminist critics since the 1970s,[27] the Convention was negotiated with the image of a Western, white, heterosexual male refugee in mind, fleeing public forms of (often political) persecution.[28] The definition was considered blind to forms of persecution in the private sphere, where most SGBV occurs.[29]

According to Krause, this was 'not merely a side effect of the political landscape at the time,'[30] but a strategic result of Western androcentric power dominating the Convention's drafting to avoid, downplay, and ultimately disregard gender-related persecution.[31] She illustrates how gender-related issues were on the agenda, but actively dismissed as irrelevant with a quote from the president of the Convention's final drafting conference (Denmark's delegate),

25 Council of Europe (CoE), 'Explanatory Report to the Council of Europe Convention on Preventing and Combating Violence against Women and Domestic Violence' (2011) para 310; Georgina Firth and Barbara Mauthe, 'Refugee Law, Gender and the Concept of Personhood' (2013) 25 International Journal of Refugee Law 470, 472.

26 Art. 1, A, (2) Convention and Protocol Relating to the Status of Refugees (UN Refugee Convention) 1951 (UNTS, vol 189, p 137).

27 Oxford (n 11) 157–158.

28 Malak Benslama-Dabdoub, 'Epistemic Violence and Colonial Legacies in the Representation of Refugee Women: Contesting Narratives of Vulnerability and Victimhood' (2024) 20 International Journal of Law in Context 54, 54; Thomas Spijkerboer, 'Gender and Refugee Status' (Routledge 2000); Georgina Firth and Barbara Mauthe, 'Refugee Law, Gender and the Concept of Personhood' (2013) 25 International Journal of Refugee Law 470, 472; Fenix Humanitarian Legal aid and others, 'A Gendered Gaze On Migration: Report on Sexual and Gender-Based Violence in the Context of the Greek Asylum Policy on Lesvos' (2024) 32; Pradip Kumar Das and Tanmoy Roy, 'Women Refugees and Their Unrecognised Plights in International Refugee Law Regime: A Critical Analysis' (2022) 1 Indian Journal of Law and Justice 78, 83.

29 World Health Organization (WHO) and United Nations Inter-Agency Working Group on Violence Against Women Estimation and Data (VAW-IAWGED), 'Violence Against Women Prevalence Estimates, 2018: Global, Regional and National Prevalence Estimates for Intimate Partner Violence against Women and Global and Regional Prevalence Estimates for Non-Partner Sexual Violence against Women' (2021) 1; Jeffrey S Jones and others, 'Comparison of Sexual Assaults by Strangers versus Known Assailants in a Community-Based Population' (2004) 22 The American Journal of Emergency Medicine 454, 454.

30 Ulrike Krause, 'Invisibilization of the Unwanted Others? Feminist, Queer, and Postcolonial Perspectives on the 1951 Refugee Convention's Drafting' (2024) 107 Women's Studies International Forum 1, 1.

31 *Ibid.* 2 & 6.

who 'doubted strongly whether there would be any cases of persecution on the grounds of sex.'[32] Since SGBV could not be attributed to the state and the violence could not be linked to any of the five persecution grounds, survivors/victims fell outside the scope of the refugee definition, as it was then interpreted in case law.[33]

Gradually, criticism on this public/private divide permeated (inter)national refugee law[34] and key actors shifted towards more SGBV-inclusive conclusions and recommendations in soft law.[35] After an initial open formulation in 1985 (exclusively focusing on female refugees), stating: 'States are free to adopt the interpretation that women applicants [...] may be considered a "special social group"',[36] UNHCR ten years later urged states to: 'recognize as refugees women whose claim to refugee status is based upon well-founded fear of [...] persecution through sexual violence or other gender-related persecution.'[37] This view was later echoed in CEDAW's General Recommendation no. 32, stating that: 'A gender-sensitive approach should be applied at every stage of the asylum

32 *Ibid.* 6.

33 Pooja R Dadhania, 'Gender-Based Religious Persecution' (2023) 4 Minnesota Law Review 1563, 3; Donna Sullivan, 'The Public/Private Distinction in International Human Rights Law' in JS Peters and Andrea Wolper (eds), *Women's Rights, Human Rights* (Routledge 1995) 126; Guy S Goodwin-Gill and Jane McAdam, *The Refugee in International Law* (Oxford University Press 2007) 81 & 351; Lore Roels, 'Rape Myths in the European Court of Human Rights' Non-Refoulement Case Law on Sexual and Gender-Based Violence' (2024) 36 International Journal of Refugee Law 77, 4; Hannah Pearce, 'An Examination of the International Understanding of Political Rape and the Significance of Labeling It Torture' (2002) 14 International Journal of Refugee Law 534, 538; Middelburg and Balta (n 8) 445; Kate Smith, 'Telling Stories of Resistance and Ruination: Women Seeking Asylum' (2016) 2 Journal of Resistance Studies 33, 57; Firth and Mauthe (n 25) 472; Lourdes Peroni, 'The Protection of Women Asylum Seekers under the European Convention on Human Rights: Unearthing the Gendered Roots of Harm' (2018) 18 Human Rights Law Review 347, 351.

34 Oxford (n 11) 157–158; UNHCR Executive Committee, 'General Conclusion on Refugee Women and International Protection No. 39 (XXXVI)' (1985) para k; UNHCR Executive Committee, 'General Conclusion on International Protection No. 77 (XLVI)' (1995) para g; CEDAW, 'General Recommendation No. 32: The Gender-Related Dimensions of Refugee Status, Asylum, Nationality and Statelessness of Women' (2014) para 25.

35 UNHCR Executive Committee, 'General Conclusion on International Protection No. 77 (XLVI)' (1995) para k; UNHCR Executive Committee, 'General Conclusion on Refugee Women and International Protection No. 39 (XXXVI)' (1985) para k; CEDAW, 'General Recommendation No. 32: The Gender-Related Dimensions of Refugee Status, Asylum, Nationality and Statelessness of Women' (2014) para 25; UNHCR, 'Guidelines on International Protection No. 1: Gender-Related Persecution within the Context of Article 1A(2) of the 1951 Convention and/or Its 1967 Protocol Relating to the Status of Refugees (HCR/GIP/02/01)' (2002) para 9.

36 UNHCR Executive Committee, 'General Conclusion on Refugee Women and International Protection No. 39 (XXXVI)' (n 34) para k. Emphasis added. Anders B Johnsson, 'The International Protection of Women Refugees: A Summary of Principal Problems and Issues' (1989) 1 International Journal of Refugee Law 221, 224.

37 UNHCR Executive Committee, 'General Conclusion on International Protection No. 77 (XLVI)' (n 34) para g.

process.'[38] However, the non-binding nature and lack of political support for these evolutions led to inadequate implementation.[39]

Today, legally binding provisions formalise the place of SGBV in international asylum (hard) law and aim not only to ensure that SGBV is recognised as a form of persecution substantively, but also to build in procedural safeguards to facilitate disclosure in and proper assessment of SGBV-related applications for international protection.[40] While this research mainly concentrates on the substantive aspects of gender sensitivity in asylum decisions, I will also highlight procedural elements with relevance to the content of SGBV-related decisions, such as special procedural guarantees, accelerated procedures, guidelines and training for (gender-specialised) asylum officials, ... In the European context, these provisions can be found in European Union (EU) Directives and Regulations, but also in the Council of Europe's Istanbul Convention.

The latter Convention procedurally includes the obligation for state parties to 'provide [...] appropriate training for [...] professionals dealing with victims [...] of [SGBV]' and to develop gender-sensitive procedures for determining international protection.[41] On the substantive level, member states of the Istanbul Convention have to recognise SGBV as a form of persecution within the meaning of the UN Refugee Convention; interpret the grounds of the UN Refugee Convention in a gender-sensitive manner; assess applications for international protection gender-sensitively; and ensure that SGBV survivors/victims in need of protection shall not be returned to a country where they risk their life or torture/inhuman or degrading treatment (non-refoulement procedures).[42] The provisions in the Istanbul Convention and the EU Directives and Regulations are intricately linked, given that the EU has been a member of the former since October 2023.[43] This means that EU refugee law must be interpreted and applied in compliance with this Convention, as explicitly confirmed by the Court of Justice of the European Union (CJEU) in the *W.S. case*.[44]

---

38 CEDAW, 'General Recommendation No. 32: The Gender-Related Dimensions of Refugee Status, Asylum, Nationality and Statelessness of Women' (n 34) para 25.

39 Querton, 'Gender and the Boundaries of International Refugee Law' (n 13) 380–381; Arbel, Dauvergne and Millbank (n 12) 14.

40 Council of Europe (CoE) (n 25) paras 310–322.

41 Art. 15 *jo.* 60 Istanbul Convention.

42 Art. 60 *jo.* 61 *ibid.*

43 Council of Europe Treaty Office, 'Chart of Signatures and Ratifications of Treaty 210 (Council of Europe Convention on Preventing and Combating Violence against Women and Domestic Violence, CETS No. 210)' (*Treaty Office*, 21 February 2025), www.coe.int/en/web/conventions/full-list; Luc Denys, *Overzicht van het migratierecht* (5th edn, Die Keure 2025) 669.

44 *WS v Intervyuirasht organ na Darzhavna agentsia za bezhantsite pri Ministerskia savet* [2024] Court of Justice of the European Union C-621/21 [46]; European Parliamentary Research Service and Anita Orav, 'The Gender Dimension of Asylum Claims' (2025) 7; Catherine

In the context of EU refugee law, the term 'international protection' refers to two different types of protection statuses: 'refugee status' and 'subsidiary protection status'.[45] This research is concerned with refugee status determination. The EU legislation on international protection is in a transition phase, as the EU has been reforming its Common European Asylum System through the EU Pact on Asylum and Migration, to establish more unified and efficient refugee status determination across member states.[46] While this Pact was adopted on June 11, 2024 and entered into force on that date, its implementation is subject to a two-year transition period. This means that it will only become applicable in member states starting from June 11, 2026. For the sake of completeness, this research will refer to both instruments.

Concretely, the instruments regulating the (procedures for) determining international protection in EU member states, the EU Qualification Directive[47] (substantively) and the EU Procedures Directive[48] (procedurally), have now been replaced by the EU Qualification Regulation[49] and the EU Procedures Regulation.[50] While EU Directives contain binding results, leaving EU member states discretion on the measures implemented in national law to achieve these, EU Regulations are binding in their entirety and are therefore directly applicable in all member states.[51]

Procedurally, both the EU Procedures Directive and Regulation oblige member states to ensure: that asylum officials conducting the personal interview

Warin and Valeria Ilareva, 'Vulnerability in the New Pact: An Empty Promise to Protect, or an Operational Concept? – EU Immigration and Asylum Law and Policy' (11 October 2024), https://eumigrationlawblog.eu/vulnerability-in-the-new-pact-an-empty-promise-to-protect-or-an-operational-concept/.

45 Art. 2, (a) *jo.* (d)-(g) Directive on standards for the qualification of third-country nationals or stateless persons as beneficiaries of international protection, for a uniform status for refugees or for persons eligible for subsidiary protection, and for the content of the protection granted (EU Qualification Directive) 2011 (Official Journal of the European Union L 337/9).

46 European Commission and EU Directorate-General for Migration and Home Affairs, 'Common Implementation Plan to Turn the Pact on Migration and Asylum into a Reality' (12 June 2024), https://home-affairs.ec.europa.eu/news/common-implementation-plan-turn-pact-migration-and-asylum-reality-2024-06-12_en.

47 EU Qualification Directive.

48 Directive on common procedures for granting and withdrawing international protection (EU Procedures Directive) 2013 (Official Journal of the European Union L 180/60).

49 Regulation on standards for the qualification of third-country nationals or stateless persons as beneficiaries of international protection, for a uniform status for refugees or for persons eligible for subsidiary protection and for the content of the protection granted, amending Council Directive 2003/109/EC and repealing Directive 2011/95/EU of the European Parliament and of the Council (EU Qualification Regulation) 2024 (Official Journal of the European Union L 2024/1347).

50 Regulation establishing a common procedure for international protection in the Union and repealing Directive (EU Procedures Regulation) 2024 (Official Journal of the European Union L 2024/1348).

51 Art. 288 Treaty on the Functioning of the European Union 2012 (Official Journal of the European Union C 326/47).

are competent to take personal circumstances into account, such as applicants' gender and vulnerability;[52] that no accelerated procedures shall be applied for applicants with special procedural needs (where an accelerated procedure would not allow for providing the guarantees responding to those needs, particularly in the case of psychological, physical or sexual violence);[53] and that asylum authorities can seek advice from experts (e.g. on medical, cultural, religious, child-related or gender issues).[54] The latter includes the possibility to order a medical examination (upon the applicant's consent),[55] in both first instance and appeal proceedings, as ruled by the CJEU in the *B.F. case*.[56]

The new EU Procedures Regulation adds a provision allowing authorities to refer applicants to trained medical/psychological/other professionals for advice on their special procedural needs and possible guarantees, prioritising cases where there are indications of SGBV.[57] Where the EU Procedures Directive provided that applicants could request an interviewer and interpreter for their personal asylum interview of the same sex to enable them to present their flight story comprehensibly,[58] the EU Procedures Regulation slightly rephrases that they may ask for 'interviewers and interpreters [...] of the sex that the applicant prefers.'[59]

Substantively, EU[60] as well as international refugee law,[61] have now established that a state may be responsible for SGBV by private actors 'if such acts are knowingly tolerated by the authorities, or if the authorities refuse or are unable to provide effective protection.'[62] The EU Qualification Directive and Regulation include the obligation to: take applicants' gender into account when individually assessing their applications for international protection;[63] consider acts of sexual violence or of a gender-specific nature as persecution;[64] and to give due consideration to gender-related aspects in the consideration of the 'particular social group'-ground for persecution.[65] It is important to note that this 'particular social group'-ground is defined more restrictively in EU refugee

52 Art. 15(3)a EU Procedures Directive; Art. 13(7)a EU Asylum Procedures Regulation.
53 Art. 24(3) EU Procedures Directive; Art. 21(2) EU Asylum Procedures Regulation.
54 Art. 10(3)d EU Procedures Directive; Art. 34(3) EU Asylum Procedures Regulation.
55 Art. 18(1) EU Procedures Directive; Art. 24(1) EU Asylum Procedures Regulation.
56 *BF v Kypriaki Dimokratia* [2025] Court of Justice of the European Union (CJEU) C-283/24 [ruling].
57 Art. 20(4) & (5) EU Asylum Procedures Regulation.
58 Art. 15(3)b & c EU Procedures Directive.
59 Art. 13(9) EU Asylum Procedures Regulation.
60 Art. 6(c) EU Qualification Directive; Art. 6(c) EU Qualification Regulation.
61 Peroni (n 33) 351.
62 UNHCR, 'Guidelines on International Protection No. 1' (n 35) para 19.
63 Art. 4(3)c EU Qualification Directive; Art. 4(3) EU Qualification Regulation; *jo.* Art. 34(2)d EU Asylum Procedures Regulation.
64 Art. 9(2)a & f EU Qualification Directive; Art. 9(2)a & f EU Qualification Regulation.
65 Art. 10(1)d EU Qualification Directive; Art. 10(1)d EU Qualification Regulation.

law than in UNHCR's Guidelines.[66] In short, while in the EU Qualification Directive/Regulation, group members have to share a common characteristic and the group should have a distinct identity in society,[67] for UNHCR, one of these two characteristics suffices.[68]

On the new EU Qualification Regulation, Warin observes that 'there is still no mention of gender in relation to the four other grounds of persecution' than the 'particular social group'-ground.[69] This is despite widespread calls to widen the latter provision in scholarship and by the CJEU's Advocate General Collins in the *K.L. case*, explicitly stating: '[The EU Qualification Directive referring] to [...] membership of a particular social group [...] does not prevent gender-related aspects from being considered within the context of the other reasons for persecution.'[70]

Interestingly, the EU Qualification Regulation, in the provision on examining whether an applicant can safely and reasonably settle in another part of the country of origin (called 'an internal flight alternative' or IFA) and is therefore in no need of international protection, adds that asylum authorities should take applicants' gender into account.[71] Another addition can be found in recital 37, where the Regulation cites specific forms of gender-specific persecution, which might include 'genital mutilation, forced marriage, [...] and trafficking for sexual exploitation.'[72]

These legislative innovations seem to codify important achievements in CJEU case law on SGBV-related determination of international protection in the run-up to the new EU Qualification and Procedures Regulations.[73] In the *W.S. case* of January 2024, an applicant from Turkey had suffered domestic violence within a forced marriage and feared honour killing by her father and

---

66 EASO (European Asylum Support Office), 'EASO Guidance on Membership of a Particular Social Group' (2020) 11.

67 Art. 10(1)d EU Qualification Directive; Art. 10(1)d EU Qualification Regulation; *X, Y and Z v The Netherlands* [2013] Court of Justice of the European Union C-199/12, C 200/12, C 201/12 [45].

68 UNHCR, 'Guidelines on International Protection No. 2: "Membership of a Particular Social Group" within the Context of Article 1A(2) of the 1951 Convention and/or Its 1967 Protocol Relating to the Status of Refugees (HCR/GIP/02/02)' (2002) 3.

69 Catherine Warin, 'Gender in European Union Asylum Law: The Istanbul Convention as a Game Changer?' (2024) 36 International Journal of Refugee Law 93, 99.

70 *Opinion of Advocate General in KL v Staatssecretaris van Justitie en Veiligheid* [2023] Court of Justice of the European Union C-646/21 Footnote 18.

71 Art. 8(5)b EU Qualification Regulation.

72 Recital (37) *ibid.*

73 Warin and Ilareva (n 44); EUAA (European Union Asylum Agency), 'Jurisprudence Related to Gender-Based Violence against Women: Analysis of Case Law from 2020–2024' (2025) 6; European Parliamentary Research Service and Orav (n 44) 7–8; Christel Querton, 'Session II: Implications of Recent Jurisprudence on Gender-Based Asylum Claims: Specific Focus on ECJ Ruling (AH & FN) on Afghan Women' (ECRE Webinar on women & girls' access to international protection, 2024).

ex-husband after obtaining a divorce.[74] Here, the CJEU emphasised asylum authorities' obligation to collect gender-specific country of origin information (COI), including information on 'the position of women before the law, their political [...], social and economic rights, the cultural and social mores [...] and consequences for non-adherence, [...] the incidence and forms of reported [SGBV], the protection available [...], any penalties imposed on [perpetrators], and the risks [...] [upon] return [...] after making such a claim.'[75] The Court also clarified that domestic violence, forced marriage, and resulting honour killing constitute 'serious harm' eligible for subsidiary protection[76] status and that women fearing such violence may in their entirety qualify as a particular social group, whether or not they share an additional common characteristic, such as having left a marriage.[77]

In the *K.L. case* in June 2024, the Court confirmed that such an additional common characteristic might consist of the fact that 'women [...] genuinely come to identify with the fundamental value of [gender] equality during their stay in a Member State.'[78] In doing so, the Court expands already established case law in sexual orientation and gender identity (SOGI) cases[79] to SGBV cases, stating that applicants cannot be expected to express restraint in their belief in gender equality[80] to avoid persecution (similar to their SOGI), rejecting the so-called 'discretion reasoning'.[81] In a third case in October 2024, *A.H. and F.N.*, initiated by Afghan women fearing SGBV, the CJEU clarified that women subjected to cumulative discriminatory measures, such as those imposed by the Taliban regime, qualify as a particular social group, merely due to their nationality and gender, without further need to examine their individual circumstances.[82] The Court hereby confirmed a selective practice of group-based refugee recognition already in place in certain Member States.[83] Throughout this research, I will cite older relevant CJEU case law where it is most appropriate.

---

74 Warin and Ilareva (n 44); *WS v. Intervyuirasht organ na Darzhavna agentsia za bezhantsite pri Ministerskia savet* (n 44) paras 19–20.

75 *WS v. Intervyuirasht organ na Darzhavna agentsia za bezhantsite pri Ministerskia savet* (n 44) para 61.

76 This case answers the eligibility question for subsidiary protection specifically, not refugee protection (being the subject of this research).

77 *WS v. Intervyuirasht organ na Darzhavna agentsia za bezhantsite pri Ministerskia savet* (n 44) paras 49–50 & (Ruling) 1 & 3.

78 *KL v Staatssecretaris van Justitie en Veiligheid* [2024] Court of Justice of the European Union C-646/21 paragraph 45 & ruling 1.

79 *X, Y and Z v. The Netherlands* (n 67) para 10? 71? 74 1 75.

80 *K.L. v. Staatssecretaris van Justitie en Veiligheid* (n 78) para 63.

81 Janna Maria Wessels, 'The Concealment Controversy : Sexual Orientation, "Discretion" Reasoning and the Scope of Refugee Protection' (University of Technology Sydney 2017) viii.

82 *AH & FN v Bundesamt für Fremdenwesen und Asyl* [2024] Court of Justice of the European Union C-608/22 & C-609/22 [47–58 & (Ruling) 1-2].

83 European Parliamentary Research Service and Orav (n 44) 7–8.

As outlined above, to prove 'persecution' within the meaning of the UN Refugee Convention, one must prove a 'risk of persecution' attributable to the state.[84] While the standard of proof in theory is the same for applications based on public and private (such as SGBV) persecution, the latter in practice face significantly more hurdles in meeting that standard.[85] This is partly due to difficulties in demonstrating a risk of private persecution. Applicants with SGBV-related flight stories may face problems in obtaining documentary evidence[86] about private actors[87] or about COI on SGBV prevalence[88] and in providing negative proof of lacking state protection[89] (e.g. in countries where SGBV complaints are formally heard but not taken seriously[90]). In particular, for applicants whose mobility and knowledge are limited to the private sphere (often women), additional obstacles may lie in demonstrating knowledge of (public) information to support their application.[91]

Moreover, access to international protection is significantly hampered by challenges in explaining traumatising SGBV experiences or fears in a detailed, consistent, timely, and 'appropriately' emotional manner (see Part II, Chapter 2),[92] sometimes even more so for male survivors/victims

---

84 Rodger Haines, 'Gender-Related Persecution' in Erika Feller, Frances Nicholson and Volker Türk (eds), *Refugee Protection in International Law: UNHCR's Global Consultations on International Protection* (Cambridge University Press 2003) 329.

85 Ali, Querton and Soulard (n 8) 43–45.

86 Baillot, Cowan and Munro, 'Reason to Disbelieve' (n 6) 105.

87 Singer (n 8) 100.

88 Mahieu, Vanheule and Timmerman (n 23) 66; Femke Vogelaar, 'The Presumption of Safety Tested: The Use of Country of Origin Information in the National Designation of Safe Countries of Origin' (2021) 40 Refugee Survey Quarterly 106, 110; Bethany Collier, 'Country of Origin Information and Women: Researching Gender and Persecution in the Context of Asylum and Human Rights Claims' (Asylum Aid 2007); Ali, Querton and Soulard (n 8) 69.

89 Christel Querton, '"I Feel like as a Woman I'm Not Welcome": A Gender Analysis of UK Asylum Law, Policy and Practice' (Asylum Aid 2012) 37; Heaven Crawley, 'Gender, "Refugee Women" and the Politics of Protection' in Claudia Mora and Nicola Piper (eds), *The Palgrave Handbook of Gender and Migration* (Palgrave Macmillan UK 2021) 364; Katie Kuschminder, 'We Interviewed 150 Women Migrants – Revealing How Their Journeys Involve Peril at Every Turn (Women and Migration: Stories of Resilience Project)' (*The Conversation*, 26 November 2021), http://theconversation.com/we-interviewed-150-women-migrants-revealing-how-their-journeys-involve-peril-at-every-turn-171238; Noemi Magugliani, 'Trafficked Adult Males and Their Recognition as Members of a Particular Social Group in the United Kingdom's Upper Tribunal' (*Refugee Law Initiative Blog*, 9 November 2020), https://rli.blogs.sas.ac.uk/2020/11/09/trafficked-adult-males-and-their-recognition-as-members-of-a-particular-social-group-in-the-united-kingdoms-upper-tribunal/; Collier (n 88) 11.

90 Deborah E Anker, 'Legal Change from the Bottom up: The Development of Gender Asylum Jurisprudence in the United States' in Efrat Arbel, Catherine Dauvergne and Jenni Millbank (eds), *Gender in Refugee Law: From the Margins to the Centre* (Routledge 2014) 61; CEDAW, 'General Recommendation No. 32: The Gender-Related Dimensions of Refugee Status, Asylum, Nationality and Statelessness of Women' (n 34) para 29.

91 UNHCR, 'Beyond Proof. Credibility Assessment in EU Asylum Systems (Full Report)' (n 19) 70; Singer (n 8) 104–106; Middelburg and Balta (n 8) 442.

92 UNHCR, 'Guidelines on International Protection No. 1' (n 35) para 35; UNHCR, 'Beyond Proof. Credibility Assessment in EU Asylum Systems (Full Report)' (n 19) 56–74; Singer

(see Part III, Chapter 1.1.2.).[93] These obstacles have led scholars to point out persistent gender insensitivities, not only in supranational (quasi) jurisprudence, like the ECtHR or the CEDAW, but also in national asylum procedures.[94]

1.2. SGBV IN BELGIAN REFUGEE LAW & POLICY

Simply outlined, the Belgian asylum procedure involves three successive stages, handled by three different authorities, which will be discussed in more detail in Part II.[95] In the first stage, the applicant submits an application for international protection to the Immigration Office (IO), which registers the application and examines whether Belgium should process it according to the EU Dublin Regulation.[96] If so, the IO interviews applicants on their identity,

(n 8) 107–112; Helen Baillot, Sharon Cowan and Vanessa E Munro, '"Hearing the Right Gaps": Enabling and Responding to Disclosures of Sexual Violence within the UK Asylum Process' (2012) 21 Social & Legal Studies 269, 281–288; Baillot, Cowan and Munro, 'Reason to Disbelieve' (n 6) 105–106; Sarah K Chynoweth and others, 'Characteristics and Impacts of Sexual Violence Against Men and Boys in Conflict and Displacement: A Multicountry Exploratory Study' (2020) 37(9–10) Journal of Interpersonal Violence 1, 20–21.

93 UNHCR, 'Working with Men and Boy Survivors of Sexual and Gender-Based Violence in Forced Displacement' (2012) 8; Chynoweth and others (n 92) 5 and 11; Sarah K Chynoweth and others, 'A Social Ecological Approach to Understanding Service Utilization Barriers among Male Survivors of Sexual Violence in Three Refugee Settings: A Qualitative Exploratory Study' (2020) 14 Conflict and Health 1, 8–10; Baillot, Cowan and Munro, 'Reason to Disbelieve' (n 6) 132; Noemi Magugliani, '(In)Vulnerable Masculinities and Human Trafficking: Men, Victimhood, and Access to Protection in the United Kingdom' (2022) 14 Journal of Human Rights Practice 1, 5 & 11–12; Sylvie Saroléa, Francesca Raimondo and Zoé Crine, 'Exploring Vulnerability's Challenges and Pitfalls in Belgian Ayslum System' (Université catholique de Louvain 2021) 94; Joke Depraetere and others, 'Big Boys Don't Cry: A Critical Interpretive Synthesis of Male Sexual Victimization' (2020) 21 Trauma, Violence, & Abuse 991, 992 and 1003.

94 Peroni (n 33) 348; Roels, 'Rape Myths in the European Court of Human Rights' Non-Refoulement Case Law on Sexual and Gender-Based Violence' (n 33); Catherine Briddick, 'Unprincipled and Unrealised: CEDAW and Discrimination Experienced in the Context of Migration Control' (2022) 22 International Journal of Discrimination and the Law 224; Middelburg and Balta (n 8) 436 and 451; Ali, Querton and Soulard (n 8) 43–45; Baillot, Cowan and Munro, 'Reason to Disbelieve' (n 6) 105; Singer (n 8) 100; Querton, '"I Feel like as a Woman I'm Not Welcome": A Gender Analysis of UK Asylum Law, Policy and Practice' (n 89) 37; Crawley, 'Gender, "Refugee Women" and the Politics of Protection' (n 89) 364; Kuschminder (n 89); Magugliani (n 89); Anker (n 90) 61; Baillot, Cowan and Munro, '"Hearing the Right Gaps"' (n 92) 292; Janna Wessels, 'The Boundaries of Universality – Migrant Women and Domestic Violence before the Strasbourg Court' (2019) 37 Netherlands Quarterly of Human Rights 336, 348; Firth and Mauthe (n 25) 472.

95 If applicants decide to appeal their negative decisions at the first instance level, which most of them do. If not, the application for international protection is only handled by two actors (registration by the IO and first instance by the CGRS).

96 Regulation establishing the criteria and mechanisms for determining the Member State responsible for examining an application for international protection lodged in one of the Member States by a third-country national or a stateless person (Dublin Regulation) 2013 (Official Journal of the European Union L 180/31); Art. 51/5, §1 Wet betreffende de toegang

origin and travel route, and collects the written answers to a questionnaire on their flight motives (for the CGRS)[97] and any special procedural needs.[98] The language of the procedure (Dutch or French) is determined when registering the application with the IO and remains the same throughout the procedure.[99] If applicants indicate that they do not need an interpreter, they can choose between French or Dutch as the procedural language. If they do, the IO determines whether the case will be handled in Dutch or French, a decision which cannot be appealed.[100]

Secondly, the application is forwarded to the CGRS, which examines it and decides whether or not to grant someone international protection on the basis of the interview at the IO, documentary evidence submitted by applicants, available COI, and (usually)[101] a personal interview at the CGRS. The first instance CGRS decisions can consist of a positive decision, 1) to recognise applicants as refugees or grant them subsidiary protection status, or a negative decision, 2) to refuse both refugee status and subsidiary protection status, 3) to declare an application manifestly ill-founded in the accelerated procedure, or 4) inadmissible.[102] The latter happens when the CGRS considers that applicants are already enjoying protection in another country, minors do not invoke flight motives that justify a separate application from their parents, or when applicants do not bring forward new elements justifying a subsequent application for international protection.[103]

In the third stage, the Council for alien law litigation (CALL) decides on appeals lodged against individual decisions taken by the CGRS.[104] The Council has the competence to subject these to a full judicial review and its judgements can: 1) confirm the CGRS' decision to deny international protection; 2) reform the CGRS' decision by granting international protection; or 3) annul the decision and send it back to the CGRS for reconsideration. The latter happens when decisions contain substantial irregularities that cannot be rectified by the Council, or lack essential elements that hinder their confirmation or reformation without additional investigative measures.[105] The

---

tot het grondgebied, het verblijf, de vestiging en de verwijdering van vreemdelingen (Belgian Aliens Act) 1980 (Belgisch Staatsblad of 31 December 1980, p 14584).

97 Art. 51/10, part 1-2 Belgian Aliens Act.

98 Art. 48/9, §1 *ibid.*

99 Art. 51/4 *jo.* 39/9, §1, part 3 *ibid.*

100 Agentschap Integratie en Inburgering (AGII), 'Opstart verzoek om internationale bescherming' (*Vreemdelingenrecht.be*, 29 January 2025), www.vreemdelingenrecht.be/verblijfsrecht/bescherming/internationale-bescherming-asiel/standaardprocedure-internationale-bescherming-0/standaardprocedure-asiel-fase-bij-dvz/opstart-verzoek-om-internationale-bescherming.

101 Art. 57/5ter, §2 Belgian Aliens Act.

102 Art. 57/6, §1, 1°-2° *jo.* §3 *ibid.*

103 Art. 57/6, §3 *ibid.*

104 Art. 39/1 *ibid.*

105 Art. 39/2, §1 *jo.* 39/76 §1–2 *ibid.*

CALL does not have the competence to take additional investigative measures itself.[106] As a result, in their assessment, judges are confined to the COI, documents, and arguments put forward by the parties in their appeal petitions.

Normally, CALL judgments are taken by one judge. When a chamber president deems it necessary to ensure the unity of jurisprudence due to the particular circumstances, legal complexity, or importance of a case, a judgement is pronounced by three judges.[107] For the same reason, cases can be assigned to the united chambers (six members)[108] or the general assembly (at least ten members),[109] upon request by the (First) President, the chambers, or both parties in a case.[110]

Lastly, against a judgement by the CALL, an appeal in cassation may be lodged with the Council of State.[111] The latter can only assess substantial procedural irregularities (but not the facts themselves).[112] When a judgement confirmed a negative CGRS decision (or if the appeal period has expired), applicants have the option to submit a new application based on new elements in their case, called a 'subsequent application for international protection'. It is again registered at the IO, upon which the CGRS first conducts an admissibility examination by assessing whether the new elements or facts significantly increase the likelihood of granting international protection.[113]

In the law, the aforementioned provisions of the EU Qualification Directive were transposed into the Belgian Aliens Act.[114] The implementation of the relevant provisions in the EU Procedures Directive in the Belgian procedure will be further explained in Part II. The CGRS' efforts to centralise the gender dimension in its asylum procedures have been noticeable,[115] for example through an internal document clarifying the CGRS' gender policy through measures in 5 areas (the personal interview, training, work tools/support, specialised protection officers (POs) and 'other').[116] Indeed, GREVIO's abovementioned evaluation report in September 2020 did commend the measures already taken by the CGRS, such as: a brochure for female applicants, the forwarding

---

106 Ellen Desmet, 'Appellate Asylum and Migration Proceedings in Belgium: Challenges for the Best Interests of the Child Principle and Unity of Jurisprudence' in Mark Klaassen and others (eds), *Safeguarding children's rights in immigration law* (Intersentia 2020) 197.

107 Art. 39/10 Belgian Aliens Act.

108 Art. 39/11-12 *jo.* 57/23bis *ibid.*

109 Art. 39/11 *jo.* 39/4 *ibid.*

110 Desmet, 'Appellate Asylum and Migration Proceedings in Belgium' (n 106) 197–198.

111 Mahieu, Vanheule and Timmerman (n 23) 49 & 56–57.

112 Art. 39/67 Belgian Aliens Act; Art. 14, §2 Gecoördineerde wetten op de Raad van State 1973 (Belgisch Staatsblad of 21 March 1973, p 3461).

113 Art. 57/6/2, §1 Belgian Aliens Act.

114 Art. 48/3, §2, a] & f); §4, d]; art. 48/5, §1, c); art. 48/6, §5, c] *ibid.*

115 Ellen Desmet, 'Gender en migratierecht in België: een decennium in vogelvlucht' in Eva Brems, Pieter Cannoot and Liesbet Stevens (eds), *Recht en gender in België: 10 jaar later* (die Keure 2021) 467–468; Mahieu, Vanheule and Timmerman (n 23) 49–51.

116 Desmet, 'Gender en migratierecht in België' (n 115) 467–468.

of vulnerability assessments from receptions centres to the CGRS to trigger special procedural guarantees,[117] the establishment of a specialist gender cell, and gender trainings and guidelines (which will be discussed in Part II, Chapter 1.2.).[118]

However, the same GREVIO report also explicitly encouraged 'the Belgian authorities to ensure that a gender-sensitive approach is applied consistently to all grounds for persecution and that women receive optimal support for disclosing the grounds on which they are applying for international protection.'[119] In addition, 'GREVIO encourage[d] [them] to [...] publish gender guidelines offering better guarantees that violence will be taken into account in the case of vulnerable women to whom [...] 'accelerated' procedures apply.'[120] The fact that Belgium was reprimanded despite the efforts by its asylum authorities, makes it a fascinating case study for analysing gender-(in)sensitive features of asylum procedures.

The policy papers of the last two Secretaries of State for Asylum and Migration in Belgium formulate an answer to this evaluation and both draw particular attention to gender-sensitive asylum policies. They state: '[more is] needed in the fight against gender-based violence and in gender mainstreaming policies. More attention to the issue is necessary'[121] and 'substantively in cases on asylum or right of residence [...] gender deserves special attention.'[122] Minister of Asylum and Migration Van Bossuyt (appointed since February 2025) no longer makes any reference to gender-related international protection in her policy note of April 2025.[123]

The note does more generally mention the continuation of a project at the CGRS on 'vulnerability and asylum' (2023–2025, co-funded by the European Asylum, Migration and Integration Fund or AMIF), based on three pillars: 'awareness raising on the importance and relevance of high-quality medical documents in the asylum procedure, additional training and tools for case

117 E.g. a shorter interview, the right to assistance from a trustee, a specially trained CGRS welfare officer conducting the interview, the separate interviewing of female applicants from their family, the confidential treatment of information shared, the option for female applicants to request female interviewers/interpreters (upon giving justified reasons), ...

118 Group of Experts on Action against Violence against Women and Domestic Violence (GREVIO) (n 22) 62.

119 Expert Group on Combating Violence against Women and Domestic Violence (GREVIO) (n 416) 62-63.

120 Expert Group on Combating Violence against Women and Domestic Violence (GREVIO) (n 416) 62-63.

121 Staatssecretaris voor Asiel en Migratie Sammy Mahdi, Beleidsnota Asiel en Migratie 2021 DOC 55 2294/022 20.

122 Staatssecretaris voor Asiel en Migratie Nicole De Moor, Algemene beleidsnota Asiel en Migratie 2022 DOC 55 2934/006 20.

123 'Anneleen Van Bossuyt | Belgium.Be', www.belgium.be/nl/anneleen_van_bossuyt; Minister van Asiel en Migratie Anneleen Van Bossuyt, Beleidsnota Asiel en Migratie 2025 DOC 56 0856/038.

workers, and the re-evaluation of a number of work processes in collaboration with [...] Fedasil[, the agency for the reception of applicants,] and the [IO].'[124]

Importantly, Belgium's National Action Plan in The Fight Against Gender-Based Violence for 2021–2025 lists as an essential pillar: 'Ensuring that gender-based violence is taken into account in asylum and migration policies.'[125] In the interim report on the implementation of this Action Plan, published in 2024, two paragraphs are devoted to the asylum procedure. These state (without further details) that: the IO submitted a grant application to better identify vulnerable persons; particular attention was paid to the gender dimension when drawing up the list of safe countries of origin to which an accelerated procedure applies; and that the CGRS continues to monitor the quality of case handling for gender-related asylum procedures.[126]

However, as I will demonstrate below (see Part II, Chapter 2.2.3 and Part IV, Chapter 3.2), many of the states on the 'safe countries of origin' list[127] offer ineffective protection against SGBV and cause (potential) survivors/victims to flee out of fear for gender-related persecution. Also, the CGRS confirmed that, apart from an initiative to monitor the quality of asylum decision making on sexual orientation in May 2022, no trajectory for quality control on SGBV decisions has been established (see Part II, Chapter 2.2.2), nor is it scheduled for the future at the time of writing.[128]

1.3. RAPE MYTHOLOGY IN THE CRIMINAL JUSTICE SYSTEM

The challenges in obtaining international protection against gender-related persecution, as voiced by GREVIO above, fit into a longer history of the legal system preserving the belief that survivors/victims fabricate accounts of sexual violence.[129] In the context of rape, criminal justice scholarship has theoretically framed this set of beliefs as 'rape mythology'. The feminist

124 Minister van Asiel en Migratie Anneleen Van Bossuyt Beleidsnota Asiel en Migratie (n 123) 19.

125 Belgian Federal Government, 'Nationaal Actieplan in De Strijd Tegen Gendergerelateerd Geweld 2021–2025: Strategische Pijlers En Belangrijkste Maatregelen' (2021) 117.

126 Instituut voor de gelijkheid van vrouwen en mannen (IGVM), 'Tussentijds verslag over de tenuitvoerlegging van het nationaal actieplan ter bestrijding van gendergerelateerd geweld 2021–2025' (2024) 44.

127 Albania, Bosnia-Herzegovina, India, Kosovo, Moldova, Montenegro, North-Macedonia, and Serbia. Art. 1 Koninklijk besluit tot uitvoering van het artikel 57/6/1, §3, vierde lid, van de wet van 15 december 1980 betreffende de toegang tot het grondgebied, het verblijf, de vestiging en de verwijdering van vreemdelingen, houdende de vastlegging van de lijst van veilige landen van herkomst 2024 (Belgisch Staatsblad of 27 May 2024, p 65231).

128 Commissioner General for Refugees and Stateless Persons (CGRS), 'Internal Communication CGRS (Part I)' (7 January 2025).

129 Edwards and others (n 9) 768.

movement in the 1970s[130] first identified the term 'rape myth' to mean: 'prejudicial, stereotyped, or false beliefs about rape, rape victims, and rapists.'[131] Like stereotypes in general, these beliefs function as (sub)conscious cognitive schemes, enabling us to understand and explain events and phenomena, like SGBV, in our social world and everyday life. However, they can also cause cognitive distortions justifying, rationalising, or minimising behaviour of perpetrators.[132]

It is important to emphasise that, contrary to what the term 'myth' might suggest, these rape myths are not necessarily or always untrue. Their harmful consequences do not lie in their untruthfulness per se, but in the fact that they are generalised across all rape cases and survivors/victims. For example, the victim precipitation myth[133] that 'it are usually women who hang out in bars, sleep around, or dress suggestively who get raped,'[134] does not imply that women with this profile never actually suffer rape.

As Lonsway and Fitzgerald put it: 'the truth value of these statements in a particular situation is not as significant as the fact they tend to be universally applied.'[135] They further specified that 'rape myths' combine the characteristics of stereotypes (i.e. ascribing generalised assumptions to individual cases) with the cultural function of myths (i.e. explaining a societal phenomenon in a way that maintains the status quo). This clarification led to rape myths' more nuanced definition as: 'prescriptive or descriptive beliefs about rape that serve to deny, downplay or justify sexual violence.'[136]

Such beliefs may stem from cultural stereotypes (e.g. traditional gender roles, acceptance of interpersonal violence, and misunderstanding of the nature of sexual assault),[137] but also from well-intended self-protection

130 Julia R Schwendinger and Herman Schwendinger, 'Rape Myths: In Legal, Theoretical, and Everyday Practice' (1974) 1 Crime and Social Justice 18; Susan Brownmiller, *Against Our Will: Men, Women and Rape* (Open Road Integrated Media, Inc 1975); Hubert S Feild, 'Attitudes toward Rape: A Comparative Analysis of Police, Rapists, Crisis Counselors, and Citizens' (1978) 36 Journal of Personality and Social Psychology 156.

131 Martha R Burt, 'Cultural Myths and Supports for Rape' (1980) 38 Journal of Personality and Social Psychology 217, 217.

132 Gerd Bohner and others, 'Rape Myth Acceptance: Cognitive, Affective and Behavioural Effects of Beliefs That Blame the Victim and Exonerate the Perpetrator' in Miranda Horvath and Jennifer Brown (eds), *Rape: Challenging contemporary thinking* (Willan Publishing 2011) 23.

133 Ben-David and Schneider (n 3) 386.

134 Diana L Payne, Kimberly A Lonsway and Louise F Fitzgerald, 'Rape Myth Acceptance: Exploration of Its Structure and Its Measurement Using the Illinois Rape Myth Acceptance Scale' (1999) 33 Journal of Research in Personality 27, 49.

135 Kimberly A Lonsway and Louise F Fitzgerald, 'Rape Myths: In Review' (1994) 18 Psychology of Women Quarterly 133, 135; Olivia Smith and Tina Skinner, 'How Rape Myths Are Used and Challenged in Rape and Sexual Assault Trials' (2017) 26 Social & Legal Studies 441, 442–443.

136 Smith and Skinner (n 135) 443; Gerd Bohner and others, 'Rape Myths as Neutralizing Cognitions: Evidence for a Causal Impact of Anti-Victim Attitudes on Men's Self-Reported Likelihood of Raping' (1998) 28 European Journal of Social Psychology 257.

137 Burt (n 131) 217; Karen Rich, *Interviewing Rape Victims: Practice and Policy Issues in an International Context* (Palgrave Pivot 2014) 22.

mechanisms, like the so-called 'just world hypothesis'. This hypothesis assumes the world to be organised in an orderly and fair manner, implying that rape survivors/victims must somehow have deserved their treatment by showing certain characteristics or behaviour. Those who avoid such characteristics or behaviour can therefore protect themselves and be safe.[138] This not only results in self-blame by survivors/victims for having provoked the violence, but also in them being blamed by others, including social services, the legal system, and society at large (so-called 'victim blaming').[139]

Thus, these myths are both consciously and subconsciously, both well- and ill-intentionally ingrained in our collective thinking. It is essential to stress that their widespread acceptance throughout all social and institutional settings, without active and targeted efforts to dismantle them,[140] can even be considered 'normal'. When a survivor/victim discloses a SGBV experience, the perceived credibility is influenced by the recipient's level of accepting rape myths as true, which is termed 'rape myth acceptance'.[141] The higher one's level of rape myth acceptance, the more likely this person will apply rape myths when assessing ambiguous SGBV stories, that is: with little evidence and more room for interpretation,[142] as is often the case in asylum procedures. I draw on the concept of 'myths' to avoid making an assessment of the intentions of those who accept them. As such, the term covers the entire spectrum: from subconscious/well-intended to conscious/ill-intended acceptance (see Part V, Chapter 3.1).

In the context of legal claims, the processing of case file information becomes selective: a decision maker will rather focus on evidence that is congruent with pre-existing beliefs or expectations about rape (the rape myths) and discard information that contradicts these[143] (also termed 'confirmation bias'[144]). As a result, 'people who score highly on [...] adherence to rape myths are more likely to make judgements in line with those myths, rather than being driven by the evidence.'[145] To measure an individual's level of rape myth acceptance, specific

---

138 Bohner and others (n 132) 27; Rich (n 137) 21–22.

139 Bohner and others (n 132) 24; Edwards and others (n 9) 761; Rich (n 137) 21; Fiona Leverick, 'What Do We Know about Rape Myths and Juror Decision Making?' (2020) 24 The International Journal of Evidence & Proof 255, 255.

140 Navi Pillay, 'Equality and Justice in the Courtroom' (*Display News OHCHR (Office of the UN High Commissioner for Human Rights)*, 5 March 2014) 20, www.ohchr.org/en/NewsEvents/Pages/DisplayNews.aspx?NewsID=14721&LangID=E.

141 Bohner and others (n 132).

142 Joke Depraetere, Charlotte Decrock and Christophe Vandeviver, 'Een factorieel survey experiment naar de aanvaarding van verkrachtingsmythes binnen de politie in België' (2020) 4 Panopticon 373, 374.

143 Bohner and others (n 132) 23.

144 Ashleigh Parsons and Dara Mojtahedi, 'Can Jurors Be Biased in Their Evaluation of Third-Party Evidence within Cases of Rape?' (2022) 85 International Journal of Law and Psychiatry 1, 2.

145 Jane Herlihy and Stuart Turner, 'Untested Assumptions: Psychological Research and Credibility Assessment in Legal Decision-Making' (2015) 6 European Journal of Psychotraumatology 1, 4.

questionnaires were developed, known as rape myth acceptance scales. These include statements or items (the specific rape myths), to which participants respond using a Likert-type scale ranging from 'strongly agree' to 'strongly disagree'.[146]

Rape myth acceptance scales have allowed a rather intangible phenomenon like gender-insensitive attitudes to be concretised and quantified. One of the most well-known and reproduced traditional scale is the Illinois Rape Myth Acceptance Scale (IRMAS, 1999).[147] It contained 45 items divided into seven categories: (1) the survivor/victim asked for it; (2) it was not really rape; (3) the perpetrator did not mean to do it; (4) the survivor/victim wanted it; (5) the survivor/victim lied; (6) rape is a trivial event; and (7) rape is a deviant event.[148] In a contemporary setting, however, an increased awareness of rape myth acceptance (and the resulting socially desirable responses), as well as the time and culture boundedness of rape myths have to be taken into account.[149]

Therefore, new scales were (and are still being) developed, such as the Acceptance of Modern Myths About Sexual Aggression (AMMSA, 2007) scale,[150] containing 30 statements on more modern rape myths and using more subtle wording.[151] These appear in five categories: (1) denial of the scope of the problem; (2) antagonism toward victims' demands; (3) lack of support for policies designed to help alleviate the effects of sexual violence; (4) beliefs that male coercion forms a natural part of sexual relationships; and (5) beliefs that exonerate perpetrators by blaming the victim or the circumstances.[152]

Next to the items in these scales, rape myths are identified in scholarship listing useful (categorisations of) rape myths, such as Ben-David and Schneider[153] (victim masochism; victim precipitation; and victim fabrication) or Leverick[154] (beliefs that blame the survivor/victim; beliefs that cast doubt on allegations; beliefs that excuse the accused; and beliefs about what real rape looks like). The phenomenon of rape myth acceptance has been widely studied in the criminal justice context (for instance, in the context

146 Sarah McMahon and G Lawrence Farmer, 'An Updated Measure for Assessing Subtle Rape Myths' (2011) 35 Social Work Research 71, 73; Agnès Schlegel and Robert Courtois, 'Scales for Evaluating the Acceptance of the Rape Myth: Benefits and Limitations' (2019) 2 International Journal of Risk and Recovery 23, 23.

147 Payne, Lonsway and Fitzgerald (n 134).

148 Ibid. 49–50.

149 Rich (n 137) 26; Schlegel and Courtois (n 146) 24.

150 Heike Gerger and others, 'The Acceptance of Modern Myths about Sexual Aggression Scale: Development and Validation in German and English' (2007) 33 Aggressive Behavior 422.

151 Schlegel and Courtois (n 146) 24.

152 Gerger and others (n 150) 439–440.

153 Ben-David and Schneider (n 3) 386.

154 Leverick (n 139) 257.

of police officers,[155] prospective lawyers,[156] juror decision making,[157] and criminal rape/sexual assault trials[158]), but to my knowledge never in the asylum context.[159]

1.4. APPLYING RAPE MYTHOLOGY TO THE ASYLUM SYSTEM: SGBV MYTHOLOGY

To make studies on the phenomenon of rape myth acceptance in the asylum context possible, the differences between the criminal justice context, on the one hand, and the asylum context, on the other need to be considered. These are mainly located on four levels. On the first, evidentiary level, persons are often fleeing in unexpected circumstances along dangerous routes, forcing them to prioritise survival over collecting possible evidence for future legal proceedings. As such, corroborative evidence in asylum procedures may be even more sparse[160] than is already the case for criminal SGBV procedures.[161]

This often results in the applicant's story being the only or dominant source of information, without it being compared to (a lack of) evidence from an alleged perpetrator (the defence). Therefore, the 'innocent vs. guilty' binary in the criminal justice system firstly shifts towards a 'credible vs. non-credible' binary in refugee status determination, with fewer evidentiary safeguards.[162] In the second state of such assessments, if applicants' credibility as such is not questioned, this binary shifts to one of 'well- vs. ill-foundedness' of their fear of persecution.

On the second, temporal level, the criminal justice system deals with past offences. While past ill-treatment can be of relevance for asylum procedures[163] (see Part III, Chapter 2.2.3 on the burden of proof reversal

155 Karl Ask, 'A Survey of Police Officers' and Prosecutors' Beliefs About Crime Victim Behaviors' (2010) 25 Journal of Interpersonal Violence 1132; Feild (n 130).

156 Barbara Krahé and others, 'Prospective Lawyers' Rape Stereotypes and Schematic Decision Making about Rape Cases' (2008) 14 Psychology, Crime & Law 461.

157 Leverick (n 139).

158 Smith and Skinner (n 135).

159 Roels, 'Rape Myths in the European Court of Human Rights' Non-Refoulement Case Law on Sexual and Gender-Based Violence' (n 33) 81–82.

160 Ali, Querton and Soulard (n 8) 60.

161 United Nations Office on Drugs and Crime (UNODC) and Eileen Skinnider, 'Handbook for the Judiciary on Effective Criminal Justice Responses to Gender-Based Violence Against Women and Girls' (2019) 82.

162 Gregor Noll, 'Credibility, Reliability, and Evidential Assessment' in Cathryn Costello, Michelle Foster and Jane McAdam (eds), *The Oxford Handbook of International Refugee Law* (Oxford University Press 2021) 607.

163 E.g. art. 4(4) EU Qualification Directive; art. 48/7 Belgian Aliens Act.

in the case of past persecution), the main question is whether the applicant is at risk of future persecution upon return. Substantiating a hypothetical future risk of gender-related harm can be an additional barrier to obtaining protection in asylum procedures. On the third, personal level, the criminal justice system primarily works toward convicting perpetrators (and thereby protecting society), while asylum procedures exclusively focus on protecting survivors/victims.

It is worth noting that in practice, when assessing applications for international protection, asylum officials are expected to distinguish between those who have a right to, and are therefore considered 'deserving' of,[164] protection and those who are not. In a sociopolitical climate emphasising such 'control' over migration by assessing deservingness,[165] decision makers might feel pressured certainly not to wrongfully recognise persons as refugees (and therefore grant them residence status) through so-called 'false positives'.[166] In the criminal justice context, such pressure does not play out for decision makers (in the same way[167]). There, the object of protection: the society in which it functions, is per definition considered 'deserving' of protection. This might have an impact on how receptive these respective contexts are to acknowledging (and challenging) the acceptance of rape/SGBV myths in their decision-making practice.[168] Fourthly and substantively, displacement is caused by more forms of SGBV than rape alone (see Chapter 2 of this Part).

As a result of these evidentiary, temporal, personal, and substantive differences, the consequences of rape myth acceptance might turn out to be even more problematic for asylum procedures than already proven for criminal procedures.[169] Taking these into account, for the purpose of this research, I translate[170] the concept of 'rape myths that exonerate the perpetrator for past rape' in the criminal justice system to 'SGBV myths that undermine the credibility/

164 Luc Leboeuf, 'Lived Vulnerabilities in Asylum and Migration: Confronting the "Vulnerability" Label with Migrants' Experiences' (VULNER 2023) VULNER Research Report 2 50–51.

165 An in-depth discussion of such sociopolitical climates, and the (Belgian) asylum and criminal justice contexts' position in and relation to it, are outside the scope of this research.

166 *College 3 Rechtspsychologie: Wie is het? Het toetsen van levensverhalen in asielzaken* (Directed by Tanja van Veldhuizen, 2021), www.youtube.com/watch?v=q_-t7M9rGlM.

167 Without disregarding the differences in deservingness assessments between individual survivors/victims who are part of the society to be protected as a whole. See for example: Miriam Ticktin, *Casualties of Care: Immigration and the Politics of Humanitarianism in France* (University of California Press 2011) 186. An in-depth discussion of these individual deservingness assessments in the (Belgian) criminal justice context are outside the scope of this research.

168 Council for Alien Law Litigation (CALL), 'Internal Communication CALL' (21 August 2025).

169 Smith and Skinner (n 135) 441; United Nations Office on Drugs and Crime (UNODC) and Skinnider (n 161) 32.

170 Baillot, Cowan and Munro, 'Reason to Disbelieve' (n 6) 106.

well-foundedness of applicants' fear of future persecution' in the asylum context. This translation can be visualised in Figure 1.

Figure 1: Translation of rape myths in the criminal justice context to SGBV myths in the asylum context

	CRIMINAL JUSTICE SYSTEM	ASYLUM SYSTEM
1) Evidentiary	(Limited) evidence → **guilty** vs. innocent binary	Flight story = only/dominant information source → **credible** vs. non-credible & **well-** vs. ill-founded binary
2) Temporal	**Past** offences	Risk of **future** persecution upon return
3) Personal	Protection society by convicting **perpetrators**	Protecting (potential) **survivors/victims** – no defence
4) Substantive	**Rape**/sexual assault	All **SGBV** types giving rise to forced displacement
=	**Rape** myths that **exonerate** the **perpetrator** for **past rape**	**SGBV** myths that undermine the **credibility/well-foundedness** of **applicants'** fear of **future persecution**

This research will use the term 'myth' in parallel to the framework of rape 'mythology' on which it builds. The term 'SGBV myth' hereby equally holds the abovementioned nuance that individual rape/SGBV myths may vary in level of truthfulness. As explained above (Chapter 1.3), it is not necessarily the untruthfulness, but the universal application of these beliefs that generate their harmful consequences. Throughout this research, I will differentiate between these levels of truthfulness by indicating those SGBV myths that are not always false with an asterisk (*). This is the case for two of the six identified SGBV myths, which I will elaborate on below (Part I, Chapter 2.5).

2. RESEARCH QUESTIONS, SCOPE & TERMINOLOGY

2.1. RESEARCH QUESTIONS

This research departs from the overarching question into how SGBV myths permeate asylum procedures and decisions (RQ). In order to answer this question, it is organised around four consecutive sub-questions and can be visualised as in Figure 2. These questions respectively aim to conceptualise (SQ1), identify (SQ2), analyse the occurrence of (SQ3), and institutionally contextualise (SQ4) SGBV myths in gender-related asylum procedures and decisions, and eventually draw conclusions & recommendations (SQ5). To answer SQ2, SQ3, and SQ4, I took the approach of data source triangulation,[171] by collecting data from multiple sources, representing different standpoints, with the purpose of getting a comprehensive and nuanced understanding of the phenomenon of SGBV mythology in the asylum context.

To answer SQ1, I conducted an (inter)national refugee/criminal law and literature analysis to conceptually translate rape mythology in the criminal justice context to SGBV mythology in the asylum context. It is important to note that this translation exercise necessarily limits the research to myths that have already been identified in the criminal justice context. I analysed both the similarities and differences of these existing myths between the criminal justice and the asylum context and expanded them to more SGBV types than rape alone, thereby examining any new forms/nuances they may encompass. However, the question of whether there exist SGBV myths that are unique to the asylum context and do not occur in any form in the criminal justice context falls outside the scope of this research.

For SQ2, I identified SGBV myths relevant in asylum procedures and examined how these can be rebutted in existing literature on rape mythology and expertise on SGBV. More importantly, I also listened to the lived experiences of persons who navigated these procedures by conducting qualitative interviews myself with applicants who fled SGBV (research interviews in Figure 2) and by reading personal interviews conducted with them by the CGRS (interviews by CGRS in Figure 2). As such, the identification and rebuttal of SGBV myths

171 Nancy Carter and others, 'The Use of Triangulation in Qualitative Research' (2014) 5 Methods & Meanings (Oncology Nursing Forum) 545, 545.

relevant to the asylum context was informed through expertise in scholarship and expertise by experience.

To answer SQ3, I relied on four data sources to examine the levels and ways of SGBV myth acceptance and rebuttal occurring in gender-related asylum decisions in Belgium. I collected data through: 1) qualitative interviews at the first instance and appeal asylum authorities (following 2) an exploratory Knowledge, Attitude and Practices (KAP) survey), 3) an analysis of the Belgian asylum case law, and 4) the (national) refugee law & literature analysis. To get a broader picture of supranational jurisprudence that could potentially influence Belgian case law, I conducted a preliminary analysis of the non-refoulement case law before the ECtHR, which as such was not used as data for this research, but served as an exploratory step towards it and was published in the International Journal for Refugee Law.[172]

For SQ4, to analyse how the Belgian procedural and institutional framework might impact asylum decisions on SGBV (SQ4), I used the same four data sources and methods as used, complemented by a fifth: the qualitative interviews with applicants. Lastly, by examining, structuring, and comparing the thematical, procedural, and institutional distribution of SGBV myth acceptance and rebuttal, I answered SQ5 and drew: 1) theoretical conclusions on the application of rape mythology from the criminal justice to the asylum context; 2) methodological conclusions on the process of doing so, 3) legal conclusions on the gender sensitivity of asylum decisions; and 4) practical conclusions on how to challenge the acceptance and support the rebuttal of SGBV myths in asylum procedures. Below, I will elaborate on each of the methods mentioned and how I employed them to answer the research question and sub-questions (Chapter 4 of this part).

Figure 2: Overview of research questions and corresponding methods employed to answer them

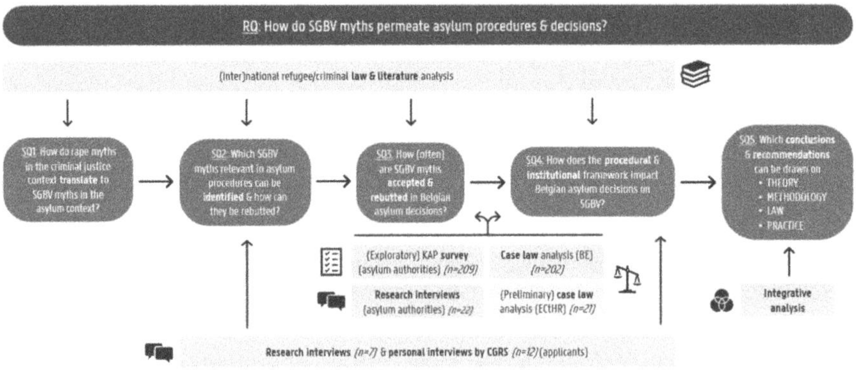

172 Roels, 'Rape Myths in the European Court of Human Rights' Non-Refoulement Case Law on Sexual and Gender-Based Violence' (n 33).

2.2. SCOPE & TERMINOLOGY

The research scope concerns persons who are outside their country of origin out of fear of becoming a survivor/victim of SGBV upon return. They arrive in a host country, where they file an application for international protection and thereby initiate an asylum procedure. I will specifically look into asylum authorities' argumentation in these procedures, leading to decisions granting or denying applicants refugee status (one form of international protection). In doing so, I will examine the levels of gender sensitivity in such SGBV-related asylum procedures, through the lens of SGBV mythology, using Belgium as a case study and 'June 2020 until June 2025' as the temporal scope. Below I will further specify the terms used to describe this scope.

This research deliberately defines SGBV survivors/victims as persons (rather than women and girls). Many studies on SGBV ignore (cisgender[173]) male, transgender, intersex and otherwise queer survivors/victims,[174] while SGBV occurs across the entire gender spectrum.[175] This makes an exclusive focus on (cisgender) female survivors/victims difficult to justify and calls for more gender-inclusive knowledge production, to which this research wants to contribute.[176]

Those who have experienced SGBV themselves disagree on the preferred term: victim or survivor, and the two terms are often used interchangeably in research and practice. For example, police and the judiciary tend to use 'victims' of crime, while health and social workers use 'survivor' or 'patient'.[177] Since the use of these terms depends on the context and on how survivors/victims see themselves and interpret the violence, I use the dual term 'survivor/victim'. The scholarship on which this research largely relies is still evolving towards more gender and trauma awareness, which is why some resources, and therefore some

[173] Designating a person whose sense of personal identity and gender corresponds to their sex at birth. Oxford English Dictionary, 'Cisgender', www.oed.com/dictionary/cisgender_adj.

[174] Chloé Lewis, 'Systemic Silencing: Addressing Sexual Violence against Men and Boys in Armed Conflict and Its Aftermath' in Gina Heathcote and Dianne Otto (eds), *Rethinking Peacekeeping, Gender Equality and Collective Security* (Palgrave Macmillan UK 2014) 203; Chynoweth and others (n 93) 2; Magugliani (n 93) 1–2; Jenna M Calton, Lauren Bennett Cattaneo and Kris T Gebhard, 'Barriers to Help Seeking for Lesbian, Gay, Bisexual, Transgender, and Queer Survivors of Intimate Partner Violence' (2016) 17 Trauma, Violence, & Abuse 585, 585.

[175] World Health Organization (WHO), 'Guidelines for Medico-Legal Care of Victims of Sexual Violence' (2003) 8.

[176] Lotte De Schrijver and others, 'Prevalence of Sexual Violence in Migrants, Applicants for International Protection, and Refugees in Europe: A Critical Interpretive Synthesis of the Evidence' (2018) 15 International Journal of Environmental Research and Public Health 1979, 9.

[177] Stacy L Young and Katheryn C Maguire, 'Talking about Sexual Violence' (2003) 26 Women and Language 40, 40 and 50; Ines Keygnaert and Leni Linthout, 'Triage Tool for Identification, Care and Referral of Victims of Sexual Violence at European Asylum Reception and Accommodation Initiatives' (ICRH, Ghent University 2020) 6.

citations used throughout the text, still refer exclusively to 'violence against women/girls' or 'victims'.

This research further includes applicants regardless of their age (see Chapter 3.1.2 of this Part for ethical aspects), able-bodiedness, country of origin, SOGI, ... Aware of the importance of intersectional research and the overlapping and mutually reinforcing types of discrimination that these characteristics may produce,[178] I consciously concentrate on an in-depth interdisciplinary analysis of the gender axis of this intersection for applicants in SGBV-based asylum procedures. In doing so, rather than focusing on the differences in intersectional oppression between cases, I aim to present a comprehensive analysis of how SGBV myth acceptance may impact all applicants, regardless of and across their intersecting characteristics and those of their flight stories (see Part V, Chapter 3.1).

The term 'SGBV' refers both to sexual and gender-based violence. For the purpose of this research, I define[179] sexual violence as violence of a sexual nature[180] and gender-based violence as violence inflicted on a person for gender-related reasons, whether of a sexual nature or not. These gender-related reasons can refer, following Crawley, to both 'gender-specific' and 'gender-related' forms of violence.[181] The former refers to violence that is targeted at individuals because of their gender and that therefore disproportionately affects one gender, such as forced marriage or domestic violence. The latter then includes any violence that is connected to gender, even if the act itself is not inherently gendered. It encompasses harm due to individuals' failure to conform to societal gender norms, such as parents refusing to subject their child to GMC, (mothers giving birth to) extramarital children, persons leaving their (forced) partner or defying restrictive dress codes, or men deviating from traditional cisgender and heteronormative[182] perceptions of masculinity.

178 Kimberle Crenshaw, 'Demarginalizing the Intersection of Race and Sex: A Black Feminist Critique of Antidiscrimination Doctrine, Feminist Theory and Antiracist Politics' (1989) 1989 University of Chicago Legal Forum 139, 140.

179 This categorisation is based on the sources listed below, but adapted to the deliberate intent of this study to go beyond the exclusive focus on female survivors/victims and include all gender identities. Heaven Crawley, *Refugees and Gender: Law and Process* (Jordan Publishing Limited 2001) 7–8; Peroni (n 33) 349; Haines, 'Gender-Related Persecution' (n 84) 326; World Health Organization (WHO), 'World Report on Violence and Health' (2002) 149–150.

180 WHO defines sexual violence as: 'Any sexual act, attempted sexual act, unwanted sexual comments or advances, act to trade in a person's sexuality, or otherwise directed, using coercion, to a person regardless of their relationship to the victim, in any setting.' World Health Organization (WHO), 'World Report on Violence and Health' (n 179) 149.

181 Crawley, *Refugees and Gender* (n 179) 7–8.

182 Assumption of a person's heterosexuality. European Institute for Gender Equality, 'Heteronormativity' (10 December 2024), https://eige.europa.eu/publications-resources/thesaurus/terms/1384?language_content_entity=en.

Violence related to one's SOGI was excluded from the scope of this research, given that the complexity and multifaceted nature of SOGI-related violence warrants stand-alone research that is informed by queer studies. Nonetheless, cases of applicants fleeing SOGI-related violence in combination with other forms of SGBV were included. This means, for example, that corrective rape[183] on grounds of SOGI is included in the research (because it coincides with sexual violence), but bullying on the basis of a person's SOGI is not. It should be emphasised that not every form of SGBV under this definition reaches the same level of severity. The question of whether an experience effectively constitutes 'persecution' in the sense of (inter)national refugee law[184] must be assessed on a case-by-case basis by asylum authorities. An in-depth discussion of such assessments is beyond the scope of this research, which uses the definitions as a selection criterion.

For the purpose of selecting, analysing, and referencing the case law and interviews with applicants in this research, I used the following six categories of SGBV (with corresponding abbreviations, as visualised in Figure 3[185]). The choice of terms was informed by the definitions of some forms of SGBV, such as forced prostitution instead of sex work, since the latter implies consensual work[186] which does not as such generate forced migration, or the double term 'genital mutilation/cutting' (GMC), mindful of postcolonial critiques on the term.[187] Other terms were informed by the aim of capturing as many relevant cases as possible, using the most commonly used terms describing the violence (based on preliminary analysis during the first months of the fieldwork for this research, see Chapter 4.2 of this part), such as 'domestic violence' instead of intimate partner violence, incest, ….

---

183 'Corrective rape is a form of rape of perpetrated against someone on the basis of their sexual orientation or gender identity. It is intended to force the victim to conform to heterosexuality or normative gender identity'. United Nations Economic and Social Commission for Western Asia (UN ESCWA), 'Corrective Rape', www.unescwa.org/sd-glossary/corrective rape.

184 Art. 1, (A) UN Refugee Convention; Art. 9 EU Qualification Directive; Art. 48/3; § 2 Belgian Aliens Act.

185 These definitions are largely based on the sources referenced below but adapted to the deliberate intent of this study to go beyond the exclusive focus on female survivors/victims and include all gender identities.

186 UNAIDS, 'UNAIDS Guidance Note on HIV and Sex Work' (2012) 3–4 & 39.

187 These critiques uncover the discriminatory double standard between GMC performed in the Global South (labelled as mutilation) and in the Global North (merely seen as genital modifications, e.g. female genital cosmetic surgery or infant intersex surgery). Nina Van Eekert and others, 'Rethinking the Definition of Medicalized Female Genital Mutilation/Cutting' (2024) 53 Archives of Sexual Behavior 441, 442.

Figrue 3: Overview of forms of SGBV and corresponding abbreviations used throughout the research

SGBV-type		Category	Further clarification
RSA	Rape and sexual assault	Sexual violence	Any (attempt to obtain a) sexual act, unwanted sexual comments or advances against a person's sexuality using coercion, by any person regardless of their relationship to the victim, in any setting,[188] including within the family or domestic unit[189]
STFP	Sex trafficking and forced prostitution		Any (transporting and/or trade in persons, with or without their initial consent, with the purpose of) forced sexual exploitation, whereby the use of force may be physical, sexual, and/or psychological, and includes intimidation and abuse of authority or a situation of dependence[190]
GMC	Genital mutilation/ cutting		A harmful intervention on (fe)male or intersex[191] genitalia, performed for non-medical reasons, to conform to societal gender norms[192]
VGNT	Violence related to gender norm transgression	Gender-based violence	Violence experienced for having transgressed gendered cultural, religious, social or traditional norms[193] (perceived as bringing dishonour to the family or community[194]), such as: extramarital relationships and/or pregnancies, refusal to wear a face veil or headscarf, refusal of or leaving a (forced) relationship/marriage, refusal to undergo or (have someone) perform GMC on others, ...[195]

(continued)

188 World Health Organization (WHO), 'World Report on Violence and Health' (n 179) 149.

189 Sexual domestic violence will be categorised as RSA and DV in the context of this research.

190 Council of Europe Parliamentary Assembly, 'Recommendation 1325: Traffic in Women and Forced Prostitution in Council of Europe Member States' (1997) para 2.

191 'Intersex individuals are born with primary and secondary sex characteristics [...] that do not fit medical or social norms for female or male bodies.' Jana Hugo and Luan Pertl, 'Intersex Refugees & Asylum Seekers Toolkit' (Organisation Intersex International Europe (OII Europe) 2023).

192 UNICEF, 'What Is Female Genital Mutilation?', www.unicef.org/protection/female-genital-mutilation; Organisation Intersex International Europe, 'What Is Intersex Genital Mutilation (IGM)?' (*OII Europe*, 4 February 2021), www.oiieurope.org/igm/.

193 Art. 42 (1) Istanbul Convention.

194 European Institute for Gender Equality, 'Crimes Committed in the Name of So-Called Honour' (10 December 2024), https://eige.europa.eu/publications-resources/thesaurus/terms/1194?language_content_entity=en.

195 Dana M Olwan, 'Gendered Violence, Cultural Otherness, and Honour Crimes in Canadian National Logics' (2013) 38 The Canadian Journal of Sociology 533, 535; Aisha Gill, 'Patriarchal Violence in the Name of "Honour"' (2006) 1 International Journal of Criminal Justice Sciences 1, 1; Her Majesty's Inspectorate of Constabulary (HMIC), 'The Depths of Dishonour: An Inspection of the Police Response to Honour-Based Violence, Forced Marriage and Female Genital Mutilation' (2015) 8; Kristen Schilt and Laurel Westbrook, 'Doing Gender, Doing Heteronormativity: "Gender Normals," Transgender People, and the Social Maintenance

FM	Forced marriage		A relationship in which (at least) one of the parties is forced and/or is not free to put an end to [it] or to leave,[196] including forced (child) marriage/cohabitation (preceded by abduction)
DV	Domestic violence		All acts of physical, psychological or economic violence that occur within the family or domestic unit or between former or current spouses or partners, whether or not the perpetrator shares or has shared the same residence with the survivor/victim[197]

In line with the terminology used in European and Belgian refugee law,[198] I call persons outside their country of origin and seeking protection from persecution 'applicants for international protection' (or applicants in short), who file an 'application for international protection'.[199] This research focuses on refugee status as a form of international protection, granted when a person meets the conditions of the refugee definition in the UN Refugee Convention (see Chapter 1.1 above).[200] The procedure in which this refugee status determination takes place is called the 'asylum procedure' and the decision makers who make these assessments in first instance or appeal are called 'asylum authorities'[201] (see chapter 5). The decisions in first instance and judgements in appeal are jointly termed 'case law' and 'decisions' for readability purposes.

Temporally, this research mainly focuses on a time frame ranging from June 2020 until June 2025. It is informed by the publication date of the abovementioned GREVIO evaluation report on Belgium (26 June 2020),[202] which marks a moment in time when the Belgian asylum authorities were formally evaluated on

of Heterosexuality' (2009) 23 Gender & Society 440, 457 and 460; Evie Browne, 'Gender Norms, LGBTQI Issues and Development: A Topic Guide' (ALiGN (Advancing Learning and Innovation on Gender Norms) 2019) 12.

196 European Institute for Gender Equality, 'Forced Marriage' (10 December 2024), https://eige.europa.eu/publications-resources/thesaurus/terms/1171?language_content_entity=en.

197 Sexual domestic violence will be categorised as RSA and DV in the context of this research. Art. 3 (b) Istanbul Convention; Claudia Garcia-Moreno and others, 'Prevalence of Intimate Partner Violence: Findings from the WHO Multi-Country Study on Women's Health and Domestic Violence' (2006) 368 The Lancet 1260, 1262.

198 Art. 2 EU Qualification Directive; EU Procedures Directive; Belgian Aliens Act.

199 Formerly called 'asylum seekers' in Belgium. Commissioner General for Refugees and Stateless Persons (CGRS), 'Omzetting Asielprocedurerichtlijn in Belgisch recht' (*CGVS*, 21 March 2018), www.cgvs.be/nl/actueel/omzetting-asielprocedurerichtlijn-belgisch-recht.

200 Art. 1, A, (2) UN Refugee Convention.

201 When not further specified, the term 'asylum authorities' (or synonyms like asylum officials or decision makers) covers both the first instance and the appeal authorities.

202 Group of Experts on Action against Violence against Women and Domestic Violence (GREVIO), 'GREVIO's (Baseline) Evaluation Report on Legislative and Other Measures Giving Effect to the Provisions of the Council of Europe Convention on Preventing and Combating Violence against Women and Domestic Violence (Istanbul Convention) Albania' (2017).

the gender-sensitive character of their asylum procedure. By then, the relevant provisions brought into existence by the Istanbul Convention[203] in 2011 were expected to be known and applied in practice. The data collection for the research was largely determined by this temporal scope. Deviations will be explicitly noted in the methodology part (see Chapter 4). Also for the purpose of readability, the quotes I use throughout the text from case law, interviews, and survey responses were freely translated into English.

It is worth noting that I do not use SGBV myth acceptance and gender sensitivity as synonyms. Gender sensitivity is a broader concept that may concern multiple aspects of asylum decision making, including procedural gender sensitivity (e.g. special procedural guarantees, trauma- and gender-sensitive interviewing techniques, ...). Instead, I examined one substantive way of interpreting and implementing gender sensitivity in the asylum context, inspired by the concept of rape mythology, leading to the identification of concrete thinking patterns that are based on 'prejudicial, stereotyped, or false beliefs'[204] about SGBV (what I call SGBV myths).

As mentioned earlier (Chapter 1.3), contrary to what the term 'myth' might suggest, these SGBV myths are not necessarily or always untrue[205] and their acceptance is not necessarily ill-intended. The harmful consequences essentially originate from their unjustified generalisation across all SGBV cases and survivors/victims[206] and SGBV myth-like beliefs may also stem from well-intended self-protection mechanisms like the 'just world hypothesis'.[207] I will use the term 'myth' in parallel to its interpretation in rape mythology, combining the characteristics of stereotypes (i.e. ascribing generalised assumptions to individual cases) with the cultural function of myths (i.e. explaining a societal phenomenon in a way that maintains the status quo).[208]

Throughout the text, I use specific case studies of applicants, some of whom I interviewed myself. These were the subject of in-depth analysis and serve as concrete illustrations of the research findings. Hereby, the research is not concerned with the factual truthfulness of the flight stories as such, but with outlining the context in which certain (decision making) practices have taken place. The flight stories are based on the information available in their case file, the interviews conducted by myself, the personal interviews conducted by the

203 Istanbul Convention art 60 *jo.* 61.
204 Burt (n 131) 217.
205 As I will explain below (chapter 4.5), the use of an asterisk/* in the figures throughout the research is used to nuance the untruthfulness level of those SGBV myths that are not always false, leaving room for these myth-based arguments to be used when explicitly supported by COI.
206 Lonsway and Fitzgerald (n 135) 135; Smith and Skinner (n 135) 442–443.
207 Bohner and others (n 132) 27; Rich (n 137) 21–22.
208 Smith and Skinner (n 135) 443; Bohner and others (n 136).

CGRS, and the first instance decisions and appeal judgements accessible to me. In describing the facts, I specifically focused on the SGBV applicants fear (and often experienced) throughout their journey, as expressed in their own statements. I want to warn that the text hereby describes experiences of SGBV and thoughts/attempts of suicide. This may trigger disturbing memories or reflections in some readers.[209]

I deliberately chose to introduce these case studies one by one throughout the text. This allowed me to integrate applicants' voices into the research at the moment when their stories seemed most meaningful. Rather than briefly discussing the cases of all 97 applicants included (see Chapter 4.2), I opted for an in-depth description of a selection of cases, based on their significance in illustrating and/or rebutting the myths discussed. These case studies are presented as follows, accompanied by a (different) name, rather than a code as a pseudonym:[210]

CASE OF [NAME]			
• Country of origin:	X	• SGBV types:	X
• Gender identity:	X	• Decisions in file:	CGRS 1 (Type) – DATE
• Birth year:	XXXX		CALL 1 (Type) – DATE – n° XXX XXX
• Interview by:	X[211]		…
[Flight story as expressed in the applicants' statements (based on the information available to me, with specific focus on the SGBV feared/experienced) and following asylum procedure]			

All case studies presented in this way are also listed in the Annex. In the text, quotes from the interviews and case files of these case studies (by applicants, authorities, lawyers, or other professionals supporting applicants)

---

209 If you, or someone close to you, had similar experiences and wish(es) to talk about it, you/they can contact the Sexual Assault Care Centres (SACC) at https://sac.belgium.be/en or the Suicide Line at www.zelfmoord1813.be/help line +32800 32 123 (in Belgium) or find a helpline at https://findahelpline.com/ (if you are based elsewhere).

210 I deliberately chose to do so, to remind the reader that these are real words from real persons with real flight stories, and to pay due attention to the singularities of the SGBV stories I encountered in my data. Echoing Kolankiewicz, 'to treat the cases as statistics – numbers and dry illustrations detached from the real lives of people – felt somehow strange' and distant. I selected names appropriate to applicants' gender identity, country of origin, and age. Marta Kolankiewicz, 'The Ethics of Renaming: On Challenges and Dilemmas of Anonymization in a Study of Anti-Muslim Racism' in The Critical Methodologies Collective (ed), *The Politics and Ethics of Representation in Qualitative Research: Addressing Moments of Discomfort* (Routledge 2022) 119.

211 Indicates whether the case description was based on interview notes or not: 'Researcher' (transcript of the interview by researcher), 'CGRS' (personal interview notes by the CGRS), '/' (none).

are highlighted as follows. As a result of the gradual mentioning of the case studies, some cases are already mentioned in the text earlier than their actual introduction as a case study (through the table above). Such citations will simply appear in quotation marks throughout the text, together with citations from other analysed case law (not selected as case studies).

'[Quote]' | CASE OF [NAME]

3. ETHICAL FRAMEWORK & POSITIONALITY

Researching how gender-stereotypical thinking patterns affect refugee status determination can reveal gendered power structures,[212] not only between the dominant asylum system and the therein marginalised applicants who flee SGBV, but also between the dominant academic system of knowledge production and the therein marginalised participants who share their stories for the sake of data collection. In academic research 'about [them] without [them],'[213] they are too often seen as producers of raw data, to be polished into scientific output through analysis by 'experts'.[214] This research wants to recognise and compensate for these power structures by centralising the realities and perspectives of experts by experience through interviews with (potential) SGBV survivors/victims who apply for international protection. This method, based on the feminist politics of listening,[215] considers participants as drivers of the knowledge that is produced.[216]

In addition, determining applicants' credibility in the asylum procedure itself is a complex, if not practically impossible (Part V, Chapter 3.2), task, fraught with the risk of being influenced by (sub)conscious harmful preconceptions. In this interactive process of telling, listening to, and assessing flight stories, both the identities of speakers and hearers are relevant to epistemic evaluations.[217] Therefore, in order to get a full and nuanced understanding of gender-related asylum decision making, next to the standpoints of applicants, those of asylum authorities should be looked at too, as sources of social power.[218] Echoing

---

212 Michelle Lokot, 'The Space between Us: Feminist Values and Humanitarian Power Dynamics in Research with Refugees' (2019) 27 Gender & Development 467, 468; Kate Ogg, 'Feminism as Method: How Do We Do Gender in International Refugee Law?' (*Refugee Law Initiative Blog*, 25 January 2023), https://rli.blogs.sas.ac.uk/2023/01/25/feminism-as-method-how-do-we-do-gender-in-international-refugee-law/, accessed 1 February 2023.

213 Veronica Fynn Bruey and others, 'Rewriting Refugee Law: Centring Refugee Knowledges and Lived Experience' (2024) 43 Refugee Survey Quarterly 115, 118.

214 Rose Jaji, 'Ethics and Intellectual Harm in Research with Refugees' (*Kujenga Amani*, 21 February 2024), https://kujenga-amani.ssrc.org/2024/02/21/ethics-and-intellectual-harm-in-research-with-refugees, accessed 20 March 2024; Fynn Bruey and others (n 45) 125.

215 Leah Bassel, 'Why a Politics of Listening?' in Leah Bassel, *The Politics of Listening: Possibilities and Challenges for Democratic Life* (Palgrave Macmillan UK 2017) 6; Ogg (n 212).

216 Lokot (n 212) 474.

217 Rachel McKinnon, 'Epistemic Injustice' (2016) 11 Philosophy Compass 437, 438.

218 Sandra Harding (ed), 'Introduction: Is There a Feminist Method?' in Sandra Harding, *Feminism and Methodology: Social Science Issues* (Highlighting edition, Indiana University Press 1988) 8–9.

Desmet's users' perspective,[219] I hereby go beyond traditional approaches in legal scholarship that consider the law, instead of the people implementing it, the subject of inquiry.[220]

The method of listening through interviews, both to applicants for international protection and the asylum authorities assessing their flight stories, does not come without ethical challenges. However, as Gardî states, legal research should have an ambition to 'not simply "recount the status quo" but also [to challenge] it, and in so doing, [to set] the future research agenda for international refugee law.'[221] She adds: 'It is critical [...] [to incorporate] a more balanced consideration of refugee voices. The methodological challenges this entails should not prevent the legal community from championing meaningful refugee participation in scholarship.'[222] Below, I will outline the ethical framework I used to 'listen' in the context of this research, as well as my internal reflections on the challenges that came with doing so. This methodological approach was described in detail in an application approved by the Law Faculty's Ethical Commission before the start of the interviews. Large parts of this section were also published as a chapter in a handbook named 'Feminist and Queer Research Methods in Law' (in Dutch).[223]

3.1. ETHICAL CONSIDERATIONS WHEN LISTENING TO APPLICANTS FOR INTERNATIONAL PROTECTION

3.1.1. ON EPISTEMIC INJUSTICE & FEMINIST STANDPOINT THEORY

a) Epistemic Injustice

Power structures in asylum procedures are governed by epistemic processes that determine what counts as knowledge.[224] When flight stories are thereby wrongly labelled non-credible, undermining applicants' capacity as knowledge

219 Ellen Desmet, 'Analysing Users' Trajectories in Human Rights: A Conceptual Exploration and Research Agenda' (2014) 8 Human Rights & International Legal Discourse 121, 122.

220 Oxford (n 11) 158.

221 Rêz Gardî, 'Foreword' in Cathryn Costello, Michelle Foster and Jane McAdam (eds), *The Oxford Handbook of International Refugee Law* (Oxford University Press 2021) viii.

222 *Ibid.*

223 Lore Roels, 'Het Cassandracomplex in Gendergerelateerde Asielprocedures: Luisteren als feministische methode in onderzoek over verkrachtingsmythologie' in Pieter Cannoot, Elise Goossens and Marie Spinoy (eds), *Feministische en queer onderzoeksmethoden in het recht* (Intersentia 2025).

224 Patricia Hill Collins, *Black Feminist Thought: Knowledge, Consciousness, and the Politics of Empowerment* (Routledge 1990) 270; McKinnon (n 217) 438.

producers, we speak of a form of epistemic injustice,[225] namely 'testimonial injustice'.[226] Sometimes, this is preceded by another kind of epistemic injustice: 'hermeneutical injustice', when one's marginalised position deprives a person of the cognitive interpretive resources to give dominantly accepted words to their own experiences.[227] For example, it appears that applicants cannot always (immediately) frame the SGBV in their flight stories as persecution that could give rise to international protection. This may be because the SGBV form is culturally embedded and/or not criminalised in their country of origin (e.g. marital rape, GMC, forced marriage, …) or because they are not familiar with the legal terms of the refugee definition.[228]

Diana, fleeing her (sexually) abusive forced ex-husband in Albania, for example explained: 'Maybe I didn't explain it properly the first time. When I did the interview, I had no help. With the lawyer I didn't have the chance to talk about it.'[229] Sofia, fleeing (child) sexual abuse by her father in Honduras, also stated: 'When I arrived here I didn't know there was such a thing as applying for asylum, I didn't want to share my story, I was ashamed and it didn't occur to me to ask.'[230] The psychological difficulties of retrieving traumatic memories in the stressful setting of a personal (asylum) interview or hearing can also lead to hermeneutical injustice, as illustrated by Vera (see Part II, Chapter 2.1), who stated that she blacked out during her interview at the IO and that she had forgotten everything, even her own name.[231]

A particular form of hermeneutical injustice occurs when marginalised groups can give words to their experiences, but dominant situated actors refuse to recognise them as knowledge. Thus, a dominant structure, such as that of the asylum procedure, can misinterpret and/or ignore (parts of) reality.[232] Pohlhaus Jr. termed this as 'wilful hermeneutical ignorance'.[233] In the case of Amani mentioned above, the CGRS (among other elements) argued that the fact that

---

225 Gayatri Chakravorty Spivak, 'Can the Subaltern Speak?' in Cary Nelson and Lawrence Grossberg (eds), *Marxism and the interpretation of culture* (University of Illinois Press 1988) 271; Enrique Galván-Álvarez, 'Epistemic Violence and Retaliation: The Issue of Knowledges in "Mother India" / Violencia y Venganza Epistemológica: La Cuestión de Las Formas de Conocimiento En Mother India' (2010) 32 Atlantis 11, 12; Benslama-Dabdoub (n 28) 55.

226 Miranda Fricker, *Epistemic Injustice: Power and the Ethics of Knowing* (Oxford University Press 2007) 5 & 30; McKinnon (n 217) 439.

227 Fricker (n 226) 1.

228 Oxford (n 11) 162 & 169–170.

229 NA001_B_1973_F_Albania_RSA_VGNT_FM_DV_NL_[01:15:52].

230 NH003_1991_F_Honduras_RSA_DV_NL_p. 3.

231 NA016_1990_F_Albania_RSA_VGNT_DV_NL_[00:06:45].

232 Rebecca Mason, 'Two Kinds of Unknowing' (2011) 26 Hypatia 294, 306.

233 Gaile Pohlhaus Jr., 'Relational Knowing and Epistemic Injustice: Toward a Theory of "Willful Hermeneutical Ignorance"' (2012) 27 Hypatia 715, 715; McKinnon (n 217) 442.

she went to her religious community alone testified to an independence difficult to reconcile with victimisation of (child) sexual abuse.[234]

However, in the personal interview with the CGRS, she made sense of her motivations in the following words: 'Because I thought [my stepfather] might come into [my room] at night, [...] I was so afraid of what might happen, that I had developed the habit of regularly going to prayer vigils at church and if there was no vigil, I went to funerals. Sometimes I didn't even know the family or the person who had died, but I would go there, out of fear of spending the night at home.'[235] This explanation is cast aside through acceptance of the myth that resourceful applicants do not need international protection against SGBV (Part III, Chapter 2).[236] The risk for applicants who fall outside the ideal 'vulnerable victim' image[237] to be denied protection is all the greater for those whom Mohanty, in her postcolonial critique, calls 'Third World Women': a group misperceived in Western (feminist) thinking as homogeneous and merely dependent and powerless.[238]

b) Feminist Standpoint Theory

There is also a danger in academic research of reproducing colonial development thinking by adopting methodologies that assume that (often white) academic 'experts', who do not share their participants' experiences, understand their problems better than they themselves do.[239] Feminist standpoint theory offers a response to this kind of epistemic violence that denies participants the right to analyse their own experiences.[240] This theory has its origins in black feminist thought and is based on the propositions that 1) knowledge is socially situated; 2) marginalised groups are more aware of oppressive structures, from both their own position and that of the dominant group; and 3) research on such power relations should start from the point of view of these marginalised groups.[241] Standpoint theories illustrate how a socio-politically disadvantaged position can result in an epistemic advantage,[242] given marginalised groups must understand

---

234 NC004_CGRS 1 (refusal)_1991_F_DRC_RSA_DV_21/12/2021_FR_NANSEN_https://www.rvv-cce.be/sites/default/files/arr/a266712.an_.pdf_p. 4.

235 NC004_ CGRS interview 1_1991_F_DRC_RSA_DV_FR_p. 15.

236 NC004_CGRS 1 (refusal)_1991_F_DRC_RSA_DV_21/12/2021_FR_NANSEN_p. 4.; Ben-David and Schneider (n 3) 386.

237 Christie (n 4); Randall (n 4).

238 Chandra Talpade Mohanty, 'Under Western Eyes: Feminist Scholarship and Colonial Discourses' (1988) 30 Feminist Review 61, 67; Eileen Pittaway and Linda Albina Bartolomei, *Only Rape! Human Rights and Gender Equality for Refugee Women: From Refugee Camps to the United Nations* (Springer Nature 2023) 119.

239 Spivak (n 225); Pittaway and Bartolomei (n 238) 119.

240 Jaji (n 214).

241 Collins (n 224) 317; Tracy Bowell, 'Feminist Standpoint Theory' (*Internet Encyclopedia of Philosophy: A Peer-Reviewed Academic Resource*, 2022), https://iep.utm.edu/fem-stan/.

242 Sandra Harding, 'The Feminist Standpoint Theory Reader: Intellectual and Political Controversies' 7–8, http://catdir.loc.gov/catdir/toc/ecip043/2003009900.html.

the systems of their oppression from the point of view of both the oppressed and the oppressor in order to survive. This understanding is neither required of, nor available to dominant groups.[243]

Similarly, applicants for international protection fleeing SGBV occupy a unique position in the asylum system. They reason not only from their own experiences, but often from the point of view of the asylum authorities who have to assess their application. This epistemic advantage is demonstrated by Nino, who tried to explain to the asylum authorities the patriarchal nature of Georgian society and the reason why she could not move away from her violent ex-husband: 'In the first year when I left my husband, I changed my address seven times and he found me every time. [...] I have not been able to explain [to the asylum authorities] the mentality in Georgia, clearly not. [...] It is a free and safe country here, they cannot understand my problem.'[244]

Patricia Hill Collins describes how such a position generates essential knowledge for informed action.[245] Thus, applicants fleeing SGBV should be at the centre of research that analyses their problems and identifies solutions.[246] On the good practice of interdisciplinary decision making in asylum procedures, Nino suggested for example: 'When they ask all these questions during the interview, during the hearing, they should also invite a psychologist. That way the psychologist can explain [...] what [it] [...] might feel [...] [like to answer] such questions for someone who comes from a country with such a [patriarchal] mentality.'[247]

c) *Positionality*

I myself was born in a Western country where I also live and work, as a white woman with the resulting gender-related experiences, but of a very different nature than the SGBV forms that applicants confided to me in our conversations. As a researcher, I cannot step outside my own social position,[248] which makes it impossible to identify, from my positionality and purely on the basis of a literature analysis, the SGBV myths that make (potential) survivors/victims fleeing SGBV feel not or misunderstood in asylum procedures.[249] However,

243 Bowell (n 241).

244 NGe014_1975_F_Georgia_RSA_DV_NL_[00:38:41].

245 Collins (n 224) 317; Michelle Van Impe, 'Narratieve criminologie meets participatief actieonderzoek' (2020) 10 Tijdschrift over Cultuur & Criminaliteit 97, 100.

246 Johnsson (n 36) 11.

247 NGe014_1975_F_Georgia_RSA_DV_NL_[00:42:09].

248 Pohlhaus Jr. (n 233) 732.

249 Harding, 'Introduction: Is There a Feminist Method?' (n 218) 9; Rebecca Campbell and others, 'Training Interviewers for Research on Sexual Violence A Qualitative Study of Rape Survivors' Recommendations for Interview Practice' (2009) 15 Violence Against Women 594, 610.

I can, what Harding refers to as, 'participate in a critical standpoint' by actively learning how this reality is shaped from the marginalised experiences of those who went through the procedure.[250]

This need for participation in critical standpoints justifies interviews with applicants about traumatic experiences such as SGBV in research contexts, provided this is done in an ethical and reciprocal way (see Chapter 3.1.2 below). Which knowledge is revealed and which is ignored thus depends on the active will to step outside one's social position, rather than on that position as such. As a result, ignorance of marginalised views is not something one is condemned to due to a dominant position, but rather something one chooses to do by not listening.[251]

d) *Listening as a Condition for Hearing*

Listening as a method does not imply, neither in research, nor in the asylum procedure, that the facts in flight stories are necessarily considered true. Instead of being concerned with their truthfulness, centralising listening must enable a setting in which the stories can first and foremost be told and heard. Only upon this condition can one's factual account in an asylum procedure be assessed against the legal conditions in the refugee definition. According to the abovementioned evaluation report of GREVIO[252] and the EU Procedures Directive and Regulation,[253] asylum authorities should indeed offer applicants fleeing SGBV optimal support for disclosure of SGBV experiences throughout the asylum procedure.

Only in this way can they fulfil their (inter)national legal obligations: to examine the subjective element in the well-foundedness of a person's fear of persecution[254] and their duty of cooperation, which binds them to assess the relevant elements in an application,[255] including the personal circumstances and statements made by applicants.[256] Precisely to make this possible, asylum authorities cannot afford to remain in the dark about applicants' marginalised views by starting to argue before starting to listen.

---

250 Sandra Harding, *Whose Science? Whose Knowledge?: Thinking from Women's Lives* (Cornell University Press 1991) 272–295; Fynn Bruey and others (n 213) 123; Linda Baker and others, 'Trauma- and Violence-Informed Interview Strategies in Work with Survivors of Gender-Based Violence' (Learning Network 2020) 2.

251 Pohlhaus Jr. (n 233) 731–732.

252 Group of Experts on Action against Violence against Women and Domestic Violence (GREVIO) (n 22) 63.

253 Art. 15(3)a EU Procedures Directive; Art. 13(7)a EU Asylum Procedures Regulation.

254 Art. 1, A, (2) UN Refugee Convention; UNHCR, *Handbook on Procedures and Criteria for Determining Refugee Status under the 1951 Convention and the 1967 Protocol Relating to the Status of Refugees* (UNHCR (United Nations High Commissioner for Refugees) 2019) paras 37–41.

255 Art. 4(1) EU Qualification Directive.

256 Art. 48/6, § 5 Belgian Aliens Act.

Nevertheless, throughout the fieldwork for this research, I experienced first-hand how difficult it is, as a researcher/interviewer, to exclude any reflections on interviewees' credibility in an interview on credibility assessments themselves (by asylum authorities). In my experience, given the ingrained nature of rape myths in our collective thinking (see Chapter 1.3 of this Part), researching rape mythology does not make you immune to its (subconscious) impact, even when the research design is built around the concept. If anything, it makes you more aware of the need for active resistance against it.[257] This realisation contributed to my personal understanding of the complexity of the task of interviewers at the CGRS and judges during a hearing, especially when applicants have difficulty accessing their memories and/or expressing themselves due to shame, trauma, or other psychological problems.

e) Limits to Listening as a Method

Another important note is that listening as a feminist method will always remain a limited way of centralising expertise by experience in research.[258] While the standpoints of SGBV survivors/victims directly shaped the hypotheses that guided this research, the analyses remained an interpretation of their words.[259] More structurally participatory methodologies are complicated by factors that practically constrain academic research in general[260] (e.g. selection procedures for funding as in the case of this research, which require research proposals to be fully developed before they can be launched), but more importantly, the precarious circumstances in which applicants navigate through the asylum procedure and the emotional toll it takes to instrumentalise traumatic experiences to advocate for change.

The applicants I listened to were often in the middle of the asylum procedure and naturally prioritised their quest for a stable residence status over the quest for more gender-sensitive asylum procedures in general. For example, at the end of our conversation, Nino stated: 'I don't want to put on a show or drama myself [and thus jeopardise my own case]. If you can make it clear [to the asylum authorities] […] I would be very grateful.'[261] However, without assuming this hierarchy of priorities, I shared the provisional research findings with all participants I interviewed, both in accessible summarised (see Figure 16 in the

257 For example, despite my awareness of the fact that traumatic memories are per definition incoherent and fragmented (see Part III, Chapter 3.2.2), it proved more difficult than expected to cancel out any thoughts on credibility when hearing stories that lacked central details and chronology.

258 Gardî (n 221) viii.

259 Linda Alcoff, 'The Problem of Speaking for Others' [1991] Cultural Critique 5, 9.

260 Aminath Nisha Zadhy-Çepoğlu, 'Reflexive Reciprocity under an Ethics of Care: Reflections from the Field for Refugee Studies' [2023] Migration Studies 1, 14.

261 NGe014_1975_F_Georgia_RSA_DV_NL_[01:03:52].

Annex) and in full format, offering to meet up and discuss them in person. This way, those who wished to do so could give their insights and help shape the final findings of the research.[262]

While some applicants simply took note of the (written) results I shared with them, others, such as Nino, preferred to discuss them in person. Interestingly, her earlier reluctance to jeopardise her own case had evolved by that point. She now spoke of being contacted by a journalist to possibly bring her case to the attention of the media. As she stated, this was after her and her daughter's first applications had been refused and their subsequent applications had been found inadmissible. This not only illustrates how applicants' priorities may shift as they navigate through asylum procedures (and thereby lose hope, as her daughter confirmed), but also serves as a reminder for researchers not to assume the ways in which participants might want to engage with research (results) in their place.

As a researcher, with no experience of the struggle to flee SGBV and navigating an asylum procedure,[263] I am bound to speak about (but not for[264]) the applicants I listened to. However, I can use my position, in a system where I am given time and resources to produce scientific knowledge, to mobilise the views of applicants as pragmatic output to generate social change.

3.1.2. ON ETHICS OF CARE & RECIPROCAL ACTION RESEARCH

While decision makers in the asylum procedure are expected to adopt trauma- and gender-sensitive methods and pursue the traditional 'do no harm' principle[265] when interacting with applicants, academic research bears the responsibility of going beyond these requirements. Feminist research is distinguished by the ways in which it applies traditional methods.[266] For this research, these ways were defined by feminist scholarship on ethics of care and reciprocal action research.

a) *Ethics of Care*

I chose to place care, empathy, and warmth for participants at its centre.[267] Both before, during and after the interviews, I built care into the methodology. First, I

262 Ulrike Krause, Franzisca Zanker and Christiane Fröhlich, 'Ethics Guidelines of the German Network for Forced Migration Studies' (German Network for Forced Migration Studies 2024) 14.

263 Bowell (n 241) 4.

264 Alcoff (n 259) 7; Ogg (n 212).

265 Richard Hugman, Eileen Pittaway and Linda Bartolomei, 'When "Do No Harm" Is Not Enough: The Ethics of Research with Refugees and Other Vulnerable Groups' (2011) 41 The British Journal of Social Work 1271, 1271.

266 Ogg (n 212); Harding, 'Introduction: Is There a Feminist Method?' (n 218) 2.

267 Lokot (n 212) 469; Jaji (n 214); Zadhy-Çepoğlu (n 260) 2; Tally Kritzman-Amir, 'Not in My Backyard: On the Morality of Responsibility Sharing in Refugee Law' (2009) 34 Brooklyn Journal of International Law 355, 11; Christina Clark-Kazak, 'Ethical Considerations: Research

attended several intensive and practice-oriented trainings on trauma and gender-sensitive interviewing of SGBV survivors/victims (with a migration background) beforehand.[268] This is the essential condition for ethically interviewing participants on SGBV experiences and responding to voices that rightly point out the risks of doing so.[269]

These trainings taught me the necessary skills to recognise and acknowledge survivors/victims in an empathetic way, to support them in their disclosures, to refer them to professional help if necessary, and to avoid re-traumatisation. Vicarious or secondary trauma[270] (see Chapter 4.4 of this part), the impact of listening to traumatic stories on the mental wellbeing and capacity to provide care of professionals and researchers, were also addressed.[271] Therefore, I made space for self-care, debriefing and sharing emotions evoked by these stories. These trainings enabled me to create a trauma-sensitive and safe setting[272] within which a kind of listening could take place that prioritised care for both interviewees and interviewer.

b) *No Active Recruitment of Participants*

I deliberately did not use an active recruitment strategy to find interview participants. In the drive for data collection, research interactions with people

with People in Situations of Forced Migration' (2017) 33 Refuge: Canada's Journal on Refugees / Refuge : revue canadienne sur les réfugiés 11, 12; Campbell and others (n 249) 595 & 610; Loraine Masiya Mponela, '"Our Wish Is To Be Human Again": Refugee Women Speaking Up and Taking Space' (2022) 41 Refugee Survey Quarterly 381, 390.

268 I.e. Leni Linthout and others, 'INHeRE E-Learning Course on Sexual Violence & Migration (International Centre for Reproductive Health at Ghent University)' (*Inclusive Holistic Care for Migrant victims of sexual violence (INHeRE)*, 2021), www.icrhb.org/storage/attachments/attachment/72.pdf?t=1633358005; Radboud universitair medisch centrum, 'Scholing Huiselijk en seksueel geweld: Over de cursus' (2022), www.radboudumc.nl/onderwijs/scholingen/huiselijk-en-seksueel-geweld/over-de-cursus; Thomas More Hogeschool, 'Postgraduaat Forensische Psychodiagnostiek en Counseling (module 8: slachtofferschap in forensische context)' (2022), https://thomasmore.be/nl/opleidingen/postgraduaat/forensische-psychodiagnostiek-en-counseling/antwerpen/basistraject; University of Strathclyde, 'Understanding Violence Against Women: Myths and Realities' (*FutureLearn*, 2022), www.futurelearn.com/courses/understanding-violence-against-women/6; Lotte De Schrijver, International Centre for Reproductive Health (ICRH), and Universiteit Gent, 'Training Voor Interviews Rond Seksueel Geweld' (2022).

269 Jasmin Lilian Diab and Dana Al-Azzeh, 'Inclusive Inquiry: A Compassionate Journey in Trauma-Informed Qualitative Research with GBV Survivors from Displaced Communities' (2024) 15 Frontiers in Psychology 1, 1; Clark-Kazak (n 267) 11–13; Baker and others (n 250) 1; Jamie Gorman, 'Beyond Extractivism in Research with Communities and Movements' (*The Commons: Social Change Library*, 23 January 2024) 4, https://commonslibrary.org/beyond-extractivism-in-research-with-communities-and-movements/; Baker and others (n 250) 2; World Health Organization (WHO), 'Ethical and Safety Recommendations for Researching, Documenting and Monitoring Sexual Violence in Emergencies' (2007) 9.

270 Gökhan Ebren, Melis Demircioğlu and Okan Cem Çırakoğlu, 'A Neglected Aspect of Refugee Relief Works: Secondary and Vicarious Traumatic Stress' (2022) 35 Journal of Traumatic Stress 891, 891.

271 Baker and others (n 250) 5.

272 *Ibid.* 1 & 3.

on the move can become exploitative and sterile, aimed at conducting as many interviews as possible in as little time as possible.[273] I did not prioritise a quantitative goal, nor did data saturation[274] constitute a target in itself. In doing so, I wanted to prevent applicants from having to recount traumatic experiences solely for the sake of achieving research goals. Instead of pursuing data saturation, I recognise, in line with third wave feminism, that an exhaustive and homogenous representation of SGBV experiences is illusory.[275] Instead of a universal truth, I consider the standpoints of a select number of applicants as essential for uncovering the power structures within their asylum procedures.[276] Thus, the objective of representative generalisability makes room for the value of expertise by experience in concrete, lived stories that can always be enriched by new standpoints in future research (see Part V, Chapter 1).

The interviews took place during sixteen months (two days a week on average) of participatory fieldwork at a Brussels-based NGO called NANSEN, a centre of legal expertise on international protection (see Chapter 4.2 of this part) providing legal assistance to applicants for international protection and/or their lawyers.[277] NANSEN NGO not only provides support by intervening in individual asylum procedures as implementing partner of UNHCR, but also works on a structural level by making expertise available to the field (e.g. through reports, training, consultations with asylum authorities, and interventions in strategic procedures). In doing so, the NGO focuses in particular on survivors/victims of torture, including SGBV.

I only organised interviews after applicants contacted the NGO on their own initiative to obtain legal support and confirmed (themselves or through their lawyer, psychologist, social worker, …) that they had sufficient mental headspace and energy to discuss their asylum procedure. One of the applicants I contacted for an interview expressed not feeling in a state to talk about her story,[278] the other eight did. The interview was thus primarily aimed at facilitating their legal support. Only secondarily, applicants could opt to include their answers in the research as data. In line with Clark-Kazak's ethical guidelines for research

273 Lokot (n 212) 467–468 & 472–473; Halleh Ghorashi, 'Giving Silence a Chance: The Importance of Life Stories for Research on Refugees' (2008) 21 Journal of Refugee Studies 117, 118.

274 Data saturation is achieved at 'the point in data collection and analysis at which new information produces little or no change […] [and] a reliable sense of thematic exhaustion and variability within [the] dataset' is achieved. Greg Guest, Arwen Bunce and Laura Johnson, 'How Many Interviews Are Enough?: An Experiment with Data Saturation and Variability' (2006) 18 Field Methods 59, 65.

275 Harding, 'Introduction: Is There a Feminist Method?' (n 218) 7.

276 Nicola Gavey, 'Feminist Poststructuralism and Discourse Analysis: Contributions to Feminist Psychology' (1989) 13 Psychology of Women Quarterly 459, 463; Bowell (n 241) 11.

277 NANSEN, 'NANSEN – Assistance and Legal Aid for Refugees – Belgium' (*NANSEN*), https://nansen-refugee.be/en/.

278 NT015_1996_F_Turkey_RSA_FM_FR.

on forced migration, I thus prioritised the applicants' wellbeing over research objectives.[279]

c) Informed Consent

In explaining[280] the research with a view to obtaining informed consent,[281] I paid particular attention to this potentially dual role of the interview and the fact that their choice to (not) participate in the research would have no impact on the NGO's legal support.[282] In doing so, I weighed the risk that applicants would nevertheless feel inclined to participate (to get legal support) against respect for their ability to make this choice for themselves based on the information given, in favour of the latter. After the first interview, it appeared more appropriate to record participants' informed consent orally instead of in writing. I experienced my own and the applicant's discomfort when using a written informed consent form in the context of research on forced displacement. As Clark-Kazak points out: '[d]isplaced people who have had negative interactions with authorities and/or from different cultural traditions may be suspicious of written consent forms.'[283] The sensitive interview topic, namely gender-related flight stories, reinforces this conclusion. Thus, I obtained an amendment allowing the use of oral informed consent from the Law Faculty's Ethical Commission.

I used an information sheet, tailored to the subject by stressing: the potential risks of recalling traumatic memories while participating; the confidentiality of the interview; the principal purpose of the questions (legal support) and that repeating the authorities' argumentation in questions did not equal my endorsement of it; applicants' full control over their (free) narrative, the details they do (not) disclose, and timing and pace of the interview; the revocability of their participation at any time without justification; and the option to receive any psychosocial or other support (upon referral) afterwards.[284]

I explained the information sheet verbally beforehand, handed a (translated) written version to the applicants, and recorded their oral informed consent. I asked about their wish to participate at the end of the interview, once they had a full view on the answers that could be included/excluded. Participants were

279 Clark-Kazak (n 267) 12.

280 Silvia Lamonaca and others, 'Good Practice Tool for Police Hearings with Migrant, Applicant for International Protection, Refugee (MAR), Trafficked, and LGBT+ Victims of Sexual Violence' (Payoke & ICRH, Ghent University 2021) 37–38.

281 *Ibid.* 30.

282 Clark-Kazak (n 267) 12.

283 *Ibid.*

284 Lamonaca and others (n 280) 20, 30 & 38; Clark-Kazak (n 267) 11–13; United Nations Office on Drugs and Crime (UNODC), 'Resource Book for Trainers on Effective Prosecution Responses to Violence against Women and Girls' (2017) 115; Baker and others (n 250) 5; Campbell and others (n 249) 596 & 611.

given the choice of having their responses written down via notes or recorded, upon which the audio recordings were destroyed after transcription (except for the part where the informed consent was expressed). All applicants invited for an interview decided to participate in the research and all interviews except one were recorded and transcribed afterwards.

When I encountered a relevant case during the fieldwork, but an interview could not be organised (e.g. because they did not feel ready to do so, the NGO could not provide useful support, or it was an archived case), I included the personal interview already conducted at the CGRS in the research. While the facts (as described in decisions/judgements) in these files are in any case made public (in a pseudonymised manner) in the CALL's online database[285] (if applicants appeal), this is not the case for the 'raw' notes of the personal interview at the CGRS. To allow this valuable representation of the applicants' standpoint during their personal interview to be included in the research, the NGO's mandate served as consent.

Each applicant whose case I analysed signed this mandate, in which they gave permission to share their data for scientific research. This was possible under the condition of confidentiality by the scientific partner, according to the legal framework of the EU General Data Protection Regulation,[286] and within the framework of a pre-agreed memorandum of understanding between the research team and the NGO. While these applicants did not risk re-traumatisation by having another conversation about their flight stories, including the CGRS' personal interviews without direct informed consent from these applicants nonetheless raised ethical questions.

In theory they agreed to the processing of their data, but a written form serving as a condition for their legal support does not equal an orally clarified informed consent form tailored specifically to the research that they are consenting to participate in. To further complicate this dilemma, the NGO's mandate does not authorise sharing their contact details, preventing me from reaching out to explain my research and obtain their direct consent. At the same time, excluding these personal interviews would mean keeping narratives silent that contribute to a full understanding of their standpoint and possibly to improving refugee status determination for applicants with similar experiences. Unable to straightforwardly resolve this tension, I acknowledge this limitation and the complexity of upholding ethical standards in research that seeks to

---

285 The CALL maintains a public online database, in which it is legally required to publish its jurisprudence, usually containing the CGRS decision against which the appeal is lodged. Art. 39/65 Belgian Aliens Act; Council for Alien Law Litigation (CALL), 'Arresten', www.rvv-cce.be/nl/arr.

286 Regulation on the protection of natural persons with regard to the processing of personal data and on the free movement of such data, and repealing Directive 95/46/EC (GDPR) 2016 (Official Journal of the European Union L 119/1).

include participants who, often only briefly and with varying priorities and mental states, come into contact with the NGO where the fieldwork took place.

d) Interpreters & Location

The Interviews I conducted myself took place in a private and quiet room at the NGO, with an interpreter (when needed) contacted through an organisation the NGO usually works with, and in the presence of a coworker of the NGO for the first two. It is important to note that, although I prepared myself thoroughly for the interviews through training on trauma and gender-sensitive interviewing, this was not the case for the three interpreters I worked with. The risk of re-traumatisation by intermediaries such as interpreters should not be underestimated, especially for flight stories concerning SGBV, as Maryns argues.[287] Also, ideally, the interview could have taken place in a warmer, less corporate setting. I gave applicants the choice to organise the interview at a location and with an interpreter (if necessary) of their choice, but none of them chose to do so, except one applicant bringing her sister to interpret. Except in this latter case, both the choice of interpreters and location were guided by the pragmatic circumstances of the fieldwork.

I followed the NGO's usual interview setting and organisation, recognising that finding interpreters was already difficult, let alone with the additional requirement of specific trauma-/gender sensitivity training. In addition, my observations of the NGO's functioning throughout the fieldwork had given me confidence in their approach, abiding to their own ethical standards and with an experienced team of professionals. They were trained to work with vulnerable persons, supported by external psychological supervision with attention to vicarious trauma, and above all approaching applicants with a warm and empathetic attitude, constituting an essential element of the ethics of care approach in my own research.

I invited an interpreter only when the conversation could not take place in French or English, I focused on my own warm reception of applicants and was attentive to possibly differing attitudes of interpreters. None of the interpreters I worked with (three in total, including the abovementioned sister) acted in a way that seemed to interfere with my own approach. One of them seemed to add information to the answers of the applicant herself, which I noted in the interview transcript.[288]

---

287 Katrijn Maryns, 'Disclosure and (Re)Performance of Gender-Based Evidence in an Interpreter-Mediated Asylum Interview' (2013) 17 Journal of Sociolinguistics 661, 682–683.

288 E.g. NGe014_1975_F_Georgia_RSA_DV_NL_[00:16:07].

e) *Minor Participants*

Applicants were free to bring a trustee to the interview, such as a friend, family member, social worker, ...[289] This happened in two cases: Vera,[290] who brought her sister, and Diana,[291] who brought her 16-year-old daughter Erina.[292] The duo interview with Diana and Erina is a telling example of how fieldwork may give rise to unpredictable situations, which an Ethical Commission application cannot always anticipate. While I did not initially intend to interview minors, Diana and Erina actively requested an interview together. At the time, I conducted the interview in any case for the purpose of their legal support by NANSEN NGO.

After their expression of wanting to participate in the research, I considered that the following circumstances could justify the inclusion of Erina in the interview sample. From the case file I read beforehand, I knew Erina's own experiences did not involve direct sexual violence but did occur within a context of domestic and sexual violence against her mother. She had the age of sexual majority and sexual self-determination according to Belgian law[293] (16 years) and Albanian law[294] (14 years) at the time of the interview. Both Diana (as her guardian) and Erina gave their written (the NGO's mandate) and verbal informed consent. This parental and individual consent is considered a best practice in the literature on ethical research with children.[295] The trainings I took in preparation of the interviews also specifically focused on SGBV against minors.[296] Erina also explicitly indicated that she wanted to tell her part of the story herself.

At the end of the conversation, Diana said about Erina: 'Sometimes I would talk to her about things like that and she would always say, "leave it, we'll talk about something else." [...] After the first negative decision [...] it was she who made the decision [to want to talk about it]', to which Erina confirmed: 'Yes, I really wanted to try [to talk about it] [...] that's why I said that if [you have]

289 Baker and others (n 250) 3.

290 NA016_1990_F_Albania_RSA_VGNT_DV_NL.

291 NA001_B_1973_F_Albania_RSA_VGNT_FM_DV_NL.

292 NA001_A_2006_F_Albania_RSA_VGNT_FM_DV_NL_MINOR.

293 Art. 417/6 Strafwetboek 1867 (Belgisch Staatsblad of 9 June 1867, p 3133).

294 Girls Not Brides, 'Albania' (*Girls Not Brides*, 1 January 2014), www.girlsnotbrides.org/learning-resources/child-marriage-atlas/regions-and-countries/albania/.

295 Anne Graham and others, *Ethical Research Involving Children* (UNICEF Office of Research – Innocenti 2013) 56.

296 Training Radboud University Medical Center: 2nd course day 'Children in distress: child abuse' and 4th course day 'Caring for sexual violence in children and adults'; Postgraduate Forensic Psychodiagnostics and Counselling Thomas More Module 8: 3rd class 'Trauma issues in minors' and 4th class 'Family Justice Centre Veilig Thuis Antwerp'. Radboud universitair medisch centrum (n 268); Thomas More Hogeschool (n 268); University of Strathclyde (n 268).

any questions about the story, don't hesitate, because I tried to say what I thought was important [in the personal interview at the CGRS], but [...] I think I didn't give enough details, maybe [...] also because of the stress since it was the first time after three years that I had to talk about it again.'[297] The inclusion of Erina's interview as data in the research was presented to and eventually validated by the Law Faculty's Ethical Commission.

f) Trauma- & Gender-Sensitive Interviewing Techniques

I collected open-ended questions for the interviews with particular care to: avoid survivor/victim-blaming[298] or suggestive questioning;[299] hand over control to applicants of their own stories;[300] and create a safe environment.[301] In conducting the semi-structured interviews, I paid specific attention to leaving room for a free narrative,[302] focusing on feelings, thought processes, and often sensorily encoded elements in traumatic memories (instead of chronology, consistency or contextual details,[303] see Part III, Chapter 3.2.2). Although SGBV-related flight stories prompted the interviews, the questions did not seek to discuss the violence itself.[304] The case files contained the notes of the CGRS' personal interview and often the facts as described in the decision(s) by CGRS (and CALL). Thanks to this prior knowledge, the interview did not focus on the details of the violence, but on the ways in which applicants felt (mis)understood by the asylum authorities.

Thus, the research tried not to add to the burden of having to repeat a flight story over and over again to different actors throughout the asylum system.[305] As Malkki stated from personal experience: in research with people on the move, it is essential to 'leave some stones unturned' and 'not pry'.[306] However, where applicants themselves insisted, I did make space for discussing details, so as not to fill in what they perceived as retraumatising and what not. For some survivors/victims, uninvolved third parties can play a role in validating feelings stemming from violence.[307] Research also shows that SGBV survivors/victims can value

297 NA001_A/B_2006/1973_F_Albania_RSA_VGNT_FM_DV_NL [01:29:37].
298 Baker and others (n 250) 4; International Association of Chiefs of Police (IACP), 'Successful Trauma Informed Victim Interviewing' (2020) 1; Keygnaert and Linthout (n 177) 21.
299 Lamonaca and others (n 280) 30.
300 *Ibid.* 38.
301 Baker and others (n 250) 1 & 3.
302 United Nations Office on Drugs and Crime (UNODC) (n 284) 115.
303 Keygnaert and Linthout (n 177) 22.
304 Clark-Kazak (n 267) 13.
305 *Ibid.* 11.
306 Liisa H Malkki, *Purity and Exile: Violence, Memory, and National Cosmology among Hutu Refugees in Tanzania* (University of Chicago Press 1995) 51.
307 Baker and others (n 250) 1.

participation in ethically conducted research into their experiences.[308] In Diana and Erina's duo interview, they spontaneously recounted in detail the domestic violence they experienced. At the end of the conversation, Diana said: 'It's good that [Erina] talks to you about it now. [...] This was [a] good [conversation], this way I can only talk to my psychologist and Erina added: '[This] felt like a conversation among friends.'[309]

When applicants expressed struggling with (how they (re)acted during or after) their SGBV experiences, I attempted to: exonerate applicants for what happened to them; stress the limits of individual impact on structural violence; normalise survivors'/victims' diverse and evolving (sub)conscious survival strategies; exculpate any reluctance to disclose and/or report SGBV; and recognise and support their accounts of resilience and coping.[310] Yet, occupying a position of comfort while engaging in these conversations sometimes left me feeling unsettled.

While 'participating in a critical standpoint'[311] is theoretically vital, in practice, the discrepancy between my own positionality and that of the applicants was confronting. Applying what I had learnt in the abovementioned trainings in practice underscored this tension: who was I to recognise their resilience, normalise their survival strategies, or tell them it was not their fault? At times, this awareness risked becoming immobilising to me. However, having colleagues and supervisors both at NANSEN NGO and at Ghent University to talk to and process these complexities with was invaluable, as was the commitment to not let discomfort dilute the broader aim of advocating for social change. Maintaining faith in the possibility of transformation, however incremental, became both a methodological and an ethical imperative.

g) Reciprocal Action Research

This aim of striving for social change lies at the heart of feminist action research,[312] seeing participants as partners who voluntarily share their stories and have the right to expect positive change as a result of their participation.[313] As with the ethics of care approach, action research reaches beyond minimising

308 *Ibid.*

309 NA001_A/B_2006/1973_F_Albania_RSA_VGNT_FM_DV_NL_[01:29:37].

310 Baker and others (n 250) 5; Keygnaert and Linthout (n 177) 23; United Nations Office on Drugs and Crime (UNODC) (n 284) 115.

311 Harding, *Whose Science?* (n 250) 272–295; Fynn Bruey and others (n 213) 123; Baker and others (n 250) 2.

312 Katrina M Powell and Pamela Takayoshi, 'Accepting Roles Created for Us: The Ethics of Reciprocity' (2003) 54 College Composition and Communication 394, 394; Lokot (n 212) 469; Pittaway and Bartolomei (n 238) 34 & 163; Van Impe (n 245) 106; Harding, 'Introduction: Is There a Feminist Method?' (n 218) 8.

313 Pittaway and Bartolomei (n 238) 5.

harm, to research that creates mutual benefit.[314] According to Van Impe, the power of telling personal and lived stories through research lies precisely in the fact that they can be a catalyst for social change.[315] The active role of researchers to initiate change within their field of research is criticised by some for allegedly compromising their neutrality and objectivity.[316]

Feminist action researchers, however, dismantle the very idea of neutrality and reciprocal action research is, in their view, the only responsible model for ethical research with marginalised groups.[317] According to this model, interviewing participants about personal and often traumatic experiences comes with the responsibility to generate research output with the aim of improving their situation. This output can take place both at individual and structural levels. The link between these two was for example expressed by Nino, who said: 'That's going to help me too, if it's going to make judges and people aware.'[318]

Researchers who want to 'give back' to participants should ask themselves what skills they can use to create added value for the target group they are researching.[319] This added value, in the form of time, care, empathy, information or practical support, can be a way of compensating for the power imbalance between researcher and participants.[320] On an individual level, I was able to use my legal training and interviewing skills to support NANSEN NGO in handling cases. For all applicants with SGBV-related flight stories who contacted the NGO during my fieldwork, I analysed the file and where possible organised the interview. I prepared the questions, conducted and recorded the interview, and provided them with the transcripts. In a number of files, I supported both the NGO and the applicants' lawyers by providing relevant source material, which I collected in my capacity as researcher, that they could use for reference in their legal advice or argumentation.

At the structural level, I opted for action suggested by the applicants with whom I spoke themselves, namely raising awareness about the causes, nature and consequences of SGBV among asylum authorities. Nino asked me to 'make it clear to [the asylum authorities], so that they can empathise with our stories, [...] do anything at all to help them understand.'[321] In addition to traditional academic output such as journal articles, book chapters, blog posts, or conference presentations, I have been committed to valorisation through lectures on SGBV and asylum to professionals working in asylum procedures and with

314 *Ibid.* 163.
315 Van Impe (n 245) 99.
316 Pittaway and Bartolomei (n 238) 33.
317 *Ibid.*
318 NGe014_1975_F_Georgia_RSA_DV_NL_[01:13:15].
319 Gorman (n 269).
320 Lokot (n 212) 469.
321 NGe014_1975_F_Georgia_RSA_DV_NL_[01:03:52].

applicants, including asylum authorities and lawyers.[322] In addition, together with a fellow researcher focusing on SOGI and asylum, I wrote a practical guide for lawyers on gender stereotyping in the Belgian asylum procedure.[323]

Lastly, next to the individual applicants, I also pursued reciprocity in my collaboration with NANSEN NGO. I did so by supporting them in their daily work during the fieldwork period, writing the abovementioned practical guide for lawyers at their request, and reporting back to them on the preliminary research results in order to obtain their input on the parts relating to the fieldwork.

To conclude, the combination of reflexivity about epistemic injustice, standpoint theory, positionality, ethics of care and reciprocity characterises the ethical framework for this research as a form of 'reflexive reciprocity'.[324] According to Zadhy-Çepoğlu, this is all the more essential in research with people fleeing SGBV, whose stories are the subject of credibility assessments at risk of epistemic injustice.

3.2. ETHICAL CONSIDERATIONS WHEN LISTENING TO ASYLUM OFFICIALS

3.2.1. KAP SURVEYS & INTERVIEWS WITH ASYLUM OFFICIALS

As mentioned above and according to Harding: 'If we want to understand how our daily experience arrives in the forms it does, it makes sense to examine critically the sources of social power,'[325] such as those who implement the law.[326] Unlike applicants, asylum officials participated in the interviews in their professional capacity and the content did not concern their own experiences with/fear of SGBV or other (traumatic) flight stories. However, the dominant position and professional capacity of these actors do not absolve research of commitment

322 E.g. Presentation on gender-related asylum procedures through NANSEN NGO (December 2022, https://nansen-refugee.be/nl/2022/11/24/intervisie-21-december-gender-en-asielprocedure/); Workshop on *safe spaces* in gender-sensitive interviews with persons fleeing SGBV through the international *Women in Refugee Law Network* (April 2024, https://wirl.org.uk/event/workshop-on-safe-spaces-in-gender-sensitive-interviews/); Internal presentation on gender and asylum to The Immigration & Protection Tribunal in Auckland, New Zealand (September 2024); Presentation to advocacy, magistrates and regional authorities in Belgium for an annual Migration and Migrant Law Chair on gender and asylum (December 2024, www.diekeure.be/professional/nl/product/leerstoel-migratie-en-migrantenrecht-2024/).

323 Lore Roels and Liselot Casteleyn, 'Practical guide for lawyers: gender-based proceedings for international protection (sexual and gender-based violence, sexual orientation and gender identity) '(Université de Gand 2023); Lore Roels and Liselot Casteleyn, 'Guide pratique pour les avocat-es: procédures de protection internationale liées au genre: violences sexuelles ou basées sur le genre, orientation sexuelle et identité de genre' (Université de Gand 2023).

324 Zadhy-Çepoğlu (n 260) 14.

325 Harding, 'Introduction: Is There a Feminist Method?' (n 218) 8–9.

326 Oxford (n 11) 159.

to ethical standards when directly involving their voices. Therefore, both the survey and interviews with asylum officials were organised and conducted in collaboration with and with approval of the Belgian asylum authorities in first instance (CGRS) and appeal (CALL), formalised through a memorandum of understanding.

To ensure individual informed consent of participants, both the KAP survey and interviews opened with an information sheet on the practicalities and purpose of the survey/interview and the research at large. It stressed the confidentiality of participation and that their answers would be processed in a pseudonymised manner. Informed consent for the survey and interviews was registered in writing. When participants consented to participate in and record the interview, the audio recordings were destroyed after transcription.

The survey finished with a call for respondents to participate in the interviews, to be answered separately from the survey form, so that the contact details submitted to this end could not be linked to the rest of the survey answers. Participants were given the opportunity to withdraw their participation without justification and (for the interviews) to read and check the transcripts for factual accuracy afterwards. 42 survey respondents initially indicated wanting to participate in an interview, of whom 22 eventually scheduled a time slot (see Chapter 4.4 of this part). No interview participants made use of the option to reread and adjust their transcripts. The interviews took place in a private and quiet room at the offices of the CGRS and CALL.

3.2.2. POSITIONALITY

Approaching these interviews with asylum authorities, I was aware of my positionality as a legal scholar with a specialisation in human rights and gender studies. These disciplinary lenses inevitably shape my standpoint as a researcher, orienting me toward the users' perspective[327] of those protected by/making use of human rights frameworks and those subjected to gendered power structures. Moreover, the research methodology led me to conduct interviews with applicants and analyse their case files during the fieldwork first, in order to identify SGBV myths relevant to the asylum context. Only thereafter did I conduct the survey and interviews with asylum officials and a case law analysis to examine the acceptance and rebuttal of these myths among asylum authorities (see Chapters 4.3 & 4.4 of this part). This meant that I was first exposed to applicants' standpoints before engaging with those of decision makers.

This chronology reinforced a critical stance towards asylum authorities' attitudes and practices. However, as conversations unfolded, several interviewed

[327] Desmet, 'Analysing Users' Trajectories in Human Rights' (n 219) 2.

asylum officials seemed to profoundly reflect on their roles within and the constraints of legal structures, as well as on the weight of their decisions. Their willingness to engage candidly, acknowledging dilemmas, inconsistencies, and the limits of their discretion, nuanced the critical standpoint with which I approached these interviews. Combined with my earlier thoughts on the challenge of hearing flight stories without instinctively reflecting on credibility myself (see chapter 3.1.1 above), these interviews deepened my understanding of the complexity of their task to determine refugee status. These encounters above all gave a balanced insight into the humans behind the asylum decisions and judgements constituting the focus of this research.

3.2.3. RECIPROCAL ACTION RESEARCH

In terms of reciprocity, asylum authorities too are entitled to expect some form of added value as a result of their participation in academic research. For example, some of the interview respondents cited: 'The [research] can also be […] useful for us. […] Maybe there will be […] things resulting from it […] [that can help] to keep improving our practices',[328] 'That is also good for us to know, where we are getting it wrong',[329] or 'I […] applaud the fact that [this] research is happening […]. It is not always comfortable for the court in question, but I think we have to dare to face that. And where improvement is needed […] I think it is […] a matter of […] getting the necessary training and […] skills.'[330] Therefore, this research was committed to formulate practically applicable recommendations alongside theoretical conclusions (see Part VI).

The (provisional) research findings were presented to the asylum authorities in order to gather their input and have it inform the final representation of the research. This gave both the CGRS and CALL the opportunity to, for example, correct any factual inaccuracies, add recent evolutions in decision making or institutional practice, or to indicate where their interpretation of the data differed from that in the research analysis, without compromising the independence of the research itself.[331] Importantly, while marking the end phase of the research, this consultation also served as a starting point and invitation to reflect on the feasibility of and steps towards implementation of the research's recommendations.

328 CB008_CGRS_Supervisor+PO_GENDER_[01:11:52].
329 CB009_CGRS_PO_GENDER_[01:11:19].
330 RB001_CALL_Judge_[00:49:20].
331 When mentioning such corrections, additions, or differences, I referred to: Commissioner General for Refugees and Stateless Persons (CGRS), 'Internal Communication CGRS (Part V)' (25 August 2025); Council for Alien Law Litigation (CALL), 'Internal Communication CALL' (n 168).

Finally, an Implementation & Community Advisory Board (ICAB) guided this research process, with representatives from the relevant government agencies (e.g. the CGRS, the CALL, and the IO), lawyers, and relevant civil society organisations. According to Clark-Kazak, ethical research with people on the move requires involving relevant partners throughout the research process, from data collection to communication and implementation of the results.[332] It was a conscious decision to collect applicants' expertise individually and separately from this ICAB, to not replicate the power dynamics present in asylum procedures between them and authorities, lawyers, …

Through setting up this ICAB, I also gathered a network of organisations to whom I could refer applicants for psychosocial or further legal support.[333] This advisory board was involved at the beginning of the research (both plenary and in groups according to their expertise) in shaping the research design, methodology, and ethical framework. At the end, the preliminary findings and recommendations were run by them to ensure their practical relevance and appropriateness.[334]

332 Clark-Clark-Kazak (n 38) 12.

333 *Ibid.*

334 Implementation & Community Advisory Board (ICAB), 'Internal Communication ICAB' (19 August 2025).

4. METHODOLOGY

4.1. LAW & LITERATURE ANALYSIS

The first and essential step in answering the abovementioned research questions (SQ1 & SQ2), was to conceptualise and identify SGBV myths relevant to gender-related asylum procedures. First, I looked into (inter)national refugee/criminal law and literature on the differences between the criminal justice context, in which the concept of rape mythology was identified, and the asylum context, in order to translate the concept to 'SGBV mythology'. Then, I collected existing literature and expertise on rape mythology and SGBV (with relevance to the asylum context). I did so in line with UNHCR's recommendation to inform refugee status determination and credibility assessments therein by 'the substantial body of relevant empirical evidence that exists in' fields exceeding legal scholarship, such as 'neurobiology, psychology, gender and cultural studies, anthropology, and sociology.'[335] In order to answer SQ3 and SQ4, I also analysed national refugee law, policy documents, and literature to examine how the procedural and institutional framework might impact Belgian asylum decisions on SGBV (SQ4) and the SGBV myth acceptance/rebuttal therein (SQ3).

This multidisciplinary literature analysis was facilitated by supervision at the Migration Law Research Group (MigrLaw)[336] at Ghent University's Faculty of Law and Criminology, and at the Gender & Violence Team in the International Centre for Reproductive Health (ICRH)[337] at the Faculty of Medicine and Health Sciences; and by my fieldwork at NANSEN NGO,[338] explicitly adopting an interdisciplinary approach. In the context of this fieldwork, I complemented the literature analysis by expert interviews with Prof. Dr Jane Herlihy[339] (clinical psychologist, co-founder of the Centre for the Study of Emotion and Law[340]) and Emilie Berghmans[341] (clinical

---

335 UNHCR, 'Beyond Proof. Credibility Assessment in EU Asylum Systems (Full Report)' (n 19) 56.

336 'Migration Law Research Group' (*Universiteit Gent*), www.ugent.be/re/epir/en/researchgroups/public-law/research/migration-law.

337 'International Centre for Reproductive Health Belgium' (*ICRH*), www.icrhb.org/en.

338 NANSEN (n 277).

339 Interview with Jane Herlihy, 'Expert Interview during Fieldwork at NANSEN NGO (Brussels, Belgium)' (17 October 2022).

340 'Centre for the Study of Emotion and Law' (*Centre for the Study of Emotion and Law*), https://csel.psychologyresearch.co.uk/.

341 Interview with Emilie Berghmans and Woman'Dō, 'Expert interview during fieldwork at NANSEN NGO (Brussels, Belgium)' (19 October 2022).

psychologist at Woman'Dō NGO,[342] a psychosocial centre specialising in post-traumatic support for exiled women fleeing violence), in support and validation of the (neuro)psychological aspects of the analysis in this research.

These sources were accessed through electronic databases and library catalogues, using search terms focusing on refugee law, rape mythology, and SGBV (and combinations of these). The data collected was organised and processed using the digital reference management software Zotero. The literature analysis was conducted in an iterative manner, resulting in a constant search for new and rereading of gathered sources according to newly gained insights on the subject throughout the entire research period.

4.2. INTERVIEWS WITH APPLICANTS FOR INTERNATIONAL PROTECTION

Next to collecting literature, in order to identify and rebut SGBV myths relevant to asylum decisions (SQ2) and to examine the procedural context in which these are shaped (SQ4), I listened to the personal experiences and expertise of those who fled SGBV and sought international protection in Belgium through interviews. Of course, this comes with ethical challenges, as addressed in Chapter 3.1. Instead of making these applicants' stories fit into a predetermined research framework, I used them to shape this framework itself. The ways in which applicants in the interviews indicated feeling misunderstood in the asylum procedure formed direct expertise for identifying the SGBV myths. These were then used to analyse the levels and ways of SGBV myth acceptance and rebuttal in asylum authorities' accounts and decisions. Only in this way can it be revealed how the asylum system is oppressive to persons fleeing SGBV and can targeted and pragmatic conclusions be developed from their narratives.[343]

As mentioned above, the interviews were organised during fieldwork at NANSEN NGO, providing legal assistance to applicants for international protection/their lawyers upon their request. Often, these requests concern factually and legally complex cases, which already contain one or more decisions by the CGRS and/or judgements by the CALL. The case files mostly include the lawyer's argumentation in appeal (when explicitly cited in the judgement(s) or sent to the NGO by the lawyer) and sometimes the written notes of the personal interview(s) at the CGRS.

As explained above, I both conducted research interviews myself with applicants who approached NANSEN NGO during the fieldwork period (between June 2022 and September 2023), and analysed the personal interview notes by the CGRS when available in the case file, for those I could not interview (see

342 'Woman'Dō', https://womando.be/nl/.
343 Johnsson (n 36) 231; Van Impe (n 245) 106.

Chapter 3.1.2 of this Part). For the latter, I went back to files with at least one decision/judgment issued after 26 June 2020, the publication date of the above-mentioned GREVIO evaluation report.[344] During the fieldwork period, between June 2022 and September 2023, I analysed the notes of 12 personal interviews by the CGRS of 7 applicants and conducted 7 research interviews with 8 applicants myself.

Because I did not actively recruit participants for the interviews, I had no control over the inclusion process, nor over the diversity of the sample. This resulted in a set of interviews involving applicants exclusively identifying as cisgender women,[345] including 1 minor (16 years old, who participated with her mother, see Chapter 3.1.2 of this Part), who fled from: Albania, the Democratic Republic of Congo, Eritrea, Ethiopia, Guinea, Georgia, Honduras, Liberia, Senegal, Syria and Turkey. They feared the following SGBV forms: rape/sexual assault (RSA), GMC, sex trafficking/forced prostitution (STFP), domestic violence (DV), forced marriage (FM), and violence related to gender norm transgression (VGNT). The sample of interviews with asylum applicants is visualised in Figure 4.

Figure 4: Sample of interviews with applicants, conducted by the researcher and by the Office of the Commissioner General for Refugees and Stateless Persons (CGRS)

Pseudonym	Case study name	Country of origin	Gender	Y of birth	RSA	STFP	GMC	VGNT	FM	DV	N° research interviews
NA001_A	Erina	Albania	F	2006	X			X	X	X	1
NA001_B	Diana	Albania	F	1973	X			X	X	X	
NA016	Vera	Albania	F	1990	X			X		X	1
NEr018	Rahel	Eritrea	F	1985	X						1
NG012		Guinea	F	1987	X		X		X		1
NGe014	Nino	Georgia	F	1975	X					X	1
NH003	Sofia	Honduras	F	1991	X					X	1
NL017	Mary	Liberia	F	1980		X	X	X	X		1
TOTAL					7	1	2	4	4	5	7
Pseudonym	Case study name	Country of origin	Gender	Y of birth	RSA	STFP	GMC	VGNT	FM	DV	N° interviews by CGRS
NC004	Amani	DRC	F	1991	X					X	2
NC006	Angele	DRC	F	1984	X						3
NE002	Aster	Ethiopia	F	1988		X					1
NEr000		Eritrea	F	1999	X	X					1
NS005		Senegal	F	2002	X					X	1
NSy019	Aya	Syria	F	1997	X						1
NT015	Zeynep	Turkey	F	1996	X				X	X	3
TOTAL					6	2			1	3	12

RSA: rape/sexual assault, STFP: sex trafficking/forced prostitution, GMC: genital mutilation/cutting, VGNT: violence related to gender norm transgression, FM: forced marriage, DV: domestic violence

344 Group of Experts on Action against Violence against Women and Domestic Violence (GREVIO) (n 22).

345 The case law analysis, in which applicants' standpoints are (partly) reflected in their lawyers' argumentation in appeal, does include files of 12 men and 1 transgender woman.

In addition to these interviews, the applicants' standpoints are also represented in the research through their lawyers' arguments in the appeal procedures. Depending on the judge, these are described to a greater or lesser extent in the judgment. Thus, in addition to the 19 interviews, the (available) argumentation of applicants' lawyers in the 202 cases of the case law analysis was also included in the analysis (see Chapter 4.3 of this part).

It is important to note that the standpoints of applicants are therefore reflected in three distinct sets of data: 1) interviews conducted by the researcher, according to the ethical framework set out above and with the double aim of facilitating NANSEN NGO's legal assistance and informing the research; 2) lawyers' argumentation in appeal before the CALL, drafted with the aim of legally representing their clients and obtaining international protection; and 3) personal interviews conducted by the Belgian asylum authorities, according to the CGRS' ethical framework and with the aim of gathering information to allow for refugee status determination. To keep this difference clear, I use different terms, 'research interviews' conducted by myself and 'personal interviews' conducted by the CGRS, throughout this research.

The first two types of data originate from a trust-based setting, encouraging disclosure of flight stories from applicants' point of view, albeit that lawyers' argumentation is inherently biased towards applicants' legal defence and the research interviews are not. The third type follows an institutional approach that should enable credibility assessments by the asylum authorities. Although these distinct objectives impact the ways in which applicants present their flight stories, all three types of data contain important insights into the ways in which they may have felt understood or misunderstood throughout their procedure. Therefore, I based the analysis on all three types, but approached them in different ways, keeping in mind their different nature (see Chapter 4.5 describing the different use of these data types).

Lastly, it is worth noting that I did not interview applicants with/about positive asylum decisions. These interviews (and the research at large) focused on the written argumentation in asylum decisions of persons fleeing SGBV. In first instance, as the CGRS' argumentation in positive decisions is not communicated to them/made public, such an interview would have been devoid of purpose.[346] In appeal, where the CALL does publish its argumentation in annulment or recognition judgments, none of the cases of the applicants I interviewed ended with a judgment annulling the CGRS decision or recognising them as refugees (during the course of the research).

In the footnotes, quotes from the research interviews and the CGRS' personal interviews with applicants will be referenced as follows. Each pseudonym

[346] While they could be interviewed about their experiences during the interviews with the IO and CGRS leading to a positive decision, these interviews are not the subject of this research.

consists of [a letter to indicate the sampling method (N for NANSEN NGO) – letter(s) to indicate country of origin – a unique identification number for each applicant – _X (addition for closely linked case files)]. In cases where an application was (initially) filed by more than one person or the flight stories are closely linked (mostly family members), the applicants and their respective decisions/judgements are distinguished in the pseudonym by adding '_A, _B_...' (these are considered as separate decisions and judgements in the visualisation of the case law samples below, since they may contain different forms of SGBV and argumentation).

	Pseudonym_ letter per related case	CGRS interview n°[347]	Birth year	Gender	Country of origin	SGBV type	Procedural language	Minor[348]
e.g.	NA001_A_		2006_	F_	Albania_	RSA_ VGNT_ FM_DV_	NL_	MINOR
e.g.	NC006_	CGRS interview 3_	1984_	F_	DRC_	RSA_	FR_	

4.3. CASE LAW ANALYSIS

The SGBV myths, identified through the law and literature analysis (see chapter 4.1) and interviews with applicants (see chapter 4.2), formed the hypotheses against which gender-related asylum decisions were assessed (SQ3). I on the one hand aimed to capture the Belgian authorities' self-reported ideas and attitudes (via a Knowledge, Attitude and Practices (KAP) survey and follow-up interviews, see Chapter 4.4). On the other hand, I examined the written arguments that ultimately shape decisions in practice, through a case law analysis of CGRS decisions and CALL judgements in Belgian asylum procedures.

It is important to stress that this research is not concerned with the factual truthfulness of the included applicants' flight stories, nor with their procedures' eventual result of (not) granting them international protection. Instead of (re)assessing these final decisions and judgments as a whole, which is the prerogative of the asylum authorities themselves, the analysis focused on the individual arguments used to (cumulatively) substantiate them. I will come back to how this multi-layered nature of refugee status determination takes shape in SGBV-related cases in Part VI, Chapter 3.1.

347 Left blank if the interview was conducted by the researcher.

348 At the time of the first (accessible) decision.

Both these decisions and judgements can be accessed through a public online database, in which the CALL is legally required to publish its jurisprudence, usually containing the CGRS decision against which the appeal is lodged.[349] It is important to note that the analysis in this research cannot include positive CGRS decisions, as only the argumentation in negative decisions is communicated to applicants (and made public) (see Chapter 4.5 for the implications on the findings).

I selected the case law sample through triangulation of three different data sources and related pathways, as further elaborated below: 1) a systematic search in the CALL database, 2) a specific search in the CALL database (judgments by more than one judge or highlighted as important by the CALL itself), and 3) the fieldwork. The decisions and judgements in the sample are part of the procedures of 97 applicants, of which 85 women (among whom 84 cisgender and 1 transgender) and 12 (cisgender) men. The age distribution cannot be accurately described, since not all decisions and judgements analysed mention the applicants' year of birth and in some cases their age is subject to discussion. For the applicants whose age is mentioned, they include 45 adults and 3 minors (at the time of the first CGRS decision I had access to).

For all three pathways, I identified which cases were relevant to include. I determined this relevance according to a substantive and a temporal inclusion criterium and a substantive exclusion criterium. Substantively, I included those cases where applicants at a certain stage in the procedure disclosed a form of SGBV as a reason to flee from and/or fear to return to their country of origin. I used the abovementioned six forms of SGBV to streamline the inclusion process (RSA, STFP, GMC, DV, FM, and VGNT). Temporally, case files included contain at least one decision/judgement taken after 26 June 2020.[350] I excluded those cases: where not the applicants themselves but others, for example their relatives, experienced/feared SGBV; that only involved SOGI-related violence and no other forms of SGBV (falling outside the scope of this research); and where the asylum authorities' argumentation did not, from a first exploratory reading, substantively engage with the SGBV experienced/feared (e.g. a decision based on merely procedural grounds).

The case files I analysed mostly included: 1) one (or more) decision(s) of the CGRS in first instance and 2) one (or more) judgement(s) of the CALL in appeal.[351] The number of decisions/judgements per case file depends on whether

349 Art. 39/65 Belgian Aliens Act; Council for Alien Law Litigation (CALL), 'Arresten' (n 285).

350 Group of Experts on Action against Violence against Women and Domestic Violence (GREVIO) (n 202).

351 For the sake of completeness, for most cases, I did not have access to the notes of the personal interview at the CGRS, except for the 15 applicants included in the fieldwork sample as mentioned in Figure 4 above. These notes helped outlining the institutional context in which SGBV-related asylum decision making in Belgium takes place (see Part II, Chapter 2.3).

or not the applicant chose to appeal and/or register subsequent applications for international protection, and whether the CALL sent the case back to the CGRS for reconsideration (annulment judgement). Consequently, the number of CGRS decisions and CALL judgements in the sample I analysed are not identical.

4.3.1. SYSTEMATIC CALL DATABASE SEARCH

The first selection pathway consisted of a systematic search in the online CALL database, adding the time limit of 1 January 2024. I used search terms based on the substantive inclusion criterium of the 6 SGBV forms mentioned above. I checked the results for relevance chronologically, starting from the most recent case. This resulted in a sample containing judgements from 1 January 2024 until 31 May 2024 in Dutch and French (the two procedural languages in asylum procedures in Belgium).[352]

The database search in French gathered enough relevant results using one set of search terms. The first search in Dutch using the same (translated) terms resulted in only 11 relevant cases and required a second search using complementary terms. I then added the general term 'gender' in order to grasp gender-related cases more broadly. For this second search in Dutch, I checked half of the results for relevance per search term, except when the number exceeded 40, in which case I reviewed results 1 to 20. For both language searches, in addition to the exclusion criteria mentioned above, I excluded those cases with too many common characteristics to cases already included in the sample (SGBV type, country of origin, wording of argumentation, case files of family members, …).

I added these criteria, aiming to construct a recent and diverse sample in terms of facts and legal argumentation. The sampling process can be visualised as in Figure 43 of the Annex (keeping in mind that most cases contain multiple forms of violence and therefore appear in multiple result sets). The cases in the sample I selected through the CALL database are each linked to one preceding negative decision by the CGRS against which an appeal is lodged.[353] The systematic CALL

However, as this research does not focus on these interviews as such, this lack of access does not constitute a limitation to its methodology, analyses, or results.

352 Art. 51/4 *jo.* 39/9, §1, part 3 Belgian Aliens Act.

353 Two Georgian cases form an exception, where the country had been taken off the list of safe countries of origin (Art. 1 Koninklijk besluit tot uitvoering van het artikel 57/6/1, §3, vierde lid, van de wet van 15 december 1980 betreffende de toegang tot het grondgebied, het verblijf, de vestiging en de verwijdering van vreemdelingen, houdende de vastlegging van de lijst van veilige landen van herkomst.) in between the decision of the CGRS and the appeal before the CALL. In these cases, the CALL found that the legal basis of the CGRS decision no longer existed and assessed the cases again in a written procedure. In both cases, the applicant requested to be heard (Art. 39/73, §3 Belgian Aliens Act.), resulting in the judgement containing a reassessment of the case based on the elements submitted at the hearing (counted

database search sample contained: 72 CGRS decisions (of which 37 in Dutch: 29 refusal, 3 manifestly ill-founded, and 5 inadmissible; and 35 in French: 32 refusal, 2 manifestly ill-founded, and 1 inadmissible) and 76 CALL judgements (of which 41 in Dutch: 36 refusal, 1 recognition, and 4 annulment; and 35 in French: 17 refusal, 7 recognition, and 11 annulment). The dates of the decisions and judgements are spread over time as follows: 2022 (6), 2023 (64), and 2024 (78).

4.3.2. SPECIFIC CALL DATABASE SEARCH

For the second pathway, I conducted a specific search in the CALL database for cases with particular importance, in order to ensure inclusion of jurisprudence deemed influential by the CALL itself. Firstly, I searched for cases that were decided by other Council compositions than a single judge, namely by: three judges, the united chambers (six judges), or the general assembly (at least ten judges). This mostly happens when it is deemed necessary to ensure unity of jurisprudence due to particular legal challenges in or importance of the case.[354] I used the general search term 'gender' (*gender* in Dutch and *genre* in French) in order to grasp as many gender-related cases as possible. I conducted this search on 3 September 2024 for both the French and Dutch procedures. Interestingly, both searches resulted in zero relevant gender-related CALL judgements issued by more than one judge over the more than 4-year time period (June 2020 – September 2024).

In addition, the CALL itself started publishing a selection of important cases on its website since January 2024, with the aim of facilitating the monitoring of its jurisprudence by highlighting notable evolutions.[355] I searched these selections, which at the moment of searching went back to May 2024, again using the

as a separate CALL judgement, instead of the omitted CGRS decision). DGe109_CALL 1&2 (refusal)_F_Georgia_RSA_FM_DV_19/12/2023_303 313_NL_Database.; DGe112_CALL 1&2 (refusal)_M_Georgia_GMC_CALL.

354 Art. 39/10-12 *jo.* 57/23bis Belgian Aliens Act.

355 Council for Alien Law Litigation (CALL), 'Maandelijkse selectie van arresten van de Raad', www.rvv-cce.be/nl/select-arr; Before systematically publishing these case law selections from January 2024 onwards, the CALL did publish important evolutions in its case law in the 'News' section on its website. This was internally communicated by the CALL at the end of the research (in August 2025), which is why these news items were not systematically included in the methodology of this research. However, for the sake of completeness, it is worth noting one relevant news item (on SGBV and international protection, in the time period relevant to this research: June 2020 until June 2025) on an applicant from Senegal, who faced persecution after she had undergone an abortion, and was recognised as a refugee. Council for Alien Law Litigation (CALL), 'Nieuws', www.rvv-cce.be/nl/actua; Council for Alien Law Litigation (CALL), 'Abortus in Senegal' (25 November 2021), www.rvv-cce.be/nl/actua/abortus-senegal.

general search term 'gender'. From this search, 11 relevant cases were selected, of which 3 were excluded due to overlap with the systematic CALL database search results. The 8 included cases are again each succeeding one appealed negative CGRS decision.

It is interesting to note that this case law sample exclusively contains positive CALL judgements of recognition and annulment, compensating for the samples collected through the systematic CALL database search and fieldwork pathways, largely including negative decisions and judgements (which does reflect refusal rates at CGRS and CALL more broadly).[356] The specific CALL database search sample contained: 8 CGRS decisions (of which 3 in Dutch: 3 refusal; and 5 in French: 4 refusal, and 1 inadmissible) and 8 CALL judgements (of which 3 in Dutch: 1 recognition, and 2 annulment; and 5 in French: 4 recognition, and 1 annulment). The decisions and judgements are temporally spread as follows: 2023 (7), and 2024 (9).

4.3.3. FIELDWORK

As a third pathway, I collected cases from persons fleeing SGBV during my fieldwork. The sample included both the relevant case files already in the archive of the NGO (going back to 20 June 2020), as well as those sent in by applicants or their social workers, lawyers, psychologists, ... during the fieldwork (from June 2022 until September 2023). It is important to note that NANSEN NGO is often only contacted for support at a stage where an asylum procedure had already proved to be challenging. Therefore, this sample at times involves subsequent applications for international protection, where the previous procedure(s) ended in a negative decision by the CGRS (and the CALL).

As a result, the analysis is subject to an inevitable sampling bias of more negative and legally and/or factually complex decisions and judgements. The fieldwork sample contained: 20 CGRS decisions (of which 12 in Dutch: 4 refusal, 3 manifestly ill-founded, and 5 inadmissible; and 8 in French: 8 refusal) and 18 CALL judgements (of which 10 in Dutch: 10 refusal; and 8 in French: 1 refusal, 1 recognition, and 6 annulment). The decisions and judgements are temporally spread as follows: ≤ 2020[357] (7), 2021 (8), 2022 (13), 2023 (7), and 2024 (1)

[356] Commissioner General for Refugees and Stateless Persons (CGRS), 'Asielstatistieken 2024: Overzicht' (2025) 1; Council for Alien Law Litigation (CALL), 'Activiteitenverslag RvV 2023' (2023) 8.

[357] Since case files included contain at least one decision/judgement taken after 26 June 2020, earlier decisions in the case file may date from before 2020.

4.3.4. TOTAL CASE LAW SAMPLE

To summarise, the sampling strategy for all three pathways can be visualised as follows (Figure 5):

Figure 5: Visualisation of sampling strategy for case law analysis

		Systematic CALL database search	Specific CALL database search: > 1 judge	Specific CALL database search: Case law selections	Fieldwork
Inclusion criteria	Substantive/procedural	**Disclosure of SGBV as reason to flee from and/or fear to return to country of origin:** - **Sexual violence:** rape/sexual assault, sex trafficking/forced prostitution & genital mutilation/cutting - **Gender-based violence:** domestic violence, forced marriage & violence related to gender norm transgression			
		/	Judgement by 3 judges, united chambers or general assembly	/	/
	Search terms	Gender(+) sex(ual)(+)rape, prostitution, mutil*, excision, domestic violence, forced(+)marriage, shame	Gender	Gender	/
	Temporal	**20/06/2020 → moment of selecting**			
		Further limited: 1/01/2024 → moment of selecting	/	Only possible for: 1/01/2024 → moment of selecting	/
Cases incl.		**CGRS: 990 CALL: 994**	**/ /**	**CGRS: 11 CALL: 11**	**CGRS: 20 CALL: 18**
Exclusion criteria	Substantive	- **Other person than applicant fleeing from/fearing SGBV** - **Exclusively sexual orientation/gender identity-related violence** - **No substantive engagement with SGBV in argumentation**			
		Commonalities with existing sample	Overlap with the systematic CALL database search results		/
Cases excl.		**CGRS: 918 CALL: 918**	**/ /**	**CGRS: 3 CALL: 3**	**/ /**
Full sample		72 (CGRS) & 76 (CALL) = **148**	**0**	8 (CGRS) & 8 (CALL) = **16**	20 (CGRS) & 18 (CALL) = **38**

CGRS: Office of the Commissioner General for Refugees and Stateless Persons & CALL: Council for Alien Law Litigation

The total case law sample selected through all three pathways included the following types and dates of decisions/judgements (Figure 6 & Figure 7):

Figure 6: Number of decisions & judgements in case law sample, according to authority, language, type & year of decision/judgement

<table>
<tr><th colspan="60">TOTAL CASE LAW SAMPLE</th></tr>
<tr><td colspan="30">CGRS decisions</td><td colspan="30">CALL judgements</td></tr>
<tr><td colspan="30">100</td><td colspan="30">102</td></tr>
<tr><td colspan="15">In Dutch</td><td colspan="15">In French</td><td colspan="15">In Dutch</td><td colspan="15">In French</td></tr>
<tr><td colspan="15">52</td><td colspan="15">48</td><td colspan="15">54</td><td colspan="15">48</td></tr>
<tr><td colspan="5">REF</td><td colspan="5">MIF</td><td colspan="5">INA</td><td colspan="5">REF</td><td colspan="5">MIF</td><td colspan="5">INA</td><td colspan="5">REF</td><td colspan="5">REC</td><td colspan="5">ANN</td><td colspan="5">REF</td><td colspan="5">REC</td><td colspan="5">ANN</td></tr>
<tr><td colspan="5">36</td><td colspan="5">6</td><td colspan="5">10</td><td colspan="5">44</td><td colspan="5">2</td><td colspan="5">2</td><td colspan="5">46</td><td colspan="5">2</td><td colspan="5">6</td><td colspan="5">18</td><td colspan="5">12</td><td colspan="5">18</td></tr>
<tr><td colspan="3">≤20</td><td colspan="3">'21</td><td colspan="3">'22</td><td colspan="3">'23</td><td colspan="3">'24</td><td colspan="3">≤20</td><td colspan="3">'21</td><td colspan="3">'22</td><td colspan="3">'23</td><td colspan="3">'24</td><td colspan="3">≤20</td><td colspan="3">'21</td><td colspan="3">'22</td><td colspan="3">'23</td><td colspan="3">'24</td><td colspan="3">≤'20</td><td colspan="3">'21</td><td colspan="3">'22</td><td colspan="3">'23</td><td colspan="3">'24</td></tr>
<tr><td colspan="3">2</td><td colspan="3">5</td><td colspan="3">6</td><td colspan="3">35</td><td colspan="3">4</td><td colspan="3">2</td><td colspan="3">2</td><td colspan="3">6</td><td colspan="3">37</td><td colspan="3">1</td><td colspan="3">2</td><td colspan="3">0</td><td colspan="3">6</td><td colspan="3">3</td><td colspan="3">43</td><td colspan="3">1</td><td colspan="3">1</td><td colspan="3">3</td><td colspan="3">3</td><td colspan="3">40</td></tr>
<tr><td colspan="60">202</td></tr>
</table>

REF: refusal, MIF: manifestly ill-founded, INA: inadmissible, REC: recognition, ANN: annulment, CGRS: Office of the Commissioner General for Refugees and Stateless Persons & CALL: Council for Alien Law Litigation

Figure 7: Visualisation of total case law sample, according to authority, language & type of decision/judgement

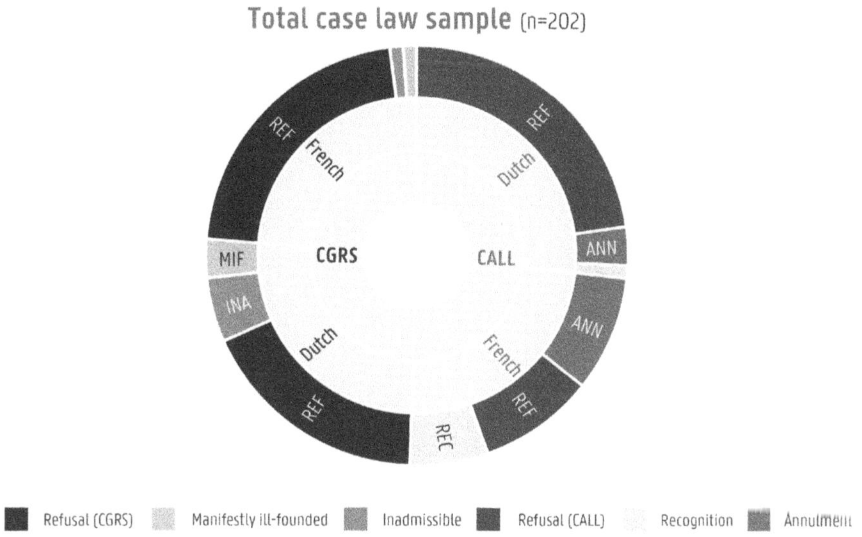

The sample contains the following SGBV forms (with according number of decisions/judgements): rape/sexual assault (136), sex trafficking/forced prostitution (19), GMC (60), violence related to gender norm transgression (84), forced marriage (100), and domestic violence (114), keeping in mind that most flight stories contain multiple types of violence. The decisions/judgements are geographically spread across the following countries of origin: Afghanistan, Albania, Algeria, Angola, Benin, Bolivia, Bosnia and Herzegovina, Burkina Faso,

Burundi, The DRC, Ecuador, Eritrea, Ethiopia, Gabon, Georgia, Ghana, Guinea, Honduras, Iran, Iraq, Ivory Coast, Kenya, Liberia, Mauritania, Moldavia, Morocco, Nigeria, North-Macedonia, Palestine, Russia, Senegal, Serbia, Somalia, Suriname, Syria, The Gambia, Turkey, and Uganda, which can be visualised in Figure 8.

While applicants from most countries of origin are consistently assigned to the Dutch or French procedural languages when the application is registered at the IO, some are treated by both language sections/chambers at the CGRS and CALL (such as Albania, Morocco, or Nigeria in this case law sample). Consequently, the language of the procedure is inherently linked to certain countries of origin and therefore to certain forms of SGBV that are more prevalent there. The geographical case law sample distribution in exact numbers of decisions/judgements, according to procedural language and type of SGBV, can be visualised in Figure 45 of the Annex.

Figure 8: Visualisation of the geographical distribution of the case law sample

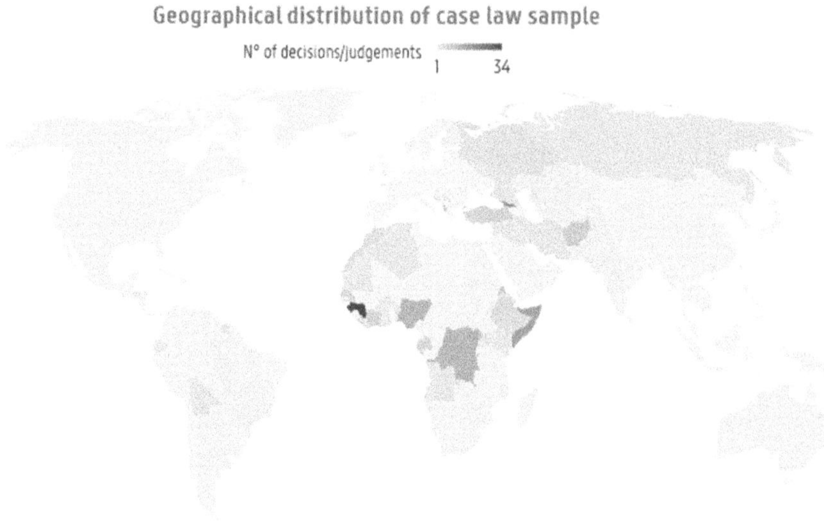

For the systematic search in the online CALL database, I made the deliberate choice to include a relatively limited number of decisions and judgements (148 of the 202 in total), feasible for substantive in-depth analysis, rather than opting for a more large-scale but more superficial analysis. As the systematically selected cases date from 1 January 2024 to 31 May 2024, it must be emphasised that this part of the analysis concerns a recent but limited time frame, unrepresentative for the CALL's decision-making practice before or after that period. Instead,

I prioritised: more recent cases; inclusion of different types of SGBV, argumentation, and countries of origin; and balance between the two procedural languages (Dutch and French) in the sample.

The latter was done in parallel with the pursued balance between procedural languages for the interviews with asylum officials (see Chapter 4.4), in order to give a truthful reflection of the decision makers working in first instance at the CGRS and in appeal at the CALL. In addition, the divergence between the Dutch-language and French-language procedures before the CALL has been demonstrated in past research on minors by Desmet (the former more strict, the latter more lax) and has been recognised by the CALL itself.[358] As will be discussed below, the CALL has taken measures to enhance its unity of jurisprudence since (Part VI, Chapter 4.2). As these findings date from 2020, it is interesting to include this language aspect in the current research to examine how this divergence has evolved since and plays out for SGBV-related cases in particular.

In sum, the case law analysis is not exhaustive. Instead, the sample is an exploratory selection with the aim of providing a factually diversified and recent analysis on a wide variety of SGBV types causing forced migration. Nonetheless, the analysis presented throughout this research is supported by established (inter)national (case) law and legal, health, and social sciences expertise. Therefore, the results can at least be considered indicative of the challenges experienced by applicants applying for international protection in the Belgian asylum procedure.

Lastly, this case law analysis concerns the Belgian national level. I did conduct a similar case law analysis for the ECtHR's non-refoulement jurisprudence on persons fearing SGBV upon return, of which the results were published separately (but were not used as data as such).[359] The conclusions drawn from this preliminary analysis will serve to outline the international jurisprudential framework throughout the discussions on the SGBV myths below, next to other relevant case law with an impact on the Belgian asylum jurisprudence (e.g. of the CJEU).

In the footnotes, quotes from case law will be referenced as follows. By doing so, I deviate from traditional ways of referring to case law in legal research, to

358 According to the CALL's press magistrate: '[t]here is a difference in approach and methodology, which has historically grown. This can partly be explained by a division between Northern European, more administrative thinking, and Southern European, more principled thinking, because of which similar cases lead to different conclusions.' Desmet, 'Appellate Asylum and Migration Proceedings in Belgium' (n 106) 214–215. This is also confirmed by interviewed asylum officials in this research, e.g. see Part V, Chapter 2.2.3.

359 Roels, 'Rape Myths in the European Court of Human Rights' Non-Refoulement Case Law on Sexual and Gender-Based Violence' (n 33).

allow for direct identification of the type of decision, number of application, procedural language, asylum authority, sampling method, country of origin, type of violence, gender identity, and age (where possible) of the applicant. For the case law analysis, I constructed pseudonyms over the course of the case law sampling process. Due to exclusion of certain case files along the way, the numbers are not always consecutive. The pseudonyms are constructed in the same way as for the interviews with applicants, adding the letter 'D' to indicate the sampling method of the CALL online Database (both for the systematic and specific search).

	Pseudonym_letter per related case_ authority, procedure n°[360] (type of decision)[361]	Birth year[362]	Gender	Country of origin	SGBV type	Decision date	CALL case n°[363]	Proc. lang.	Sampling method
e.g.	DA099_A_CALL 1 (refusal)_		M_	Albania_	DV_	21/3/2024_	303 553_	FR_	Database
e.g.	DB068_CALL 1 (annulment)_	1975_	F_	Bolivia_	RSA_ DV_	23/2/2024_	302 134_	NL_	CALL case law selection
e.g.	NC006_CGRS 2 (refusal)_	1984_	F_	DRC_	RSA_	30/8/2021_	275 955_	FR_	NANSEN

When referring to a Belgian case that was not included as such in the case law analysis, the reference will follow the OSCOLA referencing rules used for all other sources:

	[Year of judgement]	Case in Dutch (RvV)[364] or in French (CCE)[365]	CALL case n°
e.g.	[2023]	RvV	294 383

360 With new procedures starting with a subsequent application for international protection being numbered 2, 3....

361 Adding [_lawyers' argumentation] when specifically referring to the applicant's argumentation in appeal before the CALL.

362 The birth year is not consistently mentioned in the anonymised versions of case law in the online CALL database. This is left blank when not mentioned in the decision/judgement.

363 Leading to the pdf file of the CALL decision in the online database (www.rvv-cce.be/nl/arr), mostly including the contested CGRS decision and the lawyers' argumentation in the procedure.

364 For 'Raad voor Vreemdelingenbetwistingen' or CALL in Dutch.

365 For 'Conseil du Contentieux des Etrangers' or CALL in French.

4.4. SURVEY AND INTERVIEWS WITH ASYLUM OFFICIALS

As a case law analysis only includes the written legal reasoning relevant to the outcome of an asylum procedure, it is likely that certain underlying thinking patterns of asylum officials remain unnoticed. Given that there might be 'considerable gaps between what is said and what is done,'[366] this research also aimed to examine how the human beings behind asylum decisions/ judgements understand gender-based persecution and the people applying for protection against it.[367] To conduct an in-depth analysis of the diversity of knowledge, attitudes and practices of the actors involved in this decision making process, I combined an exploratory survey with in-depth qualitative follow-up interviews.

4.4.1. KNOWLEDGE, ATTITUDE AND PRACTICES (KAP) SURVEY

The case law analysis was firstly supplemented by an exploratory Knowledge, Attitude, and Practices (KAP) survey:[368] a quantitative method with predefined questions in a standardised questionnaire, meant to reach a larger sample of respondents. This method is designed to explore both quantitative and qualitative information on respondents' (self-reported) knowledge, attitudes, and practices towards a particular topic, revealing knowledge (gaps), cultural beliefs and (mis) conceptions.[369] Based on the law and literature analysis, the interviews with applicants conducted so far, and a preliminary case law analysis focusing on the Belgian asylum procedure in the context of my fieldwork,[370] I drafted questions in three categories, focusing on:

1) The profile of respondents (incl. how often they handled SGBV-related applications for international protection, which gender-related trainings (if any) they had followed (while) at the CGRS/CALL, …) and the impact of

366 Médicins du Monde, 'The Kap Survey Model (Knowledge, Attitudes, & Practices) (Tool Summary)' (USAID 2011) 1.

367 Oxford (n 11) 159; Van Impe (n 245) 98.

368 Sybille Gumucio, 'The Kap Survey Model – Knowledge Attitude and Practices' (Médecins du Monde 2011) 3.

369 Médicins du Monde (n 366) 1.

370 In preparation of: Roels and Casteleyn, 'Praktijkgids voor advocaten' (n 323); Roels and Casteleyn, 'Guide pratique pour les avocat·es' (n 323).

their professional role on their well-being (based on Vrklevski and Franklin's validated Vicarious Trauma Scale[371])

2) Knowledge and attitude questions (KA), translating the rape myths identified as relevant to the asylum context, focusing on: SGBV prevalence, the nature and risk factors of SGBV, survivors'/victims'/their environment's reactions to SGBV, evidence in SGBV-related asylum procedures, protection against SGBV, and the legal framework regulating SGBV-related asylum procedures
3) The practices (P) around SGBV-related refugee status determination, inquiring into: access to gender-related trainings, psychological support, and to what extent respondents considered themselves skilled to react to SGBV disclosures, ask appropriate questions on SGBV, meet special procedural needs of applicants, or assess SGBV-related applications accurately

The survey (fully included in E of the Annex) was developed through an iterative process of multiple feedback rounds from the supervisors of this research and with the support of an expert in quantitative analysis within the Gender & Violence Team at the International Centre for Reproductive Health (ICRH) at the Faculty of Medicine and Health Sciences at Ghent University. It was drafted and conducted online via Qualtrics survey software. It was sent out to 275 POs, supervisors, members of CEDOCA,[372] and members of the gender coordination team (see Part II, Chapter 2.2.1) at the CGRS, as well as to 83 judges and attachés supporting them, who handle cases on international protection (also called 'full jurisdiction'[373]) at the CALL. 253 respondents opened the survey, of whom 209 filled in all questions, resulting in a response rate (until the end) of 63,86% for the CGRS, 56,73% for the CALL, and 58,38% in total. The respondent sample and the answers to the profile questions in category 1 can be visualised as follows (Figure 9).[374]

371 Vicarious trauma is described as 'the negative effects that result from working with trauma survivors. These include compassion fatigue or secondary traumatic stress, countertransference, and burnout.' Vrklevski and Franklin developed an 8 question Vicarious Trauma Scale (VTS) in order to assess subjective levels of distress associated with working with traumatised persons. The VTS items are rated on a 7-point Likert-type scale, ranging from 1 (strongly disagree) to 7 (strongly agree). Lila Petar Vrklevski and John Franklin, 'Vicarious Trauma: The Impact on Solicitors of Exposure to Traumatic Material' (2008) 14 Traumatology 106, 106, 110 & 115.

372 CEDOCA is the CGRS' research service, consisting of researchers who collect, analyse and prepare reports on COI.

373 Chapter 5, Section II Belgian Aliens Act. Also called 'volle rechtsmacht' in Dutch or 'plein contentieux' in French.

374 The total number of respondents decreases as respondents stopped completing the questionnaire at a certain point. Also, some questions were only relevant for and posed to the CALL respondents.

Figure 9: Quantitative representation of responses to KAP survey questions in category 1. 'The profile of respondents'

Variable	Category	CGRS		CALL		TOTAL n° of respondents
		Dutch-speaking	French-speaking	Dutch-speaking	French-speaking	
Gender identity[375]	Female	80	36	22	16	241
	Male	44	22	9	12	
Average age		*37,4*	*39,2*	*40,1*	*42,0*	244
Role[376]	Judge			12	5	61
	Attaché			21	23	
Work experience	≤ 5 years	66	36	12	13	231
	6-10 years	19	9	9	7	
	11-15 years	13	2	9	5	
	> 15 years	18	8	2	3	
Frequency of handling SGBV-related applications	≥ 1x/week	11	16	5	18	231
	≤ 1x/month	77	37	22	9	
	≤ 1x/year	28	2	5	1	

After each section of the survey, respondents were given the opportunity to provide feedback on the questions, more information about their responses, or comments on the survey in general via free text entry. This qualitative input was processed in the same way as the interviews with asylum officials and will also be used throughout the research to substantiate the institutional analysis of the Belgian asylum procedure (Part II) and the analysis on SGBV myth acceptance/rebuttal (Part III, Part IV & Part V).

In the footnotes, quotes from these survey responses will be referenced as follows. Respondents' language and gender identity is not provided to guarantee their non-identifiability. Therefore, I will refer to them using the gender-neutral pronouns 'they/them' throughout the text.

	Pseudonym[377]	Authority	Role (current)
e.g.	R_3fSFAvlx87VK7YK_	CGRS_	PO/supervisor/gender coordinator/CEDOCA member_
e.g.	R_BR1w4qNxGb5rqkF_	CALL_	Attaché_

375 One respondent was excluded, who indicated identifying as 'a wizard'. Three respondents were not counted, since they answered 'I prefer not to say' to this question. No one indicated identifying as non-binary, transgender, or otherwise queer.

376 Six CALL participants were excluded who had indicated 'other' under 'role'. They specified other roles such as registrar and coordinator. As they do not make substantive decisions, they were excluded from the analyses.

377 These pseudonyms were automatically generated by Qualtrics survey software.

4.4.2. IN-DEPTH FOLLOW-UP INTERVIEWS

Based on the survey results, a semi-structured topic guide was prepared for the in-depth follow-up interviews, including questions on the same 3 categories as the survey: 1) profile & well-being, 2) knowledge & attitudes, and 3) practices (i.e. trainings, skills, and psychological support). All interview participants were working at the CGRS or CALL at the time the survey was conducted (January 2023), but some of them had left by the time the interview took place. It should be noted that this interview sample was subject to a selection bias, whereby only those participants who were willing to share their views and experiences, often based on a pre-existing interest in the subject, volunteered. The interview sample can be visualised as follows (Figure 10):

Figure 10: Number of participants in interviews with asylum authorities sample, according to authority, language, role, gender-specialisation, gender identity, and experience

<table>
<tr><th colspan="8">INTERVIEWS WITH ASYLUM AUTHORITIES</th></tr>
<tr><td colspan="4">CGRS</td><td colspan="4">CALL</td></tr>
<tr><td colspan="4">14</td><td colspan="4">8</td></tr>
<tr><td colspan="2">Dutch-speaking</td><td colspan="2">French-speaking</td><td colspan="2">Dutch-speaking</td><td colspan="2">French-speaking</td></tr>
<tr><td colspan="2">8</td><td colspan="2">6</td><td colspan="2">4</td><td colspan="2">4</td></tr>
<tr><td>PO</td><td>Supervisor</td><td>PO</td><td>Supervisor</td><td>Attaché</td><td>Judge</td><td>Attaché</td><td>Judge [378]</td></tr>
<tr><td>4</td><td>4</td><td>4</td><td>2</td><td>2</td><td>2</td><td>2</td><td>2</td></tr>
<tr><td colspan="8">Gender-specialised? [379]</td></tr>
<tr><td colspan="4">5</td><td colspan="4"></td></tr>
<tr><td colspan="8">F/M/X</td></tr>
<tr><td colspan="4">4 M / 10 F</td><td colspan="4">2 M / 6 F</td></tr>
<tr><td colspan="3">≤ 5y experience</td><td colspan="2">6-10y experience</td><td colspan="3">≥ 11y experience [380]</td></tr>
<tr><td colspan="3">11</td><td colspan="2">3</td><td colspan="3">8</td></tr>
<tr><td colspan="8">22</td></tr>
</table>

In the footnotes, quotes from these interviews will be referenced as follows. Each pseudonym consists of: [a letter to indicate the institution (R for RvV[381] (CALL in Dutch) and C for CGRS) – B for Belgium – a unique identification number for each participant]. For confidentiality purposes, decision makers with

---

378 Current role to my knowledge from the interview. Supervisors in some cases still fulfilled the role of PO simultaneously.

379 To my knowledge from the interview.

380 For confidentiality purposes, the exact number of years is not further specified. To my knowledge from the interview, at the current institution.

381 For 'Raad voor Vreemdelingenbetwistingen'.

any kind of gender specialisation to my knowledge (see Part II, Chapter 2.2.) are distinguished by the marker 'GENDER' but will not be further specified. Here too, I will not provide asylum officials' language and gender identity to guarantee their non-identifiability, but I will refer to them with the gender-neutral pronouns 'they/them'.

	Pseudonym	Authority	Roles (current/previous)	Specialisation[382]
e.g.	CB005_	CGRS_	Supervisor+PO_	GENDER_
e.g.	RB001_	CALL_	Judge_	

4.4.3. ROLE OF THE SURVEY AND INTERVIEWS WITH ASYLUM OFFICIALS IN THE RESEARCH (METHODOLOGY)

The survey's overall response rate (until the end: 58,38%) did not permit representative stand-alone conclusions, and most importantly, SGBV-related refugee status determination is a subject of such complexity that a survey format, as also indicated by a number of respondents, may not fully reflect the depth of their perspectives. Therefore, the survey primarily served as an exploratory step in shaping the qualitative follow-up interviews. However, the information from category 1 (profile and wellbeing) did contribute to providing direct info on the institutional context of the Belgian asylum procedure (Part II).

Although the follow-up interviews could necessarily only be conducted with a selection of asylum officials, the quantitative data from the broader survey sample did allow the interview questions and answers to be framed in their institution-wide context. For example, when an interview respondent answered that a certain thinking pattern or practice occurred frequently or not at all, this could be compared to the survey results, which enriched the interview and the analysis as such. In addition, the cases I had analysed during the fieldwork up to then also provided useful input to flesh out and illustrate certain questions with concrete examples. This allowed me to move away from more general, superficial, or socially/institutionally desirable responses throughout the interview. It was the final input from these interviews that, as data, directly shaped the results of this research.

It is important to stress that, while all asylum officials in the Belgian procedure got the chance to do a follow-up interview, those who eventually voluntarily participated constitute a limited, self-selected, and therefore non-representative sample. As such, the data collected from these interviews are not generalisable across the CGRS or CALL as a whole. Instead, the quotes used throughout the research serve to illustrate and validate the conclusions of the case law analysis.

382 See Part II, Chapter 2.2.1. This is left blank when not gender-specialised.

In contrast, the latter case law sample was representatively selected and therefore its conclusions are generalisable (for the specific time period analysed, see Chapter 4.3 above).

Lastly, the interviews with asylum officials were semi-structured, following a flexible guide of predetermined open-ended questions while allowing interviewees' input to shape the conversation through follow-ups and spontaneous discussion. As not all questions were posed to all interviewees, these interviews are not mutually comparable, making it difficult to assess whether answers were common (trends) or not (outliers). It goes without saying that no outlier statement is claimed to represent a trend throughout the text. The other way around, a trend (where similar answers were given by multiple interviewees) is often represented by only one/few quote(s) for the sake of readability and conciseness. In the latter case, this is clarified throughout the text and/or in the references.

4.4.4. TRAININGS AND GUIDELINES ON SGBV AT THE CGRS

Lastly, it is worth noting that the CGRS was willing to share, in the context of this research, the training courses and guidelines available to guide POs and supervisors in their SGBV-related decision making. According to the memorandum of understanding with the CGRS, these guidelines (partly based on the content of the training courses) could not be made public. Because this research focuses specifically on SGBV myth acceptance/rebuttal in decision making practice, regardless of the training and guidelines that precede/inform these, I have chosen not to include these confidential documents as data in the research. However, throughout the text, I will refer to how individual asylum officials experience, interpret and use these guidelines/training courses in their daily practice. In addition, I will hereafter discuss the types of training and guidelines that exist at the CGRS, in order to outline the support available for SGBV-related refugee status determination (Part II) and come back to these in the Conclusion (Part VI).

4.5. INTEGRATIVE ANALYSIS

4.5.1. CODING PROCESS

The data collected via the above-described methods were the subject of an integrative analysis, in order to draw conclusions and recommendations on SGBV myth acceptance/rebuttal in asylum procedures and decisions. For each of the identified SGBV myths (SQ3) and procedural and institutional aspects (SQ4), I created codes using the qualitative data analysis software NVivo. I employed a hybrid coding approach,[383] integrating both deductive and inductive thematic analysis. The SGBV myth codes were initially developed through a theory-driven deductive coding process,[384] drawing on the law and literature analysis (see Chapter 4.1). These were tested against a preliminary case law analysis during the fieldwork at NANSEN NGO (see Chapter 4.2), allowing for the identification of *a priori* codes representing relevant SGBV myths in the asylum context.

Thereafter, I used an inductive, grounded coding approach[385] to allow for the emergence of new, unanticipated SGBV myths from the research interviews and personal (asylum) interviews with asylum applicants (see Chapter 4.2). This combination ensured that the analysis was anchored in existing theory on rape mythology, but also in survivor/victim-applicants' lived experiences. This hybridly defined set of codes/myths served as an analytical framework for the subsequent coding of the case law (see Chapter 4.3) (and lawyers' argumentation therein) and the interviews/survey with asylum authorities (see Chapter 4.4). While here too, I allowed for instances of new SGBV myth acceptance or rebuttal to emerge from the data, no new codes/myths emerged beyond those already identified through the literature and applicant interviews.

Per myth, I distinguished between a code for SGBV myth acceptance (MA) and myth rebuttal (MR). I analysed all empirically collected data by coding fragments of MA and MR, namely: responses in research interviews and personal (CGRS) interviews with asylum applicants (MR), interview responses of asylum authorities (MA & MR), qualitative survey responses of asylum authorities (MA & MR), lawyers' argumentations in case law (representing the applicants' views) (MR), and the case law itself (MA & MR). As mentioned above (Chapter 4.3), the latter case law coding concerned individual arguments, echoing this research's focus on the separate types of reasoning (cumulatively) substantiating decisions, and not on their eventual result (not) to grant applicants international protection as a whole.

While lawyers and applicants themselves may also accept certain SGBV myths (whether or not in an internalised manner[386]), their SGBV myth acceptance and gender sensitivity towards their clients'/own SGBV-related application for international protection is not the focus of this research. Therefore, (personal)

383 Jennifer Fereday and Eimear Muir-Cochrane, 'Demonstrating Rigor Using Thematic Analysis: A Hybrid Approach of Inductive and Deductive Coding and Theme Development' (2006) 5 International Journal of Qualitative Methods 80, 82–85.

384 Andrea J Bingham, 'From Data Management to Actionable Findings: A Five-Phase Process of Qualitative Data Analysis' (2023) 22 International Journal of Qualitative Methods 1, 2.

385 Kathy Charmaz, *Constructing Grounded Theory: A Practical Guide through Qualitative Analysis* (Sage 2012) 42–43.

386 United Nations Office on Drugs and Crime (UNODC) (n 284) 95; Patricia L Fanflik, Office on Violence Against Women, and National District Attorneys Association, 'Victim Responses to Sexual Assault: Counterintuitive or Simply Adaptive' (American Prosecutors Research Institute 2007) 11.

interviews with applicants and lawyers' argumentation were not analysed on MA. The research does occasionally reflect upon their (internalised) SGBV myth acceptance where this contributes to a nuanced understanding of decision makers' practice of SGBV-related refugee status determination. Below, I will discuss the merely supportive role of lawyers' argumentation in rebutting SGBV myths (MR), given their inherently biased nature. I overlappingly coded all case law according to the six above defined categories of SGBV,[387] allowing an analysis of MA/MR distribution across different forms of gender-related persecution.

To conduct the institutional analysis of SGBV-related procedures in Belgium (Part II), I inductively identified codes within three predefined categories: 1) decision making attitudes (towards the decision making process, applicants, gender-related international protection in general, ...); 2) decision making process (focusing on procedural aspects in gender-related asylum procedures); and 3) decision making support (throughout decision makers' refugee status determination, such as trainings, guidelines, psychological support, ...). All abovementioned data sets were coded according to these categories, within which specific subcodes arose in a grounded manner. The coding tree used to code the MA/MR instances, SGBV types, and decision-making attitudes, process, and support in NVivo can be visualised in Figure 44 of the Annex. In an NVivo classification sheet, the meta data of all analysed case law was registered according to the following attributes: year of birth, gender identity, and country of origin of the applicant; type(s) of SGBV mentioned; authority (CGRS or CALL), court composition and judge (if applicable), date, number (if applicable), type, and language of the decision/judgement; number of the (subsequent) procedure; and sampling strategy (systematic or specific search in the online CALL database or fieldwork).

Throughout this coding process, I engaged in continuous comparison[388] across data sources, ensuring consistency in code application and refining definitions as needed. The codes were developed and applied individually, but this process was systematically monitored and validated with the research supervisors.[389] This approach allowed me to set the institutional scene of attitudes toward, procedural aspects of, and support throughout the assessment of gender-related applications for international protection; describe how applicants (themselves or via their lawyers' argumentation) explained the myth-like character of certain arguments from their own experience; and draw conclusions on the

[387] Rape and sexual assault (RSA), Sex trafficking and forced prostitution (STFP), Genital mutilation/cutting (GMC), Violence related to gender norm transgression (VGNT), Forced marriage (FM), and Domestic violence (DV).

[388] Margaret M Cullen and Niamh M Brennan, 'Grounded Theory: Description, Divergences and Application' (2021) 27 Accounting, Finance & Governance Review 1, 5.

[389] Allison Tong, Peter Sainsbury and Jonathan Craig, 'Consolidated Criteria for Reporting Qualitative Research (COREQ): A 32-Item Checklist for Interviews and Focus Groups' (2007) 19 International Journal for Quality in Health Care 349, 352.

distribution/cumulation of and relations between SGBV myth acceptance and rebuttal by authorities across case law with different factual and procedural attributes.

4.5.2. INTEGRATED ECOLOGICAL APPROACH

Inspired by Heise's integrated ecological approach to SGBV, I divided the identified SGBV myths across three levels: the micro, meso/exo, and macro level. Heise's approach was on its turn based on Bronfenbrenner's ecological systems theory, explaining human development as influenced by multiple interacting environmental systems, each 'nested [...] within the next.'[390] Along the same lines, Heise conceptualised SGBV as a 'multifaceted phenomenon, grounded in an interplay among personal, situational, and sociocultural factors.'[391] I expand this framing of factors impacting SGBV prevalence in several concentric levels,[392] to include the SGBV myth-like thinking patterns downplaying and perpetuating such violence. Similar to Heise's framework, this ecological structure will reveal how SGBV myths too exist in 'embedded levels of causality,'[393] where the acceptance of one myth might overlap with or generate acceptance of other myths as a ripple effect from the micro level outward to the macro level (Figure 11).

For this research, the micro level represents arguments focusing on survivors'/victims' personal characteristics (e.g. their material and non-material resourcefulness, (mental) health and its impact on their memory, their ways and timing of disclosing SGBV, their survival reactions after SGBV experiences/threats ...). The meso level moves on to the immediate interpersonal setting in which the SGBV takes place (i.e. private support network, such as family, friends, community, ...). The exo level then comprises the institutional context surrounding the survivor/victim, both formal and informal. These include both non-state organisations and service providers (e.g. doctors, teachers, NGOs, ...) and 'state actors of protection' in the sense of (inter)national refugee law (e.g. the police, the military, the judiciary, or organisations controlling (a substantial part of) the state territory[394]) Finally, the macro level encompasses the broader society and culture, as well as the attitudes towards survivors/victims installed

390 Urie Bronfenbrenner, 'Toward an Experimental Ecology of Human Development' (1977) 32 American Psychologist 513, 513–515.

391 Lori Heise, 'Violence Against Women: An Integrated, Ecological Framework' (1998) 4 Violence against women 262, 262.

392 *Ibid.* 264–265.

393 *Ibid.* 264.

394 Art. 7(1) EU Qualification Directive; Art. 7(1) EU Qualification Regulation; Art. 48/5, §2 Belgian Aliens Act.

therein (e.g. the perception of SGBV as a private issue).[395] The identified SGBV myths are categorised into these levels as follows:

- Micro level: 1) resourcefulness myths, 2) disclosure myths, and 3) survival myths, focusing on applicants' material and non-material resourcefulness (with specific focus on male resourcefulness); (alleged) shortcomings in the detailedness, consistency, or timing of and demeanour during disclosure of SGBV-related flight stories; and their short and long-term survival reactions to SGBV respectively
- Meso & exo level: 4) non-state protection myths and 5) state protection myths, focusing on applicants' help-seeking behaviour from private support networks (friends, family ...), non-state actors (NGOs, doctors ...), and state actors of protection (police, military, judiciary ...) in the country of origin
- Macro level: 6) private issue myth, qualifying SGBV as a private problem and therefore excluding it from the UN Refugee Convention scope

Figure 11: Visualisation of the ecological levels and myths used for integrative analysis

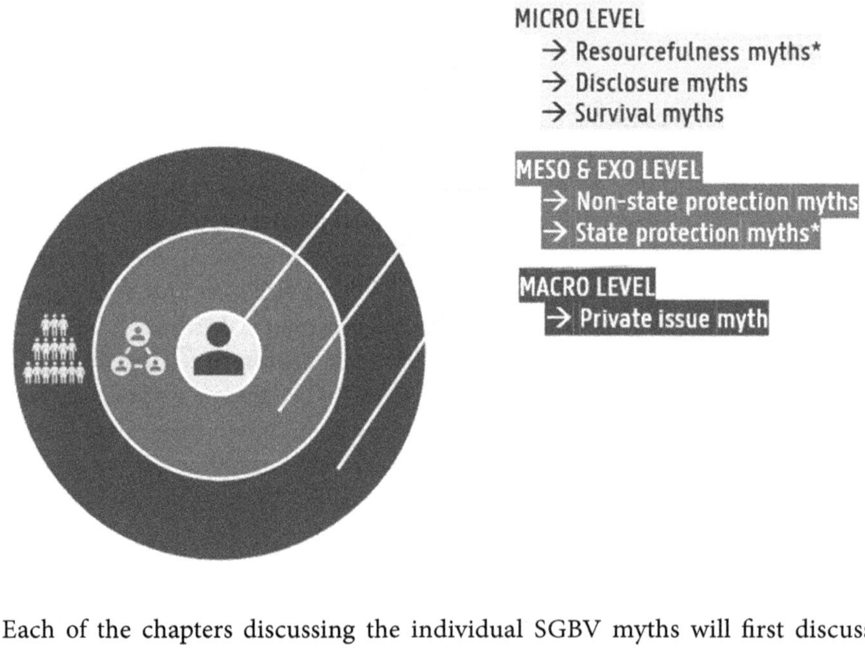

Each of the chapters discussing the individual SGBV myths will first discuss acceptance of the myth as originally described in literature on rape mythology and observed in the analysed case law and interviews/survey with Belgian asylum authorities. Thereupon, they go into the reasons why the myth can be

395 Heise (n 391) 264; Bronfenbrenner (n 390) 514–515.

rebutted, both from health/social sciences and law/legal sciences perspective, and into the ways in which such rebuttal is already reflected in Belgian asylum decision making. The chapters will conclude with a quantitative representation of the acceptance and rebuttal levels of each SGBV myth in the analysed case law sample (n=202), according to the asylum authority (CGRS and CALL) and language (Dutch and French).

As mentioned above, it is important to stress that the available CGRS decisions, because this is a first instance procedure and the argumentation of positive decisions is not made public, give virtually no reason to rebut myths explicitly. This explains the fact that these decisions generally contain no arguments rebutting the SGBV myths. Therefore, in the quantitative representation finalising each SGBV myth chapter, the CGRS' myth rebuttal levels will not be visualised. Also, only explicit rebuttal/acceptance of the myths could be coded in this analysis. Cases in which SGBV myth-based arguments were not explicitly rejected, confirmed, or repeated, but were simply not commented on, are not reflected in these figures, since absence of engagement with an argument could not be qualified as acceptance, nor as rebuttal.

The rebuttal of the SGBV myths in health and social sciences builds both on scientific and experiential knowledge. The former constitutes evidence-based research on the causes, nature, consequences, and prevalence of SGBV from disciplinary fields such as psychology, neurobiology, gender studies, anthropology, and sociology (whether or not linked to the migration/asylum context). Secondarily, this scientific knowledge is illustrated and validated by experiential knowledge from applicants directly (through their (personal) interviews) or indirectly through their statements reflected in medical certificates or lawyers' argumentation. Importantly, as the latter argumentation is inherently biased towards applicants' legal representation, it is only mentioned for illustration/supportive purposes when directly representing applicants' statements (experiential knowledge) and/or confirming empirical knowledge (e.g. medical/psychological expertise, COI, ...). This allows the standpoints of applicants for whom no interview transcripts or notes from the personal (asylum) interview were available to be represented in the research.

As for the rebuttal in law and legal sciences, these sections will first cite the most authoritative legal sources: relevant international law (e.g. UN Refugee Convention, EU Directives/Regulations, ... and preparatory works) and case law (e.g. CJEU, ECtHR, ...), followed by international guidelines on their implementation (e.g. UNHCR, CEDAW, ...), and by legal scholarship and national case law in other asylum systems that may serve as good practice examples. The latter are not based on a systematic or exhaustive case law analysis, but were collected throughout the literature analysis, via snowballing. The legal scholarship used may, like the health/social sciences rebuttal, also be empirically grounded, but does establish a link to and primarily focuses on the legal (asylum) context. Lastly, lawyers' argumentation in the analysed case law may also be cited here, purely for illustrative purposes, where they are based on undisputed case elements.

Figure 12 gives an overview of the SGBV myths I identified and analysed in the Belgian asylum procedure, categorised within their ecological levels, and linked to the existing framework of rape mythology. As mentioned earlier (Chapter 1.4), two of the six myths are indicated with an asterisk/* (the resourcefulness and state protection myths), to nuance that these beliefs are not always false, leaving room for these myth-based arguments to be used when explicitly supported by COI. I will elaborate on the conditions for this to be the case in each of these myths' separate chapters (Part III, Chapter 2.2 and Part IV, Chapter 3.2 respectively).

Figure 12: Visualisation of identified SGBV myths, corresponding ecological levels, and existing rape myths

Type of myth	RAPE MYTH IN CRIMINAL JUSTICE CONTEXT (illustrative)	SGBV MYTH IN ASYLUM CONTEXT
MICRO LEVEL		
Resourcefulness myths*	'[SGBV] is […] the problem of certain neighbourhoods […] and certain types of people',[396] 'Men cannot be raped; they can resist'[397]	Resourceful applicants do not need protection against SGBV
Disclosure myths	A real SGBV survivor/victim 'is absolutely certain about the details', 'does not change [the] account of what happened',[398] 'will disclose [the] violation at the first reasonable opportunity',[399] or is 'visibly upset by the experience'[400]	'Inappropriate' disclosure undermines SGBV flight stories' credibility
Survival myths	'Survivors never remain in contact with offenders following an assault'[401] or 'will finally be safe when [they leave] [a violent] relationship'[402]	'Inappropriate' survival reactions undermine SGBV flight stories' credibility

(continued)

396 Miriam Ticktin, 'In the Name of Violence against Women' in Miriam Ticktin, *Casualties of Care: Immigration and the Politics of Humanitarianism in France* (University of California Press 2011) 156.

397 James Lochhead and Pek Leng Tan, *Seeking Justice for Victims of Sexual Crime* (Women's Centre for Change (WCC) Penang 2009) 52.

398 Kimberly A Lonsway and others, 'False Reports: Moving Beyond the Issue to Successfully Investigate and Prosecute Non-Stranger Sexual Assault' (End Violence Against Women International (EVAWI) 2009) 4.

399 United Nations Office on Drugs and Crime (UNODC) and Skinnider (n 161) 90.

400 Hannah McGee and others, 'Rape and Child Sexual Abuse: What Beliefs Persist About Motives, Perpetrators, and Survivors?' (2011) 26 Journal of Interpersonal Violence 3580, 3586.

401 Lorna H Breen and Melissa A Boyce, '"Why Did She Talk to Him Again?" The Effects of the Justice Motive, Relationship Type, and Degree of Postassault Contact on Perceptions of Sexual Assault' (2021) 36 Journal of Interpersonal Violence 5229, 5233.

402 World Health Organization (WHO), 'Caring for Women Subjected to Violence: A WHO Training Curriculum for Health Care Providers' (2021) 5.

MESO & EXO LEVEL			
Non-state protection myths		'Rape is unlikely to happen in the [person]'s own familiar neighbourhood',[403] 'Nowadays, sexual violence [survivors/victims] receive sufficient help in the form of [...] shelters, therapy [...], and support groups'[404]	Applicants with non-state actor support do not need protection against SGBV
State protection myths*		'[A real] victim would promptly seek help and report',[405] 'Nowadays, [those] who really sexually assault [others] are punished justly'[406]	Non-exhaustion of state protection implies non-credibility or ill-foundedness of SGBV flight stories
MACRO LEVEL			
Private issue myth		'Domestic violence [is] a private matter[, e.g. because] the attack happened at the home and [...] the offender was not a danger to the public'[407]	SGBV is a private issue excluded from the UN Refugee Convention scope

403 Payne, Lonsway and Fitzgerald (n 134) 49.
404 Gerger and others (n 150) 440.
405 United Nations Office on Drugs and Crime (UNODC) and Skinnider (n 161) 36.
406 Gerger and others (n 150) 440.
407 United Nations Office on Drugs and Crime (UNODC) and Skinnider (n 161) 122.

PART II

SGBV-RELATED ASYLUM PROCEDURES IN BELGIUM

1. INTRODUCTION

This chapter presents an institutional analysis of SGBV-related asylum procedures in Belgium. It will first discuss the registration of applications for international protection at the IO. I will hereby discuss how IO case workers assess applicants' special procedural needs, how they are trained to handle SGBV-related cases, and how the 'small' registration interview takes place. Next, the first instance stage at the CGRS will be set out, where POs determine whether applicants should be granted international protection. In doing so, I will focus on procedural and institutional aspects with particular relevance to SGBV-related cases, namely: the organisation of gender specialisation, gender guidelines, psychological support, and procedural aspects in place at the CGRS. Lastly, I will describe the appeal procedure before the CALL, including awareness raising initiatives on SGBV for judges and attachés handling SGBV-related cases, psychological support available to them, and the appeal hearing.

2. INSTITUTIONAL ANALYSIS OF SGBV-RELATED ASYLUM PROCEDURES IN BELGIUM

2.1. REGISTRATION: THE IMMIGRATION OFFICE

2.1.1. REGISTRATION & SPECIAL PROCEDURAL NEEDS

The IO registers an application for international protection and starts the asylum procedure with an interview that enquires into applicants' identity, origin and travel route.[408] The IO confirms prioritising the registration of applications from minors, families, elderly persons and 'other vulnerable persons'.[409] A case worker at the IO assesses possible special procedural needs of applicants[410] and provides 'appropriate support' if these needs are sufficiently demonstrated and would hinder the applicant to fulfil their obligations in the procedure.[411] If there are indications that a flight story includes gender-related persecution, the same case worker has to verify whether applicants prefer being heard by a person of the same gender identity.[412]

2.1.2. SGBV-RELATED TRAINING

The case workers conducting the IO interviews are not necessarily legally trained. They do receive a training on the UN Refugee Convention, the human rights

408 Art. 51/10, part 1-2 Belgian Aliens Act.

409 Immigration Office (IO), 'Internal Communication IO' (20 February 2025).

410 The IO confirms registering applicants' vulnerabilities via a form including the non-exhaustive categories: 'minors, elderly persons, single women, single persons with minor children, pregnant women, LGBT, persons with medical problems, psychological problems, victims of violence or victims of trafficking.' The form also provides open space to add other vulnerability categories or details. *Ibid.*

411 Art. 48/9, §4 Belgian Aliens Act.

412 Art. 8, §2 Koninklijk besluit houdende vaststelling van bepaalde elementen van de procedure die dienen gevolgd te worden door de dienst van de Dienst Vreemdelingenzaken die belast is met het onderzoek van de asielaanvragen op basis van de wet van 15 december 1980 betreffende de toegang tot het grondgebied, het verblijf, de vestiging en de verwijdering van vreemdelingen (Belgian Royal Decree on the IO) 2003 (Belgisch staatsblad of 27 January 2004, p 4645).

conventions that bind Belgium and other legal protection grounds, intercultural communication, and interviewing vulnerable groups.[413] When it comes to support in SGBV-related procedures,[414] the IO adds in internal communication that in 2024, (some) case workers received a workshop on 'Diversity, Equality and Inclusion' (28 front-line staff members) and half a day of training on 'Gender in the IO's practice' (on a voluntary basis, 178 staff members), providing information on the definition of gender and its relationship to societal norms, intersectionality, gendered vulnerabilities, SGBV and its survivors/victims, the legal obligations to take into account special procedural needs, and relevant partners in civil society. The IO does acknowledge that 'half a day is not enough to concretely go into each of these elements,' but that the content is determined by the interaction among participants and that it contributes to creating a support platform among them.[415]

2.1.3. THE 'SMALL' REGISTRATION INTERVIEW

The first registration interview at the IO (in practice often called the 'small' interview, in preparation for the 'big' personal interview at the CGRS) takes place without the legal support of a lawyer (but in the presence of a parent or (legal) guardian if the applicant is a minor).[416] In theory, this interview mainly serves to register the application for international protection and to identify possible vulnerabilities that could lead to special procedural guarantees during the procedure before the IO, CGRS, and CALL.[417] In practice, however, it appears that whether or not certain vulnerabilities or elements in the flight story are mentioned at this preliminary stage can have an impact on the final outcome of the procedure (see Part III, Chapter 2.1.1.). This is particularly the case when these elements differ from the 'big' personal interview at the CGRS and/or the appeal documentation or hearing at the CALL. In some cases, these inconsistencies inform (among other arguments) the decision not to grant someone special procedural guarantees and/or international protection, as happened in Mary's case.[418]

---

413 Art. 13 *ibid.*; The IO confirms that this covers gender-related procedural needs and that these trainings are given prior to case workers starting to interview applicants on their own. Immigration Office (IO) (n 409).

414 Hereby not mentioning the exclusively SOGI-related trainings, which are excluded from the scope of this research.

415 Immigration Office (IO) (n 409).

416 Art. 9 Belgian Royal Decree on the IO.

417 Art. 11 *ibid.*

418 Zoes are traditional heads of the Sande 'bush schools', carrying out female genital mutilation in Liberia. Efua Dorkenoo Obe and 28 Too Many, 'Country Profile: FGM in Liberia' (FGM/C Research Initiative 2019) 14.

CASE OF MARY			
• Country of origin:	Liberia	• SGBV types:	Sex trafficking/forced prostitution, GMC, violence related to gender norm transgression & forced marriage
• Gender identity:	Woman	• Decisions in file:	CGRS 1 (refusal) – 17/02/2022
• Birth year:	1980		CALL 1 (refusal) – 10/08/2022 – n° 275 866
• Interview by:	Researcher		

According to her statements, Mary did not grow up with her parents but was raised in Liberia by guardians from the United States. When she asked why her parents left her, her guardians first replied that she wouldn't understand, and at an older age that her mother wanted to save her from GMC, but nothing more. She finished high school, left her guardians and moved to Ghana to take courses to become a tailor. She married her partner and they had a son. Later on, back in Liberia, Mary met her biological father and relatives, who invited her to a family meeting without disclosing its purpose. At the gathering, they insisted she **take on her role as a GMC practitioner, forcibly marry** an older man, and **undergo GMC** herself. She had to replace her mother, who had recently passed away, as a 'Zoe'. Opposed to the practice, she refused and left, but her relatives came back to remind her of her duties. She went into hiding at a friend's house, together with her son. However, she spotted her family around the house several times, pointing at her. Fearing for her safety but also for the dangerous migration journey, Mary left Liberia with assistance from a smuggler, leaving her son in the care of her friend. Since the Liberian government, overruled by traditional leaders, dismisses GMC as 'family business', she fled to a country that is against the practice, like Belgium. After she left, her friend sent Mary a letter reporting how her family visited her son at school to ask about her, upon which she unenrolled him.

Upon arriving in Belgium, Mary was **forced into prostitution** and repeatedly **sexually abused**. She submitted psychological certificates that describe her post-traumatic stress disorder (PTSD), resulting in memory issues, confusion, and difficulty discussing her past.

In Mary's procedure, the CGRS denied her international protection and stated in the decision that:

> 'The psychological certificate […] would show that you were the victim of sexual violence upon your arrival in Europe, that you were locked up in a house and that you were raped several times […]. However, **during your interview at the IO […] you do not indicate at all that you experienced problems upon arrival in Belgium.** You only stated to the CGRS that you stayed in a house for several months […]. […] That you failed to do so indicates that **you have no fear upon return to Liberia, if you actually suffered sexual violence.**'[419] | CASE OF MARY

419 NL017_CGRS 1 (refusal)_1980_F_Liberia_STFP_GMC_VGNT_FM_17/2/2022_NL_NANSEN_ p. 4.

Mary later explains her confusion about the IO interview in the interview:

> 'They didn't ask me what happened when I got here. […] [T]he people that brought me here, they had me in a place and they had people […] sleeping with us for some time. […] You ask this, I explain. […] But **they didn't ask. So I didn't explain**. […] I explained [my answers] while she wrote and she said, "later you go for another [interview]".'[420] | CASE OF MARY

Procedures like Mary's might lead asylum officials, like a PO I interviewed at the CGRS, to reason: 'If the person […] [gives one flight] reason to the IO, […] [and] at the CGRS […] she admits […] also fearing [SGBV], […] she has to have a good reason why she didn't tell the IO before.'[421] This risk is exacerbated by the lack of legal assistance and the fact that these interviews are often perceived by applicants as rushed and stressful, as illustrated by the case of Vera.[422]

CASE OF VERA			
• Country of origin:	Albania	• SGBV types:	Rape/sexual assault, violence related to gender norm transgression & domestic violence
• Gender identity:	Woman	• Decisions in file:	CGRS 1 (manifestly ill-founded) – 10/10/2022
• Birth year:	1990		CALL 1 (refusal) – 27/02/2023 – n° 285 363
• Interview by:	Researcher		

According to her statements, Vera was born in Shkodër (Albania), where she worked as a secondary school teacher. She met her husband at university, gave birth to a son, and married him two months later. During the five years of this marriage, her husband used constant **psychological, physical and sexual violence** against her and was addicted to alcohol and drugs. Her husband and family-in-law carried a firearm at all times due to their involvement in a blood feud and problems with the mafia. Because of this, her son was kidnapped once, leading her to not let him go to school or outside anymore. She herself was not allowed to leave the house either. With the property surrounded by surveillance cameras, she could only leave for work or when accompanied by her husband. She did not dare to report the violence, fearing her husband's threats and family-in-law's ties with the police. She sought support through a few therapy sessions on the phone when her husband, who could not know, was out of the house. She eventually fled the country with her son and filed for divorce. In these proceedings, her husband was awarded full custody and consequently filed a complaint for international child abduction, upon which she was questioned by the Belgian police. Especially in Northern-Albanian areas like Shkodër, patriarchal

(continued)

420 NL017_1980_F_Liberia_STFP_GMC_VGNT_FM_NL_[00:25:43].

421 CB004_CGRS_PO_[00:46:19].

422 William Shankley, Maria Ramanov and Yasmeen Jaber, 'Exploring the Significance of the Kanun in Young Albanian People's Asylum Journeys in the UK' (University of Liverpool, Shpresa Programme & University of Nottingham 2024) 3, 4 & 8.

cultural norms are upheld by the Kanun: a book containing traditional customary laws, for example prohibiting a woman to leave her husband. Since she **violated her family's honour** by doing so, they do not support her and she fears for her life upon return.

In her asylum procedure, she submitted: news items and police reports on her son's abduction; video recordings of the domestic violence by a surveillance camera outside their house; and medical certificates by both Albanian and Belgian psychologists and psychiatrists, documenting her PTSD, treatment with medication, insomnia, anxiety, and inability to talk about her experiences.

Vera testified about the IO interview:

> 'It went terribly because **I forgot everything. I forgot my name, my first name.** [...] I repeated ten times "What do you mean? I don't understand any of these questions." I had forgotten everything, **I cried all the time**. They just told me "It'll be all right, ma'am".'[423] | CASE OF VERA

2.2. FIRST INSTANCE: THE OFFICE OF THE COMMISSIONER GENERAL FOR REFUGEES AND STATELESS PERSONS

2.2.1. DETERMINATION OF INTERNATIONAL PROTECTION STATUS

After the registration, the case is sent to the CGRS, an independent federal administration led by the Commissioner-General and two deputies (one Dutch and one French-speaking).[424] The CGRS decides on the recognition of refugee status or the granting of subsidiary protection status on the basis of the documents submitted by applicants, available COI, and one (or more) personal interview(s) (if organised),[425] by determining whether the application meets the criteria of the refugee definition in the UN Refugee Convention[426] or the provisions on subsidiary protection.[427] In addition, it assesses whether there is an IFA available

423 NA016_1990_F_Albania_RSA_VGNT_DV_NL_[00:06:45].

424 Art. 57/2 *jo.* 57/4 Belgian Aliens Act; Commissioner General for Refugees and Stateless Persons (CGRS), 'About the CGRS', www.cgrs.be/en/about-the-cgrs.

425 The CGRS is not always obliged to do so, for example when the available evidence allows the CGRS to take a positive decision in a first asylum procedure or any decision in a subsequent asylum procedure, or when the applicant cannot be heard due to durable circumstances beyond their control. Art. 57/5*ter*, §2 Belgian Aliens Act.

426 Art. 1(A)2 UN Refugee Convention; Art. 2(d) EU Qualification Directive; Art. 48/3 Belgian Aliens Act.

427 Art. 2(f) EU Qualification Directive; Art. 48/4 Belgian Aliens Act.

to applicants in another part of the country of origin.[428] Such an IFA can be considered on the conditions that applicants have no fear of being persecuted or have access to protection against persecution, and can reasonably be expected to safely and legally travel to and settle at this alternative location.[429]

The personal interview at the CGRS is conducted by individual case workers called POs,[430] the decisions they draft are being evaluated and monitored by supervisors, who have the final say on their content, and these are finally validated and communicated to the applicant by the Commissioner-General. Similar to the IO, the POs are not necessarily legally trained,[431] but they do get training in the same fields as the IO (as provided in Belgium's Royal Decree on the CGRS).[432] Below, I will elaborate on four elements of this first instance stage with particular relevance to SGBV-related cases, namely: the organisation of gender specialisation, gender guidelines, psychological support, and procedural aspects in place at the CGRS.

2.2.2. GENDER SPECIALISATION

a) The Gender Cell & Gender-Specialised POs

In accordance with the EU Procedures Directive, the CGRS has made sure that all POs get a training on gender[433] and that they can seek advice from gender experts[434] called 'gender reference persons' (19 at the time of writing).[435] These gender reference persons assist (regular) POs in complicated gender-related cases upon their request, but also identify their need for training and information on gender-related topics. Next to this role, they mainly work in their principal

---

428 UNHCR, 'Guidelines on International Protection No. 4: "Internal Flight or Relocation Alternative" within the Context of Article 1A(2) of the 1951 Convention and/or 1967 Protocol Relating to the Status of Refugees (HCR/GIP/03/04)' (2003).

429 Art. 8 EU Qualification Directive; Art. 8 EU Qualification Regulation.

430 Art. 6, §1 Koninklijk besluit tot regeling van de werking van en de rechtspleging voor het Commissariaat-generaal voor de Vluchtelingen en de Staatlozen (Belgian Royal Decree on the CGRS) 2003 (Belgisch Staatsblad of 27 January 2004, p 4638).

431 According to the results of the KAP survey conducted in the context of this research (see Part I, Chapter 4.4) at the CGRS (63,86% response rate until the end), respondents had educational backgrounds in: law and criminology (31.75% FR, 26.71% NL); psychology and educational sciences (6.35% FR, 4.79% NL); social and political sciences (44.44% FR, 31.51% NL); linguistics, literature and philosophy (15.87% FR, 34.93% NL); and other (1.59% FR, 2.05% NL). The percentages were calculated on the total number of respondents who answered this particular question.

432 Art. 3, §2 Belgian Royal Decree on the CGRS.

433 Art. 15(3)a EU Procedures Directive; Art. 13(7)a EU Asylum Procedures Regulation.

434 Art. 10(3)d EU Procedures Directive; Art. 34(3) EU Asylum Procedures Regulation.

435 Numbers communicated at the time of writing. Commissioner General for Refugees and Stateless Persons (CGRS), 'Internal Communication CGRS (Part II)' (24 January 2025).

function: at CEDOCA (the COI research unit of the CGRS) (2), at the Legal Department (5), or as a PO/supervisor (12).[436] The gender reference persons are part of the CGRS' 'gender cell', further including: a gender coordinator, a deputy gender coordinator, a coordinator for female GMC monitoring, and an attaché to the gender coordination (taking up administrative tasks).[437] The gender coordinator and deputy coordinator also monitor the organisation of gender trainings and drafting of internal gender guidelines (see 2.2.3.).[438]

In addition, POs can also opt for further specialisation to handle complex gender-related cases, for which they get the title of 'gender PO'.[439] In January 2025, the CGRS confirmed that the group of gender POs counted 48 persons (in comparison to 24 members in 2020).[440] The assignment of cases to these specialised POs is based on the information forwarded after the interview at the IO. When an applicant discloses a fear of four or more different types of SGBV cumulatively, a case (relevant to this research[441]) is considered a 'complex gender case'. Over the course of 2024 (1 December 2023 until 30 November 2024), 7 complex SGBV cases[442] were assigned to the 48 gender POs as a whole, meaning that at least 41 gender POs did not treat any complex SGBV case at all. After several gender POs had pointed this out, discussions were initiated at the CGRS, which led to the suggestion to reduce the current criterion of 'four cumulative SGBV forms' to three. The CGRS confirmed that these discussions are still going on at the time of writing.[443]

436 Numbers communicated at the time of writing. *Ibid.*

437 *Ibid.*

438 Commissioner General for Refugees and Stateless Persons (CGRS), 'Internal Communication CGRS (Part IV)' (2 June 2025); Mahieu, Vanheule and Timmerman (n 23) 50; Commissioner General for Refugees and Stateless Persons (CGRS), 'Gender' (22 January 2015), www.cgvs.be/nl/gender.

439 Commissioner General for Refugees and Stateless Persons (CGRS), 'Internal Communication CGRS (Part I)' (n 128); Vluchtelingenwerk Vlaanderen (Flemish Refugee Action), 'Country Report: Belgium' (The Asylum Information Database (AIDA) 2023) 80; Commissioner General for Refugees and Stateless Persons (CGRS), 'Gender' (n 438).

440 Among these are the 12 gender reference persons mentioned above functioning both as gender POs and as gender reference persons for their geographical section. Commissioner General for Refugees and Stateless Persons (CGRS), 'Internal Communication CGRS (Part I)' (n 128); Commissioner General for Refugees and Stateless Persons (CGRS), 'Internal Communication CGRS (Part II)' (n 435).

441 Hereby not mentioning the exclusively SOGI-related cases, which are excluded from the scope of this research. For the sake of completeness: the CGRS confirms systematically referring all cases involving gender identity to a gender PO. Commissioner General for Refugees and Stateless Persons (CGRS), 'Internal Communication CGRS (Part I)' (n 128); Commissioner General for Refugees and Stateless Persons (CGRS), 'Internal Communication CGRS (Part II)' (n 435).

442 In addition, 14 cases on gender identity (falling outside the scope of this research) were assigned to the gender POs over the course of this same year. Commissioner General for Refugees and Stateless Persons (CGRS), 'Internal Communication CGRS (Part I)' (n 128).

443 *Ibid.*

Gender-related cases that are not considered 'complex' (involving less than four different SGBV types) are handled by all (gender-specialised and non-gender-specialised) POs. The CGRS confirmed that, in principle, all POs are sufficiently trained and therefore expected to handle gender cases.[444] However, some POs pointed out that they themselves 'don't like [...] cases involving sexual violence, because [...] [they] don't want to ask [...] questions that might [...] make [applicants] feel [...] uncomfortable'[445] or 'if [they] could, [they]'d ask not to hear any more women [with SGBV-related flight stories], [...] because it's hard.'[446]

Others state that 'not everyone is equally capable of handling gender cases'[447] and that 'it's really important [...] to have a PO who knows how to put people at ease and who is interested in this theme. Otherwise, [...] this can have a negative impact on the outcome of the procedure.'[448] According to the CGRS, there is in principle no possibility for POs to opt out from handling gender cases, except when they can provide good reasons, upon consultation of and after case by case approval by their supervisor.[449] One PO indicated that this could be the case if you have had experiences with SGBV yourself, but also mentioned: 'Someone with such experiences, who [...] would disclose this? When you've just started a new job [...] who would dare do so?'[450]

b) SGBV-Related Training

POs and supervisors get support in interviewing, drafting, and supervising decisions through the trainings they receive. As mentioned above and confirmed by the CGRS,[451] all POs and supervisors get a standard training on SGBV at the beginning[452] of their appointment, specifically on (relevant to this research[453]): 'gender' (all POs/supervisors since 2010); 'sexual violence' (all POs/supervisors since the implementation of the first sexual violence guideline at the CGRS

444 *Ibid.*
445 CB004_CGRS_PO_[00:59:16].
446 CB013_CGRS_PO_[01:29:58].
447 CB002_CGRS_PO_[00:50:17].
448 CB010_CGRS_PO_[00:16:23].
449 Commissioner General for Refugees and Stateless Persons (CGRS), 'Internal Communication CGRS (Part I)' (n 128).
450 CB014_CGRS_PO_[01:26:31].
451 Commissioner General for Refugees and Stateless Persons (CGRS), 'Internal Communication CGRS (Part I)' (n 128).
452 The general gender training is in principle planned during the first moth, while the other more specified trainings should take place during the second month. Commissioner General for Refugees and Stateless Persons (CGRS), 'Internal Communication CGRS (Part II)' (n 435).
453 Hereby not mentioning the exclusively SOGI-related trainings, which are excluded from the scope of this research.

in 2017); and 'female GMC' (only those POs/supervisors treating countries of origin where prevalent[454]).

In addition, a training on 'the impact of trauma on the memory' was followed by 80 employees at the CGRS (across different services[455]) at the time of writing, as well as one on 'interviewing vulnerable persons', by a selection of POs and supervisors (due to organisational limitations[456]). Lastly, there are trainings that are not structurally organised by the Knowledge and Learning Centre of the CGRS, but *ad hoc* according to the needs and at the request of the different geographical sections, such as a training on forced marriages that was mentioned by some interviewed POs/supervisors.[457]

Gender POs (including those who are also gender reference persons) get additional SGBV-specific trainings (relevant to this research[458]), namely on: 'gender, gender identity and sexual orientation'; 'gender and intercultural aspects'; and 'the psychological impact of SGBV'. The latter two were specifically organised in the aftermath of completing the KAP survey for this research by the CGRS' staff in early 2023.[459] These trainings are given by the 7 internal trainers[460] at the CGRS or by external experts (e.g. a doctor, midwife, psychologist ...) and last between 0,5 and 1,5 day (except for the specialised module on gender and SOGI from the EU Agency for Asylum (EUAA), lasting 45 hours of online and 2 days of in person training).

---

454 I.e. Benin, Burkina Faso, Cameroon, Central African Republic, Chad, Côte d'Ivoire, Djibouti, Egypt, Eritrea, Ethiopia, Gambia, Ghana, Guinea, Guinea-Bissau, Indonesia, Iraq, Kenya, Liberia, Maldives, Mali, Mauritania, Niger, Nigeria, Senegal, Sierra Leone, Somalia, Sudan, Tanzania, United Republic of Togo, Uganda, and Yemen. Commissioner General for Refugees and Stateless Persons (CGRS), 'Internal Communication CGRS (Part IV)' (n 438).

455 Out of ca. 580 employees at the CGRS in total (according to their 2023 annual report), of which 275 POs and supervisors treating cases (according to internal communication with the CGRS). Commissioner General for Refugees and Stateless Persons (CGRS), 'Jaarverslag 2023' (2024) 42; Commissioner General for Refugees and Stateless Persons (CGRS), 'Internal Communication on KAP Participants CGRS' (January 2023).

456 This module, developed by the EUAA, is in principle obligatory for all POs. According to internal communication in January 2025, due to organisational limitations at the CGRS, some POs have already taken the training, while others have not. Both categories deal with gender-related applications for international protection. Commissioner General for Refugees and Stateless Persons (CGRS), 'Internal Communication CGRS (Part II)' (n 435).

457 Since this is not standard training for all (gender-specialised) POs and the CGRS was unable to provide information on the frequency and geographical focus of these training courses, they are not included in the overview of gender training and guidelines below (Figure 13).

458 Hereby not mentioning the exclusively SOGI-related trainings, which are excluded from the scope of this research.

459 Commissioner General for Refugees and Stateless Persons (CGRS), 'Internal Communication CGRS (Part I)' (n 128).

460 These internal trainers followed courses provided by the EU Agency for Asylum (EUAA), namely: 'Gender, Gender Identity & Sexual orientation / Train the trainers' (all 7 trainers), 'sexual orientation, gender identity and expression, and sex characteristics (SOGIESC)' (1 trainer), and 'Victims of gender-related violence' (1 trainer). *Ibid.*

Upon request of the training manager at the CGRS, the duration of certain trainings has been shortened since the end of 2022 and some of the practical exercises that used to be conducted face-to-face have been cancelled. For the gender POs and gender reference persons, a yearly day to deepen gender-related knowledge and exchange issues encountered in gender-related cases is organised.[461] For the non-specialised POs and supervisors, the gender-related trainings are not standardly repeated or refreshed.

From interviews with POs, their experiences with both the general and specialised gender trainings are divided. On the one hand, they applaud the awareness these create and support these provide in their work. One PO, who received more training before starting to interview than usual, due to the exceptional Covid-19 circumstances, said: 'I thought [the trainings were] very relevant […] [although] we didn't go into too much detail about the practical side […] because […] practice varies greatly from one country […] to another. […] We were also told about the psychological difficulties […] for […] victims […]. I thought it was really interesting to have this information beforehand so that we could take these precautions during the interviews.'[462] However, another PO stated that for them, the training on sexual violence 'came much too late.'[463]

In the interviews, POs mentioned specific approaches they took away from trainings and guidelines, such as: using specific questioning techniques (e.g. avoiding direct questions about details of SGBV experiences or direct expression of disbelief to applicants); installing an empathic climate of trust; leaving room for applicants' free narrative (instead of closed or leading questions); explaining the purpose of certain questions; mirroring the words used by applicants to describe the violence; providing (more) breaks; understanding the impact of trauma on disclosure of SGBV (timing, memory and demeanour) and possible coping mechanisms of SGBV survivors/victims; and avoiding retraumatisation and stereotypes altogether.

On the other hand, some POs explained how the gender trainings did not suffice. 'Avoiding stereotypes altogether' is a complex task, as one PO states: 'if the [PO] is not well trained, […] they run the risk of missing the [SGBV] and […] not putting the person at ease enough to be able to confide in them.'[464] They testify having had discussions with colleagues, realising that the latter 'have prejudices that shouldn't be there and that may have had an impact on the processing of the case.'[465] Another PO called the training for POs 'largely inadequate for the topics

461 This day focused on sexual orientation in 2021, on gender identity in 2022, on sexual violence in 2023, and on domestic violence in 2024. Commissioner General for Refugees and Stateless Persons (CGRS), 'Internal Communication CGRS (Part II)' (n 435).

462 CB010_CGRS_PO_[00:09:08].

463 CB003_CGRS_PO_[00:48:16].

464 CB010_CGRS_PO_[00:16:50].

465 CB010_CGRS_PO_[00:16:50].

we cover.'[466] This PO believed it should include a practical part where they can first attend a gender-related personal interview led by an experienced colleague, allowing them to ask questions, before facing this on their own.[467] This is not currently the case. Some do not remember any gender-specific training, for instance because they started as POs a long time ago and the trainings were not yet in place or were never repeated since.[468]

Others pointed out how the gender trainings tend to focus on SGBV against girls and women in regions like Africa (e.g. GMC), a geographical section dealing with many gender cases. As a result, POs hearing applicants with other gender identities, SGBV experiences, or countries of origin (e.g. (male) survivors/applicants facing domestic violence in Eastern Europe or violence related to gender norm transgression in the Middle East) are lacking the necessary knowledge to assess their cases. For domestic violence, sex trafficking/forced prostitution, and violence related to gender norm transgression, the CGRS confirms that no training exists whatsoever.[469]

The interviews and case law analysis also revealed a lack of knowledge among some POs/supervisors about legal-technical elements, such as: the role of non-state actors (see Part IV, Chapter 2.1), the definition of state protection (see Part IV, Chapter 3.1), the scope of the UN Refugee Convention (see Part V, Chapter 2.1), ..., or a lack of guidance in assessing the credibility of traumatic SGBV experiences (see Part III, Chapter 3), which will be discussed in more detail throughout the research.

2.2.3. GUIDELINES & PSYCHOLOGICAL SUPPORT

Next to the abovementioned trainings, POs/supervisors are also guided by the COI made available by CEDOCA, against which they assess applicants' individual flight stories. CEDOCA is the CGRS' research unit, consisting of researchers who collect, analyse, and prepare reports on COI.[470] How this COI, gender-specific or not, plays a role in assessing SGBV-related applications for international protection will be discussed in more depth throughout this research. In addition, the CGRS circulates internal guidelines on different aspects of gender-related asylum procedures.

466 CB013_CGRS_PO_[00:37:01].
467 CB013_CGRS_PO_[00:39:36].
468 CB011_CGRS_Supervisor+PO_GENDER_[00:13:22].
469 Commissioner General for Refugees and Stateless Persons (CGRS), 'Internal Communication CGRS (Part I)' (n 128); Commissioner General for Refugees and Stateless Persons (CGRS), 'Internal Communication CGRS (Part III)' (28 May 2025).
470 Art. 3, §1 Belgian Royal Decree on the CGRS; Commissioner General for Refugees and Stateless Persons (CGRS), 'CEDOCA' (*CGVS*), www.cgvs.be/nl/landeninfo/over-cedoca.

a) *Gender Guidelines*

There are two types of gender guidelines at the CGRS: 'horizontal guidelines' and 'guidance notes'. According to the CGRS, a horizontal guideline is a formally validated, CGRS-wide document developed through a fixed process to ensure harmonised handling of recurring gender-related cases across multiple countries of origin. A guidance note then, is a more flexible tool, drafted upon request of specific (groups of) POs/supervisors on specific issues or profiles and does not require the same formal management endorsement as guidelines before being shared internally.[471] For the sake of readability, both types will be referred to as 'guidelines' in this research. Those (relevant to this research[472]) focus on: sexual violence and female GMC (guidelines) and honour killings and forced marriage (guidance notes).

The latter was drafted primarily for POs dealing with Guinea, the country from where the majority of applicants disclosing forced marriage flee. POs dealing with other countries whose nationals are less likely to disclose forced marriage are advised by the CGRS to use this guideline.[473] The other guidance note only concerns honour killings (i.e. 'the killing of a person (usually a woman) by a member of her family (or by her partner) in response to behaviour that is considered humiliating'[474]) but not the other forms of violence related to gender norm transgression that are categorised as such in this research. The note focuses on specific countries.[475] When assessing an application on a country of origin not included in this list, POs should resort to COI, as the CGRS confirms.[476]

One PO explained for example that the guideline on sexual violence does not allow for using questions on the act of SGBV itself, but only on the circumstances in which the applicants found themselves. However, they added: 'Honestly, [...] even asking these questions made me feel uncomfortable because, in fact, in all cases, the person has to remember the scene.'[477] Another PO indicated that, in contrast to the SOGI guideline, the sexual violence guideline does not include 'a clear set of questions [with] topics to discuss.'[478]

---

471 Commissioner General for Refugees and Stateless Persons (CGRS), 'Internal Communication CGRS (Part III)' (n 469).

472 Hereby not mentioning the exclusively SOGI-related guidelines, which are excluded from the scope of this research.

473 Commissioner General for Refugees and Stateless Persons (CGRS), 'Internal Communication CGRS (Part I)' (n 128).

474 Commissioner General for Refugees and Stateless Persons (CGRS), 'Internal Communication CGRS (Part III)' (n 469).

475 The CGRS lists: Afghanistan, Bangladesh, Turkey (especially in the Kurdish regions of Eastern Turkey), Jordan, Egypt, India, Iran, Iraq, Israel, Palestine, Syria, Lebanon, Nigeria, Pakistan, Mexico, Ecuador, Brazil, East Africa, Malaysia, Papua New Guinea, Cambodia, ... *Ibid.*

476 *Ibid.*

477 CB010_CGRS_PO_[01:10:19].

478 CB014_CGRS_PO_[00:05:35].

While a supervisor with long-standing experience at the CGRS stated: 'in the last ten years, things have changed enormously. There are [...] guidelines on sexual violence that apply across [...] all nationalities and sections,'[479] there are still gaps. There is no guidance available on: other forms of violence related to gender norm transgression than honour killings, sex trafficking/forced prostitution, and domestic violence. As such, one PO confirmed: 'For domestic violence, [...] I sometimes feel a bit helpless because there is no [...] concrete guideline.'[480] In addition, no guidelines exist on how to determine the value of medical certificates. A gender-specialised supervisor, when asked about the differences they noticed in treatment of gender cases, replied: 'With some [POs], you would think "have you even read the guideline?"' and: 'Some [supervisors] go about it [...] faster than others. [...] [In contrast to the POs, at least] they do know there is a guideline, hopefully *laughs* [...] [but] you have to repeat it often.'[481] They continued that POs hear about the gender guideline once at the beginning of their career. After that, the gender cell sends out updates of guidelines to everyone.[482] However, the same gender-specialised supervisor commented: 'Whether people take the time to read it depends more on personal interest.'[483]

The abovementioned follow-up mechanism on SOGI-related cases in May 2022 (see Part I, Chapter 1.2) led to the finding that, considering adherence to guidelines: 'Things still need to be improved, otherwise POs do what they want.'[484] In addition, the time pressure under which POs have to conduct personal interviews and draft decisions cannot be underestimated, one PO explained: 'we have to work fast. [...] And so sometimes it's very difficult to put certain things in place, to say you can take as many breaks as you want, to say [...] "we'll stop the interview, we'll invite you again." [...] [S]ometimes we [...] don't believe in [a] case at all, but [we] have to invite [applicants] again, it [...] [takes us] a long time [...] So that's [...] frustrating.'[485]

As mentioned earlier, a systematic analysis of the existing SGBV guidelines and trainings at the CGRS is beyond the scope of this research. However, throughout the text, I will illustrate individual asylum officials' interpretation and implementation thereof in practice. Figure 13 below presents the types of support (un)available for POs/supervisors at the CGRS for each of the SGBV forms included in this research. To sum up, no standardised training is provided on any form of gender-based violence. For sex trafficking/forced prostitution,

479 CB005_CGRS_Supervisor+PO_GENDER_[00:07:57].
480 CB010_CGRS_PO_[00:10:59].
481 CB015_CGRS_Supervisor+PO_GENDER_[01:03:26].
482 Commissioner General for Refugees and Stateless Persons (CGRS), 'Internal Communication CGRS (Part II)' (n 435).
483 CB015_CGRS_Supervisor+PO_GENDER_[01:04:28].
484 CB009_CGRS_PO_GENDER_[01:01:15].
485 CB007_CGRS_PO_[00:53:56].

domestic violence, and violence related to gender norm transgression (other than honour killings), there are neither trainings nor guidelines in place.[486]

Figure 13: Overview of support (un)available for POs/supervisors at the Office of the Commissioner General for Refugees and Stateless Persons (CGRS) on SGBV forms included in this research

SGBV form		Standard trainings	Guidelines
Rape & sexual assault	Sexual violence	- Training **sexual violence** (all POs)	- Guideline **sexual violence**
Sex trafficking & forced prostitution		✕	✕
GMC		- Training **female GMC** (only POs handling countries where most prevalent)	- Guidelines **female GMC**
Violence related to gender norm transgression	Gender-based violence	✕	- Guidance note **honour killing** (focused on specific countries)
Forced marriage		✕	- Guidance note **forced marriage** (focused on Guinea)
Domestic violence		✕	✕
SGBV in general		- Training on **gender** (all POs) - Training on: **gender**, gender identity & sexual orientation; gender & **intercultural aspects**; the **psychological impact** of SGBV (gender-specialised POs)	✕

PO: protection officer

b) Trauma- & Gender-Sensitive Practices

While some POs, in line with the guideline cited above, deliberately avoid detailed questions about SGBV experiences, others do not. One gender PO, in the case of an applicant forced to marry at age 13, stated: 'The most embarrassing question you have to […] ask is "and the wedding night?", and then […] she told me about it in detail and that was […] very sad.'[487] By contrast, when applicants are not able to disclose details on the SGBV itself, the same PO explained how to them, this obstructs refugee status determination altogether: 'That is very frustrating, […] you can do your best and beg as much as you want […] and stress "you can tell me anything", […] if it doesn't come[, there is not much I can do].'[488] In the case of Angele, she was interviewed three times (two times before her first negative decision and one time before her subsequent negative decision), the third time by a gender reference person.

486 In internal communication, the CGRS confirms that, at the time of writing, a guideline on domestic violence is being drafted. Commissioner General for Refugees and Stateless Persons (CGRS), 'Internal Communication CGRS (Part V)' (n 331).

487 CB011_CGRS_Supervisor+PO_GENDER_[00:27:08].

488 CB011_CGRS_Supervisor+PO_GENDER_[00:29:19].

CASE OF ANGELE			
• Country of origin:	DRC	• SGBV types:	Rape/sexual assault
• Gender identity:	Woman	• Decisions in file:	CGRS 1 (refusal) – 30/03/2020
• Birth year:	1984		CALL 1 (annulment) – 5/11/2020 – n° 243 679
• Interview by:	CGRS		CGRS 2 (refusal) – 30/08/2021
			CALL 2 (recognition) – 11/08/2022 – n° 275 955

According to her statements, Angele was born in the DRC, where she lived with her husband, a lawyer, and their two children. While she was abroad for work, her husband had participated in a political march where he went missing. During her absence, her maid reported that armed men had come to the home to steal documents and jewellery. After Angele's return, several men, dressed in civilian clothes (she recalled trainers, no military shoes) and carrying weapons, came back looking for documents allegedly in possession of her husband. They beat up her brother-in-law, chased the maid away, and **raped** Angele while her children were hiding in the house. The neighbours called the police, but were told that they were understaffed and could not get there. No investigation was ever launched afterwards. From then on, she recounted fearing the return of these men, since the home had now become 'their battlefield'. The day after the rape, she went to live at her parents' house with the children. There, she took medication used for abortions and when the pain in her genital area had not stopped after two days, she went to the hospital. She did not dare to go to her gynaecologist, who was a family friend, but visited another doctor. The doctor wanted to know what happened, seeing her injuries, but Angele did not disclose the rape to her, nor to anyone else. Afterwards, she was contacted by a man who confirmed that her husband was safe and she agreed for him to organise the whole family's flight out of the country.

In Belgium, they applied for international protection. In support of her application, she submitted (among other elements) medical documents from the hospital in the DRC, as well as from her psychologist in Belgium, stating that she shows symptoms corresponding to those of sexual violence survivors/victims and of PTSD.

Throughout the personal interviews by the gender reference person, Angele was questioned about specific details of her sexual violence experience, such as the number of persons that raped her, where her children were at the time, where in the house it happened, what the offenders said to her during the rape, … The gender reference person at one point asked her: 'Tell me about the circumstances of the attack, how it happened […] I need you to be as precise as possible […]. I wasn't there, so you need to give me as much information as possible so that I can understand. […] I'm listening, please? Have you understood what I'm asking you here?,' upon which the notes of her response state '*tears*'. The notes further read:

'<u>PO</u>: Yes, I'm listening?

<u>Angele</u>: *Silence*

> PO: You don't have to go into details, but I do need to understand what happened to you?
>
> Angele: I took off my loincloth, he covered my face. *Silence*
>
> PO: And you were sexually assaulted?
>
> Angele: He ripped off my underwear. *Silence, cries*
>
> PO: Have you been sexually assaulted? Do I understand correctly?
>
> Angele: Yes. By him and by the other one
>
> [...]
>
> PO: I don't have any more questions for you; Do you want to add anything? [...]
>
> Angele: *Madam raises her voice, gets angry* I repeat that this is the 3rd hearing! In 2018 for 4 hours and then I already talked about the assault! There was a first person from the CGRS! The 2nd time in 2019, for 3 hours! By another person! And today a 3rd person! *Still angry*. I think you've got what you want! **Every time I have to talk about this story it's like putting a knife in the wound! While I'm trying to chase it away and forget about it!** Here I'm obliged to talk about it!
>
> PO: Madam, please calm down. I would like to remind you of the context in which we find ourselves: you have decided to make an application for international protection, so it's only natural that you should tell us the reasons for your decision. [...]
>
> Angele: *Raises her voice* [...] **I've never spoken about this with anyone else, I don't want to talk about it anymore!** [...] *Raises her voice very loudly* I wonder if I should end my life?! Every time I have to answer! Should I end my life?!'[489] | CASE OF ANGELE

Personal interviews with survivors/victims prying into SGBV details that are peripheral to the refugee status determination process dangerously risk having a (re)traumatising effect,[490] as in the case of Angele. However, it is essential to note that this should not lead to questions on SGBV being avoided altogether, as for Mary's abovementioned experience. The sex trafficking/forced prostitution she (partly) disclosed was not further questioned and therefore not included in the assessment of her case.

Another PO stated: 'For example, typically [the sexual violence] happening in Libya is difficult [to hear]. So, [in the interview] I'm not going to focus on what happened there.'[491] Enquiring into relevant details of SGBV experiences must not be avoided, but should be conducted in a caring, ethical, trauma- and

489 NC006_CGRS interview 3_1984_F_DRC_RSA_FR_p.12 & 19-20.
490 Malkki (n 306) 51.
491 CB013_CGRS_PO_[00:04:42].

gender-sensitive manner (see Part I, Chapter 3.1.2). The challenges that come with interviewing applicants about their lived experiences should not prevent their flight stories from being heard.[492] As such, conducting personal interviews (and refugee status determination based on these) proves to be a difficult task for decision makers, whether gender-specialised or not, requiring in-depth and adapted sensitisation on trauma-sensitive interviewing (see Part VI, Chapter 4.2).

Discrepancies in personal interview practices concern other aspects of refugee status determination too, such as applicants' exhaustion of state protection against SGBV. Some asylum officials stated that, for countries where no state protection against SGBV is available, they do not even ask the question,[493] in line with the CGRS' official policy.[494] One PO confirmed this lack of state protection against SGBV for the DRC.[495] However, the POs interviewing Angele and Amani, another Congolese applicant, demonstrated an opposite practice, asking them: 'Did you think of going to the police?'[496] after their rape. Others confirmed this practice, stating that they deliberately do ask that question, even in the absence of state protection against SGBV. In doing so, some stated not necessarily expecting applicants to have sought state protection,[497] but rather to be able to explain their inner thought process on this decision.[498] When choosing whether or not to pose this question, it is important to stress that asking about (help-seeking) behaviour after SGBV risks being perceived as 'victim blaming'[499] and therefore potentially retraumatising by survivors/victims.[500]

c) *Psychological Support*

Moreover, it is important to note that these personal interviews risk not only to traumatise interviewees, but also interviewers in a secondary manner. Their

492 Gardî (n 221) viii.
493 CB011_CGRS_Supervisor + PO_GENDER_[00:35:18].
494 Commissioner General for Refugees and Stateless Persons (CGRS), 'Internal Communication CGRS (Part V)' (n 331).
495 CB007_CGRS_PO_[00:35:37].
496 NC004_CGRS interview 2_1991_F_DRC_RSA_DV_FR_NANSEN_p. 10., NC006 CGRS interview 3_1984_F_DRC_RSA_FR_NANSEN_p. 16.
497 CB009_CGRS_PO_GENDER_[00:44:01]., CB014_CGRS_PO_[00:32:32].
498 CB002_CGRS_Supervisor + PO_[00:12:06].
499 Madeleine van der Bruggen and Amy Grubb, 'A Review of the Literature Relating to Rape Victim Blaming: An Analysis of the Impact of Observer and Victim Characteristics on Attribution of Blame in Rape Cases' (2014) 19 Aggression and Violent Behavior 523, 524; Fanflik, Office on Violence Against Women, and National District Attorneys Association (n 386) 11.
500 Lore Roels, 'The Use of Rape Myths and Resulting Victim-Blaming Mechanisms in Asylum Interviews and Decisions on the Grounds of Sexual and Gender-Based Violence (SGBV)' (Women in Refugee Law (WiRL) Workshop: Gender sensitivity in asylum interviews, 2025).

attitude, such as illustrated in Angele's case, might for example be explained by compassion fatigue[501] and/or vicarious traumatisation. Both terms clarify how 'the recounting of traumatic events also indirectly transmits trauma from the [applicant] to the decision maker,' leading to psychological stress, for example expressed through avoidance, denial, trivialisation of horror, cynicism, lack of empathy, or anger.[502]

The KAP survey included a validated scale measuring vicarious trauma (designed by Vrklevski and Franklin[503]), which was completed with a response rate of 62.29% and measured an average vicarious trauma level of 4,5 (Dutch-speaking respondents) and 4,7 (French-speaking respondents) out of 7 at the CGRS (where 1 indicates no vicarious trauma at all and 7 indicates a very high degree). This psychological load of continuously hearing applicants' traumatising flight stories is articulated by one PO who admitted: 'The subjects that these women [who flee SGBV] broach are not easy to listen to. [...] I confess that I have left certain interviews [thinking] "[...] I am not equipped to hear these stories".'[504] A PO with gender specialisation added: 'I've found that only talking to people who have been sexually abused has exhausted me [...] at some point [...] I couldn't take it anymore.'[505]

POs and supervisors appear to seek psychological support in a variety of ways. Some develop individual coping mechanisms, such as distancing themselves from the process by: 'draw[ing] a clear line between [themselves] and what goes on in the interview room';[506] becoming 'emotionally numb when [they] don't believe in the case from the start';[507] 'just [...] [doing] your interview and [...] [saying] [...] "personally, I would want to give protection [...] but I can't because that's not covered by the guideline' [which is put in place for a reason]';[508] or believing that 'very few [applicants] are sent back to their country, [...] which makes our job very comfortable. If [...] every time I refused [...] a human being was put on a plane [...], I'd find it harder [...] but that's not the case, [...] in fact [...] I don't know, but I think [...] it's very rare.'[509]

Another PO expressed more victim-blaming emotions like anger when an Indian applicant, who claimed to have been gang-raped, did not give the answers needed to be granted protection. They stated: 'I was just really pissed at the

501 Rachel S Rauvola, Dulce M Vega and Kristi N Lavigne, 'Compassion Fatigue, Secondary Traumatic Stress, and Vicarious Traumatization: A Qualitative Review and Research Agenda' (2019) 3 Occupational Health Science 297, 303–304.

502 Rousseau and others (n 7) 49 & 58–59.

503 Vrklevski and Franklin (n 371) 115.

504 CB013_CGRS_PO_[00:04:42].

505 CB005_CGRS_Supervisor+PO_GENDER_[00:56:49].

506 CB001_CGRS_PO_[00:58:24].

507 CB007_CGRS_PO_[00:51:00].

508 CB003_CGRS_PO_[00:41:32].

509 CB013_CGRS_PO_[01:38:42].

applicant [...] like dammit, had you done this right, [...] you would've had a recognition. [...] I [thought] "are you really going to force me to [write] a refusal [for] the clearest case where everyone thought [it would] be a recognition?" [...] [T]o remain calm at that moment [...] is [...] difficult.'[510]

Others seek support from peers, in an informal manner by venting to colleagues or supervisors (depending on their attention to the mental well-being of their (fellow) POs). The CGRS adds that peer support is also formalised through the Critical Incident Team and group sessions. The former provides peer-to-peer debriefing, reception, and referral for and by colleagues in cases of impactful experiences at the CGRS.[511] None of the interviewed POs/supervisors mentioned (experiences with) this Team. The latter are organised for POs focusing on first-line contact with applicants and for supervisors on leadership and coaching skills.[512]

Concentrating on the substance of cases, rather than the mental health of those handling them, these group sessions are not guided by a psychological professional, but by colleagues at the CGRS who followed a course in peer coaching. Attendance is optional,[513] leading for example to larger attendance by the French than the Dutch-speaking POs.[514] One PO comments on these group sessions: 'I think [...] psychological support should be in place, [...] maybe that is now too much expected of colleagues among themselves. [...] It would be interesting to have [people] who [are] actually trained for that.'[515]

The CGRS does indicate some external pathways to psychological supervision,[516] but these do not always appear clear or suitable, as one PO stated: 'I felt the need for psychological counselling [...] [but] the information was hard to find and [...] the steps to take were difficult to reconcile with the need for confidentiality. [...] [I]n my opinion, management should communicate on this and give us access to support from professionals who know the specific work context, which didn't seem to be the case.'[517]

In contrast to this PO identifying their need for support themselves, others might never reflect upon or signal this. Some POs found that learning to deal with difficult cases is a self-taught skill that comes with age and experience, leading those who prove unable to do so to eventually drop out: 'If you can't

---

510 CB014_CGRS_PO_[01:12:01].

511 Commissioner General for Refugees and Stateless Persons (CGRS), 'Internal Communication CGRS (Part I)' (n 128).

512 *Ibid.*

513 *Ibid.*

514 CB005_CGRS_Supervisor+PO_GENDER_[01:03:56].

515 CB006_CGRS_PO_[01:07:01].

516 E.g. trustees, prevention advisors, the social service, an Employee Assistance Program, the Federal Public Service 'Policy and Support', or coaching and career counselling services (e.g. Lumen or Talent Plus) at one's own initiative. Commissioner General for Refugees and Stateless Persons (CGRS), 'Internal Communication CGRS (Part I)' (n 128).

517 R_215mekDbAHvOGHc_CGRS_ PO/supervisor/gender coordinator/CEDOCA member.

put up a shield against it, you will succumb to it.'[518] As a result, 'There are really good POs who are capable and then drop out or say "I don't want to do this anymore because I take it home" [...]. You have a problem if you can't keep those [people].'[519]

At the time of writing, no individualised psychological supervision at the CGRS itself is available, let alone encouraged or standardly included in POs' and supervisors' periodic follow-up. In contrast, this for example is the case for police inspectors working on sexual violence cases in the Belgium's Sexual Assault Care Centres, which provide holistic care and advice to survivors/victims and their support persons. The model that establishes the functioning of these centres provides for annual individual supervision by an external psychologist for these inspectors (as well as (quarterly) group supervision for forensic nurses and psychologists working there) and recommends multidisciplinary consultation between them.[520]

2.2.4. PROCEDURAL ASPECTS

a) Separate Personal Interviews, Case Files & Assessments

Apart from the abovementioned forms of guidance for POs and supervisors handling gender-related cases (through trainings, guidelines, or peer support), several procedural safeguards should ensure gender sensitivity in the CGRS' case processing. For families who flee together, they can submit separate asylum applications and be interviewed individually. In gender-related procedures, this may enable SGBV survivors/victims to tell their story independently, especially when they fear family members and/or do not want them to know about their fears or experiences.[521]

Applications for international protection by family members are usually joined in one asylum file, unless applicants explicitly state their wish to split the file to the IO at the start of the procedure.[522] Of course, to do so, applicants have to disclose their fear of/experiences with SGBV immediately at the IO interview,

518 CB011_CGRS_Supervisor+PO_GENDER_[00:51:29].

519 CB014_CGRS_PO_[01:19:53].

520 Ines Keygnaert and Saar Baert, 'Zorgcentra Na Seksueel Geweld in België: Het ZSG-Model – Nationale Criteria En Standaardprocedures' (Instituut voor de gelijkheid van vrouwen en mannen (IGVM) 2024) 20; Instituut voor de gelijkheid van vrouwen en mannen, 'Zorgcentra Na Seksueel Geweld (ZSG)', https://igvm-iefh.belgium.be/nl/themas/geweld/seksueel-geweld/zsg; Art. 2, 10° *jo.* Chapter 3 Wet betreffende de Zorgcentra na Seksueel Geweld 2024 (Belgisch Staatsblad of 31 May 2024, p 68926).

521 Mahieu, Vanheule and Timmerman (n 23) 57.

522 Commissioner General for Refugees and Stateless Persons (CGRS), 'Women, Girls and Asylum in Belgium Brochure' (2020) 6; Mahieu, Vanheule and Timmerman (n 23) 58; Vluchtelingenwerk Vlaanderen (Flemish Refugee Action) (n 439) 84.

which is not always possible in practice (see Part II, Chapter 3.3.2). The option to split the file is only mentioned explicitly in the CGRS brochure 'Women, girls and asylum in Belgium'[523] for applicants, but not in the general one.[524] However, men and boys encounter similar or even higher hurdles to disclose (see Part I, Chapter 2.1.3). For example, a male applicant who had fled Egypt after being raped with the aim of converting him to Islam, answered the question whether he had new elements to support his subsequent asylum application with: 'Yes, but I really don't dare say this. I also don't want my wife or anyone else to find out, but I was raped in Egypt.'[525]

Angele's case testifies of the reality that the administrative separation of family members' case files does not necessarily guarantee the independent assessment of the case or confidentiality of the facts disclosed. She repeated several times that she had not told her husband and children about the rape and that she did not want them to know.[526] Nonetheless, one of her decisions was communicated to her husband directly (as her lawyer pointed out during the third personal interview).[527] The CALL also annulled the CGRS' decision denying her international protection because the latter assessed her experience as coinciding with and dependent on her husband's flight story. The judge validated Angele's counter-argumentation as follows:

> '[T]he applicant explained, as far as possible given her psychological state, that she had been **raped by armed persons** [...]. However, the applicant's statements were not analysed by the CGRS [...]. **The [...] decision does not contain any analysis of the facts personally experienced by the applicant**: indeed, virtually all the complaints relied on are based on matters not experienced by the applicant herself [but by her husband].'[528] | CASE OF ANGELE

b) *Special Procedural Guarantees*

Next to a separate personal interview and case file, applicants in gender-related procedures can object to being heard by a person of a different gender than their own.[529] The same applies to the interpreter, if another interpreter speaking the same language is available at the CGRS and the applicant's reason is considered

523 Commissioner General for Refugees and Stateless Persons (CGRS), 'Women, Girls and Asylum in Belgium Brochure' (n 522).

524 Commissioner General for Refugees and Stateless Persons (CGRS), 'The Asylum Procedure at the CGRS' (2019).

525 [2023] RvV 294 383 18.

526 NC006_CGRS interview 3_1984_F_DRC_RSA_FR_p. 7 & 10.

527 NC006_CGRS interview 3_1984_F_DRC_RSA_FR_p. 20.

528 NC006_CALL 1 (annulment)_1984_F_DRC_RSA_5/11/2020_243 679_FR_NANSEN_p. 2.

529 At the time of writing, not yet taking into acount the new EU Pact on Migration and Asylum reforming the CEAS. Art. 15 Belgian Royal Decree on the CGRS; Mahieu, Vanheule and Timmerman (n 23) 58; Vluchtelingenwerk Vlaanderen (Flemish Refugee Action) (n 439) 84.

valid.[530] The CGRS can take other procedural guarantees when the information in the case file indicates that an applicant may not be able to fully participate in the asylum procedure without such guarantees. These special procedural needs are assessed on the basis of the answers given at the IO, any documents submitted to the CGRS (e.g. medical certificates), and other recommendations from medical examinations or the reception centre.[531]

Examples of guarantees responding to these needs given by the CGRS itself are: adjusting the timing or location of the personal interview/procedure, allowing submission of written answers, requesting a medical examination, involving a guardian for unaccompanied minors, assigning a specialised PO, providing the option of a PO or interpreter of the same gender identity, ...[532] However, some of these guarantees already are inherent safeguards provided by the Aliens Act to all applicants, regardless of their special procedural needs. In gender-related cases, the guarantees installed often intend to facilitate the practical course of the personal interview, rather than installing a gender-sensitive approach to the content of the assessment.

Although the granting of special procedural guarantees in individual cases is not appealable as such,[533] the CALL does exceptionally comment on which guarantees are (not) adequate in general. In the case of Angele, the CALL stated:

> '[T]he measures taken by the [CGRS], namely the decision to **administratively separate** the handling of the applicant's case from that of her husband, the fact that **breaks** were provided, that the applicant was offered a **glass of water**, and that she was given the opportunity to **speak with her lawyer**, are procedural safeguards **inherent in any interview conducted by the [CGRS] and in no way demonstrate that the applicant's vulnerability was taken into account**.'[534] | CASE OF ANGELE

c) *The Personal Interview*

Applicants are in principle invited at least once by the CGRS for a personal interview, with the aim of gathering the information necessary for refugee or subsidiary protection status determination. Exceptionally, the CGRS is not obliged to do so, for example when the available evidence allows to take a positive decision in a first asylum procedure or any type of decision in a subsequent asylum procedure, or when the applicant cannot be heard due to durable

530 Art. 21 Koninklijk besluit betreffende de toegang tot het grondgebied, het verblijf, de vestiging en de verwijdering van vreemdelingen (Belgian Aliens' Royal Decree) 1981 (Belgisch staatsblad of 27 October 1981, p. 13740).

531 Art. 48/9 Belgian Aliens Act.

532 Commissioner General for Refugees and Stateless Persons (CGRS), 'Special Procedural Needs' (*CGVS*, 1 October 2019), www.cgrs.be/en/asylum/special-procedural-needs.

533 Art. 48/9, §4 Belgian Aliens Act.

534 NC006_CALL 2 (recognition)_1984_F_DRC_RSA_11/8/2022_275 955_FR_NANSEN_p. 14.

circumstances beyond their control.[535] In contrast to the IO interview, applicants may be assisted by a lawyer and/or trustee during the personal interview at the CGRS. However, the absence of the lawyer or of the trustee does not prevent the PO from interviewing applicants[536] (unless they are minors, who should always be assisted by their lawyer, guardian, and trustee if applicable[537]).

Applicants or their lawyer may request a copy of the personal interview notes made by the PO.[538] As such, they can comment on factual inaccuracies[539] and avoid the risk that inconsistencies would later be used against them. These notes are drafted in Dutch or French, languages that applicants usually do not master, making them reliant on help from their lawyer or others assisting them throughout the procedure. Mary for example never got the chance to correct her personal interview notes, she says:

> **'I honestly don't get *Nederlands*.**[540] **I speak *een beetje***[541] [...] **so** [...] **I couldn't understand.** [...] **We didn't [go through] it.** I [sent] it to the lawyer expecting a call because I think the lawyer is supposed to call for us to go through it. [...] **And [the notes] have a mistake.** They have, there's things that were [...] not [...] correct.'[542] | CASE OF MARY

The CGRS later denied her international protection based (among other arguments) on inconsistencies about her places of residence,[543] which she indicated in our interview were noted incorrectly.[544] In the decision, the CGRS stated:

> **'You failed to respond to the notes of the personal interview, which means that it can be assumed that you agree** [...]. In the asylum procedure, you bear a responsibility; [...] you are expected to indicate [inaccuracies] during the personal interview or at least when you were sent the notes.'[545] | CASE OF MARY

In another case, Diana, a mother fleeing Albania with her daughter in fear of (sexual) domestic violence by her ex-husband, testified on the challenges of making sense of one's own SGBV experiences in a personal interview: 'I didn't

535 Art. 57/5ter Belgian Aliens Act.
536 Art. 19 Belgian Royal Decree on the CGRS.
537 Art. 19, §1, part 2 *jo.* 14, §2 *ibid.*; Art. 57/1, §3, part 2 Belgian Aliens Act.
538 Art. 57/quater, §1-2 Belgian Aliens Act; Art. 16, §1 Belgian Royal Decree on the CGRS.
539 Art. 57/quater, §3 Belgian Aliens Act.
540 'Dutch' in Dutch.
541 'a little' in Dutch.
542 NL017_1980_F_Liberia_STFP_GMC_VGNT_FM_ NL_ [00:12:49].
543 NL017_CGRS1(refusal)_1980_F_Liberia_STFP_GMC_VGNT_FM_17/2/2022_NL_NANSEN_ p. 3.
544 NL017_1980_F_Liberia_STFP_GMC_VGNT_FM_ NL_ [00:41:26].
545 NL017_CGRS1(refusal)_1980_F_Liberia_STFP_GMC_VGNT_FM_17/2/2022_NL_NANSEN_ p. 5.

have the opportunity to talk about it [with the lawyer] before [the interview]. But afterwards, with time, with the psychologist, I see things a bit better and I've tried to clarify things, what I've been through.'[546]

Both cases illustrate how the aforementioned provisions do not necessarily result in effective legal support throughout the personal interview and procedure in general. It is important to note that the same time constraints and psychological pressure experienced by POs/supervisors at the CGRS count for lawyers, who report dealing with high workloads and numbers of clients, the complex legal field of refugee law,[547] the hopelessness of a system where clients' chances to recognition are slim, legal aid cuts,[548] and similar risks to vicarious traumatisation.[549]

Despite the legal provisions on special procedural needs and legal assistance, applicants testify on the stressful circumstances of a personal interview in similar ways as for the IO interview. Mary explained:

> 'Honestly, the day of the interview [...] [I was] [...] **stressed and afraid.** I don't know why [...], it made me afraid. I [got] nervous. [...] I would always like go to the bathroom. [...] I did what I could do. [...] But I don't know if she, she understood me really.'[550] | CASE OF MARY

While applicants or their lawyer can make comments after the personal interview,[551] for example about the extent to which they felt (un)comfortable telling their story, these are not necessarily taken into account. In the case of a Nigerian applicant fleeing forced marriage and domestic violence, the CGRS stated:

> '[Your lawyer] mentioned a "disrespectful attitude" of the [PO], [...] you told your social worker [...] that you did not "feel at ease" or "listened to" [...] you felt judged by the [PO] [...] he "often" "rolled" his eyes [...] you had the "impression" that you were "disturbing" him and that [...] you didn't "dare say" that you didn't fully understand the questions [...]. You added that you "felt trapped in this situation" and had [...] "no choice but to reveal" your "story in a setting that was not benevolent" [...]. [...]

546 NA001_B_1973_F_Albania_RSA_VGNT_DV_ NL_ [01:16:28].

547 Zoé Crine, Christine Flamand and Francesca Raimondo, 'Time(S), Space(S) and Shapes of Vulnerabilities in the Belgian Asylum System' in Luc Leboeuf and others (eds), *Between Protection and Harm: Negotiated Vulnerabilities in Asylum Laws and Bureaucracies* (Springer Nature Switzerland 2025) 183–184.

548 Neil Graffin, 'The Emotional Impacts of Working as an Asylum Lawyer' (2019) 38 Refugee Survey Quarterly 30, 30.

549 Line Rønning, Jocelyn Blumberg and Jesper Dammeyer, 'Vicarious Traumatisation in Lawyers Working with Traumatised Asylum Seekers: A Pilot Study' (2020) 27 Psychiatry, Psychology and Law 665, 665.

550 NL017_1980_F_Liberia_STFP_GMC_VGNT_FM_ NL_ [00:18:57].

551 Art. 19, §2 *jo.* 17, §3 Belgian Royal Decree on the CGRS.

> [A]ll of your observations [...] are based on subjective feelings which are not reflected in [...] the notes [...]. [...] [A]t the beginning of the [...] interview, the [PO] gave you the opportunity to explain how you were feeling: you mentioned a feeling of "stress". In response, the [PO] informed you that you could express any feeling of discomfort at any time [...]; you refrained from doing so.'[552]

In some cases, the impact of trauma can even result in an amount of stress hindering applicants to accept the personal interview invitation(s) altogether. After Vera's aforementioned experience at the IO interview, she was unable to accept the following four invitations by the CGRS. Each time, she provided a medical certificate from her psychiatrist, showing her severe PTSD diagnosis that involved cognitive dysfunction with memory impairment and emotional instability, making it impossible for her to share her flight story in the context of a personal interview.[553] According to the Belgian Royal Decree on the CGRS, if the reason for not accepting the invitation is considered valid, the CGRS can request written information from applicants or re-invite them at a later date.[554] The same Decree allows the CGRS to take a decision based on the elements available in the case file, if the applicant again provides a valid reason for not accepting the re-invitation.[555]

In Vera's case, the CGRS opted to re-invite her three times and then took a decision based on her answers provided at the IO, despite her 'very fragile condition and [the fact] that she was unable to answer the questions asked,'[556] according to her lawyer and as reflected in the quote about this interview above. Vera nevertheless found the strength to participate in an interview for this research and, of all the survivors/victims I spoke to, showed most physical signs of difficulty when speaking about her experiences. Even more than a year after leaving Albania, in the presence of her sister who supports her and with psychiatric and psychological counselling, she trembled incessantly and could barely whisper when recalling the SGBV she experienced.

d) Accelerated Procedure

Vera's application for international protection was found 'manifestly ill-founded' due to the fact that she fled Albania, a so-called 'safe country of origin', leading her application to be assessed in an accelerated procedure.[557] A country of

---

552 DN100_CGRS 1 (refusal)_1993_F_Nigeria_VGNT_FM_DV_6/10/2022_FR_p. 3-4.

553 NA016_CGRS 1 (manifestly ill-founded)_1990_F_Albania_RSA_VGNT_DV_10/10/2022_NL_NANSEN_p. 2-3.

554 Art. 18, §2, part 1-4 Belgian Royal Decree on the CGRS.

555 Art. 18, §2, part 5 *ibid.*

556 NA016_CALL 1 (refusal)_lawyers' argumentation_1990_F_Albania_RSA_VGNT_DV_27/2/2023_285 363_NL_NANSEN_p. 6-7.

557 Art. 57/6/1, §1-2 Belgian Aliens Act.

origin is considered 'safe' when, based on the legal situation, the rule of law in a democratic system and the general political circumstances, it can be shown that there is generally and durably no risk of persecution or serious harm.[558] It is important to mention the *C.V.* case by the CJEU, confirming that a country can only be designated as a safe country of origin when its entire territory satisfies the conditions to be considered 'safe', and not when certain parts of its territory fail to meet this standard.[559] At the time of writing, the list of safe countries of origin in Belgium consists of: Albania, Bosnia and Herzegovina, India, Kosovo, Moldova, Montenegro, North-Macedonia, and Serbia.[560]

Apart from India, these are all countries in Eastern Europe, a region with concerning rates of SGBV prevalence, according to WHO statistics.[561] Amnesty International also signals the lack of protection against domestic violence in this region, which is exacerbated by a patriarchal and openly misogynistic society.[562] A judge confirmed this for Albania, stating that it is a society that is 'more than patriarchal.'[563] In the case of India, one PO (with experience as a CEDOCA researcher) in the above case on gang rape, explained how the CGRS had doubted the necessity of a personal interview because the applicant was likely to be recognised, since 'gang rape in India [...] is very sensitive. It is also often in the news, that [it] leads to death.'[564] NGOs like Amnesty International and Equality Now confirm that perpetrators continue to commit SGBV with impunity[565] and that survivors/victims face huge barriers in accessing justice in India.[566]

558 Art. 57/6/1, §3, part 2 *ibid.*

559 *CV v Ministerstvo vnitra České republiky, Odbor azylové a migrační politiky* [2024] Court of Justice of the European Union C-406/22 Ruling 2.

560 Art. 1 Koninklijk besluit tot uitvoering van het artikel 57/6/1, §3, vierde lid, van de wet van 15 december 1980 betreffende de toegang tot het grondgebied, het verblijf, de vestiging en de verwijdering van vreemdelingen, houdende de vastlegging van de lijst van veilige landen van herkomst.

561 World Health Organization, 'Global and Regional Estimates of Violence against Women: Prevalence and Health Effects of Intimate Partner Violence and Non-Partner Sexual Violence' (World Health Organization 2013) 47–48. Safe countries of origin on the Belgian list that are included in this WHO analysis are: Albania, Moldova, Serbia, and Kosovo. With regions such as: Central and East Asia and Southern Latin America measuring lower prevalence for intimate partner violence than Eastern Europe (26,13%); and regions such as: Central, East, South and South-East Asia, Southern Latin America and North Africa/Middle-East measuring lower prevalence for non-partner sexual violence than Eastern Europe (6,97%).

562 Amnesty International, 'Eastern Europe and Central Asia: Protect Women from Violence in Crises and Beyond' (2022).

563 RB006_CALL_Judge_[00:31:12].

564 CB014_CGRS_PO_[00:36:42].

565 Amnesty International, 'Amnesty International Report 2022/2: The State of the World's Human Rights: India 2022' (2023) 7.

566 Equality Now, 'Sexual Violence in South Asia: Legal and Other Barriers to Justice for Survivors' (2021).

In asylum procedures of applicants fleeing these countries, the standard of proof is higher. International protection is only granted when applicants can provide fundamental reasons as to why their country of origin is not safe in their specific circumstances.[567] Another reason for applying an accelerated procedure, is when applicants submitted false or withheld relevant information or (identity) documents with a potentially negative impact on their decisions.[568] This is the case, for example, when individuals need false identity documents to flee from their country of origin at short notice, arrive at the airport, and are intercepted by Belgian authorities. In these accelerated procedures, the CGRS has to take a decision within 15 working days after receiving the file from the IO.[569]

In cases where the CGRS identifies special procedural needs in applicants, in particular because of torture, rape or other serious forms of psychological, physical or sexual violence, it in principle does not apply the accelerated procedure, if these needs are not compatible with such a procedure.[570] In Vera's case, her medical certificates diagnosed PTSD due to SGBV experiences, determined that the personal interview had to be postponed, and were considered a valid justification by the CGRS not to attend the personal interview. Nonetheless, she was not granted any special procedural guarantees and the accelerated procedure was applied. The CGRS stated:

> '[Y]ou declared to the IO that you are having mental difficulties. You are unable to sleep and are anxious […]. […] Your psychiatrist's certificate […] states that you have severe PTSD […] [and] therefore considers you unfit for an interview at the [CGRS]. Your psychologist's follow-up certificate also mentions that you are taking medication. However, **these summary attestations do not allow to determine how you were examined and diagnosed […], nor what specific implications […] this may have** on your participation in the procedure. Moreover, […] **you did not mention** [any **special procedural needs to the IO yourself**] […]. **Nor can any further indications in this sense be derived from the interaction […] at the IO**.'[571] | CASE OF VERA

In the abovementioned case of Amani, a Congolese applicant who fled sexual violence by her stepfather and by unknown perpetrators, the CGRS did accord her special procedural guarantees due to attested psychological difficulties related to the abuse. Nonetheless, the accelerated procedure was applied because she had arrived at a Belgian airport with false identity documents.[572]

---

[567] Art. 57/6/1, §3 Belgian Aliens Act.

[568] Art. 57/6/1, §1, c] *ibid.*

[569] Art. 57/6/1, §1, part 1, b] *jo.* part 3 *ibid.*

[570] Art. 48/9, §5 *ibid.*; Commissioner General for Refugees and Stateless Persons (CGRS), 'Special Procedural Needs' (n 532).

[571] NA016_CGRS 1 (manifestly ill-founded)_1990_F_Albania_RSA_VGNT_DV_10/10/2022_NL_NANSEN_p. 2-3.

[572] NC004_CGRS 1 (refusal)_1991_F_DRC_RSA_DV_21/12/2021_FR_NANSEN_p 3.

2.3. APPEAL: THE COUNCIL FOR ALIEN LAW LITIGATION

2.3.1. APPEAL

The CALL is responsible for ruling on appeals filed against individual decisions made by the CGRS. It has the authority to conduct a full judicial review and may either confirm the CGRS' decision, reform it by granting international protection, or annul it and refer the case back to the CGRS for reconsideration. The Council counts eleven chambers, handling Dutch, French, and bilingual cases,[573] and is chaired by Chamber Presidents, among whom the First President and President of the CALL.[574] Each chamber counts at least three judges,[575] who are usually[576] assisted by attachés, who make proposals for handling the case and write draft judgments under the responsibility of the judge.[577] Judges assess cases in an independent and impartial manner and are therefore not bound by internal guidelines like POs/supervisors at the CGRS. The CALL's case law is only guided by the principle of unity of jurisdiction.[578] Also in contrast to the case workers at the IO, and POs/supervisors at the CGRS, both the judges and attachés at the CALL are legally educated.[579]

2.3.2. AWARENESS RAISING ON SGBV

Judges and attachés can undergo further voluntary training by taking internal (organised by the CALL itself) or external courses.[580] The CALL has a gender coordinator appointed, who is also responsible for organising the trainings that judges can voluntarily attend. The courses in the CALL's yearly activity reports going back to 2020 do occasionally mention courses on vulnerabilities in general

573 For the sake of completeness, the CALL also handles cases in German (another official language in Belgium), but no asylum procedures in 'full jurisdiction' (see Part I, Chapter 4.4).

574 Art. 39/9, §1, part 1 Belgian Aliens Act; Council for Alien Law Litigation (CALL), 'Organogram RvV/CCE/CALL' (29 October 2014), www.rvv-cce.be/nl/rvv/organogram.

575 Art. 39/9, §1, part 5 Belgian Aliens Act.

576 Not all judges have attachés assisting them. One judge for example stated: 'But we don't all have attachés. I don't have any at the moment.' RB008_CALL_Judge_[00:51:37]. The CALL clarifies in internal communications that, in theory, the Council has sufficient resources to assign an attaché to every judge. However, at the time of writing, it appears that it is not easy to find enough Dutch-speaking attachés, even though there are open vacancies. Council for Alien Law Litigation (CALL), 'Internal Communication CALL' (n 168).

577 Council for Alien Law Litigation (CALL), 'Over de Raad' (29 October 2014), www.rvv-cce.be/nl/rvv/over-de-raad.

578 Art. 39/12 Belgian Aliens Act.

579 Art. 39/9, §1, part 4 *ibid.*

580 Council for Alien Law Litigation (CALL), 'Activiteitenverslag RvV 2022' (2022) 11.

or SOGI-related international protection. However, until recently, these did not list any training specifically focusing on SGBV.[581] In September 2023, a first-of-its-kind pilot project was coordinated by NANSEN NGO, testing an awareness raising module on 'The role of judges in moving towards a more gender-sensitive asylum procedure.' It included presentations on: the Istanbul Convention, the definition of SGBV, its psychological consequences, sexual violence experiences of male migrants in transit ...[582]

Several judges/attachés confirmed that this was the first SGBV-related module they ever attended. They stressed the importance of information on the psychological impact of gender-based trauma for their work: 'The psychological [part] ... [has] provided a lot of context that we ... cannot get from legal texts';[583] 'I would now be much more understanding [of shame to disclose SGBV]. [...] [Also,] some colleagues [reason] [...] "if you have experienced something very bad ... it is engraved in your memory". [...] [Since the module] we know it's exactly the opposite';[584] 'I've been told in this training: there are a thousand reasons why a [SGBV] victim [...] might not disclose. [...] [Also,] I used to think that all stories without details were made-up.'[585]

On SGBV prevalence, participants to the module also valued the sensitisation on male victimisation along migration routes or in their country of origin, sometimes wrongly framed as homosexual practices; the increased risk of revictimisation for survivors/victims who have already experienced SGBV in the past; or on survivors'/victims' profiles: 'NANSEN's training [...] told us [that] victims of sexual violence [...] can even be [...] highly educated people. [...] [Before] I took this training [...] when someone told me "I'm a woman, I have my own shop and I'm the victim [...] of a violent husband", I didn't believe her.'[586]

Some participants appreciated the psychological expertise but labelled the module peripheral to their legal-technical work, for example by stating: '[The content] about gender, [...] forced marriage, [GMC], I think we're [...] the experts in fact. And it's going to be [...] difficult to come and teach us something [about this].'[587] Another judge stated: '[The pendulum] shouldn't swing too far either [...] sometimes there is an excessive focus [on gender], I think.'[588] By contrast, others testified: 'Everyone was shocked to learn about certain aspects

581 Council for Alien Law Litigation (CALL), 'Activiteitenverslag RvV 2020' (2020) 12; Council for Alien Law Litigation (CALL), 'Activiteitenverslag RvV 2021' (2021) 10 & 33; Council for Alien Law Litigation (CALL), 'Activiteitenverslag RvV 2022' (n 580) 11 & 33–34; Council for Alien Law Litigation (CALL), 'Activiteitenverslag RvV 2023' (n 356) 50–52.
582 Council for Alien Law Litigation (CALL), 'Activiteitenverslag RvV 2023' (n 356) 51; Instituut voor de gelijkheid van vrouwen en mannen (IGVM) (n 126) 31.
583 RB001_CALL_ Judge_[00:06:16].
584 RB005_CALL_Judge_[00:24:44] & [00:38:32].
585 RB007_CALL_Attaché_[00:55:55] & [00:57:37].
586 RB007_CALL_Attaché_[00:34:26] & [00:35:27].
587 RB006_CALL_Judge_[01:20:21].
588 RB005_CALL_Judge_[00:59:43].

[of] rape victim[isation]. And if you are shocked, [it means] you weren't really aware of it. I think it would be really interesting to do this [...] on a regular basis';[589] 'There are many people who wanted to follow [the NANSEN module]. There were more people registered than places available. So there is a demand';[590] and 'I [...] would [...] advocate to make it compulsory.'[591] Attendance at this module was purely voluntary, with some participants further committing to join a steering committee of the pilot project to help shape and evaluate it.

Interestingly, there are no standard modules on gender in place for all judges and attachés at the appeal level of the CALL. In contrast, all Belgian judges in criminal, family and juvenile law must undergo in-depth training on SGBV within one year of their first appointment, according to the Judicial Code.[592] Given that proceedings before the CALL, an administrative court, do not fall within the scope of this Judicial Code, the judges in refugee law escape the obligation in this provision.[593] However, in the KAP survey, 90% of the French-speaking and over 45% of the Dutch-speaking judges and attachés reported dealing with gender-related cases at least once a month.[594]

Nevertheless, none of the parliamentary documents[595] on the legislative changes[596] introducing the training on SGBV in the Judicial Code mention the CALL, the CGRS, or the relevance of such trainings in asylum procedures. The documents do mention how training on SGBV is essential 'for those whose role involves dealing concretely with cases of sexual and intra-family violence'[597] and

---

589 RB007_CALL_Attaché_[01:06:20].

590 RB008_CALL_Judge_[00:53:25].

591 RB001_CALL_Judge_[00:50:42].

592 Art. 78, part 10 Gerechtelijk Wetboek 1967 (Belgisch Staatsblad of 31 October 1967, p 11360).

593 Johan Vande Lanotte, Geert Goedertier and Yves Haeck, *Handboek Belgisch Publiekrecht. Deel 2: Basiskenmerken van de Belgische Staatstructuur* (die Keure 2015) 329.

594 According to the results of the KAP survey conducted in the context of this research (see Part I, Chapter 4.4) with the judges and attachés at the CALL (56,73% response rate until the end). The percentages were calculated on the total number of respondents who answered this particular question.

595 Belgische Kamer van Volksvertegenwoordigers, Wetsvoorstel houdende diverse bepalingen inzake justitie, onder meer in het kader van de strijd tegen de verspreiding van het coronavirus: Amendementen 2020 [DOC 55 1295/007] 6–9; Belgische Kamer van Volksvertegenwoordigers, Wetsvoorstel houdende diverse bepalingen inzake justitie, onder meer in het kader van de strijd tegen de verspreiding van het coronavirus: Verslag van de tweede lezing 2020 [DOC 55 1295/008] 13–14; Belgische Kamer van Volksvertegenwoordigers, Wetsontwerp inzake de preventie en de bestrijding van feminicides, gendergerelateerde dodingen en het geweld dat daar aan voorafgaat: Voorstel van resolutie betreffende de officiële telling van het aantal vrouwenmoorden en de oprichting van een observatorium voor vrouwenmoorden in België: Verslag 2023 [DOC 55 3400/004] 5 & 8.

596 Art. 48-53 Wet houdende diverse dringende bepalingen inzake justitie 2020 (Belgisch Staatsblad of 7 August 2020, p 58048); Art. 18 Wet voor de preventie en de bestrijding van feminicides en gendergerelateerde dodingen 2023 (Belgisch Staatsblad of 31 August 2023, p 70960).

597 Belgische Kamer van Volksvertegenwoordigers Wetsvoorstel houdende diverse bepalingen inzake justitie, onder meer in het kader van de strijd tegen de verspreiding van het coronavirus: Amendementen (n 595) 7.

that the legislative change 'aims to provide a general framework for the control and prevention of feminicides and gender-based killings [...] [for] all persons in the public sector, including government agencies, and all administrative and judicial authorities.'[598]

2.3.3. PSYCHOLOGICAL SUPPORT

Similar to the CGRS, irrespective of the trainings they followed, there is no option for judges/attachés handling cases on international protection to opt for handling more or less gender-related cases.[599] Judges and attachés across all chambers assess these applications, with some of them admitting: 'I'm glad I don't do these files regularly, [...] it's very violent [...] for your mind'[600] or '[gender-related cases] weigh me down.'[601] In line with the CGRS, no standardised professional psychological support is offered within the CALL to potentially relieve some of this mental load.

In the KAP survey, almost all judges and attachés indicated that their job involves exposure to disturbing material, experiences, and traumatised applicants.[602] Up to 70% of the French-speaking and 44,11% of the Dutch-speaking respondents indicated they feel distressed when listening to the stories and situations of applicants.[603] Similar to the CGRS, the vicarious trauma scale included in the survey[604] measured an average vicarious trauma level of 4,7 (French-speaking) and 3,9 (Dutch-speaking) out of 7 at the CALL.[605]

Some judges and attachés expressed their wish to get psychological support within the CALL explicitly: 'We don't have any psychological support at the CALL and I think there should be (as is the case, for example, at the Brussels

598 Art. 3 *jo.* 5 Wet voor de preventie en de bestrijding van feminicides en gendergerelateerde dodingen. Emphasis added.

599 If they want to keep handling appeals against individual CGRS decisions, of course. Alternatively, they could become judges in the CALL's 'annulment jurisdiction', which rules on appeals unrelated to international protection. Council for Alien Law Litigation (CALL), 'FAQ', www.rvv-cce.be/nl/faq.

600 RB007_CALL_Attaché_[01:04:33].

601 RB005_CALL_Judge_[00:56:08].

602 Specifically, 88,23% (Dutch-speaking) and 93,33% (French-speaking) of respondents answered between 5 and 7 on a 7-point Likert Scale from 'totally disagree (1)' to 'totally agree (7)' concerning traumatised applicants; and 73,53% (Dutch-speaking) and 86,67% (French-speaking) of respondents concerning exposure to disturbing material and experiences. The percentages were calculated on the total number of respondents who answered this particular question.

603 The percentages were calculated on the total number of respondents who answered this particular question.

604 Vrklevski and Franklin (n 371) 115.

605 Where 1 indicates no vicarious trauma at all and 7 indicates a very high degree. The percentages were calculated on the total number of respondents who answered this particular question.

Public Prosecutor's Office).'[606] Like the POs and supervisors at the CGRS, some judges and attachés demonstrated individual coping mechanisms to emotionally distance themselves from the decision making process, such as: '[For] a forced marriage [...] there's always that little comfort that I can tell myself "maybe she's making it up to get papers" [...] on the other hand, infibulation?[607] [...] That's a proven fact.'[608]

At the CALL too, decision makers seek support from peers, as one judge related: 'What helps me with [gender-related] cases is [talking] to colleagues, [...] having attachés helps [...]. I think it's dangerous to have only one opinion on this type of cases, but we don't all have attachés. I don't have anyone left at the moment.'[609] As the CALL internally communicated, it is worth mentioning that the Council has started systematically organising such peer support, by training colleagues as trustees for its attachés (and that it is in the course of doing so for its judges at the time of writing).[610]

2.3.4. THE HEARING

The weight of gender-related cases also manifests itself during the hearings at the CALL. The asylum procedure before the CALL is essentially a written and a public one, but there is (usually) a hearing where parties and their lawyers may make oral comments.[611] Also, the case can be handled behind closed doors if the CALL decides or the parties request so.[612] One attaché explained how the hearing provides an opportunity to 'confront the person with the [...] contradictory information [...] found, so that they can explain themselves.'[613] At the hearing, applicants are legally represented by their lawyer. If applicants are not present themselves, nor represented by their lawyer, their appeal is dismissed.[614]

If they are present, the hearing might lead to discomfort for both decision makers and applicants. One attaché explained: 'Gender cases [...] [are] more difficult, [...] because, for example, if someone said to me "I've been beaten up by bandits", I wouldn't mind asking a lot of questions, but questions

606 R_3LXa1xWZookEix6_CALL_Judge_1976.

607 Female GMC type 3: the narrowing of the vaginal opening through the creation of a covering seal. The seal is formed by cutting and repositioning the labia minora, or labia majora, sometimes through stitching, with or without removal of the clitoral prepuce/clitoral hood and glans. World Health Organization (WHO), 'Female Genital Mutilation', www.who.int/news-room/fact-sheets/detail/female-genital-mutilation.

608 RB007_CALL_Attaché_[01:04:50].

609 RB008_CALL_Judge_[00:51:37].

610 Council for Alien Law Litigation (CALL), 'Internal Communication CALL' (n 168).

611 Art. 39/60 Belgian Aliens Act.

612 Art. 39/64 *ibid.*

613 RB002_CALL_Attaché_[00:22:42].

614 Art. 39/59, §2 Belgian Aliens Act.

[on SGBV] are often taboo in many cultures, [so] in the hearing [...] you're a bit uncomfortable.'[615] A judge added, when asked about important details in cases on SGBV: 'Indeed [...] I don't feel equipped at all to assess the credibility of the story. I'd rather avoid the person having to talk about it and [...] intuitively I'd prefer to focus on the circumstances.'[616]

Naturally, for applicants, a hearing in a 'last chance' appeal procedure is stressful too, for example when lawyers do not show up on the day of the hearing but send a colleague to represent them, as was the case in Mary's[617] and happens in many others' procedure. Rahel, an Eritrean applicant, articulated her feeling of helplessness at the hearing: 'I didn't speak some things I wanted to speak [at the CALL], but I don't know. *Starts crying more heavily* So this is my mind. It's like [...] how can I explain to you? It's like, I wish. I wish you see me. I wish I [could] put [you] inside. *Points at her chest* I will show you!'[618] The ongoing challenges at all three abovementioned stages call for research that digs deeper into the causes and concrete forms of gender insensitivity occurring in the procedure, going beyond an exclusively refugee law-centred analysis.[619]

615 RB007_CALL_Attaché_[00:30:01].

616 RB008_CALL_Judge_[00:46:22].

617 NL017_1980_F_Liberia_STFP_GMC_VGNT_FM_ NL_ [00:21:02].

618 NEr018_1985_F_Eritrea_RSA_NL_[00:17:03].

619 UNHCR, 'Beyond Proof. Credibility Assessment in EU Asylum Systems (Full Report)' (n 19) 16.

3. CONCLUSION

Part II discussed the procedural aspects relevant to SGBV-related asylum decision making, according to their institutional stage (registration at the IO, first instance at the CGRS, and appeal at the CALL). In terms of SGBV-related training, I mentioned the IO case workers' limited training, by the IO itself acknowledged as insufficient to foster in-depth understanding of the topic but establishing support among participants. At the CGRS, I described the (gaps in the) offer of standard SGBV-related trainings for all POs, as well as specific trainings for gender POs and gender reference persons further specialising in gender-related cases.

However, I pointed out how the vast majority of gender cases are handled by non-gender-specialised POs, partly due to the high threshold for qualifying cases as 'complex gender cases'. The opinions on these trainings of POs and supervisors interviewed are divided. While some highly value the expertise and awareness these bring, others indicate that they come late, are not refreshed, are selective in terms of geographical scope and types of SGBV discussed, or do not address all necessary skills for SGBV-related interviewing and refugee status determination.

POs and supervisors at the CGRS are further supported in their work by gender guidelines, although there is a guidance gap on sex trafficking/forced prostitution, domestic violence, violence related to gender norm transgression, and medical/psychological certificates. So far, there has been no follow-up mechanism installed at the CGRS as to how these SGBV-related trainings and guidelines are being taken into account in practice. At the CALL, in contrast to all Belgian judges in criminal, family and juvenile law, no standard training on gender is in place. However, a first-of-its-kind pilot project, testing an awareness raising module on gender-sensitive asylum procedures, was considered highly relevant by several asylum officials at the CALL.

In terms of the psychological load and risk of vicarious traumatisation coming with treating SGBV cases, both at the CGRS and CALL, there is no possibility to opt out from or downscale handling gender-related cases. POs, supervisors, judges, and attachés report coping with this load individually or among peers, mentioning a risk of dropout for those who cannot 'put up a shield'. Some explicitly express their need for individual psychological supervision, which is not available internally at the CGRS or at the CALL at the moment.

The procedural guarantees mentioned above are meant to facilitate disclosure during and assessment of SGBV-related asylum procedures, but do not always seem to have the desired effect. For example: family members' case files are not always kept confidential or assessed separately; special procedural needs or comments about a trauma- or gender-insensitive interview conduct are not always accurately taken into account; applicants do not always receive effective legal support; applicants' inability to accept the personal interview invitation(s) might lead to decisions based on their inaccurate IO interview; the safe countries of origin list includes countries with concerning rates of SGBV prevalence; and the provision not to apply the accelerated procedure in SGBV cases involving special procedural needs is not consistently applied.

Finally, the 'small' IO interview is conducted by case workers who are not necessarily legally trained and without the legal support of a lawyer. However, whether or not certain fears or vulnerabilities are mentioned at this stage may substantially impact the final outcome of the procedure. This is further complicated by applicants often experiencing these interviews as rushed and stressful. The same counts for the personal interview at the CGRS, where POs do receive SGBV-specific training and applicants normally are supported by a lawyer. Still, not all personal interviews seem to be conducted in an equally gender- and trauma-sensitive manner, as in Angele's example. The CALL hearing, in a 'last chance' appeal procedure, is also stressful for applicants. Some judges, who are legally, but not necessarily trauma- and gender-sensitively trained, report discomfort around asking questions on SGBV during these hearings, which might lead applicants' cases to be assessed in an incomplete or inaccurate manner.

To conclude, although this research mainly focuses on the substantive assessment of SGBV-related applications for international protection, the abovementioned procedural and institutional aspects are of relevance to the final outcome of such procedures. Therefore, they should be taken into account when drawing conclusions and recommendations on gender sensitivity in asylum procedures and decisions on SGBV, as aimed at by this research.

PART III

RESOURCEFULNESS, DISCLOSURE & SURVIVAL MYTHS ON THE MICRO LEVEL

1. INTRODUCTION

In this chapter on SGBV mythology on the micro level, I will go into three types of SGBV myths, focusing on applicants' resourcefulness, disclosure of SGBV, and survival reactions post-SGBV. The first one, that 'resourceful applicants do not need protection against SGBV' (the resourcefulness myth), relies on the existing victim precipitation myth that SGBV normally happens to persons with limited material and/or non-material resources. The second and third myth hold the beliefs that 'inappropriate' disclosure (the disclosure myth) and 'inappropriate' survival reactions (the survival myth) undermine SGBV flight stories' credibility. These can be respectively traced back to the victim fabrication myth that persons tend to lie about or exaggerate SGBV and to the perception of certain reactions to SGBV as 'normal' and others not, leading to denial or minimisation of the violence when applicants' behaviour deviates from this norm.

First, in discussing acceptance of the resourcefulness myth, I will specifically go into how both material (e.g. education, financial means, ...) and non-material (e.g. social network, age, ...) resourcefulness are taken into account in refugee status determination (Chapter 2.1.2) and how male applicants' gender identity is at times perceived as a form of non-material resourcefulness rendering them less vulnerable to future SGBV (Chapter 2.1.3). A particular feature of the resourcefulness myth is that it appears to be accepted by asylum authorities in both a stand-alone and intersecting manner (Chapter 2.1.4). Therefore, I will discuss the ways in which this myth is often linked to other myths at the different ecological levels, reflecting the idea that applicants' resourcefulness enhances their ability of disclosing in a complete and consistent manner, showing active survival reactions, or seeking help from (non-)state actors of protection (meso/exo level). For male applicants, their resourcefulness is at times also linked to the macro level myth that their SGBV falls outside the scope of the UN Refugee Convention.

Second, the disclosure myth unfolds in four specific aspects of disclosure, namely: detailedness and consistency (Chapter 3.2), timing (Chapter 3.3), and demeanour (Chapter 3.4). In discussing the detail myth, I will go into how the types of details (central vs. circumstantial) and the level of detail (too little vs. too much) expected from applicants, as well as details not given by or not accessible to them may play a role in their refugee status determination. For the consistency myth, the discussion distinguishes between internal inconsistency (within and between applicants' own statements) and external inconsistency (between these statements and external information, such as COI and medical/psychological certificates) and sets out the types of elements found inconsistent by asylum authorities, as well as their position towards possible justifications for inconsistency.

A specific form of internal inconsistency, namely between previous and current statements of applicants, is discussed as the delayed disclosure myth. Here, I go into the several procedural stages at which this myth is accepted by asylum authorities (when submitting the first application, within the same personal interview, within the same procedure, or across procedures), as well as their positions towards justifications for such delays. Finally, in the part on the demeanour myth, I will elaborate on the ways in which the Belgian authorities assess applicants' demeanour while disclosing SGBV experiences/fears, namely by using the concept of 'sense of experience' or 'lived-throughness'.

Third, I will go into (potential) SGBV survivors'/applicants' short-term (e.g. freeze, appease, flight, and fight) reactions to and long-term (e.g. avoidance and approach) coping with SGBV (threats) and their perpetrators. Arguments based on such survivor/victim behaviour reason that survival reactions perceived as inappropriate undermine the credibility of survivors'/victims' SGBV story. I will demonstrate how, in contrast to the criminal justice context (where active survival reactions, i.e. fight/flight reactions and approach coping, are still considered credible in certain circumstances), asylum authorities seem to qualify both applicants' active (Chapter 4.1.2) and passive (Chapter 4.1.3) survival reactions (freeze/appease reactions and avoidance coping) as non-credible. This leaves applicants fleeing SGBV in a behavioural minefield, where any survival reaction they show(ed) might negatively impact their future/current refugee status determination.

For each of these myths on the micro level, I will go into the reasons for and ways of their rebuttal. As such, I will rebut the resourcefulness (Chapter 2.2), disclosure (Chapters 3.2.1, 3.2.2, and 3.3.2), and survival myths (Chapter 4.2) by setting out relevant expertise from social and health sciences, authoritative refugee (case) law, legal scholarship, and the ways in which the myths are at times explicitly rebutted by asylum officials in the Belgian asylum procedure. To visualise the acceptance and rebuttal levels of these myths, each section concludes with an overview of the percentage of analysed case law (n=202) in which the myths are explicitly accepted (CGRS and CALL) or rebutted (CALL), according to asylum authority and procedural language in Belgium (Chapters 2.3 on the resourcefulness myth, 2.4 on the disclosure myths, and 4.3 on the survival myths).

2. THE MYTH THAT RESOURCEFUL APPLICANTS DO NOT NEED PROTECTION AGAINST SGBV

CASE OF AMANI			
• Country of origin:	DRC	• SGBV types:	Rape/sexual assault & domestic violence
• Gender identity:	Woman	• Decisions in file:	CGRS 1 (refusal) – 21/12/2021
• Birth year:	1991		CALL 1 (annulment) – 17/01/2022 – n° 266 712
• Interview by:	CGRS		

According to Amani's statements, after her father had died, her mother remarried her stepfather, a teacher involved in local politics. From the age of 14, her stepfather started **raping** her when her mother was away for work. He made her drop out of school, wanting to prioritise his own children's education first. She never returned, explaining she had lost all self-confidence and the few friends she had, because the abuse had isolated her. She did work as a braider and sold goods, and found a religious community, the only place she really felt safe. When she was not out for these activities, she avoided her stepfather by staying in her room, since she could not bear facing him. In 2016, Amani fell ill, leading her to discover that she was **pregnant as a result of the sexual abuse**. As her stepfather threatened to kill her if she told anyone, she lied to her mother that she was no longer in contact with the child's father. From her son's birth onwards, fearful that her stepfather would come back to rape her at night, Amani avoided spending the night at home. When her son fell ill and had to go to hospital, Amani felt compelled to tell someone the truth and confided in her cousin. To protect her, the latter wanted to take the baby away from Amani's mother and stepfather. When her mother asked why, the cousin told her about the abuse. The next day, Amani was **abducted** and **raped** by 2 men dressed as policemen and a third. They left her in a graveyard. Upon returning home, her stepfather threatened her with a gun for bringing out the truth and locked her in the house. Finding the door open in the morning, she fled to her maternal cousin in Congo-Brazzaville. After receiving anonymous phone calls there, she travelled on to Turkey, where she collected money to travel to Belgium by working in a night club.

She was apprehended at the airport for travelling with false identity documents, applied for international protection and was detained in a closed centre. In support of her application, Amani submitted two psychological reports, attesting her difficulties in recounting her experiences and her wish to be heard by a female PO and interpreter.

As mentioned above, the CGRS refused Amani refugee status and, while according her special procedural guarantees in theory, did so in an accelerated procedure. This goes against the Belgian Aliens act prescribing not to do so in cases of torture, including rape.[620] In its decision, the CGRS used (among others) the argument:

> '[You] have been working since you were 17 [...], are financially independent, [...] [sell] goods on credit [...], [are a member of a] religious community [...], the choir [...], the majorettes [...], [you participate] in multi-day retreats [...], and [...] financed part of your trip yourself [...]. These elements demonstrate an [...] **independence**, which is **difficult to reconcile with** your [...] status as a young woman alone and without resources, **at the mercy of a [sexually] abusive stepfather**.'[621] | CASE OF AMANI

This type of reasoning boils down to the idea that only persons without certain resources run a risk of being subjected to SGBV. In the criminal justice context, Ben-David and Schneider have categorised this resourcefulness argument as the 'victim precipitation myth': SGBV only happens to certain types of persons.[622] In the asylum context, I will discuss how acceptance of this SGBV myth involves different forms of material and non-material resourcefulness of applicants. In addition, it does not only impact the well-foundedness of applicants' fear of SGBV as such but also intersects with the assessment of other aspects of refugee status determination and other SGBV myths. Concerning the disclosure myths for example, the CGRS also linked Amani's resourcefulness to her perceived ability to disclose the violence she experienced.

> '[W]hile your psychologist mentions your difficulty in recounting the sexual violence of which you claim to have been a victim, the questions you were asked, far from [...] limited to [this], concerned your entire experience in your family home [...]. [Y]our level of independence and **resourcefulness** [...] [is] **difficult to reconcile** with your **inability to provide a detailed account** of the events you claim to have experienced.'[623] | CASE OF AMANI

After going into the acceptance of this resourcefulness myth, I will set out the reasons for and instances of its rebuttal. Throughout the interviews, several asylum officials expressed dissenting opinions when confronted with the abovementioned reasoning in Amani's case, stating for example: 'Anyone can be a victim [...] I don't know if there are any figures [...] but I think that there are

620 Art. 48/9, §5 Belgian Aliens Act; Commissioner General for Refugees and Stateless Persons (CGRS), 'Special Procedural Needs' (n 532).

621 NC004_CGRS 1 (refusal)_1991_F_DRC_RSA_DV_21/12/2021_FR_NANSEN_p. 4.

622 Ben-David and Schneider (n 3) 386.

623 NC004_CGRS 1 (refusal)_1991_F_DRC_RSA_DV_21/12/2021_FR_NANSEN_p. 4.

just as many well-educated victims. [...] So I don't know if I would dare to write that.'[624] Throughout this chapter, I will pay specific attention to male applicants, for whom the resourcefulness myth can take on the form of male SGBV myths, such as: 'Men cannot be raped; they can resist.'[625] Both acceptance and rebuttal of this male resourcefulness myth will be illustrated below.

2.1. ACCEPTANCE OF THE RESOURCEFULNESS MYTH

2.1.1. FROM CRIMINAL JUSTICE TO ASYLUM CONTEXT

Ben-David and Schneider's victim precipitation myth has been further concretised in the criminal justice context as: 'Nice girls do not get sexually assaulted; only a certain type of women does,'[626] '[V]ictims of trafficking are usually young girls who are naïve, vulnerable, poor and uneducated,'[627] '[SGBV] is [...] the problem of certain neighbourhoods [...] and certain types of people'[628] or '[U]sually it is only [persons] who do things like hang out in bars, sleep around or dress suggestively who get raped.'[629] These types of reasoning also may assume that vulnerability to SGBV stems from a lack of individual strength, independence and resourcefulness, which is personally generated and thus 'correctable through individual self-improvement'[630] (also theorised as the neoliberal victimisation theory[631]).[632] Both thinking patterns (reproaching someone for being either too resourceful or not resourceful enough) are the flip sides of the same victim blaming phenomenon focusing on a person's static characteristics, called 'characterological blame' in the literature.[633]

As a result, the persons considered survivor/victim-worthy are being limited to those who Christie calls 'ideal victims' in the criminal justice context. He defined an ideal victim as 'a person or a category of individuals who [...] most readily are given the complete and legitimate status of being a victim'[634] with the following

624 CB015_CGRS_Supervisor+PO_GENDER_[00:26:25].
625 Lochhead and Tan (n 397) 52.
626 *Ibid.* 51.
627 Linthout and others (n 268).
628 Ticktin, 'In the Name of Violence against Women' (n 396) 156.
629 Payne, Lonsway and Fitzgerald (n 134) 49.
630 Rebecca Stringer, *Knowing Victims: Feminism, Agency and Victim Politics in Neoliberal Times* (Routledge 2014) 9.
631 *Ibid.*; Elizabeth Comack and Tracey Peter, 'How the Criminal Justice System Responds to Sexual Assault Survivors: The Slippage between "Responsibilization" and "Blaming the Victim."' (2005) 17 Canadian Journal of Women & the Law 283, 283.
632 Peroni (n 33) 361.
633 van der Bruggen and Grubb (n 499) 524; Fanflik, Office on Violence Against Women, and National District Attorneys Association (n 386) 11.
634 Christie (n 4) 18.

characteristics: 1) weak, 2) carrying out a noble task, 3) located in a respectable place and harmed by 4) malign and 5) unknown forces or actors.[635] Those with characteristics and/or in situations falling outside this ideal image, risk being assessed as 'too agentive to be innocent',[636] disbelieved as survivors/victims, and eventually left unprotected. This risk is even higher for adult men, who are seen as almost *a priori* invulnerable[637] 'authors of their own destiny',[638] assumed to be more resilient[639] to SGBV in the so-called hierarchy of suffering.[640] Their gender is considered a form of non-material resourcefulness, giving rise to a specific form of male rape myths, such as: 'Men cannot be raped; they can resist',[641] '[S]exual abuse of boys by women is not sexual violence',[642] '[M]en would not be [as] traumatised by rape [as women]',[643] and '[P]erpetrators of male-on-male sexual violence are gay or [...] heterosexual male survivors become gay through penile-anal rape.'[644]

Similarly, (inter)national refugee case law portrays an image of the 'ideal SGBV refugee' as a passive, dependent, and vulnerable female and/or child victim[645] with minimal public/political agency. To maximise the chance of a successful application for international protection, Barsky explains that applicants must fit into a story that is sought by the authorities.[646] This story

635 *Ibid.* 19.

636 Miriam Ticktin, 'Innocence: Shaping the Concept and Practice of Humanity' in Michael N Barnett (ed), *Humanitarianism and Human Rights: A World of Differences?* (Cambridge University Press 2020) 9.

637 Saroléa, Raimondo and Crine (n 93) 93.

638 Magugliani (n 93) 4.

639 Depraetere and others (n 93) 1002.

640 Magugliani (n 93) 5.

641 Lochhead and Tan (n 397) 52; Women's Refugee Commission and UNICEF Europe & Central Asia, 'Supporting Young Male Refugees and Migrants Who Are Survivors or at Risk of Sexual Violence: A Field Guide for Frontline Workers in Europe' (2021) 10; Siobhan Weare, '"Oh You're a Guy, How Could You Be Raped by a Woman, That Makes No Sense": Towards a Case for Legally Recognising and Labelling "Forced-to-Penetrate" Cases as Rape' (2018) 14 International Journal of Law in Context 110, 124; Chynoweth and others (n 93) 8; Paula S Kerr Melanson, 'Belief in Male Rape Myths: A Test of Two Competing Theories' (Queen's University 1998) 61; Cindy Struckman-Johnson and David Struckman-Johnson, 'Acceptance of Male Rape Myths Among College Men and Women' (1992) 27 Sex Roles 85, 86.

642 Women's Refugee Commission and UNICEF Europe & Central Asia (n 354) 10; Weare (n 354) 124; Melanson (n 354) 61.

643 Michelle Davies, Jennifer Gilston and Paul Rogers, 'Examining the Relationship Between Male Rape Myth Acceptance, Female Rape Myth Acceptance, Victim Blame, Homophobia, Gender Roles, and Ambivalent Sexism' (2012) 27 Journal of Interpersonal Violence 2807, 2810; McGee and others (n 400) 3586.

644 Chynoweth and others (n 93) 8.

645 Megan Denise Smith, 'Rethinking Gender in the International Refugee Regime' (2016) 53 Forced Migration Review 65, 65.

646 Robert F Barsky, *Constructing a Productive Other: Discourse Theory and the Convention Refugee Hearing* (John Benjamins Publishing Company 1994) 84; Loes Verhaeghe, 'To be or not to be believed: discoursanalyse van het geloofwaardigheidsonderzoek tijdens asielprocedures van lesbische, biseksuele en transgender vrouwen' (Ghent University 2018) 13.

is based on their own specific world view and the assumption that 'we can recognize suffering wherever we see it.'[647] As such, an (ideally female) victim must demonstrate to behave 'properly' according to societal gender roles, as a preferably apolitical, voiceless victim of an oppressive, dysfunctional and patriarchal culture.[648]

In the case of Amani, she does not fit the ideal of the suffering 'Third World Woman', as coined by Mohanty.[649] She cannot be considered passive nor voiceless and therefore cannot, in the view of the CGRS, represent what Ticktin calls a 'morally legitimate suffering body'.[650] With this term, she reveals how human compassion is not static, but is dependent on both survivors/victims' personal characteristics (such as resourcefulness) and the ways in which they disclose their experiences (see Chapter 3). Whether survivors/victims succeed to 'perform gendered affect in the courtroom'[651] or interview room (both in the content of their story and the way they present it), matching asylum authorities' gendered expectations, will determine their deservingness of benevolence and protection.[652] In the context of the Belgian asylum procedure, this 'ideal of the female SGBV victim'[653] gives rise to specific forms of characterological victim blaming, serving as arguments to refuse refugee status.

2.1.2. MATERIAL VS. NON-MATERIAL RESOURCEFULNESS

a) Material Resourcefulness

Characterological victim blaming in the asylum context may involve both material resources and non-material resources. Concerning the former, both national and supranational decision makers seem to assume that certain forms of material resourcefulness render applicants less vulnerable to SGBV. In the UK asylum procedure for example, Baillot, Cowan, and Munro uncovered

647 Ticktin, *Casualties of Care: Immigration and the Politics of Humanitarianism in France* (n 167) 11.

648 Firth and Mauthe (n 25) 481.

649 Mohanty (n 238) 67–68.

650 Ticktin, 'In the Name of Violence against Women' (n 396) 130.

651 Sara L McKinnon, 'Citizenship and the Performance of Credibility: Audiencing Gender-Based Asylum Seekers in U.S. Immigration Courts' (2009) 29 Text & Performance Quarterly 205, 215.

652 Ticktin, 'In the Name of Violence against Women' (n 396) 129–130.

653 Lore Roels, 'How Joining a Majorette Group Can Lead You to Being Denied International Protection: On Rape Mythology in Asylum/Non-Refoulement Procedures' (*Völkerrechtsblog*, 7 March 2023), https://voelkerrechtsblog.org/how-joining-a-majorette-group-can-lead-you-to-being-denied-international-protection/; Lore Roels, 'Hoe lid worden van de majorettes ertoe kan leiden dat je verzoek om internationale bescherming wordt geweigerd' (*Tijd voor Mensenrechten*, 8 March 2023), https://tijd.mensenrechten.be/2023/03/08/hoe-lid-worden-van-de-majorettes-ertoe-kan-leiden-dat-je-verzoek-om-internationale-bescherming-wordt-geweigerd/.

how (higher) education might be seen as a characteristic reducing applicants' chances at international protection, where it is perceived as lowering the risk to experience SGBV upon return.[654] In the ECtHR's non-refoulement case law, I illustrated that the Court's case law 'seems to assume that educated and/or professionally experienced applicants are less vulnerable (or even invulnerable) to ill-treatment.'[655] Also, applicants' financial means and ability to for example afford a large house, cars, a house help, or travels abroad are perceived as enabling them to protect themselves and/or their children from SGBV.[656]

In the Belgian asylum procedure, authorities have expressed similar types of reasoning for applicants' education level, professional experience, housing (and the urbanisation level of its location), and financial means (including access to social security[657]). One PO for example mentioned a case of a woman who had a university diploma and work experience at international organisations, earned a good living, bought her own house, and 'was leading a perfectly normal life,'[658] despite the fact that she had been abused by her husband for years. Consequently, the PO stated: 'I thought that she could [...] simply leave her husband.'[659] The PO categorised the applicant's explanation that this is not so simple for women in Guinea as 'general statements [that fail] to explain why [...] she didn't [do] anything.'[660]

Another PO confirmed that the CGRS' refugee status determination relies on a typical profile of women being more at risk of forced marriages. They testified how some colleagues 'start from the assumption that a woman who is educated, [...] from an urban environment [...] where there is certain [...] financial wealth, cannot be subject to [...] well, [...] may be less likely to be believed.'[661] A gender-specialised PO also explained that women fleeing forced marriage in Guinea often mention they could study. This leads the PO to conclude that such family contexts are open and progressive and that, if the same applicant had not studied and did come from a conservative family, she would have been credible. They added that someone who is economically independent will be expected to break ties with a violent or abusive family.[662]

654 Baillot, Cowan and Munro, 'Reason to Disbelieve' (n 6) 114.

655 Roels, 'Rape Myths in the European Court of Human Rights' Non-Refoulement Case Law on Sexual and Gender-Based Violence' (n 33) 88.

656 *Izevbekhai and Others v Ireland* [2011] ECtHR 43408/08 [80].

657 CB002_CGRS_PO_[00:20:50].

658 CB004_CGRS_PO_[00:09:37].

659 CB004_CGRS_PO_[00:44:53].

660 CB004_CGRS_PO_[00:44:53].

661 CB010_CGRS_PO_[00:19:52].

662 CB009_CGRS_PO_GENDER_[00:18:59].

On appeal level at the CALL, certain asylum officials illustrated a similar reasoning, for example: 'If someone said, "I'm a doctor", we thought it's not possible for this person to undergo a forced marriage because she can move to another town.'[663]

b) *Non-Material Resourcefulness*

When it comes to non-material resourcefulness, scholarship has pointed out acceptance of this form of the resourcefulness myth in international refugee decision making.[664] Peroni for example explains how the ECtHR has perceived applicants' strength, independence, resourcefulness, initiative to take legal steps, organisation of their flight out of the country, and even application for international protection as such as 'indications of women's independence and strength to protect themselves or their children.'[665] Similarly, the Belgian asylum authorities demonstrated acceptance of the myth that applicants are less or invulnerable to SGBV when they can draw on non-material resources, such as: being older/an adult, having a social/family network, taking a (public) stance against certain SGBV forms, being progressive/assertive/independent as such, having taken legal steps in the past, or having travelled (alone) or fled as such.

As with the material resourcefulness myth, acceptance of the non-material resourcefulness myth occurs with both first instance and appeal decision makers in Belgium. One PO described the case of an applicant who had travelled several times to other countries on her own and asked her: 'Why didn't you take the opportunity to run away if your husband had been beating you for years?'[666] A judge confirmed: '[If applicants are independent and have a wide social network] [...] you're going to consider them stronger.'[667] Sometimes, applicants' self-reported lack of material resources was overruled by asylum officials' perception that they were in fact (non-materially) resourceful. One

---

663 RB007_CALL_Attaché_[00:33:53].

664 Eva Brems, 'Strong Women Don't Need Asylum (the European Court on FGM)' (*Strasbourg Observers*, 19 August 2010), https://strasbourgobservers.com/2010/08/19/%e2%80%98strong-women-don%e2%80%99t-need-asylum%e2%80%99-the-european-court-on-fgm/; Thomas Spijkerboer, 'European Sexual Nationalism: Refugee Law after the Gender & Sexuality Critiques.' (Social Science Research Network 2015) 4; Wessels (n 94) 9–10; Roels, 'Rape Myths in the European Court of Human Rights' Non-Refoulement Case Law on Sexual and Gender-Based Violence' (n 33) 88–89; Elena Ghidoni, 'The Nexus between Gender Stereotypes and Evidence: Insights from the CEDAW Committee' (Unpublished 2023).

665 Peroni (n 33) 359; Roels, 'Rape Myths in the European Court of Human Rights' Non-Refoulement Case Law on Sexual and Gender-Based Violence' (n 33) 88–89.

666 CB004_CGRS_PO_[00:44:53].

667 RB005_CALL_Judge_[00:28:35].

PO for example explained how an applicant, claiming to have fled a forced marriage with very little resources, 'raises questions: how could this person [who claims to have no schooling or network] [...] have left on her own [...] and come to Europe?'[668]

Interestingly, the non-material resourcefulness argument is not only made on the basis of real life social networks as described in the personal interview, but also online social networks through social media screenings.[669] This was demonstrated by a gender-specialised supervisor at the CGRS, mentioning a case where a Facebook search showed that an applicant was a university student with 'an incredible network of friends, [...] in contact with her parents, who seem rather westernised, [...] an objective observation [preventing] us from believing [...] in [her forced marriage].'[670]

c) *Material and Non-Material Resourcefulness Myth Acceptance in Case Law*

Acceptance of both the material and non-material resourcefulness myths is not only reflected in the Belgian asylum officials' self-reported reasoning but also occur in their written arguments shaping decisions and judgements. In the analysed case law sample, both the CGRS and the CALL have found applicants' fear of SGBV to be non-credible and/or ill-founded due to (among other arguments) all the above-mentioned forms of material and non-material resourcefulness. One specific example is the case of Carmen.

CASE OF CARMEN			
• Country of origin:	Ecuador	• SGBV types:	Rape/sexual assault & domestic violence
• Gender identity:	Woman	• Decisions in file:	CGRS 1 (refusal) – 8/12/2023
• Birth year:	1981		CALL 1 (refusal) – 28/04/2024 – n° 305 805
• Interview by:	/		

(continued)

668 CB007_CGRS_PO_[00:26:45].

669 For an in-depth analysis of the legal issues with social media screenings in the context of the Belgian asylum procedure, see: Lore Roels, 'Socialemedia- en smartphonescreenings tegen misbruik in Belgische verzoekprocedures om internationale bescherming : een doel dat de middelen niet wettigt' (2020) 4 Tijdschrift voor Vreemdelingenrecht 329.

670 CB005_CGRS_Supervisor+PO_GENDER_[00:33:50]. This reasoning was also confirmed in the case law analysis, e.g. DG094_CGRS 1 (refusal)_F_Guinea_RSA_GMC_VGNT_FM_DV_5/5/2023_FR_Database_p. 4., DK152_CALL 2 (refusal)_1997_F_Kenya_RSA_VGNT_FM_DV_4/4/2024_304 367_NL_Database_p. 7 and 19.

According to her statements, Carmen is a pharmacist who owned and afterwards worked for a pharmaceutical business in Ecuador. She had to quit her job in 2019 after her ex-husband had attacked her with a knife over an alimony dispute. She got married to him in 2007, but his **mental, physical, and sexual abuse** started one year earlier, after their daughter was born. The next child, her son, was the result of **intramarital rape**. She sought help from a foundation supporting domestic violence survivors/victims, filed a complaint with the police, and obtained a protection order. She reported his first violation of the order, upon which he was detained for 8 days instead of 60 as provided. After being released, his threats got worse. After this, she dared not report the violations again. She managed to divorce him, but alimony for her children was denied. Unable to accept the divorce, her husband **hit Carmen with a car** in 2010, **attacked her with a knife in the chest** in 2018, and **poured burning liquid in her face** in 2020, forcing her to quit her job again. In 2021, he **threatened to kill her** on the phone, whereupon she fled the country fearing he would succeed.

With the help of a friend, she flew to Turkey and then to Brussels, where she applied for international protection. She supported her application with legal documents, such as the protection order, the divorce petition, and her ex-husband's criminal record, as well as medical documents, such as photographs and medical attestations of her injuries, and a psychological report confirming her need of long-term psychological support.

The CGRS refused Carmen refugee status with (among others) two arguments, later confirmed by the CALL in appeal, focusing both on her material (financial means, housing, and professional experience) and non-material (social network, being independent, and having taken legal steps in the past) resourcefulness:

> '[I]t [cannot] be assumed that you did not have the **financial means** to move […], you have a **house** that you rent out […], had your **own pharmacy** and **worked** for several pharmaceutical companies […]. After your divorce, you **rented a house** […] a short distance from your former residence, so it cannot be explained that you could [not] have done so elsewhere […]. Moreover, you **managed to find someone willing to finance your trip** to Europe […], which could have supported you in building a new life.'[671]
>
> 'Your own statements have clearly shown your **independence and resourcefulness**, as well as your ability to assert your rights through the Ecuadorian **legal system** […]. Nothing shows that you would not be able to do so again upon return.'[672] | CASE OF CARMEN

671 DEc120_CGRS 1 (refusal)_1981_F_Ecuador_RSA_DV_ 8/12/2023_NL_Database_p. 3., DEc120_CALL 1 (refusal)_1981_F_Ecuador_RSA_DV_ 29/4/2024_ 305 805_NL_Database_ p. 7–8.

672 DEc120_CGRS 1 (refusal)_1981_F_Ecuador_RSA_DV_ 8/12/2023_NL_Database_p. 4., DEc120_CALL 1 (refusal)_1981_F_Ecuador_RSA_DV_ 29/4/2024_ 305 805_NL_Database_ p. 10.

2.1.3. MALE RESOURCEFULNESS MYTH

a) *Acceptance of the Male Resourcefulness Myth*

Specifically for male applicants, their gender is at times seen as a form of non-material resourcefulness. As mentioned in the introduction (see Part I, Chapter 1), this form of male SGBV myth acceptance has been observed in the ECtHR's non-refoulement case law.[673] As shown by the interviews for this research, this is also the case in the Belgian asylum procedure. On the one hand, respondents described perceiving male applicants seeking protection from SGBV as internally incompatible. One PO estimated sexual violence being committed by men in 'perhaps 98% of the cases,' concluding that male victimisation of sexual violence is not impossible, but that it is 'essential that [...] [they] should be able to explain why [...] it happened,' putting them in a disadvantaged position.[674] Another PO found applicants' likelihood of successful reintegration after sexual violence to depend on their gender identity, clarifying that: 'For a woman, it's always going to be complicated. So [their] need for protection is much more obvious.'[675]

When male applicants are seen as potential survivors/victims of SGBV, other respondents found their physical appearance to impact their risk to SGBV: the more fragile and/or feminine male applicants appear, the more credible their flight story might be. One gender-specialised supervisor stated about the practice of *bacha bazi* in Afghanistan, a form of sex trafficking/forced prostitution where (pre)adolescent boys are enslaved for sexual abuse by powerful male patrons:[676] 'Victims [...] behave a bit younger [...] and [...] have more feminine sides. [...] you can put two Afghans next to each other and [...] say [...] "this one is much more likely to be abused". [...] [T]hey are usually [...] beautiful boys[, nicely shaven and dressed,] [...] versus a less beautiful [...] Afghan with a full beard.'[677] A judge at the CALL described a male applicant fleeing sexual violence due to his sexual orientation as a small and thin boy, who 'certainly wouldn't be able to protect himself physically.' This observation rendered their consideration of an IFA in a big city without a social network less likely, since: '[For] a weaker person, [...] a network does become important.'[678]

---

673 Roels, 'Rape Myths in the European Court of Human Rights' Non-Refoulement Case Law on Sexual and Gender-Based Violence' (n 33) 88–89.

674 CB004_CGRS_PO_[00:54:54].

675 CB001_CGRS_PO_[00:08:57].

676 Amalendu Misra, 'Men on Top: Sexual Economy of Bacha Bazi in Afghanistan' (2023) 60 International Politics 350, 350.

677 CB011_CGRS_Supervisor+PO_GENDER_[00:30:18].

678 RB005_CALL_Judge_[00:33:05].

b) *Wrong or Lack of Qualification as Persecution*

In the analysed case law, SGBV-related persecution in flight stories of male applicants runs a risk of being wrongly or not qualified as such. This is for example illustrated by the case of Yusuf.

CASE OF YUSUF			
• Country of origin:	Afghanistan	• SGBV types:	Rape/sexual assault
• Gender identity:	Man	• Decisions in file:	CGRS 1 (refusal) – 5/10/2023
• Birth year:	/		CALL 1 (refusal) – 8/03/2024 – n° 302 900
• Interview by:	/		

According to his statements, Yusuf grew up in Afghanistan, where he was educated up to sixth grade and lived with his parents, four sisters, and four brothers. His father was approached several times by a known Taliban member (or *talib*), asking that Yusuf join the Taliban. His father refused this request, arguing that he was too young and still needed to study. Without his father knowing, the same *talib* had also repeatedly approached Yusuf directly with **unwanted sexual advances, by trying to touch him, telling him he loved him, and asking him to have sexual intercourse.** Yusuf managed to escape these but was ashamed and dared not tell his father anything, as he feared he would bring shame to the family and be rejected by them. Yusuf understood from the *talib's* advances that his request to join the Taliban to his father was only a false motive. The last time the *talib* approached Yusuf's father, he informed him that he would come and get Yusuf the next day, upon which his father decided it was safer to send Yusuf away.

He eventually fled Afghanistan with his uncle and arrived in Belgium, where he applied for international protection.

Both the CGRS and the CALL denied Yusuf refugee status on the grounds that his profile and story did not match the COI on forced recruitment by the Taliban. Nowhere did the decisions mention any COI or standalone assessment regarding *bacha bazi* or other forms of exploitation of boys within the ranks of the Taliban.[679] Instead, the unwanted sexual advances were not qualified as stand-alone gender-related persecution eligible for refugee status protection, but were dismissed as a hypothetical fear of something that never actually occurred and as merely peripheral to the alleged forced recruitment. The CGRS argued:

> '[The *talib*] showed romantic and/or sexual interest in you, but this was not desired by you and you therefore rejected him [...]. [Y]ou [...] have **neither voluntarily nor**

679 Maria Gevorgyan and Armen Matevosyan, 'Bacha Bazi: Unraveling Debate between Crime Against Humanity and Regional Tradition' (2023) 2 European Journal of Law and Political Science 38, 38–40.

> **against your will performed acts** with this person [...]. [Y]our statements regarding the [...] **forced recruitment** are already considered non-credible, which makes any link between [the *talib's*] behaviour towards you and this [recruitment] [...] **bare allegations** that you cannot further substantiate.'[680] | CASE OF YUSUF

It is important to note that whether acts of persecution were effectively completed or not (e.g. when an applicant managed to flee in time) is not relevant to refugee status determination, as this is a future-oriented assessment based on a person's fear of persecution upon return.[681] Further, the risk of trivialising sexual exploitation of young men (*bacha bazi*) in parts of Afghanistan and Pakistan has been recognised by UNICEF Europe & Central Asia and the Women's Refugee Commission, warning that both service providers and survivors themselves may fail to qualify the practice as rape/sexual assault.[682]

Similarly, in a Nigerian rape/sexual assault case, the grooming[683] and rape of a male applicant by a man in a position of power were wrongly qualified as a homosexual relationship. The applicant was raped during a camp when he was 14, by a person in the military. After this, he did not speak to this man for two months. The decision states: '[Y]ou reconnected and became friends with benefits [...]. He bought gifts for you and you had sex with him. This relationship lasted for seven months.'[684] This case was complicated by the fact that for the applicant, the rape confirmed his homosexual orientation, as he got an erection. However, he experienced confusion and guilt in the process due to the contradiction between his physical reaction and the fact that he was forced into these acts.[685]

This case shows how male rape myths, such as 'obtaining an erection during rape denotes enjoyment or event consent' (while it actually is a common physiological response)[686] or 'a man who is sexually assaulted by another

---

680 DAf150_CGRS 1 (refusal)_M_Afghanistan_RSA_5/10/2023_NL_Database_p. 3–4., DAf150_CALL 1 (refusal)_M_Afghanistan_RSA_8/3/2024_302 900_NL_Database_p. 14.

681 Art. 1(A)2 UN Refugee Convention; UNHCR, 'Guidelines on International Protection No. 12: Claims for Refugee Status Related to Situations of Armed Conflict and Violence under Article 1A(2) of the 1951 Convention and/or 1967 Protocol Relating to the Status of Refugees and the Regional Refugee Definitions (HCR/GIP/16/12)' (2016) para 24.

682 Women's Refugee Commission and UNICEF Europe & Central Asia (n 641) 10.

683 'Broadly, [Grooming] refers to how some perpetrators interact with and engage a child, and sometimes others around the child, to enable sexual abuse while decreasing the likelihood of disclosure', for example by buying them gifts. Afrooz Kaviani Johnson, 'Grooming and Child Sexual Abuse in Organizational Settings – an Expanded Role for International Human Rights Law' (2024) 16 Journal of Human Rights Practice 355, 357.

684 DN149_CGRS 1 (refusal)_1997_M_Nigeria_RSA_VGNT_CGRS_19/6/2023_NL_Database_p. 3. Emphasis added.

685 DN149_CALL 1 (annulment)_lawyers' argumentation_1997_M_Nigeria_RSA_VGNT_29/2/2024_302 605_NL_Database_p. 6.

686 Weare (n 641) 125; Chynoweth and others (n 93) 11; Melanson (n 641) 61; Women's Refugee Commission and UNICEF Europe & Central Asia (n 641) 10.

man must be homosexual,[687] occur in both internalised (by survivors/victims themselves) and externalised forms. These phenomena are challenged by some asylum authorities in the interviews: 'Sometimes [we] [...] frame [something] as homosexual practices[, but it might] rather have been rape,'[688] but replicated by others: 'You come across [...] stories [...] [for example] "I was sexually abused as a child so I have now become homosexual" [...] that really puts me off [...] those are really stereotypical statements, which [...] don't reflect [...] how someone develops in their childhood.'[689]

In addition, the SGBV brought up by male applicants seems to be more rigorously scrutinised than for female applicants. For instance, the question of whether a forced marriage or GMC is serious enough to fulfil the legal qualification of 'persecution' is usually not raised in women's cases. For female applicants, the sufficient severity of such violence has long been established.[690] This is not the case for male applicants, a double standard that can be illustrated by two Georgian cases.

In the first, a bisexual male applicant was forced to marry a woman by her family after she became pregnant of him. After his wife told both their families and friends about his sexual orientation against his will and he wanted to file for divorce, he was on several occasions abducted and severely beaten by his family-in-law, who forbade him to see his daughter. The CGRS did not include the forced marriage in its assessment at all, and the CALL stated in appeal: 'Apart from the two incidents with his ex-in-laws, the applicant cited [...] no incidents [...] due to his sexual orientation. [...] [D]iscriminatory treatment [does] not in itself involve persecution in the sense of refugee law.'[691] In doing so, both the CGRS and CALL failed to acknowledge male forced marriage as a severe enough form of persecution eligible for international protection, as they normally do in female cases.

The second case revolves around a male applicant who feared GMC by his family. In this way, they wanted to convert him to Islam and had almost succeeded to abduct him to this end in the past. The CALL dismissed these fears in the judgment by stating that: '[The] problems with [his] parents [...] are not sufficiently serious in nature, intensity and scope to be considered acts of persecution within the meaning of the Refugee Convention.'[692] Here too, a form of SGBV (forced GMC) is considered insufficiently serious to be qualified as persecution, which is generally not the case when invoked for female applicants.

687 McGee and others (n 400) 3585.
688 RB001_CALL_Judge_[00:06:16].
689 CB011_CGRS_Supervisor+PO_GENDER_[00:39:14].
690 UNHCR, 'Guidelines on International Protection No. 1' (n 35) para 9.
691 DGe110_CALL 1 (refusal)_1986_M_Georgia_FM_VGNT_27/3/2024_303 889__NL_Database_p. 16.
692 DGe112_CALL 2 (refusal)_M_Georgia_GMC_29/3/2024_304 208_NL_Database_p. 15.

c) *Stricter Plausibility Assessment*

In addition, the plausibility of both the physical feasibility of the violence and the motives of perpetrators tend to be questioned in male applicants' cases. By contrast, this generally does not apply to female applicants. For example, an Iraqi applicant sought international protection in fear of being ostracised by his family. His aunt had repeatedly raped him during six months (which was again described by the asylum authorities as 'a relationship'[693]) under the threat that she would tell the family that he had sexually assaulted her if he did not do exactly what she requested. In the first instance decision, the CGRS raised questions about how this woman could have forced a man into a 'sexual relationship' and the fact that he had 'lost his self-control' in the process[694] (similar to the uncontrollable physical reactions to rape/sexual assault as mentioned in the Nigerian case above).

Thereupon, the CGRS deemed it totally implausible that this female perpetrator could have blackmailed him, in light of the available COI on honour crimes against women, showing that 'rape is taboo and [...] it would be very complicated for a woman to [lie about her sexual victimisation] to her family because she would risk [...] death.'[695] The rape myth that men can resist is used here to question not only the physical feasibility of the sexual violence itself, but also the means by which coercion can be exercised by female perpetrators. It is telling how the authorities questioned this aunt's ability to pressure the applicant, since she puts herself at risk in the process, while the same could be said of male perpetrators who pressure their victims to stay silent, such as in Amani's case,[696] while risking prison sentences due to their acts.

2.1.4. STAND-ALONE RESOURCEFULNESS MYTH VS. INTERSECTING WITH OTHER SGBV MYTHS

The case law and interviews include examples of acceptance of the resourcefulness myth in its stand-alone form, where applicants' resourcefulness impacts the well-foundedness of their fear of SGBV. In addition, authorities' thinking patterns also demonstrate how the resourcefulness myth may intersect with other SGBV myths concerning other aspects of the refugee status

693 DIq095_CGRS 1 (refusal)_M_Iraq_RSA_DV_20/1/2023_FR_Database_p. 2.
694 DIq095_CGRS 1 (refusal)_M_Iraq_RSA_DV_20/1/2023_FR_Database_p. 3.
695 DIq095_CGRS 1 (refusal)_M_Iraq_RSA_DV_20/1/2023_FR_Database_p.3–4.
696 '[My stepfather] threatened me. He was telling me clearly that he was going to kill me [...] if I dared to tell the truth [...]. [...] [B]before [I had to tell my cousin], I didn't see how I could [...], I was [...] very ashamed" (NC004_CGRS interview 2_1991_F_DRC_RSA_DV_FR_NANSEN_p. 5 & 8.).

determination process (e.g. disclosure, survival reactions, seeking (non-)state protection, …).

a) *Stand-Alone Resourcefulness Myth*

In its stand-alone form, resourcefulness is directly linked to applicants' risk to experience SGBV and thus the well-foundedness of their fear. This was observed both with asylum officials from the CGRS, where one PO testified how some colleagues used applicants' profile to call into question their reported SGBV by starting 'from the premise that she wasn't credible, but without even trying to find out what she had to say.'[697] At the CALL too, this stand-alone resourcefulness myth is accepted, but not without internal debate on the topic. One attaché explained: 'If the person […] has a well-developed social network, […] this partly reduces the risk of future persecution, whereas conversely, if the person is totally isolated and has extremely limited socio-economic resources, this will [aggravate] the risk.'[698]

Also, this stand-alone myth is accepted based on the perceived resourcefulness not only of applicants themselves, but also of their parents, for example in GMC cases, where the risk of external pressure to subject their children to the practice is assessed. One judge reasoned: 'You have to look at the […] socio-economic profile [of the parents] in general, […] as long as they are the financial providers [to other people in the family], they are not going to be pressured.'[699] However, as ECtHR judge Power-Forde once concluded in a separate opinion to an SGBV-related non-refoulement judgement, these types of reasoning risk to reduce the protection of applicants' fundamental human rights to 'a question of currency'.[700]

b) *Resourcefulness Myth Intersecting with Other SGBV Myths*

Additionally, the resourcefulness myth is accepted in combination with other SGBV myths that will be discussed throughout this research. The intersection with the disclosure myths, leading to the assumption that higher education implies more complete and consistent disclosure of SGBV, will be elaborated on below (see Chapter 3.2.1). Next, resourceful applicants are expected to show more active survival reactions to distance themselves from the perpetrator more readily (see Chapter 4.1), for example by moving to an IFA. In contrast to UNHCR's position that applicants' traceability by actors of persecution should

697 CB010_CGRS_PO_[00:58:06].
698 RB002_CALL_Attaché_[00:37:59].
699 RB006_CALL_Judge_[00:36:59].
700 *AA and Others v Sweden* [2012] ECtHR 14499/09 29.

be part of IFA assessments,[701] one judge explicitly considered such traceability irrelevant. Instead, they stated basing such assessments on applicants' level of education and autonomy, not seeing a problem for 'someone who's a doctor [or] an academic [...] to practice her profession in another part of the country and create a new social network.'[702]

In addition, the resourcefulness myth co-occurs with both the state protection and the non-state protection myths. First, resourceful applicants are expected to be able to seek state protection more quickly and easily (see Chapter 3.1). As such, one judge found it less understandable that someone did not seek help from state actors of protection, if they benefit 'from a social network and an education, which should have drawn her attention to this possibility.'[703] Second, authorities also seem to more readily demand from resourceful applicants to seek help from non-state actors (see Chapter 4.1): '[For] women who have little education, who are dependent on their family, etc. [...] it's complicated to go to NGOs when they may not even know what these are doing.'[704]

Specifically for male SGBV victimisation, the male resourcefulness myth is also linked to the myth qualifying SGBV as a private issue. As such, male applicants fleeing SGBV-related persecution are at times placed outside the scope of the UN Refugee Convention (see Part V, Chapter 2). Resulting from the above described tendency to wrongly or not qualify male SGBV as persecution, some decision makers at the CGRS (one of them gender-specialised) have concluded in the interviews that for male SGBV survivors/victims, who have for example been stigmatised in the context of *bacha bazi* or domestic violence, the link to the UN Refugee Convention is not always clear[705] or even non-existent.[706]

c) *Acceptance of the Stand-Alone & Intersecting Resourcefulness Myth in Case Law*

These accounts of resourcefulness myth acceptance in its stand-alone form and intersecting with other SGBV myths can also be observed in the analysed case law, such as Amani's[707] and Carmen's cases. Illustrating the overlap between the resourcefulness and survival myths, the fact that Carmen

701 UNHCR, 'Guidelines on International Protection No. 4' (n 428) para 14; Ali, Querton and Soulard (n 8) 72.
702 RB008_CALL_Judge_[00:26:21].
703 RB008_CALL_Judge_[00:32:42].
704 CB004_CGRS_PO_[00:19:30].
705 CB011_CGRS_Supervisor+PO_GENDER_[00:09:56].
706 CB014_CGRS_PO_[00:42:23].
707 NC004_CGRS 1 (refusal)_1991_F_DRC_RSA_DV_21/12/2021_FR_NANSEN_p. 4.

had for example rented a house for herself[708] and had navigated the Ecuadorian legal system in the past[709] was seen as proof of her resourcefulness. Regardless of the severe violence her ex-husband had persistently committed in the meantime, this resourcefulness should have enabled her, according to the authorities, to do so again and protect herself in the future.

When it comes to the overlap between the resourcefulness and non-state protection myths, a Senegalese forced marriage case can serve as an example. The applicant fled mental, physical, and sexual violence at the hands of her forced husband, who, according to her testimonies, carried out mystical practices involving human sacrifices. She succeeded to do so by escaping to her mother's house and selling sewing machines and fabrics to pay a smuggler. In the decision to refuse her refugee status, the CGRS considered these preparatory measures to collect money to flee proof of her resourcefulness, incompatible with her inability to disclose the violence to and seek help from non-state actors like her family, before fleeing the country.[710]

Lastly, the two Georgian cases mentioned above are examples of the intersection between the male resourcefulness myth and the private issue myth, excluding male SGBV from the scope of the UN Refugee Convention. The forced marriage (and resulting violence by his family-in-law)[711] and the fear of GMC[712] of these applicants were both considered not sufficiently serious to qualify as acts of persecution.

2.2. REBUTTAL OF THE RESOURCEFULNESS MYTH

This part will go into the lack of evidence for material and non-material resourcefulness as SGBV predictors. I will discuss the relative irrelevance of individual resourcefulness against socially and culturally embedded structural SGBV, as will be illustrated by several applicants' testimonies. This expertise has (partly) found its way into legal scholarship and (case) law, with the CJEU having rebutted both the stand-alone resourcefulness myth, as well as its intersecting form with the state protection myth. Finally, I will focus on the ways in which this myth is rebutted in the Belgian asylum procedure itself, both in interviews with decision makers and in case law. In doing so, I will also focus on male victimisation, the relevance of past SGBV experiences as a predictor of

708 DEc120_CGRS 1 (refusal)_1981_F_Ecuador_RSA_DV_ 8/12/2023_NL_Database_p. 3., Dec120_CALL 1 (refusal)_1981_F_Ecuador_RSA_DV_ 29/4/2024_ 305 805_NL_Database_p. 7–8.

709 DEc120_CGRS 1 (refusal)_1981_F_Ecuador_RSA_DV_ 8/12/2023_NL_Database_p. 4., Dec120_CALL 1 (refusal)_1981_F_Ecuador_RSA_DV_ 29/4/2024_ 305 805_NL_Database_p. 10.

710 NS005_CGRS 1 (refusal)_2002_F_Senegal_RSA_DV_FM_13/05/2022_FR_NANSEN_p. 5–6.

711 DGe110_CALL 1 (refusal)_1986_M_Georgia_FM_VGNT_27/3/2024_303 889__NL_Database_p. 16.

712 DGe112_CALL 2 (refusal)_M_Georgia_GMC_29/3/2024_304 208_NL_Database_p. 15.

SGBV for future-oriented refugee status determination, and decision makers' cautious use of gender-specific COI.

2.2.1. REBUTTAL IN HEALTH & SOCIAL SCIENCES

Both the material and non-material resourcefulness arguments lack evidence. It has long been established that SGBV occurs across all socio-economic backgrounds and that 'no personal attribute of the victim is sufficient in itself to offer protection.'[713] Research in health and social sciences has confirmed that individuals' level of: education, social support, self-esteem, substance (ab)use, or economic resourcefulness as such, are unreliable SGBV predictors.[714] Keygnaert et al.'s study (on sexual violence in Belgium) for example confirmed that: 'The level of respondents' completed education was not significantly related to the likelihood of sexual victimisation.'[715]

Instead of absolute income or objective changes therein, a study by Benson et al. demonstrated that it are elements like residential and employment instability, subjective financial strain (i.e. interpreting one's financial situation pessimistically through dissatisfaction with finances and worries about income sufficiency), and differing employment statuses between partners that drive SGBV.[716] In addition, the research of Haselschwerdt and Hardesty specifically concerns financially resourceful domestic violence survivors/victims, who are often presumed to be less at risk of SGBV and/or more capable of coping with it. It points at the specific disclosure barriers such survivors/victims face 'due to the pervasive emphasis on privacy in the culture of affluence.'[717]

---

713 Judith Lewis Herman, *Trauma and Recovery: The Aftermath of Violence – from Domestic Abuse to Political Terror* (Basic Books/Hachette Book Group 1992) 57 & 59–60; Megan L Haselschwerdt and Jennifer L Hardesty, 'Managing Secrecy and Disclosure of Domestic Violence in Affluent Communities' (2017) 79 Journal of Marriage and Family 556, 556; Elizabeth Dozois and Kathy Germann, 'No One Deserves To Be Abused: An Inquiry to Inform the Development of Supports for Affluent Survivors: Highlights from a Literature Review, Environmental Scan & Qualitative Research' (Sagesse 2017) 2; Heise (n 391) 266–267 & 273–274; Ines Keygnaert and others, 'UN-MENAMAIS: Understanding the Mechanisms, Nature, Magnitude and Impact of Sexual Violence in Belgium, Final Report' (Belgian Science Policy 2021) 38; Michael L Benson and others, 'Neighborhood Disadvantage, Individual Economic Distress and Violence Against Women in Intimate Relationships' (2003) 19 Journal of Quantitative Criminology 207, 957; Garcia-Moreno and others (n 197) 1265; World Health Organization (WHO), 'Caring for Women Subjected to Violence' (n 402).

714 Heise (n 391) 266–267; Benson and others (n 713) 213, 224–226.

715 Keygnaert and others (n 713) 38.

716 Benson and others (n 713) 207, 213, 224–225 & 230.

717 Haselschwerdt and Hardesty (n 713) 556.

What does appear to be the strongest predictor for SGBV victimisation (such as rape/sexual assault or domestic violence), are past experiences with SGBV. Research on SGBV predictors consistently demonstrates how persons with a history of childhood, adolescent, and adult SGBV victimisation (both directly and indirectly through witnessing) are at increased risk of revictimisation, by rape/sexual assault and domestic violence in particular.[718] According to Viejo et al., SGBV can become a 'normalization scheme of the life of affective relationships' for these persons, potentially rendering them less capable of identifying such violence in future contexts.[719] In terms of the psychological impact afterwards, in her work on trauma and recovery, Herman confirms: 'The most powerful determinant of psychological harm is the character of the traumatic event itself. Individual personality characteristics count for little in the face of overwhelming events.'[720]

In the interviews, many applicants talked at length about their education, work experience, or housing, at times to demonstrate the urgency of their flight and fear of persecution. Mary for example explained that, in Liberia, she had a shop, had a place to live, went to school and had some money, she 'was not [...] sitting [around] not doing anything.'[721] Nino, a Georgian applicant fearing her violent ex-partner, had to flee with her husband, who worked at a well-known television agency. She stated: '[In Belgium] we are nobody, there we still had our career, we were somebody.'[722]

For some applicants, like Nino's daughter, her education was even motivated by the violence she experienced or witnessed. She explained: '[My daughter] started studying criminology at university because of the family violence she experienced, to protect me after her studies, that is what she said.'[723] Zeynep, an applicant from Turkey, recounts how her university studies precisely facilitated the grooming and sexual violence she experienced.

718 Jonathan C Waldron and others, 'Sexual Victimization History, Depression, and Task Physiology as Predictors of Sexual Revictimization: Results From a 6-Month Prospective Pilot Study' (2015) 30 Journal of Interpersonal Violence 622, 622; Kate Walsh and others, 'A Preliminary Examination of Sexual and Physical Victimization 6 Months after Recent Rape' (2023) 26 Archives of women's mental health 495, 6; Carmen Viejo, Gema Linde Valenzuela and Rosario Ortega Ruiz, 'Adult Partner Violence and Previous Violence Experiences: Retrospective Study with Women Victims of Gender-Based Violence' (2018) 18 International journal of psychology and psychological therapy 179, 189; Maria Testa, Carol VanZile-Tamsen and Jennifer A Livingston, 'Prospective Prediction of Women's Sexual Victimization by Intimate and Nonintimate Male Perpetrators' (2007) 75 Journal of Consulting and Clinical Psychology 52, 1.

719 Viejo, Linde Valenzuela and Ortega Ruiz (n 718) 188.

720 Herman (n 713) 57.

721 NL017_1980_F_Liberia_STFP_GMC_VGNT_FM_NL_[00:29:04].

722 NGe014_1975_F_Georgia_RSA_DV_NL_[00:30:13].

723 NGe014_1975_F_Georgia_RSA_DV_NL_[00:12:04].

CASE OF ZEYNEP			
• Country of origin:	Turkey	• SGBV types:	Rape/sexual assault, forced marriage & domestic violence
• Gender identity:	Woman	• Decisions in file:	CGRS 1 (refusal) – 22/12/2022
• Birth year:	1996		CALL 1 (annulment) – 12/1/2023– n° 283 107
• Interview by:	CGRS		CGRS 2 (refusal) – 1/2/2023
			CALL 2 (annulment) – 23/2/2023– n° 285 279

According to her statements, Zeynep is of Kurdish ethnicity and was born in Turkey, where she obtained a university degree in web design, against the wishes of her conservative father. During her studies, she attended Gülen study centres, inspired by the religious teachings of a political opponent of president Erdoğan. The Gülen movement is deemed a terrorist organisation by the government, with many of its member persecuted through unfair trials.[724] In 2017, Zeynep's university residence was searched, she was detained at the police station for four days, and she was questioned again two months later. One of the police officers involved (in his fifties) also worked as a security guard on her university campus and contacted her afterwards. This contact gradually evolved into a friendship, but in 2018, he confessed romantic feelings to her, which she rejected. He began **stalking and harassing** her, forcing Zeynep to move to another city. He tracked down her address and contacted her again in 2020. Hoping he would leave her alone after rejecting him one last time, she got into his car, where he **raped** her. He kept threatening her afterwards, upon which she stayed inside and isolated herself. She tried to take her own life at the end of 2020. In 2021, she learnt about a legal procedure running against her, aggravated by her previous police custody. Next to this, Zeynep's family had started pressuring her into a **forced marriage** with her cousin. She refused, as she considered this incest, but was **beaten** several times by her father when doing so. Knowing the value of a woman's virginity in Kurdish culture and that rape survivors/victims risk being blamed for having provoked the violence, she never told anyone about the rape. She feared that her experience would be revealed by this marriage due to the fact that she was no longer a virgin. She eventually fled the country in 2022.

Once arrived in Belgium, she applied for international protection and was detained in a closed centre. She submitted documents on several doctors' and psychologists' consultations in Belgium and Turkey (e.g. attesting her suicide attempt in 2020 and current medication prescriptions).

Zeynep was not accorded any special procedural guarantees and her case was handled in an accelerated procedure due to her use of false identity documents to flee. In her personal interview at the CGRS, she articulately explained how her (official) education provided the setting that facilitated

724 Human Rights Watch, 'World Report 2024: Türkiye' (11 January 2024), www.hrw.org/world-report/2024/country-chapters/turkey.

the grooming, and how her material resourcefulness resulting from it was undermined by fundamental attachment issues in her childhood and the cultural gender norms she was taught informally:

> 'He knew I was **studying computer science** and wanted to teach in that field, so when we met he would prepare the next meeting on the pretext of a problem with his computer. A friendship grew out of these meetings over time.'[725]
>
> 'The **education** we receive convinces us of our guilt, even if we are not, [they teach us:] "If [a female victim] had not done anything, the [male perpetrator] would not have acted in this way." [...] I knew very well that if [my family] found out, they would have accused me of the rape. [...] [W]hen you are raised [...] in these **rules and fears**, [...] you grow up **submissive**.'[726] | CASE OF ZEYNEP

In another forced marriage case, a Kenyan applicant stressed (in a direct statement presented by her lawyer) the relativity of formal education for SGBV victimisation. She explained how, despite her successful education and career, she was seen as useless by her parents, who 'believe in the traditional way of valuing marriage and having children [...] [and] in ancestors living on through the memorial sacrifices of their children. So they need children to keep their memory alive after their death.'[727]

Moreover, the resourcefulness myth underestimates the complex nature of SGBV as a structural issue, deeply rooted in the interaction between 'personal, situational and socio-cultural factors,' as Heise explains.[728] The cases of Zeynep and Mary illustrate this structural dimension through the family and community pressure they experienced. Concerning the continued practice of female GMC in Liberia, Mary explained that despite her own clear opposition to GMC:

> '[My **family** was] forcing, telling me [...] to **take this role** [...] **because [I am the] first** [...] **girl child**, [...] this is my position, [...]. [The CGRS doesn't] understand [that] [...] **the tradition is the tradition**. What will change the tradition? [...] It stays there. [...] You won't go against the **traditional leaders** in Liberia [...] [and] when my people come and get [...] me to [become a Zoe, a female GMC practitioner[729]], the government [...] won't do anything about it. The only thing they will tell you [is:] "It's **family business**".'[730] | CASE OF MARY

725 NT015_CGRS interview 1_1996_F_Turkey_RSA_FM_DV_FR_p. 14.
726 NT015_CGRS interview 1_1996_F_Turkey_RSA_FM_DV_FR_p. 13 & 20.
727 DK152_CALL 2 (refusal)_lawyers' argumentation_1997_F_Kenya_RSA_VGNT_FM_DV_4/4/2024_304 367_NL_Database_p. 9.
728 Heise (n 391) 262.
729 Traditional heads of the Sande 'bush schools', carrying out female genital mutilation in Liberia. Obe and 28 Too Many (n 418) 14.
730 NL017_1980_F_Liberia_STFP_GMC_VGNT_FM_NL_[01:09:49].

Male applicants, whose gendered non-material resourcefulness results in their exclusion from the 'ideal female SGBV victim', risk ending up without international protection against SGBV, such as: (forcibly executing or witnessing) rape/sexual assault, sex trafficking/forced prostitution, male GMC (such as castration or circumcision), ...[731] As literature on help-seeking barriers for male SGBV survivors/victims explains, their road to care and protection is often preceded by an initial barrier: (self-)recognition as a survivor/victim,[732] making it even harder for them to come forward or seek help. The aforementioned confusion and self-blame about normal biological reactions during sexual violence, such as getting an erection, further complicate this process. Psychoeducation on these reactions by actors at each stage of their help-seeking journey is therefore essential to overcome this barrier.[733]

At the next stage, male survivors/victims may experience specific personal, relational and socio-cultural difficulties in disclosing the violence, both in their country of origin and in a host country.[734] Their help seeking is hindered by barriers, such as: gender restrictions on access to protection; the criminalisation of same-sex relationships; negative attitudes of caregivers; lack of community awareness; and social/self-stigma.[735] For rape, according to Chynoweth et al., the latter can be explained as follows: 'Their identity is compromised. The rape has hurt their personal [...] masculine identity. [...] [S]urvivors spontaneously described struggling with feelings of guilt, anger, shame, and self-blame. [...] The impact [...] starts an endless loop of confusion, shame, isolation, frustration, and exhaustion.'[736] In Yusuf's case, his lawyer illustrates this social/self-stigma as follows:

> '[Yusuf] stresses that he is **ashamed** of these facts and he also did not and **still does not dare to talk** about this situation with his father. He states that it would have been

[731] Jane Herlihy, 'Psychological Barriers to Fair Refugee Status Determination Related to Our Understanding and Expression of Gender' in Efrat Arbel, Catherine Dauvergne and Jenni Millbank (eds), *Gender in Refugee Law* (Routledge 2014) 127; Chynoweth and others (n 93) 2; UN Voluntary Fund for Victims of Torture, 'Report on Expert Panel & Workshop – Surviving Torture and Fighting Stigma: The Road to Recovery for Victims of Sexual and Gender-Based Torture' (2019) 10; Rose Jaji, '"Aberrant" Masculinity: Men, Culture and Forced Migration' in Claudia Mora and Nicola Piper (eds), *The Palgrave Handbook of Gender and Migration* (Palgrave Macmillan UK 2021) 373.

[732] UNHCR, 'Working with Men and Boy Survivors of Sexual and Gender-Based Violence in Forced Displacement' (n 93) 4 and 8; Herlihy (n 731) 129.

[733] Regina Kakhnovets and Dana R Holohan, 'Initial Steps in Treating the Male Patient' (2007) 24 Federal Practitioner 16, 23.

[734] Herlihy (n 731) 129; Women's Refugee Commission and UNICEF Europe & Central Asia (n 641) 10.

[735] Chynoweth and others (n 93) 1; Herlihy (n 731) 129; UN Voluntary Fund for Victims of Torture (n 731) 10.

[736] Chynoweth and others (n 92) 20–21.

a **disgrace** to the family, which might have ostracised him, and that if his father found out today, they would never talk to him again.'[737] | CASE OF YUSUF

Eventually, this low level of disclosure, reporting, and help-seeking behaviour leads to statistical underestimates.[738] Therefore, documenting and finding relevant information (e.g. COI) on SGBV victimisation may be even more problematic for male survivors/victims than it already is for female survivors/ victims. Due to this underreporting of SGBV in general, and for male survivors/victims in particular, decision makers risk assuming that the latter are hardly at risk of such violence. However, SGBV occurs across all gender identities, rendering the myth that masculinity as non-material resourcefulness makes applicants less vulnerable to SGBV cannot be confirmed.[739]

As a result, the general idea that resourceful persons are less at risk of SGBV and therefore less in need of protection must be firmly rebutted. However, as mentioned above (see Part I, Chapter 1.3), it must be recognised that the resourcefulness myth (echoing rape mythology's 'victim precipitation myth') is not necessarily or always untrue. When thinking of SGBV under the Taliban's regime in Afghanistan (at the time of writing), which highly targets against women,[740] being a man (or male resourcefulness) does in fact lower one's risk to such violence. Therefore, asylum decision making must leave room for this myth-based argument to be used exceptionally, which is why it is indicated with an asterisk/* in the figures of this research.

However, it is essential to stress that such argumentation requires extreme caution, for two main reasons. Firstly, a lower risk to SGBV does not imply its impossibility. Yusuf for example did flee Afghanistan as a man out of fear of *bacha bazi*, a well-documented form of SGBV specifically perpetrated against boys and young men,[741] despite the Taliban's discriminatory policies primarily targeting women. Secondly, this exceptional use can only be justified under the strict condition that (accurate and up-to-date) COI, linking specific resourcefulness types to low(er) prevalence of specific SGBV types in the relevant region, is available.

However, when it comes to SGBV, such information is extremely difficult to find. Asylum officials must take into account the inherent limitations of

737 DAf150_CALL 1 (refusal)_lawyers' argumentation_M_Afghanistan_RSA_8/3/2024_302 900_ NL_Database_p. 10.

738 Herlihy (n 731) 128.

739 World Health Organization (WHO), 'Guidelines for Medico-Legal Care of Victims of Sexual Violence' (n 175) 8–9; UNHCR, 'Working with Men and Boy Survivors of Sexual and Gender-Based Violence in Forced Displacement' (n 93) 6.

740 Amnesty International and International Commission of Jurists (ICJ), 'Afghanistan: The Taliban's War on Women: The Crime against Humanity of Gender Persecution in Afghanistan' (2023) 1–4.

741 Misra (n 676) 350.

SGBV-related COI due to the private, intangible, difficult to measure, and sensitive nature of this type of violence, leading to systematic underreporting and underestimation of its actual prevalence (as described above and further in Part IV, Chapter 3.2.2.). If no such COI is available, decision makers should recognise that, generally, the resourcefulness myth is an assumption lacking any evidence-based grounds in SGBV expertise.

2.2.2. REBUTTAL IN LAW & LEGAL SCIENCES

The CJEU has clearly translated this evidence-based expertise to the asylum context in the *O.A. case*, confirming the irrelevance of both non-material and material resourcefulness in refugee status determination: 'Mere social and financial support [...] is inherently incapable of either preventing acts of persecution or of detecting, prosecuting and punishing such acts and, therefore, cannot be regarded as providing [...] protection.'[742] Next to dispelling the stand-alone resourcefulness myth, the CJEU also rebutted the myth linked to the state protection myth: '[S]ocial and financial support is of no relevance to the assessment of the effectiveness or the availability of the protection provided by the State.'[743] Specifically on the argument that travel experience would constitute non-material resourcefulness (namely: 'if you manage to flee, you can protect yourself from SGBV'[744]), the UN Committee on the Rights of the Child has noted: '[Applicants'] departure could similarly be understood as an inability to resist pressure.'[745]

As mentioned above, (accurate and up-to-date) COI, linking specific resourcefulness types to low(er) prevalence of specific SGBV types in the relevant region, might justify exceptional use of the resourcefulness myth. Assessing individual SGBV cases in light of such COI aligns with the provision to individually assess applications for international protection as prescribed in the Belgian Aliens Act[746] (in line with the EU Qualification Directive/Regulation[747]). In doing so, decision makers should take into account applicants' individual situation and personal circumstances (i.e. their background, gender, and age).

742 *Secretary of State for the Home Department v OA* [2021] Court of Justice of the European Union C-255/19 [46] (EN).

743 *Ibid.* 48.

744 Brems (n 664).

745 *IAM (on behalf of KYM) v Denmark* [2018] UN Committee on the Rights of the Child 3/2016 [11.8].

746 Belgian Aliens Act art 48/6 §5, c).

747 Art. 4(3)c EU Qualification Directive; Art. 4(3) EU Qualification Regulation; *jo.* Art. 34(2)d EU Asylum Procedures Regulation.

On this need for asylum authorities to base their SGBV decisions on gender-specific COI, the CJEU has also pronounced itself in the *A.H. & F.N.*, *K.L.*, and *W.S. cases* (but hereby exclusively focusing on female survivors/victims). The Court concretely ruled that, instead of making assumptions on SGBV risk factors and profiles (including resourcefulness elements), 'precise and up-to-date information'[748] should be taken into account, 'that has relevance for the examination of women's applications for refugee status,' specifically naming information on: prevalence and forms of SGBV reported; women's position before the law; and their political, social, and economic rights.[749]

However, given the scarcity of such information, UNHCR has urged (Belgian) asylum authorities to recognise that, in gender-related cases, 'the usual types of evidence[, statistical data or reports] [...] may not be as readily available [...] due to under-reporting [...] or lack of prosecution'[750] and that: '[t]he absence or lack of [gender-specific COI] does not mean that there is no persecution (or that state protection is effective).'[751] Both legal scholarship,[752] as well as the UN Inter-Agency Standing Committee[753] and Asylum Aid,[754] have echoed this caution, by pointing out the often hidden, sensitive, and intangible nature of gender-related norms, power relations, and persecution, rendering information on SGBV difficult to document and access.

For male survivors/victims specifically, UNHCR, in line with the evidence in health/social sciences available, reiterates the barriers that might hinder their disclosure. This might be caused by entrenched gender norms in combination with cultural/religious taboos, scarce services, and communities' reluctance to acknowledge their SGBV experiences, since this may be seen as weak and/or shameful. Therefore: '[M]ale survivors rarely report SGBV incidents immediately, and frequently do so only when the physical effects of attacks require urgent intervention.'[755] The UN Special Rapporteur on the

748 *AH & FN v. Bundesamt für Fremdenwesen und Asyl* (n 82) para 52; *K.L. v. Staatssecretaris van Justitie en Veiligheid* (n 78) para 60.

749 UNHCR, 'Guidelines on International Protection No. 1' (n 35) para 36; *WS v. Intervyuirasht organ na Darzhavna agentsia za bezhantsite pri Ministerskia savet* (n 44) para 61.

750 UNHCR, 'Guidelines on International Protection No. 1' (n 35) para 37.

751 UNHCR, 'Note Du Haut Commissariat Des Nations Unies Pour Les Réfugiés Relative à l'évaluation Des Demandes d'asile Introduites Par Des Femmes' (2012) 2.

752 Ali, Querton and Soulard (n 8) 69; Vogelaar (n 88) 110; Crawley, 'Gender, "Refugee Women" and the Politics of Protection' (n 89) 364; Herlihy (n 731) 128.

753 'Sexual violence is under-reported even in well-resourced settings worldwide [...]. [We] should therefore assume [...] that [S]GBV [...] is taking place [...], regardless of the presence or absence of concrete and reliable evidence.' UNHCR and Inter-Agency Standing Committee (IASC), 'Guidelines for Gender-Based Violence Interventions in Humanitarian Settings: Focusing on Prevention of and Response to Sexual Violence in Emergencies' (2005) 12.

754 'Information on women's human rights in country reports often constitutes only a paragraph unless the report is specifically focused on women.' Collier (n 88) 11.

755 UNHCR, 'Working with Men and Boy Survivors of Sexual and Gender-Based Violence in Forced Displacement' (n 93) 4 and 8.

independence of judges and lawyers further comments on male SGBV victimisation, for example male rape by female perpetrators as in the Iraqi case mentioned above (Chapter 2.1.3.c)). A 2011 report states that judges must be able to challenge male gender stereotyping, such as 'their ability, in cases of male rape, to have defended themselves; and about women as perpetrators of crimes of violence against men.'[756]

In legal scholarship, Peroni aptly summarises the shortcomings of the material resourcefulness argument for female survivors/victims. She argues that they may be highly educated, 'but still not be able to secure a job if [they relocate] to an area where widespread discrimination excludes women from job opportunities' or still risk SGBV because: actors of persecution can still trace and pressure them, survivors/victims may suffer psychological consequences of the violence (e.g. PTSD or depression), or have become isolated from their social network.[757] They may be wealthy, 'but still fail to secure protection if the police systematically see domestic violence as a private affair.'[758]

On domestic violence among financially resourceful survivors/victims specifically, Bellew has highlighted the risk for legal professionals to exclusively associate domestic violence with 'poor' women, thereby perpetuating the misconception that such violence does not occur in mid- and high-income settings.[759] As such, accepting the resourcefulness myth overshadows the broader social and institutional structures that determine individual capability to cope with (threats of) SGBV, including cultural attitudes, family/community pressure, and the gender sensitivity of a legal system.[760] Therefore, the idea that individuals 'strong enough to stand up against cultural oppression [are] too strong for outsider protection'[761] is unsubstantiated, according to Brems.

The additional hurdles for male applicants towards care and protection, such as difficult (self-)recognition as a survivor/victim, are recognised in legal scholarship too.[762] A recent report on the Belgian asylum system specifically highlights the narrow interpretation of the term 'vulnerability' as only applying to women and children. It argues that male applicants' vulnerabilities are

756 Gabriela Knaul, 'Report of the Special Rapporteur on the Independence of Judges and Lawyers (UN Doc. A/66/289)' (United Nations General Assembly 2011) 20, www.icj.org/wp-content/uploads/2014/06/UNDoc-A-66-289.pdf.

757 Peroni (n 33) 361.

758 *Ibid.*

759 Kara Bellew, 'Silent Suffering: Uncovering and Understanding Domestic Violence in Affluent Communities Note' (2005) 26 Women's Rights Law Reporter 39, 39–40.

760 Wessels (n 94) 345; Peroni (n 33) 358–366.

761 Brems (n 664).

762 UNHCR, 'Working with Men and Boy Survivors of Sexual and Gender-Based Violence in Forced Displacement' (n 93) 4 and 8; Depraetere and others (n 93) 1003; Magugliani (n 93) 5; Herlihy (n 731) 129.

less visible because of gender bias and the image of 'the strong man'.[763] On male forced marriage in particular, such as in the Georgian case above, the same report states: '[T]here are also men who want to have their choice with regard to [a] marriage, which is not in fact theirs. [...] [T]here are men who don't accept forced marriage.'[764] For (sex) trafficking specifically, Magugliani points out how female survivors/victims are still more likely to fall under the Convention ground of 'particular social group' than adult men.[765] For these men, large gaps have also been identified in the COI available to asylum authorities, requiring caution in analysing (a lack of) such information.[766]

This legal rebuttal is also of relevance to the specific dimension of the resourcefulness myth that 'resourceful applicants can more actively react to SGBV, for example by moving to an IFA'. As this reasoning strongly overlaps with the non-state and state protection myths (that 'applicants can, whether or not supported by non-state actors, find state protection against SGBV at an IFA'), its rebuttal will be discussed in more depth there (see Part IV, Chapter 2.2.2).

2.2.3. REBUTTAL BY BELGIAN ASYLUM AUTHORITIES

In line with the CJEU case law, some Belgian asylum authorities too (partly) rebutted the stand-alone resourcefulness myth in the survey and interviews. Some did so implicitly,[767] by stating: 'Violence against women in Europe is not just perpetrated by poor men, it happens in all environments. [...] [And a woman], who is very well educated, is going to find it just as difficult to get out of this dynamic, this marriage, etc.'[768] Others do so explicitly, for instance in the words of an attaché: 'The example that, because the person enjoyed a certain [...] autonomy, they could not possibly have suffered sexual violence within the family, is quite problematic, [...] even in Belgium, it would be absolutely absurd to say that.'[769]

The resourcefulness myth intersecting with other SGBV myths is also rebutted by some asylum officials. On state protection, one PO mentioned the example of a highly-educated woman, who lives in a city and therefore potentially has access to the police, and argued: 'If she has no family support, [...] in reality she still runs a fairly heightened risk. Especially as we know very well that authorities [...] often say "It's a family affair, so we're not

763 Saroléa, Raimondo and Crine (n 93) 100.
764 *Ibid.* 96.
765 Magugliani (n 89).
766 *Ibid.*
767 E.g. R_3fSFAvlx87VK7YK_CGRS_PO/supervisor/gender coordinator/CEDOCA member.
768 CB013_CGRS_PO_[01:03:48].
769 RB002_CALL_Attaché_[00:47:56].

interfering".'[770] On the impact of resourcefulness on SGBV disclosure, one PO clarified: 'From someone who has studied, we are not going to [expect] being able to explain things better or [...] having more knowledge of the legislation.'[771] However, another PO differentiated this myth rebuttal according to the content. They explained: when talking 'around' the SGBV experienced, an educated person is expected to use more precise words and understand questions more easily. When going into the SGBV itself, one's education level 'won't particularly have an influence.'[772]

Further, the literature on past SGBV experiences as predictors of future SGBV victimisation is of particular relevance to refugee status determination, namely when applying article 48/7 of the Aliens Act. This provision reverses the burden of proof where applicants have already experienced or feared persecution in the past.[773] In such cases, previous threats/acts of persecution directly aimed at applicants indicate the well-foundedness of their fear, unless asylum authorities substantiate good reasons to believe that this will not recur.[774] One judge recognised this relevance explicitly by explaining how they learnt from the pilot module organised by NANSEN NGO (see Part II, Chapter 2.3) that '[previous victimisation] increases the risk of becoming a victim again. [...] That is very important for [applying article] 48/7, to be given that context, because it apparently makes you less resilient.'[775]

These forms of rebuttal at times trickle down into case law, where refusal of refugee status argued through the resourcefulness of applicants (or their parents) is labelled superficial[776] or incomprehensible.[777] In one analysed case, the judge specifically referred to the abovementioned CJEU case law in doing so.[778] In Amani's case, the CALL annulled the decision of the CGRS, by explicitly rebutting the resourcefulness myth as follows:

> 'The applicant's level of independence and **resourcefulness**, as put forward by the [CGRS], **cannot lead to** the conclusion that it is **not credible** that she was at the mercy of a **violent stepfather**.'[779] | CASE OF AMANI

---

770 CB010_CGRS_PO_[00:21:09].

771 CB009_CGRS_PO_GENDER_[00:20:34].

772 CB001_CGRS_PO_[00:12:44]. Why not only statements about abuse itself, but also broader contextual and autobiographical elements may be inaccurately memorised and disclosed, regardless of one's level of education, will be elaborated below (see Chapter 3.2.2).

773 Denys (n 43) 626.

774 Art. 48/7 Belgian Aliens Act; Art. 4(4) EU Qualification Directive; Art. 4(4) EU Qualification Regulation.

775 RB001_CALL_Judge_[00:45:51].

776 E.g. DBF101_CALL 1 (recognition)_1988_F_Burkina Faso_RSA_GMC_VGNT_FM_DV_23/4/2024_305 334_FR_Database_p. 10.

777 E.g. DIC074_CALL 1 (annulment)_F_Ivory Coast_GMC_VGNT_11/03/2024_302 979_FR_Case law selection by CALL_p. 9.

778 DS103_CALL 1 (annulment)_F_Senegal_GMC_FM_DV_30/4/2024_305 927_FR_Database_p. 11.

779 NC004_CALL 1 (annulment)_1991_F_DRC_RSA_DV_17/1/2022_266 712_FR_NANSEN_p. 7.

The resourcefulness myth excluding (potential) male survivors/victims from the UN Refugee Convention scope is also challenged in case law, such as the CALL's judgements in the Nigerian case mentioned above and Iraqi case mentioned above. In the former, the CALL dismantled the idea that the applicant's homosexual orientation would originate from being raped (which rendered it the main and non-credible flight motive). The judge challenged the CGRS' interpretation that the applicant had 'discovered' he was homosexual as a result of being raped, by stating: '[I]t is clear from his statements [...] that this actually confirmed [...] that he was homosexual.'[780]

In the latter Iraqi case, where the applicant had been raped by his aunt under threat that she would expose him as her rapist, the CALL recognised him as a refugee. The judge here argued that, while the COI on honour killings in the Kurdistan region of Iraq indeed showed that the aunt's blackmail entailed serious risks for herself as a (perceived) rape survivor/victim, that same information revealed the applicant's risk of violence as a survivor/victim himself.[781] The judgement concluded: 'While women are the primary victims of [honour-related] violence [...], it cannot be ruled out that men may also be targeted because they are perceived to have transgressed [social norms], thereby bringing shame on their families, or that [...] there is no refuge in the Iraqi Kurdistan region [for male survivors/victims].'[782]

As described above, besides the resourcefulness myth rebuttal, it is important to recognise that applicants' personal profile, including their material and non-material characteristics, still is of relevance to refugee status determination. It does not only allow for appropriate questions and interviewing techniques, but also for an individual assessment of their applications. Both good practices were described by asylum officials in this research.[783]

Next to the Iraqi rape/sexual assault case mentioned above, this individual assessment through reliance on gender-specific COI is illustrated by a judge, who disproved the CGRS' argument that a Kurdish girl, coming from an educated family since her mum was a nurse, was at a lower risk of GMC. They (partly) based an annulment judgement on the fact that 'the [COI] showed that the prevalence was the same regardless of [the educational level of mothers] [...] [and] that [female GMC] was really so pervasive that this didn't matter at all.'[784] However, in cases where no such gender-specific COI is available, this gap still risks to lead to a conclusion that 'it just [doesn't] happen very often.'[785]

780 DN149_CALL 1 (annulment)_1997_M_Nigeria_RSA_VGNT_29/2/2024_302 605_NL_Database_p. 12. Emphasis added.

781 DIq095_CALL 1 (recognition)_ M_Iraq_RSA_DV_29/2/2024_302 595_FR_Database_p. 10.

782 DIq095_CALL 1 (recognition)_ M_Iraq_RSA_DV_29/2/2024_302 595_FR_Database_p. 11.

783 E.g. R_2vcXK3qiYvk544g_CGRS_PO/supervisor/gender coordinator/CEDOCA member.; CB008_CGRS_Supervisor+PO_GENDER_[00:13:15].

784 RB001_CALL_Judge_[00:13:01].

785 RB003_CALL_Attaché_[00:26:19].

This reasoning was demonstrated by an attaché working on a case of an Egyptian applicant, who had been raped with the aim of converting him to Islam. The attaché had started actively searching for information on this phenomenon, asking themselves: 'Is this really a conversion strategy?', 'Could it be that [he] […] had [kept silent] for so long?', and 'Is it […] true what this man said?'[786] They concluded that literature existed about female survivors/victims, but 'about men, there […] was nothing at all. […] Indeed, COI may […] not be complete, but I would imagine that it just wasn't that common.'[787] Such cases demonstrate the importance of empirical information to carry out refugee status determination in an evidence-based manner.

Still, if such gender-specific COI is available, it should be treated with extreme caution. One PO warned: 'Just because one profile is more at risk does not mean that other profiles are not.' They considered not believing someone from the outset, because they do not match the 'typical profile', a stereotypical thinking pattern.[788] Another PO went as far as to say: '[Statistics on SGBV prevalence according to education level for example,] I don't think you can put a number on that.'[789] In the judgment of Clarisse on female GMC in Ivory Coast, a judge emphasised that, just because there are statistics on certain risk factors in a person's profile, this does not mean that only the narrow group that cumulatively features all these characteristics is at real risk.[790] The same Iraqi rape/sexual assault judgement mentioned above, explicitly alerted that such violence is 'difficult to assess quantitatively because of the low level of reporting combined with the fear of stigma and/or [reprisals].'[791]

2.3. OCCURRENCE OF THE RESOURCEFULNESS MYTH

How the extent of acceptance vs. rebuttal of the resourcefulness myth in the analysed case law sample is divided, between asylum authorities at first instance (negative CGRS decisions) and in appeal (all CALL judgments), according to the procedural language, can be visualised as follows:

786 RB003_CALL_Attaché_[00:26:19].
787 RB003_CALL_Attaché_[00:26:19].
788 CB010_CGRS_PO_[00:19:52].
789 CB001_CGRS_PO_[00:29:11].
790 DIC074_CALL 1 (annulment)_F_Ivory Coast_GMC_VGNT_11/03/2024_302 979_FR_Case law selection by CALL_p. 8.
791 DIq095_CALL 1 (recognition)_ M_Iraq_RSA_DV_29/2/2024_302 595_FR_Database_p. 11.

Figure 14: % of decisions in the case law sample including at least one resourcefulness myth acceptance/rebuttal argument, according to asylum authority & language

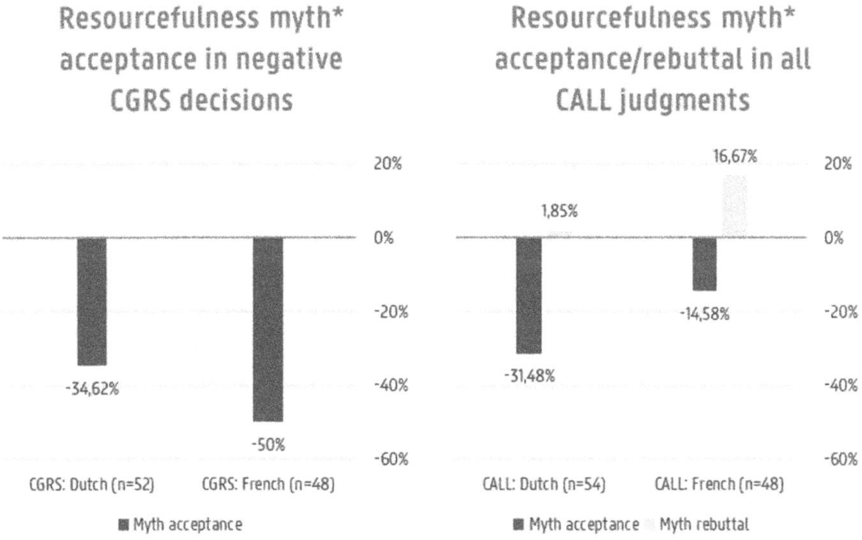

In the total case law sample, ca. **one out of three** (32,67%) of the 202 decisions and judgements included at least one argument based on **acceptance of the resourcefulness SGBV myth**. For the procedures in French in first instance (CGRS), this amounts to half of the decisions. Interestingly, in the French-speaking chambers of the CALL, the myth rebuttal level amounts to 16,67% and hereby far exceeds the Dutch-speaking chambers. Focusing on the smaller case law sample of male applicants, 6 of the 24 decisions and judgements accepted the male resourcefulness myth at least once. 5 of these are decisions in Dutch (3 by the CALL and 2 by the CGRS). Two CALL judgements explicitly rebutted the male resourcefulness myth.

3. THE MYTH THAT 'INAPPROPRIATE' DISCLOSURE UNDERMINES SGBV FLIGHT STORIES' CREDIBILITY

Mary, who fled her family's pressure to replace her mother as a Zoe[792] in Liberia and whose case was introduced in Part II, illustrates the asylum authorities' acceptance of a set of disclosure myths, next to the resourcefulness myths at the micro level. These specifically focus on four aspects: 1) the level of detail, 2) consistency, 3) delay, and 4) demeanour of/during disclosure of applicants' SGBV experiences/fears. Firstly, despite the fact that Mary was raised by two American guardians who never explained her mother's role or reasons to give up her child for protection (even after her repeatedly asking), the CGRS and CALL both reproached her for her inability to give details about the cultural traditions surrounding female GMC in Liberia:

> '[Y]ou **could have known** that there are **traditions** where the eldest daughter would be supposed to succeed the mother after the latter's death. Your **failure to inform yourself** properly is a **negative** indication on the **credibility** of your account.'[793]
> | CASE OF MARY

Secondly, the CGRS and CALL found inconsistencies in her disclosures, concerning her stay with her uncle (which she clearly stated was a factual error in the personal interview notes, as she had never lived there[794]) and concerning the forced prostitution she experienced upon arrival in Belgium. The inconsistencies were respectively found between (and within) the IO and CGRS interviews, and between her IO interview, CGRS personal interview, and submitted medical

---

792 Traditional heads of the Sande 'bush schools', carrying out female genital mutilation in Liberia. Obe and 28 Too Many (n 418) 14.

793 NL017_CALL 1 (refusal)_1980_F_Liberia_STFP_GMC_VGNT_FM_10/08/2022_275 866_NL_NANSEN_p. 10.; NL017_CGRS 1 (refusal)_1980_F_Liberia_STFP_GMC_VGNT_FM_17/2/2022_NL_NANSEN_p. 3.

794 NL017_1980_F_Liberia_STFP_GMC_VGNT_FM_ NL_ [00:12:49].

certificate. The latter was illustrated above (see chapter 5.1). The former was voiced by the CGRS and CALL,[795] stating:

> 'It does come as a great surprise that you **failed to declare to the IO** that you were **living with your uncle**, especially considering that is where all your problems started.'[796] | CASE OF MARY

Thirdly, according to the CGRS, her credibility was further affected as she only applied for international protection eight months after her arrival in Belgium. Conclusions were drawn from this delay without taking into account the period during which she was forced into prostitution upon arrival:

> '[Y]ou submitted your first **application** [...] **[on]** [...] **31 January 2020**. The fact that you applied [...] at the same time [as your husband's sixth application] may indicate **procedural abuse**, [...] [e]specially given that [...] you had already been **in Belgium since 18 June 2019** [...]. [Y]ou may reasonably be expected, if you are in actual need of protection, to apply [...] as soon as possible. That you [did not do so] raises **concerns about the veracity** of your account.'[797] | CASE OF MARY

Fourthly, although the decisions in her case made no mention of her demeanour during disclosure in the interviews/at the hearing, she herself stated feeling:

> '**Stress** and **afraid**. I don't know why [...] interviews like that, it made me afraid [and] I got **nervous**. [...] I did what I could do. [...] But I **don't know if she** [...] **understood me** really.'[798] | CASE OF MARY

It is important to note that Mary, whose mother tongue is English with a distinct Liberian accent, was not assisted by an interpreter during her personal interview at the CGRS. She was only made aware after her personal interview that she could have asked for this by her psychologist.[799]

---

795 E.g. 'The Council further notes in this context that the applicant makes inconsistent statements as to why she went to live at her uncle's house [...]' (NL017_CALL 1 (refusal)_1980_F_Liberia_STFP_GMC_VGNT_FM_10/08/2022_275 866_NL_NANSEN_ p. 10–11.).

796 NL017_CGRS 1 (refusal)_1980_F_Liberia_ STFP_GMC_VGNT_FM _17/2/2022_NL_ NANSEN_p. 3.

797 NL017_CGRS 1 (refusal)_1980_F_Liberia_ STFP_GMC_VGNT_FM _17/2/2022_NL_ NANSEN_p. 4.

798 NL017_CGRS 1 (refusal)_1980_F_Liberia_ STFP_GMC_VGNT_FM _17/2/2022_ NL_NANSEN_p. 4.

799 NL017_1980_F_Liberia_STFP_GMC_VGNT_FM_NL_[00:11:58].

In this chapter, I will go into the ways in which each of these aspects lead to acceptance of SGBV disclosure myths in the asylum context, both in asylum officials' interview responses and decisions/judgements. For each disclosure myth, I will focus on the reasons for and ways of rebuttal, both in literature and international (case) law. I will also illustrate how such rebuttal is at times confirmed by Belgian asylum officials themselves.

3.1. FROM CRIMINAL JUSTICE TO ASYLUM CONTEXT

The idea that only a certain (level of) detail, consistency, timing, and demeanour in SGBV disclosure is considered appropriate and therefore indicative of a truthful account, is represented in several existing rape myths. These include: a real SGBV survivor/victim 'is absolutely certain about the details,'[800] 'does not change [the] account of what happened,'[801] 'will disclose [the] violation at the first reasonable opportunity,'[802] is 'visibly upset by the experience,'[803] and: 'Overgeneral memories [are] viewed as less credible, false or exaggerated.'[804]

Apart from the effect of shame, which is very specific to the experience of SGBV survivors/victims,[805] it is important to note that these disclosure myths are relevant to most trauma-related applications for international protection. For SGBV in particular, this type of reasoning largely fits into the more general victim fabrication myth that '[(alleged) survivors/victims] lie or exaggerate,'[806] also formulated as: 'many [individuals] tend to exaggerate the problem of [SGBV]',[807] '[survivors/victims] tend to exaggerate how much rape

---

800 Lonsway and others (n 398) 4.

801 *Ibid.*

802 United Nations Office on Drugs and Crime (UNODC) and Skinnider (n 161) 90.

803 McGee and others (n 400) 3586.

804 Jane Herlihy, Laura Jobson and Stuart Turner, 'Just Tell Us What Happened to You: Autobiographical Memory and Seeking Asylum' (2012) 26 Applied Cognitive Psychology 661, 673.

805 Anna Papoutsi and others, 'Geographies of Shame: Diachronic and Transnational Shame in Forced Migrants with Experiences of Sexual and Gender-Based Violence' (2022) 35 Journal of Refugee Studies 1221, 1221; Herlihy (n 731) 117; Allen Kiconco and Martin Nthakomwa, 'Wartime Captivity and Homecoming: Culture, Stigma, and Coping Strategies of Formerly Abducted Women in Post-Conflict Northern Uganda' (2022) 46 Disasters 654, 670; Sherene Razack, 'Domestic Violence as Gender Persecution: Policing the Borders of Nation, Race, and Gender' (1995) 8 Canadian Journal of Women and the Law 45, 63.

806 Ben-David and Schneider (n 3) 386.

807 Gerger and others (n 150) 439.

affects them',[808] and 'false [SGBV] accusations out of revenge or regret are common',[809] which have been confirmed by the UN Office on Drugs and Crime in their handbook for the judiciary on responses to SGBV.[810]

Acceptance of the four aspects of the SGBV disclosure myth can also be observed in the tendency of asylum authorities to treat SGBV stories, expressed with too much/little detail, inconsistency, delay, and/or 'inappropriate' demeanour, with suspicion. As such, decision makers repeatedly qualify such limitations as evidence of fabrication rather than as indicators of genuine trauma, fear, or shame, for example.[811] Following my preliminary case law analysis at the ECtHR level, this Court has also shown to adhere to these disclosure myths in its non-refoulement case law.[812]

How these rape myths precisely translate to the national asylum context, is illustrated aptly by a Swiss judge who spoke at a Conference for French-speaking asylum judges in the EU in 2022, organised by the EUAA. Taking part in a roundtable on 'Assessing credibility and evidence on gender issues', her contribution qualified an implausible flight story on SGBV as 'short, with many contradictions, especially on key elements [...], not reconstructing important scenes, [with] caricatural [and unrealistic] descriptions [...], [told without] feeling emotions.'[813] Below, I will illustrate in more detail the ways in which each of the four aspects of the SGBV disclosure myth take shape in the Belgian asylum procedure.

808 Payne, Lonsway and Fitzgerald (n 134) 49.

809 Leverick (n 139) 257.

810 United Nations Office on Drugs and Crime (UNODC) and Skinnider (n 161) 25, 26 and 92.

811 Baillot, Cowan and Munro, '"Hearing the Right Gaps"' (n 92) 283; McKinnon (n 651) 205, 210 and 213; Keygnaert and Linthout (n 177) 22; Lamonaca and others (n 280) 19; Marie Jacobs and Katrijn Maryns, 'Managing Narratives, Managing Identities: Language and Credibility in Legal Consultations with Asylum Seekers' (2022) 51 Language In Society 1, 20; Magugliani (n 93) 16; Herlihy, Jobson and Turner (n 804) 667; Jane Herlihy and Stuart Turner, 'Should Discrepant Accounts given by Asylum Seekers Be Taken as Proof of Deceit' (2006) 16 Torture 81, 91.

812 Roels, 'Rape Myths in the European Court of Human Rights' Non-Refoulement Case Law on Sexual and Gender-Based Violence' (n 33) 89–92.

813 Emilia Antonioni Luftensteiner (Judge at the Federal Administrative Court in Switzerland), 'Les enjeux actuels du régime d'asile européen commun à travers la pratique des juridictions et magistrats francophones des pays membres et associés de l'Union européenne – 3ème table ronde: L'évaluation de la crédibilité et des éléments de preuve sur les questions liées au genre et échange avec l'auditoire' (Conférence de Agence de l'Union européenne pour l'asile et de la Cour nationale du droit d'asile, en collaboration avec le Conseil d'Etat, Paris, 2022) 37.

3.2. DETAIL AND CONSISTENCY IN SGBV DISCLOSURE

3.2.1. ACCEPTANCE OF THE DISCLOSURE MYTHS ON DETAIL & CONSISTENCY

a) Acceptance of the Detail Myth

CASE OF NELLA			
• Country of origin:	Burundi	• SGBV types:	Rape/sexual assault
• Gender identity:	Woman	• Decisions in file:	CGRS 1 (refusal) – 29/6/2023
• Birth year:	/		CALL 1 (recognition) – 11/4/2024 – n° 304 646
• Interview by:	/		

According to her statements, Nella is engaged to a taxi driver who is also involved in a political Movement for Solidarity and Democracy. She supported this movement upon request of her fiancé but was never a party member. He regularly invited taxi passengers and friends over to spend one or more nights at their house, but the names of the latter were never registered. When Nella asked about the reason for this or their identities, he refused to answer. In October 2021, several visitors spent the night and left the next day. Five days later, at around 9pm, three men in uniforms and five Imbonerakure members (the youth league of Burundi's ruling party)[814] came to the house. They arrested her fiancé and questioned him on his membership of a rebel party fighting for the rule of law in Burundi (RED Tabara),[815] given his incorrect visitor registrations and involvement in demonstrations. Two of the men **raped** Nella. After they left, she managed to get to her neighbour's house, who took her to the hospital. There, she received medication and care. The next day, her neighbour noticed two individuals loitering near their homes. Fearing for her safety and that of her family, she suggested that Nella moved in with a widow further away. Her parents' house was searched the same day. After staying with the widow for one month, her uncle helped her to flee the country via a smuggler.

She arrived in Belgium in December 2021 and immediately applied for international protection, supported by a medical report attesting the rape and care she received at the hospital.

Nella's application was refused by the CGRS, stating that, in the absence of any objective evidence, they were entitled to expect detailed statements,

814 Lewis Mudge and Human Rights Watch, '"We Will Beat You to Correct You": Abuses Ahead of Burundi's Constitutional Referendum' (Human Rights Watch 2018) 1.

815 UN Special Rapporteur on the situation of human rights in Burundi, 'Report of the Special Rapporteur on the Situation of Human Rights in Burundi (A/HRC/57/58)' (2024) 2.

which she failed to provide.[816] The decision both referred to details central to the traumatic experiences provoking her flight (in this case the rape) and details circumstantial to it.

Central Details

In terms of central details, the CGRS pointed out gaps in her statements about her hospital visit immediately after the rape. The CGRS focused on the name of a doctor in her medical report, attesting 'tears in the cervix and the vaginal wall with moderate bleeding',[817] as well as the medicines she was given:

> 'You […] were given paracetamol and […] other medicines […]. When asked about these **medicines**, you reply that there were many, but you are unable to mention their **names** […]. Nor can you remember **how long you stayed** in the hospital. Your statements, which **lack any detail** or precision […] once again **undermine the credibility** of the events you claim to have experienced.'[818] | CASE OF NELLA

In the interviews, asylum officials at both the CGRS and the CALL confirmed this expectation from applicants to give detailed accounts on central aspects of their SGBV-related flight stories in order to be found credible. One judge explained clearly how the standard reasoning used to be (and with some colleagues still is): 'If you've been through something really bad, you can retell it perfectly from A to Z […] because […] it is engraved in your memory.'[819] Decision makers mentioned several types of central details expected from applicants in the interviews, such as: temporal and geographical details,[820] details about their living context for long-term forms of SGBV such as forced marriage or domestic violence,[821] or personal details about the perpetrator(s).[822] The latter was illustrated by the CGRS decision in Nella's case too:

> 'When asked about the [**identities** of the] people who stayed at your home […], you state that you asked your partner […] but that he did not […] reply [and told you that "[…] women cannot keep secrets […]" and that you therefore gave up] […].

816 DBu083_CGRS 1 (refusal)_F_Burundi_RSA_29/6/2023_FR_Database_p. 3.

817 E.g. '[T]he [medical rape report] […] is signed by […] a stamp of a general practitioner called "Dr B. O.". Although it attests to '[…] tears in the cervix […] and the vaginal wall with moderate bleeding', it is surprising that this document is not signed by a gynaecologist […] [and] when asked to give the name of this doctor, you do not give any […].' (DBu083_CGRS 1 (refusal)_F_Burundi_RSA_29/6/2023_FR_Database_p. 4.).

818 DBu083_CGRS 1 (refusal)_F_Burundi_RSA_29/6/2023_FR_Database_p. 5.

819 RB005_CALL_Judge_[00:38:54].

820 E.g. CB011_CGRS_Supervisor+PO_GENDER_[00:23:48]; CB006_CGRS_PO_[00:14:10].

821 E.g. CB001_CGRS_PO_[00:07:08].

822 E.g. RB007_CALL_Attaché_[00:07:03].

Since these elements are directly linked to the persecution [...], it is **reasonable** [...] to think that your statements would be **more detailed**.'[823] | CASE OF NELLA

In Yusuf's abovementioned case too, the CALL and CGRS both negatively assessed his credibility due to the insufficiently detailed account of the *talib's* sexual advances, despite his expressions of shame and fear to talk about these central elements:

'The Council [finds it] reasonable to expect an applicant [...] to make accurate and **detailed** statements on matters at the heart of his fears, in this case **the *talib's* alleged sexual advances** and forced recruitment. The fact that [...] he stated [...] **not feeling comfortable** [...] **to talk** about all the reasons for his flight, cannot invalidate the finding that he also made deficient statements [...] at the CGRS [...], **affecting his credibility**.'[824] | CASE OF YUSUF

Amani's credibility was also discredited by a lack of detail in her statements on both the long-term abuse she suffered from her stepfather, and the abduction and rape she experienced right before fleeing. On the former, despite her efforts to systematically avoid him and her comprehensive answers during the personal interview,[825] the CGRS considered her knowledge vague concerning the stepfather's: political activities and connections, (the name of his) work(place), family and children, acquaintances, habits, relationship with her mother, or 'what he loved to do and what not.'[826] On the abduction and rape by men pretending to be police officers, the CGRS stated:

'You say that **the men** were strong, but you can't say anything more about them. When asked about your memories of **the journey** to this unknown place, you simply reply that the men didn't say anything and, as for **the place** where you were taken, you simply mention a dark place and a house under construction. You offer nothing more [...]. It is clear from [the concise nature of your comments] that this abduction and assault [...] have **not been established**.'[827] | CASE OF AMANI

Similarly, the applicant from Senegal mentioned above was denied refugee status by the CGRS, based on (among other arguments) her lack of detailed knowledge on her forced husband's job, family members, friends, and relationship to her father, as well as his reasons for staying unmarried in his premarital life, for wanting to marry her, and for getting angry before abusing her.[828]

823 DBu083_CGRS 1 (refusal)_F_Burundi_RSA_29/6/2023_FR_Database_p. 3.
824 DAf150_CALL 1 (refusal)_M_Afghanistan_RSA _8/3/2024_302 900_NL_Database_p. 15.
825 NC004_ CGRS interview 1_2_1991_F_DRC_RSA_DV_FR_NANSEN.
826 NC004_CGRS 1 (refusal)_1991_F_DRC_RSA_DV_21/12/2021_FR_NANSEN_p. 3–4.
827 NC004_CGRS 1 (refusal)_1991_F_DRC_RSA_DV_21/12/2021_FR_NANSEN_p. 5.
828 NS005_CGRS 1 (refusal)_2002_F_Senegal_RSA_DV_FM_13/05/2022_FR_NANSEN_p. 3–5.

Interestingly, the expectation from applicants to provide detailed information on forced and often violent partners shows strong parallels with the requirements in SOGI cases for voluntarily chosen partners. There too, applicants are expected to provide info on a partner's 'professional life, family, romantic past, social contacts, [and other interests].'[829] It should go without saying that in forced marriage cases, where applicants by definition did not choose their partner and mostly experienced severe violence from them, no similar interest or knowledge can be expected, let alone any evidence of intimacy.

However, some files in the case law sample proved the contrary, such as two forced marriage cases (Gambian and Senegalese), with the Gambian applicant being a minor at the time. Both applicants were asked to explain their forced partner's behaviour or resentful nature. Due to a perceived lack of detail in their answers, the CGRS refused them protection, arguing: 'Your comments are [...] vague and unclear, specifying at most that "if he says he's going to kill me or hit me, he does it", without any further details revealing any proven intimacy'[830] and 'You are clearly unable to provide any [...] information revealing any intimacy between you [...]. In fact, you recount in an abstract manner and after a silence: 'every time [...] I refuse to [...] have sex with him [...]. He's someone who, if he wants something, goes all the way.'[831]

When it comes to central details of SGBV in flight stories, asylum officials explained how the abovementioned sexual violence guideline at the CGRS (see Part II, Chapter 2.2.1) instructs not to ask questions on the act of SGBV itself, but only on the circumstances in which it occurred.[832] However, the case law analysed at times revealed an opposite practice,[833] leading to disbelief of applicants' insufficiently detailed responses. Where POs did seem to follow the guideline and would therefore be expected not to rely on lacking detail on these central elements in the credibility assessment, this appears no guarantee either.

---

829 DS088_CGRS 1 (refusal)_F_Senegal_RSA_GMC_VGNT_FM_DV_19/7/2023_FR_Database_p. 8.

830 DGa102_CGRS 1 (refusal)_F_The Gambia _FM_DV_10/10/2023_FR_Database_p. 4. Emphasis added.

831 DS103_CGRS 1 (refusal)_F_Senegal_GMC_FM_DV_17/7/2023_FR_Database_p. 5. Emphasis added.

832 CB010_CGRS_PO_[01:10:19].

833 E.g. 'You have been asked several times to give a precise, concrete and detailed account of a situation in which you were a victim of abuse' (DG073_CGRS 2 (inadmissible)_F_Guinea_RSA_FM_DV_23/6/2023_FR_Case law selection by CALL_p. 4.); "[T]he [CGRS] twice encourages you to talk about what happens afterwards, even though you say you were raped and your hands and feet were tied up" (NS005_CGRS 1 (refusal)_2002_F_Senegal_RSA_DV_FM_13/05/2022_FR_NANSEN_p. 5.).

In a Georgian case of an applicant raped by a police officer, whose name she did not want to give out of fear for the regime, the PO explicitly voiced that she understood how difficult the personal interview was, assuring her that it was not necessary to provide details about the rape.[834] However, both the CGRS[835] and the CALL afterwards based their negative decision (among other elements) on a contradiction about whether or not she knew the name of her perpetrator. The CALL added: 'It cannot be understood why [she did not] already indicated during her first [...] interview that she knew the name but did not want to share it].'[836]

The aforementioned thinking pattern, that SGBV experiences would be 'engraved in one's memory', was echoed in a variety of ways in the analysed case law. Several decisions stated that the more 'crucial', 'central', 'severe', or 'significant' an SGBV experience is deemed or the longer it lasted, the more details about it can be expected. One judgement explicitly stated: 'Since the events [...] constitute a manifest deviation from everyday life and had a determining influence on her subsequent life, they can reasonably be regarded as having been engraved in her memory' and concluded that her alleged stress or the time passed since the experiences could not alter the CGRS' refusal of international protection.[837] Other interviewed decision makers asked themselves the question: 'Why would an applicant be able to say that there has been abuse, [...] but be unable to get into the details?'[838]

Circumstantial Details

One PO linked the expectation from applicants to provide details central to their flight story to those circumstantial to it. They reasoned: if applicants can make clear general statements circumstantial to the SGBV, they should also be able to disclose the elements central to it.[839] These details circumstantial to the traumatic experiences are the other type of details, next to the central ones, focused on by decision makers. One PO went as far as stating that refugee status determination largely depends on applicants' ability to credibly recount the context in which persecution took place, concluding: 'If they fail [...] then it ends there.'[840] An attaché at the CALL upheld a firm distinction between central and circumstantial details. While, according to them, applicants will never be criticised for not describing their traumatic experiences in sufficient

834 DGe137_CALL 1 (refusal)_F_Georgia_RSA_DV_23/5/2024_307 106_NL_Database_p. 17.
835 DGe137_CGRS 1 (refusal)_F_Georgia_RSA_DV_27/12/2023_NL_Database_p. 6.
836 DGe137_CALL 1 (refusal)_F_Georgia_RSA_DV_23/5/2024_307 106_NL_Database_p. 24.
837 DE132_CALL 1 (refusal)_1998_F_Ethiopia_RSA_FM_ 15/5/2024_306 550_NL_Database_ p. 14. Emphasis added.
838 CB001_CGRS_PO_[00:12:44].
839 CB006_CGRS_PO_[00:23:08].
840 CB014_CGRS_PO_[00:11:52] & [01:05:23].

detail, which '[the CALL] won't ask, and hopefully the CGRS won't either,' descriptions of the events before and after these experiences should be detailed and coherent.[841]

The types of circumstantial details mentioned by decision makers as relevant and necessary range from personal details of other actors than perpetrators to information on the preparation/organisation of and reactions after SGBV, or broader autobiographical information. One PO gave the abovementioned example of an Indian applicant who became the survivor/victim of a gang rape by her father's creditors within a pyramid scheme. The PO mentioned the difficult process of the personal interview, in part because the applicant had been diagnosed with a brain tumour. She had failed to provide information on the company that had addressed her father or provide other evidence and 'didn't know half the things her father had done.' Instead, the applicant had kept replying that her father never told her anything. The PO explained they had expected more, especially since the applicant had a bachelor's degree in accounting, concluding there was nothing they could do to give her international protection.[842]

In the abovementioned Georgian case of a bisexual man forced to marry a woman by her family, the CALL discredited his flight story by pointing out his lack of knowledge on the precise time when he was publicly outed by his wife (while he was not there) and his stepfather's job at the Georgian Security Service (including how long he already worked there, his studies, his previous jobs, his influential colleagues, or when exactly he had showed him his badge).[843] In Nella's case, the CGRS argued:

> 'When asked about your **partner's job**, you say that he has been a driver since he was 20 […]. Asked to give a **precise date when he started** working, you […] can't remember […]. […] You do not know why [the men who raped you] **turned up so late**, five days after the visitors had left […]. The [CGRS] can only note your statements […] lack any circumstantial evidence that would […] ground this event in reality.'[844] | CASE OF NELLA

Level of Detail & Details not Given by or not Accessible to Applicants

The interview answers and case law differed in terms of the expected level of detail, the person to whom the details are accessible, and the person giving

841 RB002_CALL_Attaché_[00:25:47].
842 CB014_CGRS_PO_[00:36:42].
843 DGe110_CALL 1 (refusal)_1986_M_Georgia_VGNT_FM_27/3/2024_303 8891_NL_Database_p. 13 & 18.
844 DBu083_CGRS 1 (refusal)_F_Burundi_RSA_29/6/2023_FR_Database_p. 3.

the details. First, while most asylum authorities label a lack of detail as non-credible, a few oppositely do so when applicants provide too much detail. One PO for example found stories that are set out too clearly and too explicitly less credible,[845] and a judge and attaché confirmed that applicants should not give too many details, since it might look like they learnt them by heart[846] or made them up, since they could not know certain information about perpetrators they didn't know beforehand.[847]

Secondly, the details expected by decision makers are not always those experienced by applicants themselves, but also those accessible to other actors, or to no one at all. These other actors may be applicants' partner,[848] mother,[849] or father.[850] The information expected from applicants for example concerned the latter's opinion about the harmful (sexual) rituals his children-applicants were subjected to. This occurred in the case of a Gabonese girl, who was a minor at the time of her CGRS decision. Asked what her father thought of these practices, she stated not knowing, but having 'the impression that he agreed because he did nothing to defend [her].' The CGRS concluded that her 'lack of interest in communicating [her] distress to [her] father is not consistent with the behaviour of someone driven by fear.'[851]

While barriers to SGBV disclosure will be discussed in-depth below (see Chapter 3.3.2. and Part IV, Chapter 2.2.1), it is already important to note here that this conclusion lacks empirical grounds. In fact, research on such barriers for children towards their parents for example mentions 'trying not to burden them'.[852] It also shows how parents' reactions are less often supportive than not, and that children's accurate estimates about this may

---

845 CB003_CGRS_PO_[00:17:53].

846 RB005_CALL_Judge_[00:49:04].

847 RB007_CALL_Attaché_[00:22:35].

848 On their political activities, arrest, detention, or searches for them, as in Angele's case (NC006_CGRS 1 (refusal)_1984_F_DRC_RSA_30/3/2020_FR_NANSEN_p. 3–4.; NC006_CGRS 2 (refusal)_1984_F_DRC_RSA_30/8/2021_FR_NANSEN_p. 6–7.) and Nella's case (DBu083_CGRS 1 (refusal)_F_Burundi_RSA_29/6/2023_FR_Database_p. 4.).

849 On her reasons for giving up her child to guardians to protect her from female GMC in Mary's case (NL017_CALL 1 (refusal)_1980_F_Liberia_STFP_GMC_VGNT_FM_10/08/2022_275 866_NL_NANSEN_p. 10.; NL017_CGRS 1 (refusal)_1980_F_Liberia_ STFP_GMC_VGNT_ FM _17/2/2022_NL_NANSEN_p. 3.).

850 On the times he was approached by the *talib* who made sexual advances in Yusuf's case (DAf150_CGRS 1 (refusal)_M_Afghanistan_RSA_5/10/2023_NL_Database_p. 3., DAf150_ CALL 1 (refusal)_M_Afghanistan_RSA_8/3/2024_302 900_NL_Database_p. 14 & 16.).

851 DC079_C_CGRS 1 (refusal)_2006_F_Gabon_RSA_20/2/2023_FR_Database_p. 6.

852 Ramona Alaggia, Delphine Collin-Vézina and Rusan Lateef, 'Facilitators and Barriers to Child Sexual Abuse (CSA) Disclosures: A Research Update (2000–2016)' (2019) 20 Trauma, Violence & Abuse 260, 265.

also withhold them from disclosing.[853] Reluctance to disclose child sexual abuse specifically increases with for example: the severity of the violence, the familiarity of the perpetrator, and when children perceive their parents as highly overprotective on the one hand or less protective on the other,[854] such as was the case for the abovementioned Gabonese girl.

In some cases, the details expected from applicants are not (yet) accessible to anyone at all, as in Esmeralda's Moldovan domestic violence case. She did not inquire about her ex-husband (the perpetrator) since her arrival in Belgium, neither herself nor through her mother who was still in Moldova, because she was afraid he might find out her whereabouts. The CGRS argued: 'Since you feared being killed by him, you could be expected to [inform yourself]. [...] [Your justifications for not doing so are] unconvincing. After all, you have every interest – if you actually have such fear – in knowing where your ex-husband is.'[855] This reasoning sharply conflicts with the confidentiality principle in asylum procedures concerning state actor-perpetrators,[856] meaning that applicants and asylum authorities are precisely expected not to contact or inquire into the actor of persecution when it (directly) concerns a government (official).

Thirdly, non-credibility is found by decision makers when insufficient details can be given by applicants themselves, as well as by others, such as relatives. The latter occurred in the abovementioned case where a Gabonese girl, together with her brother, fled harmful (sexual) rituals they were subjected to by their paternal family. In both of the children's cases, aged 8 and 16 at the time, the CGRS refused them refugee status arguing (among others) that their mother could not give sufficient details about the perpetrators. Apart from the first name of one of them, their 'mum [knew] neither the surname, [...] first name, [...] [or] nickname of any of [them].'[857]

Intersection of the Resourcefulness and Disclosure Myth

When it does concern lack of detail in the applicants' own statements, case law often uses a standard wording that expects detailed statements from applicants, regardless of their age, education level, or mental and/or physical well-being for example. This can be illustrated by Binta's case.

---

853 Irit Hershkowitz, Omer Lanes and Michael E Lamb, 'Exploring the Disclosure of Child Sexual Abuse with Alleged Victims and Their Parents' (2007) 31 Child Abuse & Neglect 111, 113; Alaggia, Collin-Vézina and Lateef (n 852) 269.

854 Alaggia, Collin-Vézina and Lateef (n 852) 268.

855 DMol140_CGRS 1 (refusal)_1971_F_Moldavia_DV__30/11/2023_NL_Database_p. 4.

856 UNHCR, *Handbook on Procedures and Criteria for Determining Refugee Status under the 1951 Convention and the 1967 Protocol Relating to the Status of Refugees* (n 254) para 33.

857 DC079_B_CGRS 1 (refusal)_2014_M_Gabon_RSA_VGNT_20/2/2023_303 320_FR_Database_MINOR_p. 8.; DC079_C_CGRS 1 (refusal)_2006_F_Gabon_RSA_20/2/2023_303 320_FR_Database_MINOR_p. 7.

CASE OF BINTA			
• Country of origin:	Guinea	• SGBV types:	Rape/sexual assault, GMC, violence related to gender norm transgression, forced marriage & domestic violence
• Gender identity:	Woman	• Decisions in file:	CGRS 1 (refusal) – 20/6/2023
• Birth year:	/		CALL 1 (refusal) – 11/4/2024 – n° 304 652
• Interview by:	/		

According to her statements, after Binta's father had died, her mother remarried her paternal uncle. She was circumcised at the age of eight, **forced** by her uncle **to marry** at the age of 14, and therefore never got any higher education. During this marriage, she was **verbally, physically and sexually abused** by her husband regularly, and gave birth to a daughter. She shared the house with her husband's mother and three sisters, who had started accusing her of bringing bad luck, and **attacking her**. She suspected them of having **attempted to poison her**. When her husband left for Mozambique in 2018, her sisters-in-law blamed her for having chased him out of the house. Their attacks intensified by **threatening to kill her**. Out of fear they might succeed, Binta eventually fled the country in 2021, travelling via Morocco, Spain and France before arriving in Belgium.

She applied for international protection, fearing for herself to be sent back to her husband's house and to be killed by her family-in-law, and for her **daughter to be circumcised**. In support of her applications, she submitted medical reports on her own circumcision and her injuries following the abuse. She also provided proof of her registration/treatment with an organisation specialising in female GMC and with a psychologist, since she had difficulties accessing her memory of the experiences.

One of the arguments advanced by the CGRS and CALL[858] to refuse Binta protection, was:

> 'Although you are **poorly educated** and state having **memory problems** [...], these are central elements of your personal [marital] life, which **do not explain** such a **lack of [...] detail** [...]. [This] cannot be justified by your **young age** [(14 years old when marrying)], as you were 21 years old when you left [...], and it is up to you to provide [...] concrete information concerning [your flight story] in your own words, which does not require any cognitive education.'[859] | CASE OF BINTA

[858] E.g. '[W]hile the Council can understand that it is difficult for a domestic violence victim to talk about their marital life and [...] the perpetrator [...], it nevertheless considers that this alone cannot explain the gaps in her statements, especially since she claims to have lived with [him] for four years and to have had a child with him. Neither the contextual explanations [...], nor the applicant's age [...] [or] lack of education can mitigate these findings.' (DG082_CALL 1 (refusal)_F_Guinea_RSA_GMC_VGNT_FM_DV_11/4/2024_304 652_FR_Database_p. 11.).

[859] DG082_CGRS 1 (refusal)_F_Guinea_RSA_GMC_VGNT_FM_DV_20/6/2023_304 652_FR_Database_p. 3.

In the abovementioned similar Gambian forced marriage case, the CGRS confirmed this reasoning by pointing out the unlikeliness of the applicant's lack of interest into the buildup to and organisation of her forced marriage. The CGRS refused her refugee status, despite her age at the time (13 years old) and her 'vague claims' that she never thought about this, was simply forced to stay with him, and: 'You know, at the moment, I didn't know what I wanted, I didn't know anything, I knew that I got married, but it was only two years later that I got my first period.'[860]

This intersection of the resourcefulness and disclosure myth is also reflected in several decision makers' interviews, with some claiming that more details are expected from higher-educated applicants,[861] but others discarding education level as irrelevant altogether, reckoning that 'if the person has really experienced violence, then they should be able to explain [what happened to them], no matter what their level of education. I mean, these are things that they have experienced themselves, it's not theory.'[862]

A similar expectation of detailedness, this time regardless of applicants' physical and/or mental well-being, can be detected in the case law, for example in an Ethiopian forced marriage, forced labour, and rape case. While the applicant pointed to her psychological vulnerability at the time of the personal interview, as she was breastfeeding, tired and stressed and had to give statements about sensitive subjects, the CALL generally concluded that every personal interview at the CGRS involves some degree of stress. Nonetheless, 'an applicant [...] can reasonably be expected to [...] make sufficiently clear, accurate and coherent statements.'[863]

This line of reasoning also applies in cases where medical certificates of the violence suffered are available, such as Nella's medical report of rape,[864] or Binta's injury report:

> 'Your **report** mentions [...] a scar on your right buttock, [...] on the outside of your left thigh and [...] on your left knee. When asked about these [...], you say that the [first] was caused by a beating with a lighted piece of wood [...] and [...] the [second] with an electric cord [...]. However, you later say that [it] was caused by a burn [...]. Without questioning the existence of these scars, [...] the **lack of details** as to [...]

860 DGa102_CGRS 1 (refusal)_F_The Gambia_FM_DV_10/10/2023_305 436_FR_Database_ p. 4.

861 E.g. 'if [...] a highly educated person were to be forced into an arranged marriage, it might be expected that this person could say [...] more than someone who has had no education" (CB015_CGRS_Supervisor+PO_GENDER_[00:21:33].).

862 CB004_CGRS_PO_[00:31:21].

863 DE132_CALL 1 (refusal)_1998_F_Ethiopia _RSA_FM_15/5/2024_306 550_NL_Database_ p. 14.

864 DBu083_CGRS 1 (refusal)_F_Burundi_RSA_29/6/2023_FR_Database_p. 4.

these injuries **do not allow [the CGRS] to believe the circumstances** in which you got them.'[865] | CASE OF BINTA

When it comes to the impact of trauma or other psychological issues on one's ability to disclose details, some asylum officials at the CALL reported having acquired knowledge on this through the pilot module organised by NANSEN (see Part I, Chapter 3.3), such as an attaché stating: 'Personally, I thought that anyone who didn't give details was lying. And it was at this training that it was said that one's psychological state could prevent people from giving details.'[866] Others seem to lack knowledge on how details are registered in traumatic memories, such as the relative importance of sensory details (e.g. a colour, fabric, sound, smell, …) versus poorly remembered contextual details (also called the tunnel memory, see Chapter 3.2.2).

One PO for example had based a negative decision about an applicant who was abducted and raped on the element (among others) that she could not locate the place of the rape, especially since she was in the car for ten minutes beforehand. The fact that she mentioned the colour of the walls of the room where she was raped, was irrelevant to this PO.[867] A rape case where the applicant provided details of the trousers worn by her perpetrator, but no further contextual details, was found non-credible by the CGRS along the same lines.[868] One gender-specialised supervisor was unable to say what kind of details, if any, would be of importance to refugee status determination in SGBV-related cases at all.[869]

Furthermore, asylum authorities deal differently with medical/psychological certificates on trauma-related psychological problems, such as PTSD. One interviewee stated that POs themselves do not analyse applicants' psychological problems because they 'really have no way of doing so.'[870] On the contrary, a gender-specialised supervisor with long-standing experience stated that they accept such certificates in principle, but are able to qualify them as outdated themselves if applicants 'appear' to pass the personal interview 'normally'. They testified having had persons in front of them who submitted PTSD certificates of a few years old, estimating after two half-day

865 DG082_CGRS 1 (refusal)_F_Guinea_RSA_GMC_VGNT_FM_DV_20/6/2023_304 652_FR_Database _p. 3.

866 RB007_CALL_Attaché_[00:55:20].

867 CB004_CGRS_PO_[00:39:45].

868 E.g. 'When […] asked [on several occasions] to talk in more detail about the assault […], what you said was particularly vague […], merely describing [his] trousers […], but nothing more – not exactly how you were injured, […] what the other people […] [did], or how you reacted.' (DG104_CGRS 1 (refusal)_F_Guinea_RSA_GMC_FM_1/9/2023_305 941_FR_Database_ p. 5.).

869 CB011_CGRS_Supervisor+PO_GENDER_[00:21:35].

870 CB007_CGRS_PO_[00:20:54].

personal interviews that they no longer 'felt' any PTSD. Since the applicants' chronology was well organised and they 'didn't seem […] that vulnerable' anymore, the only explanation they could see was that their PTSD diagnosis was outdated.[871]

This reasoning is reflected in the analysed case law too, where the CALL for example judged an Angolan gang rape and sex trafficking case non-credible. While the applicant's PTSD diagnosis was not in itself questioned, her 'mental health did not always affect her with the same intensity and [continuity], and it [did] not appear from the [personal interview notes] that […] it was impossible […] to [disclose] in a […] detailed […] manner.'[872] However, the credibility assessment in this case was based on, among other things, insufficient details about: where she was abducted to, how she and others were forced into prostitution there, her abductors and rapists, the care she received after her rape, her clientele, and her escape.[873] This judgement went on to use a standard argument regularly observed in the CALL's jurisprudence that psychologists' and psychiatrists' diagnoses are necessarily based on applicants' accounts and are therefore of no relevance to outlining the factual circumstances causing the trauma and/or flight.[874]

An attaché added that the CALL also in a standardised manner devalued certificates that are drafted by psychologists, who are no doctors, in contrast to psychiatrists[875] and placed asylum officials' own credibility assessment on the same level as these medical diagnoses. They assumed that every applicant has been traumatised in some way and 'they all have PTSD'. However, they stated: 'I have to assess to what extent I believe that this is so impactful that that person really can't explain why they [fled]' and stressed that this standard is 'fairly high'.[876]

One PO demonstrated how this standard of expected detail in memories appears higher for applicants than for decision makers themselves. Asked to describe a case, they replied not remembering some of the cases they dealt with a fortnight ago. They might remember that a case concerned a rape, but not the exact circumstances. They gave the example of an applicant who had given a 'weak' description of her stay in camps in Tanzania and had made a 'mistake' concerning a travel route. They concluded: 'this episode in Tanzania was

871 CB005_CGRS_Supervisor+PO_GENDER_[00:48:37].
872 DAn114_CALL 1 (refusal)_1997_F_Angola_RSA_STFP_18/4/2024_305 003_NL_Database_ p. 17.
873 DAn114_CALL 1 (refusal)_1997_F_Angola_RSA_STFP_18/4/2024_305 003_NL_Database_ p. 13–14.
874 DAn114_CALL 1 (refusal)_1997_F_Angola_RSA_STFP_18/4/2024_305 003_NL_Database_ p. 17.
875 RB003_CALL_Attaché_[00:15:44].
876 RB003_CALL_Attaché_[00:15:44].

not true and that had an impact on the rest of her story. […] But it's extremely complicated to give you the precise details.'[877]

b) *Acceptance of the Consistency Myth*

The Consistency Heuristic

Next to too little or too many details, credibility assessments are also based on inconsistencies between details each time a version of a (part of the) flight story is presented. One judge even stated that the CGRS is trained to look for contradictions and that 'there are many'.[878] Another judge confirmed how contradictions are part of credibility assessments and that in everyday life, this is also 'how you can tell if someone is lying to you.'[879] As such, the abovementioned belief that bad experiences are engraved in applicants' memories, so that they 'can retell it perfectly from A to Z', is completed by: 'Another version is never going to creep in, even if you [retell] it four or five times.'[880]

This belief has been framed in the literature as 'the consistency heuristic', explained by Granhag and Strömwall as the idea that 'inconsistency implies deception and consistency implies truth.'[881] While some expect more consistency the more central to traumatic experiences[882] or significant[883] certain details are, others put more emphasis on consistent circumstantial details.[884] Reliance on the consistency heuristic in the asylum context can be illustrated by Nyakato's case.

CASE OF NYAKATO			
• Country of origin:	Uganda	• SGBV types:	Rape/sexual assault
• Gender identity:	Woman	• Decisions in file:	CGRS 1 (refusal) – 22/6/2023
• Birth year:	/		CALL 1 (refusal) – 5/4/2024 – n° 304 388
• Interview by:	/		

(continued)

877 CB013_CGRS_PO_[01:29:04].
878 RB005_CALL_Judge_[00:07:55].
879 RB006_CALL_Judge_[00:17:12].
880 RB005_CALL_Judge_[00:38:54].
881 Pär Anders Granhag and Leif A Strömwall, 'Repeated Interrogations – Stretching the Deception Detection Paradigm' (1999) 7 Expert Evidence 163, 163.
882 CB006_CGRS_PO_[00:23:08].; CB013_CGRS_PO_[00:27:17].
883 DG092_CALL 1 (refusal)_F_Guinea_RSA_VGNT_FM_DV_4/1/2024_299 471_FR_Database_ p. 14.
884 E.g. 'I would be very wary of inconsistencies in statements about the hours and days surrounding a potentially traumatic event, but I would obviously expect solid statements about the situation […] a year before or after.'(R_3KZba7RYvtc7NX5_CGRS_PO/supervisor/ gender coordinator/CEDOCA member.); RB002_CALL_Attaché_[00:25:47].

According to her statements, Nyakato was sent to live with her mother's stepsister at the age of 12. This aunt **forced her to marry** a man from Dubai, by whom she was repeatedly **raped**. She managed to escape and ended up on the streets, where she was found by a nun. The nun offered her shelter, education, and work at an Italian orphanage. It was there that she met her husband, an Italian businessman operating in Uganda. Around the age of sixteen, in 2017, she obtained her mother's approval to marry him. Two years in, her husband became involved in financial disputes with business partners, though he did not disclose the details to her. In September 2019, Nyakato fell pregnant and discovered that her husband had been arrested. She managed to bail him out, upon which he went into hiding. His business associates started searching for him. During this period, she felt increasingly unsafe in their marital home, but because she had dogs that had to be fed, she still went there a few times a week. On those visits, she first noticed that someone had tried to break-in, and later that her large dog had been killed and her small dog had been hanged. She filed a complaint with the police and, following the advice of a friend, paid three men working as police officers to protect her home. While taking a shower, Nyakato was **raped** by one of the officers. Being pregnant at the time and losing a lot of blood, she went to the hospital, where they confirmed that she had lost the baby and that the remains had to be removed. Her sister drove her to another clinic so that the procedure could be performed by her family doctor, the only person to whom she confided the rape.

Fearing for her safety, she left Uganda and applied for international protection in Belgium in April 2020.

Concerning the circumstantial inconsistencies in Nyakato's case, the CALL stated:

> 'The unsubstantiated claim that [her experiences] have left "**deep traces**", which "**do not facilitate** the proper functioning of the **memory**" and that they concern matters from her "**early childhood**" **cannot** [**explain**] the many **discrepancies** and improbabilities regarding the applicant's account of her stay in an orphanage [...] and (forced) marriage.'[885] | CASE OF NYAKATO

The CGRS also found inconsistencies in her flight story on elements central to the persecution she fled, such as the date of her miscarriage,[886] the chronology of her pregnancy,[887] or the number of perpetrators who raped her:

> 'your [...] [rape] [...] is not convincing, as it contains serious contradictions. Whereas at the IO you still stated that you were **raped by two police officers** [...], at the CGRS you say [it was] **one of the three** officers present [...]. Faced with this [...], you stated: "I never said [this]. [...] [T]here was an argument, when [the first one] raped me, he said, when **the** [**second**] **one came in** and shouted angrily 'what are you doing!', that he should do it too, but [the second one] [...] **didn't rape me**." However,

885 DU113_CALL 1 (refusal)_F_Uganda_RSA_5/4/2024_304 388_NL_Database _p. 9.
886 DU113_CGRS 1 (refusal)_F_Uganda_RSA_22/6/2023_304 388_NL_Database_p. 5.
887 DU113_CGRS 1 (refusal)_F_Uganda_RSA_22/6/2023_304 388_NL_Database_p. 5.

> your explanation **does not justify the contradiction**, as you merely stick to the latest version of your statements.'[888] | CASE OF NYAKATO

This excerpt raises the question whether this constitutes a real or 'false' inconsistency, due to misinterpretation or miscommunication. This also counts for another of the CGRS' arguments, namely:

> 'Although [at the IO] you [...] clearly **link [the rape and miscarriage]** [...] **[to] your husband's problems** [...], you state at the CGRS that the rape incident could have **nothing to do with your husband** [...] as you had contacted the officers [...] yourself to serve as a private security guards.'[889] | CASE OF NYAKATO

What are presented here by the CGRS as two inconsistent statements, could equally be interpreted as complementary ones. It may both be true that the perpetrators of the rape had no direct links to her husband and that appointing them as guards was indirectly caused by her feeling unsafe due to her husband's problems. Besides interpretatively false inconsistencies, decisions also risk containing factually false inconsistencies, where the applicants' words were not captured or understood correctly. This is illustrated by the inconsistencies in Mary's abovementioned case about her residence with her uncle.[890] She claimed never to have lived there and never to have stated otherwise during her interviews.

Van Veldhuizen distinguishes two forms of inconsistency: internal inconsistency (within and between the statements given by applicants themselves) and external inconsistency (between the statements and information from other sources, such as COI, medical/psychological certificates, and witness or family members' statements).[891] The interviews with Belgian asylum authorities and the case law analysis contain instances of both types. As one PO put it, refugee status determination is a matter of assessing whether the person provides consistent information with the available COI, but also with what they said earlier in an interview, for example at the IO.[892]

Internal Inconsistency

Internally, refugee status determination relies (among other arguments) on applicants' inconsistencies within the same interview or between current and previous interviews, both during other asylum procedures abroad[893] and in

888 DU113_CGRS 1 (refusal)_F_Uganda_RSA_22/6/2023_304 388_NL_Database_p. 5.

889 DU113_CGRS 1 (refusal)_F_Uganda_RSA_22/6/2023_304 388_NL_Database_p. 5.

890 NL017_CGRS 1 (refusal)_1980_F_Liberia_ STFP_GMC_VGNT_FM _17/2/2022_NL_NANSEN_p. 3.

891 Tanja van Veldhuizen, 'Effectief Horen in Asielzaken: Niet Inperken Maar Uit Laten Weiden' (2017) 16 Journaal Vreemdelingenrecht 48, 49.

892 CB004_CGRS_PO_[00:35:09].

893 CB013_CGRS_PO_[00:29:25].

Belgium[894] at the IO or the CGRS (also when these were for example organised a year apart[895]). Inconsistencies between interviews were used in the case of the abovementioned Angolan applicant fleeing gang rape and sex trafficking. She was refused international protection because both the CGRS and the CALL found inconsistencies between her statements (on how she and others were forced into prostitution, her abductors, rapists, guards, and clientele) in the first and second personal interview at the CGRS.[896]

Inconsistencies within the same interview are often negatively labelled 'evolutive answers'. One PO explained how applicants might discredit their story by 'making their answers evolve according to the questions asked.' They illustrated this with an example of an applicant who said that her cousin had abducted and raped her. In her first version, she 'was in the street, [her] cousin came, he picked [her] up, he opened the door, he put [her] in the car and then he […] sat down and [they] drove off.' The PO found this inconsistent with her second version, that 'he put [her] in the car and locked the door, […] he took [her] bag and phone and then [they] drove off.' Because this PO had asked her in between these versions whether she had tried to escape in the time her cousin walked to the driver's seat, she warned the applicant that she noticed how she changed her story a bit each time new questions were asked.[897]

Similarly, in the abovementioned Iraqi case (of the applicant who had been sexually abused by his aunt under the threat that she would spread that he raped her), the CGRS argued that in explaining how the abuse was discovered, his statements evolved throughout the interview. He changed from thinking that his grandfather saw them through an open window, to doubting whether he saw or heard it and admitting not knowing how, to 'contradictorily stat[ing] that the window was closed but the curtains were open,'[898] to thinking the curtains were closed as always, but that this time he must have left a few centimetres open allowing his grandfather to see. Confronted by the PO with these uncertain statements, he finally answered that he might not have seen his grandfather but only heard him shout. The decision concluded that these discrepancies, changing as he was questioned, 'cast doubt on […] the […] sexual relationship with [his] aunt. Consequently, [he had] not managed to substantiate [his] fears […] upon returning.'[899]

---

894 RB005_CALL_Judge_[00:49:04].

895 NG012_CALL 1 (refusal)_1987_F_Guinea_RSA_GMC_FM_8/6/2021_255 907_FR_NANSEN_p. 11.

896 DAn114_CGRS1(refusal)_1997_F_Angola_RSA_STFP_30/10/2023_305003_NL_Database_p. 6–7.; DAn114_CALL 1 (refusal)_1997_F_Angola_RSA_STFP_18/4/2024_305 003_NL_Database_p. 12–14.

897 CB004_CGRS_PO_[00:41:18].

898 DIq095_CGRS 1 (refusal)_M_Iraq_RSA_DV_20/1/2023_FR_Database_p. 4.

899 DIq095_CGRS 1 (refusal)_M_Iraq_RSA_DV_20/1/2023_FR_Database_p. 4.

Next to internal inconsistencies between and within interviews, these are also found between applicants' stated knowledge/experiences and their self-reported or attributed profile/living conditions. Again, this is an example of how both SGBV myths on the micro level, the resourcefulness and disclosure myths, are intersectingly accepted by decision makers in the Belgian asylum procedure. To illustrate this form of inconsistency, I refer to the abovementioned cases in Chapter 2.1 on resourcefulness and to a telling quote in the abovementioned Nigerian forced marriage decision. In the latter, the applicant explained her father's initial open-minded and caring stance towards her, which gradually evolved into violent and authoritarian severity once she refused a forced marriage. The CGRS refused her refugee status, finding (among others) her descriptions of the father's profile and his change in mentality 'incoherent, contradictory, evolving, stereotypical, vague, evasive[,]redundant' and incapable of explaining what led him to forcibly marry her after having financed her studies and taken care of her for years.[900]

External Inconsistency

When it comes to external inconsistency, Belgian asylum authorities support their negative credibility assessments with contradictions between applicants' (ways of) SGBV disclosure and: 1) COI, 2) medical/psychological certificates or other submitted documents, and 3) other applicants' flight stories. Firstly, the authorities in the interviews stated to identify inconsistencies between applicants' statements on SGBV and available COI.[901] However, there was only one case in the analysed case law sample that explicitly mentioned inconsistencies with relevant (but not gender-specific) COI.

This was a Somali forced marriage and domestic violence case, in which the CALL joined 'the [CGRS in finding] that the applicant's knowledge of the security situation in her region of origin appears incoherent, inaccurate and flawed.'[902] The judge saw no justification for this lack of knowledge in the fact that she was married off at age 12 or suffered an uneducated, illiterate and socially isolated life. The judgement generally stated: '[E]ven an uneducated woman with such a profile can reasonably be expected to [...] situate simple matters in time,' hereby stressing the 'certain maturity' she had when fleeing (at age 27)'.[903] The judge added, possibly conflating social with literal physical isolation, that

900 DN100_CGRS 1 (refusal)_1993_F_Nigeria_VGNT_FM_DV_6/10/2022_304 410_FR_Database_ p. 7.

901 CB004_CGRS_PO_[00:35:09].; RB003_CALL_Attaché_[00:09:30].

902 DSo122_CALL 1 (refusal)_1992_F_Somalia_FM_DV_2/05/2024_305 966_NL_Database_ p. 18.

903 DSo122_CALL 1 (refusal)_1992_F_Somalia_FM_DV_2/05/2024_305 966_NL_Database_ p. 18.

the applicant did leave her house and went outside, since she sold milk in the surrounding area.[904]

On the social position of women in Somali society, the CGRS and CALL do mention gender-specific COI in another judgement, but this time to discredit the agency of a woman challenging her husband's authority: 'It seems unlikely that your mother could go against your stepfather's will as there is a patriarchal society in Somalia.'[905] As already mentioned above, Yusuf's declarations were also found to be inconsistent with COI, but this concerned forced recruitment by the Taliban, which was irrelevant to the gender-specific persecution he was fleeing, namely sexual exploitation of young men (e.g. *bacha bazi*).[906] Cases where applicants' fear of SGBV was (indirectly) contrasted with COI on the availability of state protection against such violence, will be discussed below (see Part IV, Chapter 3.1).

Secondly, applicants' statements and/or appearances during the personal interview are also found to be inconsistent with the medical/psychological certificates they submitted. The CALL for example, in the same Somali forced marriage and domestic violence case mentioned above, found the applicant's psychological difficulties, medically attested through a PTSD diagnosis, inconsistent with a reading of the personal interview notes, which did not 'show' that she was unable to explain her story in an independent and functional manner. The diagnosis was therefore unable to justify the identified inconsistencies in her story, according to the CALL.[907]

As mentioned earlier, Mary's case too testifies to such inconsistencies, where the CGRS interestingly connected the incoherence between a psychological report describing her forced prostitution upon arrival in Belgium and her conciseness about this during her interviews to the conclusion that she has no genuine fear of returning to Liberia.[908] Further, in Nella's case, the CGRS found that her statements inconsistent with her medical rape report (further) undermined her story:

> '[T]he document mentions that 'the patient was **brought by her family** on 30/10/2021 at 11:00 p.m.' [...] [while] you claim to have been **accompanied by your neighbour** [...]. Confronted with this, you reply that [...] she was **speaking**

[904] DSo122_CALL 1 (refusal)_1992_F_Somalia_FM_DV_2/05/2024_305 966_NL_Database_ p. 18.

[905] DSo125_CALL 1 (refusal)_1996_F_Somalia_VGNT_FM_3/05/2024_306 071_NL_Database_ p. 12.

[906] DAf150_CALL 1 (refusal)_M_Afghanistan_RSA_8/3/2024_302 900_NL_Database_p. 13.-14.; DAf150_CGRS 1 (refusal)_M_Afghanistan_RSA_5/10/2023_302 900_NL_Database_ p. 3.

[907] DSo122_CALL 1 (refusal)_1992_F_Somalia_FM_DV_2/05/2024_305 966_NL_Database_ p. 17.

[908] NL017_CGRS 1 (refusal)_1980_F_Liberia_STFP_GMC_VGNT_FM_17/2/2022_NL_NANSEN_ p. 4.

for you [when she took you to the hospital] […] so that you could **receive care quickly** […]. In view of all these findings, this **document** has **no probative force** capable of reversing the meaning of this [refusal] decision.'[909] | CASE OF NELLA

The case law sample contained no illustrations of inconsistency between applicants' statements or appearance with other submitted documents than medical/psychological certificates.

A third type of external inconsistencies concern applicants' own words versus those of other applicants. The abovementioned Georgian case of an applicant raped by a police officer, whose name she refused to mention out of fear for the regime, can serve as an example,[910] as well as another Georgian case, where such inconsistencies were concluded in an identical decision to that of the applicant's husband:

CASE OF ANA			
• Country of origin:	Georgia	• SGBV types:	Rape/sexual assault & domestic violence
• Gender identity:	Woman	• Decisions in file:	CGRS 1 (refusal) – 27/10/2023
• Birth year:	1985		CALL 1 (refusal) – 29/05/2024 – n° 307 462
• Interview by:	/		

According to her statements, Ana met her husband in 2003 and aspired to open a household goods store in the same year, leading them to borrow money from an acquainted prosecutor. Her business suffered financially and was ultimately destroyed in a fire caused by faulty electrical wiring. When they were unable to repay the loan, the prosecutor began threatening them. In 2006, her husband was first sentenced to three years in prison under false charges of theft by the prosecutor and afterwards, in 2009, again to another six years. Although he was granted amnesty in 2012 following a political shift, the prosecutor lost his position but never ceased his threats against them. Fearing for their safety, Ana and her husband left Georgia for Turkey, where they lived for seven years, but the threats persisted. In 2021, her husband returned to Georgia briefly, hiding with family before fleeing to Poland and then Belgium, where his application for international protection was rejected twice. Meanwhile, Ana was left behind in Georgia to secure travelling documents for their daughter.

(continued)

909 DBu083_CGRS 1 (refusal)_F_Burundi_RSA_29/6/2023_FR_Database_p. 4.

910 E.g. 'You stated in your first interview that something happened to your partner after your rape, but curiously you did not know what […], while your partner […] stated that he had told you that he was beaten up at the police station […]. Your partner's statements that he […] heard from your friends that you were insulted by a police officer are also curious, since you [first] say you had […] not told anyone about this incident […], [but later] […], contrary to your partner's statements, […] that you had immediately told him […]. […] Confronted with [this] […], your partner adjusted his previous statements and claimed that he did know from the beginning that you had been raped […], which does not appear convincing' (DGe137_CALL 1 (refusal)_F_Georgia_RSA_DV_23/5/2024_307 106_NL_Database_p. 25.).

She finally managed to flee with her daughter, arriving in Belgium in December 2022, where she filed her own asylum application. Despite mentioning she was **raped** by the prosecutor in Georgia in the questionnaire (to be read by the CGRS) at the IO, the CGRS copied her husband's refusal decision in her procedure, stating that their flight stories rested on identical grounds and making no mention of the sexual violence in the argumentation. In the appeal procedure before the CALL, Ana disclosed that she had continuously suffered **domestic violence** from her husband, both in Georgia and Belgium. Her husband was arrested and imprisoned in Belgium, but the violence started over upon his release. While she never filed a complaint in Georgia, having no trust in the Georgian authorities' response to gender-based violence, she did do so in Belgium. At the time of the appeal, she learnt through others that he was back in prison. At the hearing, she confirmed fearing for herself and for her child should they be forced, along with her husband, to return to Georgia.

Consequently, the inconsistencies raised in this case existed between Ana's words and those of her continuously abusive husband, with the CGRS arguing in the decision (still written as addressed to the husband):

> 'You claim that the prosecutor continued to make threats during your first [...] imprisonment [...] [, visiting your wife] every week and [sending] her messages every day[,] [...] during your second prison stay [...] [, and] [...] by telephone and [...] [harassing] your mother-in-law in Georgia [when you were in Turkey] [...]. However, your wife stated that threats were only made during [...] three months in 2009 [...] [and] [...] that [...] you heard nothing more [...]. until you returned [...] from Turkey. She also says that your family members were never contacted [...]. Confronted with [these inconsistencies], **your wife only said that she did not understand why you would have hidden something like that** [...]. Your **contradictory statements** [...] further **damage the credibility of your story**.'[911] | CASE OF ANA

Type of Elements Found Inconsistent

As illustrated throughout this chapter, the type of elements that are found to be inconsistent by the authorities vary. Temporal inconsistency for example concerned: the timing of a wedding and divorce in the abovementioned forced marriage and domestic violence case of an uneducated and illiterate Somali applicant;[912] the date of a miscarriage and chronology of a pregnancy in Nyakato's case;[913] or the exact date of the rape in Nella's case:

> 'The CGRS highlights several **discrepancies** [...] in your asylum story, once again **undermining the veracity** of your claims [...]. [O]n the one hand you say that you

911 DGe144_CGRS 1 (refusal)_ 1985_F_Georgia_RSA_27/10/2023_307 462_NL_Database_p. 4.
912 DSo122_CALL 1 (refusal)_1992_F_Somalia_FM_DV_2/05/2024_305 966_NL_Database_p. 18.
913 DU113_CGRS 1 (refusal)_F_Uganda_RSA_22/6/2023_304 388_NL_Database_p. 5.

> went to your neighbour's house [...] during the **night of 30 to 31 October 2021** [...] and, on the other hand, **on 31 October 2021** [...]. [Y]ou claim that your parents were informed of your assault on **30 October** [...] **or later on 1 November 2021.** However, you also state that your parents learnt what had happened to you on **30 or 31 October 2021**.'[914] | CASE OF NELLA

In other cases, the inconsistencies concern numbers of persons, such as: perpetrators in Nyakato's case[915] or other women forced into prostitution, guards, abductors, perpetrators, and nurses treating the applicant after her rape in the abovementioned Angolan gang rape and sex trafficking case.[916] Further, inconsistent details about perpetrators are brought up in the authorities' argumentation, such as: (knowledge of) the name of the police officer who raped the Georgian journalist mentioned above;[917] or their clothing in Nella's case:

> 'Firstly, you say [...] that people in **military uniform** as well as [...] in civilian clothes, Imbonerakure [(members of the youth league of Burundi's ruling party)] [...], entered your home and then that they were **police officers** and Imbonerakure [...]. Moreover, you repeat six times that they were **police officers** [...]. The [CGRS] can only note these **discrepancies** [...], which further **discredit the [rape]**.'[918] | CASE OF NELLA

Assessment of Justifications for Inconsistency

Some interviewed asylum authorities (partially) accepted justifications for the inconsistencies set out above, for example: trauma[919] or low education level, as explained by a PO as follows: 'The more educated someone is, the [...] more concretely you can use contradictions,' adding that, in their argumentation, they looked at what are 'logical' mistakes given applicants' educational level.[920] In the case law, justifications were often cast aside. Yusuf for example experienced problems during his personal interview and with the interpreter. Nonetheless, the CALL confirmed the CGRS' argumentation that:

---

914 DBu083_CGRS 1 (refusal)_F_Burundi_RSA_29/6/2023_FR_Database_p. 5.

915 DU113_CGRS 1 (refusal)_F_Uganda_RSA_22/6/2023_304 388_NL_Database_p. 5.

916 DAn114_CGRS 1 (refusal)_1997_F_Angola_RSA_STFP_30/10/2023_305003_NL_Database_p. 6–7.; DAn114_CALL 1 (refusal)_1997_F_Angola_RSA_STFP_18/4/2024_305 003_NL_Database_p. 12–14.

917 DGe137_CGRS 1 (refusal)_F_Georgia_RSA_DV_27/12/2023_NL_Database_p. 6.; DGe137_CALL 1 (refusal)_F_Georgia_RSA_DV_23/5/2024_307 106_NL_Database_p. 24.

918 DBu083_CGRS 1 (refusal)_F_Burundi_RSA_29/6/2023_FR_Database_p. 4.

919 E.g. 'We know that trauma can have an effect [...], but we do need to know, in general terms, the order in which things happened' (CB015_CGRS_Supervisor+PO_GENDER_[00:11:37].); 'if everything is correct and the chronology is not fully accurate, then I know it will probably be because of the trauma' (CB014_CGRS_PO_[00:09:41].).

920 CB014_CGRS_PO_[00:40:21].

> '[T]he applicant stated to the IO that he [...] was personally approached by the Taliban [...], but [...] [at the CGRS] [...] that it was always his father [...]. Confronted with this, [he] said that **he had mentioned [...] his father [at the IO] [...], but that he was told to be brief.** This is **not a satisfactory explanation,** [...] since there are no traces in the IO report which was read to [him] of this statement, which he clearly tried to **add later to make his story seem more serious.** [...] Although [...] he was assisted by a **Pashtou interpreter while Dari is his mother tongue,** it must be pointed out that [...] the motives set out above show conclusively that **no credibility** can be given to [...] his **inadequate statements.**'[921] | CASE OF YUSUF

Concerning education level or age, the abovementioned Somali forced marriage and domestic violence case illustrates how no justification for the applicant's inconsistencies was found in her young age, lack of education, or illiteracy.[922] A similar conclusion was drawn in the abovementioned case of Binta.[923] Another notable explanation, having been drugged at the time of the disclosed facts, is also rejected in two cases: for Nella (who received paracetamol and other medicines in the hospital after her rape)[924] and for the abovementioned Angolan applicant fleeing gang rape and sex trafficking (who stated being drugged 'during sexual, physical and psychological attacks'[925]). In the latter case, the Council bluntly stated: 'While the applicant claims that she was drugged, [...] she was not drugged at the time of her [CGRS] interview.'[926]

When it comes to psychological difficulties, several of the cases described throughout this chapter illustrate the authorities' rejection of such issues as a justification for inconsistency. A concrete example is the case of Fatou, a Guinean applicant whose psychiatric and psychological certificates diagnosed PTSD and elaborately described the relevant symptoms.[927] The CGRS argued, having taken these certificates into account, that it did not 'appear' from her personal interview that she had any difficulty relating her experiences. Therefore, 'the CGRS considers that the disorders from which you suffer are not sufficient to explain the contradictions and deficiencies in your

921 DAf150_CALL 1 (refusal)_M_Afghanistan_RSA_8/3/2024_302 900_NL_Database_p. 14–15.
922 DSo122_CALL 1 (refusal)_1992_F_Somalia_FM_DV_2/05/2024_305 966_NL_Database_p. 18.
923 DG082_CALL 1 (refusal)_F_Guinea_RSA_GMC_VGNT_FM_DV_11/4/2024_304 652_FR_Database_p. 10.
924 DBu083_CGRS 1 (refusal)_F_Burundi_RSA_29/6/2023_FR_Database_p. 5.
925 DAn114_CALL 1 (refusal)_1997_F_Angola_RSA_STFP_18/4/2024_305 003_NL_Database_p. 15.
926 DAn114_CALL 1 (refusal)_1997_F_Angola_RSA_STFP_18/4/2024_305 003_NL_Database_p. 17.
927 Such as: suppression, avoidance, dissociation when evoking traumatic memories, orientation/temporal errors, minimisation of the facts, indifference to defending oneself, sleep disorders, nightmares, flashbacks, reliving the experience, hypervigilance, concentration and memory disorders, and visual and auditory hallucinations (the latter related to the grieving process over her deceased son).

account.'[928] This reasoning gives the impression that authorities consider the effects of such a diagnosis to be practically observable. Thus, if applicants manage to complete the personal interview and appear to behave and disclose 'normally', the relevance of the entire diagnosis for their refugee status determination, including any consequences for the content of the story such as inconsistencies, is cast aside.

3.2.2. REBUTTAL OF THE DISCLOSURE MYTHS ON DETAIL & CONSISTENCY

The health and social sciences rebuttal of the detail and consistency myths will distinguish between internal (related to the memory itself) and external (apart from the memory) explanatory factors. I will illustrate how traumatic memories, impaired through the effects of for example PTSD and depression, as well as 'normal memories', characterised by 'natural inconsistency', are difficult to access or rely on. This applies to both central and contextual elements of the SGBV itself, as well as broader autobiographical elements in someone's life/ flight story. Disclosing in a consistent way is further complicated by our memory tending to mix up multiple similar instances of long-term SGBV and by the impact of time passing between repeated interviews.

Next, I will discuss available evidence on the impact of external factors, apart from our memory, on capacity to disclose in a detailed and consistent way, such as shame, stigma, fear, stress, concentration issues, distrust, or isolation (and the importance of applying a cross-cultural lens to these factors). In addition, focusing on consistency between applicants' behaviour/statements and their psychological diagnoses or profile may be a fruitless attempt. The effects of such diagnoses are often not physically observable during an interview and might lead applicants to minimise violence or idealise perpetrators.

In a limited way, this expertise has been taken up by the ECtHR in its non-refoulement case law, accepting certain vagueness and inconsistency in flight stories if these do not undermine the overall credibility. Many of the empirically established internal and external factors impacting detailedness and consistency of disclosure have been translated to legal scholarship on (inter)national refugee law. The Belgian asylum authorities too demonstrated a certain level of rebuttal of these myths, with some officials even emphasising the importance of allowing a free narrative in interviews, the risk that the effect of social isolation on disclosure might lead to education-based discrimination in the procedure, or the need to interpret special procedural guarantees as shaping the substantive assessment of an application.

---

928 DG070_CGRS 1 (refusal)_F_Guinea_RSA_FM_DV_30/3/2023_300 255_FR_Case law selection by CALL_p. 8.

a) *Rebuttal in Health & Social Sciences*

On an internal level,[929] related to the memory, survivors/victims often have to fall back on impaired memories when testifying on their SGBV experiences/fears.[930] This can not only result from PTSD developed after a specific traumatic event, but also from symptoms of depression over longer periods of time (particularly relevant for long-term forms of SGBV such as forced marriage or domestic violence). Although greater emphasis is often placed on the former in asylum procedures, both have an undeniable and distinct impact on a person's ability to disclose such violence.

For traumatic memories, this damage manifests itself, for example, in distorted temporal or geographical information.[931] From neurobiological and psychological research on the traumatic memory, we know that the amount and type of information captured by the memory depends on attentional disturbances in the processes of information encoding, retention (at the moment of the experience) and retrieval (at a later stage).[932] However, it is precisely the part of the brain that regulates attention (the prefrontal cortex) that is affected when the brain's defence circuitry is activated (e.g. during intensely traumatic experiences).[933] Traumatic memories (like SGBV in particular[934]) therefore differ from normal or narrative memories[935] in that they are affected by 'sensory encoding, dissociation, circumscribed memory retention, recall deficit, avoidance and poor concentration,'[936] all of which are symptoms of PTSD if they persist for more than a month after the SGBV experience.[937]

---

929 van Veldhuizen (n 891) 27.

930 Lamonaca and others (n 280) 8 and 18–19.

931 Rousseau and others (n 7) 49.

932 van Veldhuizen (n 891) 49–50; Eric Vermetten, Wijnand Raaijmakers and Berthold Gersons, 'Trauma, dissociatie en het geheugen: neurobiologische aspecten' (1998) 18 Directieve therapie 275, 283; Evert Bloemen and Riëtte Mellink, '"Ik Kan Niet Alles Vertellen ..." Asielzoekers Met Psychische Problemen in de Asielprocedure' (2008) 11 Maandblad geestelijke volksgezondheid 890, 894; Lamonaca and others (n 280) 21–22.

933 Department of Justice of the Government of Canada, 'The Impact of Trauma on Adult Sexual Assault Victims: PART II – The Neurobiological Impact of Trauma on the Brain' (10 January 2017) 3–4, www.justice.gc.ca/eng/rp-pr/jr/trauma/p3.html.

934 Diana Bögner, Jane Herlihy and Chris R Brewin, 'Impact of Sexual Violence on Disclosure during Home Office Interviews' (2007) 191 The British Journal of Psychiatry 75, 75; Baillot, Cowan and Munro, 'Reason to Disbelieve' (n 6) 120.

935 Bessel A van der Kolk and Onno van der Hart, 'Het Binnendringend Verleden: De Flexibiliteit van Het Geheugen En de Inprenting van Trauma's' (1992) 8 ICODO–INFO 1, 1.

936 Vermetten, Raaijmakers and Gersons (n 932) 275; Evelyne Josse, '"They Came with Two Guns": The Consequences of Sexual Violence for the Mental Health of Women in Armed Conflicts' (2010) 92 International Review of the Red Cross 177, 190.

937 American Psychiatric Association, *Diagnostic and Statistical Manual of Mental Disorders, Fifth Edition* (APA Publishing 2013) 271–272; Josse (n 936) 183 and 189; GAMS België vzw, 'Impact van gendergerelateerd geweld op de gezondheid (Transversale fiche 3)' (2019) 6; Keygnaert and Linthout (n 177) 18 and 22; Lamonaca and others (n 280) 8 and 18–19.

The medical documentation submitted in the case of Fatou clearly and elaborately explained the abovementioned impact of a PTSD diagnosis on the extent to and ways in which applicants can be expected to disclose their SGBV experiences.

CASE OF FATOU			
• Country of origin:	Guinea	• SGBV types:	Rape/sexual assault, forced marriage & domestic violence
• Gender identity:	Woman	• Decisions in file:	CGRS 1 (refusal) – 30/3/2023
• Birth year:	/		CALL 1 (recognition) – 18/1/2024 – n° 300 255
• Interview by:	/		

According to her statements, Fatou was born in Conakry and never knew her father, who had passed away. At the age of four, her mother abandoned her with a neighbour. Later, her paternal aunt took her in. At five years old, she was subjected to female GMC, an experience that took the life of one of her friends. That same year, her aunt died, leaving her to live with her cousin, where she faced **domestic violence**. The husband of her cousin, an influential man involved in drug trafficking, never accepted her presence. One night, while she was sleeping, he **poured hot water on her leg**. At age 11, Fatou began experiencing severe pain in her leg, but she only received painkillers, **never proper medical care**. In sixth grade, her cousin took her out of school to take care of her children. At age 12, her cousin's husband **sexually abused** her, resulting in pregnancy, which was terminated by a befriended doctor. Later that year, she became pregnant again and underwent another **forced abortion**. While being forced to sell clothes and water in markets, Fatou met a man in whom she confided and they started a relationship. When she became pregnant of him, her cousin's husband forced her again to take abortion pills and **confined her at home**. In 2013, her cousin, also pregnant, was beaten severely by her husband, leading to her death. Fearing for her life, Fatou escaped during the mourning period and sought refuge with her boyfriend, whom she later married in 2014. Their son was born with health issues. At a certain point, her husband decided to leave Guinea and travel to Europe. Although he initially contacted her from Italy, their communication became scarce after he moved to Belgium. After this, Fatou was **forced** by her cousin's husband into **marriage** with a wealthy and influential gold miner. Since she had no other means of support and was financially dependent on her cousin's husband, Fatou was pressured into accepting the marriage despite her strong objections.

In 2019, she eventually managed to flee Guinea and reached Belgium, where she reunited with the father of her daughter and applied for international protection. Fatou submitted, among other documents, several psychological and psychiatric reports to support her application. In 2021, she received the news that her son had died in unknown circumstances.

Her psychiatric report identified:

> 'a patient in a state of extreme trauma. The symptoms are very worrying and go beyond those currently defined […] for **chronic PTSD**: […] **re-experiencing**; […]

> **avoidance** (**withdrawal** and seeking **solitude**); [...] persistent **negative** alterations in **cognition and mood**; [...] **hyper-reactivity** [...] related to the multiple sexual abuses [...] and the severe mistreatment of which she has been a victim and a witness on numerous occasions. She is at high risk of **suicide**. Her mental state is **fragile**. She shows episodes of **suppression, avoidance, dissociation** when these traumatic memories are evoked, and **disorientation, misplacing dates, minimising** the facts or **indifference** to defending herself [...]. One of [her] symptoms [...] [also] is the tendency to **idealise the aggressor** [...]. It should be remembered that recalling the violence experienced requires **memory**, a cognitive skill that can be **impaired** [...]. [The applicant] has memories of the traumatic events that may **seem accurate**, but **the context is often unclear** to her.'[938] | CASE OF FATOU

The fact that recalling sensitive SGBV details can be painful, at times leading to avoidance or suppression, is also explained by applicants such as Angele. As mentioned in Part II, Chapter 2.2.1, she ended her personal interview in despair with the words: 'Every time I have to talk about this story it's like putting a knife in the wound! While I'm trying to chase it away and forget about it.'[939] Mary testified:

> 'I'm **trying to** [...] **forget** some of the things, even though it's difficult [...] but [...] now, [...] when I start to talk about it, **everything will come back**.'[940] | CASE OF MARY

The concrete bits of information that remain in one's traumatic memory (often fragments, e.g. a ticking clock or the colour of a carpet, also called the 'tunnel memory'[941]) are accurate, but can be disorganised and incomplete.[942] Herlihy explains in an expert interview how the elements of the traumatic memory are not context-, nor time-related. We therefore may not be able to remember them as a chronological and geographical narrative.[943] On the one hand, our body needs us to be ready if we ever encounter a certain sensory detail (e.g. smell, sound, colour ...) again in a different context. Therefore, these memories do not have a context but are built around sensory triggers, functioning as a future-oriented protection mechanism.[944] Bloemen and Mellink confirm

938 DG070_CALL 1 (recognition)_F Guinea_RSA_FM_DV_18/1/2024_300 255_FR_Case law selection by CALL_p. 21–22.

939 NC006_CGRS interview 3_1984_F_DRC_RSA_FR_p. 19.

940 NL017_1980_F_Liberia_STFP_GMC_VGNT_FM_NL_NANSEN_[01:07:07].

941 Bloemen and Mellink (n 932) 894; Ingrid Candel and Harald Merckelbach, 'Het Geheugen Voor Negatieve Gebeurtenissen' (2002) 57 Nederlands Tijdschrift voor de Psychologie en haar Grensgebieden 1, 1; Herlihy and Turner (n 811) 86.

942 Vermetten, Raaijmakers and Gersons (n 932) 277 and 283; Keygnaert and Linthout (n 177) 22; Lamonaca and others (n 280) 22.

943 Herman (n 713) 37–38 & 43.

944 Interview with Herlihy (n 339) [00:14:27].

that the traumatic memory tends to be more accurate for central sensory details, but poor for contextual details, such as 'rooms, times, duration of travel or stay, number of people present and clothing of guards.'[945] Personal interviews focusing on such contextual details might therefore lead to credibility assessments that are not evidence-based.[946]

On the other, traumatic events may activate our 'capacity of trance', serving as a natural mechanism to literally numb (parts of) otherwise unbearable suffering. Spiegel even comments: '[I]t would be surprising indeed If people did not spontaneously use this capacity to reduce their perception of pain during acute trauma.'[947] Herman notes the apparent contradiction whereby survivors/victims in a state of 'ordinary awareness' may remember little or nothing at all due to post-traumatic amnesia, but in a state of reliving the events may replicate them in exquisite detail.[948] As such, trauma survivors/victims find themselves in a 'dialectic of trauma', 'caught between the extremes of amnesia or of reliving the trauma.'[949]

Besides memories of a specific traumatic event per se, symptoms of depression (often overlapping with PTSD)[950] can also affect a person's ability to describe more general autobiographical memories. This phenomenon is called 'Autobiographical Memory Overgenerality'[951] and is widely observed in individuals with Major Depressive Disorder (MDD).[952] Moore and Zoellner clarify that 'when instructed to describe specific memories, individuals with MDD instead tend to describe broader, more general categories of events rather than a particular instance, even with repeated prompting.'[953] This is all the more relevant when credibility assessments are based on inconsistencies in circumstantial elements, such as autobiographical information, rather than details central to the persecution feared.

Graham et al. confirm that for SGBV survivors/victims specifically, 'higher post-traumatic symptoms are associated with greater overgenerality.'[954] Herlihy therefore advocates for more attention to symptoms of depression and their impact on the ability to disclose detailed flight stories. She points at how, in contrast to PTSD, depression is not talked about in the asylum procedure,

---

945 Bloomon and Mellink (n 932) 894.

946 *Ibid.*

947 D Spiegel and others, 'Dissociation, Hypnotizability and Trauma' (Annual meeting of the American Psychiatric Association, San Francisco, 1989); Herman (n 713) 43.

948 Herman (n 713) 45.

949 *Ibid.* 47.

950 Belinda Graham, Jane Herlihy and Chris R Brewin, 'Overgeneral Memory in Asylum Seekers and Refugees' (2014) 45 Journal of Behavior Therapy and Experimental Psychiatry 375, 376.

951 *Ibid.* 378.

952 Sally A Moore and Lori A Zoellner, 'Overgeneral Autobiographical Memory and Traumatic Events' (2007) 133 Psychological bulletin 419, 420.

953 *Ibid.*

954 Graham, Herlihy and Brewin (n 950) 379.

while it has an undeniable influence on how people can present themselves. Therefore, she stresses that asylum authorities, 'when testing hypotheses to assess the veracity of an individual flight story, should keep in mind the hypothesis that someone might have symptoms of depression [...], resulting in severe difficulties in giving details about their life.'[955]

Zeynep and her lawyer illustrated the practical impact of depression at the time of a personal interview on one's ability to disclose in a detailed and consistent manner. At the beginning of her personal interviews, they signal to the PO:

> Lawyer: 'I can see that she is extremely **tense** and a little **disoriented** [...] there's a lot of **stress**, it's very **difficult** for her to get to the bottom of the story, but we'll see'
>
> Zeynep: 'I don't feel well, I'm **depressed**, I **sleep badly**, I have **nightmares**, I'm **afraid** of everyone, I'm constantly **anxious** [...] as I said last time, I am taking **medication**, I am a little **confused**, my ideas are **not clear**, I am **eating very little** at the moment, if an answer is not clear enough, I ask for your understanding'[956] | CASE OF ZEYNEP

Even when memories are not distorted by trauma, their reproduction is characterised by a certain degree of 'natural inconsistency'.[957] This retrieval is a process of reconstruction[958] rather than duplication, making the 'consistency heuristic' a strategy to be used with great caution.[959] In contrast to the scepticism towards inconsistencies illustrated above, psychological evidence instead shows that persons making up a story tend to try and repeat their initial statement, whereas those telling a true story try to reconstruct it.[960] In doing so, they do not naturally remember events chronologically. On the contrary, different memories, not always following logically from those previously disclosed, might surface by association while (re)telling an experience.[961] As a result, the idea that evolutive answers indicate non-credibility cannot be confirmed and, especially for traumatic memories, Lamonaca et al. advise authorities to 'not assume that changes in memory necessarily indicate lying, but may be an effect of traumatic memory.'[962]

Survivors/victims who have experienced/witnessed multiple repeated instances of SGBV over the course of longer periods, 'may appear less reliable

---

955 Interview with Herlihy (n 339) time 0:27:4-0:27:7.

956 NT015_CGRS interview 1_2_3_1996_F_Turkey_RSA_FM_DV_FR_NANSEN_p. 4–5 (interview 1) & 3-4 (interview 2).

957 Granhag and Strömwall (n 881) 170.

958 Herlihy, Jobson and Turner (n 804) 671.

959 Granhag and Strömwall (n 881) 170.

960 *Ibid.* 163 & 170.

961 van Veldhuizen (n 891) 55.

962 Lamonaca et al (n 29) 19.

in their reports than [those] who have witnessed a single event.'[963] This impact of experiencing a series of similar events on memory completeness and consistency is particularly relevant for long-term SGBV, such as domestic violence, forced marriage, or forced prostitution/sex trafficking. Inconsistencies also seem likely to arise in repeated interviews and increase the more time passes between them, especially for elements circumstantial to the traumatic event. Therefore, '[f]or refugees showing symptoms of high levels of post-traumatic stress, the length of the application process may also affect the number of discrepancies,'[964] which should therefore not be relied on to make credibility assessments.

One lawyer in the case law sample specifically illustrated this impact of time passing between repeated interviews on consistency: '[M]ention must be made of the delay in hearing the applicant [...], as [she] was heard [by the CGRS] two and a half years after her case had been transferred [...] by the IO. In the meantime, the applicant had had two children in Belgium and had tried to find peace of mind. It is impossible to remember and recall traumatic events over such a long period of time.'[965] Zeynep also very articulately rebutted the SGBV disclosure myth on internal consistency between/within interviews. She especially described the evolutive nature of the process of recalling her experiences throughout the personal interviews:

> 'I **didn't go into detail**, [the IO] told me it was normal, that I could express myself later. [...] **[I]t is possible that I may give information that I did not communicate at that time**, that I may **remember things** that I did not remember when I submitted my application.'[966]
>
> '[I]t feels like I have already been here for a very long time. **My memory is erasing my past.** [...] I feel like my head is full and that **as you ask questions it becomes clearer**.'[967] | CASE OF ZEYNEP

Apart from the memory itself, external factors such as: shame,[968] stigmatisation, fear of rejection by family/community, stress, lack of concentration, distrust

---

963 Tjeu PM Theunissen and others, 'Adult Eyewitness Memory for Single Versus Repeated Traumatic Events' (2017) 31 Applied Cognitive Psychology 164, 164.

964 Jane Herlihy, Peter Scragg and Stuart Turner, 'Discrepancies in Autobiographical Memories – Implications for the Assessment of Asylum Seekers: Repeated Interviews Study' (2002) 324 the British Medical Journal 324, 324–325.

965 DE132_CALL 1 (refusal)_lawyers' argumentation_1998_F_Ethiopia_RSA_FM _15/5/2024_306 550_NL_Database_p. 13–14.

966 NT015 CGRS interview 1_2_3_1996_F_Turkey_RSA_FM_DV_FR_NANSEN_p. 7 (interview 1).

967 NT015 CGRS interview 1_2_3_1996_F_Turkey_RSA_FM_DV_FR_NANSEN_p. 11 (interview 3).

968 Bögner, Herlihy and Brewin (n 934) 75; Herlihy (n 731) 117–119.

in the authorities,[969] fear of reprisals from persecutors,[970] and isolation[971] can significantly hinder applicants' narratives and justify partial disclosure. For example, in human trafficking cases, applicants experience significant difficulties in denouncing the networks in which they were recruited for fear of reprisals (e.g. when breaking moral promises after voodoo rituals or when traffickers threaten to publish (audio)visual recordings of the abuse).[972]

For forced marriages in particular, Berghmans in an expert interview stressed the importance of assessing these cases through a cross-cultural lens. She illustrated the case of a patient who was not aware of her husband's public activities, although he held regular meetings with political friends at their home. She did not hear what was discussed because she had to make food in the kitchen. Berghmans explained how in forced marriages, the husband's public life and the wife's private life are often organised separately and (mutual) interest in each other's daily activities may be completely absent. Therefore, she states: 'In a context of domestic violence, priorities often shift from cohabitation to survival.'[973]

Vera demonstrated these external factors, such as stress, fear, concentration issues, and (physical) isolation, in our interview:

> 'I've been very **stressed**, very **nervous**. [...] I **can't sleep** at night. I have a lot of **fear** [...] [and] **nightmares** [...] all the time, [...] if I'm asleep at 11 o'clock, 12 o'clock. After 1am, I'm awake. [...] [They] **didn't ask** [at the IO **if I felt ready or able to do the interview**].'
>
> Her sister, interpreting during the interview, added, replying to a question about her ex-husband's family members: 'I ask "are there any others that you know about?" *directed at Vera*, because she knows everything, she's just **not concentrated**.'
>
> '[I **couldn't**] **go out**, [I couldn't] go to friends, [I couldn't] go to [my] parents. [I had] to **stay at home**. A few times I went [out] with [my husband] [...] *not understandable because she is whispering* his hand, **never alone. Always accompanied**.'[974] | CASE OF VERA

Next to literal (physical) isolation, other applicants testified to a societal position isolated from the information they are expected to give during the

969 Bloemen and Mellink (n 932) 891; Ines Keygnaert and others, 'Sexual Violence and Sub-Saharan Migrants in Morocco: A Community-Based Participatory Assessment Using Respondent Driven Sampling' (2014) 10 Globalization and Health 1, 13–14; Lamonaca and others (n 280) 13–14.

970 Bloemen and Mellink (n 932) 891.

971 Josse (n 936) 177–186; GAMS België vzw (n 937) 4.

972 Lamonaca and others (n 280) 14.

973 Interview with Berghmans and Woman'Dō (n 341) [00:24:27].

974 CB010_CGRS_PO_[01:14:59].

personal interview. Mary's societal isolation for example originated from her upbringing. She was criticised for not knowing the specific succession traditions for practitioners of female GMC, even though she was raised by two white American missionaries:

> 'The whole **culture [around female GMC] [...] I really don't know much about it.** [...] **[My guardians] didn't explain** in detail. [...] [When] I said: "You people, we are not the same, like you are different from me, so why?," I always used to ask, they would say: "You won't understand." [...] [Eventually] she told me: [...] **"Your mother [...] wanted you to be safe** from this [(GMC)]." **That was all.** But I kept asking, she said: "The day you meet any one of them, you gon' understand." But **she didn't explain, like "because your mother is a Zoe, this is why [...]" or "the day your mother dies[...]"**'.[975] | CASE OF MARY

Next to lacking the social position to gather specific details about one's forced partner, in line with Berghmans' comments above, applicants might also cope with this type of SGBV in an avoidant manner (see Chapter 4.2.1 below). As in Fatou's case, such avoidance can come with complete disinterest and reluctance to gather information on this person as a whole. She declared that

> 'she had lived with him for about a month and a half. She had **neither the time nor the desire to find out anything about him** and although she explained that he was well known in the region, that did not mean that people also knew about any wives [...] or [...] children he had.'[976] | CASE OF FATOU

Apart from forced marriage, survivors/victims of other forms of SGBV may also show reluctance to gather information about their perpetrators. In the case of Aster, who fled Ethiopia and was forced into prostitution in Greece for example stated: 'I have no communication or information about [the trafficker]. I don't want to know anything about him.'[977]

External factors like stress and lack of concentration are also illustrated by Fatou's case. Her psychologist pointed at the fact that applicants might feel pressured to answer 'anything' during interviews, even when they are not sure of an answer.[978] Also, the duration of the interviews might lower

975 NL017_1980_F_Liberia_STFP_GMC_VGNT_FM_NL_[00:37:09] & [00:47:31].

976 DG070_CALL 1 (recognition)_lawyers' argumentation_F_Guinea_RSA_FM_DV_18/1/2024_300 255_FR_Case law selection by CALL_p. 16.

977 NE002_CGRS interview 1_1988_F_Ethiopia_STFP_NL_NANSEN_p. 11.

978 '[During the IO interview] she already presented all the symptoms of PTSD [...]. In this sense, she was not in a good [...] psychological condition to answer questions [...]. It should be noted that [...] [after the interview] she stated several times [...] that when she took this interview, she just answered "anything".' (DG070_CALL 1 (recognition)_lawyers' argumentation_F_Guinea_RSA_FM_DV_18/1/2024_300 255_FR_Case law selection by CALL_p. 15.).

concentration and therefore negatively impact applicants' consistency, as Fatou's lawyer explained:

> 'Regarding [...] the contradiction noted by the [CGRS], [...] [these answers were given] just before the end of the interview [...] [at a time when she] had been at the CGRS [**for four hours**].'[979] | CASE OF FATOU

When it comes to fear of or mistrust in authorities, both in the country of origin and in the Belgian asylum procedure, the lawyer of the abovementioned (p. 171) Georgian journalist (who refused to share the name of the police officer who raped her out of fear) expressed this poignantly in appeal. The argumentation explained that her mistrust originated from being raped by a police officer. The fact that her statements during the Belgian asylum procedure are confidential and will not be shared with the Georgian authorities does nothing to alter her fear for the figures representing power in her country. Therefore, she 'cannot be blamed for [not giving her perpetrator's name] [...] [, her] attitude [...] during her personal interview [...] had nothing to do with her unwillingness to cooperate.'[980]

Further, Zeynep's case nuanced the idea that (the absence of) psychological issues might be practically observable during an interview or from the mere fact that an applicant succeeds to complete it. For her, participating in the personal interview was an obligatory step towards obtaining protection, instead of proof of her psychological fitness to do so.

> 'I constantly want to cry [...] [but] I want to do [the interview] because [...] **it is inevitable, I have to complete this interview.**'[981] | CASE OF ZEYNEP

Conclusions drawn from inconsistencies between medical certificates and applicants' behaviour/statements during this interview may therefore be unfounded.

Concerning inconsistencies between applicants' experiences or knowledge and their (self-reported or attributed) profile or living context, it is important to point at the abovementioned symptoms of trauma to minimise the facts and idealise the aggressor.[982] In cases where this leads applicants to downplay the brutality of perpetrators or circumstances, the violence experienced might be found inconsistent with their living conditions. For domestic violence in

979 DG070_CALL 1 (recognition)_lawyers' argumentation_F_Guinea_RSA_FM_DV_18/1/2024_300 255_FR_Case law selection by CALL_p. 16–17.

980 DGe137_CALL 1 (refusal)_lawyers' argumentation_F_Georgia_RSA_DV_23/5/2024_307 106_NL_Database_p. 12–13.

981 NT015_CGRS interview 1_2_3_1996_F_Turkey_RSA_FM_DV_FR_NANSEN_p. 4 (interview 2).

982 DG070_CALL 1 (recognition)_F Guinea_RSA_FM_DV_18/1/2024_300 255_FR_Case law selection by CALL_p. 21–22.

particular, violent relationships may be characterised by what is called 'the cycle of violence' in literature. The concept explains long-term SGBV as a cyclical pattern in which abusive behaviour escalates through distinct phases (tension building, acute violence, and reconciliation), highlighting that no violent relationship is explicitly violent 24/7.[983]

Decision makers also risk finding inconsistencies that are factually or interpretationally false. These factually false inconsistencies were already illustrated in Mary's case, who did not manage to rectify factual errors in her personal interview notes.[984] Another applicant, through her lawyer, argued before the CALL that the inconsistencies between her IO and CGRS interviews unjustly had led to a negative credibility assessment. They concerned the names of family members, such as her mother, husband, and son, 'which she could not explain other than an [...] error, [...] [since] such basic information is so fundamental that she cannot see how it is possible that she could be mistaken.'[985]

When it comes to interpretationally false inconsistencies, Nyakato, via her lawyer, rectified her allegedly inconsistent statements on the number of perpetrators during her rape as follows:

> '[T]he CGRS questionnaire [...] states: "[...] **2 policemen** [...] raped me and I lost my child." This in no way contradicts the more thorough account given [...] to the CGRS at a later date[...]. The only nuance she made is that **only one agent carried out the physical act** of rape, while **the other was summoned** by the previous one to participate, **but refused.** Thus, there were indeed two policemen present during the rape. The foregoing thus **does not affect the credibility** of the applicant's story.'[986] | CASE OF NYAKATO

b) *Rebuttal in Law & Legal Sciences*

It is established case law of the ECtHR that it accepts a certain degree of vagueness and inconsistency in the statements and documents submitted by applicants, provided they do not jeopardise the overall credibility of their story.[987] The Court has illustrated this holistic approach to credibility

983 David Axlyn McLeod and others, 'The Model of Systemic Relational Violence: Conceptualizing IPV as a Method of Continual and Enforced Domination' (2021) 1 Trauma Care 87, 90.

984 NL017_CALL 1 (refusal)_1980_F_Liberia_STFP_GMC_VGNT_FM_10/08/2022_275 866_NL_NANSEN_p. 10–11.; NL017_CGRS 1 (refusal)_1980_F_Liberia_ STFP_GMC_VGNT_FM _17/2/2022_NL_NANSEN_p. 3.

985 DSo069_CALL 1 (recognition)_F_Somalia _GMC_VGNT_FM_DV_8/3/2024_302 889_NL_Case law selection by CALL_p. 9.

986 DU113_CALL 1 (refusal)_lawyers' argumentation_F_Uganda_RSA_5/4/2024 304 388_NL_Database_p. 6.

987 UNHCR, 'Note Du Haut Commissariat Des Nations Unies Pour Les Réfugiés Relative à l'évaluation Des Demandes d'asile Introduites Par Des Femmes' (n 751) 3; UNHCR, 'Avis Du

assessments[988] in several non-refoulement cases (unrelated to SGBV). In *R.C. v. Sweden*, the Court found the applicant's basic story consistent, 'notwithstanding some uncertain aspects [...] [which] do not undermine the overall credibility of his story.'[989] In *A.F. v. France* and *A.A. v. France*, it further clarified that 'a mere discrepancy in the chronological sequence of events does not constitute a major inconsistency,'[990] neither do inconsistencies concerning dates or the manner in which the applicant left his country.[991]

This approach is echoed by UNHCR, recalling that applicants' 'inability to recall dates or small details, minor contradictions, evasive or incorrect statements that do not go to the heart of the matter should not be considered as decisive factors for the credibility.'[992] It is important to emphasise that these positions of both the ECtHR and UNHCR only partially recognise the impact of trauma on memories, by still expecting detailed and consistent accounts on elements 'at the heart of' flight stories.

Nonetheless, UNHCR, together with other international bodies and organisations (such as the UN Office on Drugs and Crime, EUAA, and Amnesty International) do more generally recognise the impact of both the abovementioned internal[993] and external[994] factors on one's ability to disclose SGBV in a detailed and consistent manner. Consequently, UNHCR's Guidelines on International Protection No. 1 on gender-related persecution explicitly rebut the victim fabrication myth by stating that, rather than exaggerating SGBV experiences, survivors/victims 'may be reluctant to identify the true extent of the persecution suffered or feared.'[995]

In addition, EUAA explicitly recognises that applicants' fear to disclose might be triggered by cultural taboos surrounding SGBV, especially when interpreters share the same cultural background. The Agency's practical guide for

HCR Relatif à l'évaluation Des Demandes d'asile de Personnes Ayant Des Besoins Particuliers et En Particulier de Personnes Qui Ont Subi Des Tortures, Des Viols Ou d'autres Formes Graves de Violence Psychologique, Physique Ou Sexuelle' (2012) 3.

988 EUAA (European Union Asylum Agency), 'Evidence and Credibility Assessment in the Context of the Common European Asylum System, Judicial Analysis, Second Edition' (2023) 123.

989 *RC v Sweden* [2010] ECtHR 41827/07 [52].

990 *AA v France* [2015] ECtHR 18039/11 [54].

991 *AF v France* [2015] ECtHR 80086/13 [56].

992 UNHCR, 'Note Du Haut Commissariat Des Nations Unies Pour Les Réfugiés Relative à l'évaluation Des Demandes d'asile Introduites Par Des Femmes' (n 751) 1.

993 United Nations Office on Drugs and Crime (UNODC) and Skinnider (n 161) 25–26; UNHCR, 'Beyond Proof. Credibility Assessment in EU Asylum Systems (Full Report)' (n 19) 61–66 & 153; EUAA (European Union Asylum Agency) (n 988) 123; Amnesty International Nederalnd and instituut voor Mensenrechten en Medisch Onderzoek (iMMO), 'Slachtoffers seksueel geweld: blinde vlek in asielprocedure?' (2023) 24; EASO (European Asylum Support Office), 'EASO Practical Guide: Evidence Assessment' (2015) 15.

994 UNHCR, 'Beyond Proof. Credibility Assessment in EU Asylum Systems (Full Report)' (n 19) 70–72; United Nations Office on Drugs and Crime (UNODC) (n 284) 81.

995 UNHCR, 'Guidelines on International Protection No. 1' (n 35) para 35.

interpreters therefore stresses that 'people subjected to [SGBV] may feel ashamed or guilty, fear that their experiences become known to their families, be afraid of being rejected or have problems trusting others.'[996] This was also confirmed in research into the UK asylum procedure.[997] In Vera's case for example, this fear was voiced by an accompanying letter from her lawyer to the authorities:

> '[T]he mere fact that the applicant is confronted with an **interpreter who speaks her mother tongue causes anxiety and panic attacks.**'[998] | CASE OF VERA

The expertise from health and social sciences rebutting the detail and consistency myths has also found its way into legal scholarship, highlighting its relevance for refugee status determination. Such scholarship points at the same internal and external barriers for SGBV survivors/applicants to recount their flight story in an asylum procedure setting, for example: the difficult access to memories impaired by trauma,[999] the temporal/geographical distortion of such memories,[1000] SGBV-related stigmatisation, fear of reprisals by persecutors or rejection by family/community, stress, concentration problems, distrust in authorities,[1001] isolation,[1002] and low education levels or illiteracy.[1003]

Evans Cameron confirms the inaccuracy of 'normal' human autobiographical memory, even apart from the impact of trauma and stress. She points at decades of psychological research (as mentioned above) demonstrating that such memories change over time and that truth-tellers are more often disbelieved than those instructed to lie, hereby using specific conceiving strategies (e.g. including details, sticking to/repeating the same story, imitating spontaneity, ...).[1004] Linking such knowledge directly to the asylum context, she confirms that narrative gaps or inconsistencies are

996 EUAA (European Union Asylum Agency) and IGC (Intergovernmental Consultations on migration, asylum and refugees), 'Practical Guide on Interpretation in the Asylum Procedure' (2024) 60.

997 Sandra Pertek, Jenny Phillimore and Lisa Goodson, 'Forced Migration and Sexual and Gender-Based Violence: Findings from the SEREDA Project in the UK' (University of Birmingham 2021) 15.

998 NA016_CALL 1 (refusal)_lawyers' argumentation_1990_F_Albania_RSA_VGNT_DV_27/2/2023_285 363_NL_NANSEN_p. 7.

999 Thomas Spijkerboer, 'Asylum Decision-Making, Gender and Sexuality' in Evangelia Tsourdi and De Bruycker (eds), *Research Handbook on EU Migration and Asylum Law* (Edward Elgar Publishing 2022) 203; Pertek, Phillimore and Goodson (n 997) 19.

1000 Baillot, Cowan and Munro, '"Hearing the Right Gaps"' (n 92) 283; McKinnon (n 651) 214.

1001 Middelburg and Balta (n 8) 443; Baillot, Cowan and Munro, '"Hearing the Right Gaps"' (n 92) 281; Pertek, Phillimore and Goodson (n 997) 18; Magugliani (n 93) 5 and 11.

1002 Saroléa, Raimondo and Crine (n 93) 80–81.

1003 Middelburg and Balta (n 8) 442.

1004 Hilary Evans Evans Cameron, 'Refugee Status Determinations and the Limits of Memory' (2010) 22 International Journal of Refugee Law 469, 469 & 508–509.

misleading credibility indicators that should never be used mechanically to assess applicants' credibility.[1005]

c) *Rebuttal by Belgian Asylum Authorities*

The above described impact of trauma on applicants' ability to disclose, such as blocked access to memories during interviews, are (selectively) acknowledged by the decision makers in the Belgian asylum procedure. One PO for example expects applicants 'to be able to talk about [things that will hugely impact their life], unless it's been so traumatic that the brain has completely blacked out, as can happen in cases of rape.'[1006] Others rebutted the myth more firmly, such as this PO considering inconsistency and level of detail as subjective elements, especially in gender cases, where 'the person might not want to go into details because it is too hard for them, or [they are] confused because it is such a traumatic memory.'[1007]

Two POs even demonstrated specific knowledge on tunnel memory and the importance of sensory details. One did so implicitly, stating: 'For me, when you're going through a trauma, you're not necessarily analysing everything that's going on around you. So [...] I will perhaps focus more on what the person felt, [...] heard, [or] thought.'[1008] Another more explicitly explained having learnt from a training that sensory details are strong indicators of credibility, for example 'if an applicant spontaneously says "it smelled like this, it was cold, it was hot".'[1009]

The expectation that applicants can provide details central to traumatic memories, such as timing/chronology, locations, or information on perpetrators, was also rebutted by some decision makers. They for example considered stories that are not chronologically told more credible, while still acknowledging that chronological stories might also be credible 'because applicants have simply prepared it well.'[1010] On details of perpetrators, an attaché pointed out a practice of the CGRS to reproach applicants for not knowing such information. They replied: 'The opposite would have been surprising! [...] When she's being attacked, it's normal that she doesn't try to decipher the faces of her attackers.'[1011]

Speaking of the observed practice of asking applicants to recount specific episodes of violence in detail, contrary to what is prescribed in the CGRS' gender guidelines (see Part II, Chapter 2.2.2.), several earlier mentioned quotes

---

1005 *Ibid.* 510.
1006 CB010_CGRS_PO_[01:12:51].
1007 CB010_CGRS_PO_[01:09:26].
1008 CB004_CGRS_PO_[00:38:27].
1009 CB010_CGRS_PO_[01:16:11].
1010 CB008_CGRS_Supervisor+PO_GENDER_[00:27:42].
1011 RB007_CALL_Attaché_[00:22:39].

testified to the potentially retraumatising nature of doing so. While being forced to reveal painful details about SGBV is consistently described as destabilising by applicants, others also indicated that they were not given sufficient opportunity to talk about it (under the right circumstances), as this applicant did in her appeal argumentation, criticising 'the PO for interrupting her [...], consider[ing] that, "given the traumatic nature of the events [...], [she] needs to tell her story at her own pace and with the necessary context [...]. [T]he fact that she was unable to structure her story as she wished [did] not allow her to feel listened to and drastically shortened the various episodes that she intended to recount spontaneously." She also regretted that she was not asked more questions [...] about the reported acts of rape [...] and the attempted abductions of her son.'[1012] A similar feeling was described by Mary, who regretted not being asked about the forced prostitution she experienced upon arrival in Belgium,[1013] which was later held against her.[1014]

In contrast to these experiences, one PO did emphasise the importance of allowing applicants' free narrative, deeming it 'important [...] to go into the violence, but [...] to let [the narrative] come from [applicants] themselves [...] to ask what they can tell about the violence, and then possibly ask more questions to find out exactly what happened [...] without explicit details.'[1015] Others confirmed this good practice of allowing and encouraging free narrative in personal interviews,[1016] explaining that 'the trick is to let [applicants talk] and not interrupt them to demand that they tell the story in chronological order.'[1017]

When it comes to expecting applicants to provide autobiographical details that are not directly relevant to the persecution feared, one PO described feeling uncomfortable with the behaviour of a colleague, who was 'really annoyed' after a personal interview with an applicant: 'I thought he was very violent in his words [...] he expected a lot from this person, he said "she doesn't even know her father's job" [...] But there may have been a lot of reasons [explaining this].'[1018] As to autobiographical details in the context of long-term SGBV, a judge denounced the CGRS' practice of concluding non-credibility from lack of detail or inconsistency in forced marriage or domestic violence cases, that for example 'started 40 years ago', rhetorically asking: 'Do they realise what they are asking?' In this case, they recognised the person as a refugee, since 'the

1012 DC096_CALL 1 (refusal)_lawyers' argumentation_F_DRC_RSA_VGNT_11/3/2024_302961_FR_Database_p. 12.

1013 NL017_1980_F_Liberia_STFP_GMC_VGNT_FM_NL_[00:25:43].

1014 NL017_CGRS 1 (refusal)_1980_F_Liberia_STFP_GMC_VGNT_FM_17/2/2022_NL_NANSEN_p. 4.

1015 CB006_CGRS_PO_[00:11:32].

1016 CB005_CGRS_Supervisor+PO_GENDER_[00:39:13].

1017 CB008_CGRS_Supervisor+PO_GENDER_[00:27:42].

1018 CB007_CGRS_PO_[00:55:37].

inaccuracies were understandable given the age of the facts [...] and the young age of the woman at the time.'[1019]

The same PO demonstrating knowledge on sensory details from a training mentioned above, also learnt about repeatedly experiencing similar scenes over and over, and how this might result in applicants mixing details from several episodes into one. They therefore found it 'difficult to ask a person to recount a single episode' and said they could use this expertise from the training in her argumentation for positive decisions.[1020] By contrast, a judge I interviewed, while recognising themselves the difficulty to place specific instances of long-term violence in time, did find that the CGRS trains 'POs precisely to focus more on these specific facts.'[1021]

Lack of insight in the nature and consequences of such long-term violence, including the cycle of violence as explained above, might for example lead authorities to conclude: 'You say that your husband treated you well at the beginning of your marriage and that there were no problems [...], [the CGRS] cannot therefore believe in a situation where he would lock you up [at the end] as you claim'[1022] as was the case in an abovementioned (p. 147) Senegalese forced marriage, rape, and domestic violence case. What can also lead to such conclusions is a lack of knowledge about minimising violence as a trauma symptom. This risk is especially present when perpetrators are known to survivors/victims, as acknowledged by one judge. In particular for SGBV cases, often touching on intimate subjects and occurring between people known to each other, they stated: 'I think for the victim herself, designating the person she fears as a persecutor is not easy.'[1023]

When it comes to the abovementioned cross-cultural aspects in long-term violence such as forced marriages, an attaché echoed Berghmans' insights into the nature of the relation between survivor/victim and perpetrator. This attaché indeed considered the argumentation credible that 'in some countries, women['s] husbands are not their friends, [...] it's not a relationship like we imagine here in Belgium, [...] it's more of a relationships to procreate [...] or husbands don't tell their wives about their private lives.'[1024]

On external factors impacting SGBV disclosure, a Guinean applicant specifically voiced the impact of her socially isolated position on her ability

---

1019 RB006_CALL_Judge_[00:20:45].

1020 CB010_CGRS_PO_[01:17:04].

1021 RB008_CALL_Judge_[00:45:18].

1022 NS005_CGRS 1 (refusal)_2002_F_Senegal_RSA_DV_FM_13/05/2022_274 056_FR_NANSEN_p. 4.

1023 RB008_CALL_Judge_[00:07:56]. As illustrated above, these factors might for example have influenced a CGRS' decision to refuse protection to a Nigerian applicant, whose father's initial caring behaviour eventually evolved into violent and authoritarian severity once she refused a forced marriage (DN100_CGRS 1 (refusal)_1993_F_Nigeria_VGNT_FM_DV_6/10/2022_304 410_FR_Database_p. 7.).

1024 RB007_CALL_Attaché_[00:08:38].

to explain herself: 'I'm not used to questions like that, [...] I try to answer as much as I know. But afterwards I always have doubts. I don't know [...] it's difficult.'[1025] These difficulties might impact how well-articulated a flight story comes out, which is key for some POs: 'It all depends on how the applicant explains it. [...] [If] she explains that she wasn't interested at all because in her head she was in denial [...], that can be a perfectly valid explanation. But if [she] keeps saying 'I don't know, I don't know, I don't know', it will be different.'[1026]

However, an attaché warned that such reasoning can lead to discrimination based on one's level of intelligence. They explained how highly educated applicants might more easily be perceived as convincing 'because they will know more, explain, recount facts, while people who are poorly educated know less how to explain themselves.'[1027] For applicants fleeing rural areas for example, they acknowledged that an interview or hearing 'may be more intimidating than [for] women who have been to university, for example. I find that they are more easily believed.'[1028] This impact of education and age on one's ability to disclose in a detailed and consistent manner was also recognised by other asylum officials. One PO explained how it is easier to understand the living circumstances of a person who is well-educated and that this is a question of common sense. However, they stated: 'Unfortunately I don't think everyone knows what they may expect as a response [...]. If it's a girl who is not at all educated, [...] [I do] not ask the same questions as to a more educated person.'[1029]

In line with the ECtHR case law above, the CALL at times indeed makes a positive credibility assessment, regardless of remaining vagueness or inconsistencies in applicants' statements. In a case that the CALL itself highlighted as important, it for example stated: '[N]otwithstanding some remaining grey areas [...], the main facts of the alleged persecution can be considered sufficiently established and, consequently, the alleged fear well-founded.'[1030] In Fatou's recognition judgement, equally highlighted as important,[1031] the CALL even explicitly called out the CGRS' acceptance of the SGBV disclosure myth:

> 'Unlike the [CGRS], [the CALL] considers that the findings of the psychologist [...] [and] psychiatrist [...] are such as to **explain a whole series of deficiencies, inconsistencies, implausibilities and other shortcomings noted in the applicant's**

1025 NG012_1987_F_Guinea_RSA_GMC_FM_FR_NANSEN_[00:10:25].
1026 CB010_CGRS_PO_[01:14:59].
1027 RB007_CALL_Attaché_[00:31:15].
1028 RB007_CALL_Attaché_[00:31:15].
1029 CB010_CGRS_PO_[01:12:51].
1030 DG073_CALL 2 (recognition)_F_Guinea_RSA_FM_DV_11/3/2024_302 978_FR_Case law selection by CALL_p. 9.
1031 Council for Alien Law Litigation (CALL), 'Maandelijkse selectie van arresten van de Raad' (n 355).

> **statements** […]. By **disregarding such elements**, the [CGRS] has carried out an **analysis particularly inadequate and lacking in thoroughness**.'[1032] | CASE OF FATOU

Angele's first CGRS decision was annulled by the CALL for similar reasons:

> 'The applicant **explained, as far as possible given her psychological state, that she had been raped by armed persons**, presumably belonging to the authorities.'[1033] | CASE OF ANGELE

While both Fatou and Angele were able to provide medical/psychological certificates to substantiate their vulnerabilities, it should be acknowledged that this is not an (immediate) option for all applicants. However, this should not prevent decision makers from taking into account such vulnerabilities based on the facts of the flight story and/or impressions during the interview, as illustrated by the CGRS in an Algerian case. The PO identified special procedural needs in this applicant, arguing: 'It is clear from your statements at the beginning of the interview that [your experiences] caused you to suffer psychological problems characterised by flashbacks […]. Later […] you added that you feel uncomfortable talking about certain subjects in front of your lawyer and the interpreter, that you would have liked to discuss it first with a psychologist, but that you did not have the opportunity.'[1034]

For some asylum officials, these special procedural needs play a role not only in the procedural but also in the substantive assessment of an application. This position was confirmed in the recognition judgement of Fatou's case (highlighted by the CALL as important):

> 'While the [CGRS] has recognised that the applicant has certain **special procedural needs**, it does not appear from the **grounds of** [**its decision**] that the defendant has duly taken the applicant's state of health into account in **assessing the credibility of her account**.'[1035] | CASE OF FATOU

This 'standard of proof adapted to applicants' profile' is also demonstrated by the CALL in the case of the abovementioned Gabonese minor girl, who fled forced harmful (sexual) rituals by her paternal family. Here, the CGRS' decision was annulled by the CALL, arguing that her description of the violence reflected

1032 DG070_CALL 1 (recognition)_F_Guinea_RSA_FM_DV_18/1/2024_300 255_FR_Case law selection by CALL_p. 22.
1033 NC006_CALL 1 (annulment)_1984_F_DRC_RSA_5/11/2020_243 679_FR_NANSEN_p. 2.
1034 DAlg076_CGRS 1 (refusal)_M_Algeria_RSA_VGNT_8/12/2023_305 949_FR_Database_p. 3.
1035 DG070_CALL 1 (recognition)_F_Guinea_RSA_FM_DV_18/1/2024_300 255_FR_Case law selection by CALL_p. X.

'a certain sense of reality', taking into account her young age at the time of the events and personal interview, where she had stated: 'It's a lot of emotions. Even telling it today took courage because [...] I've tried not to think about it for a long time.'[1036]

In a Burundian rape case, the CALL explicitly dismantled the CGRS' expectation of applicants to provide geographical details on their SGBV experiences/fears. The applicant in this case was unable to describe the road towards and location where she was raped. The Council 'consider[ed] that [she could] not be expected to carefully observe the return journey in order to provide the elements enabling to locate the place of [her attempted rape].'[1037] On details of SGBV perpetrators, in Nella's case for example, the CALL recognised her as a refugee, disregarding the inconsistencies on her rapists' clothing as alleged by the CGRS:

> 'The fact that the applicant is **confused about the identity of the security men**, sometimes referring to **police officers** and sometimes to **soldiers**, is **not sufficient** to conclude that her statements on this subject **lack credibility**. When questioned at the hearing [...] regarding [their] identity [...], [she] makes convincing statements and again insists on the presence of the **Imbonerakure militia**.'[1038] | CASE OF NELLA

Occasionally, applicants' reluctance to gather details on their perpetrators was also explicitly validated in case law. In the same Burundian abduction and rape case mentioned above, the CALL considered it plausible and credible that a survivor/victim of an (attempted) rape would not want to disclose or discuss this with others to find out information about the perpetrator(s), location, ..., especially if these are strangers, regardless of their rank or prerogatives. The Council further concluded that the CGRS 'did not explain why it would be "legitimate to think that a person who had been helped by a high-ranking member of the police could find out about the identities of the [perpetrators]"'.[1039]

The risk that multiple similar instances of SGBV might be muddled in applicants' memories on long-term violence, was also recognised in a Guinean annulment judgement, where the CALL argued that it 'cannot agree with [...] the argument [...] calling into question [the applicant's] relationship [...] because of the concise nature of her statements, given [it] dates back more than

1036 DC079_C_CALL 1 (annulment) 2006_F_Gabon_RSA_18/3/2024_303 320_FR_Database_MINOR_p. 12.
1037 DBu089_CALL 1 (recognition)_F_Burundi_RSA_30/5/2024_307 576_FR_Database_p. 17.
1038 DBu083_CALL 1 (recognition)_ F_Burundi_RSA_11/4/2024_304 646_FR_Database_p. 13.
1039 DBu089_CALL 1 (recognition)_F_Burundi_RSA_30/5/2024_307 576_FR_Database_p. 17.

twenty years.'[1040] The conclusion that certain details expected from applicants are simply irrelevant for the legal analysis of their application for international protection is reflected in some CALL judgements too. In Nella's case for example, the CALL argued:

> 'Although [...] there are still some grey areas in the applicant's statements, [...] she was nevertheless able to provide relevant and detailed information that testifies to actual experiences. [...] [T]he fact that [she] did not know the **exact date** on which [her partner] began **working as a taxi driver** is **not decisive**, [...]. The Council also considers that the **reason why the Burundian authorities** did not **visit** her partner's home until **five days after** his friends [(who raped her)] had left is also **irrelevant**.'[1041] | CASE OF NELLA

Similarly, in the abovementioned Iraqi case (of the applicant who had been sexually abused by his aunt under the threat that she would spread that he raped her), the CALL pointed out how the issue whether, upon discovery of the sexual abuse, the bedroom window and curtain were open, closed, or ajar, or whether he only heard his grandfather's screams before fleeing, 'relates to a completely marginal element in the applicant's statements.'[1042] The Council drew the same conclusion for two other contradictions found by the CGRS, namely whether or not he had shoes on when he fled and the number of rapes he suffered from his aunt. The Council stated: '[T]hese elements are [...] matters of detail [...] [which] alone cannot justify the refusal of his application for international protection.'[1043]

Finally, it should be noted that in certain cases, the CALL has also simply rejected the CGRS's finding that a story was insufficiently detailed as such, as in Amani's case:

> 'The Council was **not convinced by the grounds of the** [CGRS'] **decision**, which called into question the reality of the sexual abuse inflicted by the applicant's stepfather over a period of years. It noted that **the applicant had been able to provide information about this person and details of their life under the same roof**.'[1044] | CASE OF AMANI

1040 DG094_CALL 1 (annulment)_F_Guinea_RSA_GMC_VGNT_FM_DV_22/2/2024_302 063_FR_Database_p. 8.

1041 DBu083_CALL 1 (recognition)_ F_Burundi_RSA_11/4/2024_304 646_FR_Database_p. 12–13.

1042 DIq095_CALL 1 (recognition)_M_Iraq_RSA_DV_29/2/2024_302 595_FR_Database_p. 10 & 12.

1043 DIq095_CALL 1 (recognition)_M_Iraq_RSA_DV_29/2/2024_302 595_FR_Database_p. 10 & 12.

1044 NC004_CALL 1 (annulment)_1991_F_DRC_RSA_DV_17/1/2022_266 712_FR_NANSEN_p. 7.

3.3. DELAYED (DISCLOSURE IN) SGBV-RELATED ASYLUM PROCEDURES

3.3.1. ACCEPTANCE OF THE MYTH ON DELAYED DISCLOSURE

a) Delayed (Disclosure During) SGBV-Related Asylum Procedures

A specific type of internal inconsistency occurs when applicants do not immediately disclose their fears and/or experiences of SGBV during their asylum procedure or wait to introduce a SGBV-related procedure in the first place. This results in an inconsistency between the earlier situation in which SGBV was not invoked, and a later application or version of the facts in which it was. In the Belgian asylum procedure, the law in principle requires applicants for international protection to submit their application as soon as possible (at the time of entry or at least within 8 working days).[1045]

Delayed submission of an application can also be a reason for the authorities to apply an accelerated procedure, when applicants entered the territory or prolonged their stay unlawfully and, without good reasons, did not submit an application as soon as possible.[1046] Further, the benefit of the doubt that may be granted to applicants under certain conditions requires in any case that applicants have submitted their application as soon as possible, or provided good reasons why they failed to do so.[1047] While authorities can assess such 'good reasons' in a discretionary manner, the interviews and case law analysis for this research uncovered how they are often inclined to consider delayed (disclosure in) SGBV-related asylum procedures as an indication of non-credibility.[1048]

1045 Art. 50, §1 Belgian Aliens Act.

1046 Art. 57/6/1, §1, h] *ibid.*; E.g. DSu147_CGRS 1 (refusal)_F_Suriname_RSA_VGNT_FM_DV_9/5/2023_301 074_NL_Database_p. 2.

1047 Concretely, when applicant's statements are not supported by evidence, these do not need confirmation when (cumulatively): (a) the applicant has made a genuine effort to substantiate the application; (b) all relevant elements at the applicant's disposal have been submitted (or a satisfactory explanation has been given for the lack thereof); (c) the applicant's statements are found to be coherent, plausible, and in line with COI; (d) the applicant has applied at the earliest possible time (or good reason are given for not having done so); and (e) the general credibility of the applicant has been established. Interestingly, in the new EU Qualification Regulation, conditions d] and e) have been rephrased to 'the general credibility of the applicant has been established, taking into account, inter alia, the time at which the applicant applied for international protection'. Art. 48/6, §4, d] *ibid.*; Art. 4(5]d EU Qualification Regulation; Art. 4(5]e EU Qualification Directive.

1048 Lore Roels, 'How Protecting Your Daughter Can Lead You to Being Denied International Protection in Belgium: On Rape Mythology, Delayed Disclosure, and Asylum' (*Refugee Law Initiative Blog*, 11 May 2023), https://rli.blogs.sas.ac.uk/2023/05/11/how-protecting-your-daughter-can-lead-you-to-being-denied-international-protection-in-belgium/.

In doing so, they demonstrated another form of acceptance of the SGBV disclosure myth, namely the one on delayed disclosure.

Although this reasoning too is relevant outside gender-specific asylum procedures, for SGBV in particular, it embodies a certain scepticism with which (alleged) survivors/victims of SGBV are generally treated in legal contexts and again reflects the belief that SGBV stories are regularly fabricated.[1049] They resonate with established rape myths, such as: 'an ideal victim would tell immediately,'[1050] '[a sexual violence survivor/victim] will disclose [...] at the first reasonable opportunity,'[1051] and 'delays in disclosure [should] be associated with dishonesty.'[1052]

In the Belgian asylum procedure, acceptance of the delayed disclosure myth focuses both on 1) delays in submitting the first application and delays: 2) within the same interview, 3) within the same procedure, or 4) across (subsequent) procedures (in Belgium or abroad). The first type was voiced by a PO, who explained that the credibility of applicants claiming to have fled their country because of sexual violence, is impacted when they did not apply for international protection as soon as possible.[1053] In the case law, this delay was at times associated with 'passive behaviour that is hardly compatible with a well-founded fear of persecution.'[1054] The argument is also used for (relatively) shorter delays, like three,[1055] four,[1056] six[1057] or eight[1058] months after arriving in Belgium. The latter was the case for Mary, who was forced into prostitution upon arrival in Belgium as mentioned above.

Secondly, delayed disclosure within the same interview, already framed as 'evolutive answers' above, is found to undermine applicants' credibility.

1049 International Commission of Jurists (ICJ), 'Sexual Violence Against Women: Eradicating Harmful Gender Stereotypes and Assumptions in Laws and Practice' (2015) 14; Council of Europe (CoE) and Louise Hooper, 'Gender-Based Asylum Claims and Non-Refoulement: Articles 60 and 61 of the Istanbul Convention: A Collection of Papers on the Council of Europe Convention on Preventing and Combating Violence against Women and Domestic Violence' (2019) 38; Keygnaert and Linthout (n 177) 22; Rousseau and others (n 7) 57.

1050 United Nations Office on Drugs and Crime (UNODC) and Skinnider (n 161) 102.

1051 Elaine Craig, 'The Relevance of Delayed Disclosure to Complainant Credibility in Cases of Sexual Offence' (2011) 36 Queen's Law Journal 1, 2; United Nations Office on Drugs and Crime (UNODC) and Skinnider (n 161) 90.

1052 Pertek, Phillimore and Goodson (n 997) 15.

1053 CB007_CGRS_PO_[00:31:00].

1054 DA099_A_CGRS 1 (manifestly ill-founded)_M_Albania_DV_6/7/2023_303 553_FR_Database_p. 2.

1055 DGa102_CALL 1 (refusal)_F_The Gambia_FM_DV_24/4/2024_305 436_FR_Database_p. 9.

1056 NGe014_CALL 1 (manifestly ill-founded)_1975_F_Georgia_RSA_DV_16/3/2022_269 856_NL_NANSEN_p. 20.; NGe014_CGRS 1 (manifestly ill-founded)_1975_F_Georgia_RSA _DV_31/8/2021_269 856_NL_NANSEN_p. 4.

1057 DS088_CGRS 1 (refusal)_F_Senegal_RSA_GMC_VGNT_FM_DV_19/7/2023_307 398_FR_Database _p. 10.

1058 NL017_CGRS 1 (refusal)_1980_F_Liberia_ STFP_GMC_VGNT_FM _17/2/2022_NL_NANSEN_p. 4.

One PO explained that stories are considered stereotypical when 'the person will give one tiny element of response at a time, but [they] already had the opportunity to express themselves before.'[1059] A Guinean domestic violence case illustrated this reasoning. The CGRS noted the applicant's 'evolving statements,' since she first only mentioned forced labour as domestic violence, 'only to say, later, when asked about [her] submitted documents [...], that this man also hit [her].' Consequently, the decision concludes that the evolutive nature of her account 'completely destroys' the credibility of these experiences.[1060]

Thirdly, when SGBV is only disclosed later in the same asylum procedure (at the stage of the CGRS or the CALL), one PO clearly stated that the earlier the violence is mentioned, preferably at the IO, the better.[1061] By contrast, the CALL (in the Burundian rape case mentioned on p. 207) stressed that 'the purpose of the hearings at the IO is not to obtain a full and detailed account of the applicant's story, but rather to provide an opportunity for the applicant to present their case.'[1062] However, this delayed disclosure reasoning was used at the appeal stage in another Afghan case of an applicant who feared being killed by persons from Jamaat Tablighi, a transnational missionary movement where he attended religious studies, he was trained as a suicide bomber, and fellow students were sexually abused.[1063] The CGRS refused to grant him refugee status because 'the applicant did not refer in any way to the problems he was having [...] at Jamaat Tablighi during his first interview at the IO.'[1064]

Fourthly, delayed disclosure is also identified across subsequent procedures in Belgium or abroad. The latter was confirmed by an attaché naming as a major reason for disbelief, in particular in gender-related cases, 'discrepancies with the story in another European member state.'[1065] While the interviewed asylum officials claimed negative credibility assessments might be drawn from late SGBV disclosure in the fifth/sixth[1066] or seventh/eighth[1067] procedure, all

1059 CB001_CGRS_PO_[00:17:37].

1060 DG087_CGRS 1 (refusal)_F_Guinea_RSA_GMC_VGNT _DV_2/10/2023_305 819_FR_Database_p. 14.

1061 CB004_CGRS_PO_[00:46:19].

1062 DBu089_CALL 1 (recognition)_F_Burundi_RSA_30/5/2024_307 576_FR_Database_p. 16.

1063 DAf142_CGRS 3 (inadmissible)_M_Afghanistan_RSA_15/9/2022 307 178_NL_Database_p. 13.

1064 DAf142_CGRS 3 (inadmissible)_M_Afghanistan_RSA_15/9/2022 307 178_NL_Database_p. 13.

1065 E.g. 'For example, a woman [...] who had first [...] gone to France [basing her application on] political affiliation [...] and then to Belgium and said that it was because [her] ex-boyfriend hit her. '(RB003_CALL_Attaché_[00:08:4].).

1066 CB001_CGRS_PO_[00:43:26].

1067 RB002_CALL_Attaché_[00:50:48].

examples in the case law analysis already concerned the second procedure. One of these was the case of Diana and Erina, mother and daughter.

CASE OF DIANA & ERINA			
• Country of origin:	Albania	• SGBV types:	Rape/sexual assault, violence related to gender norm transgression, forced marriage & domestic violence
• Gender identity:	Women	• Decisions for Diana:	CGRS 1 (manifestly ill-founded) – 29/05/2019
• Birth year:	1973 (D)		CALL 1 (refusal) – 7/04/2020 – n° 234 950
	2006 (E)		CGRS 2 (inadmissible) – 21/10/2021
• Interview by:	Researcher		CALL 2 (refusal) – 21/03/2022 – n° 270 155
		• Decisions for Erina:	CGRS 1 (inadmissible) – 2/12/2021
			CALL 1 (refusal) – 7/09/2022 – n° 276 951
			CGRS 2 (inadmissible) – 14/9/2023
			CALL 2 (refusal) – 8/5/2024 – n° 306 251

According to their statements, Diana and Erina, a mother and her 14-year-old daughter at the time, fled Albania in 2019 to escape severe **verbal, psychological, physical, and sexual violence** inflicted by their ex-husband/father. During her parents' forced marriage, Erina was born out of **marital rape**. Apart from Erina and her brother, Diana's ex-husband had prevented previous pregnancies through **forced abortion** and physical violence, leading to miscarriages. He was a convicted criminal for fraud, assault, and attempted murder, but never for the violence towards his family. Upon his release from prison, he returned home, once again abusing Diana while pregnant. When Erina was five months old, he abandoned the family and left for the UK, only to be extradited back to Albania twice, in 2011 and 2012. Upon his return, their home became a site of constant violence and psychological terror. Erina and her brother faced daily **beatings, death threats** – including threats with a **knife** – and exposure to their father's **exhibitionism**. They witnessed their mother being **raped, strangled, and threatened with firearms**. Meanwhile, their father refused to work, drank a lot, engaged in human trafficking, stole from Diana, and accumulated significant debt. As a result, their family home was repeatedly targeted by criminal associates seeking retribution. Desperate for protection, Diana and Erina sought help from authorities at least 16 times, filing complaints and requesting protection orders. Diana only managed to secure temporary protection orders for herself, but never for her children and parents, who also suffered violence. Nonetheless, the Albanian authorities consistently failed to enforce these orders, allowing the abuse to continue. Police on several occasions dismissed their complaints, refusing to document property damage or collect evidence.

(continued)

After years of **legal battles sabotaged** by her husband, Diana was finally granted a divorce in 2015. However, the ruling allowed Erina's father **unsupervised visitation rights** with her every weekend and during school holidays. In 2018, while Diana was briefly away in Switzerland, Erina stayed with her maternal grandparents. During this time, her father violently broke into their home, changed the locks, and repeatedly threatened them. He even filed a police report accusing the grandparents of kidnapping Erina, prompting law enforcement to actively pressure her into meeting him. This led to an attempted **abduction**, during which the father and his sisters tried to take Erina to his hometown, where he planned to hide and **force her into marriage** at age 13. With the help of her maternal aunt, Erina managed to escape. Despite multiple **kidnapping attempts** afterwards, including at her school, the authorities failed to act. A month before fleeing Albania, Diana encountered her ex-husband in court while another temporary protection order was still in place. He openly threatened her, but despite an alleged arrest warrant and her contacting the police, he remained free. The police advised Diana to change the locks and stay indoors. Having been forced to **quit her job** due to the ex-husband's threats at her workplace and to eventually **take Erina out of school** for safety, Diana saw no choice but to flee.

In March 2019, Diana and Erina left Albania for Belgium, where Diana initially applied for international protection alone. After her case was found manifestly ill-founded in an accelerated procedure due to Albania being a safe country of origin (which was confirmed in appeal), Diana applied a second time, and Erina a first time in her own name in 2021. In between these procedures, Belgian police questioned Diana following an **international child abduction complaint** filed by Erina's father from Albania. He continued to harass their relatives in Albania, demanding to know their whereabouts. In support of their applications, Erina and Diana submitted multiple documents, such as the divorce certificate including visitation rights, multiple medical and psychological certificates, the invitation letter from the Belgian police, and an official document stating the ex-husband's convictions.

Diana only mentioned the attempted abductions of and forced marriage threats towards Erina in her second (or first subsequent) procedure, in an attempt to protect Erina – upon her request – from having to talk about this in a personal interview. The CALL judged this delay as follows:

> '[I]f the applicant really harbours a fear that her ex-husband will take her daughter away and marry her off […], it may reasonably be expected of her that she would have already **mentioned [this] during her first application**. […] [T]he fact that [she] […] fails to [do so], **merely because her daughter asked her not to go into detail about her**, is **by no means serious** and **in no way proportional** to the risk she claims they would both run if they returned to Albania. The fact that the applicant did

not mention this during her initial request certainly undermines its credibility.'[1068] | CASE OF DIANA

Acceptance of the delayed disclosure myth is detected at all the abovementioned procedural stages. As a result, applicants who are unwilling or unable to talk about their SGBV fears/experiences immediately, risk to find themselves in a catch-22 situation. When they immediately apply for international protection, but disclose the violence later in this procedure, they might be found not credible, as happened with Diana. When they postpone the personal interview to avoid this, for example through medical certificates confirming their inability to talk about the facts, as in Vera's aforementioned case,[1069] a negative decision might be based solely on the (in her case incomplete and inaccurate) IO interview and lead to a refusal too. When they delay their first application until they feel ready to disclose, this passivity too might be found irreconcilable with a genuine fear of SGBV.[1070] When they attempt to disclose the violence in a first procedure, but in a limited way due to the disclosure barriers they face, and feel ready to provide more information at a later stage in a subsequent procedure, this might lead to an inadmissibility decision because no new elements (i.e. significantly increasing the likelihood of granting international protection) are provided.

The latter was the case in Erina's second procedure, where the CGRS argued:

'Although you stated that you **wanted to tell more details about what had happened** to you, you did **not cite elements that you could not mention before** [...]. You did not shine any new light on the main element of the decision taken in the context of your previous application.'[1071] | CASE OF ERINA

The decision in her previous procedure found her application inadmissible too, based on the conclusion that her story fully aligned with the problems already mentioned by her mother and that she did not cite any elements of her own that would justify a separate application.[1072] This practice was termed the 'transfer of non-credibility' by one attaché,[1073] but appears to be a contested practice among authorities.

1068 NA001_B_CALL 2 (refusal)_1973_F_Albania_RSA_VGNT_FM_DV 21/3/2022 270 155_NL_NANSEN_p. 11.

1069 Art. 18, §2, part 1-4 Belgian Royal Decree on the CGRS.

1070 E.g. DA099_A_CGRS 1 (manifestly ill-founded)_M_Albania_DV_6/7/2023_303 553_FR_Database_p. 2.

1071 NA001_A_CGRS 2 (inadmissible)_2006_F_Albania_RSA_VGNT_FM_DV_14/9/2023_306 251_NL_NANSEN_MINOR_p. 4.

1072 NA001_A_CGRS 1 (inadmissible)_2006_F_Albania_RSA_VGNT_FM_DV_2/12/2021_276 951_NL_NANSEN_MINOR_p. 4.

1073 RB002_CALL_Attaché_[00:21:08].

One PO stated that if applicants for example belatedly '[weave] a rape into [other] events that they had invoked [before, but] that were considered non-credible, confirmed by the CALL, [...] we are talking about *res judicata*, [...] that is impossible.'[1074] However, an attaché at the CALL nuanced this, explaining that they used to transfer non-credibility of one part of a narrative to the other parts that were not substantiated, arguing that previously given false information 'will compromise the overall credibility of the story.' Now, according to them, the CALL avoids making such transfers of non-credibility altogether.[1075] Indeed, the reasoning that if someone first only concisely discloses an SGBV experience/fear, this automatically renders any subsequent application offering more details inadmissible, raises substantial questions.

b) *Assessment of Justifications for Delayed Disclosure/Procedures*

The Belgian asylum officials themselves indicated a number of factors that could (partially) justify applicants' delayed disclosure, such as: how the person arrived in Belgium,[1076] how delayed the disclosure is,[1077] how well articulated the reasons for the delay are,[1078] or which type of SGBV they disclose. One interview[1079] and one KAP survey respondent[1080] believed that disclosure of sexual violence would be more difficult and justified more delay than forced marriage for example. It should be noted that such reasoning risks trivialising marital rape, present in most forced marriages, which in turn can be linked to other existing rape myths, such as: 'Husbands cannot rape their wives.'[1081]

In contrast, other asylum officials and cases analysed did not see a justification for delayed disclosure at all. One PO for example stated bluntly: 'I find it hard to see how, in front of a stupid civil servant like me, a woman would not dare to tell me "I'm afraid I'm going to be circumcised".'[1082] Some labelled it a sign of procedural abuse, estimating that false gender cases are more prevalent for specific countries of origin. One PO for example claimed that Iraqi applicants, if their first application has been rejected, tend to 'suddenly mention something about sexual violence.'[1083]

1074 CB001_CGRS_PO_[00:43:26].
1075 RB002_CALL_Attaché_[00:21:08].
1076 CB007_CGRS_PO_[00:31:00].
1077 RB002_CALL_Attaché_[00:50:48].
1078 RB006_CALL_Judge_[00:50:15].; RB007_CALL_Attaché_[00:59:35].; CB001_CGRS_PO_[00:47:04].; CB007_CGRS_PO_[00:34:12].
1079 CB015_CGRS_Supervisor+PO_GENDER_[00:19:26].
1080 R_3fSFAvlx87VK7YK_CGRS_PO/supervisor/gender coordinator/CEDOCA member.
1081 Edwards and others (n 9) 763; McGee and others (n 400) 3587.
1082 CB013_CGRS_PO_[01:10:31].
1083 CB002_CGRS_PO_[00:08:04].

Others casted justifications aside, qualifying immediate disclosure as a legal duty of applicants to cooperate in accordance with the burden of proof resting on them.[1084] One attaché explained finding delayed disclosure instantly suspicious, because refugee law is based on the idea of asking protection in another country, implying that applicants must therefore 'make explicit [...] what [they] need protection from'[1085] This reasoning was followed in the case for Ana, who only disclosed the continuous domestic violence she suffered from her husband, accompanying her to Belgium, at the stage of the CALL. The judge refused her refugee status, stating:

> 'that the **burden of proof** [...] rests with the applicant [...], who should provide all useful elements [...] as soon as possible. The fact that [she] **hoped** [...] **that the violence would stop** [**in Belgium**] **does not detract from this** in any way. [...] [A]n applicant is **obliged to cooperate** fully from the start of the procedure [...]. Moreover, the fact that someone turns to the authorities of a particular country in order to have their status as a refugee recognised inherently involves **trust in the authorities** from whom protection is sought. [...] [T]he applicant was explicitly informed [at the CGRS] ... of her duty to cooperate [...] and that correct statements were expected from her. [...] The [...] applicant could reasonably be expected to have mentioned the problems with her husband that occurred prior to her departure from Georgia, given the guarantees of **privacy and confidentiality** during her interview at the [CGRS]'[1086] | CASE OF ANA

Justifications put forward by applicants themselves for delayed disclosure were also met with scepticism by Belgian decision makers. Fear of or coping with perpetrators or authorities was for example rejected as a justification in both the cases of Ana[1087] and the abovementioned (p. 171) Georgian journalist (who out of fear refused to share the name of the police officer who raped her[1088]). An attaché, trying to put themselves in applicants' shoes, stated: 'If I were to ask for protection from Belgium or France, the idea of protection would prevail and I would be less afraid [to disclose]'[1089] Problems during an interview, such as

1084 Art. 4(1) EU Qualification Directive. This article states: 'Member States may consider it the duty of the applicant to submit as soon as possible all the elements needed to substantiate the application for international protection'.

1085 RB003_CALL_Attaché_[00:17:32].

1086 DGe144_CALL 1 (refusal)_1985_F_Georgia_RSA_DV_29/05/2024_307 462_NL_Database_ p. 7–8.

1087 DGe144_CALL 1 (refusal)_1985_F_Georgia_RSA_DV_29/05/2024_307 462_NL_Database_ p. 7–8.

1088 DGe137_CALL 1 (refusal)_F_Georgia_RSA_DV_23/5/2024_307 106_NL_Database_p. 24.

1089 RB003_CALL_Attaché_[00:17:32].

applicants not being heard in their mother tongue[1090] or not feeling comfortable to talk about SGBV in front of a male PO,[1091] have also been rejected as justifications for delayed disclosure in the analysed data.

Applicants bringing up problems accessing their traumatic memories as a justification are also met with disbelief, such as in Mary's CALL judgement.[1092] In some cases, applicants only later disclose SGBV while/after receiving psychological support, such as a Guinean applicant whose psychologist told her that, over the years, 'she had buried something deep inside her' and had eventually helped her to talk about it. However, the CGRS pointed at the time passed since the psychological treatment started (in 2018) and the lack of clarification as to why she was only able to talk about the sexual violence now, during her second asylum procedure.[1093]

On wanting to protect others as a justification, like Diana who wanted to shield Erina from having to recall difficult memories during a stressful interview, a gender-specialised supervisor at the CGRS replied: 'If you really want to protect someone, it is better to disclose […], so that is actually a reverse reasoning.'[1094] Diana's[1095] and Yusuf's cases both testify to some asylum authorities' tendency to also discard shame or taboo around SGBV disclosure as a reason for delays:

> 'Although the Council can understand that the applicant **did not dare to speak** to the IO about the sexual advances because of the **sensitivity** of the situation, together with the [CGRS], it **cannot be seen why the applicant initially made no mention** of his father being approached when the forced recruitment attempts were brought up.'[1096]
> | CASE OF YUSUF

Marjorie's case below illustrates the dismissal of two more explanations for delayed submission of applications, namely a lack of knowledge about the asylum procedure and a sense of safety for the period of the delay.

1090 For example the fact that in Yusuf's interview, he was told to be brief and was assisted by a Pashtou interpreter while Dari is his mother tongue. These problems were discarded as a justification in his case (DAf150_CALL 1 (refusal)_M_Afghanistan_RSA_8/3/2024_302 900_NL_Database_p. 14–15.).

1091 CB013_CGRS_PO_[01:14:09].

1092 NL017_CALL 1 (refusal)_1980_F_Liberia_STFP_GMC_VGNT_FM_10/08/2022_275 866_NL_NANSEN_p. 9.

1093 DG073_CGRS 2 (inadmissible)_F_Guinea_RSA_FM_DV_23/6/2023_302 978_FR_Case law selection by CALL_p. 3.

1094 CB008_CGRS_Supervisor+PO_GENDER_[00:34:27].

1095 'With regard to the [threats of forced marriage towards her daughter], the applicant [stated] she had not mentioned this because her daughter […] was ashamed [of talking about this violence] […]. However, the applicant never concealed that her ex-husband was violent towards herself and her children […] [and] she could reasonably be expected to have already mentioned [this] during her initial application.' (NA001_B_CALL 2 (refusal)_1973_F_Albania_RSA_VGNT_FM_DV_21/3/2022_270 155_NL_NANSEN_p. 10.).

1096 DAf150_CALL 1 (refusal)_M_Afghanistan_RSA_8/3/2024_302 900_NL_Database_p. 15.

CASE OF MARJORIE			
• Country of origin:	Suriname	• SGBV types:	Rape/sexual assault, violence related to gender norm transgression, forced marriage & domestic violence
• Gender identity:	Woman	• Decisions in file:	CGRS 1 (refusal) – 9/5/2023
• Birth year:	/		CALL 1 (refusal) – 5/2/2024 – n° 301 074
• Interview by:	/		

According to her statements, Marjorie was forcibly married off by her parents to a man who repeatedly **physically and sexually abused** her, including through **death threats**. He was also physically violent towards her daughter and son. She could not find support with her family, since they felt that once married, she had to stay with her husband. In January 2019, Marjorie took her children and secretly fled the home to move in with acquaintances, to whom she had explained the situation and who wanted to help. She managed to divorce her husband in April 2019. Because of this, her family cut off all contact, except for her brother, who called and threatened her for **disgracing the family**. She received similar **death threats** from her ex-husband's family. Fearing retaliations, she left Suriname with her daughter in October 2019.

After arriving in Belgium, she met someone, with whom she started a relationship and gave birth to another daughter in January 2021. However, the father did not want to take care of this child and left Marjorie. After a failed attempt at family reunification with her brother, who lives in the Netherlands, Marjorie applied for international protection in August 2022. Upon return to Suriname, she feared being killed by her ex-husband, his family, or her brother, and that her youngest daughter would be at risk of ostracism as an extramarital child. Due to this delayed application, for which her reasons were not considered a justification, her case was assessed in an accelerated procedure.

When Marjorie's oldest daughter mentioned, during the personal interview, that they were not aware of the procedure and conditions for being recognised as a refugee, the CGRS rejected this explanation by arguing:

> '[You] can reasonably be expected, after arrival **in countries that have signed and implement the Geneva Convention**, to **gather information about and to invoke the protection options provided therein** […] as soon as possible […]. The fact that you did not do this seriously calls the validity of your application into question.'[1097] | CASE OF MARJORIE

This reasoning was confirmed in the interview with a gender-specialised PO, naming as an insufficient justification for delay: having only just arrived in

[1097] DSu147_CGRS 1 (refusal)_F_Suriname_RSA_VGNT_FM_DV_9/5/2023_301 074_NL_Database_p. 2–3.

Belgium or not yet being familiar with the procedure.[1098] As mentioned before (see Part I, Chapter 3.1.1), this lack of procedural knowledge is described in the literature as a form of 'hermeneutical injustice', when a marginalised position deprives persons of the resources to fit their own experiences in dominantly accepted frameworks and make (in this case legal) sense of them.[1099]

Another example of such hermeneutical injustice occurs when applicants are unable to (immediately) frame the SGBV they experienced/fear as persecution (in the sense of the UN Refugee Convention) that could give rise to international protection. An attaché at the CALL illustrated their incomprehension on such inability through a case of a Rwandese woman, who 'was a victim of violence and they [had] burnt [her] thighs with an iron.' She had only disclosed this experience when she was about to be deported, upon which the attaché asked themselves: 'Why didn't she say it the first time? Because she had a better chance of getting the status? [...] When you have such serious facts that you can invoke, why don't you invoke them?'[1100]

Another example is the case of a Georgian applicant, who only at the end of her personal interview, as a side matter, mentioned the attempted sexual violence she experienced, by a family friend and on the metro, both as a child and as an adult. Both the CALL and CGRS argued that, although such incidents are deeply regrettable, 'after having had several opportunities, you [...] only brought [this] up at the end of your interview after the question of whether you were ever physically assaulted.'[1101] In light of asylum authorities' duty to collaborate in asylum procedures,[1102] it could be argued that they also have a responsibility to identify possible fears of persecution that are not framed as such by the applicants (and questioned, other than that, what the purpose of this last question in the personal interview would be).

A similar reflection arises concerning the expectation that applicants immediately and actively request special procedural guarantees themselves. In Marjorie's case, although she disclosed the violence she experienced from the start of the procedure on, she only made her trauma-related vulnerabilities explicit in the appeal procedure. The CALL concluded:

> '[T]he applicant has made **no mention** [at the CGRS] **of any traumatic vulnerability factors** [...]. [Her] general, unsubstantiated [...] **accusation that the [CGRS] did not**

1098 CB015_CGRS_Supervisor+PO_GENDER_[00:17:25].

1099 Fricker (n 226) 1.

1100 RB007_CALL_Attaché_[00:56:14].

1101 DGe138_CALL 1 (refusal)_1998_F_Georgia_RSA_DV_23/5/2024_307 108_NL_Database_p. 15.; DGe138_CGRS 1 (refusal)_1998_F_Georgia_RSA_DV_27/12/2023_307 108_NL_Database_ p. 4.

1102 Art. 4(1) EU Qualification Directive. This article states: 'In cooperation with the applicant, it is the duty of the Member State to assess the relevant elements of the application'.

> **take her vulnerability sufficiently into account can hardly suffice.** The applicant's **late application** for international protection thus constitutes a **counter-indication of the seriousness** of her [case].'[1103] | CASE OF MARJORIE

Additionally, Marjorie explained that she only applied for international protection after the father of her youngest daughter had left her and she no longer felt protected from having to return to Suriname. The CALL replied:

> 'The argumentation [...] that [...] she **saw no other way out** [...] **only after [her daughter's father] abandoned her, cannot be accepted as a sufficient excuse** [for the applicant's late application]. Nor can it condone why, all this time, she failed to make at least an attempt to secure permanent protection against the alleged fears that forced her to leave her country of origin.'[1104] | CASE OF MRAJORIE

Oppositely, a sense of insecurity and vulnerability may also cause an applicant to delay an application for international protection. In the abovementioned Georgian case (of a bisexual man forced to marry a woman by her family), the applicant's homelessness, due to the ongoing reception crisis in the Belgian asylum system,[1105] was also rejected as a justification for his delayed application by the CALL. The latter stressed the 'complete irreconcilability' between the urgency of his flight out of Georgia in search of safety on the one hand and his delay of almost a year and a half to apply for international protection on the other. He explained that there were long waiting lines to register, that others told him that he would not be granted shelter, and that he then looked for other solutions to avoid becoming homeless and seek (immediate physical) safety. Regardless, the Council argued that these explanations 'can offer no excuse [...] [since s]ubmitting an application for international protection [...] creates (or at least should create) the right to reception.'[1106]

3.3.2. REBUTTAL OF THE MYTH ON DELAYED DISCLOSURE

Below, I will set out the rebuttal in both health/social sciences and law/legal sciences of the delayed disclosure myth, as well as its reflection in the interviews

---

1103 DSu147_CALL 1 (refusal)_F_Suriname_RSA_VGNT_FM_DV_5/2/2024_301 074_NL_Database_ p. 7.

1104 DSu147_CALL 1 (refusal)_F_Suriname_RSA_VGNT_FM_DV_5/2/2024_301 074_NL_Database_ p. 7.

1105 Leni Linthout and others, 'Hoe het migratiebeleid van Nicole de Moor discrimineert: "Eerst vrouwen en kinderen, dan de honden. Pas daarna de mannen"' (*MO* Magazine*, 4 September 2023), www.mo.be/opinie/eerst-vrouwen-en-kinderen-dan-de-honden-pas-daarna-de-mannen.

1106 DGe110_CALL 1 (refusal)_1986_M_Georgia_VGNT_FM_27/3/2024_303 889_NL_Database_ p. 12.

and case law of the Belgian authorities. I will first demonstrate the lack of evidence for a link between delayed disclosure and truthfulness of SGBV, which can be explained by both internal and external factors, such as: recall deficit, avoidance, suppression, minimisation, fear, stigma, shame, distrust, (self-) accusation, or lack of self-identification as a survivor/victim.

In EU refugee (case) law, the Procedures Directive provides that refusal of international protection cannot solely rely on applicants' delayed application. Also, the CJEU has already judged that false statements by applicants, when clarified and withdrawn as soon as possible, cannot in themselves undermine applicants' overall credibility.[1107] The health/social sciences expertise on delayed disclosure can also be found translated to the asylum context in legal scholarship. The Belgian asylum authorities too partly recognise explanatory factors for delays, such as: the short duration of the IO interview, getting bad advice, homelessness, not being immediately threatened with deportation, or cultural embeddedness of SGBV leading applicants to only later identify their experiences as persecution.

a) *Rebuttal in Health & Social Sciences*

Considering late statements about SGBV as non-credible lacks scientific justification,[1108] as there is no evidence of a link between delays in disclosing SGBV and truthfulness. On the contrary, the EU Agency for Fundamental Rights' EU-wide survey on violence against women found that 35% of survivors/victims of sexual violence never spoke to anyone about the incident.[1109] A Belgian study showed that, among applicants for international protection specifically, '62% [...] did not talk to anyone about the sexual violence [they experienced]. If they did, they most often confided in an acquaintance (70%).'[1110]

Like the level of detail and consistency, the timing of (disclosure of SGBV during) an asylum procedure may be explained by both internal and external factors. Related to the memory, the abovementioned effects of trauma (see Chapter 3.2.2. above), such as recall deficit, avoidance, suppression, or minimisation of the facts, might also result in applicants' failure or reluctance

1107 *International Protection Appeals Tribunal and Others (Attentat au Pakistan)* [2023] Court of Justice of the European Union C-756/21 [96].

1108 Magugliani (n 93) 12; Saroléa, Sylvie, Raimondo, Francesca and Crine, Zoé, 'Through the Eyes of the "Vulnerable": Exploring Vulnerabilities in the Belgian Asylum System' (Zenodo 2022) 47.

1109 European Union Agency for Fundamental Rights (FRA), 'Violence against Women: An EU-Wide Survey. Main Results Report' (2014) 115.

1110 Keygnaert and others (n 713) 74; Lotte De Schrijver and others, 'Victimization of Applicants for International Protection Residing in Belgium: Sexual Violence and Help-Seeking Behavior' (2022) 19 International Journal of Environmental Research and Public Health 12889, 13.

to promptly disclose.[1111] External factors causing delays in disclosure include: fear, stigma, shame, distrust in the authorities, possible (self-)accusation, lack of self-identification as a survivor/victim (especially for men), fear of the perpetrator, effects of PTSD/other mental health problems, ...[1112]

Specifically, the element of shame, preventing applicants from disclosing, is typical for SGBV-related flight stories. According to Herman, in her work on trauma and recovery, such shame originates from survivors'/victims' feelings of 'helplessness, the violation of bodily integrity, and the indignity suffered in the eyes of another person.'[1113] Bloemen and Mellink confirm that the power of shame and honour 'can be so great that an asylum applicant will sometimes choose to remain silent [...] for the sake of safety, their own future and position in the family or community,' which is further reinforced by avoidance as a core trauma symptom.[1114]

This results in applicants being directed by a 'power of silence' at odds with the requirement to disclose all elements of a flight story immediately in the asylum procedure.[1115] Bögner et al. confirm this specificity of SGBV-related procedures, explaining how applicants with a SGBV history report 'more difficulties in disclosing personal information during [asylum] interviews, [are] more likely to dissociate during these interviews and [score] significantly higher on measures of post-traumatic stress symptoms and shame' than applicants with no SGBV history.[1116]

In light of this expertise, it seems more logical to assume that such barriers cause survivors/victims of SGBV to avoid, or at least postpone, disclosing the violence to anyone,[1117] regardless of how important the outcome of an asylum procedure is to their survival. Amani,[1118] Angele, and Zeynep illustrated the impact of fear, shame, and guilt on disclosure in their personal interviews as follows:

> '**No one knows** [about the rape]. [...] I **haven't even told my lawyer.** If [my husband] finds out, **he'll reject me.** [...] I'm **afraid** of men, I cannot even sleep with my husband. He thinks it's related to his experiences [...] I cry every day when I'm in the bathroom. [...] [I haven't contacted a psychologist. If I do, my husband] may know,

1111 Herlihy (n 731) 116; Keygnaert and Linthout (n 177) 22; Rousseau and others (n 7) 50.

1112 Herlihy (n 731) 116; Keygnaert and Linthout (n 177) 22; Rousseau and others (n 7) 50.

1113 Herman (n 713) 53.

1114 Bloemen and Mellink (n 932) 891–893.

1115 *Ibid.*

1116 Bögner, Herlihy and Brewin (n 934) 75.

1117 Craig (n 1051) 7.

1118 "[My stepfather] threatened me. He was telling me clearly that he was going to kill me ... if I dared to tell the truth .... [B]before [I had to tell my cousin], I didn't see how I could ..., I was ... very ashamed" (NC004_CGRS interview 2_1991_F_DRC_RSA_DV_FR_NANSEN_p. 5 & 8.).

he may realise it's a problem for me. He is a lawyer and has already had to deal with sexual violence.'[1119] | CASE OF ANGELE

'In our culture, virginity is very important *she cries* [...]. I find it very **humiliating** to explain [...], if you're raped, you're not [seen as] the victim but [as] **the guilty one**. [...] I was forced [...] to destroy all [evidence] [...] I was very very **afraid** of him [...] [and] that my family would find out because [...] they would say "god only knows **what you did to provoke him**," that's why [...] **I didn't tell anyone**. [...] I have **panic attacks** when I talk about it, so I couldn't.'[1120] | CASE OF ZEYNEP

One male applicant also linked this fear to male rape mythology, by explaining (through his lawyer in appeal) 'not having previously told about the sexual assault he suffered in Greece out of shame and fear that he would be accused of provocative behaviour and perceived as homosexual.'[1121]

b) Rebuttal in Law & Legal Sciences

The EU Procedures Directive is very clear on the matter that applications for international protection should 'neither [be] rejected nor excluded from examination on the sole ground that they have not been made as soon as possible.'[1122] However, it is important to note that this provision was not incorporated in the same explicit manner in the new EU Procedures Regulation. The CJEU ruled on the issue of delayed statements within asylum procedures in the *Attentat au Pakistan case*. This case concerned a Pakistani man showing serious indications of mental health problems, which may have resulted from traumatic events in his country of origin.[1123] Here, the Court confirmed that Article 4(5)e of the EU Qualification Directive (benefit of the doubt and the role of credibility therein) should be understood to mean that a false statement by an applicant in their 'initial application for international protection, which was clarified and withdrawn [...] at the first opportunity, does not in itself preclude a finding that the applicant can be considered broadly credible.'[1124]

In the European context, the Council of Europe therefore advises asylum authorities not to automatically take late disclosure as an indicator of non-credibility.[1125] UNHCR confirms this advice, both for delayed statements during

[1119] NC006_CGRS interview 1_2_3_1984_F_DRC_RSA_FR_NANSEN_p. 1 (memo).
[1120] NT015_CGRS interview 1_2_3_1996_F_Turkey_RSA_FM_DV_FR_p. 1, 7 & 9 (memo).
[1121] DP134_CALL 2 (annulment)_lawyers' argumentation_1989_M_Palestine_RSA_16/5/2024_306 755_NL_Database_p. 4.
[1122] Art. 10(1) EU Procedures Directive.
[1123] *International Protection Appeals Tribunal and Others (Attentat au Pakistan)* (n 1107) paras 14–24.
[1124] *Ibid.* 96.
[1125] Council of Europe (CoE) and Hooper (n 1049) 38–39.

an asylum procedure[1126] and for delayed asylum procedures as such, stressing that applicants may be found credible, regardless of whether their application was made at the earliest possible opportunity. In the case of late application or disclosure, asylum authorities should consider whether this delay could be explained by 'a desire to achieve security, [...] the effects of disorientation, language barriers, anxiety, [...] fear or mistrust of the authorities, [...] doubts about the procedure [...] [or] the effect of any trauma experienced, ... including avoidance, dissociation, and shame, [...] [which] may mean that an applicant does not [apply] until compelled by circumstances such as the threat of forced return.'[1127] This 'desire to achieve security' was demonstrated by the abovementioned Georgian man forced to live on the streets due to the Belgian asylum reception crisis.[1128] Delaying one's application until feeling a 'threat of forced return' was illustrated by Marjorie.

These internal and external barriers to timely disclosure are also recognised by other international actors (such as the Council of Europe, UNHCR, and the UN Voluntary Fund for Victims of Torture: in general[1129] and for men specifically[1130]) and in legal scholarship (in general[1131] and for men specifically[1132]). Phillimore and Pertek add that the #MeToo-movement has brought to light how survivors/victims in their country of origin (surrounded by friends/family, in their mother tongue) often take years to open up, while applicants for international protection are usually given neither time nor support.[1133]

Along the same lines as the CJEU, the Supreme Court of Canada for example has ruled that immediate SGBV disclosure can no longer be assumed, as the timing of disclosure is, alone, of no significance to a [sexual assault survivor/victim]'s credibility.[1134] The International Commission of Jurists

1126 UNHCR, 'Note Du Haut Commissariat Des Nations Unies Pour Les Réfugiés Relative à l'évaluation Des Demandes d'asile Introduites Par Des Femmes' (n 751) 2.

1127 UNHCR, 'Beyond Proof. Credibility Assessment in EU Asylum Systems (Full Report)' (n 19) 201–202.

1128 DGe110_CALL1(refusal)_1986_M_Georgia_VGNT_FM_27/3/2024_303889_NL_Database_ p. 12.

1129 UNHCR, 'Beyond Proof. Credibility Assessment in EU Asylum Systems (Full Report)' (n 19) ch 2.1 Delay in applying for asylum; Council of Europe (CoE) and Hooper (n 1049) 38–39; UN Voluntary Fund for Victims of Torture (n 731) 9.

1130 UNHCR, 'Working with Men and Boy Survivors of Sexual and Gender-Based Violence in Forced Displacement' (n 93) 11.

1131 Papoutsi and others (n 805) 1221; Craig (n 1051) 7.

1132 Magugliani (n 93) 11.

1133 Jenny Phillimore and Sandra Pertek, 'The Interests and Vulnerabilities of Female Forced Migrants Need to Be Recognised and Integrated within the National Strategy for Tackling Violence against Women and Girls' (*British Politics and Policy at LSE*, 30 November 2021), https://blogs.lse.ac.uk/politicsandpolicy/forced-migrants-sgbv/.

1134 Craig (n 1051) 7.

confirmed, by citing the Supreme Court of California: '[T]he overwhelming body of current empirical studies, data, and other information establishes that it is not inherently "natural" for the victim to confide in someone or to disclose, immediately following [...] [sexual assault]. Instead, survivors are often afraid of reporting the crime because of stigma and shame. If the perpetrator is someone the survivor knows personally, as is often the case, it can be even more difficult.'[1135]

c) *Rebuttal by Belgian Asylum Authorities*

In line with the evidence-based expertise set out above, one judge in the Belgian asylum procedure firmly categorised the idea that 'disclosing rape five years after it happened is implausible' as a stereotype.[1136] Other asylum officials, both at the CGRS[1137] and the CALL, also rebutted the delayed disclosure myth. One attaché, commenting on applicants who after confrontation at the hearing admit they lied about certain elements, went as far as stating: 'I've never seen a judgement stating "you lied here, so we don't believe you"'.[1138] When confronted with the reasoning in Diana's case, rejecting her explanation for delayed disclosure because she wanted to protect her daughter upon her request, several asylum officials expressed their dissenting opinion, stating for example: 'It will depend from judge to judge [...] [but] I think the majority [of judges] will accept this [as an explanation].'[1139] However, some asylum officials nuanced their myth rebuttal, by having it depend on how well the justifications for the delay are explained[1140] or on the context and individual background of the applicant.[1141]

Several asylum officials acknowledged that the fear, shame, guilt, trauma, taboo, or sensitivity around SGBV might explain delayed disclosure. One PO validated applicants' reluctance to disclose to protect themselves, by using an example very similar to Ana's case. They explained how an Algerian woman had initially applied for international protection with her husband but was refused. She applied a second time once she had separated from her husband, after the police had to intervene for domestic violence in Belgium. This PO acknowledged the epistemic injustice (see Part I, Chapter 3.1.1) applicants might face by only later identifying their experiences as violence that qualifies for international

1135 International Commission of Jurists (ICJ) (n 1049) 14.
1136 RB006_CALL_Judge_[00:13:33].
1137 CB014_CGRS_PO_[00:23:50].
1138 RB002_CALL_Attaché_[00:22:42].
1139 RB005_CALL_Judge_[00:43:44].
1140 RB006_CALL_Judge_[00:50:15].
1141 R_1Fsp6plXnoJCROB_CGRS_PO/supervisor/gender coordinator/CEDOCA member.

protection, often with help from professionals. The positive decision in this case was based on the fact that all her female family members had been forcibly married, leading the applicant to believe that 'this was just the way people got married in Algeria.'[1142] Once her husband had assaulted her in Belgium, 'she had been in contact with psychologists [...] and social workers who had made her realise that it was not normal and [...] she [...] hadn't understood that it could also be a reason for asylum.'[1143]

Other explanatory factors were recognised in the interviews too, such as: the short duration of the IO interview,[1144] getting bad advice[1145] (such as, brought up by applicants, from: lawyers,[1146] perpetrators,[1147] acquaintances,[1148] or non-legal advice[1149]), being homeless, or feeling no immediate threat to be deported. The latter is particularly relevant for 'people who are allowed to travel visa-free [...] [and] to stay [in Belgium] for 90 days, [mostly Georgians,] [...] they have no risk of being deported during that [...] period,' as one gender-specialised supervisor at the CGRS mentioned.[1150] However, other factors brought up by applicants, such as: mistrust in authorities, negative past experiences with SGBV disclosure, lack of knowledge on the procedure itself, or problems during the interview, are not mentioned as valid explanations throughout the interviews with authorities or analysed case law.

Similar to the Algerian case described by the PO above, but focusing on the practice of GMC, the CALL (in a judgement highlighted as important), took into account the widespread prevalence rate and cultural embeddedness of female GMC in Somalia. Therefore, the Council considered that 'the applicant could not be criticised for not [immediately] having made further statements on her own initiative [on her female GMC-related fears].'[1151] Another analysed judgement explicitly rejected the argument on delayed disclosure as irrelevant in the case of an applicant from Ivory Coast who

1142 CB004_CGRS_PO_[00:47:40].
1143 CB004_CGRS_PO_[00:47:40].
1144 R_3fSFAvlx87VK7YK_CGRS_PO/supervisor/gender coordinator/CEDOCA member.
1145 RB006_CALL_Judge_[00:10:07].
1146 DAf141_CALL 2 (refusal)_lawyers' argumentation_F_Afghanistan_RSA_307 173_NL_Database_p. 8.
1147 DN146_CALL 1 (refusal)_lawyers' argumentation_1993_F_Nigeria_STFP_NL_Database_p. 2.
1148 DGe110_CALL 1 (refusal)_lawyers' argumentation_1986_M_Georgia_27/3/2024_303 889_NL_Database_p. 7.
1149 DN108_CALL 1 (refusal)_lawyers' argumentation_F_Nigeria_GMC_FM_14/3/2024_303 213_NL_Database_p. 3.
1150 CB008_CGRS_Supervisor+PO_GENDER_[00:36:08].
1151 DSo067_CALL 1 (annulment)_1986_F_Somalia_GMC_FM_20/2/2024_301 914_NL_Case law selection by CALL_p. 22.

faced domestic violence because she was accused of sorcery and bringing misfortune. Here, the Council saw no valid reason to question the applicant's sincerity, arguing 'the mere fact that [she] has belatedly invoked [her fear] [...] does not constitute sufficient reason to challenge its reality,'[1152] in line with the CJEU *Attentat au Pakistan* case law.[1153]

3.4. DEMEANOUR DURING SGBV DISCLOSURE

3.4.1. ACCEPTANCE OF THE DISCLOSURE MYTH ON DEMEANOUR

Lastly, as mentioned above, asylum authorities might expect applicants to be 'visibly upset,'[1154] 'explicitly emotional'[1155] or 'angry but not too angry and [...] distressed but not excessively'[1156] when recalling an SGBV experience in order to be credible. This might lead decision makers to interpret certain (lack of) emotions or distress as signs of fabrication.[1157] Literature on female rape in the criminal justice context specifically has described how 'the perceived credibility of a [...] victim is strongly influenced by social stereotypes regarding [their] appropriate emotional expression.'[1158]

Interestingly, the Belgian asylum authorities use a specific term to describe applicants' demeanour and perceived authenticity while disclosing, namely: '*sentiment de vécu*' in French, or '*doorleefdheid*' in Dutch. Literally translated, these terms mean 'sense of experience' or 'lived-throughness'. While their use in decisions is widespread, the exact meaning and authorities' position towards them appear to be contested. On the one hand, one judge exceptionally interpreted the term from the point of view of decision makers, explaining: 'In the end, this

---

1152 DIC153_CALL 2 (recognition)_1979_F_Ivory Coast_RSA_GMC_VGNT_FM_DV_29/5/2024_307 471_FR_Case law selection by CALL_p. 14.

1153 *International Protection Appeals Tribunal and Others (Attentat au Pakistan)* (n 1107) para 96.

1154 McGee and others (n 400) 3586.

1155 Linda Alcoff and Laura Gray, 'Survivor Discourse: Transgression or Recuperation?' (1993) 18 Signs 260, 285.

1156 *Ibid.*

1157 Rousseau and others (n 7) 51.

1158 Ellen Wessel and others, 'Credibility of the Emotional Witness: A Study of Ratings by Court Judges' (2006) 30 Law and Human Behavior 221, 222.

'sense of experience' is the body of our intimate conviction.[1159] In fact, it's our job as judges to be convinced, to form our own convictions.'[1160]

On the other hand, most asylum officials attribute the terms 'sense of experience' or 'lived-throughness' to applicants. Some stated what it (could) mean, relating it to a personal/inner feeling or reflection, which this PO explained as: 'Deep down […] it doesn't sink in […] they don't feel it inside. And so what they say […] doesn't make sense at all.'[1161] Others linked it to applicants' emotions[1162] or level of detail[1163] while disclosing. The latter was reflected in Nella's case, where the CGRS concluded, right after mentioning the lack of detail on her stay in the hospital after being raped:

> 'Your comments **do not reflect any personal experience** and do not contain any information that could establish that you were the victim of an assault in the circumstances you have described.'[1164] | CASE OF NELLA

Other asylum officials explained what the term does not mean to them, namely a disclosure that is: short/dry,[1165] too clear/explicit,[1166] or that sounds like 'a little story'.[1167]

Interestingly, in contrast to the established rape myth on demeanour (that true SGBV survivors/victims are visibly upset[1168]), in the asylum context, some decision makers believe that showing (too many) emotions is not indicative of truthfulness either. One PO stated that 'just [showing] emotions won't

---

1159 Interestingly, this notion of 'intimate conviction' originates from the French-language (continental) criminal law tradition and stands for decision makers' 'free evaluation of evidence according to conscience' or 'moral certainty'. In criminal law, the standard of proof requires decision makers to presume innocence unless they are convinced 'beyond reasonable doubt' of the defendant's guilt. However, in administrative law, applied in asylum procedures, this standard is brought back to a 'balance of probabilities'. Asylum authorities, based on the available evidence, must find an applicant's claim 'likely [to be] credible' or 'more probable than not to have occurred', but not credible beyond reasonable doubt according to their 'intimate conviction'. Therefore, the use of 'intimate conviction' in the asylum context risks to raise the standard of proof higher than required in refugee law. Demetra Fr Sorvatzioti and Allan Manson, 'Burden of Proof and L'intime Conviction: Is the Continental Criminal Trial Moving to the Common Law?' (2018) 23 Canadian Criminal Law Review 107, 107; Jacopo Della Torre, 'Taking the Evolution of the Standards of Proof for a Criminal Conviction Seriously' (2024) 8 Quaestio facti. Revista internacional sobre razonamiento probatorio 155, 180; UNHCR, 'Note on Burden and Standard of Proof in Refugee Claims' (1998) para 8.

1160 RB006_CALL_Judge_[01:08:25].

1161 CB001_CGRS_PO_[00:54:20].

1162 CB004_CGRS_PO_[00:33:21].; CB011_CGRS_Supervisor+PO_GENDER_[00:37:15].

1163 CB004_CGRS_PO_[00:32:02].

1164 DBu083_CGRS 1 (refusal)_F_Burundi_RSA_29/6/2023_FR_Database_p. 5.

1165 CB002_CGRS_PO_[00:08:04].

1166 CB003_CGRS_PO_[00:17:53].

1167 CB003_CGRS_PO_[00:17:53].

1168 McGee and others (n 400) 3586.

be enough,'[1169] since many applicants arrive in complicated circumstances, sometimes live on the streets, are away from home, ... which can also cause them to feel emotional or unwell. Another PO stated feeling moved if applicants are crying very heavily, but if their story 'is not "lived-through", then their crying is not going to change anything.'[1170]

Some interviewed decision makers approached the term positively, stating that it comes with experience,[1171] is useful to detect fraudulent stories,[1172] is used a lot,[1173] or even is 'the number one argument'[1174] in refugee status determination. One judge elaborated how it plays an extremely important role, since the majority of cases depend on the credibility of the statements. They admitted their reluctance to use the term at the beginning, associating it with subjectivity. However, later on, they evolved into admitting that 'this is true, [...] we are not machines.'[1175] In contrast, an attaché thought the notion was 'mainly [used by] the CGRS' and linked it to interviewers' impressions 'when they find themselves face to face with the person for several hours during the interview,' information to which the CALL has no access.[1176] The same judge who evolved into using the term did nuance that it requires caution by the CALL, since it is not guaranteed that non-verbal cues are written down in the personal interview notes.[1177]

The analysed case law illustrated how the term (or expressions similar to it)[1178] is in practice mainly linked to the three other aspects of SGBV disclosure mentioned above, namely the: detailedness[1179] (and applicants' attitude towards gathering details or ability to deliver details spontaneously[1180]), consistency,[1181]

1169 CB004_CGRS_PO_[00:33:21].
1170 CB014_CGRS_PO_[01:05:43].
1171 CB014_CGRS_PO_[01:07:25].; CB011_CGRS_Supervisor+PO_GENDER_[00:37:15].
1172 CB001_CGRS_PO_[00:54:20].
1173 CB003_CGRS_PO_[00:17:53].
1174 CB014_CGRS_PO_[01:03:40].
1175 RB006_CALL_Judge_[01:07:07].
1176 RB002_CALL_Attaché_[00:57:06].
1177 RB006_CALL_Judge_[01:10:17].
1178 Such as 'force de conviction', 'vécu spontané', 'ressenti personnel', 'dépourvu de vécu', réflection de votre vécu', 'empreint de vécu', 'sensation de vécu'.
1179 E.g. DG092_CGRS 1 (refusal)_F Guinea_RSA_VGNT_FM_DV_27/4/2023_299 471_FR_Database_p. 3.; DG073_CGRS 2 (inadmissible)_F_Guinea_RSA_FM_DV_23/6/2023_302 978_FR_Case law selection by CALL_p. 4.; DG097_CGRS 1 (refusal)_F_Guinea_RSA_GMC_FM_DV_5/4/2023_303 242_FR_Database_p. 3.; DGa102_CALL 1 (refusal)_F_The Gambia_FM_DV_24/4/2024_305 436_FR_Database_p. 9.; DGa102_CGRS 1 (refusal)_F_The Gambia_FM_DV_10/10/2023_305 436_FR_Database_p. 2–5.
1180 DG106_CGRS 1 (refusal)_F_Guinea_RSA_GMC_VGNT_FM_DV_4/9/2023_306 929_FR_Database_p. 4.
1181 E.g. DG092_CALL 1 (refusal)_F_Guinea_RSA_VGNT_FM_DV_4/1/2024_299 471_FR_Database_p. 14.; DN100_CGRS 1 (refusal)_1993_F_Nigeria_VGNT_FM_DV_6/10/2022_304 410_FR_Database_p. 7–8.

and delayed/evolutive nature[1182] of statements. Interestingly, while some authorities qualified 'evolutive answers' as non-credible (as mentioned in Chapter 3.2.1. above), one decision labelled the applicant's statements about her forced husband as 'incomplete [...] not very reflective of [her] experience. [...] [lacking] spontaneity [...] inflexible and poorly substantiated,'[1183] preventing them from being considered credible too.

The acceptance of the demeanour myth, linked to applicants' level of detail, can be illustrated by the case of Binta, where the CALL[1184] and CGRS argued:

> 'When asked about your husband, your concise remarks [...] do not give a **sense of experience** in your marriage. You do not know his age [...], and explain that he sold palm oil [...]. Asked more about him, you say that you 'did not observe him, not managing to look him in the eye' [...]. **Your comments about him remain general.** [...] Even when asked specifically about the fights you mentioned when talking about your scars [...] in more detail, [...] you only say that you kept a straight face when he hit you after coming home [...]. As for your reaction, you explain that you cried and screamed [...]. Even when asked to describe your **personal feelings,** you explain that you felt uncomfortable and upset, **without giving further details.**'[1185] | CASE OF BINTA

3.4.2. REBUTTAL OF THE DISCLOSURE MYTH ON DEMEANOUR

The rebuttal of the demeanour myth will first go into the empirically established range of emotional responses of survivors/victims during SGBV disclosure, going from hyper-reactivity to indifferent affect, making it practically impossible to base credibility assessments on such (non-)verbal cues. While, to my knowledge, no higher case law in the European context so far discusses the issue of demeanour during SGBV disclosure, the available expertise is taken up in legal scholarship in the field of refugee law. In the Belgian asylum context, I will illustrate rebuttal of this myth through the reluctance of some decision makers to use the terms 'sense of experience' or 'lived-throughness'

1182 DG106_CGRS 1 (refusal)_F_Guinea_RSA_GMC_VGNT_FM_DV_4/9/2023_306 929_FR_Database_p. 4.

1183 DG106_CGRS 1 (refusal)_F_Guinea_RSA_GMC_VGNT_FM_DV_4/9/2023_306 929_FR_Database_p. 4. Emphasis added.

1184 '[T]hat the applicant's statements were particularly lacking in detail, were incomplete and did not reflect a sense of experience [...], particularly about [her forced husband], their marital life, but also their arguments.' (DG082_CALL 1 (refusal)_F_Guinea_RSA_GMC_VGNT_FM_DV_11/4/2024_304 652_FR_Database_p. 11.).

1185 DG082_CGRS 1 (refusal)_F_Guinea_RSA_GMC_VGNT_FM_DV_20/6/2023_304 652_FR_Database _p. 3.

due to their subjective nature or the lack of definition or guidance on how to use them.

a) *Rebuttal in Health & Social Sciences*

The SGBV disclosure myth on demeanour has been elaborately rebutted in health and social sciences. Although asylum authorities seem to assume that recalling SGBV experiences in a stressful and emotionally triggering environment will facilitate memory,[1186] the direct question/answer method and stressful circumstances during a face-to-face interview seem to have a rather inhibiting effect on the already rigid access[1187] to such memories.[1188] More specifically, the forced recollection and talking about a traumatic event may return survivors/victims to the state they were in during victimisation, which may trigger the biological responses they had at that time, such as: fighting, fleeing, freezing or appeasing (see Chapter 4.2.1 below). This is particularly true for individuals who were in a state of dissociation during the event and did not receive any care afterwards.[1189]

As mentioned above (see chapters 3.2.2. & 3.3.2. above), symptoms of trauma, that might determine someone's demeanour while disclosing, include: re-experiencing, avoidance, negative cognition and mood, hyper-reactivity, suppression, avoidance, minimisation of the facts, idealisation of the perpetrator, indifference to defend oneself, and dissociation. Especially the latter 'can contribute to creating a situation of emotional control,' as expressed by the psychologist in Fatou's case and repeated by the CALL.[1190] Herman notes, in her work on trauma and recovery, that traumatic events may be encoded as 'truncated memor[ies], devoid of emotion,' whereby survivors/victims do not 'allow' themselves to think about the meaning behind these memories, since doing so would trigger too much suffering.[1191]

The same 'dialectic of trauma' as described above (see Chapter 3.2.2. above), leads trauma survivors/victims to be caught 'between floods of intense, overwhelming feeling and arid states of not feeling at all.'[1192] The implications for applicants' demeanour in disclosing trauma-related flight stories are explained by Rousseau et al. A claimant's mental vulnerability during an

1186 Herlihy, Jobson and Turner (n 804) 664; Middelburg and Balta (n 8) 443.

1187 Vermetten, Raaijmakers and Gersons (n 932) 283; Bloemen and Mellink (n 932) 894; Keygnaert and Linthout (n 177) 22.

1188 van Veldhuizen (n 891) 27; Bögner, Herlihy and Brewin (n 934) 79–80.

1189 Ellert Nijenhuis, Onno van der Hart and Kathy Steele, 'Trauma-Related Structural Dissociation of the Personality' (2010) 52 Activitas Nervosa Superior 1, 1; Lamonaca and others (n 280) 23.

1190 DG070_CALL 1 (recognition)_FGuinea_RSA_FM_DV_18/1/2024_300 255_FR_Case law selection by CALL_p. 21–22.

1191 Herman (n 713) 46.

1192 *Ibid.* 47.

interview or hearing may result in emotional responses or signs of distress that are misunderstood, ranging 'from nervous laughter to a blank and indifferent affect. Such anxiety is often expressed through cultural idioms unfamiliar to the decision maker, can result in hesitance or contradiction, and may be interpreted as a lack of credibility.'[1193]

Applicants (themselves in the interviews or via their lawyer or psychologist/psychiatrist in the appeal argumentation) have described their own demeanour throughout the procedure as: silent (incl. being unable to give spontaneous answers), emotional, scared, panicky, stressed (e.g. trembling or fidgeting), tired, depressed, apathic, confused, avoidant, detached, indifferent, or short. Research on the impact of SGBV on mental health has confirmed these possible emotional responses.[1194] This renders attempts to draw any credibility conclusions from someone's demeanour during SGBV disclosure futile. To complicate matters even further, as pointed out by Given-Wilson et al., 'decision makers' own beliefs, past experiences, and emotional state also affect their decision-making processes.'[1195]

b) Rebuttal in Law & Legal Sciences

Higher case law in the European context does not specifically deal with the issue of demeanour during disclosure of SGBV (or other trauma), nor on the use of the term 'sense of experience', to my knowledge at the time of writing. However, the EUAA does mention 'emotion at the oral hearing' in its judicial publication on evidence and credibility assessments. It hereby translates the abovementioned expertise to the asylum procedure, highlighting how interviews and hearings are interactive processes between individuals showing distress along a spectrum from 'openly distressed to withdrawn.'[1196] As such, asylum authorities should be aware of the fact that such physical signs are poor indicators of credibility and should 'take responsibility for their own emotional responses at hearings and when considering cases before them in purely written procedures.'[1197]

Amnesty International further divides this spectrum of possible demeanour while disclosing SGBV in verbal and non-verbal cues, confirming those described by applicants above. Verbally, applicants might: reply more slowly or suddenly not understand questions when they concern (possible) SGBV,

1193 Rousseau and others (n 7) 51.

1194 Josse (n 936) 184–193.

1195 Zoe Given-Wilson, Jane Herlihy and Matthew Hodes, 'Telling the Story: A Psychological Review on Assessing Adolescents' Asylum Claims.' (2016) 57 Canadian Psychology / Psychologie canadienne 265, 265.

1196 EUAA (European Union Asylum Agency) (n 988) 54.

1197 *Ibid.*

mention an unclear or non-specific physical complaint such as a headache, answer only part of the question or skip phases in the timeline in order to circumvent possibly difficult elements of the story, … Non-verbal signs might include: looking away, staring, freezing, crying, increasing nervousness, or physical unrest.[1198]

A report from the American Prosecutors Research Institute (APSI) confirms that SGBV survivors/victims might be 'unable to effectively answer questions regarding how and why the event happened and what meaning and implications the event has for a person's life' while being interviewed about their SGBV experiences.[1199] The fact that negative feelings or emotional numbness can complicate applicants' responsiveness in interviews/during hearings is also emphasised by the UN Office on Drugs and Crime.[1200] The same APSI report mentions possible emotional reactions like hyper-alertness, irritability, restlessness, outbursts of anger, but also mood swings (e.g. crying then laughing), minimisation of the violence, or emotional numbing.[1201]

McKinnon in her work uncovers how asylum authorities might expect applicants to 'perform gendered affect in the courtroom' matching the judge's gendered expectations of appropriate emotion. McKinnon and others, like Spijkerboer,[1202] describe the dichotomy whereby applicants must 'demonstrate enough emotionality to fit their gender and claim […], but not too much to be [seen as a] "hysterical woman" […] as [they] must also embody rationality and reason.'[1203] Both McKinnon[1204] and others such as Skrifvars et al. point out another layer of complexity to be added to decision makers' task: the one of intercultural communication. They stress that the ways in which individuals present their stories vary in 'verbal directness (direct or indirect) and emotional expressiveness (restrained or articulate),' according to their cultural background.[1205]

Hathaway and Hicks point out how this wide range of (non-)verbal emotional expressions further complicate the assessment of the subjective

1198 Amnesty International Nederalnd and instituut voor Mensenrechten en Medisch Onderzoek (iMMO) (n 993) 27.

1199 Fanflik, Office on Violence Against Women, and National District Attorneys Association (n 386) 10.

1200 United Nations Office on Drugs and Crime (UNODC) (n 284) 82.

1201 Fanflik, Office on Violence Against Women, and National District Attorneys Association (n 386) 5.

1202 Thomas Spijkerboer, 'Stereotyping and Acceleration – Gender, Procedural Acceleration and Marginalised Judicial Review in the Dutch Asylum System' in Gregor Noll (ed), *Proof, Evidentiary Assessment and Credibility in Asylum Procedures* (Brill Nijhoff 2005) 70.

1203 McKinnon (n 651) 215.

1204 *Ibid.*

1205 Jenny Skrifvars and others, 'Psychological Assumptions Underlying Credibility Assessments in Finnish Asylum Determinations' (2022) 76 Nordic Psychology 1, 4.

element in the UN Refugee Convention's requirement of 'well-founded fear'.[1206] They even argue that no subjective element can be read into the well-founded fear standard in the UN Refugee Convention, which was not 'intended [...] to require an examination of the emotional reaction of the claimant.'[1207] In line with this conclusion, some national asylum authorities have drafted guidelines regarding the concept of demeanour,[1208] such as the UK Home Office, stating that 'demeanour should never be used for the basis of a decision on plausibility.'[1209]

c) Rebuttal by Belgian Asylum Authorities

In the Belgian context, some asylum officials demonstrated awareness around the impact of trauma symptoms on demeanour, by normalising applicants who 'put up distance [...] in order not to hurt themselves any more'[1210] or 'remain very strong [...] as a defence mechanism.'[1211] One CALL judgement in the analysed sample annulled the CGRS' refusal of refugee status to a (trans) woman from North-Macedonia, stating: '[D]espite the fact that [she] does not submit any medical or psychological certificates, [...] her lack of education, her statements during the [...] procedure, the application, the statement of her social assistant, and her <u>general appearance at the hearing</u> [...] <u>raise questions about her mental state</u> and intellectual capacity. [...] [T]he possibility cannot be ruled out that [these factors] may constitute a (partial) justification [...] for her rather vague and ambiguous statements.'[1212] Other asylum officials in general emphasised the irrelevance of emotion or body language for credibility assessments or refugee status determination, for example: 'You can't tell everything from emotion because people are in such a stressful situation. Body language actually says very little to me.'[1213]

Two other CALL judgements used the concept of 'sense of experience' to argue in favour of the applicants' credibility, without further specifying the

---

1206 James Hathaway and William Hicks, 'Is There a Subjective Element in the Refugee Convention's Requirement of "Well-Founded Fear"?' (2005) 26 Michigan Journal of International Law 505, 519–520.

1207 *Ibid*. 507.

1208 Abigail Stepnitz, 'Believing Asylum-Seeking Women: Doing Gender in Legal Narratives of Sexual and Gender-Based Violence' (2023) (forthcoming) Social & Legal Studies 1, 2.

1209 UK Home Office, 'Asylum Policy Instruction: Assessing Credibility and Refugee Status' (2015) 18; Magugliani (n 93) 12.

1210 CB011_CGRS_Supervisor+PO_GENDER_[00:20:26].

1211 CB014_CGRS_PO_[01:05:43].

1212 DNM117_CALL 1 (annulment) 1974_F (trans)_North-Macedonia_RSA_VGNT_DV_24/04/2024_305 445_NL_Database_p. 10–11. Emphasis added. In light of the quantitative information at the end of this chapter, this case was counted as a decision including an argument based on 'Myth rebuttal' of the demeanour myth.

1213 CB003_CGRS_PO_[00:19:29].

demeanour expressed *in casu*.[1214] In one of these, the CALL did so by explicitly labelling the CGRS' reasoning, relying on 'sense of experience' to refuse the applicant protection, as 'result[ing] essentially from [a] subjective assessment.'[1215] Apart from these, no other decisions analysed explicitly pointed at the limited relevance of applicants' demeanour during SGBV disclosure for their credibility/well-foundedness assessment.

Some of the asylum authorities interviewed reported their reluctance to use the term 'sense of experience', due to its subjective nature[1216] or lack of any definition or guidance on how to use it. One PO admitted: 'Don't ask me to describe it because that's very difficult and they didn't really explain it to me concretely [...] when we started.'[1217] Lastly, one judge very firmly rejected the use of the term altogether, by stating: 'I don't use that expression [of 'sense of experience'] [...] in my judgements [...]. I've always been uncomfortable with that expression [...] especially as I know that psychologically, it's not easy for a person who has been traumatised to talk about traumatic events again and that they may tend to tell it as if it happened to someone else [...] as a defence mechanism.'[1218]

3.5. OCCURRENCE OF THE DISCLOSURE MYTHS

To conclude, argumentation based on 'inappropriate' level of detail, consistency, timing, or demeanour of/during SGBV disclosure may reflect an inadequate understanding of the disclosure barriers experienced by applicants with a gender-based need for international protection.[1219] This understanding is reflected in the extent of acceptance vs. rebuttal of the four disclosure myths in the analysed case law sample. These levels of disclosure myth acceptance and rebuttal, divided between asylum authorities at first instance (negative CGRS decisions) and in appeal (all CALL judgments), according to the procedural language, can be visualised as follows:

1214 DG106_CALL 1 (recognition)_F_Guinea_RSA_GMC_VGNT_FM_DV_21/5/2024_306 929_FR_Database_p. 8.; DC079_C_CALL 1 (annulment)_2006_F_Gabon_RSA_18/3/2024_303 320_FR_Database_MINOR _p. 12. In light of the quantitative information at the end of this chapter, these cases were counted as a decision including an argument based on 'Myth rebuttal' of the demeanour myth.

1215 DG106_CALL 1 (recognition)_F_Guinea_RSA_GMC_VGNT_FM_DV_21/5/2024_306 929_FR_Database_p. 8.

1216 CB011_CGRS_Supervisor+PO_GENDER_[00:37:15].; CB013_CGRS_PO_[01:18:00].

1217 CB014_CGRS_PO_[01:07:25].

1218 RB008_CALL_Judge_[00:47:08].

1219 Baillot, Cowan and Munro (n 5) 131.

Figure 15: % of decisions in the case law sample including at least one detail myth acceptance/rebuttal argument, according to asylum authority & language

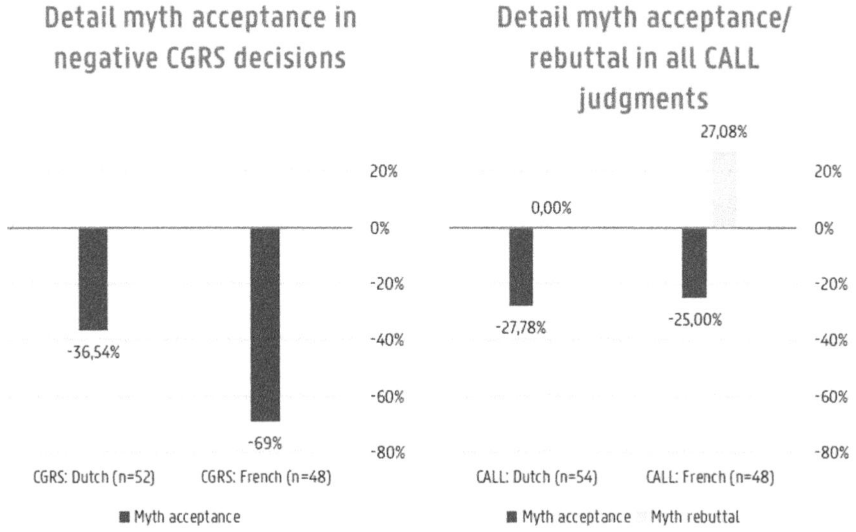

Figure 16: % of decisions in the case law sample including at least one consistency myth acceptance/rebuttal argument, according to asylum authority & language

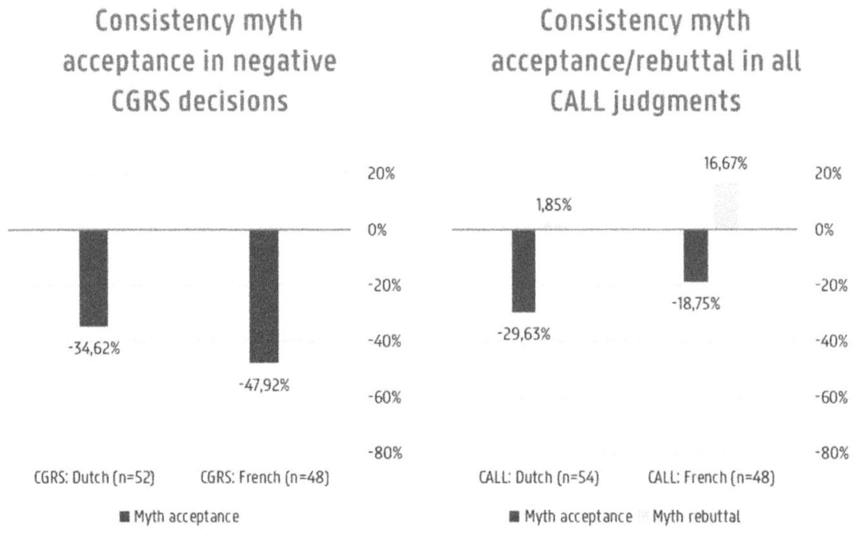

Figure 17: % of decisions in the case law sample including at least one delayed disclosure myth acceptance/rebuttal argument, according to asylum authority & language

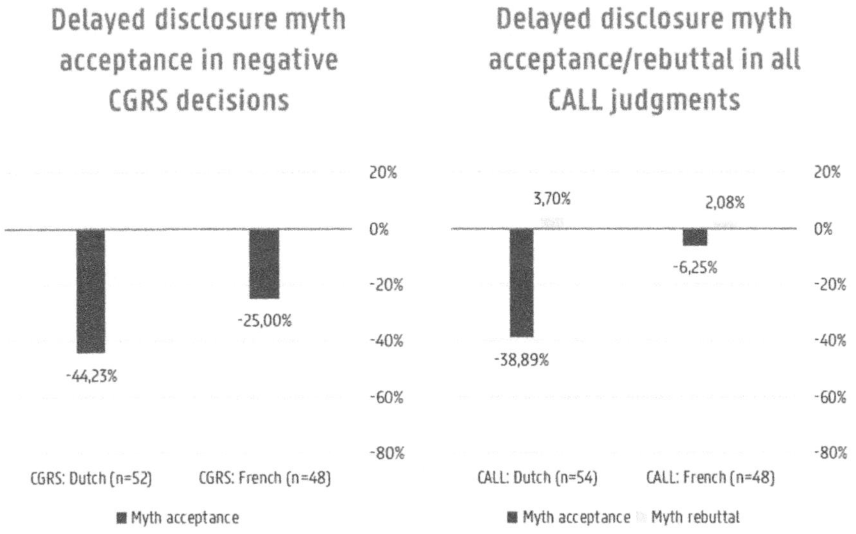

Figure 18: % of decisions in the case law sample including at least one demeanour myth acceptance/rebuttal argument, according to asylum authority & language

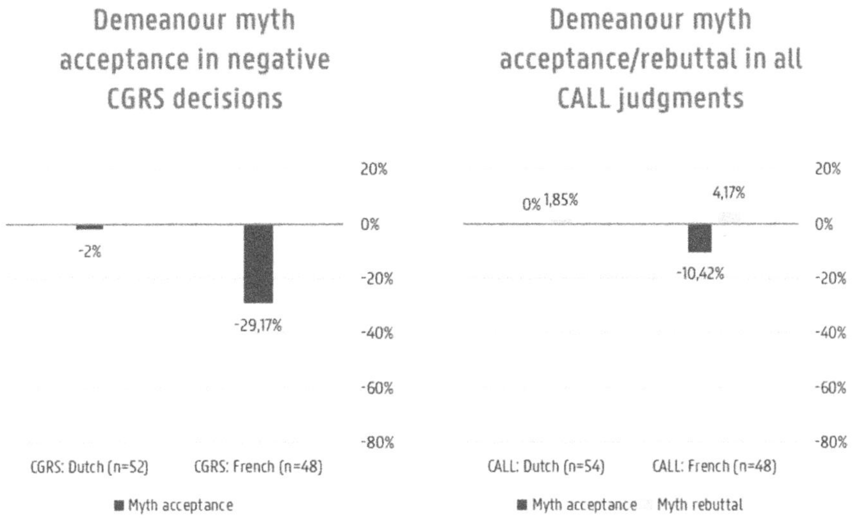

In the total case law sample (n=202), the percentage of decisions and judgements including at least one argument based on acceptance of a disclosure SGBV myth, amounted to: 39,11% for the detail myth, 32,67% for the inconsistency myth, 29,21% for the delayed disclosure myth, and 9,9% for the demeanour myth. For the procedures in French in first instance (CGRS), this amounts to ca. 70% for the detail myth, and ca. 50% for the consistency myth. Interestingly, acceptance is particularly low(er) for the delayed disclosure myth in French CALL judgements (6,25%). For the demeanour myth, acceptance is particularly high(er) in French CGRS decisions (29,17%) and particularly low(er) in both the Dutch CGRS decisions (2%) and CALL judgements (0%). The highest rates of myth rebuttal can be found in the French CALL judgements, with ca. 30% for the detail myth and ca. 15% for the consistency myth. Taking the four separate disclosure myths together across the whole case law sample, this comes down to an **acceptance** level of the **SGBV disclosure myth** in **almost 60% of the decisions/judgements** (57,92%).

4. THE MYTH THAT 'INAPPROPRIATE' SURVIVAL REACTIONS UNDERMINE SGBV FLIGHT STORIES' CREDIBILITY

4.1. ACCEPTANCE OF THE MYTHS ON SURVIVAL REACTIONS

4.1.1. FROM CRIMINAL JUSTICE TO ASYLUM CONTEXT

Another micro level element, next to applicants' resourcefulness and way of disclosing SGBV, concerns their short- and long-term survival reactions to deal with SGBV (threats). Arguments based on such survival behaviour reason that (re)actions perceived as abnormal or inappropriate undermine the credibility of survivors'/victims' SGBV story. Existing literature on reactions to and coping with SGBV and its perpetrators links this type of reasoning to a criminal justice tradition that minimises or denies sexual violence through expectations about 'normal' victim behaviour. Throughout this chapter, I will use the term 'survival reactions' to cover both short-term reactions and long-term coping mechanisms to SGBV experiences/threats.

Before going into the different types of survival reactions, it is important to highlight the misconception that people make rational assessments as to which survival reaction to 'use'. When under threat, for example of SGBV, our capacity for conscious calculation is minimised or impaired. Instead, stress hormones can rapidly cause dramatic loss of cognitive abilities in our prefrontal cortex (i.e. 'the center of executive functions in the brain [...] involved in [...] reason, logic, problem solving, planning and memory').[1220] This automatic and subconscious process results in survivors/victims making split-second instinctive decisions, reacting in ways that might seem illogical or irrational.[1221] As such, there

[1220] Department of Justice of the Government of Canada (n 933).

[1221] United Nations Office on Drugs and Crime (UNODC) (n 284) 80.

are four scientifically proven short-term survival reactions that occur as 'natural' and subconscious survivor/victim behaviour: fight, flight, freeze, and appease.[1222]

In the (short-term) acute phase, during and shortly after the event,[1223] active reactions such as fighting back or fleeing (fight or flight) are seen as more credible than freezing or appeasing the perpetrator to prevent escalation (freeze or appease).[1224] In the reorganisation phase, longer-term active coping mechanisms[1225] that seek to eliminate or confront the source of violence (approach coping) are considered more 'normal' than passive ones that seek to avoid or ignore the violence (avoidance coping).[1226] These assumptions manifest themselves in existing rape myths, such as: 'It can't be that bad, otherwise [the survivor/victim] would have fled,'[1227] 'If it was really serious [the survivor/victim] would have taken legal action and provided evidence',[1228] or '[Survivors/victims] never stay in contact with perpetrators after sexual assault'.[1229]

In contrast to existing rape myths in the criminal justice context, which consider active reactions to SGBV as 'normal' in certain circumstances, asylum authorities seem to qualify both applicants' active and passive reactions as non-credible. Both these active and passive types of reactions can be illustrated by Rahel's case.

CASE OF RAHEL			
• Country of origin:	Eritrea	• SGBV types:	Rape/sexual assault
• Gender identity:	Woman	• Decisions in file:	CGRS 1 (refusal) – 30/5/2022
• Birth year:	1985		CALL 1 (refusal) – 25/11/2022 – n° 280 827
• Interview by:	Researcher		

(continued)

1222 Zoe Lodrick, 'Psychological Trauma – What Every Trauma Worker Should Know.' (2007) 2 The British Journal of Psychotherapy Integration 1, 4–6; United Nations Office on Drugs and Crime (UNODC) (n 284) 80; United Nations Office on Drugs and Crime (UNODC) and Skinnider (n 161) 23; Lamonaca and others (n 280) 23.

1223 Fanflik, Office on Violence Against Women, and National District Attorneys Association (n 386) 125.

1224 Lodrick (n 1222) 5–6; United Nations Office on Drugs and Crime (UNODC) (n 284) 79 & 96.

1225 Fanflik, Office on Violence Against Women, and National District Attorneys Association (n 386) 125.

1226 Aysun Babacan Gümüş, Sevinç Şıpkın and Özden Erdem, 'The Prevalence of Intimate Partner Violence against Women and Women's Methods of Coping with Partner Violence*' (2020) 11 Journal of Psychiatric Nursing 79, 80; Fanflik, Office on Violence Against Women, and National District Attorneys Association (n 386) 8.

1227 United Nations Office on Drugs and Crime (UNODC) (n 284) 98.

1228 *Ibid.* 99.

1229 Breen and Boyce (n 401) 5233.

According to her statements, Rahel was born in 1985 in Eritrea, where she worked in a beauty salon. Rahel met a man, who she said was a spy for the Eritrean government and who asked to marry her multiple times, but she refused. Unable to accept this, he warned her that she would 'face the consequences'. One day, Rahel was attacked on her way home from work and was **raped** by a masked man, who later turned out to be him. After her mother found her, she was hospitalised because of her injuries, turned out to be pregnant, and gave birth to a daughter. She initially wanted to confront him after her police complaint was left without consequences, but could not find him. For a long time, Rahel heard nothing from this man, but in 2018, he resurfaced. He demanded that she hand over his daughter to him, or he would kill her. He threatened her both verbally on the phone and physically by **stalking** her along her commuting route. Rahel's initial anger made room for fear of escalation, eventually leading her to go into hiding at her aunt's house, quitting her job, and taking her daughter out of school. Having stayed hidden and having blocked her phone, she heard nothing more from him during this period. After a year in hiding, realising that they could not go on living like this, she saw no other way out than to flee the country, a journey she considered so dangerous that she left her daughter in the care of her mother, to later rescue her through legal migration pathways. She left Eritrea with a smuggler in January 2020.

She arrived in Belgium in August 2020 and submitted an application for international protection in November 2020. While she was already in Belgium, she learnt that someone had seen her rapist in a shop in her neighbourhood. Aside from her fear of him, she also stated that she feared the Eritrean government, as she had left the country irregularly.

Rahel employed both active (wanting to confront the perpetrator and eventually flee the country) and passive (staying in the country for another year, in hiding) survival reactions that evolved and overlapped over time. During our interview, she explained her urge to seek justice and confrontation with the perpetrator, while at the same time wanting and needing to forget him. She also articulated her inner conflict of having to leave her daughter behind:

> '[**I wanted to find him**,] [...] I reported it to the police [...] [after giving birth,] **I wanted him to go to jail** because he had left me like that! *lifts voice* [...] How can I explain it, even though **maybe I was going to die, he left me there**! [...] I didn't find him [...] and then [...] **I had to forget him**. [...] When I think about him, I feel so much stress. [...] I have to forget him. *says this resolutely* **Completely**.'[1230]

> 'I fled illegally. No, **I could not take my daughter with me**. [...] maybe I would [...] die, maybe he would kill me, it was better if I went alone. [...] **I feel sad**. [...] *starts crying harder* [...] If I had fled [and] taken my daughter [...] with me, [...] **maybe the army would come**. [...] They would tell you 'stop'. If you don't stop, **they will kill**

[1230] NEr018_1985_F_Eritrea_RSA_NL_NANSEN_[00:36:33].

> you. **And I was scared.** [...] But I'm here. If I'm alone, it's okay. **Even if I say I'll die, it's fine.** [...] **It's better that I go alone. I am a mother.** [...] I have no choice. [...] **It was better that I left my daughter with my mum.**'[1231] | CASE OF RAHEL

In Rahel's case, both the CGRS and the CALL refused her international protection, relying on argumentation that (among others) focused on her post-rape survival reactions:

> 'It [...] is remarkable [...] that [she], after learning that she was pregnant, went to track down [the perpetrator] on her own initiative [...]. It is **incomprehensible that the applicant, having been raped by this man, tried to contact him herself.** [...] [I]t is also **questionable that the applicant chooses to flee the country herself but leaves her 15-year-old daughter behind** in her home.'[1232]

> '[The] threats [from the perpetrator] date back to 2018 after all, but nothing else has happened. **You lived with your aunt for another year before your departure** but did not even receive phones from him during that period.'[1233] | CASE OF RAHEL

Below, I will illustrate asylum authorities' tendency to label not only survivors'/victims' passive survival reactions as abnormal and therefore non-credible, but their active survival reactions as well, in contrast to the existing criminal justice rape myths. I will discuss short- and long-term responses to SGBV jointly, first focusing on passive survival reactions (freeze/appease reactions and avoidance coping, see Chapter 4.1.2.), and second on active ones (flight/fight reactions and approach coping, see Chapter 4.1.3.). Hereby, I will pay particular attention to an important difference with freeze and flight reactions in the criminal justice context. In the asylum context, all applicants seeking international protection have ultimately decided to flee, resulting in a broader geographical interpretation of the freeze and flight reaction (not only at/from the crime scene, but also at/from a certain region or country of origin as a whole).

Then I will set out why the belief that certain responses to SGBV are considered more legitimate than others cannot find support in health and social sciences. Since a person's survival reactions depend on numerous and evolving personal and circumstantial factors, it is impossible to predict how SGBV survivors/victims will 'normally' react. I will discuss how this rebuttal has (partially) entered into (case) law and legal sciences. Finally, I will illustrate the ways in which the Belgian asylum authorities themselves occasionally rebut

1231 NEr018_1985_F_Eritrea_RSA_NL_NANSEN_[00:55:58].
1232 NEr018_CALL 1 (refusal)_1985_F_Eritrea_RSA_25/11/2022_280 827_NL_NANSEN_p. 15.
1233 NEr018_CGRS 1 (refusal)_1985_F_Eritrea_RSA_30/5/2022_280 827_NL_NANSEN_p. 4.

the myth that 'inappropriate' survival reactions undermine the credibility of an SGBV flight story. Parts of this chapter are also published in a handbook on 'Feminist and Queer Research Methods in Law' (in Dutch).[1234]

4.1.2. PASSIVE SURVIVAL REACTIONS

a) Freeze Reactions & Avoidance Coping

The myth on freeze reactions and avoidance coping specifically relates to existing rape myths such as: 'Why don't victims leave at the first instance of physical violence?',[1235] 'If [survivors/victims] stay with a violent partner, it is [their] fault',[1236] and '[Survivors/victims] will finally be safe if [they] leave [a violent] relationship'.[1237] In the asylum context, authorities demonstrate a similar scepticism towards applicants who 'froze' in response to SGBV and therefore did not leave a 1) situation (e.g. relationship or area) or 2) country of origin (sooner). Instead of actively leaving (immediately), applicants' choice to initially stay might also negatively impact their refugee status determination when 3) they did not experience additional SGBV (threats) in the period prior to their eventual flight. This is also the case when they managed to avoid or minimise the risk of further violence/threats by going into hiding during that time. Asylum authorities also appear sceptical towards 4) justifications for freeze-survival reactions, such as physical or mental dependence on perpetrators. Below, I will discuss each of these aspects in acceptance of the 'freeze myth' in the Belgian asylum context.

Firstly, asylum authorities have found it non-credible that applicants froze and did not leave a situation or area (instead of the country as such). As for violent situations/relationships, one attaché wondered 'why [a] woman, who is a doctor for example, stayed with a husband who hit her for years [...] I've already found this non-credible.'[1238] This argument also occurred in the abovementioned case (p. 219) of a Senegalese applicant forced to marry a man carrying out human sacrifices. She explained feeling like she had no choice and could not leave, telling herself it would pass. Nonetheless, the CGRS found

[1234] Roels, 'Het Cassandracomplex in Gendergerelateerde Asielprocedures: Luisteren als feministische methode in onderzoek over verkrachtingsmythologie' (n 223).
[1235] United Nations Office on Drugs and Crime (UNODC) and Skinnider (n 161) 18–19.
[1236] World Health Organization (WHO), 'Caring for Women Subjected to Violence' (n 402) 5.
[1237] *Ibid.*
[1238] RB007_CALL_Attaché_[00:31:15].

the fact that she stayed in the marriage for so long (among other elements) to undermine her credibility.[1239]

In other cases, it was found implausible that an applicant stayed with her psychologically violent family for too long,[1240] that the applicant's husband still lived with his mother who wanted to excise their daughter, regardless of his financial dependence on her,[1241] or that the applicant did not escape a sex trafficking network sooner, despite the fact that she had sworn a voodoo oath, endangering her family if she would flee.[1242] When applicants initially stayed in the area where the SGBV (threats) occurred, authorities in several cases[1243] 'expected that [applicants] would try to move as far away from [their] problems as possible [...] [and] that [they] would opt for a hiding place as far away as possible from [the perpetrator].'[1244]

Secondly, the Belgian asylum authorities at times also argue that applicants fearing SGBV fled the country too late. This reasoning was reflected in the personal interview of Aya, a Syrian applicant fleeing sexual assault by a military official, where the PO literally asked her: 'Why did you not flee sooner?'[1245] The degree of belatedness perceived as 'abnormal' varies greatly,[1246] with the analysed case law containing examples from 16 years to one month and a half 'late'. The latter occurred in a Georgian and Bosnian case. In the former, an abovementioned (p. 219) Georgian applicant, who was fleeing domestic violence, booked her flight tickets out of the country one month and a half in advance. Both the CGRS and the CALL responded by arguing: 'If the applicant really was a victim of daily psychological violence [...], she could be expected to buy a flight ticket allowing her to leave as soon as possible

---

1239 NS005_CGRS 1 (refusal)_2002_F_Senegal_RSA_DV_FM_13/05/2022_274 056_FR_NANSEN_p. 5.

1240 DGe138_CALL 1 (refusal)_1998_F_Georgia_RSA_DV_23/5/2024_307 108_NL_Database_p.11.

1241 DIC074_CGRS 1 (refusal)_F_Ivory Coast_GMC_VGNT_13/6/2023_302 979_FR_Case law selection by CALL_p. 3.

1242 DN146_CGRS 1 (refusal)_1993_F_Nigeria_STFP_14/11/2023_307 592_NL_Database_p. 4., DN146_CALL 1 (refusal)_1993_F_Nigeria_STFP_31/5/2024_307 592_NL_Database_p. 11.

1243 DGa102_CGRS 1 (refusal)_F_The Gambia_FM_DV_10/10/2023_305 436_FR_Database_p. 5., DSo125_CALL 1 (refusal)_1996_F_Somalia_VGNT_FM_3/05/2024_306 071_NL_Database_p. 13., DSo125_CGRS 1 (refusal) 1996_F_Somalia_VGNT_FM_26/09/2023_306071_NL_Database_p. 5., DEc120_CALL 1 (refusal)_1981_F_Ecuador_RSA_DV_29/4/2024_305 805_NL_Database_p. 8., DEc120_CGRS 1 (refusal)_1981_F_Ecuador_RSA_DV_8/12/2023_NL_Database_p. 3., DIC153_CGRS 2 (refusal)_1979_F_Ivory Coast_RSA_GMC_VGNT_FM_DV_3/8/2023_307 471_FR_Case law selection by CALL_p. 6.

1244 DB068_CGRS 1 (refusal)_1975_F_Bolivia_RSA_DV_25/1/2024_302 134_NL_Case law selection by CALL_p. 5–7.

1245 NSy019 CGRS interview_1997_F_Syria_RSA_FR_NANSEN_p. 16.

1246 (7 months) DGe110_CALL 1 (refusal)_1986_M_Georgia_VGNT_FM_27/3/2024_303 889_NL_Database_p. 11., (5 years) DGa102_CGRS 1 (refusal)_F_The Gambia_FM_DV_10/10/2023_305 436_FR_Database_p. 6., (16 years) DS103_CGRS 1 (refusal)_F_Senegal_GMC_FM_DV_17/7/2023_305 927_FR_Database_p. 6.

and not only a month and a half later, even if it was at a lower fare.'[1247] The latter Bosnian case concerned the flight story of Lejla.

CASE OF LEJLA			
• Country of origin:	Bosnia-Herzegovina	• SGBV types:	Rape/sexual assault & sex trafficking/forced prostitution
• Gender id:	Woman	• Decisions in file:	CGRS 1 (manifestly ill-founded) – 23/5/2023
• Birth year:	/		CALL 1 (annulment) – 30/4/2024 – n° 305 882
• Interview by:	/		

According to her statements, Lejla was born in Transnistria (part of the Soviet Union at the time), where she was **abducted and forced into prostitution** by the mafia and was repeatedly **sexually abused** in this context. When two undercover police officers came to a club where she was forced to work, the mafia leader ordered to attack them. One of them died and Lejla helped the other escape, for which she was severely punished (e.g. with **beatings** that **broke her teeth**). Eventually, the police arrived and she was taken to the hospital first and to a safe house later. However, the mafia leader found her and **attacked** her again, including **with a glass bottle**, marking her with scars that remain to this day. She was moved to another safe house and eventually testified at a trial in 2002. The mafia leader was sentenced to 20 years in prison and **threatened** Lejla that he would come back for her upon his release.

In 2001, Lejla met her current husband, with whom she moved to Bosnia-Herzegovina. They both obtained international protection, got married and raised five children (three boys and two girls). They spent much of their lives in reception centres, only moving to private accommodation in 2019. Shortly after the mafia trial, a YouTube video was published in which Lejla shared her life story, revealing how she had been abducted and who had abused her. While they immediately reported it and it was removed, they began receiving **threats** from the convicted mafia leader and his associates, continuing until 2007. In 2018 or 2019, while still living in a reception centre, Lejla was **raped and beaten** by a man who had locked her in a barrack. She kept this a secret from her husband until 2022.

In 2021 or 2022, while having coffee with her husband in Sarajevo, Lejla suddenly saw the mafia leader again. Shortly after, her **daughter was abducted** 50 metres from their home. They heard screams and her husband saw their daughter being dragged into a car. After informing the police, the kidnappers were intercepted. At the police station, they were placed in the same room as the four kidnappers, with one of them giving Lejla **'greetings' from the mafia leader**. Lejla, her husband, and her daughter were eventually questioned for five minutes and told to wait for the chief inspector, who never came. A police officer advised them to file a complaint, which they did not do, not wanting to fight these people again. The perpetrators were released. The day after the abduction, in April 2022, her husband brought both their daughters into safety with family in Poland.

(continued)

[1247] DGe138_CALL 1 (refusal)_1998_F_Georgia_RSA_DV_23/5/2024_307 108_NL_Database_p.11, DGe138_CGRS 1 (refusal)_1998_F_Georgia_RSA_DV_27/12/2023_307 108_NL_Database_p. 3.

Right before they fled, the whole family obtained Bosnian citizenship. They eventually travelled together to Belgium in June 2022, where they applied for international protection. In support of her application, Lejla submitted various legal and medical documents, attesting her forced prostitution, her PTSD, the abduction of her daughter, her hospitalisation after the rape in the reception centre, and other proof of the threats they received. Lejla could not be interviewed by or provide written information to the CGRS, as her psychiatrist declared her unfit to do so. After several declined interview invitations (supported by a medical certificate) for that reason, the CGRS made a decision identical to her husband's, since their applications were deemed to rely on the same facts. As Bosnia-Herzegovina is listed as a 'safe country of origin', her husband's application was assessed via the accelerated procedure. Lejla herself had indicated at the IO that 'her husband and children were not aware of everything and that she wished to keep it that way'.

Lejla and her family spent one month and a half (after the abduction of her daughter) organising their flight out of the country. The CGRS found their application manifestly ill-founded (in the accelerated procedure), by arguing, regardless of their precautions to go to the police and take their daughters to Poland:

> '[Y]ou have **not acted in any way in accordance with the fears you raised**. It appears that after [your daughter's] abduction, you continued to **live in Bosnia-Herzegovina for another month and a half** and that you **took hardly any precautions** to protect yourselves. [...] When asked **why you did not leave [...] sooner**, you indicated that you had waited until all of your family had citizenship [...] [and your son was] graduated [...]. Your [...] **passive attitude** [and] **lack of precautions** in your daily life, **call the credibility of your alleged fear into question**.'[1248] | CASE OF LEJLA

Thirdly, a freeze response can also negatively impact applicants' refugee status determination if they no longer experienced direct violence or threats in the period prior to their eventual flight. Asylum authorities specifically invoke such situations to argue that applicants' fear of SGBV persecution is no longer present and/or that there are no reasons to assume that history would repeat itself.[1249] One gender-specialised supervisor stressed the importance of 'the time between the incident and the departure. [...] [An applicant who left] immediately [...] is different from someone who [still lived there for years without any significant problems].'[1250] At times, this argument is combined with resourcefulness elements. In an abovementioned Guinean rape case,

1248 DBH121_CGRS 1 (manifestly ill-founded)_F_Bosnia and Herzegovina_RSA_STFP_23/5/2023_305 882_NL_Database_p. 5–6.

1249 RB006_CALL_Judge_[01:03:59]., CB005_CGRS_Supervisor + PO_GENDER_[00:11:09]., CB007_CGRS_PO_[00:25:16].

1250 CB015_CGRS_Supervisor + PO_GENDER_[00:34:40].

the CALL for example stated: '[T]he particularly old nature of these events, combined with the applicant's profile as a mother now aged over 30, constitute in any event good reason to believe that the [rape] will not occur again.'[1251]

In the cases analysed, this time period without direct SGBV experiences/threats ranged from one year to more than 18 years.[1252] In Lejla's case for example, the argument concerned a period of three to four years after her rape in the reception centre, with the CGRS arguing (in a decision directed at her husband:

> 'With regard to the **rape of your wife** [...], it should first of all be pointed out that this event dates from **three or four years before your departure** and that your wife **did not know any problems with this person thereafter** [...]. In view of the fact that you subsequently remained in Bosnia-Herzegovina for a considerable time without knowing any problems with him, [...] it is **not** possible to conclude [...] that there was a **need for international protection**.'[1253] | CASE OF LEJLA

Some asylum officials extend this line of reasoning to applicants who tried to actively avoid perpetrators, for example by going into hiding, during that time.[1254] One gender-specialised PO gave the example of an applicant who was raped, but was sheltered by family for years, without being revictimised after that. This PO reasoned: 'Simply the fact that [someone] didn't experience anything because [they were] in hiding, [...] that's not an element [I] would take into account' and concluded that this applicant had nothing left to fear.[1255] In the case of Sofia, an applicant from Honduras, who had been sexually abused by her father since the age of 12, the CGRS (in a later withdrawn

1251 DG087_CALL 1 (refusal)_F_Guinea_RSA_GMC_VGNT_DV_29/4/2024_305 819_FR_Database_p. 28.

1252 (two years) NT015_CGRS 2 (refusal)_1996_F_Turkey_RSA_FM_DV_1/2/2023_285 279_FR_NANSEN_p. 6., (more than a year) DA099_A_CGRS 1 (manifestly ill-founded)_M_Albania_DV_6/7/2023_303 553_FR_Database_p. 3., (more than 10 years) DAlg076_CGRS 1 (refusal)_M_Algeria_RSA_VGNT_8/12/2023_305 949_FR_Database_p. 5., (more than 18 years) DB068_CGRS 1 (refusal)_1975_F_Bolivia_RSA_DV_25/1/2024_302 134_NL_Case law selection by CALL_p. 5–6., (two years) DG094_CGRS 1 (refusal)_F_Guinea_RSA_GMC_VGNT_FM_DV_3/3/2023_302 063_FR_Database_p. 3., (eight years) DG097_CGRS 1 (refusal)_F_Guinea_RSA_GMC_FM_DV_5/4/2023_303 242_FR_Database_p. 3., (three years) DGe112_CALL 2 (refusal)_M_Georgia_GMC_29/3/2024_304 208_NL_Database_p. 4., (three years) DN108_CALL 1 (refusal)_F_Nigeria_GMC_FM_14/3/2024_303 213_NL_Database_p. 4., (17 years) DS088_CALL 1 (refusal)_F_Senegal_RSA_GMC_VGNT_FM_DV_28/5/2024_307 398_FR_Database_p. 21., (1 year) DS088_CGRS 1 (refusal)_F_Senegal_RSA_GMC_VGNT_FM_DV_19/7/2023_307 398_FR_Database_p. 5.

1253 DBH121_CGRS 1 (manifestly ill-founded)_F_Bosnia and Herzegovina_RSA_STFP_23/5/2023_305 882_NL_Database_p.7.

1254 CB008_CGRS_Supervisor + PO_GENDER_[00:42:13].

1255 CB009_CGRS_PO_GENDER_[00:21:41] & [00:24:53].

decision[1256]) stressed the period of three years before her flight, in which she had not faced any more problems. However, the CGRS hereby disregarded the fact that her father 'continued to seek contact [...] by asking for hugs or telling [her] to sit on his lap, but [she] tried to make sure that [she was] always busy when he came home so that [she] had to spend as little time as possible with him.'[1257]

While she tried to avoid her father but did not go into literal hiding, other applicants did. In the Burundian (attempted) rape case mentioned above for example, the CGRS 'emphasises that [the applicant did] not mention any problems between [her] release [after being abducted] [...] and the date of [her] flight [...], mentioning at most that [she] moved in with [her] grandmother's friends in order to hide.'[1258] Similarly, this reasoning was used in the CGRS' refusal decision of Rahel, who went into hiding with her daughter early 2019 and blocked her phone number.[1259]

Lastly, applicants may (in)directly give explanations as to why they (initially) 'froze' in a violent situation or location, such as social, financial, or emotional dependence on or coercion by perpetrators, as part of a possible cycle of violence[1260] (see Chapter 4.2.1 below), preventing them from leaving. However, asylum officials reported not taking this into account,[1261] because 'it is hard to assess'[1262] or '[such dependence] is not going to change by coming to Belgium.'[1263] For others, such statements seemed to be cancelled out by the applicants' (non-)material resourcefulness. For example, one PO dismissed an applicant's (perceived) impossibility to file for divorce in Guinea by stating that this 'can't explain why [...] with their profile, education, financial level, [solo travel experience,] she didn't do anything.'[1264] A gender-specialised PO

1256 Upon refusal of her application by the CGRS, Sofia's appeal with the CALL was not registered, since her insufficient bank balance had caused an error in the payment of the registration fee. Despite a letter from her lawyer explaining this, the situation could not be rectified and she could not appeal against her refusal decision by the CGRS. Eventually, the CGRS decided to withdraw the initial refusal of Sofia's application and, after reconsidering her case (the reasoning of which is not made public), to recognise her as a refugee.

1257 NH003_CGRS 1 (refusal)_1991_F_Honduras_RSA_DV 12/8/2021_NL_NANSEN_p. 2.

1258 DBu089_CGRS 1 (refusal)_F_Burundi_RSA_14/11/2023_307 576_FR_Database_p. 7.

1259 'After all, [your rapist's] threats date back to 2018, but nothing else happened. You lived with your aunt for another year before your departure, but did not even get phone calls from him during that period. Your only explanation for this is that [...] since he no longer encounters you, he can no longer threaten you. However, this cannot be considered [a] serious [explanation]' (NEr018_CGRS 1 (refusal)_1985_F_Eritrea_RSA_30/5/2022_280 827_NL_NANSEN_p. 4.).

1260 McLeod and others (n 983) 90.

1261 CB004_CGRS_PO_[00:11:07].

1262 CB007_CGRS_PO_[00:43:28].

1263 RB007_CALL_Attaché_[00:39:53].

1264 CB004_CGRS_PO_[00:45:32].

added: 'You can expect someone who has studied to [break ties with their family].'[1265]

Sometimes, the fact that applicants did not flee the situation (sooner) is used against them, even if the violence only became imminent after a while[1266] or they realised the situation's violent nature only later on. For example, in a Ghanaian forced marriage case, the CGRS argued: 'Despite staying in your parents' house for the rest of the day after the wedding ceremony […] at no time did you make any attempt to escape.'[1267] The applicant's explanation that 'it did not occur to [her] that [she] had to escape […] [since she] felt that the marriage would set [her] free from [the violence in her] parental home'[1268] was not accepted as a justification for her freeze reaction and she was refused international protection by both the CGRS and the CALL.

b) *Appease Reactions & Avoidance Coping*

Next to freezing, SGBV survivors/victims might appease perpetrators as a short-term reaction to or long-term coping with SGBV (threats), which might equally be labelled as an 'abnormal' and therefore non-credible survival reaction. Appease reactions and avoidance coping mechanisms may manifest themselves as: 1) not acting upon threats/experiences of SGBV, 2) carrying on as usual (e.g. continuing to work or keeping up appearances on social media[1269]), 3) remaining in or seeking contact with the perpetrator, 4) returning to the perpetrator's surroundings, or 5) pleasing the perpetrator (e.g. by dropping charges or even 'accepting' SGBV). I will discuss how each of these forms are discredited in asylum authorities' argumentation in SGBV asylum decisions.

Firstly, asylum authorities seem to reason that applicants who appeased the perpetrator by not acting (sufficiently, effectively, or immediately) upon

1265 CB009_CGRS_PO_GENDER_[00:19:58].

1266 '[T]he applicant explicitly stated that she would not have fled her uncle's home if she had not been pregnant […] [and] said that "[a]t the time I didn't know if I was going to flee, but if they insisted on the marriage I was definitely going to leave the house", the Council […] considered that this highlighted the applicant's lack of interest in […] the alleged marriage plan, which reinforced the Council's conviction that her fear was not credible.'(DMa090_CALL 1 (annulment)_F_Mauritania_RSA_GMC_VGNT_FM_DV_30/5/2024_307 565_FR_Database_p. 9.).

1267 DGh115_CGRS 1 (refusal)_1999_F_Ghana_RSA_FM_DV_26/3/2024_305 147_NL_Database_p. 4., DGh115_CALL 1 (refusal)_1999_F_Ghana_RSA_FM_DV_19/4//2024_305 147_NL_Database_p. 9.

1268 DGh115_CGRS 1 (refusal)_1999_F_Ghana_RSA_FM_DV_26/3/2024_305 147_NL_Database_p. 4., DGh115_CALL 1 (refusal)_1999_F_Ghana_RSA_FM_DV_19/4//2024_305 147_NL_Database_p. 9.

1269 For an in-depth analysis of the legal issues with social media screenings in the context of the Belgian asylum procedure, see: Roels, 'Socialemedia- en smartphonescreenings tegen misbruik in Belgische verzoekprocedures om internationale bescherming' (n 669).

SGBV (threats) can hardly be considered credible. This lack of action can take the form of refraining to file charges against perpetrators,[1270] as in Carmen's case:

> '[T]he [CGRS] does not question that you were a victim of domestic violence in Ecuador. [...] However, [...] it cannot be followed that you, already having a protection order since 2008 and already having appealed to the Ecuadorian legal system, **would not have used this order after other attacks. [...] Given your past history with your ex-partner and the severity of the alleged attack you faced, some action could be expected.**'[1271] | CASE OF CARMEN

In addition, applicants' lack of opposition to and/or lack of interest in the organisation of a forced marriage[1272] or the identity of the sender of threatening messages[1273] have also been seen as non-credible appease reactions. In a Guinean forced partnership case mentioned above, the applicant justified her 'passivity' by explaining that she thought it safer not to oppose her father because he 'had already hurt [her] too much' and thought that he chose her forced partner because '[this man] needed a little girl to do the household chores.' Nevertheless, the CGRS argued that these reactions lacked a 'sense of experience' and undermined her credibility.[1274] In the abovementioned Ghanaian case, the CGRS even concluded that, due to a similar lack of opposition or interest, 'we cannot speak of a forced marriage' at all.[1275]

This lack of interest in perpetrators appears relevant to asylum authorities, even after applicants have fled the country.[1276] They for example argued: 'Some interest in your alleged persecutors could be expected, especially since you had been in Belgium for quite some time. That you did not even attempt to find out more about [them, because you did not want to remember it,] is incompatible with the seriousness of your alleged fear.'[1277] As I will explain below, this

1270 DGe151_CALL 1 (refusal)_2003_F_Georgia_VGNT_DV_27/03/2024_303 891_NL_Database_p. 16.

1271 DEc120_CGRS 1 (refusal)_1981_F_Ecuador_RSA_DV_ 8/12/2023_NL_Database_p. 2–3., Dec120_CALL 1 (refusal)_1981_F_Ecuador_RSA_DV_ 29/4/2024_ 305 805_NL_Database_p. 7–8.

1272 DG072_CALL 2 (recognition)_F_Guinea_STFP_GMC_VGNT_FM_DV_12/2/2024_301 330_FR_Database_p. 10., DG097_CGRS 1 (refusal)_F_Guinea_RSA_GMC_FM_DV_5/4/2023_303 242_FR_Database_p. 3.

1273 DGab075_CALL 1 (refusal)_M_Gabon_RSA_5/4/2024 304 393_FR_Database_p. 8.

1274 DG087_CGRS 1 (refusal)_F_Guinea_RSA_GMC_VGNT_DV_2/10/2023_305 819_FR_Database_p. 14.

1275 DGh115_CGRS 1 (refusal)_1999_F_Ghana_RSA_FM_DV_26/3/2024_305 147_NL_Database_p. 4.

1276 E.g. DMol140_CGRS 1 (refusal)_1971_F_Moldavia_DV_30/11/2023_307 172_NL_Database_p. 4.

1277 DN108_CALL 1 (refusal)_F_Nigeria_GMC_ FM_14/3/2024_303 213_NL_Database_p. 8., DN108_CGRS 1 (refusal)_F_Nigeria_GMC_FM_10/7/2023_303 213_NL_Database_p. 3.

reasoning is difficult to reconcile with authorities' belief that staying in contact with perpetrators also constitutes 'abnormal' and non-credible behaviour.

Secondly, applicants who carried on with their lives as usual after SGBV (threats) have equally been found non-credible. One gender-specialised supervisor illustrated the relevance of such 'carry on'-behaviour[1278] as follows: 'If a person explains that [after a] rape, they have basically resumed their normal life, [...] and at some point left her country – perhaps for another reason – the fear assessment is different [...] than a woman who [...] was so scarred after the rape that she never left her house again.'[1279] In case law, this reasoning has alternatively been phrased as: '[I]f you really were under constant threat from your ex-husband [...] requiring you to stay under the radar, it can be expected that you would not participate freely in the labour market [...] and guard every piece of [on- or offline] information.'[1280]

As in the latter case, (potential) survivors/victims indeed report having 'carried on as usual' by continuing to work and/or (let their children) go to school.[1281] This was also the case for Lejla and her family. Again regardless of their complaint to the police and sheltering their daughters in Poland, the CALL argued:

> 'Even after [your daughter's] abduction, you did not take any special precautions. [...] [Y]ou only advised [your sons] to lock the door of the room and not to open it to anyone. Although [...] you took your daughters [...] to relatives in Poland [...], the lack of serious precautions for the other family members is remarkable [...]. [Your son] was still **attending school** [by bus] [...], [which] was 17km away from where you lived and [...] you and your wife **continued to work**. [...] **It is not at all plausible that you would continue your usual life and that you would continue to go out and live in the same house** that was already on the mafia's radar if you actually believed that [they were] on your heels.'[1282] | CASE OF LEJLA

It is important to note that the judge did not consider bringing their daughters into safety abroad and fleeing the country one month and a half after the abduction 'special precautions'.

1278 CB006_CGRS_PO_[00:51:15].

1279 CB005_CGRS_Supervisor + PO_GENDER_[00:25:16].

1280 DB068_CGRS 1 (refusal)_1975_F_Bolivia_RSA_DV_25/1/2024_302 134_NL_Case law selection by CALL_p. 5–6.

1281 ("a normal life") DAlg076_CGRS 1 (refusal)_M_Algeria_RSA_VGNT_8/12/2023_305 949_FR_Database_p. 5.? ("simply continue to live in the same house ... and work") DGe110_CALL 1 (refusal)_1986_M_Georgia_VGNT_FM_27/3/2024_303 889_NL_Database_p. 11., ("working with other people") DL119_CALL 1 (refusal)_1987_F_Liberia_FM_DV_26/4/2024_305 790_NL_Database_p. 7., DL119_CGRS 1 (refusal)_1987_F_Liberia_FM_DV_18/7/2023_305 790_NL_Database_p. 3.

1282 DBH121_CALL 1 (annulment)_F_Bosnia and Herzegovina_RSA_STFP_30/4/2024_305 882_NL_Database_p. 5–6.

Another type of 'carry on'-behaviour might consist in keeping up appearances on social media to avoid escalation, as was the case for Fatou:

> '[T]he [CGRS] considers that this **sexual violence has not been established** because, on the one hand, the applicant did not mention it during her interview at the IO and, on the other hand, **because she has been "liking" her perpetrator's Facebook posts since 2018.**'[1283] | CASE OF FATOU

In another Congolese forced marriage, domestic violence, and rape case, the applicant's non-credible appease behaviour was identified through 'the happy expressions and smiles on the faces [of a social media photo, which] are very different from the image of the forced marriage that [she] is trying to paint.'[1284] In addition to the likes or expressions of applicants themselves, asylum authorities have also identified non-credible appeasing behaviour from the likes of others on Facebook photos of a perpetrator, failing to prove that he wanted to 'hide' his forced partner.[1285]

Thirdly, remaining in or seeking contact with perpetrators after SGBV (threats) has also been perceived as non-credible behaviour. Asylum officials at both the CGRS[1286] and the CALL confirmed this belief, with one judge illustrating a Colombian domestic violence case, where the applicant had obtained a protection order against her husband. However, 'her Facebook account showed that she still had contact with that man about their daughter and that he was liking pictures of her [...]. Based on this, it was decided [...] "you should not seek protection from your husband here if you are still in contact with him yourself"'.[1287]

In addition to (forced) (ex-)partners (whether or not about parenting arrangements[1288]), applicants' credibility has also been undermined due to contact with their parent-perpetrators,[1289] as in Elene's case.

1283 DG070_CALL 1 (recognition)_F_Guinea_RSA_FM_DV_18/1/2024_300 255_FR_Case law selection by CALL_p. 14.

1284 DC098_CALL 1 (refusal)_F_DRC_RSA_FM_DV_21/3/2024_303 543_FR_Database_p. 6.

1285 DG094_CGRS 1 (refusal)_F_Guinea_RSA_GMC_VGNT_FM_DV_5/5/2023_302 063_FR_Database_p. 4.

1286 CB015_CGRS_Supervisor + PO_GENDER_[00:51:23].

1287 RB005_CALL_Judge_[00:20:52].

1288 E.g. 'It may come as a surprise that you would contact him about your daughter, despite your alleged fears. It is to be expected that you would avoid any contact or reason to have contact.' (DB068_CGRS 1 (refusal)_1975_F_Bolivia_RSA_DV_25/1/2024_302 134_NL_Case law selection by CALL_p. 7.).

1289 DGe138_CALL 1 (refusal)_1998_F_Georgia_RSA_DV_23/5/2024_307 108_NL_Database_p. 11., DK152_CALL 2 (refusal)_1997_F_Kenya_RSA_VGNT_FM_DV_4/4/2024_304 367_NL_Database_p.19. DK152_CGRS 2 (refusal)_1997_Kenya_RSA_VGNT_FM_DV_7/3/2024_304 367_NL_Database_p. 7.

CASE OF ELENE			
• Country of origin:	Georgia	• SGBV types:	Violence related to gender norm transgression & domestic violence
• Gender identity:	Woman	• Decisions in file:	CGRS 1 (refusal) – 27/07/2023
• Birth year:	2003		CALL 1 (refusal) – 27/03/2024 – n° 303 891
• Interview by:	/		

According to her statements, Elene was born in Georgia in 2003, studied law, and lived with her parents. She described the domestic violence taking place by her father and brothers, both **threatening and abusing her and her mother**. Her parents got divorced, but her father kept stalking and abusing her mother. As a result, her mother fled the country. From then on, Elene was left living with her father, sister, and two brothers. While her father had forbidden her to contact her mother in an attempt to manipulate her and turn them against each other, they kept in touch in secret. Elene had always identified as lesbian, but never dared to tell anyone. She had a few brief relationships in secret and eventually told a few friends about her sexual orientation. While in Georgia, Elene never dared to tell her family, including her mother, because she feared they would reject her. Elene explained thinking that her father and brothers suspected her **sexual orientation**, because they asked questions about her playing football with boys or her clothes. Eventually, she fled Georgia in 2022, fearing that her father and brothers might kill her if they found out about her sexual orientation or her contact with her mother.

After fleeing the country seven years earlier, Elene's mother applied for international protection in Belgium, stating that she feared her ex-husband and son, because of her marriage to another man and her ex-husband's continuous stalking and abuse. The Belgian asylum authorities refused her international protection in March 2022. A cassation appeal against the appeal judgement was pending at the time of Elene's own procedure. Elene's mother and maternal uncle helped her travel to Belgium, where she too applied for international protection in December 2022. Meanwhile, her father and brothers believe she was in Sweden for an Erasmus exchange program and she was still in contact with them so as not to cause suspicion. In support of her application, she submitted a psychological report attesting that she had to grow up in an extremely unsafe and violent environment.

In Elene's case, both the CGRS and the CALL argued:

> 'Surely we can reasonably **expect that, if you feared** that **your father or your brothers** would kill you, **you would no longer contact them** once you are staying abroad. That you [do so] because you want to **prevent your sister from getting into trouble** [or **do not know how to explain** why you would break off contact], is **hardly convincing** [...] [and] make it unlikely that you fear such serious persecution.'[1290] | CASE OF ELENE

As mentioned above, asylum authorities seem to expect genuine SGBV survivors/victims to show interest in their perpetrators (whether before or

1290 DGe151_CALL 1 (refusal)_2003_F_Georgia_VGNT_DV_27/03/2024_303 891_NL_Database_p. 12., DGe151_CGRS 1_(refusal)_2003_F_Georgia_VGNT_DV_27/7/2023_303 891_NL_Database_p. 3.

after fleeing the country),[1291] while at the same time breaking off all contact with them. When applicants have few other means of gathering information about perpetrators than through direct contact, they should, so it seems, keep interacting with them after all, provided it is strictly aimed at obtaining information on their whereabouts and activities. Whether such a distinction is feasible in practice, is yet another question.

Fourthly, asylum authorities seem to infer lack of credibility from the fact that applicants at a certain point (temporarily) returned to their perpetrators' surroundings.[1292] Possible explanations for this are hereby rejected, such as: being 'hopeful that things had changed [under a new president and,] just having left your husband, […] [needing] to earn money, despite your colleagues telling you that you were still sought';[1293] being 'unable to live with your spouse, out of fear of being killed, [and therefore] returning to your [violent] family';[1294] or caring for ill family members.[1295]

The latter occurred in the abovementioned Georgian case of a bisexual man forced to marry a woman by his family-in-law, where the applicant returned to take care of his mother (with whom he had a very strong bond) after she suffered a cerebral haemorrhage. The CALL named his return 'praiseworthy, but […] difficult to reconcile with the alleged fear for his life.'[1296] Once in Georgia, he legally had to stay in the country for three months, but the CGRS expected him to 'even if illegal, find ways to have left earlier.'[1297] The argument was also used in the case of another Georgian applicant, Nino.

CASE OF NINO			
• Country of origin:	Georgia	• SGBV types:	Rape/sexual assault & domestic violence
• Gender identity:	Woman	• Decisions in file:	CGRS 1 (manifestly ill-founded) – 31/08/2021
• Birth year:	1975		CALL 1 (refusal) – 16/3/2022 – n° 269 856
• Interview by:	Researcher		

(continued)

[1291] DC096_CGRS 1 (refusal)_F_DRC_RSA_VGNT_30/11/2022_302 961_FR_Database_p. 4., DL119_CALL 1 (refusal)_1987_F_Liberia_FM_DV_26/4/2024_305 790_NL_Database_p. 7., DL119_CGRS 1 (refusal)_1987_F_Liberia_FM_DV_18/7/2023_305 790_NL_Database_p. 3.

[1292] E.g. DGa102_CGRS 1 (refusal)_F_The Gambia_FM_DV_10/10/2023_305 436_FR_Database_p. 5., DGa102_CALL 1 (refusal)_F_The Gambia_FM_DV_24/4/2024_305 436_FR_Database_p. 10., DGe138_CGRS 1 (refusal)_1998_F_Georgia_RSA_DV_27/12/2023_307 108_NL_Database_p.3.

[1293] DC096_CGRS 1 (refusal)_F_DRC_RSA_VGNT_30/11/2022_302 961_FR_Database_p.4.

[1294] DSo069_CGRS 1 (refusal)_F_Somalia_GMC_VGNT_FM_DV_23/8/2023_302 889_NL_Case law selection by CALL_p.5.

[1295] DB068_CGRS 1 (refusal)_1975_F_Bolivia_RSA_DV_25/1/2024_302 134_NL_Case law selection by CALL_p.6., DGe110_CGRS 1 (refusal)_1986_M_Georgia_VGNT_FM_28/9/2023_303 889_NL_Database_p.3–4.

[1296] DGe110_CALL 1 (refusal)_1986_M_Georgia_VGNT_FM_27/3/2024_303 889_NL_Database_p. 12.

[1297] DGe110_CGRS 1 (refusal)_1986_M_Georgia_VGNT_FM_28/9/2023_303 889_NL_Database_p.4.

According to her statements, Nino was born in 1975 and was initially married to a man with whom she had four children and lived in Georgia. During this marriage, he **abused her both physically, psychologically and sexually**. She managed to divorce him in 2013, but he continued to **stalk and physically assault** her afterwards. Between 2013 and 2016, she changed her address seven times, but was tracked down by him each time. She obtained three temporary protection orders (each for one month) against him, but these offered no effective protection. No criminal investigation was ever opened and the police and courts repeatedly told her that nothing could be done against her ex-husband as long as he had not been caught red-handed. Having obtained the last one-month protection order in November 2015, she eventually felt forced to flee to Turkey in order to find safety. She lived in Istanbul from 2016 to 2019 without legal residence status or protection. In January 2019, she met her current husband and decided to return to Georgia, where she could go into hiding with him. They stayed there for nine months, but ultimately fled to France, when this situation was no longer tenable. While in France, Nino's eldest son found out about her remarrying and her current location. Being warned by her daughter that he was **on his way to France to kill them**, they left the country and travelled on.

Nino arrived in Belgium and applied for international protection in September 2020. While in Belgium, she learnt from acquaintances at the French reception centre that unknown men had been asking about her. To support her asylum application, Nino submitted several legal and medical documents attesting her divorce, protection order rulings, and her scars caused by physical abuse.

In Nino's judgement, the CALL focused on her decision to return to Georgia to go into hiding with her husband, after her stay without legal residence status in Turkey, arguing:

> 'The applicant [...] repeats that [she] was **forced to flee to Turkey** [...], where she **resided illegally and enjoyed no protection** [...]. Apart from the fact that she was **living in hiding** – albeit in [her husband's] home – and **strictly limiting her contacts**, it is **surprising that [she], claiming to have been living in fear of her ex-husband since the 1990s, would return to the city where he lives**, as well as her son, who threatened her.'[1298] | CASE OF NINO

A similar argument was put forward in Lejla's judgement (directed at her husband):

> '[Your wife] **repeatedly leaving [...] and subsequently returning to Bosnia-Herzegovina** without applying for international protection [abroad], **cannot be reconciled with** [...] **a need for international protection** [...]. [Y]ou had **agreed to apply for international protection together** once the whole family obtained their [Bosnian] nationality [and s]**he did not want to leave you and the children**. [...]

1298 NGe014_CALL 1 (manifestly ill-founded)_1975_F_Georgia_RSA_DV_16/3/2022_269 856_NL_NANSEN_p. 17.

> [S]uch an attitude raises **serious questions**. Once again, [...] it can be **expected that she** [...] **would try to get to safety as quickly as possible**. [...] [This] leads to the conclusion that the abduction [and] [...] fear for [the mafia] cannot be believed.'[1299] | CASE OF LEJLA

Interestingly, the argument on returning to the perpetrator's surroundings, as it was used in Lejla's case, is diametrically opposed to another often-used argument, namely that mothers who leave their child in the country of origin are either bad mothers or non-credible, which I will discuss further below (see Chapter 4.1.3).

Fifthly, some SGBV survivors/victims reported trying to 'please' (potential) perpetrators as a form of appeasing survival reaction. These acts have also been qualified by asylum authorities as deviating from expected responses to SGBV (threats) and therefore found non-credible. Examples of such pleasing behaviour include: withdrawing statements on a violent partner once explained that qualifying him as an actor of persecution would exclude the option of family reunification;[1300] agreeing to hand over a child to a violent ex-partner in the future, hoping to (temporarily) avoid escalation;[1301] or as a man, obeying an older woman demanding sexual acts to avoid being falsely accused of rape and being publicly ostracised.[1302] In all three examples, these applicants' pleasing behaviour led them to be found non-credible and to be denied international protection.

4.1.3. ACTIVE SURVIVAL REACTIONS

Unlike the passive survival reactions discussed above (freeze/appease reactions and avoidance coping), the criminal justice context traditionally shows itself more lenient towards applicants who employed active survival reactions. Thus, SGBV survivors/victims in criminal proceedings are typically more readily believed if they fled, fought back, or employed approach coping mechanisms. These beliefs manifest themselves in existing rape myths such as: 'When a woman's chastity is threatened, she will violently resist, attempt to escape or scream for help' or 'If it was really serious she would come to court to provide evidence'.[1303]

1299 DBH121_CALL 1 (annulment)_F_Bosnia and Herzegovina_RSA_STFP_30/4/2024_305 882_NL_Database_p.6.

1300 DG094_CGRS 1 (refusal)_F_Guinea_RSA_GMC_VGNT_FM_DV_5/5/2023_302 063_FR_Database_p. 4., DG094_CALL 1 (annulment)_F_Guinea_RSA_GMC_VGNT_FM_DV_22/2/2024_302 063_FR_Database_p. 8.

1301 DIC153_CGRS 2 (refusal)_1979_F_Ivory Coast_RSA_GMC_VGNT_FM_DV_3/8/2023_307 471_FR_Case law selection by CALL_p.5.

1302 DIq095_CGRS 1 (refusal)_M_Iraq_RSA_DV_20/1/2023_302 595_FR_Database_p. 3.

1303 United Nations Office on Drugs and Crime (UNODC) (n 284) 80 & 99.

However, even active survival reactions, such as fleeing the situation/country or fighting back (physically, legally, ...), seem to be approached with scepticism in asylum contexts.

a) *Flight Reactions & Approach Coping*

An important difference between the criminal justice and the asylum context is that applicants for international protection have, by definition, already employed active survival reactions by fleeing, in order to arrive in the host country. Asylum authorities at times qualify these flight reactions as non-credible too, due to: 1) the flight as such, its timing (too soon, without exhausting other options, or too late), or its successful/well-prepared character, 2) the location of the flight (too far, instead of moving within the country, or too near), or 3) the fact that mothers fled without their children. I will also discuss 4) asylum authorities' dismissal of possible justifications to flee the country instead of the region, such as survivors'/victims' (perception of) traceability by perpetrators throughout the entire country.

Firstly, asylum authorities sometimes label applicants' flight reactions to SGBV as non-credible in and of itself. In Amani's case for example, the fact that she left on a one-week retreat the day after her mother found out about her stepfather's sexual abuse via her cousin was seen as reinforcing her non-credibility.[1304] In a Somali forced marriage case, both CGRS and CALL found it 'unlikely that [the applicant], as a young, uneducated woman, would leave [her town] all by herself to escape to [a nearby city].'[1305] Her explanation that she received material and moral support of the women in her family and that the journey only took two days, could not alter this conclusion.

Next to fleeing the area, asylum authorities consider fleeing one's country of origin, often via life-threatening migration routes, as a 'drastic decision'.[1306] The fact that applicants took this risk, leaving everything behind, is often seen as proof of mendacity, rather than urgency or severity of the SGBV feared.[1307] Applicants who flee relatively soon, often without seeking/exhausting (all) other options for support within their country's borders, are approached with suspicion.[1308] In the abovementioned Nigerian forced marriage and domestic violence case, the CGRS for example argued that, regardless of the applicant's decision to go into hiding with her aunt, she could not explain why '[she] did not

1304 NC004_CGRS 1 (refusal)_1991_F_DRC_RSA_DV_21/12/2021_266 712_FR_NANSEN_p. 5.

1305 DSo067_CALL 1 (annulment)_1986_F_Somalia_GMC_FM_20/2/2024_301 914_NL_Case law selection by CALL_p. 18., DSo067_CGRS 1 (refusal)_1986_F_Somalia_GMC_FM_27/2/2023_301 914_NL_Case law selection by CALL_p. 8.

1306 CB011_CGRS_Supervisor + PO_GENDER_[00:48:44]., RB003_CALL_Attaché_[00:15:44].

1307 RB003_CALL_Attaché_[00:15:44]., CB013_CGRS_PO_[01:05:10].

1308 RB008_CALL_Judge_[00:19:48]., NS005_CGRS 1 (refusal)_2002_F_Senegal_RSA_DV_FM_13/05/2022_274 056_FR_NANSEN_p. 6.

try other avenues to find help in Niger, [such as proposing a reconciliation to her father,] and why the only option was to leave the country.'[1309]

Along the same lines, one gender-specialised supervisor found it hard to empathise, but did not consider immediately leaving the country after sexual abuse 'the most logical step.' Instead, they said: 'If it happened to me, I would first try something else, because people are sometimes very casual about leaving their country, everything and everyone behind.' They concluded that, if applicants first took intermediary steps by seeking protection elsewhere in the country of origin, this would benefit their case.[1310] A judge confirmed that this reasoning applies all the more to resourceful applicants who leave a lot behind.[1311]

In other cases, applicants' flight from SGBV was considered either too well-prepared or too successful to be plausible. In contrast to the case of Lejla, from whom more serious precautions (than for example finding shelter for their daughters abroad with family) were expected before fleeing Bosnia-Herzegovina,[1312] the opposite reasoning was observed in the abovementioned Burundian rape case. There, the CGRS found that the applicant's precautions to flee the country were too meticulously prepared to be credible and did 'not correspond to the hasty departure of a person who fears persecution by their national authorities.'[1313]

In the same Nigerian forced marriage and domestic violence case as mentioned above, the applicant's escape attempts from her father's home were considered too successful to be credible. The first time, after her father had beaten her and had turned around to grab a stick, she ran and jumped into a taxi, not knowing why her father had not followed her. After her brothers had found her hiding at her aunt's, she had waited to escape a second time until dawn, when people would go out for prayer, leaving her unsupervised. Finding these statements 'incoherent, contradictory, evolving, evasive, incomplete, vague[,] stereotypical [...] and lacking spontaneity and objective evidence', the CGRS concluded her alleged forced marriage unsubstantiated.[1314] Importantly, such reasoning contrasts with asylum authorities' aforementioned disbelief of appease reactions, such as not trying to escape or resist a forced marriage, equally labelling these as non-credible.

1309 DN100_CGRS 1 (refusal)_1993_F_Nigeria_VGNT_FM_DV_6/10/2022_304 410_FR_Database_p. 8.

1310 CB011_CGRS_Supervisor + PO_GENDER_[00:48:44].

1311 'If a person directly leaves for the airport after a rape, it may seem, [...] completely crazy not to have tried other things depending on the profile. A person who is strong, who has everything in his or her own country, possibly children, etc., if someone like that fled, [...] it may be something that [...] will play a part in terms of credibility.'(RB006_CALL_Judge_[00:32:08].).

1312 DBH121_CGRS 1 (manifestly ill-founded)_F_Bosnia and Herzegovina_RSA_STFP_23/5/2023_305 882_NL_Database_p. 5.

1313 DBu089_CGRS 1 (refusal)_F_Burundi_RSA_14/11/2023_307 576_FR_Database_p. 7.

1314 DN100_CGRS1(refusal)_1993_F_Nigeria_VGNT_FM_DV_6/10/2022_304410_FR_Database_p.8–9.

Secondly, the location of flight seems to play a major role in the asylum context, namely whether applicants fled inside or outside their country of origin's borders. In refugee status determination, the reasoning comes down to: 'If you [have] a well-founded fear [of SGBV] […], you are expected to try to get away from [your perpetrator], to bring distance between you,'[1315] as long as this distance is not too far (i.e. abroad). Thus, the analysed case law demonstrated how applicants are far and foremost expected to relocate internally. Apart from the safety and reasonability assessment of such IFAs (see Part IV, Chapter 2.2.2), asylum authorities also tend to base credibility assessments on applicants' attempts to test these internal 'solutions' or not.

One attaché explained this reasoning by stating: '[Fleeing one's country] still remains a very difficult step, that brings up [the question whether] I can believe that a person who had [less difficult to reach] options [internally], would then still decide to [flee their country].'[1316] Other asylum officials confirmed that they expect an applicant fleeing SGBV: to 'simply leave her husband and settle elsewhere'[1317] or to not have 'stay[ed] with a husband who beats her for all those years [while she could have had] her own little clinic and moved elsewhere, […] [therefore] I thought she was lying.'[1318]

The analysed case law reflects the idea that 'true' SGBV survivors/victims would have simply fled the region[1319] (or even the room[1320]), instead of the country. In Carmen's case for example, the CALL argued:

> 'Regarding her **failure to move [internally]**, the applicant argues […] that her ex-husband did not live in [her city,] but still managed to hurt her on several occasions

---

1315 DN108_CALL 1 (refusal)_F_Nigeria_GMC_ FM_14/3/2024_303 213_NL_Database_p. 9., DN108_CGRS 1 (refusal)_F_Nigeria_GMC_FM_10/7/2023_303 213_NL_Database_p. 4.

1316 RB003_CALL_Attaché_[00:45:13] & [00:47:37].

1317 CB004_CGRS_PO_[00:09:37], [00:11:29] & [00:44:53].

1318 RB007_CALL_Attaché_[00:32:11].

1319 DA118_CGRS 1 (manifestly ill-founded)_F_Albania_STFP_DV_22/12/2022_305 447_NL_Database_p. 5., DA118_CALL 1 (refusal)_F_Albania_STFP_DV_24/4/2024_305 447_NL_Database_p. 15., DGe151_CALL 1 (refusal)_2003_F_Georgia_VGNT_DV_27/03/2024_303 891_NL_Database_p. 12., DGe151_CGRS 1_(refusal)_2003_F_Georgia_VGNT_DV_27/7/2023_303891_NL_Database_p.6., DIC105_CGRS 1 (refusal)_1999_F_IvoryCoast_RSA_VGNT_DV 26/10/2023 306 239_FR_Database_p. 6., DM116_CALL 1 (refusal)_1999_F_Morocco_VGNT_FM_DV_24/04/2024_305 429_NL_Database_p. 15, DM116_CGRS 1 (refusal)_1999_F_Morocco_VGNT_FM_DV_3/4/2024_305 429_NL_Database_p. 4., DR145_CGRS 1 (inadmissible)_2003__Russia_RSA_VGNT_30/3/2023_307 559_NL_Database_p. 3., NA016_CGRS 1 (manifestly ill-founded)_1990_F_Albania_RSA_VGNT_DV_10/10/2022_285 363_NL_NANSEN_p. 6.

1320 'Finally, you mention several times that you were the victim of attempted assault, both by a family friend and on the metro. Both as a child and later in life when you already had a child of your own. […] It later appears that these were always attempts, which apparently could be avoided by, for example, going to another room. Nowhere does it appear that you were physically touched in this context.' (DGe138_CGRS 1 (refusal)_1998_F_Georgia_RSA_DV_27/12/2023_307 108_NL_Database_p. 4., DGe138_CALL 1 (refusal)_1998_F_Georgia_RSA_DV_23/5/2024_307 108_NL_Database_p. 15.).

> despite the eight-hour drive and thus it must be concluded that [he] can reach her anywhere. […] [As such,] **she never thought of settling elsewhere in Ecuador** […]. With this argument, the applicant […] gets no further than persisting in previous statements found to be **non-credible**.'[1321] | CASE OF CARMEN

Like Carmen, applicants often justified their flight outside (instead of inside) state borders through the risk (whether perceived or real) that they could be found by their SGBV perpetrators, especially if there is a history of stalking or abduction. For asylum authorities, this traceability plays a role in refugee status determination, especially in assessing whether applicants would still fear persecution at the location of an IFA.[1322] The extent to which this traceability is evaluated differs according to the asylum official. Some of them do not take into account the traceability of applicants by their perpetrators at all.[1323]

Another judge more cryptically stated that 'it is not the traceability that is important, but the opportunity to settle [at an IFA],' which is largely determined by applicants' (non-)material resourcefulness.[1324] For the CGRS, one PO more concretely mentioned the often-used argument: 'Dakar is a huge city and Senegal is a big country, they don't really have the means to find you […] and even if the [SGBV is] proven […], you can always go and live in another city.'[1325]

This fear of traceability by SGBV perpetrators has been dismissed by the authorities in the analysed case law.[1326] In the abovementioned forced marriage and rape case of an Ivorian applicant accused of sorcery, whose perpetrator had stalked and threatened her before, the CGRS argued: '[Y]ou say that he would find you in another part of the [country] and that you therefore left Ivory Coast altogether […]. [However,] there is nothing to indicate that he would be willing or able to find you outside […] this metropolis of more than five million inhabitants, where the population density allows a certain form of anonymity.'[1327] In the abovementioned Georgian case of a bisexual applicant

---

1321 Dec120_CALL 1 (refusal)_1981_F_Ecuador_RSA_DV_ 29/4/2024_ 305 805_NL_Database_ p. 8.

1322 Art. 8(1)a EU Qualification Directive; Art. 8(1)a EU Qualification Regulation.

1323 CB004_CGRS_PO_[00:12:42]., CB007_CGRS_PO_[00:44:41]., RB005_CALL_Judge_ [00:34:36].

1324 RB008_CALL_Judge_[00:26:21].

1325 CB010_CGRS_Supervisor + PO_[00:21:03] & [00:23:31].

1326 E.g. 'The fact that you did not want to move to another place because [the perpetrator] could find you anywhere and something could still happen to you there is not serious.' (DB068_ CGRS 1 (refusal)_1975_F_Bolivia_RSA_DV_25/1/2024_302 134_NL_Case law selection by CALL_p. 5–6.), 'The fear expressed during the personal interview that her father would find them everywhere is no more than a bare allegation, for which there are no concrete indications' (DGe139_CALL 1 (refusal)_lawyers' argumentation_2005_F_Georgia_DV_23/5/2024_307 109_NL_Database_p. 10.).

1327 DIC153_CGRS 2 (refusal)_1979_F_Ivory Coast_RSA_GMC_VGNT_FM_DV_3/8/2023_307 471_FR_Case law selection by CALL_p.6.

forced to marry a woman, he considered moving within Georgia pointless, given that his stepfather (as a colonel) and family-in-law (with their criminal activities and contacts in police and criminal circles) could find him if they wanted to. Nevertheless, the CALL found the fact that he initially continued to live and work in the same house and eventually fled Georgia altogether non-credible.[1328]

Interestingly, in the Ghanaian forced marriage and rape case mentioned above, the CGRS and CALL oppositely argued that the applicant fled to a location too near (instead of too far/abroad) to be found credible: 'it is unlikely that, if you truly feared that [your perpetrator] would take your life after the argument you had, you simply fled to [a] neighbouring village [...], only six kilometres away [...]. Such behaviour completely contradicts [and renders non-credible] [...] your fear of persecution.'[1329]

Thirdly, applicants who flee without their children are often labelled as non-credible too.[1330] This reasoning was reflected in the personal interview of Aya, the Syrian applicant fleeing threats of sexual assault by a military official, where the PO asked her: 'I'm not sure I understand why you fled. From what I understand, this man threatened those around you in order to put pressure on you. Why did you leave on your own?'[1331] This argument, that mothers fleeing without their children cannot be considered credible, was also used in the decisions of Qawtar, a Moroccan applicant,[1332] and of Rahel:

> '[Y]ou **fled** [...] **alone, but left your daughter behind**[, giving as a] reason that fleeing the country illegally is dangerous because you can be shot, and that you **did not dare to risk your daughter's life** [...]. [T]hat you would leave your daughter [...] at home with your mother and your niece, [forbidding her to leave the house or go to school, fearing that her father would abduct her], **purely out of fear of illegal border crossing** [...], **severely damages your credibility.**'[1333] | CASE OF RAHEL

1328 DGe110_CALL1(refusal)_1986_M_Georgia_VGNT_FM_27/3/2024_303889_NL_Database_p. 11.

1329 DGh115_CALL 1 (refusal)_1999_F_Ghana_RSA_FM_DV_19/4//2024_305 147_NL_Database_p. 9., DGh115_CGRS 1 (refusal)_1999_F_Ghana_RSA_FM_DV_26/3/2024_305 147_NL_Database_p. 3–4.

1330 E.g. DB068_CGRS 1 (refusal)_1975_F_Bolivia_RSA_DV_25/1/2024_302 134_NL_Case law selection by CALL_p. 6–7.

1331 NSy019 CGRS interview_1997_F_Syria_RSA_FR_NANSEN_p. 16.

1332 '[Y]ou left your two-year-old child in Morocco, where it has since been raised by your family, because you first wanted to [...] find a permanent place to live before bringing [her] to Europe [...]. This explanation very seriously clashes with your alleged fear of not being able to care for [her, due to your father's and ex-husband's violence and the risk of stigmatisation in Moroccan society after your divorce].' (DM116_CALL 1 (refusal)_1999_F_Morocco_VGNT_FM_DV_24/04/2024_305 429_NL_Database_p. 14, DM116_CGRS 1 (refusal)_1999_F_Morocco_VGNT_FM_DV_3/4/2024_305 429_NL_Database_p. 4.).

1333 NEr018_CGRS 1 (refusal)_1985_F_Eritrea_RSA_30/5/2022_280 827_NL_NANSEN_p. 5., NEr018_CALL 1 (refusal)_1985_F_Eritrea_RSA_25/11/2022_280 827_NL_NANSEN_p. 15.

As mentioned above, it is important to note that in the case of Lejla, the authorities oppositely criticised her for returning to Bosnia-Herzegovina to flee together with her children. While Lejla's husband explained that they had agreed to apply for international protection as a family and that Lejla did not want to leave her children by fleeing alone, the CALL argued that 'such an attitude raises serious questions […] [as] it can be expected that she […] would try to get to safety as quickly as possible.'[1334]

b) *Fight Reactions & Approach Coping*

Finally, applicants fleeing SGBV might have tried to 'fight back' or confront the perpetrator through approach coping before eventually fleeing their country of origin. In contrast to the criminal justice context, asylum authorities have also called into question this second form of active survival reactions. One gender-specialised supervisor for example called the need that survivors/victims might feel to confront SGBV perpetrators 'an illogical response.'[1335] Below, I will illustrate how asylum authorities at times discredit: 1) applicants' reaction to fight back as such (and what forms such resistance might take) and 2) the fact that they did so in a way considered too radical, insufficiently persistent, or too successful.

Firstly, fighting back as a short- or long-term response to SGBV (threats) in asylum contexts may take multiple forms. As mentioned above, Rahel initially wanted to 'fight back' by actively tracking down and confronting her rapist, after her complaint to the police remained without effect. The CALL labelled it 'incomprehensible that [she] […] tried to contact [her rapist] herself.'[1336] In a Senegalese case, the applicant's resistance against her forced marriage was more subtle. Feeling unable to oppose the marriage itself, she refused to give birth to children 'whose father [she] detested.' While her family-in-law put pressure on her, she told them she was getting fertility treatments at the hospital, but in reality went there to get contraceptives. Hereupon, the CGRS found it 'unlikely that [she] had managed to dismiss [her] in-laws' pressure […] to have offspring from their eldest son […]. [T]he way in which [she did so] clearly [clashed with the image of a] religious and traditionalist family […] [and] undermined [her] credibility.'[1337]

In the case of Aya, her resistance to the attempted sexual assault by a military official came closest to the traditional meaning of physically 'fighting back'.

1334 DBH121_CALL 1 (annulment)_F_Bosnia and Herzegovina_RSA_STFP_30/4/2024_305 882_NL_Database_p.6.

1335 CB015_CGRS_Supervisor + PO_GENDER_[00:36:49].

1336 NEr018_CALL 1 (refusal)_1985_F_Eritrea_RSA_25/11/2022_280 827_NL_NANSEN_p. 15.

1337 DS103_CGRS 1 (refusal)_F_Senegal_GMC_FM_DV_17/7/2023_305 927_FR_Database_p. 5–6.

CASE OF AYA			
• Country of origin:	Syria	• SGBV types:	Rape/sexual assault
• Gender identity:	Woman	• Decisions in file:	CGRS 1 (refusal) – 8/8/2023
• Birth year:	1997		CALL 1 (annulment) – 31/8/2023 – n° 293 489
• Interview by:	CGRS		

According to her statements, Aya was born in 1997 in Syria. Her husband was forced to do military service, where she visited him in March 2023. Upon arriving, she noticed an officer stepping out of his office to look at the queue of visitors. He spoke to a guard while pointing at her. After meeting her husband, the same guard ordered Aya to follow him to his superior. She found herself alone with the officer (who turned out to be a colonel) in his office, upon which he began making **sexual advances** towards her. She categorically refused these, but he became more insistent and **grabbed her** by the arm to **prevent her from leaving**. She tried to intimidate him by lying that she knew a general in the army. The colonel appeared to be deterred by this, which allowed her to leave, though he warned her that he would find a way to make her return. Two months later, Aya received a phone call from her husband's phone. The caller said that her husband had been injured and that she needed to come to sign documents for his hospital treatment. She went there again, but this time, the guard took her firmly by the arm and led her directly to the colonel's office. Before he could force her inside, she resisted and loudly warned that if he touched her again, she would scream. The colonel then asked if she had been mocking him by lying about the general and **threatened** that he would harm her daughter, her husband, her family, and Aya herself for not obeying him. He then pushed her and ordered her to leave. One to two weeks later, her husband was transferred to another region, which Aya saw as a retaliation from the colonel. She lived in constant fear that something would happen to her or her family.

In May 2023, she saw an opportunity to leave while she was in Lebanon with family, using her sister's passport. She arrived in Belgium without legal travel documents and submitted an application for international protection, upon which she was placed in a detention centre.

In Aya's refusal decision, the CGRS argued:

> 'According to the objective information available to the CGRS, women who are **victims of** [...] **abuse receive no support** whatsoever from the Syrian authorities [...] [and] in Syria and other Middle Eastern countries, **male-female relationships are far from** [...] **equal** [...]. It therefore seems particularly **implausible that such a "monster" would be intimidated by a woman who brings up a random [general's] name and openly threatens to scream to draw attention to him and humiliate him.**'[1338] | CASE OF AYA

[1338] NSy019_CGRS 1 (refusal)_1997_F_Syria_RSA_8/8/2023_293 489_FR_NANSEN_p. 3–4.

Another form of 'fighting back' (legally) might consist of filing a complaint with the authorities. In most cases, applicants' failure or delay to seek state protection seems to weaken their credibility (see Part IV, Chapter 3.1). By contrast, a Bolivian applicant's complaint for domestic violence to the police was considered implausible. The CGRS refused her international protection, arguing: 'For someone who claims to be living in hiding, it cannot be understood that she would appeal to a commissariat where she claims the officer present would collude with her attacker.'[1339]

Secondly, some non-credibility assessments are also based on applicants' fight reactions being either too radical, not persistent enough, or too successful to be plausible. The abovementioned Nigerian forced marriage case can serve as an example of the first. In this case, after learning she would be forcibly married, the applicant immediately confronted her father, telling him: 'I'd rather die than marry him!' Upon the PO's question why she had not tried to set up a long-term dialogue with her father, with whom she previously had a good relationship, she replied that he had recently undergone a 'moral transformation', becoming much stricter towards her. However, the CGRS considered 'this part of [her] story vague, imprecise and devoid of any element of real experience.'[1340] In other cases, the insufficiently persistent nature of applicants' 'fight' response proved to be a credibility issue. The abovementioned Bolivian applicant, who on the one hand was found non-credible because she filed a (risky) police complaint, was on the other hand disbelieved because '[she] did not follow up on [...] [this] complaint[,] [...] showing a lack of interest.'[1341]

Other applicants' initiatives to 'fight back' were perceived as unrealistically successful. This is specifically the case with forced marriages,[1342] such as a Somali case where both the CGRS and CALL found it 'remarkable that after [the applicant's] father's death, [her] mother was able to marry a man of her own choosing and successfully resisted marrying [her late husband's] brother [...], given that Somalia is a patriarchal society.'[1343] In Zeynep's case, the 'successful' nature of her resistance to being forcibly married to her cousin (e.g. through

1339 DB068_CGRS 1 (refusal)_1975_F_Bolivia_RSA_DV_25/1/2024_302 134_NL_Case law selection by CALL_p.4.

1340 DN100_CGRS 1 (refusal)_1993_F_Nigeria_VGNT_FM_DV_6/10/2022_304 410_FR_Database_p. 7.

1341 DB068_CGRS 1 (refusal)_1975_F_Bolivia_RSA_DV_25/1/2024_302 134_NL_Case law selection by CALL_p. 7.

1342 DG097_CALL 1 (refusal)_F_Guinea_RSA_GMC_FM_DV_14/3/2024_303 242_FR_Database_p. 9., DGa102_CGRS 1 (refusal)_F_The Gambia_FM_DV_10/10/2023_305 436_FR_Database_p. 5., DI131_CALL 1 (refusal)_F_Iran_VGNT_FM_DV_14/5/2024_306 520_NL_Database_p. 9., DI131_CGRS 1 (refusal)_F_Iran_VGNT_FM_DV_27/7/2023_306 520_NL_Database_p. 3.

1343 DSo125_CALL 1 (refusal)_1996_F_Somalia_VGNT_FM_3/05/2024_306 071_NL_Database_p. 12., DSo125_CGRS 1 (refusal) 1996_F_Somalia_VGNT_FM_26/09/2023_306 071_NL_Database_p.4.

a suicide attempt attested by a medical report[1344]) cynically led the CGRS to conclude that her fears were purely hypothetical:

> '[Y]ou have regularly **opposed this marriage by threatening to take your own life,** which has allowed you to **escape it until now.** We therefore note that **the fears** associated with this marriage to your cousin are **hypothetical** and you have **not provided any concrete evidence** to substantiate them. You state that your family has been putting pressure on you for two years, yet no wedding date had been set.'[1345] | CASE OF ZEYNEP

4.2. REBUTTAL OF THE MYTHS ON SURVIVAL REACTIONS

Above, I illustrated how both applicants' passive (short-term freeze and appease reactions or long-term avoidance coping) and active survival reactions (short-term flight and fight reactions or long-term approach coping) are at times considered abnormal and therefore non-credible behaviour in response to SGBV (threats). In refugees status determination, this ultimately means that any of applicants' survival reactions can be called into question, whether these involve fleeing, not fleeing (freezing), fighting back, not fighting back (appeasing), avoiding/ignoring the SGBV/perpetrator (avoidance coping), or not doing so (approach coping). Below, I will go into the expertise from health, social, and legal sciences and (case) law rebutting expectations about 'normal' vs. 'abnormal' survivor/victim behaviour. I will pay specific attention to how such expectations might result in minimisation or denial of SGBV, when its survivors/victims show behaviour that is considered 'deviant'.[1346]

4.2.1. REBUTTAL IN HEALTH & SOCIAL SCIENCES

As demonstrated in studies on SGBV and domestic violence in particular, active survival reactions after SGBV may for example include: seeking help from private networks, filing a complaint to state actors, or planning an escape. Survivors/victims showing passive reactions often cannot move past the first step towards help-seeking: acknowledgement of one's experiences as SGBV. Such passive survival reactions can consist of: refusing to believe the SGBV took

---

1344 NT015_CGRS interview 1_2_3_1996_F_Turkey_RSA_FM_DV_FR_p. 3–4 (memo)., NT015_CGRS 2 (refusal)_1996_F_Turkey_RSA_FM_DV_1/2/2023_285 279_FR_NANSEN_p. 2 & 6.

1345 NT015_CGRS 2 (refusal)_1996_F_Turkey_RSA_FM_DV_1/2/2023_285 279_FR_NANSEN_p. 6.

1346 Breen and Boyce (n 401) 5232.

place, keeping feelings to oneself, blaming oneself, … with the aim of preventing escalation and/or the (often futile) hope of improving the situation.[1347] While active survival reactions are generally considered more credible than passive ones, research across different SGBV forms shows that, in reality, passive coping is more common than active coping.[1348] More important than precise statistics, is the observation that both types of short-term reactions and long-term coping mechanisms (active and passive) may constitute 'normal survivor/victim behaviour'.

As mentioned earlier, for short-term reactions specifically, stress hormones can cause a drastic loss of prefrontal cognitive abilities, limiting SGBV survivors'/victims' decision making and strategising capacities in the face of violence.[1349] Therefore, asking survivors/victims to rationally 'account for the decisions [they] made around a traumatic sexual assault is not a reasonable request.'[1350] In the asylum interview setting, already prone to (perceived) victim blaming, such questions may force applicants 'to offer explanations […] [that expose] feelings of shame and vulnerability [when challenged] […] [or to] make what appear to be inconsistent statements about what they think they were doing.'[1351]

For long-term survival reactions, it is essential to stress that avoidance is one of the key criteria to diagnose PTSD (when lasting for over one month), according to the Diagnostic and Statistical Manual of Mental Disorders (DSM). Concretely, PTSD comes with survivors'/victims' persistent avoidance of stimuli associated with the trauma, such as SGBV, including the people and places involved, conversations on what happened, and other distressing memories, thoughts, or feelings.[1352] This recognition of avoidance coping as a manifestation of PTSD rather than an illogical reaction to be scrutinised, is essential to accurate refugee status determination for applicants fleeing SGBV.

Moreover, according to the intra-individual approach in literature,[1353] the coping mechanisms used depend on the characteristics of a stressful situation

---

1347 Angela E Waldrop and Patricia A Resick, 'Coping Among Adult Female Victims of Domestic Violence' (2004) 19 Journal of Family Violence 291, 292; Erin L Foster and others, 'Coping with Intimate Partner Violence: Qualitative Findings from the Study of Dynamics of Husband to Wife Abuse' (2015) 33 Families, Systems, & Health 285, 290.

1348 Zeynep Zonp and others, 'Coping Strategies among Women Exposed to Gender-Based Violence in Turkey' (2022) 78 Journal of Advanced Nursing 4236, 4237; Babacan Gümüş, Şıpkın and Erdem (n 1226).

1349 Department of Justice of the Government of Canada (n 933); United Nations Office on Drugs and Crime (UNODC) and Skinnider (n 161) 23.

1350 Department of Justice of the Government of Canada (n 933).

1351 *Ibid.*

1352 American Psychiatric Association (n 937) 271–272.

1353 '[T]wo primary methodological perspectives that commonly appear in the literature on coping [are t]he inter-individual approach[, describing] responses to stress in terms of coping "styles" that a person is expected to use across different types of stressors[, and] […] the

(e.g. severity, frequency, or type of abuse[1354] and whether or not an abusive relationship has been terminated).[1355] The personal and material resources SGBV survivors/victims (perceive to) have at their disposal, as well as their past experiences with certain coping also impact these choices. For example, positive responses from institutional actors and non-avoidant responses from private networks have been linked to higher use of active coping with intimate partner violence.[1356] Also, survivors/victims who perceive their situation as changeable tend to adopt active survival reactions, while those who perceive it as unchangeable mostly adopt passive ones.[1357]

Further, coping mechanisms are employed in a flexible and evolving manner, especially in the case of SGBV forms that take place over a longer period of time and in a cyclical manner[1358] (e.g. domestic violence, stalking, forced marriage, ...).[1359] Particularly because they are variable in frequency, duration, and nature over time, survivors'/victims' survival reactions are often approached with disbelief.[1360] However, survivors'/victims' personal characteristics,[1361] combined with the external circumstances of a threatening situation,[1362] make it almost impossible to predict how a person will react after

---

intra-individual approach, suggest[ing] that people change their coping strategies according to the stressor'. Waldrop and Resick (n 1347) 292.

[1354] E.g. 'The women who were exposed to partner violence physically, sexually and economically were less likely to use the self-confident and optimistic approaches, and the effective coping method of seeking social support. The women who were exposed to emotional violence used ineffective coping methods such as submissive approach more often.' Babacan Gümüş, Şıpkın and Erdem (n 1226) 85.

[1355] E.g. 'Women appear to use more avoidance strategies when they are still in abusive relationships and trying to cope with ongoing violence. However, the more severe and frequent the abuse becomes, the more likely battered women are to try to take active steps to leave the relationship.' Waldrop and Resick (n 1347) 292 & 300; E.g. 'women were more likely to report that they responded assertively to a sexual assault situation, rather than diplomatically when they were less concerned about preserving the relationship.' Christine A Gidycz, John R McNamara and Katie M Edwards, 'Women's Risk Perception and Sexual Victimization: A Review of the Literature' (2006) 11 Aggression and Violent Behavior 441, 451.

[1356] Foster and others (n 1347) 286; Waldrop and Resick (n 1347) 300.

[1357] Babacan Gümüş, Şıpkın and Erdem (n 1226) 84.

[1358] Sharelle Aitchison, 'The Temporality of Intimate Partner Violence – How an Understanding of Time and Gendered Threats Can Foster Protection-Positive Outcomes' (2024) 43 Refugee Survey Quarterly 73, 84.

[1359] Waldrop and Resick (n 1347) 300; Babacan Gümüş, Şıpkın and Erdem (n 1226) 84; Fanflik, Office on Violence Against Women, and National District Attorneys Association (n 386) 14; Lodrick (n 1222) 10.

[1360] Fanflik, Office on Violence Against Women, and National District Attorneys Association (n 386) 14.

[1361] E.g. mental health, developmental level and self-image before the violence, desire to maintain relationship with perpetrator, past experiences with SGBV, spiritual beliefs, genetic predisposition, internalisation of (blame for) the violence, ...

[1362] E.g. social support network, (nature and continuation of) relationship with perpetrator, severity/frequency/type of violence, resources available to victims, responsiveness of potential resources, societal or cultural responses to victimisation of SGBV, ...

an experience of sexual violence.[1363] As Fanflik confirms: 'Given the number of possible influences on a victim's reaction after sexual assault, there is no comprehensive model of coping mechanisms in victims of sexual violence.'[1364]

On top of this, literature on risk theory (in SGBV or general contexts) exposes that survivors/victims rarely respond with 'reasonable' steps expected to keep themselves safe.[1365] This is reinforced by the optimism bias at play in human responses to risk in general, and to SGBV in particular.[1366] Research shows for example that 'women in general perceive themselves as less likely than their peers to be sexually assaulted.'[1367] As Evans Cameron states: '[H]uman response to danger can be "bewildering" even to the experts, and much of its well-documented variance still remains unexplained.'[1368] As a result of the above findings in research on survival reactions and risk theory, it is senseless for asylum authorities to prioritise one type of survival reaction as 'normal behaviour of genuine SGBV survivors/victims' over another type.

Instead, decision makers must recognise the wide range of potential human responses to such violence,[1369] which depend on evolving individual and circumstantial characteristics and are therefore almost impossible to predict. Below, I will demonstrate that each of the above discussed (short- or long-term) passive and active survival reactions may occur and may constitute 'normal' responses to SGBV (threats). As such, the myth that 'inappropriate' survival reactions undermine SGBV flight stories' credibility cannot be supported by empirical evidence.

a) *Freeze Reactions & Avoidance Coping*

Contrary to what asylum authorities have demonstrated to believe above, there are many reasons why (potential) SGBV survivors/victims might freeze and fail to leave a violent situation (sooner). Literature on coping with domestic violence for example describes many barriers to planning and envisioning a way out of SGBV, rendering survivors/victims unable or even unwilling to escape.

1363 Fanflik, Office on Violence Against Women, and National District Attorneys Association (n 386) 2; Gidycz, McNamara and Edwards (n 1355) 451.

1364 Fanflik, Office on Violence Against Women, and National District Attorneys Association (n 386) 7.

1365 Hilary Evans Cameron, 'Risk and the Reasonable Refugee: Exploring a Key Credibility Inference in Canadian Refugee Status Rejections' (2023) 35 International Journal of Refugee Law 10, 15.

1366 Gidycz, McNamara and Edwards (n 1355) 452; Hilary Evans Cameron, 'Risk Theory and "Subjective Fear": The Role of Risk Perception, Assessment, and Management in Refugee Status Determinations' (2008) 20 International Journal of Refugee Law 567, 573.

1367 Gidycz, McNamara and Edwards (n 1355) 450.

1368 Evans Cameron, 'Risk Theory and "Subjective Fear"' (n 1366) 585.

1369 Barbara Krahé, 'Cognitive Coping With the Threat of Rape: Vigilance and Cognitive Avoidance' (2005) 73 Journal of Personality 609, 610.

These include: financial dependence, health problems, fear of escalation or increased danger upon separation, social values and policies discouraging leaving, lack of opportunity or service provision, or other psychological and situational factors.[1370] These barriers may cause survivors/victims to remain in a violent but known situation rather than expose themselves to unknown and unpredictable escalation. The avoidant coping mechanisms resulting from these barriers might, within violent relationships for example, take the form of 'sleeping in separate rooms [...], staying at work for longer hours, [...] [or] "[if a violent partner] doesn't go, [packing a] night bag and [...] [spending] the weekend with [family] just [to] get away [temporarily]"'.[1371]

These barriers to leaving a violent situation or the country as a whole are also demonstrated by the applicants included in this research. Diana for example initially demonstrated an optimism bias[1372] preventing her from thinking about leaving Albania. Although she did not experience the divorce procedure as just, she told herself she would at least be separated from her husband and was hoping that after this 'it would be over, but this wasn't the case.'[1373] Long after the divorce, after the stalking, attempted abduction of her daughter, and further escalation of physical and psychological violence of her ex-husband, the police quite literally forced Diana and Erina into avoidant coping, by forbidding them to go out (incl. to school), until they could arrest him (which eventually never happened).[1374]

Other applicants initially stayed because they first had sought other means to resolve their problems. Some sought ways to avoid their perpetrator, such as Sofia, the abovementioned Honduran applicant who was sexually abused by her father, who spent as much time as possible with her grandmother,[1375] or Amani, who avoided having to sleep at home by going to funerals and vigils at the church, sometimes of people she did not even know.[1376] Others went into complete hiding, such as Mary with her friend[1377] or Zeynep[1378] and Rahel[1379] with their aunt. The fact that they were not directly threatened by their perpetrators anymore since going into hiding, does not mean that their fear/risk of SGBV had passed. Mary for example almost immediately arranged her flight out of Liberia after she had seen her perpetrators in town one day.[1380]

1370 Foster and others (n 1347) 292; Jennifer L Dunn, '"Victims" and "Survivors": Emerging Vocabularies of Motive for "Battered Women Who Stay"*' (2005) 75 Sociological Inquiry 1, 5.
1371 Foster and others (n 1347) 291.
1372 Evans Cameron, 'Risk Theory and "Subjective Fear"' (n 1366) 574.
1373 NA001_B_1973_F_Albania_RSA_VGNT_FM_DV_NL_NANSEN_[00:34:17].
1374 NA001_A_B_2006_F_Albania_RSA_VGNT_FM_DV_NL_NANSEN_MINOR_[01:00:42].
1375 NH003_1991_F_Honduras_RSA_DV_NL_NANSEN_p.2.
1376 NC004_CGRS interview 1_1991_F_DRC_RSA_DV_FR_NANSEN_p. 15.
1377 NL017_1980_F_Liberia_STFP_GMC_VGNT_FM_NL_NANSEN_[01:02:52].
1378 NT015_CGRS interview 1_2_3_1996_F_Turkey_RSA_FM_DV_FR_p. 8 (memo).
1379 NEr018_1985_F_Eritrea_RSA_NL_NANSEN_[00:53:12].
1380 NL017_1980_F_Liberia_STFP_GMC_VGNT_FM_NL_NANSEN_[01:02:52].

Rahel, who was living in hiding with her daughter (no longer going to school) and who was only going out to work in a salon close to the house, argued through her lawyer:

> '[T]he only **reason the applicant did not receive any threats** after 2018 was that she **managed to hide without him finding her**, she **no longer had a telephone** and no [other] means of communication or contact.'[1381] | CASE OF RAHEL

In addition, SGBV survivors/victims might perceive it practically, mentally, or legally impossible to leave a violent situation (immediately). Practical barriers brought up by applicants for example included: wanting/having to take up care for family members (such as Aya for her parents[1382] or the abovementioned Georgian bisexual applicant for his mother[1383]), insufficient financial resources[1384] (such as Carmen[1385] and Aya[1386]), camera surveillance monitored by the perpetrator around the house (such as Vera[1387]), or the administrative organisation of a flight out of the country for an entire family (such as Lejla).

> '[B]esides the fact that the **departure of a family of five could not be organised overnight**, they explained that they were bound by **employment contracts** and [...] still had to give notice [...], [t]hat [they] were about to obtain Bosnian **nationality**, which they needed before they could consider leaving[, and t]hat from the moment they had taken the decision to leave Bosnia, it **did not make sense to move for six weeks** [...], so they remained in their home, but were very **cautious**.'[1388] | CASE OF LEJLA

Mental barriers to leaving might be installed through the interpersonal dynamics at play in violent relations. Often, after a 'violent phase', abusers may use emotional manipulation (the so-called 'honeymoon phase') by behaving apologetically and promising improvement, and then resort to violence again (constituting a 'cycle of violence').[1389] Due to the coercive control resulting from

1381 NEr018_CALL 1 (refusal)_lawyers' argumentation_1985_F_Eritrea_RSA_25/11/2022_280 827_NL_NANSEN_p. 9.

1382 NSy019 CGRS interview_1997_F_Syria_RSA_FR_NANSEN_p. 16.

1383 DGe110_CALL 1 (refusal)_lawyers' argumentation_1986_M_Georgia_VGNT_FM_27/3/2024_303 889_NL_Database_p. 6–7.

1384 DIC074_CALL 1 (annulment)_lawyers' argumentation_F_Ivory Coast_GMC_VGNT_11/3/2024_302 979_FR_Case law selection by CALL_p. 5.

1385 DEc120_CALL 1 (refusal)_lawyers' argumentation_1981_F_Ecuador_RSA_DV_29/4/2024_305 805_NL_Database_p. 8.

1386 NSy019 CGRS interview_1997_F_Syria_RSA_FR_NANSEN_p. 16.

1387 NA016_1990_F_Albania_RSA_VGNT_DV_NL_NANSEN_[00:30:48].

1388 DBH121_CALL 1 (annulment)_lawyers' argumentation_F_Bosnia and Herzegovina_RSA_STFP_30/4/2024_305 882_NL_Database_p. 16.

1389 United Nations Office on Drugs and Crime (UNODC) and Skinnider (n 161) 18; Herman (n 713) 79.

this cycle,[1390] survivors/victims may become emotionally dependent on their abuser (called 'trauma bonding') as a survival mechanism.[1391] Zeynep described her relationship with the policeman who raped her in similar terms:

> '[O]**ne day he was a friend and the next an enemy, one day he apologised** saying that it wasn't possible given our age difference, **and another day, that I belonged to him and that I couldn't belong to anyone else, he threatened me** [...], said that I would not be able to press charges against him.'
>
> 'I was [adopted by] my maternal aunt, [but I only realised after six years that she was not my real] mother. [...] [A]s I didn't really have a [male figure] in my childhood and afterwards, and as **this man had shown interest in me, I agreed to see him. I didn't get much love from my family, but as he was very nice, I felt close to him.**'[1392]
> | CASE OF ZEYNEP

As a result, according to research on cognitive distortions in domestic violence survivors/victims, they may on the one hand become convinced of their own helplessness,[1393] fail to respond to violence,[1394] and/or continue their relationship with a perpetrator, even post-assault.[1395] On the other hand, survivors'/victims' might also overestimate their own control over the situation, believing that the violence depends on their behaviour and that they could save or change the perpetrator, making them choose to stay in a violent relationship too.[1396]

For short-term reactions to SGBV, the goals of survival and maintaining attachment are neurologically intertwined. This means that, '[w]hen confronted with a significant threat from someone depended upon, most people respond in a way that best ensures continued attachment to that person[,] [...] even when escape is objectively possible.'[1397] Thus, for survivors/victims who are threatened by someone on whom they depend, the likelihood of fight or flight responses is low. As Herman states: 'In domestic captivity, physical barriers to escape are rare. In most homes, even the most oppressive, there are no bars on the windows, no barbed wire fences [...] [but t]he barriers to escape are generally invisible.'[1398]

1390 Herman (n 713) 74–75 & 77.

1391 Dunn (n 1370) 6; Herman (n 713) 81; University of Strathclyde, 'Developing a Trauma-Informed Response' (*FutureLearn: Understanding Violence Against Women*, 2022), www.futurelearn.com/courses/understanding-violence-against-women/6/steps/1415956.

1392 NT015_CGRS interview 1_2_3_1996_F_Turkey_RSA_FM_DV_FR_p. 2 & 8 (memo).

1393 Dunn (n 1370) 5.

1394 Babacan Gümüş, Şıpkın and Erdem (n 1226) 84.

1395 Veronica Shepp, Erin O'Callaghan and Sarah E Ullman, 'Interactions with Offenders Post-Assault and Their Impacts on Recovery: A Qualitative Study of Sexual Assault Survivors and Support Providers' (2020) 29 Journal of aggression, maltreatment & trauma 725, 727.

1396 Marta Badenes-Sastre and others, 'Cognitive Distortions and Decision-Making in Women Victims of Intimate Partner Violence: A Scoping Review' (2025) 34 Psychosocial Intervention 23, 29.

1397 Lodrick (n 1222) 8.

1398 Herman (n 713) 74.

Individuals' psychological entrapment, both in the short and long term, can only be altered 'through a redefinition of the relationship as violent and of themselves as [survivors/victims].'[1399] Zeynep articulated how she felt psychologically entrapped within her violent family structure as follows:

> 'You know, when you grow up, from your earliest childhood, in these rules and fears, […] **you grow up submissive.** It's like this cartoon with the elephant, who is born in a circus, he is tied up and as he grows up, the rope breaks but he **doesn't think of leaving because that is all he has ever known, that explains my story with my family.**'[1400] | CASE OF ZEYNEP

Apart from the interpersonal dynamics within violent relationships, mental barriers to leaving might also be installed by external factors, such as societal gender norms or obedience sworn by oath. The latter may occur in flight stories on sex trafficking, such as a Nigerian case where the applicant 'did not try to run away […] because she took a voodoo oath. [She] was threatened [and was] told [the perpetrator] would go to her family should she escape.'[1401] SGBV survivors/victims might also be 'held captive' in violent situations through societal gender norms, such as the traditional marriage system and patriarchal (customary) legal systems, including rules and actors (both in law enforcement and social services) inadequately responding to or even excusing SGBV and discouraging (potential) survivors/victims who seek help.[1402] This was for example demonstrated in Moroccan society (by Qawtar[1403]), in Albanian society (by Vera), and in Georgian society (by Nino):

> 'Everything is explained in the **Kanun[, a set of traditional Albanian laws[1404]]**. […] There is this rule that **a woman cannot […] leave her husband. If she does, she must be killed** either by her husband or the family because she has **betrayed their honour**. […] In the past […] a bullet […] was given to a bride [at the wedding, to kill her with] in case she ever did anything "stupid", so she would be reminded to always obey to the rules.'[1405] | CASE OF VERA

> '[Y]ou don't understand, but in **Georgian [age-old] mentality**, […] **the husband decides, the husband can kill**, the husband […]. [A]nd it will remain that way for a

---

1399 Dunn (n 1370) 5.

1400 NT015_CGRS interview 1_2_3_1996_F_Turkey_RSA_FM_DV_FR_p. 4 (memo).

1401 DN146_CALL 1 (refusal)_lawyers' argumentation_1993_F_Nigeria_STFP_31/5/2024_307 592_NL_Database_p. 9.

1402 Dunn (n 1370) 6.

1403 '[T]he situation of women in Morocco is still very different from […] men and […], although Moroccan women can divorce their husbands, their situation after this divorce is characterised by great difficulties.' (DM116_CALL 1 (refusal)_lawyers' argumentation_1999_F_Morocco_VGNT_FM_DV_24/4/2024_305 429_NL_Database_p. 7.).

1404 Shankley, Ramanov and Jaber (n 422) 3, 4 & 8.

1405 NA016_1990_F_Albania_RSA_VGNT_DV_NL_NANSEN_[00:37:36].

long time to come.' *Georgian interpreter adds* 'It is passed down **from generation to generation. Women are always in an oppressed position, always have to obey.**'[1406] | CASE OF NINO

In contrast to countries of origin where women are theoretically (but not necessarily practically) able to divorce, Binta reminded the CALL of the legal barriers she faced to leave her husband in Guinea, a Muslim country where divorce can only be granted in extremely limited cases and upon agreement of the husband.[1407]

b) Appease Reactions & Avoidance Coping

Next to freezing, research on survival reactions to SGBV also normalises survivors/victims who appease perpetrators or 'go into a state of surrender.'[1408] Such literature describes avoidant behaviour by appeasing for example as: cognitively changing the meaning of a stressful situation (e.g. by perceiving more positive aspects to a violent relationship), neutralising perpetrators' anger before it erupts into violence (e.g. by trying to calm them down, preparing food, or 'walking on eggshells'), creating breathing space, engaging in constant negotiations and trade-offs, 'maintaining' and surviving day-to-day, or seeking/staying in contact with perpetrators.[1409] In contrast, this body of research has shown that others 'are more likely to endorse victim blaming myths when a survivor of a sexual assault maintains contact with an offender after[wards].'[1410]

Reported motivations for such appeasing reactions are for example: preventing escalation; minimising harm; avoiding future SGBV; protecting 'things that are too costly to risk'; managing emotions (e.g. avoiding stressful feelings by denying the victimisation altogether); safeguarding residency in the same household as, financial support from, or complex emotional ties with perpetrators; or wishfully thinking that the situation will resolve itself.[1411] As such, it might be perfectly plausible that survivors/victims chose not to act upon a violent situation, continued to act as normal, remained in or sought contact with perpetrators, returned to their surroundings, or even actively pleased them or consented to the violence. Several applicants included in this research confirmed this.

1406 NGe014_1975_F_Georgia_RSA_DV_NL_NANSEN_[00:17:06].
1407 DG082_CALL 1 (refusal)_lawyers' argumentation_F_Guinea_RSA_GMC_VGNT_FM_DV_11/4/2024_304 652_FR_Database_p. 9.
1408 Herman (n 713) 42.
1409 Foster and others (n 1347) 286, 291 & 292; Breen and Boyce (n 401) 5233–5234.
1410 Breen and Boyce (n 401) 5245.
1411 Foster and others (n 1347) 286, 291 & 292; Evans Cameron, 'Risk Theory and "Subjective Fear"' (n 1366) 573; Breen and Boyce (n 401) 5233–5234.

The idea that 'when [a survivor/victim] withdraws her complaint or refrains from participating in the criminal justice system, the violence could not really be so serious'[1412] was disproved in Diana's and Elene's cases. Although Diana had always feared going to the police, years of abuse made her realise her husband wouldn't change. One day, when he was deported from the UK back to Albania, she promised herself to finally act if he hurt her or her children again. The moment he did, she sought a protection order and filed for divorce immediately. However, the judge urged her to forgive him the first time. Uninformed of the next hearing, the Court decided in her absence that she wanted to halt the divorce proceedings.[1413] In Elene's case, she explained through her lawyer:

> 'If she had **contacted the authorities to file a complaint** against her father and brothers, she believes this would have **merely escalated things** and [...] she would also have been **accused** of ruining her family's honour and/or having relations with women, resulting in **serious consequences**.'[1414] | CASE OF ELENE

Fear of the consequences of resisting SGBV might even lead survivors/ victims to actively accept the violence, such as the abovementioned Senegalese applicant, stating: 'My father was fooled, he believed that [my forced husband] was a good person. [I did not oppose the marriage], I accepted. I didn't dare defy my father, [...] I couldn't refuse.'[1415]

Next, seeking or staying in contact with SGBV perpetrators has been identified as a common survivor/victim response too.[1416] The reasons for doing so might include being manipulated by or dependent on perpetrators, or wishfully thinking the situation would improve. Aster, an Ethiopian applicant, for example recounted that she was homeless, unemployed and vulnerable to sexual violence on the streets of Athens, Greece. She accepted a job offer to clean and make beds in a guesthouse. While she initially got a room and two meals a day, two weeks later, she was forced to sign a contract she could not read, consenting to work in a sex trafficking network.[1417]

Erina, Mary, and Zeynep were also exposed to SGBV (threats) under false pretences. Erina's father wanted to abduct her to his hometown, where he wanted to forcibly marry her off at age 13. Her aunts called her and told her: 'You'll be better off here. Without your mother, we'll find you someone and you'll be happy.'[1418] Mary's family had invited her to a meeting, without saying anything

---

1412 United Nations Office on Drugs and Crime (UNODC) (n 284) 81.
1413 NA001_B_1973_F_Albania_RSA_VGNT_FM_DV_NL_NANSEN_[00:56:09].
1414 DGe151_CALL1(refusal)_lawyers'argumentation_2003_F_Georgia_VGNT_DV_27/3/2024_303 891_NL_Database_p. 8.
1415 NS005_CGRS interview_2002_F_Senegal_RSA_DV_FM_FR_NANSEN_p. 10.
1416 Breen and Boyce (n 401) 5233–5234.
1417 NE002_CGRS interview_1988_F_Ethiopia_STFP_NL_NANSEN_p. 7.
1418 NA001_A_2006_F_Albania_RSA_VGNT_FM_DV_NL_NANSEN_MINOR_[01:13:01].

about their plan to force her into performing female GMCs. Therefore, the questions during her personal interview about why she had put herself in danger by visiting them left her puzzled: 'So why would I, knowing that my people want to do this to me, […] [go there] and say: "Okay, I have come, so you [can] take me", why?'[1419] The police officer who raped Zeynep would initially find excuses to see her by pretending to have computer problems she might be able to solve. Later on, after she had ended the relationship, she explained:

> '[H]e wanted to see me again, and **I thought maybe he wanted to talk to me one last time and leave me alone.** He came to collect me by car, but I refused to get in, saying that he could tell me what he had to say right there. **He insisted that we couldn't talk like that in the middle of the street, so I had to get in.** He took me to an unknown place where there was no-one. I was in a state of panic. That's when what I told you happened *she cries*.'[1420] | CASE OF ZEYNEP

In Fatou's case, where the CGRS labelled her sexual violence unsubstantiated because she was still 'liking' her perpetrator's Facebook posts, her lawyer, based on her medical certificates, argued:

> '[She] was abused […] when she was **13 years old**; […] lived her **entire adolescence in fear**, […] was sexually abused in the greatest **secrecy without receiving any help**; [and] her attacker was the husband of her "big sister", […] on whom she was completely **dependent for her survival**. […] The **obedience towards her aggressor** as well as phenomena […] [like] **suppression** […] can easily **explain why a victim likes the posts of her sexual aggressor** […]. [I]t appears from the psychological certificate […] that […] her tendency to **idealise** [him] […] could explain why [she] seems to have **remained in contact**.'[1421] | CASE OF FATOU

Applicants further explained their choice to (temporarily) return to the surroundings of their perpetrators for example by the aim to: go and get their children to flee together as a family (as Lejla and her husband[1422]), go into hiding instead of continuing to live abroad without any protection (as Nino[1423]), or care for ill family members (as the abovementioned Georgian bisexual applicant).[1424] In contrast to him, other applicants, never managed to return to care for or bid

[1419] NL017_1980_F_Liberia_STFP_GMC_VGNT_FM_NL_NANSEN_[00:31:01].

[1420] NT015_CGRS interview 1_2_3_1996_F_Turkey_RSA_FM_DV_FR_p. 3 (memo).

[1421] DG070_CALL 1 (recognition)_lawyers' argumentation_F_Guinea_RSA_FM_DV_18/1/2024_300 255_FR_Case law selection by CALL_p. 14.

[1422] DBH121_CALL 1 (annulment)_lawyers' argumentation_F_Bosnia and Herzegovina_RSA_STFP_30/4/2024_305 882_NL_Database_p. 16.

[1423] NGe014_CALL 1 (manifestly ill-founded)_lawyers' argumentation_1975_F_Georgia_RSA_DV_16/3/2022_269 856_NL_NANSEN_p. 10.

[1424] DGe110_CALL 1 (refusal)_lawyers' argumentation_1986_M_Georgia_VGNT_FM_27/3/2024_303 889_NL_Database_p. 6–7.

farewell to their loved ones. Nino for example testified: 'My father passed away. I couldn't even [go to the] funeral. [...] If one day [my mother] dies, I won't be able to go either. Do you think all this is normal, that I have chosen to live like this?'[1425]

c) *Flight Reactions & Approach Coping*

When it comes to active survival reactions, such as short-term flight reactions and long-term approach coping, these too are scientifically supported survivor/ victim reactions to SGBV (threats). As such, applicants might decide to flee a violent situation (even without initially bringing their children or with well-considered planning) on the advice of others, including authorities, or on their own initiative, because they for example considered it impossible to find safety elsewhere in the country.

This (perceived) unsafety throughout the country of origin is often informed by applicants' feeling that they risk SGBV again in the future, by the same or other perpetrators. They may feel traceable by perpetrators anywhere in the country, for instance due to past threats, stalking, or abduction, or societal cohesion that allows information to circulate quickly. Sometimes, this traceability is even enforceable due to court-ordered custody/visitation rights of violent parents towards their children. In addition, patriarchal gender norms that paved the way for past SGBV are often equally prevalent in other locations throughout the country of origin.

The fear of SGBV revictimisation by the same perpetrator is far from speculative, as research on SGBV risk assessment has shown that such violence often continues or even increases after leaving a relationship. In fact, as pointed out by research on risk factors for intimate partner violence and feminicide, '[t]he most dangerous time period is the days and months after the alleged perpetrator discovers that the victim might attempt to separate from him [or] terminate the relationship'[1426] and the 'risk of being murdered is greatest immediately after separation.'[1427] When it comes to other/new perpetrators, as mentioned above (see Chapter 2.2.1), past SGBV victimisation is the strongest predictor for revictimisation, whether directly or indirectly experienced through witnessing.[1428] This is because past SGBV might have become a normalisation

1425 NGe014_1975_F_Georgia_RSA_DV_NL_NANSEN_[00:49:48].

1426 United Nations Office on Drugs and Crime (UNODC) (n 284) 173.

1427 World Health Organization (WHO), 'Caring for Women Subjected to Violence' (n 402) 5; Jacquelyn C Campbell and others, 'Risk Factors for Femicide in Abusive Relationships: Results From a Multisite Case Control Study' (2003) 93 American Journal of Public Health 1089, 1089.

1428 Waldron and others (n 718) 622; Walsh and others (n 718) 6; Viejo, Linde Valenzuela and Ortega Ruiz (n 718) 189; Testa, VanZile-Tamsen and Livingston (n 718) 1.

scheme for future affective relationships, potentially rendering survivors/victims less capable of identifying such danger in new contexts.[1429]

Among the applicants included in this research, Nino fled Georgia because 'the police advised [her] to leave the country, to go and save [herself].'[1430] Amani simply motivated her own choice to flee during her personal interview as follows:

> 'Why do you keep asking the same questions over and over again? **If I hadn't lived through all these problems, I wouldn't have fled my country.**'[1431] | CASE OF AMANI

A refugee and activist talking from experiential knowledge strikingly described the decision to (initially) flee without your children as a 'heartbreaking pain. The emptiness. The heaviness. The disconnection. A decision no one should ever have to make. Can you imagine having to leave your child behind?'[1432] Both Rahel[1433] and Mary, who wanted to save their children from the dangers on illegal migration routes, in the hope to be later reunited through safer pathways such as family reunification, confirmed this feeling:

> '**Emotionally, it's eating me every day**. Every day. [...] And **if the possibility was there to bring [him], I [would have]**, but I, I left my son. I was in tears. [...] I can't imagine that I'm here and [he] is not with me. I tried to, like, picture the whole scenario, [thinking] "[Mary], you really left your s ... is this real?" [...] **No one would be like in peace in a normal situation, [...] [and] you just pack up and leave your child.** No, nobody [...] I [only did] it because I [knew] **when I [got] there, I will be able to get my son** [...]. So [...] even though it was hard [...] [I told myself] **"Let me just be brave and do it"** [...], from [...] the minute I left there [...] **I cried for my life** "God, what happened? What is going on?" [...] I feel so bad, [...] because if anything happened to [him], I will be responsible.'[1434] | CASE OF MARY

This testimony illustrates that fleeing without your child might just as well be proof of the urgency and seriousness of SGBV (threats), rather than of a lack of credibility, as the authorities often seem to assume.

The choice of applicants to flee the country, instead of a region, might also be explained by their (perceived) impossibility to build a safe life at an IFA. Several

---

1429 Viejo, Linde Valenzuela and Ortega Ruiz (n 718) 188.

1430 NGe014_1975_F_Georgia_RSA_DV_NL_NANSEN_[00:07:49].

1431 NC004_CGRS interview 2_1991_F_DRC_RSA_DV_FR_NANSEN_p. 9.

1432 Loraine Masiya Mponela, 'Women for Refugee Women: Loraine's Story' (*Women for Refugee Women*, 22 February 2024), www.refugeewomen.co.uk/loraines-story/.

1433 NEr018_1985_F_Eritrea_RSA_NL_NANSEN_[00:55:58].

1434 NL017_1980_F_Liberia_STFP_GMC_VGNT_FM_NL_NANSEN_[00:02:23], [00:09:50] & [00:27:58].

applicants reported being forced (sometimes literally by the authorities[1435] or driven by their own fear) to go and live 'underground',[1436] unable to work and earn money,[1437] unable to go to school,[1438] and/or having to block all means of communication.[1439]

To Sofia, the Honduran applicant, who had been sexually abused by her father since the age of 12, the CGRS suggested (in a later withdrawn decision[1440]) she could go live with her sister and her husband to avoid her father. As her sister only lived a few minutes away from her paternal home and her husband lived there too, she responded: 'I have no one except [my] sister, but [...] I cannot see myself living with a man [again],' and directly directed at the CGRS: 'How could they possibly think that I would go [live there], trapped between four walls? [...] Neither my father and mother's house is safe, nor the small community.' If she were to move somewhere else, she explained, she cannot be a 100% certain, but chances are high that they would find her, since people travel, talk, and she would be easily identified as a 'newcomer'.[1441]

Like Sofia, others fled the country because they were afraid that they could still be traced in another part of the country by perpetrators. This fear might be prompted by the belief that perpetrators: have the necessary means/connections to do so,[1442] have explicitly threatened to do so,[1443] or already stalked[1444] or

1435 E.g. NA001_A_B_2006_F_Albania_RSA_VGNT_FM_DV_NL_NANSEN_MINOR_[01:09:54].

1436 E.g. NA001_A_B_2006_F_Albania_RSA_VGNT_FM_DV_NL_NANSEN_MINOR_[01:09:54]., NL017_1980_F_Liberia_STFP_GMC_VGNT_FM_NL_NANSEN_[01:02:00]., DB068_CALL 1 (annulment)_lawyers' argumentation_1975_F_Bolivia_RSA_DV_23/2/2024_302 134_NL_Case law selection by CALL_p. 8., NEr018_CALL 1 (refusal)_lawyers' argumentation_1985_F_Eritrea_RSA_25/11/2022_280 827_NL_NANSEN_p. 9.

1437 E.g. NA001_A_B_2006_F_Albania_RSA_VGNT_FM_DV_NL_NANSEN_MINOR_[01:09:54]., NT015_CGRS interview 1_2_3_1996_F_Turkey_RSA_FM_DV_FR_p. 10 (memo).

1438 E.g. NA001_A_B_2006_F_Albania_RSA_VGNT_FM_DV_NL_NANSEN_MINOR_[01:09:54]., NL017_1980_F_Liberia_STFP_GMC_VGNT_FM_NL_NANSEN_[00:05:56].

1439 E.g. NEr018_CALL 1 (refusal)_lawyers' argumentation_1985_F_Eritrea_RSA_25/11/2022_280 827_NL_NANSEN_p. 9.

1440 Upon refusal of her application by the CGRS, Sofia's appeal with the CALL was not registered, since her insufficient bank balance had caused an error in the payment of the registration fee. Despite a letter from her lawyer explaining this, the situation could not be rectified and she could not appeal against her refusal decision by the CGRS. Eventually, the CGRS decided to withdraw the initial refusal of Sofia's application and, after reconsidering her case (the reasoning of which is not made public), to recognise her as a refugee.

1441 NH003_1991_F_Honduras_RSA_DV_NL_NANSEN_p. 5.

1442 E.g. NS005_CGRS interview_2002_F_Senegal_RSA_DV_FM_FR_NANSEN_p. 7., NE002_CGRS interview_1988_F_Ethiopia_STFP_NL_NANSEN_p. 8.

1443 E.g. NA016_1990_F_Albania_RSA_VGNT_DV_NL_NANSEN_[00:31:36]., NGe014_1975_F_Georgia_RSA_DV_NL_NANSEN_[00:12:38]., NC006_CGRS interview 1_2_1984_F_DRC_RSA_FR_NANSEN_p. 3 (memo)., NEr018_1985_F_Eritrea_RSA_NL_NANSEN_[00:26:29].

1444 NEr018_1985_F_Eritrea_RSA_NL_NANSEN_[00:25:46]., NT015_CGRS interview 1_2_3_1996_F_Turkey_RSA_FM_DV_FR_p. 2–3, 7 & 10 (memo)., DEc120_CALL 1 (refusal)_lawyers' argumentation_1981_F_Ecuador_RSA_DV_29/4/2024_305 805_NL_Database_p. 8.

(tried to) abduct applicants or their children[1445] in the past, sometimes despite address[1446] or telephone number changes.[1447] Both in Aya's and Zeynep's cases, such threats came from a perpetrator in a position of power, respectively an army official and a police officer:

> 'He said "I'm going to make you beg me to sleep with you. [...] And remember: when you send your daughter to nursery school [...] she won't be coming back to your house. And be careful, when you're walking down the street, anyone can attack you. [...] **I'm going to find you wherever you are. What you didn't give me willingly, I'm going to take by force. And who's going to pay the price? Your husband, your daughter and your family**".'[1448] | CASE OF AYA

> 'He said I should sleep with him, that I shouldn't do it with anyone else, he said **he has a lot of connections, that I don't know who he is, that he can destroy my life**, he said that kind of thing. He tried to scare me, saying he was very strong and **capable of anything**. That's how he behaved.'[1449] | CASE OF ZEYNEP

For some applicants, settling in an IFA is also legally impossible, in particular when parent-perpetrators have obtained custody and/or visitation rights over their children. This was the case for Diana and Erina, as well as for Vera[1450] and her son. In the divorce judgement of Diana and her ex-husband, it was stipulated that Erina had to spend every weekend with her abusive father, without supervision. This was decided by the judge, despite Erina's explicit opposition to the court-appointed psychologist: 'I didn't want to have any contact with him, not on the phone or in person.'[1451] In addition, the ex-husbands of both Diana and Vera[1452] filed complaints for international child abduction after they fled Albania, as a result of which they had already been questioned by the police in Belgium and run the risk of being arrested upon return to Albania.[1453]

1445 NA001_A_B_2006_F_Albania_RSA_VGNT_FM_DV_NL_NANSEN_MINOR_[00:42:48]., NA016_1990_F_Albania_RSA_VGNT_DV_NL_NANSEN_[01:01:31].

1446 NGe014_1975_F_Georgia_RSA_DV_NL_NANSEN_[00:38:41].

1447 NA001_A_B_2006_F_Albania_RSA_VGNT_FM_DV_NL_NANSEN_MINOR_[00:55:02]., NEr018_1985_F_Eritrea_RSA_NL_NANSEN_[01:03:09].

1448 NSy019 CGRS interview_1997_F_Syria_RSA_FR_NANSEN_p. 12.

1449 NT015_CGRS interview 1_2_3_1996_F_Turkey_RSA_FM_DV_FR_p. 8 (memo).

1450 'The Albanian judge gave the father 100% custody of the child.'(NA016_1990_F_Albania_RSA_VGNT_DV_NL_NANSEN_[00:13:46].).

1451 NA001_A_2006_F_Albania_RSA_VGNT_FM_DV_NL_NANSEN_MINOR_[00:45:03] & [01:10:20].

1452 NA001_A_2006_F_Albania_RSA_VGNT_FM_DV_NL_NANSEN_MINOR_[01:02:03]., NA016_1990_F_Albania_RSA_VGNT_DV_NL_NANSEN_[00:18:00].

1453 This issue raises complex questions of private international law that are beyond the scope of this research. However, see a recent judgment of the CALL that deals with a similar situation in Spain: [2024] RvV 309 148.

Applicants' fear, hindering them to install elsewhere in the country of origin, might be reinforced by the social cohesion in their societies, causing news about people moving, newcomers, or interpersonal relationships to spread quickly.[1454] This for example explains Nino's determination to change her surname, even if she were allowed to stay in Belgium. She explained:

> 'Georgia [...] is twice the size of Belgium, but the mentality is [different], [...] **people are very connected [...] they will always find you**'. – *Georgian interpreter adds* '**Finding [Nino] wouldn't be difficult at all**, absolutely not [...], **unless she changes her appearance**.' – 'For now, I have no choice, I am using my real surname, but after [the procedure], we are all planning to change our surnames [...] **in the hope of blending into the mass [...] with a false name [...] maybe that way I will feel safe**.'[1455] | CASE OF NINO

Lastly, applicants mentioned the fact that patriarchal power structures and gender norms that made them vulnerable to SGBV apply across the entire state territory, discouraging the solution of moving internally. For example, Vera pointed to the customary Kanun rules that are still applied today in Albania,[1456] Angele to the heavy stigma attached to rape survivors/victims in the DRC,[1457] and Sofia, who experienced child sexual abuse, to the fact that sexual violence and feminicide are omnipresent in Honduras.[1458] How such informal norms and power structures might overrule formal state regulation meant to protect citizens from SGBV, will be discussed in greater detail when discussing the state protection myth (see Part IV, Chapter 3.2).

d) *Fight Reactions & Approach Coping*

Next to fleeing, other active survival reactions, such as (literally or legally) fighting back or confronting perpetrators, have been validated in research on coping with SGBV too. Such literature describes how survivors/victims might provoke perpetrators, threaten with calling the police/resisting/drawing attention,[1459] or seek (restorative) justice in order to get them to leave, settle down, 'mend or dismantle the abusive relationship',[1460] or 'gain insight and

1454 NEr018_1985_F_Eritrea_RSA_NL_NANSEN_[01:02:44]., NH003_1991_F_Honduras_RSA_DV_NL_NANSEN_p. 4., DG078_CALL 1 (refusal)_lawyers' argumentation_F_Guinea_RSA_GMC_VGNT_FM_DV_14/3/2024_303 273_FR_Database_p. 11.

1455 NGe014_1975_F_Georgia_RSA_DV_NL_NANSEN_[00:39:02] & [01:00:31].

1456 NA016_1990_F_Albania_RSA_VGNT_DV_NL_NANSEN_[00:37:09].

1457 NC006_CGRS interview 3_1984_F_DRC_RSA_FR_NANSEN_p. 6.

1458 NH003_CGRS 1 (refusal)_1991_F_Honduras_RSA_DV_12/8/2021_NL_NANSEN_p. 3.

1459 Foster and others (n 1347) 289.

1460 *Ibid.*

justice for themselves, with the hope that the interaction would benefit and change the offender.'[1461]

Where asylum authorities point to the implausible riskiness of fighting back or confrontation, a thorough understanding of risk theory is essential. This theory uncovers how, in fact, 'most people sometimes take unnecessary risks [...] naively, in ignorance of danger, or rebelliously, in defiance of danger.'[1462] Here too, as Herman points out, optimism bias might play a role, in that (potential) survivors/victims do not necessarily recognise (potential) perpetrators' hostility towards them.[1463] As such, credibility assessments of individuals' risk management strategies have to consider: the familiarity and appeal of the risk, to what extent someone initially perceived it as controllable, someone's personal risk tolerance, optimism bias, previous experiences with this type of risk, emotional response, risk assessment (incl. information used, weighing of competing dangers, psychological and cultural factors involved), and their decision making pace.[1464] 'If considering [these] factors sounds like a lot of work, it should,' Evans Cameron concludes.[1465]

When it comes to cultural factors involved in this process, Aya's response to the PO's astonishment about her fight reaction towards the army colonel is insightful:

> 'In Syria, when you're in a situation like that, **you try to use the same methods as them** [...], [**you try to intimidate** by implying that] you know someone in higher ranks. [Even if] he doesn't know [the person] [...], **it calms things down** a bit. [...] [The second time] I knew very well that if I went in, he would get his way. **I would still rather be** [...] **mistreated in front of everyone** than go into his office and let him have his way with me. **Looking back, I wonder where I found the courage to shout and raise my voice.**'[1466] | CASE OF AYA

Arguments rejecting applicants' 'risky' fight reactions or approach coping as implausible lack a scientific basis if they are not built on a correct assessment of applicants' risk management strategies, including all of the aforementioned factors. When authorities specifically argue that successful persistence against SGBV (threats) eliminates their risk, it should also be emphasised that the most high-risk period involves the days and months after survivors/victims disclose the violence to others, especially state actors.[1467]

1461 Shepp, O'Callaghan and Ullman (n 1395) 728.
1462 Herman (n 713) 69.
1463 *Ibid.*
1464 Evans Cameron, 'Risk Theory and "Subjective Fear"' (n 1366) 568.
1465 *Ibid.* 585.
1466 NSy019 CGRS interview_1997_F_Syria_RSA_FR_NANSEN_p. 11.
1467 United Nations Office on Drugs and Crime (UNODC) (n 284) 173.

Finally, as mentioned above, (potential) survivors'/victims' survival reactions might evolve over time, in function of how changeable they perceive their situation to be (whereby a greater perception of changeability implies more active reactions).[1468] This evolution is for example illustrated in a Guinean forced marriage case, where the applicant initially employed a fight reaction, which eventually evolved towards appeasement. Since her father was weakened by illness, not primarily seeking conflict with his daughter but reconciliation, the applicant had initially managed to oppose her forced marriage without suffering major consequences. However, after his death, this family context enabling her to delay the marriage had disappeared and she eventually felt forced into accepting a marriage imposed by her paternal uncle.[1469]

4.2.2. REBUTTAL IN LAW & LEGAL SCIENCES

The abovementioned expertise from health and social sciences normalising a wide range of human survival reactions in the face of SGBV has partially found its way into (inter)national case law and legal literature. As such, the myth that 'inappropriate' survival reactions undermine SGBV flight stories' credibility can be legally rebutted too. While there is no authoritative case law on this specific theme, to my knowledge, two CJEU cases may be indirectly relevant for assessing the credibility of applicants' responses to SGBV-related persecution.

To assess applicants' choice (not) to initially stay/freeze in order to seek other solutions, the CJEU case of *O.A.* discussed earlier (see Chapter 2.2.2 above) is equally relevant. The Court clearly stated that it is irrelevant whether or not applicants sought help from non-state actors, since these cannot protect them from persecution.[1470] Furthermore, according to the CJEU's *X, Y, and Z* and *K.L. cases*, it cannot be expected of applicants that they avoid their own persecution or behave discreetly by, for example, going into hiding (as already confirmed in the Court's discretion case law on applicants' SOGI[1471] or belief in gender equality[1472]). Whether or not applicants can be expected to take steps towards non-state and state actors before fleeing will be explored in greater depth below (see Part IV, Chapters 2 and 3). As mentioned earlier in Chapter 2.2.2, for applicants who decided to flee the country from female GMC specifically, the UN Committee on the Rights of

---

1468 Babacan Gümüş, Şıpkın and Erdem (n 1226) 84; Fanflik, Office on Violence Against Women, and National District Attorneys Association (n 386) 14.

1469 DG097_CALL 1 (refusal)_lawyers' argumentation_F_Guinea_RSA_GMC_FM_DV_14/3/2024_303 242_FR_Database_p. 8.

1470 Ruling 2. *Secretary of State for the Home Department v. O.A.* (n 742).

1471 *X, Y and Z v. The Netherlands* (n 67) paras 10, 71, 74 & 75.

1472 *K.L. v. Staatssecretaris van Justitie en Veiligheid* (n 78) para 63.

the Child has also noted in a Somali case that, while it was argued that the applicant's flight out of the country demonstrated her ability to resist social pressure, '[her] departure could similarly be understood as an inability to resist pressure.'[1473]

More guidance on applicants' survival reactions after SGBV is provided by international actors such as the UN Office on Drugs and Crime. Their resource book on effective responses to SGBV generally confirms that SGBV survivors/victims 'may not behave like victims of other crimes [and] might not react to the violence in ways we think is "correct".'[1474] It goes on to emphasise that SGBV survivors'/victims' short-term reactions constitute instinctive 'split-second decisions [...] given priority over all other brain functioning.'[1475] This might result in reactions that seem illogical or irrational, but are, in the perception of the survivor/victim at the time, necessary in order to survive.[1476]

Legal scholarship too has adopted some of the existing expertise on 'normal' SGBV survivors'/victims' survival reactions. When it comes to applicants' decision to (temporarily) stay in a violent situation or appease to perpetrators, Evans Cameron again refers to the importance of optimism bias for refugee status determination. Due to this natural bias, applicants tend to delay their flight or choose to return home, wishfully thinking the risk of SGBV might diminish or disappear. She writes: 'Faced with two unpleasant options – live in danger or live in exile – [applicants often] imagined a third, more optimistic, possibility: with time, the problem will resolve itself.'[1477] In contrast, asylum authorities are by definition confronted with cases where this optimism proved unjustified, leading to a 'competing normalisation bias' that most SGBV threats escalate. As a result, applicants' natural optimism seems implausible to them.[1478]

The particular dimension of the survival reactions myth when mothers flee without their children has also received special attention in legal scholarship. This dimension is based on the assumption that '"real" mothers would never leave their family.'[1479] Those who do are either labelled as 'bad mothers'[1480] or as non-credible.[1481] Oxford hereby criticises the gendered double standards in credibility assessments of applicants' survival reactions, stating: 'I have never

1473 *I.A.M. (on behalf of K.Y.M.) v. Denmark* (n 745) para 11.8.

1474 United Nations Office on Drugs and Crime (UNODC) (n 284) 79.

1475 *Ibid.* 80.

1476 *Ibid.* 80–81.

1477 Evans Cameron, 'Risk Theory and "Subjective Fear"' (n 1366) 574.

1478 *Ibid.*

1479 Oxford (n 11) 168.

1480 John R Parsons and Sara Riva, 'Innocence and Danger at the Border: Migrants, "Bad" Mothers, and the Nation's Protectors' (2024) 12 Comparative Migration Studies 1, 9 & 12.

1481 Oxford (n 11) 168; Spijkerboer, 'Stereotyping and Acceleration – Gender, Procedural Acceleration and Marginalised Judicial Review in the Dutch Asylum System' (n 1202) 77.

observed an immigration official chastise male applicants for leaving their family' (whether or not the reasons were gender-related).[1482]

This legal rebuttal as a whole is also of relevance to the specific dimension of the survival myth that 'applicants can find protection against SGBV at an IFA instead of fleeing the country'. As this reasoning strongly overlaps with the non-state and state protection myths (that 'applicants can, whether or not supported by non-state actors, find state protection against SGBV at an IFA'), its rebuttal will be discussed in more depth there (see Part IV, Chapter 2.2.2).

4.2.3. REBUTTAL BY BELGIAN ASYLUM AUTHORITIES

The myth that 'inappropriate' survival reactions undermine SGBV flight stories' credibility is rebutted to a limited extent by some asylum officials in the Belgian asylum procedure. One gender-specialised supervisor specifically commented: 'Sexual violence [...] stereotypes are often related to how applicants should have reacted. There is freeze, flight, fight, but some [decision makers] might expect applicants to have reacted in a certain way (although I hope this is no longer the case).'[1483] Below, I will go into asylum officials' instances of myth rebuttal for each of the four above discussed short-term reactions and long-term coping mechanisms.

Firstly, some interviewed asylum officials normalised applicants' freeze reactions and avoidance coping by recognising the mental, practical, and legal barriers applicants might face to leave a violent situation. One PO emphasised how having children may complicate this: 'In Chechnya, the father is always assigned child custody, so a woman [who] wants to leave her husband, [...] will lose [her] children [...]. This is a huge barrier.'[1484] However, a judge pointed at very poor argumentation from other POs, where these criticised applicants for not leaving their violent husband sooner, especially when there are children involved.[1485]

Other authorities rather recognised gender norms or threats preventing women from leaving their husband[1486] or emotional, social, or financial dependence on SGBV perpetrators[1487] as barriers to leaving. In the case law, one CALL judgement explicitly recognised financial dependence on perpetrators as a justification for freezing in a violent relationship, namely in the case of

1482 Oxford (n 11) 166.
1483 CB015_CGRS_Supervisor + PO_GENDER_[Additional info in follow-up e-mail after the interview].
1484 CB002_CGRS_Supervisor + PO_[00:26:22].
1485 RB006_CALL_Judge_[00:20:52].
1486 CB004_CGRS_PO_[00:43:27].
1487 CB007_CGRS_PO_[00:42:16]., RB006_CALL_Judge_[00:57:29].

Clarisse, an Ivorian applicant, and her husband (marked as important by the CALL itself). She feared that her daughter would be subjected to GMC by her mother-in-law, who had even filed a complaint against her for opposing the excision. The CALL annulled the CGRS' refusal decision, by arguing it 'does not see how the applicant could [protect] her daughter from [...] [female GMC] [...], given her profile[, being economically dependent on her mother-in-law] and her family environment which is favourable to excision.'[1488]

Secondly, two gender-specialised supervisors at the CGRS also explicitly normalised appeasing behaviour of applicants towards their SGBV perpetrators, for example because: they were captivated by them,[1489] the perpetrator was a family member,[1490] or to keep up appearances on social media.[1491] In the abovementioned Burundian abduction and (attempted) rape case, the judge validated the applicant's choice not to try and find out the identity of her perpetrators. In the recognition judgement, it was considered 'likely and even credible that an attempted rape victim would not want to talk to a stranger about it, regardless of their prerogatives [...] [such as in this case,] a high-ranking police officer[, in order] find out the identities of the people who had detained [the applicant].'[1492]

Thirdly, asylum officials at times seemed to accept certain justifications for fleeing the country of origin (instead of the area) 'without going to the authorities, even if they function well, because [...] there is no other way out.'[1493] In contrast to abovementioned colleagues, some did assess applicants' traceability to an IFA by perpetrators, taking into account: the time and events since the escape from or last contact with the perpetrator, the contract signed (in sex trafficking/forced prostitution cases),[1494] whether there are children and custody/visitation rights requiring continued exposure to the perpetrator,[1495] perpetrators' investigative means,[1496] past (dis)obedience to protection orders,[1497] whether the perpetrator works in law enforcement,[1498]

1488 DIC074_CALL 1 (annulment)_lawyers' argumentation_F_Ivory Coast_GMC_VGNT_11/3/2024_302 979_FR_Case law selection by CALL_p.9.
1489 CB008_CGRS_Supervisor + PO_GENDER_[00:43:09].
1490 CB015_CGRS_Supervisor + PO_GENDER_[00:36:34].
1491 CB008_CGRS_Supervisor + PO_GENDER_[00:43:29].
1492 DBu089_CALL 1 (recognition)_F_Burundi_RSA_30/5/2024_307 576_FR_Database_p. 16–17.
1493 RB006_CALL_Judge_[00:46:28].
1494 CB006_CGRS_PO_[00:56:12].
1495 CB008_CGRS_Supervisor + PO_GENDER_[00:44:34].
1496 RB001_CALL_Judge_[00:47:30].
1497 RB005_CALL_Judge_[00:35:34].
1498 RB006_CALL_Judge_[00:58:39].

and whether this alternative location evokes new fears of persecution.[1499] One supervisor did nuance that traceability will only be considered when applicants make it plausible by proving it, 'because [traceability is] of course easy [...] to claim.'[1500]

One PO briefly mentioned the relevance of informal gender norms to justify (potential) SGBV survivors'/victims' flight out of the country, such as discrimination for being subjected to SGBV.[1501] Furthermore, a supervisor at the CGRS and a judge at the CALL emphasised the role of social cohesion in assessing the reasonability and safety of IFAs, stating: 'people who know the African context really well [...] say "Africa is a village because everyone knows someone who knows someone, so [...] women can easily be found".'[1502] The judge cited a case of an Afghan boy who had been raped (and recorded) in Belgium and who they recognised as a refugee '*sur place*'.[1503] They explained: 'I can well imagine that both perpetrator and victim have told [others about the rape in Belgium], and that in his hometown, they know what happened [...]. If that story is going to circulate there [...] and he returns, it won't end well.'[1504]

Other asylum officials accepted in certain cases that the impossibility of building a safe life elsewhere in the country may justify applicants' flight abroad. For example, they clarified that (potential) SGBV survivors/victims are entitled to 'a normal life'[1505] and therefore cannot be expected to: live in hiding for years on end,[1506] no longer use any social media,[1507] or (as a woman) rely on a husband or brother for all administrative formalities.[1508] One PO squarely stated: 'In the countries I treat,[1509] [...] if [a female domestic violence survivor/victim] tries to escape, it is not possible for her to [...] start a new life on her own in another city.'[1510] Another supervisor stressed that

1499 RB006_CALL_Judge_[00:59:34].
1500 CB002_CGRS_Supervisor + PO_[00:23:45].
1501 CB006_CGRS_PO_[00:29:27].
1502 CB010_CGRS_Supervisor + PO_[00:21:03].
1503 'The requirement that a person must be outside [the] country to be a refugee does not mean that [they] must necessarily have left that country illegally, or even that [they] must have left it on account of well-founded fear. [...] [P]erson[s] who [were] not a refugee when [they] left [their] country, but who [become] a refugee at a later date, [are] called a refugee "sur place".' UNHCR, *Handbook on Procedures and Criteria for Determining Refugee Status under the 1951 Convention and the 1967 Protocol Relating to the Status of Refugees* (n 254) 26.
1504 RB005_CALL_Judge_[00:15:09].
1505 CB006_CGRS_PO_[00:54:19].
1506 CB008_CGRS_Supervisor + PO_GENDER_[00:42:13].
1507 CB015_CGRS_Supervisor + PO_GENDER_[00:51:23].
1508 RB008_CALL_Judge_[00:27:23].
1509 i.e. Turkey, Egypt, Algeria, Guinea, and Palestine (self-reported in the interview).
1510 CB004_CGRS_PO_[00:43:27].

IFAs as solutions in SGBV cases 'underestimate the trauma that women may have experienced.'[1511]

Two judges even confirmed that severe psychological problems[1512] and past experiences with SGBV[1513] can increase the risk of revictimisation, which is highly relevant when applying the burden of proof reversal when applicants experienced past persecution (Article 48/7 of the Aliens Act) (see Chapter 2.2.3 above). In such cases, previous threats/experiences of persecution directly aimed at applicants clearly indicate the well-foundedness of their fear, unless the asylum authorities establish good reasons that such persecution will not recur.[1514] While most of the applicants included in this research already experienced SGBV before they fled, the CALL only exceptionally seems to apply article 48/7 Aliens Act (explicitly) in its SGBV case law.

In the analysed sample, this was the case for one Bolivian domestic violence (of the applicant whose police complaint was found risky, as mentioned above), one Somali female GMC, and one Guinean forced marriage case (of Fatou). Interestingly, all three cases are marked as important by the CALL. In the risk assessment that such persecution might recur, the judge in the Bolivian case argued: 'While there are indications that the applicant has not seen [the perpetrator] for a long time, it is also certain that [he] is still alive, [...] that he has a criminal past and has recently been accused of crimes in Bolivia.'[1515] In the Somali case, the judge found 'no good reasons [...] to believe that the genital mutilation (disinfibulation and then reinfibulation) will not recur, for example after sexual intercourse, pregnancy, childbirth or because of [...] complications during menstruation.'[1516]

For Fatou, the fact that she had experienced violence in the past because she was a woman (an inalterable characteristic) was in itself proof that she would continue to run this risk upon return to Guinea:

> '[The applicant] has suffered **ill-treatment related to her status as a woman** [(i.e. the domestic violence, sexual abuse, forced abortions, confinement, and forced

1511 CB010_CGRS_Supervisor + PO_[00:23:31].

1512 RB005_CALL_Judge_[00:27:30].

1513 RB001_CALL_Judge_[00:43:31].

1514 This provision reverses the burden of proof where applicants have experienced or feared persecution in the past. In such cases, previous threats with or acts of persecution or serious harm directly aimed at applicants clearly indicate the well-foundedness of their fear, unless the asylum authorities substantiate that there are good reasons to believe that such persecution or serious harm will not recur. Art. 48/7 Belgian Aliens Act; Art. 4(4) EU Qualification Directive; Art. 4(4) EU Qualification Regulation; Denys (n 43) 626.

1515 DB068_CALL 1 (annulment)_1975_F_Bolivia_RSA_DV_23/2/2024_302 134_NL_Case law selection by CALL_p. 11.

1516 DSo069_CALL 1 (recognition)_F_Somalia_GMC_VGNT_FM_DV_8/3/2024_302 889_NL_Case law selection by CALL_p. 15.

> marriage)] which is sufficiently serious to constitute persecution [...], the Council considers that **this circumstance constitutes serious evidence that she has a well-founded fear of being subjected to further persecution if she returns** to her country.'[1517] | CASE OF FATOU

In one other case, the CALL recognised the applicant, a single mother with a young extramarital child, as a refugee in her second (first subsequent) asylum procedure. As customary discrimination in Guinea might severely affect single mothers' ability to organise their livelihood independently, their access to justice, and their risk to being ostracised by their family, the judge argued: '[I]t cannot be ruled out that the applicant, if she returns to Guinea, will not be mistreated and/or rejected by members of her family and community because she gave birth to a child out of wedlock.'[1518]

Fourthly, only one KAP survey respondent actively recognised 'fighting back' as a credible SGBV response, by qualifying 'defending [oneself] on the spot, filing a complaint immediately [...] etc' as actions that may occur, but cannot be expected of survivors/victims.[1519] No case law actively rebutted this 'fight reaction myth'.

4.3. OCCURRENCE OF THE MYTHS ON SURVIVAL REACTIONS

How the level of acceptance vs. rebuttal of the survival myths in the analysed case law sample is divided, between the CGRS (negative decisions) and the CALL (all judgments), according to the procedural language, can be visualised as follows. Each figure represents the acceptance/rebuttal level of the myths that: 1) applicants' freeze reactions/avoidance coping (Figure 19), 2) applicants' appease reactions/avoidance coping (Figure 20), 3) applicants' flight reactions/approach coping (Figure 21), and 4) applicants' fight reactions/approach coping (Figure 22) undermine their SGBV flight stories' credibility.

1517 DG070_CALL 1 (recognition)_F_Guinea_RSA_FM_DV_18/1/2024_300 255_FR_Case law selection by CALL_p. 23.

1518 DG072_CALL 2 (recognition)_F_Guinea_STFP_GMC_VGNT_FM_DV_12/2/2024_301 330_FR_Database_p. 14–16.

1519 R_1N94UZT5x9U3Ied_CALL_Attaché.

Figure 19: % of decisions in the case law sample including at least one freeze/avoidance myth acceptance/rebuttal argument, according to asylum authority & language

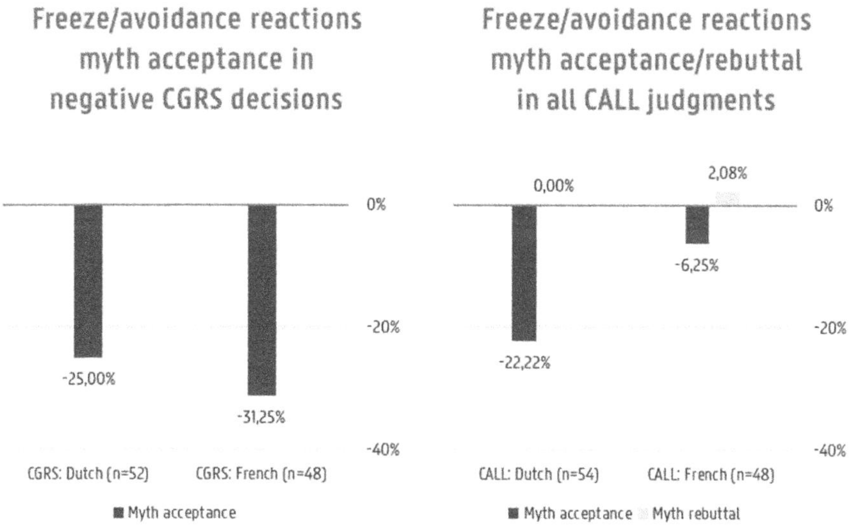

Figure 20: % of decisions in the case law sample including at least one appease/avoidance myth acceptance/rebuttal argument, according to asylum authority & language

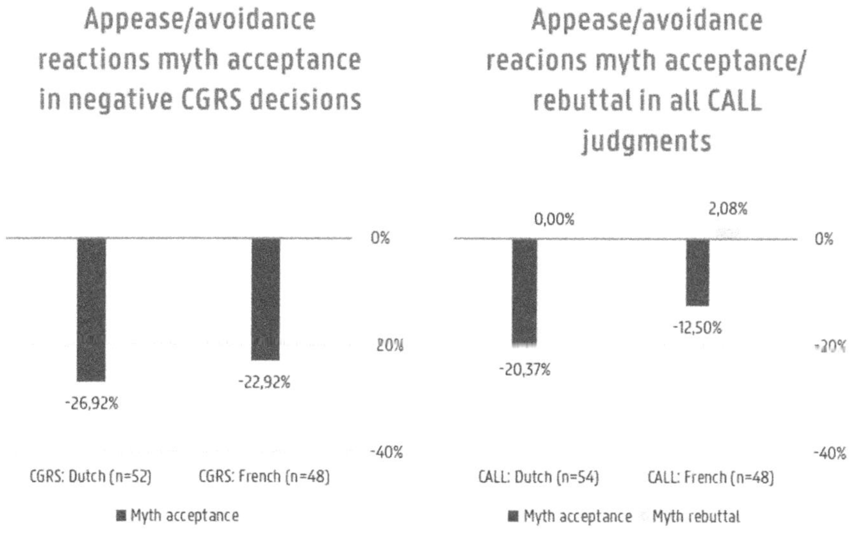

Figure 21: % of decisions in the case law sample including at least one flight/approach myth acceptance/rebuttal argument, according to asylum authority & language

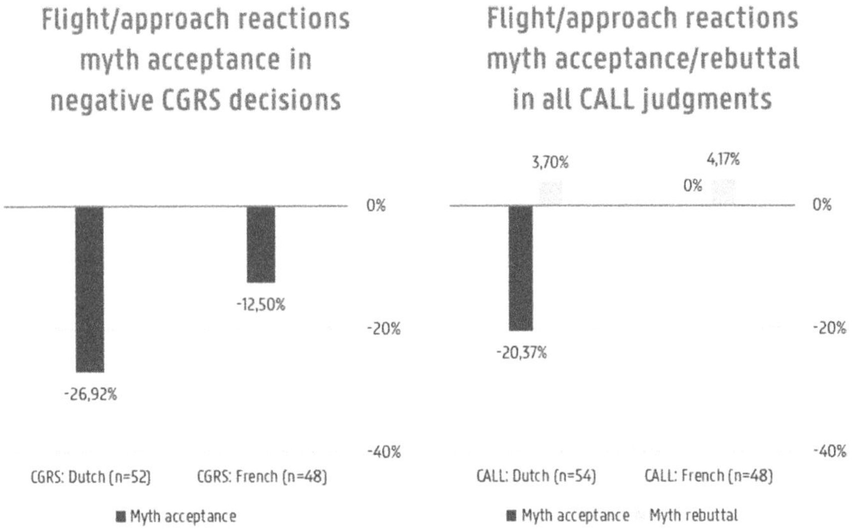

Figure 22: % of decisions in the case law sample including at least one fight/approach myth acceptance/rebuttal argument, according to asylum authority & language

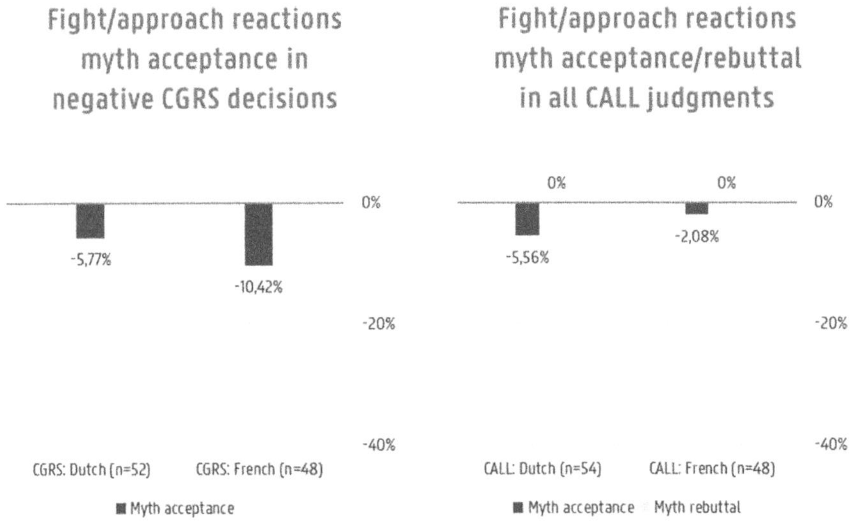

In the total case law sample, 38,61% of the 202 decisions and judgements included at least one argument based on acceptance of one of the four survival myths. This acceptance level is divided over the specific reactions as follows: 21,29% (freeze/avoidance myth), 20,79% (appease/avoidance myth), 15,35% (flight/approach myth), and 5,94% (fight/approach myth). It is important to emphasise that this overall acceptance level (across all survival reactions) is reduced considerably by the remarkably lower acceptance in the French-language CALL judgements (18,75%), in comparison to the Dutch-language CALL judgements (38,89%) as well as the CGRS decisions in both Dutch (48,08%) and French (47,92%). These percentages are contrasted by an almost non-existent rebuttal level. The highest rebuttal level at the CALL concerns the flight myth, both in Dutch (3,70%) and French judgements (4,17%). To conclude, **almost 40% of all 202 analysed decisions and judgements accepted** (among others) a **survival myth**-based argument qualifying applicants' freeze/appease/flight/fight reaction to or avoidance/approach coping with SGBV as non-credible, eventually contributing to their denial of international protection.

Figure 23 on the following page visualises how all three SGBV myths on the micro level may be accepted in argumentation across the stages of refugee status determination in SGBV cases, namely: the assessment of credibility, well-foundedness, and IFAs. It summarises the most important reasons for the rebuttal of these myths in health and social sciences, as well as in international refugee (case) law.

Figure 23: Visual of most important rebuttal reasons of the micro myths

	MYTH-BASED ARGUMENTATION	REBUTTAL in health & social sciences	REBUTTAL in international refugee (case) law
	→ APPLICANTS FLEEING SGBV DO **NOT QUALIFY FOR REFUGEE PROTECTION** BECAUSE: [not applicable]		
	→ SGBV QUALIFIES FOR REFUGEE PROTECTION, BUT IS **NOT CREDIBLE** BECAUSE:		
CREDIBILITY	**'Inappropriate' disclosure undermines SGBV flight stories' credibility**	- SGBV **disclosure barriers**	
	→ Too much/little detail → Inconsistency	- **Trauma & mental health issues impair** traumatic & autobiographical **memory** (retrieval) - **Memory retrieval** through **reconstruction** explains inconsistency	- **Lack of detail/consistency** is **accepted** when overall credibility is not jeopardised (e.g. *R.C. v. Sweden*, *A.F. v. France* & *A.A. v. France*, ECtHR)
	→ Delayed (disclosure in) SGBV procedures	- **No link** between **timing** of SGBV disclosure & **truthfulness** - Trauma-specific **disclosure barriers**	- **Refusal** of international protection **cannot** solely rely on **delayed application** (art. 10 EU ProcDir) - **Initial false statements** are **accepted**, when withdrawn as soon as possible (*Att. au Pakistan*, CJEU)
	→ 'Inappropriate' demeanour	- **Emotional responses** while disclosing SGBV are **inaccurate credibility indicators**	
	'Inappropriate' survival reactions undermine SGBV flight stories' credibility	- **Survival reactions** to SGBV vary, evolve & are **inaccurate credibility indicators** - **Optimism bias** hampers 'rational' **risk assessment** & protective measures	- Applicants should **not** seek **non-state support** (*O.A.*, CJEU) or behave discreetly (e.g. by **hiding**) (*X, Y & Z* and *K.L.*, CJEU)
	→ Short-term freeze/appease/flight/fight	- **Subconscious** nature **hampers** a **rational account** on reactions afterwards	
	→ Long-term avoidance/approach coping	- **Avoidance** coping is most common (but both occur) & is a key **PTSD** symptom	
	→ SGBV QUALIFIES FOR REFUGEE PROTECTION, IS CREDIBLE, BUT THE FEAR IS **ILL-FOUNDED** BECAUSE:		
WELL-FOUNDEDNESS	**Resourceful applicants do not need protection against SGBV***	- SGBV occurs across **all socio-economic backgrounds** - (Non-)material resourcefulness is an **inaccurate SGBV predictor** - Individual resourcefulness cannot protect against **structural SGBV**	- **Social/financial support** is **irrelevant** for refugee status determination (*O.A.*, CJEU) - SGBV-related decisions should be based on **up-to-date & gender-specific COI** (country of origin information) (*A.H. & F.N.* and *K.L.*, CJEU)
	→ Masculinity as non-material resourcefulness	- SGBV occurs across **all gender identities** - **Reporting & help-seeking barriers** may be even higher for male survivors/victims	
	→ SGBV QUALIFIES FOR REFUGEE PROTECTION, IS CREDIBLE, THE FEAR IS WELL-FOUNDED, BUT THERE IS AN **IFA** (internal flight alternative):		
IFA	**(Resourceful) applicants can find protection against SGBV at an IFA (instead of fleeing the country)***	See ↑ & PART IV	See ↑ & PART IV

CJEU: Court of Justice of the EU & ECtHR: European Court of Human Rights

5. CONCLUSION

To conclude, as visualised above (Figure 23), this part demonstrated the ways and levels of acceptance and rebuttal of the micro level myths that seem to play a role at the credibility, well-foundedness, and IFA stage of SGBV-related refugee status determination. Concretely, I discussed the myth-based reasoning that resourceful applicants do not need protection against SGBV (resourcefulness myth)[1520] and that 'inappropriate' disclosure (disclosure myths) and survival reactions (survival myths) undermine SGBV flight stories' credibility. On the resourcefulness myth, I first discussed acceptance of the belief linking material, non-material, and male resourcefulness to lesser risk of SGBV (stand-alone form), as well as to a better ability to talk about the violence, to seek help, to avoid the perpetrators, or to cope with the violence as such (intersecting form). I paid specific attention to the dimension of this myth where masculinity is perceived as a form of non-material resourcefulness, supposedly rendering male applicants more resilient towards SGBV.

On acceptance of the disclosure myths, I illustrated how authorities tend to accept the idea that 'true SGBV survivors/victims' will have the violence 'engraved in their memory' and therefore disclose it in a detailed, consistent, and timely manner, while displaying appropriate emotions. Importantly, the latter demeanour myth in the asylum context differs from the criminal justice context, as it risks qualifying all levels of emotionality (too much and too little) as non-credible (instead of only too little in rape mythology). Next, I uncovered how acceptance of the survival myths in the asylum context differs from the criminal justice context too. Applicants for international protection are not only considered non-credible for their freeze/appease/avoidant reactions, but also for their fight/flight/approach reactions. This leaves applicants fleeing SGBV in a behavioural minefield, where whatever survival reaction they (sub)consciously choose, might negatively impact their refugee status determination.

Concretely, I illustrated how applicants have been criticised for: staying in a violent situation for too long; fleeing a violent situation (too drastically or too successfully); fleeing the region but staying in the country for too long; fleeing the country instead of fleeing the region; fleeing with children;

[1520] Whereas some asylum authorities framed this argument as a credibility issue, the reasoning in practice mostly boiled down to ill-foundedness of the fear of SGBV.

fleeing without children; not acting upon the violence/threats (sufficiently, effectively, or immediately); acting upon the violence/threats by fighting back (too radically, persistently, or successfully); contacting perpetrators; hiding from perpetrators (while managing to avoid direct threats/violence for too long); and (temporarily) returning to the perpetrator's surroundings or pleasing them. It is important to note that identification of the survival myths in the asylum context constitutes a prominent contribution of this research, as this topic is virtually unexplored terrain in refugee law scholarship so far.

Relying on existing expertise in health and social sciences, I demonstrated how neither applicants' resourcefulness, level of detail, consistency, delay, or demeanour in SGBV disclosures, or survival reactions are trustworthy credibility indicators or SGBV predictors. In rebutting the resourcefulness myths through this expertise, I demonstrated how SGBV occurs across all socio-economic backgrounds and gender identities, including men. In contrast to (non-)material resourcefulness, only past SGBV experiences seem to be a consistent predictor for future victimisation. Asylum authorities should recognise the irrelevance of individual resourcefulness as a protective factor against structurally embedded SGBV, as well as the structural underreporting by survivors/victims, and men in particular.

Focusing on disclosure, applicants' retrieval of traumatic and broader autobiographical memories is a reconstructive process, hampered by factors inherent to the human brain and by symptoms of mental health issues, such as PTSD or depression, often arising from trauma such as SGBV. The details and consistency in, timing of, and emotions during disclosure are also hindered or even prevented by external SGBV-related factors, such as shame, stigma, fear of rejection or retaliation, stress, concentration issues, distrust in authorities/the system, or isolation and may vary greatly.

Also varying greatly are survivors'/victims' survival reactions to SGBV (threats), which evolve over time (especially for repetitive SGBV), according to the resources they (perceive to) have at their disposal and their past coping experiences. Moreover, calculated risk assessment, help-seeking behaviour, and the ability to rationally account for survival reactions after SGBV are hampered by the subconscious nature of short-term reactions and our optimism bias towards victimisation of such violence. Asylum authorities should recognise that, while both forms occur, avoidance coping is generally more common than approach coping, that it is a key symptom of PTSD (often resulting from SGBV), and above all that no comprehensive model to predict survival reactions to SGBV exists. Therefore, relying on applicants' individual resourcefulness as protection against SGBV and on expectations about their disclosure of and survival reactions to SGBV in refugee status determination is senseless.

I illustrated how this evidence-based expertise partially found its way into legal scholarship and international refugee (case) law. As such, the CJEU has selectively rebutted the resourcefulness myth by declaring applicants' social or financial support irrelevant for refugee status determination and demanding that SGBV-related decisions are based on gender-specific COI. As for the disclosure myths, EU refugee law prohibits refusal of international protection for the sole reason of delayed application. The ECtHR judged that a certain lack of detail/consistency is accepted, as long as it does not jeopardise applicants' overall credibility, and the CJEU that their initial false statements, when clarified and withdrawn as soon as possible, may uphold applicants' credibility. The CJEU has partially rebutted the survival myths too, by confirming that applicants are not expected to actively cope by turning to non-state actors or passively cope by behaving discreetly (e.g. going into hiding), albeit only for cases related to applicants' SOGI and belief in gender equality so far.

For the Belgian asylum procedure, I illustrated how this literature and (case) law rebutting the resourcefulness, disclosure, and survival myths at times was replicated by some asylum officials. However, **over a third** (32,67% for the **resourcefulness myth** and 38,61% for the **survival myths**) **and over half** (57,92% for the **disclosure myths**) of the 202 decisions and judgements analysed were (among other elements) based on arguments accepting these micro level myths. In order for the available health, social, and legal expertise rebutting these SGBV myths to be taken into account in refugee status determination, asylum authorities should move away from relying on these SGBV myth-like thinking patterns. Instead, their reasoning should be informed by: refugee (case) law; cautious use of recent, region-, and gender-specific COI and psychological/medical evidence in the case; and training/guidance on the causes, nature, and consequences of SGBV relevant to asylum procedures.

PART IV

NON-STATE & STATE PROTECTION MYTHS ON THE MESO & EXO LEVEL

1. INTRODUCTION

The UN refugee definition is built around states' ability and willingness to protect applicants from persecution. Next to these state actors of protection (such as the police, military, judiciary, ...), non-state actors (such as NGOs, doctors, ... but also private networks) seem to play a role in refugee status determination too. Hereby, asylum authorities at times rely on the idea that applicants with non-state actor support do not need protection against SGBV (the non-state protection myth) and that non-exhaustion of state protection implies non-credibility or ill-foundedness of SGBV flight stories (the state protection myth).

Applicants' help-seeking behaviour from (non-)state actors takes place in the immediate interpersonal and institutional (both formal and informal) setting, locating these ideas on the meso and exo level.[1521] In discussing the acceptance of both the non-state and state protection myths, I will go into the role applicants' help-seeking behaviour from these actors plays in refugee status determination and asylum authorities' position towards justifications for not seeking such (non-)state protection.

For the non-state protection myth, I will specifically elaborate on which types of actors/networks (and protection they provide) are deemed relevant in asylum decision making. I will hereby distinguish between non-state actors *sensu stricto* (e.g. NGOs, doctors, ..., Chapter 2.1.2) and private support networks (e.g. friends, family, ..., Chapter 2.1.3). For state protection, I will distinguish between three forms this myth may take, namely that non-exhaustion of state protection against SGBV: 1) undermines applicants' credibility, 2) is a condition for refugee status determination and/or recognition as such, and 3) implies ill-foundedness of their application for international protection (Chapter 3.1). Going into the latter form, I will specifically discuss asylum authorities' interpretation of the conditions for 'reasonable state protection' that applicants can be expected to exhaust, namely that these are accessible (Chapter 3.1.3), effective (Chapter 3.1.4), and non-temporary (Chapter 3.1.5).

For each of these myths on the meso/exo level, I will go into their rebuttal in law and health, social, and legal sciences and I will illustrate the ways in which Belgian asylum authorities at times already implement such rebuttals in

1521 Heise (n 391) 264; Bronfenbrenner (n 390) 514–515.

their decisions and judgements (Chapter 2.2 on the non-state protection myths and 3.2 on the state protection myth). To visualise the acceptance and rebuttal levels of these myths, each section concludes with an overview of the percentage of analysed case law (n=202) in which the myth is explicitly accepted (CGRS and CALL) or rebutted (CALL), according to language and asylum authority in Belgium (Chapter 2.3 on the non-state protection myths and 3.3 on the state protection myth).

2. THE MYTH THAT APPLICANTS WITH NON-STATE ACTOR SUPPORT DO NOT NEED PROTECTION AGAINST SGBV

2.1. ACCEPTANCE OF THE NON-STATE PROTECTION MYTHS

2.1.1. FROM CRIMINAL JUSTICE TO ASYLUM CONTEXT

In refugee status determination of applicants fleeing SGBV, asylum authorities seem to focus on applicants' (inter)action with/towards non-state actors. In discussing this focus, I will go into two types of non-state actors separately, namely 'non-state actors *sensu stricto*' (such as NGOs or doctors) and private support networks (such as family or friends). The former will refer to actors/organisations who do not represent the state, nor control (substantial parts of) its territory, nor form applicants' private support networks. This distinction is justified by the different forms of rape myths to which these non-state actors *(sensu lato)* can be related.

First, the idea that support from NGOs or doctors for example might suffice to protect applicants from SGBV, demonstrates an overreliance on non-state actors' ability to effectively protect (potential) survivors/victims against SGBV. In rape mythology, this overreliance has been voiced as: 'Victims of sexual violence today receive sufficient help in the form of refuges, therapy offers and support groups.'[1522] Second, I will discuss the idea that the mere presence of family members/acquaintances in survivors'/victims' private surroundings would sufficiently protect them against SGBV upon return. This idea of 'the home as a safe place'[1523] relates to several other rape myths, namely: 'Rape only occurs between strangers in public places',[1524] 'Rape is unlikely in the [person's] own familiar neighbourhood', '[Persons] are almost never raped by their [partners]',

1522 Gerger and others (n 150) 425.

1523 Patricia Hill Collins, 'It's All In the Family: Intersections of Gender, Race, and Nation' (1998) 13 Hypatia 62, 67–68.

1524 Leverick (n 139) 257.

or 'Rape almost never happens in the [person's] own home',[1525] or alternative phrasings such as given by the WHO and the UN Office on Drugs and Crime.[1526]

Both for the non-state actor *sensu stricto* and private support network myths, it is relevant to refer back to the disclosure and resourcefulness myths discussed on the micro level (see Part III, Chapter 2 and 3), since seeking support from such actors/networks first requires disclosure to them and a social network can be seen as a form of non-material resourcefulness. Therefore, the myths that 'an ideal victim would tell immediately' and 'resourceful applicants do not need protection against SGBV' also play a role here. How these rape myths translate to the asylum context, can be illustrated by the case of Elene mentioned above. In her refusal decision and judgement, the CALL and the CGRS argued (in combination with the SGBV resourcefulness myth) that, upon returning to Georgia, she could seek protection from non-state actors, such as NGOs or *pro bono* lawyers, providing social, psychological, and legal assistance. They point at:

> 'the applicant's profile as a **young resourceful woman** who grew up in Tbilisi and started **law studies**, who indicates to be familiar with the existence of ***pro bono* lawyers** as well as **NGOs** in Georgia that advocate for victims of domestic violence and the LGBTQI+ community. Therefore, it is reasonable to assume that the applicant would have recourse, or at least know how to find her way to organisations that could **offer her help or protection** [...] [and from whom she] can also expect **social, psychological and legal assistance**.'[1527] | CASE OF ELENE

In addition, the authorities argued she could find protection with her private support network, including her mother (who had left the country by then) and not further specified 'LGBT friends and acquaintances':

> '[Y]ou can expect support from your **mother** and [...] **uncle**, who **financially helped** you to come to Belgium [...]. [Also,] both your **sister** and your mother are aware of your sexual orientation and [you] therefore also have a **family network** that can support you [...]. [Your] **father and brothers [...] are not aware** [...] [but if they would learn about it], [...] [you are] an **adult woman** [...] [who] could **settle elsewhere** upon return [...]. [You also] have a network of **LGBT friends and acquaintances** [...] [and] are therefore not alone and could also reasonably **expect support** [from them] [...] in the event of a negative reaction [...] by your family.'[1528] | CASE OF ELENE

1525 Payne, Lonsway and Fitzgerald (n 134) 49–50.

1526 World Health Organization (WHO), 'Caring for Women Subjected to Violence' (n 402) 5 and 7; United Nations Office on Drugs and Crime (UNODC) and Skinnider (n 161) 11–12; United Nations Office on Drugs and Crime (UNODC) (n 284) 96.

1527 DGe151_CALL 1 (refusal)_2003_F_Georgia_VGNT_DV_27/03/2024_303 891_NL_Database_p. 15–16., DGe151_CGRS 1_(refusal)_2003_F_Georgia_VGNT_DV_27/7/2023_303 891_NL_Database_p. 6.

1528 DGe151_CALL 1 (refusal)_2003_F_Georgia_VGNT_DV_27/03/2024_303 891_NL_Database_p. 15–16., DGe151_CGRS 1_(refusal)_2003_F_Georgia_VGNT_DV_27/7/2023_303 891_NL_Database_p. 6.

These excerpts already hint at the role non-state actor support might play in SGBV-related refugee status determination (e.g. to provide protection against persecution and to substantiate the reasonableness or safety of an IFA). In addition, they illustrate the types of actors (NGOs, lawyers, family, friends …) and forms of protection (social, psychological, legal, financial …) taken into account by asylum authorities. Importantly, from the preliminary ECtHR case law analysis, not only national authorities, but also the ECtHR itself seems to accept the non-state actor support myth in its non-refoulement case law.[1529]

However, as I will illustrate below, literature rebutting these myths underscores the unique societal perception surrounding SGBV, often leading to negative responses from the people to whom survivors/victims might go for support. In anticipation of such responses or after negative experiences with them, survivors/victims 'often strive to cope with the experience of sexual victimization without legal, medical, or mental health support.'[1530] Above all, the refugee definition is clearly built around the notion of 'state protection'.[1531] In order to be recognised as a refugee, applicants have to demonstrate their unwillingness or inability to seek protection against persecution from state actors or from non-state actors 'controlling the state or a substantial part of its territory'[1532] (which, for readability, I will both refer to as 'state protection' throughout this chapter). However, as I will demonstrate below, decision makers[1533] often appear to assign a role to non-state actors without such state control, sometimes at the expense of any assessment of the state protection available to applicants.

Below, I will discuss the roles both non-state actors *sensu stricto* and private support networks play in refugee status determination: as actors of protection; facilitators to obtaining state protection; or indicators of safety/reasonability of an IFA, applicants' credibility, or their risk/fear of SGBV. I will further go into the types of actors and protection deemed relevant in authorities' reasoning (e.g. NGOs, lawyers, doctors, teachers, family, friends … and physical, psychological, financial, legal, … support) and into their rejection of applicants' justifications for not relying on non-state protection (i.e. applicants' or non-state actors' unwillingness/inability to seek or provide protection). Importantly, assessing the effective protective qualities of these non-state actors seems anything but a standard element in the refugee status determination of Belgian asylum authorities.

1529 Roels, 'Rape Myths in the European Court of Human Rights' Non-Refoulement Case Law on Sexual and Gender-Based Violence' (n 33) 86.

1530 Fanflik, Office on Violence Against Women, and National District Attorneys Association (n 386) 3.

1531 Art. 1(A)2 UN Refugee Convention.

1532 Art. 7(1) EU Qualification Directive; Art. 7(1) EU Qualification Regulation.

1533 Spijkerboer, 'Asylum Decision-Making, Gender and Sexuality' (n 999) 199; Middelburg and Balta (n 8) 450.

2.1.2. NON-STATE ACTORS *SENSU STRICTO*

a) *Role of Non-State Actors* Sensu Stricto *in Refugee Status Determination*

In the Belgian context, one supervisor at the CGRS described 'protection' against persecution as 'a very broad word' and pathways towards it as 'simply options to find a solution for your situation in the country of origin before you decide to flee.'[1534] One of these solutions seems to consist of seeking protection from non-state actors to: 1) protect applicants from persecution directly, 2) facilitate their access to state protection, or 3) render their relocation to an IFA safe and/or reasonable. In addition, 4) applicants' help-seeking behaviour towards non-state actors is used as a credibility indicator in refugee status determination.

Several POs at the CGRS confirmed that the SGBV guidelines prescribe to inquire during the personal interview into whether applicants did or could seek protection from non-state actors like NGOs in their country of origin.[1535] Specifically, POs are expected to ask questions such as 'Could you contact an NGO? Do you know if there are any NGOs in your country working to tackle [SGBV]? Would you have the means to contact these NGOs?'[1536] The relevance of the answers to these questions varies across the four aspects mentioned above.

Firstly, some asylum officials seemed to assess protection from non-state actors in a similar way as from state actors.[1537] One attaché explained the subsidiary nature of international protection, meaning that applicants first have to establish why their country of origin is unable to protect them. However, they added, 'if we suspect that [...] there is effective protection by NGOs, [...] we'll say: you should have gone to that NGO first.' Depending on the type and effectiveness of this NGO protection, if 'it is really capable of protecting the person, [...] it's normal to say that the NGO could have protected [applicants].'[1538]

This line of reasoning is also used in cases where it is explicitly evident that applicants cannot find effective state protection against SGBV. As one gender-specialised supervisor explained: '[When] the state doesn't provide [...] help to victims, [...] NGOs taking over that task [...] come into play, [provided that], from the [COI] we have, they are effectively offering help.'[1539] Similarly, various POs and supervisors at the CGRS, both gender-specialised and not, explicitly stated that support from non-state actors, like NGOs, can replace or compensate for a lack of state protection.[1540] It is important to already stress that this reasoning

1534 CB002_CGRS_Supervisor + PO_[00:36:29].
1535 CB003_CGRS_PO_[00:37:57].
1536 CB010_CGRS_Supervisor + PO_[00:24:23].
1537 RB003_CALL_Attaché_[00:45:13].
1538 RB007_CALL_Attaché_[00:42:16].
1539 CB015_CGRS_Supervisor + PO_GENDER_[00:30:39].
1540 E.g. CB004_CGRS_PO_[00:19:30].

flagrantly violates (inter)national refugee law, which requires protection against persecution to be provided by state actors exclusively.[1541]

In other statements, asylum authorities accepted the myth while the lack of state protection was indirectly evident, for example because: applicants could not obtain help from the police,[1542] there are NGOs working mainly on denouncing police violence against survivors/victims,[1543] or the prevalence rates of certain SGBV forms are very high (e.g. gang rape in India, as one PO mentioned above[1544]).

At times, the limitations of state protection are apparent from the argumentation itself. A standardised argument used in Georgian decisions and judgements by the CGRS and the CALL,[1545] such as Elene's, argues for non-state actors' protective qualities, while at the same time stating:

> 'A questionnaire is in place since 2018 to assist police officers in making **risk assessments in domestic violence cases**, although it is **not always filled in carefully** and **further processing is often ineffective**. [...] Both the government and NGOs run shelters with a **limited number of places** for women and their minor children in **five of Georgia's 10 regions** [...], **provided they have officially reported** the violence [...]. However, **support** [...] **after leaving a shelter** remain[s] an **issue**, as does **coordination between the various actors** who detect, follow up or accompany victims of [SGBV].'[1546] | CASE OF ELENE

For some applicants, like Carmen, the ineffectiveness of non-state actor support was demonstrated through their own past attempts at obtaining it, which could not prevent them from fleeing. Still, both the CGRS and the CALL used the argument that Carmen should return and seek help from an NGO or a doctor against domestic violence:

> '[Y]ou **found access to an organisation** after being **referred by a doctor** [...] showing your independence and **resourcefulness**, as well as your ability to assert your rights

---

1541 Art. 7(1)–(2) EU Qualification Directive; Art. 7(1)–(2) EU Qualification Regulation; Art. 48/5, §2, part 2 Belgian Aliens Act.

1542 CB002_CGRS_Supervisor + PO_[00:19:04].

1543 CB002_CGRS_Supervisor + PO_[00:37:03].

1544 CB014_CGRS_PO_[00:53:00].

1545 DGe109_CALL 1 (refusal)_F_Georgia_RSA_FM_DV_19/12/2023_303 313_NL_Database_p. 4., DGe138_CALL 1 (refusal)_1998_F_Georgia_RSA_DV_23/5/2024_307 108_NL_Database_p.12., DGe138_CGRS 1 (refusal)_1998_F_Georgia_RSA_DV_27/12/2023_307 108_NL_Database_p. 5., DGe139_CALL 1 (refusal)_2005_F_Georgia_DV_23/5/2024_307 109_NL_Database_p. 9., DGe144_CALL 1 (refusal)_1985_F_Georgia_RSA_DV_29/05/2024_307 462_NL_Database_p.9.

1546 DGe151_CALL 1 (refusal)_2003_F_Georgia_VGNT_DV_27/03/2024_303 891_NL_Database_p. 13, DGe151_CGRS 1_(refusal)_2003_F_Georgia_VGNT_DV_27/7/2023_303 891_NL_Database_p. 5.

through the Ecuadorian legal system [...]. Nothing shows that you would not be able to **do so again upon return**.'[1547] | CASE OF CARMEN

A similar reasoning was used in Diana's case, where the CALL stated:

> 'While the [applicant] argues that there is hardly any legal protection for victims (of domestic violence) in Albania, [her] previous statements [...] confirm that she could turn to an **organisation** [...] **offering free legal aid**. The applicant could therefore [...] rely on this for any **assistance and/or protection**.'[1548] | CASE OF DIANA

Secondly, next to replacing or compensating for a lack of state protection, asylum officials also see non-state actors as facilitators to obtaining state protection. One attaché hereby rightly mentioned established case law by the CJEU (*O.A. case*),[1549] confirming that non-state actors are not capable of protecting applicants against persecution, nor relevant to the assessment of the effectiveness or availability of state protection (see Chapter 3.1.3). Nonetheless, *contra legem*, the same attaché claimed: 'It is not because the [CJEU] says that we should not [...] qualify [NGOs] [...] as actors of protection, that they are not still relevant to our [...] assessment. Certainly not, because [...] this still affects whether you will be able to call on [state] protection.'[1550] Similarly, in reply to an abovementioned Georgian applicant who argued that the Belgian Aliens Act does not qualify NGOs as actors of protection, the CALL stressed: '[T]he fact that NGOs are no actors of protection [...] does not mean that applicants are not expected to rely on them for assistance in obtaining protection from national authorities.'[1551]

Thirdly, according to the authorities, non-state actors may play a role in the safety and reasonability assessment of an IFA where applicants could return to. Here too, applicants' resourcefulness appears to play in conjunction with their access to non-state actor support. A gender-specialised supervisor illustrated how, in the case of an Indian applicant and rape survivor/victim, an IFA was considered, taking into account her higher education and resourcefulness. While recognising that 'the state in India doesn't really help much towards victims,' this supervisor nonetheless stated: 'We had done some research in that region and there were many organisations that had helped the victims, especially the women.'[1552]

1547 DEc120_CGRS 1 (refusal)_1981_F_Ecuador_RSA_DV_ 8/12/2023_NL_Database_p. 4, Dec120_CALL 1 (refusal)_1981_F_Ecuador_RSA_DV_ 29/4/2024_ 305 805_NL_Database_ p. 10.

1548 NA001_B_CALL 1 (refusal)_1973_F_Albania_RSA_VGNT_FM_DV_7/4/2020_234 950_ NL_NANSEN_p. 6.

1549 Ruling 2. *Secretary of State for the Home Department v. O.A.* (n 742).

1550 RB004_CALL_Attaché_[00:13:48].

1551 DGe137_CALL 1 (refusal)_F_Georgia_RSA_DV_23/5/2024_307 106_NL_Database_p. 24.

1552 CB015_CGRS_Supervisor + PO_GENDER_[00:29:20].

Fourthly, applicants' help-seeking behaviour from non-state actors is also used as an indicator for their credibility. One supervisor was of the opinion that it is not necessarily relevant whether or not NGOs provide effective protection. Rather, applicants' internal thought process on seeking such support before fleeing is relevant for their credibility assessment.[1553] In cases where applicants did seek such support before fleeing, their credibility is at times still challenged due to the type of actors they approached or the insufficiently persistent way in which they did so.

In the abovementioned case of the minor Gabonese sister and brother who were subjected to harmful sexual rituals by their paternal family, the CGRS argued that their mother sought help from an organisation called '*La main sur la cœur*', but that this was a social project, providing basic necessities such as groceries. Questioning the use of this organisation in finding protection for them, the CGRS concluded that this (and other elements) '[does] not allow to establish the credibility of [the] fears invoked.'[1554] In Carmen's case, the CALL found her attempts to seek NGO support insufficiently persistent:

> 'It is [...] clear that opportunities were available from **organisations dealing with victims of domestic violence**. Apparently, **you did not even inform yourself** [this time before fleeing] [...], which is **completely at odds with your attitude in 2008 and in 2011 when you apparently did** find your way to available services and organisations.'[1555] | CASE OF CARMEN

Similar to the case of Elene, whose law studies prompted higher expectations for her to seek non-state actor support,[1556] a gender-specialised supervisor confirmed this link between resourcefulness and expectations on help-seeking behaviour. They explained asking questions such as: 'Have you taken any steps to [...] get concrete help from NGOs?' because this is important information to assess applicants' fear. To them, this assessment depends on their profile: 'I'd be much more demanding with a university couple than with [a single, illiterate woman].'[1557] As with the disclosure myths on detailedness and consistency, here too, some asylum officials pointed at the importance of well-articulated answers. As such, applicants might be expected to name NGOs, explain what these do,

1553 CB002_CGRS_Supervisor + PO_[00:34:37].

1554 DC079_B_CGRS 1 (refusal)_2014_M_Gabon_RSA_VGNT_20/2/2023_303 320_FR_Database_MINOR_p. 9.; DC079_C_CGRS 1 (refusal)_2006_F_Gabon_RSA_20/2/2023_303 320_FR_Database_MINOR_p. 7.

1555 DEc120_CGRS 1 (refusal)_1981_F_Ecuador_RSA_DV_ 8/12/2023_NL_Database_p. 3., Dec120_CALL 1 (refusal)_1981_F_Ecuador_RSA_DV_ 29/4/2024_ 305 805_NL_Database_p. 8.

1556 DGe151_CALL 1 (refusal)_2003_F_Georgia_VGNT_DV_27/03/2024_303 891_NL_Database_p. 15–16, DGe151_CGRS 1_(refusal)_2003_F_Georgia_VGNT_DV_27/7/2023_303 891_NL_Database_p. 6.

1557 CB005_CGRS_Supervisor + PO_GENDER_[00:31:08].

or why they have not contacted them,[1558] which again may involve a risk of discrimination based on level of intelligence (see Part III, Chapter 3.2.1).[1559]

b) *Types of Non-State Actors & Protection*

The most frequently mentioned non-state actors are NGOs that support (potential) SGBV survivors/victims, and safe houses or shelters in particular.[1560] Support from these actors is described by authorities in the form of physical protection, but also psychosocial support (as mentioned in Elene's case[1561]), including guidance towards economic independence (as in a Serbian domestic violence case[1562]), or general public awareness raising, as in Marjorie's case:

> 'Moreover, the Victim Support Office takes a leading role in **raising awareness on domestic violence**, including by **spreading messages through public television channels**. The bureau also runs a refuge for female victims of domestic violence and children under 12. […] In view of the totality of the foregoing findings, […] you have **not exhausted all reasonable steps** […] to obtain national […] protection […] and not sufficiently demonstrated that obtaining international protection was the only remaining way out for you.'[1563] | CASE OF MARJORIE

Also frequently mentioned as relevant non-state actors are lawyers and other organisations providing legal support. This often, but not always, concerns *pro bono* or free legal aid,[1564] which was also suggested as a (facilitator towards) protection against SGBV in Ana's[1565] and Diana's case:

> 'You state that you never had recourse to a **lawyer** because it would **cost too much** […] but as you also say yourself, there are opportunities in Albania to obtain **free legal assistance through certain [NGOs]** which should certainly allow you to **lodge a complaint** in the future if you feel that the police are not acting adequately.'[1566] | CASE OF DIANA

1558 CB002_CGRS_Supervisor + PO_[00:38:52].

1559 RB007_CALL_Attaché_[00:31:15].

1560 CB002_CGRS_Supervisor + PO_[00:34:37].

1561 DGe151_CALL 1 (refusal)_2003_F_Georgia_VGNT_DV_27/03/2024_303 891_NL_Database_p. 15–16, DGe151_CGRS 1_(refusal)_2003_F_Georgia_VGNT_DV_27/7/2023_303 891_NL_Database_p. 6.

1562 DSe093_CGRS 3 (manifestly ill-founded)_F_Serbia_DV_12/2/2022_301 311_FR_Database_p. 5.

1563 DSu147_CGRS 1 (refusal)_F_Suriname_RSA_VGNT_FM_DV_9/5/2023_301 074_NL_Database_p. 3, DSu147_CALL 1 (refusal)_F_Suriname_RSA_VGNT_FM_DV_5/2/2024_301 074_NL_Database_p. 9.

1564 CB008_CGRS_Supervisor + PO_GENDER_[00:39:26] & [00:41:13], DSe093_CGRS 3 (manifestly ill-founded)_F_Serbia_DV_12/2/2022_301 311_FR_Database_p. 5.

1565 DGe144_CALL 1 (refusal)_1985_F_Georgia_RSA_DV_29/05/2024_307 462_NL_Database_p. 9.

1566 NA001_B_CALL 1 (refusal)_1973_F_Albania_RSA_VGNT_FM_DV_7/4/2020_234 950_NL_NANSEN _p. 5, NA001_B_CGRS 1 (manifestly ill-founded)_1973_F_Albania_RSA_VGNT_FM_DV_29/5/2019_234 950_NL_NANSEN_p. 5.

It is important to assess the CALL's proposed solution of filing a complaint with the Albanian authorities through free legal assistance against the specific background of Diana and Erina's case. They sought help from authorities at least 16 times, only resulting in temporary protection orders for Diana (not for her children/parents), which were consistently violated by her ex-husband. The authorities on several occasions dismissed their complaints, refused to document evidence, failed to arrest the perpetrator, tried to persuade Diana to abandon her divorce proceedings, and actively encouraged Erina to visit her abusive father, which led to a (failed) attempt to abduct her.

In addition, private persons in authoritative positions towards applicants, such as doctors or teachers, are also mentioned as relevant non-state actors of protection. For example, one attaché mentioned having heard about a doctor in Bukavu (the DRC), who takes care of raped women and with whom (potential) survivors/victims can 'hide'. They stated that 'if similar safe houses exist in other countries, we can say that [...] [applicants should have gone to that doctor as a replacement for lacking state protection].'[1567] In the abovementioned Ghanese rape, forced marriage, and domestic violence case, the CGRS and the CALL simply stated: 'You made no attempt to seek help [...] in your country of origin. You did not go to the doctor nor to the police.'[1568] The expected role of teachers in (indirectly) helping to protect applicants from SGBV can be illustrated by the case of Qawtar.

CASE OF QAWTAR

• Country of origin:	Morocco	• SGBV types:	Violence related to gender norm transgression, forced marriage & domestic violence
• Gender identity:	Woman	• Decisions in file:	CGRS 1 (refusal) – 3/04/2024
• Birth year:	1999		CALL 1 (refusal) – 24/04/2024 – n° 305 429
• Interview by:	/		

According to Qawtar's statements, she was born in Morocco in 1999. She grew up under the authority of her father, who **forbade his daughter to study, work, or own a phone, and obliged her to wear a hijab.** Without him knowing and with the help of a teacher, she obtained a baccalaureate. When she turned 20, Qawtar was **forced to marry** a wealthy man, eleven years older. He too **forbade her to work** and was **physically violent.** She **gave birth** to a daughter, in whom her husband had never shown any interest. She sought support from an organisation helping domestic violence survivors/victims but gave up out of fear that they would pass on information to her husband. With the help of a lawyer, she managed to divorce him in 2022 but ended up in a legal battle over child support. Without any work experience, money,

(continued)

[1567] RB007_CALL_Attaché_[00:44:52].

[1568] DGh115_CALL 1 (refusal)_1999_F_Ghana_RSA_FM_DV_19/4//2024_305 147_NL_Database_p. 8, DGh115_CGRS 1 (refusal)_1999_F_Ghana_RSA_FM_DV_26/3/2024_305 147_NL_Database_p. 4.

or a place to live with her daughter, Qawtar was forced to go back to her parents' home. Her father **blamed her for causing the divorce** and **hit her** for leaving the house without a hijab. She received **death threats** from her ex-husband's brother, and was almost **hit by a car**, presumably by her ex-husband. Two years before fleeing the country, Qawtar met her current fiancé, who has a Dutch nationality.

She travelled to Belgium with a short-stay visa to get married to him. In December 2023, the Belgian authorities found Qawtar to be residing irregularly in the territory and therefore detained her in a closed centre. A first repatriation was postponed since she refused to return to Morocco. A second attempt was cancelled because she eventually applied for international protection in February 2024. She submitted fearing to be abused by her father and ex-husband and being stigmatised in Moroccan society because of her divorce. In support of her application, she submitted, among other documents, a certificate attesting her divorce and two photos of her with a black eye.

In Qawtar's case, regardless of her initial steps towards a domestic violence NGO, the CGRS and the CALL focused on the help she received from a teacher:

> '[Y]**ou did receive help in Morocco**[, since] it was **with the support of a teacher** that you **obtained your baccalaureate at a state school free of charge**. [...] By no means did you make plausible your impossibility to seek any support in Morocco. [...] [Y]our **manifest** [...] **lack of initiative** to get out of your presented situation appears so implausible that it further **undermines the credibility** of your statements.'[1569] | CASE OF QAWTAR

Lastly, asylum officials also mention non-state actor support in the form of helplines or smartphone apps (especially in Albanian and Georgian cases such as Diana's or Vera's).[1570] In other cases, they do not further specify the non-state actors, for example describing them as 'women or men who are there to repair the person in some way'[1571] or 'other people who can help you.'[1572]

When it comes to the actual protective qualities of the above listed non-state actors in practice, one attaché at the CALL expected the CGRS, when suggesting

1569 DM116_CALL 1 (refusal)_1999_F_Morocco_VGNT_FM_DV_24/04/2024_305 429_NL_Database_p. 16, DM116_CGRS 1 (refusal)_1999_F_Morocco_VGNT_FM_DV_3/4/2024_305 429_NL_Database_p. 5.

1570 DA099_A_CGRS 1 (manifestly ill-founded)_M_Albania_DV_6/7/2023_303 553_FR_Database_p. 3–4., DGe109_CALL 1 (refusal)_F_Georgia_RSA_FM_DV_19/12/2023_303 313_NL_Database_p. 4., DGe138_CGRS 1 (refusal)_1998_F_Georgia_RSA_DV_27/12/2023_307 108_NL_Database_p. 5., DGe138_CALL 1 (refusal)_1998_F_Georgia_RSA_DV_23/5/2024_307 108_NL_Database_p. 12., NA001_B_CGRS 2 (inadmissible)_1973_F_Albania_RSA_VGNT_FM_DV_21/10/2021_270 155_NL_NANSEN_p. 5., NA016_CALL 1 (refusal)_1990_F_Albania_RSA_VGNT_DV_27/2/2023_285363_NL_NANSEN_p.14.,NA016_CGRS1 (manifestly ill-founded)_1990_F_Albania_RSA_VGNT_DV_10/10/2022_285 363_NL_NANSEN_p. 4.

1571 CB001_CGRS_PO_[00:37:03].

1572 DS103_CGRS 1 (refusal)_F_Senegal_GMC_FM_DV_17/7/2023_305 927_FR_Database_p. 6.

such support as a solution, to rely on 'information on how [this actor] functions and how [applicants] can effectively appeal on that protection.'[1573] However, two supervisors (one of them gender-specialised) acknowledged not really delving into the difference in protective qualities of NGOs, since the guidelines lack clarity about 'how far we should go',[1574] nor does COI standardly include information on the concrete support provided by the non-state actors it mentions.[1575]

The CALL does not have the competence to take investigative measures itself.[1576] As a result, two attachés reported accepting the non-state protection myth in their argumentation,[1577] while at the same time acknowledging that they lack the resources to answer questions such as: 'Would this woman have found her way to these [SGBV] organisations? Are they as [...] accessible as we think?,'[1578] admitting their lack of sufficient information on the nature and actual protective qualities of SGBV NGOs.[1579]

c) *Assessment of Justifications for not Seeking Non-State Protection*

The asylum officials sometimes also commented on justifications provided by applicants for their choice (not) to seek non-state actor support. Firstly, applicants mention the ineffectiveness of such support to protect them from SGBV. Two Georgian applicants for example perceived NGO support as useless because 'no one could protect [them]'[1580] or 'NGOs themselves need protection.'[1581] These justifications were dismissed by the CGRS and the CALL as mere allegations. Diana's explanation, namely that legal assistance could not protect her from her ex-husband's abuse, was accepted by neither the CGRS nor the CALL:

> 'Your dissatisfaction with the fact that [the organisation you turned to] **only provides legal assistance** [...] does not alter the fact that you had access to this organisation, and **nothing prevents you from appealing to other organisations** that provide other

1573 RB004_CALL_Attaché_[00:16:46].

1574 CB010_CGRS_Supervisor + PO_[00:26:32].

1575 CB015_CGRS_Supervisor + PO_GENDER_[00:28:05].

1576 Art. 39/2 §1, 2°Belgian Aliens Act; Desmet, 'Appellate Asylum and Migration Proceedings in Belgium' (n 106) 197.

1577 '[I]f we suspect that [...] there is effective protection by NGOs, [...] we'll say: you should have gone to that NGO first' and, depending the type and effectiveness of this NGO protection, if 'it is really capable of protecting the person, [...] it's normal to say that the NGO could have protected [applicants]' (RB003_CALL_Attaché_[00:45:13].), RB007_CALL_Attaché_[00:42:16].

1578 RB003_CALL_Attaché_[00:43:26].

1579 RB007_CALL_Attaché_[00:43:30].

1580 DGe137_CALL 1 (refusal)_F_Georgia_RSA_DV_23/5/2024_307 106_NL_Database_p. 24, DGe137_CGRS 1 (refusal)_F_Georgia_RSA_DV_27/12/2023_307 106_NL_Database_p. 6.

1581 DGe110_CALL1(refusal)_1986_M_Georgia_VGNT_FM_27/3/2024_303889_NL_Database_p.18, DGe110_CGRS 1 (refusal)_1986_M_Georgia_VGNT_FM_28/9/2023_303 889_NL_Database_p. 6.

> types of assistance [...] such as **housing, protection, and financial assistance.**'[1582] | CASE OF DIANA

Other applicants, such as Carmen, mentioned their lack of access to certain organisations. While having relied on NGOs in the past, Carmen pointed at their limited capacity (stating: 'There are one or two shelters for abused women, but [...] few places available'[1583]) as a barrier to seeking their support again. In response, the CALL stated:

> 'Recent [COI] indicates that [support] initiatives are being further expanded to include a 24/7 emergency "hotline", shelters, and a support programme enabling a fresh start. [...] However, you should take the necessary steps to [call on such initiatives] and inform yourself. That you may have **run out of time to go to the organisation, or that they had few facilities at that time, is not representative of how these types of organisations operate today or the facilities they offer.**'[1584] | CASE OF CARMEN

One gender-specialised supervisor at the CGRS acknowledged, on access to SGBV-related NGOs, (with a neocolonial undertone[1585]) that they themselves 'wouldn't know how to suddenly go to an NGO either, if [they] had problems here. Let alone having just survived something like [SGBV] and growing up in a country that is still, well, [...] a bit less advanced than here so to speak.'[1586] Nonetheless, they still qualified these difficulties only as 'attenuating circumstances'[1587] for not seeking non-state actor support, which in principle is still expected of applicants.

Lastly, Qawtar refrained from seeking non-state actor support to protect her from her forced husband's domestic violence, as she feared that the organisation would not guarantee her confidentiality. Both the CGRS and the CALL dismissed this justification:

> '[H]ad [you] so wished, there would have been occasions when [you] could have escaped the authority of [your] father and ex-husband. [You] can be expected [...] to have sought an effective solution to escape the pressure [you] alleged. [...] That **you pretended you could not turn to any organisation in Morocco for help is by**

1582 NA001_B_CALL 1 (refusal)_1973_F_Albania_RSA_VGNT_FM_DV_7/4/2020_234 950_NL_NANSEN_p. 5, NA001_B_CGRS 1 (manifestly ill-founded)_1973_F_Albania_RSA_VGNT_FM_DV_29/5/2019_234 950_NL_NANSEN_p. 5.

1583 Dec120_CALL 1 (refusal)_1981_F_Ecuador_RSA_DV_ 29/4/2024_ 305 805_NL_Database_p. 11.

1584 DEc120_CGRS1 (refusal)_1981_F_Ecuador_RSA_DV_8/12/2023_NL_Database_p.4, DEc120_CALL 1 (refusal)_1981_F_Ecuador_RSA_DV_ 29/4/2024_ 305 805_NL_Database_p. 10.

1585 Fiorenza Picozza, *The Coloniality of Asylum: Mobility, Autonomy and Solidarity in the Wake of Europe's Refugee Crisis* (Rowman & Littlefield Publishers 202145) 8.

1586 CB011_CGRS_Supervisor + PO_GENDER_[00:48:44].

1587 CB011_CGRS_Supervisor + PO_GENDER_[00:48:44].

no means plausible. You […] approached **only one organisation**, but further **refused** their help because, according to you, they **'passed on all information to your husband'**. […] By no means did you make it plausible that it was impossible for you to seek help.'[1588] | CASE OF QAWTAR

2.1.3. PRIVATE SUPPORT NETWORKS

A specific form of non-state actors *sensu lato*, referred to by asylum authorities in the interviews and case law, are applicants' private support networks. Interestingly, these private support networks seem to play a different role from the non-state actors *sensu stricto* discussed above. As one attaché clearly put it, in discussing the case of a girl forced to marry a friend of her father's, 'I don't see how an NGO can protect anyone […] I can say that [she] could have gone to [her] grandmother's, but I cannot say that [she] could have gone to an NGO, no.'[1589] Also, as discussed in Part III, Chapter 2.1.2, private support networks seem to act as a form of non-material resources in asylum authorities' argumentation.

a) *Role of Private Support Networks in Refugee Status Determination*

Similar to the non-state actor *sensu stricto* myth above, private support networks are brought up in decisions/judgements: 1) to protect applicants from persecution directly, 2) to facilitate their access to state protection, 3) to render their relocation to an IFA safe/reasonable, and 4) as a credibility indicator. Additionally, 5) private support networks at times seem to neutralise applicants' fear or risk of SGBV as such, especially in GMC cases where the private support networks of applicants are opposed to the practice.

Firstly, in SGBV-related refugee status determination, the assessment of state protection at times seems to (partly) shift to one on family protection.[1590] One gender-specialised supervisor at the CGRS described their task as: 'We'll look into whether [applicants] had any form of protection, either from other family members or from the authorities.'[1591] This shift even takes place when the family sphere is the context in which the SGBV occurred in the first place. This can be illustrated by the case of Sofia, who fled Honduras from child sexual abuse by her father.

1588 DM116_CALL 1 (refusal)_1999_F_Morocco_VGNT_FM_DV_24/04/2024_305 429_NL_Database_p. 16, DM116_CGRS 1 (refusal)_1999_F_Morocco_VGNT_FM_DV_3/4/2024_305 429_NL_Database_p. 5.

1589 RB007_CALL_Attaché_[00:41:06].

1590 CB008_CGRS_Supervisor + PO_GENDER_[00:37:09].

1591 CB005_CGRS_Supervisor + PO_GENDER_[00:22:58].

CASE OF SOFIA			
• Country of origin:	Honduras	• SGBV types:	Rape/sexual assault & domestic violence
• Gender identity:	Woman	• Decisions in file:	CGRS 1 (refusal) – 12/8/2021 (withdrawn)
• Birth year:	1991		/ (error in paying registration fee prevented an appeal)[1592]
• Interview by:	Researcher		CGRS 2 (recognition) – 15/03/2023

According to Sofia's statements, she was born in 1991 in Honduras, where she lived with her family. Her father was only home every two weeks, but when he was, he **sexually abused** her when he came in at night, often drunk. This happened the first time when she was 12 years old and continued for five years. When she was 17, she found the courage to tell her cousin. The latter confronted Sofia's father and threatened to contact the police if the abuse did not stop. While her father thereupon blamed Sofia and told her he would have stopped if she had asked him, the **assault continued** in more subtle forms. He asked her to sit on his lap or touched her 'as a woman and not as his daughter'. She coped with the abuse by feeling angry and sad all the time but not knowing where else to seek help. She never thought of contacting the police herself, as she was young, she dared not talk to anyone about this (not even to her mother), there was no proof, and she normalised her father's behaviour as 'consistent with how men approach girls in Honduras.' While she used to avoid her home by visiting her grandmother, the latter eventually died. Sofia's aunt, who was living in Belgium, arranged her flight on the pretext that she would learn French and then return.

She left Honduras in 2012 for Belgium, where she took French courses and found work through the church. In Belgium, Sofia started having nightmares and feeling guilty that her silence might put her sisters (still in Honduras) at risk of the same violence. Supported by someone in church, she eventually told her mother about the abuse on the phone. While her mother believed Sofia, she kept protecting her husband and stayed with him. Only years later, after receiving psychological support in Belgium, Sofia realised the gravity of the child sexual abuse she had suffered, and that this could be a reason to obtain international protection. In 2019, she applied and supported her demand with (among other documents) a psychological certificate attesting her PTSD and news articles/reports on the widespread violence against women in Honduras.

In Sofia's (later withdrawn) refusal decision, the CGRS argued that she could find protection within the private support network of her family:

> 'Your **mother** believed you immediately and apologised. You also have [...] a **sister**, [...] who no longer lives at home [...]. Your statements thus show that **you have**

[1592] Upon refusal of her application by the CGRS, Sofia's appeal with the CALL was not registered, since her insufficient bank balance had caused an error in the payment of the registration fee. Despite a letter from her lawyer explaining this, the situation could not be rectified and she could not appeal against her refusal decision by the CGRS. Eventually, the CGRS decided to withdraw the initial refusal of Sofia's application and, after reconsidering her case (the reasoning of which is not made public), to recognise her as a refugee.

family members in Honduras with whom you have a good relationship and there is **no evidence at all that they would not support you.**'[1593] | CASE OF SOFIA

Like with non-state actors *sensu stricto*, absence of state protection does not seem to prevent asylum officials from considering private support networks as actors of protection, as confirmed by one PO for the CGRS.[1594] An attaché explicitly explained the same counts for the CALL: 'If state protection is not available, [...] then we have to go into the question whether [there is family protection] [...] and whether it is effective.'[1595] Another attaché acknowledged that state actors in the DRC do not interfere with 'family matters' like forced marriages, but at the same time asked themselves: 'But why come to Belgium? Because you have aunts, uncles and grandmothers who could protect you there? [...] I've already written [in a judgement:] [...] "[The applicant] doesn't show that her aunts, her grandmothers couldn't help her".'[1596]

In the interviews for this research, asylum officials seemed to disagree on the role of private support networks in two countries of origin specifically: Guinea and Afghanistan. For female GMC in Guinea, one judge confirmed that the prevalence rates are so high (95%), that there is no state protection available.[1597] A gender-specialised PO nuanced that, for a country like Guinea where female GMC prevalence is so high, the CGRS will not suggest parents as actors of protection, 'unless the mother has not experienced [female GMC] herself.'[1598] Yet another PO claimed the opposite and said: 'The family context is really too safe for [refugee recognition,] [...] even [...] [for] Guinea for example, [with] an extremely high incidence rate.'[1599]

Asked to give an example of a country of origin lacking state protection from SGBV persecution, one judge could think of only one: Afghanistan. Female SGBV survivors/victims cannot be expected to seek protection there, they stated, not even with the help from male chaperones,[1600] since this would require them to disclose the SGBV to their brother or father, potentially putting them at further risk.[1601] Oppositely, a gender-specialised PO and another judge did argue that applicants should rely on family networks for (seeking) protection,

1593 NH003_CGRS 1 (refusal)_1991_F_Honduras_RSA_DV_12/8/2021_NL_NANSEN_p. 2.
1594 CB014_CGRS_PO_[00:49:40].
1595 RB003_CALL_Attaché_[00:45:02].
1596 RB007_CALL_Attaché_[00:37:35].
1597 RB006_CALL_Judge_[00:35:07]. Confirmed by: 'In Guinea,97 per cent of women and girls, aged 15-49, have undergone some form of [female genital mutilation] 'in UN Population Fund (UNFPA), 'Female Genital Mutilation Dashboard (FGM) – Guinea' www.unfpa.org/data/fgm/GN.
1598 CB009_CGRS_PO_GENDER_[00:23:12].
1599 CB001_CGRS_PO_[00:23:54].
1600 Amnesty International and International Commission of Jurists (ICJ) (n 740) 9.
1601 RB001_CALL_Judge_[00:24:47].

as women without any network are easily preyed upon in Afghanistan.[1602] The judge added that, for male applicants specifically,[1603] the importance of private support networks 'depends from country to country [...], in Afghanistan, family is very important. So [...] if there is a network there, we do say "if you go back [...], you don't run as much risk".'[1604]

Secondly, some asylum officials explicitly rejected the role of private support networks as actors of protection, but did consider them as facilitators of applicants' access to state protection.[1605] They for example clearly distinguished: 'The social network is not an actor of protection, [but] it can facilitate access to an actor of protection'[1606] or 'Private [...] networks [...] cannot provide protection as such, but may be able to help obtain state protection.'[1607]

This reasoning illustrates how private networks are seen as a form of non-material resourcefulness,[1608] leading to the idea that 'if [a woman] has a social network and an education, which should have drawn her attention to this possibility,' it will be less understandable that she did not seek state protection.[1609] A judge made this more concrete with the example of an applicant who felt ashamed about the SGBV she suffered, but did tell her best friend about it. The judge concluded that she 'could have gone to the police with [her] best friend.'[1610] Here too, an attaché maintained that this reasoning is consistent with the abovementioned CJEU *O.A.* judgment[1611] (establishing the irrelevance non-state actors for assessing the effectiveness or availability of state protection).

Thirdly, private support networks are seen as relevant to the safety and/or reasonability assessment of an IFA.[1612] One gender-specialised supervisor for example explained, intersecting with the resourcefulness myth, that such an alternative will more readily be suggested to 'someone with a large network who is not rejected by their family [...], who is highly educated, who has always had a job, who is resourceful, who comes from a wealthier background.'[1613] In practice, this solution may expect applicants to return to their private support network for protection from the SGBV perpetrators they fear, what often comes down to going into hiding.

1602 CB008_CGRS_Supervisor + PO_GENDER_[00:37:30].
1603 Council for Alien Law Litigation (CALL), 'Internal Communication CALL' (n 168).
1604 RB005_CALL_Judge_[00:31:20].
1605 RB001_CALL_Judge_[00:23:10].
1606 RB008_CALL_Judge_[00:32:42].
1607 R_1N94UZT5x9U3Ied_CALL-Attaché.
1608 CB008_CGRS_Supervisor + PO_GENDER_[00:38:47].
1609 RB008_CALL_Judge_[00:32:33].
1610 RB001_CALL_Judge_[00:23:10].
1611 Ruling 2. *Secretary of State for the Home Department v. O.A.* (n 742)., RB004_CALL_Attaché_[00:13:48].
1612 CB002_CGRS_Supervisor + PO_[00:34:11], RB002_CALL_Attaché_[00:39:48].
1613 CB015_CGRS_Supervisor + PO_GENDER_[00:22:32].

Fourthly, applicants' help-seeking behaviour from private support networks is also relied upon as a credibility indicator.[1614] A gender-specialised PO explained that, if applicants can demonstrate their help-seeking attempts from private networks (e.g. by talking to parents or relatives in the case of family violence 'to solve it'), this plays in their favour.[1615] Reacting[1616] to the private support network argument in Sofia's (later withdrawn[1617]) decision, an attaché set out the relevance for her credibility assessment. They stated: 'It shows that [she] had both access to [and knowledge about] a protection alternative.' The fact that she still fled the country, to them prompted the question: 'Can I believe that a person [...] would then still decide to flee?'[1618] Similarly, in the abovementioned Senegalese case of a woman forcibly married to a man carrying out human sacrifices, the CGRS expressed the disbelief 'that [she] would not turn to anyone, whether national authorities, family members or close friends, to protect [her] or report the crimes [she says she] witnessed.'[1619]

Fifthly, applicants' access to a private support network at times seems to weaken or completely cancel out their risk of SGBV persecution altogether.[1620] Such risk assessments were illustrated by an attaché[1621] and two gender-specialised CGRS officials (one supervisor and one PO), the latter two respectively commenting on a forced marriage and sexual violence case. The first argued that, if the applicant 'could have returned to her family, who would have accepted her escape, [...] in essence, what is she still afraid of?'[1622] The second described the situation where a rape survivor's/victim's family had been aware of what happened for years and never said anything about it or, even though there is 'a huge taboo in the country,' never rejected the applicant.[1623]

Another attaché rejected both the role of private support networks as actors of protection and as a credibility indicator on the one hand but confirmed their relevance to assess applicants' future risk of persecution on the other. Although they believed there is disagreement about this within the CALL, they stated: 'If the person [...] has a well-developed social network, [...] we could consider

1614 RB008_CALL_Judge_[00:32:42].

1615 CB011_CGRS_Supervisor + PO_GENDER_[00:48:44].

1616 Which I brought up during some of the interviews with asylum authorities.

1617 Upon refusal of her application by the CGRS, Sofia's appeal with the CALL was not registered, since her insufficient bank balance had caused an error in the payment of the registration fee. Despite a letter from her lawyer explaining this, the situation could not be rectified and she could not appeal against her refusal decision by the CGRS. Eventually, the CGRS decided to withdraw the initial refusal of Sofia's application and, after reconsidering her case (the reasoning of which is not made public), to recognise her as a refugee.

1618 RB003_CALL_Attaché_[00:47:37].

1619 NS005_CGRS 1 (refusal)_2002_F_Senegal_RSA_DV_FM_13/05/2022_274 056_FR_NANSEN_ p. 5.

1620 CB005_CGRS_Supervisor + PO_GENDER_[00:27:15].

1621 RB004_CALL_Attaché_[00:13:48].

1622 CB005_CGRS_Supervisor + PO_GENDER_[00:27:31].

1623 CB009_CGRS_PO_GENDER_[00:21:41].

that this partly reduces the risk of future persecution, whereas conversely, if the person is totally isolated and has extremely limited socio-economic resources, this will be a factor that increases the risk.'[1624] It is important to refer back to Part III, Chapter 2.2 on rebuttal of the resourcefulness myth, where I illustrated how applicants' social networks are inaccurate SGBV predictors.

Especially in GMC cases where parents are opposed to the practice, some asylum authorities circumvented the question of state or private protection against SGBV, by arguing that there is no fear for such violence at all.[1625] One PO described the case of a well-educated couple with good jobs, living in a big city, who are opposed to GMC and explain that their daughter's grandparents want to abduct her to have her circumcised in the village. In response, they cynically stated: 'Yes, the grandparents could turn up in the street and kidnap the child, put her in a car and drive off to the village. But this is Abidjan? I mean!'[1626] A judge confirmed that in cases where parents are opposed to GMC, their children's fear of persecution is generally not established[1627] because no one else but parents (or close relatives like aunts or mothers-in-law at most) decide on GMC and that therefore 'there is no fear.'[1628] The judge hereby referred to Guinea as a country they often dealt with, where GMC prevalence numbers rise up to 95%, as mentioned above.[1629]

b) *Types of Private Support Networks & Protection*

There are various categories of private support networks mentioned in refugee status determination, such as family, partners, friends, or communities.

1624 RB002_CALL_Attaché_[00:37:59].

1625 CB001_CGRS_PO_[00:26:02], RB006_CALL_Judge_[00:35:49].

1626 CB013_CGRS_PO_[00:19:41].

1627 RB006_CALL_Judge_[00:34:25].

1628 RB006_CALL_Judge_[00:34:25], [00:35:49] & [00:38:23]. Interestingly, this statement clearly contrasts with another judge's statement on page 339, stating that Belgian asylum authorities systematically recognise children who fear female GMC, even if the parents oppose the practice. In internal communication, the CALL added that this contradiction might originate from a change in CGRS policy or a difference between the procedural languages (and countries of origin these treat). In any case, at the time of writing, the CALL and CGRS internally communicated being of the position that, for Guinea specifically, 'the principle is that the CGRS systematically recognises Guinean girls who have not been circumcised. It is only in very exceptional cases that it does not recognise them, particularly when it considers that the parents' profile suggests that their daughter(s) will not be exposed to this practice (educated parents, relatively high socio-economic status, mother herself not circumcised, etc.).' It is important to note the combination of the resourcefulness and non-state actor myth at play in the latter reasoning, as elaborated on page 318. Commissioner General for Refugees and Stateless Persons (CGRS), 'Internal Communication CGRS (Part V)' (n 331); Council for Alien Law Litigation (CALL), 'Internal Communication CALL' (n 168).

1629 RB006_CALL_Judge_[00:35:07]. Confirmed by: 'In Guinea,97 per cent of women and girls, aged 15-49, have undergone some form of [female genital mutilation] 'in UN Population Fund (UNFPA) (n 1597).

Asylum officials have pointed at 'the family' as a private support network for offering/facilitating access to protection against SGBV, for rendering IFAs safe/ reasonable, and for establishing credibility, risk, or fear of SGBV persecution.[1630] One case law example concerned a Guinean applicant who had given birth after she was raped in Morocco. The CGRS called her fear of violence related to the extramarital status of her child 'purely hypothetical' and unconvincing, since she had not told anyone about the rape except her brother and that '[her] sister and brother could help [her] in Guinea.'[1631] One PO for example asked themselves: if an applicant's 'entire family is against [female GMC], [...] why would she not be able to protect herself?'[1632]

In other cases, this opposition against GMC was not explicitly stated by applicants, but decision makers derived it from the fact that the applicants were not (re)circumcised when they stayed with family. This was the case in a Somali case, where the CGRS stated: '[Y]ou gave birth twice in Somalia without having [...] been circumcised [...] again. After your first birth, you lived with your family the entire time, which supports the fact that your own family will not be the actors of persecution for a new circumcision.'[1633] Similar to Sofia's case, families designated as private support networks might be those related to perpetrators themselves.[1634]

Partners too are at times found to constitute private support networks, especially in GMC cases.[1635] One example is the case of Clarisse:

1630 E.g. CB001_CGRS_PO_[00:23:14], CB004_CGRS_PO_[00:06:59], CB008_CGRS_Supervisor+PO_GENDER_[00:37:30].

1631 DG092_CGRS 1 (refusal)_F_Guinea_RSA_VGNT_FM_DV_27/4/2023_299 471_FR_Database_p. 4, DG092_CALL 1 (refusal)_F_Guinea_RSA_VGNT_FM_DV_4/1/2024_299 471_FR_Database_p. 17. It is important to note that this judgement is in sharp contrast to an earlier CALL judgement on extramarital children in Guinea, stating: 'asylum bodies must exercise caution when analysing applications for international protection made by women who, such as the applicant, have given birth to a child in an extramarital relationship. It considers, on the basis of the information in its possession, and following the example of what it had ruled in its three-judge judgment no. 128 221 of 22 August 2014, that Guinean society's perception of the phenomenon of single mothers is very nuanced and gives rise to contrasting reactions ranging from tolerance to social exclusion. While the general situation of these women remains delicate overall, the perception of this birth out of wedlock by the girl's family and community must be taken into account in each individual case, depending on the degree of openness to the modern way of life, ethnic origin, prevalence of religion and region of origin.' (DG072_CALL 2 (recognition)_F_Guinea_STFP_GMC_VGNT_FM_DV_12/2/2024_301 330_FR_Database_p. 15.).

1632 CB006_CGRS_PO_[00:29:27].

1633 DSo069_CGRS 1 (refusal)_F_Somalia_GMC_VGNT_FM_DV_23/8/2023_302 889_NL_Case law selection by CALL_p. 6.

1634 DA099_A_CGRS 1 (manifestly ill-founded)_M_Albania_DV_6/7/2023_303 553_FR_Database_p. 5.

1635 DG082_CALL 1 (refusal)_F_Guinea_RSA_GMC_VGNT_FM_DV_11/4/2024_304 652_FR_Database_p. 12, DN154_CGRS 1 (refusal)__F_Nigeria_GMC_VGNT_16/10/2023_303 239_NL_Database_p. 5, DN154_CALL 1 (refusal)_1988_F_Nigeria_GMC_VGNT_14/3/2024_303 239_NL_Database_p. 9–10.

CASE OF CLARISSE			
• Country of origin:	Ivory Coast	• SGBV types:	GMC & violence related to gender norm transgression
• Gender identity:	Woman	• Decisions in file:	CGRS 1 (refusal) – 13/6/2023
• Birth year:	/		CALL 1 (annulment) – 11/03/2024 – n° 302 979
• Interview by:	/		

According to her statements, Clarisse was born in Ivory Coast and was subjected to female GMC at the age of six. In her family, all young girls endured this practice. In 2002, her family relocated to Abidjan. Clarisse started a job in financial services, but had to abandon this when a marriage was arranged for her with her current husband. She moved into his family's compound and gave birth to three children, but the effects of her GMC made childbirth incredibly painful. Her husband, having already realised the distress she suffered during intimate relations, gradually came to understand the unjust nature of this practice. Over time, their shared opposition to GMC (among other factors) transformed their forced union into a genuine partnership. As their daughter's sixth birthday approached, Clarisse's mother-in-law announced she would **subject the child to female GMC**, in the name of tradition, despite both parents' clear disapproval. In 2020, Clarisse learnt that the excision was planned for August. Clarisse and her husband made urgent arrangements, placing their youngest child in the care of a childhood friend, and organising the escape of Clarisse and her oldest daughter (at immediate risk of GMC). Clarisse's husband would stay behind, regularly visiting their other daughter in secret.

In August 2020, Clarisse and her almost six-year-old daughter fled Ivory Coast by plane to Tunisia. Shortly thereafter, her mother-in-law filed a complaint against Clarisse. They undertook a sea journey to Italy and after transiting through France, they reached Belgium in May 2021. Five days later, they submitted an application for international protection. Clarisse feared for her daughters' GMC and for the consequences of her own opposition to this practice. In support of her demand, Clarisse provided several documents, including medical certificates attesting Clarisse's GMC and her daughter's lack thereof, as well as a police letter following her mother-in-law's complaint, dated 29 August 2020.

In its refusal decision of Clarisse and her daughter's case, the CGRS argued:

> '[T]he father's consent is the key element that makes any excision possible [...]. [Y]ou have failed to demonstrate being unable to protect [your daughters] from such a risk. In fact, you have the **support of your husband** and your second daughter is currently staying with **your friend** [...], who has helped you from the start by offering you her **unconditional support**. In addition, your husband has **continued to visit** your daughter [...] [from which can be concluded] that [he] considers **the risk that his mother finds out limited**, in fact, **your daughter's [hiding place is] a few minutes' walk from your in-laws' house**.'[1636] | CASE OF CLARISSE

[1636] DIC074_CGRS 1 (refusal)_F_Ivory Coast_GMC_VGNT_13/6/2023_302 979_FR_Case law selection by CALL_p. 3.

Not only did the CGRS point out Clarisse's husband's ability to protect their daughter from GMC, but it also designated her friend as a private actor of protection, expecting her daughter to stay hidden at a location in the immediate proximity of the perpetrator. A similar but slightly more nuanced reasoning was demonstrated in a Nigerian case by the CALL. While the Council recognised that the decision to have a girl circumcised is a family (and not a public or state) issue, it stated: 'Although refusing to perform [female GMC] can lead to social exclusion and stigma, certainly within the Yoruba ethnic group, [the COI] does not show that it would be impossible for parents to prevent the [GMC] of their daughters, which is also confirmed by the declining prevalence figures.'[1637]

Like in Clarisse's case, friends or communities also seem to function as private support networks,[1638] especially in SOGI cases like Elene's,[1639] where asylum authorities sometimes suggest 'a network of like-minded people [...] [or] a friend group consisting of LGBT people'[1640] as actors/facilitators of protection against SGBV. One gender-specialised PO brought up the example of a trans applicant who was raped in a rural area of Pakistan. They mentioned having considered: 'Okay, you have been abused in the countryside [...] but couldn't you just live in the city? Where there [...] is a very large community of *Hijras*,[1641] transgender people?'[1642] Besides 'in the real world', these networks can also be located online, with asylum authorities for instance identifying Facebook networks[1643] as actors of protection from SGBV[1644] or credibility indicators.[1645]

The types of protection that these private support networks are expected to offer vary from physical to mental support. Physically, many asylum officials

---

1637 DN154_CALL 1 (refusal)_1988_F_Nigeria_GMC_VGNT_14/3/2024_303 239_NL_Database_p. 11.

1638 CB004_CGRS_PO_[00:06:59].

1639 DGe151_CALL 1 (refusal)_2003_F_Georgia_VGNT_DV_27/03/2024_303 891_NL_Database_p. 15–16, DGe151_CGRS 1_(refusal)_2003_F_Georgia_VGNT_DV_27/7/2023_303 891_NL_Database_p. 6.

1640 DR145_CALL 1 (refusal)_2003_F_Russia_RSA_VGNT_30/5/2024_307 559_NL_Database_p. 8–9, DR145_CGRS 1 (inadmissible)_2003__Russia_RSA_VGNT_30/3/2023_307 559_NL_Database_p. 3.

1641 "Hijra is an umbrella term used for those men who are transgender, eunuch, transvestites, hermaphrodites or intersexed, bisexuals or homosexuals with feminine behaviour, loosely defined as third gender, and neither man nor woman, but containing characteristics of both". Humaira Jami and Anila Kamal, 'Measuring Attitudes toward Hijras in Pakistan: Gender and Religiosity in Perspective' (2015) 1 Pakistan Journal of Psychological Research 151, 151.

1642 CB011_CGRS_Supervisor + PO_GENDER_[00:46:45].

1643 For an in-depth analysis of the legal issues with social media screenings in the context of the Belgian asylum procedure, see: Roels, 'Socialemedia- en smartphonescreenings tegen misbruik in Belgische verzoekprocedures om internationale bescherming' (n 669).

1644 DSe093_CGRS 3 (manifestly ill-founded)_F_Serbia_DV_12/2/2022_301 311_FR_Database_p. 4.

1645 DK152_CALL 2 (refusal)_1997_F_Kenya_RSA_VGNT_FM_DV_4/4/2024_304 367_NL_Database_p. 19–20, DK152_CGRS 2 (refusal)_1997_Kenya_RSA_VGNT_FM_DV_7/3/2024_304 367_NL_Database_p. 7.

suggested that applicants might find literal 'shelter'[1646] or 'go into hiding'[1647] with their private networks. One PO illustrated this with a Palestinian case of a woman who was subjected to domestic violence for years but finally was able to get a divorce. While the domestic violence had been proven, the applicant did not live with her ex-husband anymore and since her family supported her, she could move back in with them.[1648] Commenting on a similar situation, a gender-specialised PO added: 'Even if she is very dependent […] financially or for food [on this family] […], is she at risk of persecution if she returns to her country? I would say no.'[1649]

When it comes to mental support, the CGRS in a Serbian domestic violence case for example suggested the solution that, while the applicant's father and brother refused to take her and her children in, she could count on 'the moral support of [her] mother and sister, as well as – contrary to what [she said] – the support of a social network, according to […] [her] Facebook account.'[1650] The latter was derived from the positive comments on her Facebook publications from people with an 'Albanian-sounding' or similar surname as her own, leading the CGRS to conclude that her risk to become isolated upon return to Serbia was not established.[1651]

When asked how the effective protective qualities of private support networks are evaluated, a gender-specialised supervisor vaguely replied that 'it's not really about whether the family offers protection, but rather about whether you still have support.'[1652] A judge added that their research does not go that far. Instead of the authorities being responsible for evaluating these protective qualities,[1653] they believed it is applicants' task to prove such private protection to be insufficient, for example by demonstrating that an actor of persecution 'constantly threatens them or could, so to speak, knock on their door every night.'[1654]

Others do evaluate the effective protective qualities of private support networks, hereby for example taking into account their (non-)material

---

1646 DB068_CGRS 1 (refusal)_1975_F_Bolivia_RSA_DV_25/1/2024_302 134_NL_Case law selection by CALL_p. 7.

1647 CB008_CGRS_Supervisor + PO_GENDER_[00:42:13], CB013_CGRS_PO_[00:50:57].

1648 CB004_CGRS_PO_[00:11:29].

1649 CB005_CGRS_Supervisor + PO_GENDER_[00:29:38].

1650 DSe093_CGRS 3 (manifestly ill-founded)_F_Serbia_DV_12/2/2022_301 311_FR_Database_p. 4.

1651 DSe093_CGRS 3 (manifestly ill-founded)_F_Serbia_DV_12/2/2022_301 311_FR_Database_p. 4.

1652 CB008_CGRS_Supervisor + PO_GENDER_[00:39:16].

1653 It is important to note that the new EU Qualification Regulation stipulates that 'The burden of demonstrating that an internal protection alternative is available to the applicant shall fall on the determining authority. The applicant shall be entitled to present evidence and submit any element which indicates that such an alternative is not available to him or her. The determining authority shall take into account the evidence presented and elements submitted by the applicant.' Art. 8(3) EU Qualification Regulation.

1654 RB005_CALL_Judge_[00:39:16].

resourcefulness. As one PO explained: 'The socio-economic level is [...] super important, [...] the level of education, the husband, and so on [...] because, [...] officially in any case, Guinea is raising awareness more and more about [female GMC], so that probably is an environment where this message has been understood.'[1655] Other elements seen as relevant are for example families' expenses for their children, progressiveness, university education level, permission for their daughters to study, work, or leave the home without a veil, as well as the female GMCs already performed within the family.[1656] Interestingly, one CGRS decision demonstrated an opposite reasoning on the latter element, namely: '[T] he rigorist profile of your family [...] is in no way [...] established, [...] even if you were personally circumcised in your country of origin.'[1657]

c) *Assessment of Justifications for not Relying on Private Support Networks*

In designating private support networks as actors/facilitators of protection, IFAs, or indicators of SGBV credibility/risk/fear, asylum authorities at times also comment on applicants' justifications for not wanting or being able to rely on them. As such, both the CGRS and the CALL have dismissed family members'/ friends' inability to protect applicants as a justification not to seek their help. In an Albanian domestic violence and in Rahel's rape case for example, the authorities did not accept the explanation that the applicants' father or aunt was unable to (further) shelter them with their children, since they had a very small house or their own (grand)children living there.[1658]

In the abovementioned Gabonese case where two minor children fled harmful sexual rituals by their paternal family, not their father's inability, but his unwillingness to protect them was dismissed by the CGRS as a justification. While their mother had stated she could not ask their father for help, since 'he didn't care', the CGRS countered that it showed from her visa file that he did administratively cooperate to enable medical care for the children in Belgium. Consequently, the CGRS stated: '[Y]our father's alleged lack of interest in this matter is not corroborated by his proactivity in facilitating your access to medical care in Europe.'[1659]

1655 CB001_CGRS_PO_[00:23:59].

1656 CB004_CGRS_PO_[00:14:33], CB001_CGRS_PO_[00:23:59].

1657 DS103_CGRS 1 (refusal)_F_Senegal_GMC_FM_DV_17/7/2023_305 927_FR_Database_ p. 103.

1658 DA118_CGRS 1 (manifestly ill-founded)_F_Albania_STFP_DV_22/12/2022_305 447_NL_ Database_p. 5, DA118_CALL 1 (refusal)_F_Albania_STFP_DV_24/4/2024_305 447_NL_ Database_p. 15, NEr018_CGRS 1 (refusal)_1985_F_Eritrea_RSA_30/5/2022_280 827_ NL_NANSEN_p. 6, NEr018_CALL 1 (refusal)_1985_F_Eritrea_RSA_25/11/2022_280 827_ NL_NANSEN_p. 15.

1659 DC079_B_CGRS 1 (refusal)_2014_M_Gabon_RSA_VGNT_20/2/2023_303 320_FR_Database_ MINOR_p. 8-9., DC079_C_CGRS 1 (refusal)_2006_F_Gabon_RSA_20/2/2023_303 320_ FR_Database_MINOR_p. 7.

In Sofia's case, she herself refused to seek protection within the family context that enabled the year-long child sexual abuse by her father. Her explanation too was dismissed by the CGRS, firstly pointing at her mother as a private support actor, who, despite knowing about the abuse, stayed living with Sofia's father. Secondly, the CGRS stated (in a later withdrawn decision[1660]):

> 'You claim that you cannot go and live with [your sister] because she lives with her husband. When asked why she would not be able to help you, you vaguely state that it would not change much because **she only lives 10 minutes away**. [...] [T]here is **no evidence at all that [your family members] would not support you.**'[1661] | CASE OF SOFIA

2.2. REBUTTAL OF THE NON-STATE PROTECTION MYTHS

First of all, it should be recognised that non-state actors *sensu lato* can effectively play a facilitating role in SGBV survivors'/victims' search for formal state protection (the second role of non-state actors discussed above), e.g. by reporting to the police.[1662] In fact, most SGBV survivors/victims turn to informal rather than formal support systems. Research on such informal help-seeking behaviour shows that benefits from doing so include 'fewer signs of depression and anxiety and higher self-esteem.'[1663] However, this does not mean that these non-state actors are per definition willing, capable, and obliged to provide support/ protection to (potential) SGBV survivors/victims, nor that the latter always want to or can seek help from them. In fact, while social support might influence the eventual outcome of trauma, it cannot prevent it from happening.[1664] As such, the idea that the private sphere is necessarily a safe place from SGBV[1665] should

1660 Upon refusal of her application by the CGRS, Sofia's appeal with the CALL was not registered, since her insufficient bank balance had caused an error in the payment of the registration fee. Despite a letter from her lawyer explaining this, the situation could not be rectified and she could not appeal against her refusal decision by the CGRS. Eventually, the CGRS decided to withdraw the initial refusal of Sofia's application and, after reconsidering her case (the reasoning of which is not made public), to recognise her as a refugee.

1661 NH003_CGRS 1 (refusal)_1991_F_Honduras_RSA_DV_12/8/2021_NL_NANSEN_p. 2.

1662 Saar Baert and others, 'Factors Related to Police Reporting in Sexual Assault Care Centers: Are We Underestimating the Role of Support Persons?' (2024) 30 Violence Against Women 3943, 3960; Valérie Pijlman and others, '"Sometimes It Seems Easier to Push It Away": A Study Into the Barriers to Help-Seeking for Victims of Sexual Violence' (2023) 38 Journal of Interpersonal Violence 7530, 7534.

1663 Ramón Flecha, 'Second-Order Sexual Harassment: Violence Against the Silence Breakers Who Support the Victims' (2021) 27 Violence Against Women 1980, 1983.

1664 Herman (n 713) 61.

1665 Hill Collins (n 1523) 67–68.

be rebutted, from the perspective of both health/social sciences and law/egal sciences, as I will demonstrate below.

2.2.1. REBUTTAL IN HEALTH & SOCIAL SCIENCES

Acceptance of the non-state protection myth does not only rely on an overestimation of available support for survivors/victims of SGBV in general, as already identified in rape mythology.[1666] It also reveals a lack of understanding of the range of 'normal' (re)actions of survivors/victims and the non-state actors around them to SGBV. The non-state protection myth assumes: 1) that (potential) survivors/victims are able and willing to rely on non-state actors and 2) that such actors are able and willing to protect them from SGBV or assist them in seeking state protection. I will explain the rebuttal of both aspects of the non-state protection myth below.

When it comes to applicants' willingness and ability to be supported by non-state actors, authorities expect them not only to disclose SGBV (threats) to them, but also to adopt active survival reactions to deal with it. Barriers to this disclosure and survivors'/victims' tendency to show passive/avoidant survival reactions were already set out in a more detailed manner above (see Part III, Chapter 3.3.2 and 4.2). Talking about SGBV disclosure to non-state actors *sensu stricto* specifically, the abovementioned EU-wide survey on violence against women by the EU Agency for Fundamental Rights showed that 35% of survivors/victims never disclose to 'anyone'.[1667] Of the 63%[1668] 'who spoke to somebody [...], less than 1% spoke to a lawyer [...] [or] approached a victim support organisation.'[1669] The UN-MENAMAIS study by Keygnaert et al. showed how, for Belgian citizens, '[o]nly 7% sought formal help, most of [whom] turned to a mental health care professional.'[1670] Focusing on applicants for international protection in Belgium specifically, this number drops to 38,5% who disclosed the SGBV to somebody and only 3,8% who sought professional help (i.e. a medical or mental health care professional).[1671]

On disclosure to doctors for example, both Angele and Zeynep articulated the barriers they experienced as follows:

> '[T]he one [**gynaecologist**] I normally went to **knows the family** so I went to see a general practitioner, I said I wasn't feeling well, [...] **I didn't say I'd been sexually assaulted.** *Silence* [...] She wanted to know what happened but I didn't say. *Silence*

1666 Gerger and others (n 150) 425.
1667 European Union Agency for Fundamental Rights (FRA) (n 1109) 115.
1668 2% did not answer the question in the survey.
1669 European Union Agency for Fundamental Rights (FRA) (n 1109) 116.
1670 Keygnaert and others (n 713) 40.
1671 *Ibid.* 74; De Schrijver and others (n 1110) 13.

[...] **I didn't ask for an HIV test. Because if I had, it would have raised more questions.**'[1672] | CASE OF ANGELE

'No, **I didn't go [to the doctor** after the rape] [...] I lived with a lot of fear, not knowing what to do [...]. This may sound absurd, but especially among Kurds, **seeing a gynaecologist before marriage is frowned upon.** Many women I know who needed care were afraid that their families would interpret the visit [...] as something else. [...] I followed online therapy. Apart from that, **I tried to treat myself.**'[1673] | CASE OF ZEYNEP

Disclosure to private support networks is more common.[1674] Of the 63% of survivors/victims who disclosed to somebody in the EU Fundamental Rights Agency survey, 28% talked to a friend, 24% to a relative, and 14% to their partner.[1675] Of the 39,72% who disclosed to someone in the UN-MENAMAIS study, ca. half of men and ca. two thirds of women talked to someone in their personal network.[1676]

However, barriers to disclosing SGBV to non-state actors, both *sensu stricto* and private support networks, cannot be underestimated, as these networks might be embedded in a patriarchal environment where the stigmatisation of survivors/victims erodes the honour of the family and may lead to further victimisation.[1677] In addition, survivors/victims might be hesitant to disclose to family members, out of fear that 'they will not be understood but also [...] that [their] reactions will overshadow their own.'[1678] As such, Angele and Zeynep explained keeping silent to their husband and family/friends because they felt like having lost their dignity as a woman and respectively feared stigma, rejection,[1679] or blame.[1680]

Similarly, the abovementioned Senegalese woman, forcibly married to a man carrying out human sacrifices, explained not having told her parents about his domestic and sexual abuse because 'you have to accept all your parents' decisions[, such as a forced marriage] [...]. I was really afraid [...] of reprisals, I kept it secret, I couldn't tell anyone.'[1681] Amani and Sofia too expressed their disclosure

[1672] NC006_CGRS interview 1_2_1984_F_DRC_RSA_FR_NANSEN_p. 1 (memo), NC006_CGRS interview 3_1984_F_DRC_RSA_FR_NANSEN_p.16.

[1673] NT015_CGRS interview 1_2_3_1996_F_Turkey_RSA_FM_DV_FR_p. 9 (memo).

[1674] Flecha (n 1663) 1983.

[1675] European Union Agency for Fundamental Rights (FRA) (n 1109) 116.

[1676] Keygnaert and others (n 713) 40.

[1677] Ines Keygnaert, Nicole Vettenburg and Marleen Temmerman, 'Hidden Violence Is Silent Rape: Sexual and Gender-Based Violence in Refugees, Asylum Seekers and Undocumented Migrants in Belgium and the Netherlands' (2012) 14 Culture, Health & Sexuality 505, 512; Kiconco and Nthakomwa (n 805) 654.

[1678] Herman (n 713) 65.

[1679] NC006_CGRS interview 1_2_1984_F_DRC_RSA_FR_NANSEN_p. 1–2 (memo).

[1680] NT015_CGRS interview 1_2_3_1996_F_Turkey_RSA_FM_DV_FR_p. 1 (memo).

[1681] NS005_CGRS interview_2002_F_Senegal_RSA_DV_FM_FR_NANSEN_p. 12–13.

barriers to family or friends, as well as their reluctance to take their fate into their own hands and 'adopt' approach coping mechanisms to seek protection:

> '[I could not ask my family for help] out of **fear** and [...] **shame**. And when I saw [the CGRS'] arguments, if they don't even care about it, imagine what [the reaction] would [have been] in Honduras. At the time, I was still [...] **young**, it absolutely **did not occur to me** to ask for help.'[1682] | CASE OF SOFIA

> 'I'd **lost my self-confidence**, [...] at school [...] **I couldn't see friends** anymore, with what I was going through, I really couldn't stand it. It was as if I was **overwhelmed by shame** [...]. I was in a **state of weakness**, [...] **I didn't have the courage** [**to seek help**] from family or church. I could also have [...] [**left** and looked] for a place to rent, [but] **my mother wasn't going to accept that** [...]. With us Africans, even if your daughter is [40], she can stay with her parents. [...] [If I would've left,] my mother would want to find out why.'[1683] | CASE OF AMANI

Next to these barriers to disclosing and showing active survival reactions, applicants reported not relying on non-state actors because of their (perceived) ineffectiveness or inaccessibility. Diana for example explained why she refrained from contacting a lawyer to get legal support:

> 'I made an appointment with a **legal association** to help me to take full custody of [my daughter], and they told me "you can just apply [...] [but] **it's not certain** [**that we can help**,] [...] if there are free lawyers, they'll come to the judge". Until then I had [...] done all the procedures on my own and **maybe it would have been better to have taken a lawyer** but I **didn't have a lot of money** and I know how these things go, you have to [pay first], then you have to [pay] more [...]. And **I knew I was right** and I had to win this.'[1684] | CASE OF DIANA

Apart from applicants' own unwillingness or inability to seek help from non-state actors, these actors themselves might lack the will or capacity to protect them from SGBV. For non-state actors *sensu stricto*, applicants have for example brought up (directly or via their lawyers, based on COI or applicants' statements): the limited capacity of one or two available domestic violence shelters in Ecuador[1685] or threats by the Georgian government to 'crack down' on domestic violence NGOs receiving foreign support (similar to practices in Russia).[1686]

1682 NH003_1991_F_Honduras_RSA_DV_NL_NANSEN_p. 3.

1683 NC004_CGRS interview 2_1991_F_DRC_RSA_DV_FR_NANSEN_p. 4 & 9.

1684 NA001_B_1973_F_Albania_RSA_VGNT_FM_DV_NL_NANSEN_[00:34:17].

1685 DEc120_CALL 1 (refusal)_lawyers' argumentation_1981_F_Ecuador_RSA_DV_29/4/2024_305 805_NL_Database_p. 11.

1686 DGe139_CALL 1 (refusal)_lawyers' argumentation_2005_F_Georgia_DV_23/5/2024_307 109_NL_Database_p. 3. Institute for War and Peace Reporting (IWPR) and European Country of Origin Information Network, 'Draft Law on Foreign Agents Sparks Outcry in Georgia and Abroad' (3 March 2023), www.ecoi.net/en/document/2088225.html.

Research on coping with SGBV also shows how private support networks like 'families and friends have refused to aid [SGBV survivors/victims] in a violent situation.'[1687] This might be explained through bystander theory, laying out the factors influencing bystanders' decision to intervene, remain passive, or ignore an event entirely.[1688] Such bystander intervention might occur in three stages, identified in literature as: primary (pre-assault, actions designed to prevent SGBV from happening), secondary (mid-assault, recognising a potentially dangerous situation and taking action to prevent/minimise harm), or tertiary (post-assault, helping survivors/victims afterwards) intervention.[1689] In the secondary phase, intervention may take the form of 'the five D's of bystander intervention', namely: 1) direct intervention, 2) distracting the perpetrator, 3) delegating the intervention, 4) delaying the intervention, or 5) documenting the situation.[1690]

According to the 'Bystander Decision making Model', bystanders (e.g. both non-state actors *sensu stricto* and private support networks) move through five steps before (not) intervening, namely: 1) noticing an event, 2) interpreting it as concerning, 3) taking intervention responsibility, 4) having self-efficacy (feeling capable and confident to intervene effectively[1691]) and 5) eventually deciding to intervene.[1692] Importantly, this eventual decision (not) to intervene is impacted by numerous external factors[1693] and intervention barriers may occur at all of these five stages.[1694]

1687 Waldrop and Resick (n 1347) 297.

1688 Flecha (n 1663) 1983.

1689 Jennifer Cassandra Hawkinberry, 'Examining the Perceived Role of Empathy and Self-Efficacy among College Students That Have Completed Bystander Training and Intervened to Prevent a Potential Sexual Assault Situation: A Phenomenological Study' (Liberty University 2022) 36; Sarah McMahon and Victoria L Banyard, 'When Can I Help? A Conceptual Framework for the Prevention of Sexual Violence Through Bystander Intervention' (2012) 13 Trauma, Violence, & Abuse 3, 3–4.

1690 Nicole L Johnson, Ruth V Walker and Elsa E Rojas-Ashe, 'A Social Justice Approach to Measuring Bystander Behavior: Introducing the Critically Conscious Bystander Scale' (2019) 81 Sex Roles 731, 733–734; Hawkinberry (n 1689) 21.

1691 Sarah McMahon and others, 'Predicting Bystander Behavior to Prevent Sexual Assault on College Campuses: The Role of Self-Efficacy and Intent' (2015) 56 American Journal of Community Psychology 46, 46.

1692 Chelsea Mainwaring, Fiona Gabbert and Adrian J Scott, 'A Systematic Review Exploring Variables Related to Bystander Intervention in Sexual Violence Contexts' (2023) 24 Trauma, Violence & Abuse 1727, 1728.

1693 'relationship privacy, factors relevant to the situation (e.g. if the event occurred once or repeatedly), perceptions that help was needed (e.g. if the victim was hurt), and the bystander's relationship with the victim (i.e. friend or not) were important to consider when thinking about the decision to intervene' Ashley E Ermer and others, 'Deconstructing Attitudes About Intimate Partner Violence and Bystander Intervention: The Roles of Perpetrator Gender and Severity of Aggression' (2021) 36 Journal of Interpersonal Violence NP896, NP897; 'knowledge of the issue – Relationship With the Victim or Attacker – Perception of What Might Happen After Helping: Risk and Safety' Flecha (n 1663) 1984.

1694 Tiffany L Marcantonio and others, 'Sexual and Gender Minority Men's Bystander Behaviors and Barriers in Response to Witnessing Minor Sexual Aggression' (2023) 13 Psychology of

Assuming that non-state actors do notice the SGBV (1) and unambiguously perceive it as threatening (2), their support can still be inhibited at the three other stages. As mentioned above, lack of skills or capacity to intervene (4) (e.g. having insufficient space to shelter applicants, as in the Albanian domestic violence and Eritrean rape case above[1695]) can inhibit effective intervention. Also, as mostly brought up by applicants, significant barriers occur at the stages of responsibility- (3) and action-taking (5).

Non-state actors' feeling of responsibility to protect and support (both pre-, mid-, and post-SGBV) might be impacted by their own rape myth acceptance, victim blaming attitudes, or acceptance of interpersonal violence.[1696] In Sofia's case for example, her mother somehow did or could not take responsibility for intervening, accepted the situation, and kept living with and supporting Sofia's father.

> '[Telling **my mom**] was terrible. [She] **continues to protect him**. She was sad though and cried, but **she didn't do anything and stayed with him** and so I have no family in Honduras. I love her because she is my mum, but **she is not separated from him**, that would have been different. Imagine I had told her in Honduras, I would have been all alone there.'[1697] | CASE OF SOFIA

A similar situation occurred in Amani's case where, after being told about the sexual abuse of her husband, her mother even expressed hatred towards her.

> '[M]y cousin came to the house to take the child, and my mother asked him why [...], so he took the opportunity to tell my mother the whole truth, and from that day on **my mother hated me**.'[1698] | CASE OF AMANI

In Vera's case, her parents did not want to support her due to reasons echoing rape myth acceptance on intramarital violence:[1699]

> '[My family **no longer wanted to support me** because they felt that I had **violated the family honour**,] they never agreed to our marriage. [...] [But since we married, they

Violence 319, 2; Sihyun Park, Hyunji Woo and Sin-Hyang Kim, 'A Systematic Review and Meta-Analysis of Bystander's Barriers to Intervene in Gender-Based Violence and the Role of Failed Prior Attempts' (2024) 25 Trauma, Violence, & Abuse 1998, 1998.

1695 DA118_CGRS 1 (manifestly ill-founded)_F_Albania_STFP_DV_22/12/2022_305 447_NL_Database_p. 5, DA118_CALL 1 (refusal)_F_Albania_STFP_DV_24/4/2024_305 447_NL_Database_p. 15, NEr018_CGRS 1 (refusal)_1985_F_Eritrea_RSA_30/5/2022_280 827_NL_NANSEN_p. 6, NEr018_CALL 1 (refusal)_1985_F_Eritrea_RSA_25/11/2022_280 827_NL_NANSEN_p. 15.

1696 Park, Woo and Kim (n 1694) 2000.

1697 NH003_1991_F_Honduras_RSA_DV_NL_NANSEN_p. 3.

1698 NC004_CGRS interview 2_1991_F_DRC_RSA_DV_FR_NANSEN_p. 7.

1699 E.g. 'the believe that a husband's use of physical force to have sex with his wife does not constitute rape', Edwards and others (n 9) 763.

believe that] **a woman should stay at home**, [...] **do everything [her husband] says** [...]. These [ideas] have not changed.'[1700] | CASE OF VERA

In addition, private support networks' decision to intervene might also be inhibited by acceptance of gender norms (both by themselves or their peers), leading them to 'fear criticism of their actions for not conforming to societal norms.'[1701] This is especially true for male bystanders, who may be impacted by constructions of masculinity including 'beliefs, attitudes, and power relationships that support [SGBV].'[1702] This for example led Marjorie's and Diana's families to refrain from supporting them:

(As described in the facts by the CGRS) 'You received **no support from your family**. They felt that **once you got married, you should stay together** with your spouse. [...] **After [your divorce], your family rejected and no longer contacted you**. Except your **brother** [...], [he] called and **threatened you because you had disgraced the family**.'[1703] | CASE OF MARJORIE

Diana: '**[M]y father never wanted the divorce** [...] **"because of the children, they would grow up without a family"**.' – Erina: 'But we never had a father, we only had a mother.' – Diana: '**He actually abducted me, but they didn't accept that either**. It's [...] I understand them but [...] It's not easy. When you want to be [...] with your family, your parents [...], when you need *inaudible*.'[1704] | CASE OF DIANA & ERINA

Diana's and Erina's case testifies to another barrier for bystander intervention, namely negative past experiences with providing support (e.g. verbal threats or actual violence).[1705] Such negative consequences are labelled 'Second-Order Sexual Harassment' or 'Isolating Gender Violence' in health and social sciences literature. These terms are respectively defined as 'physical and/or psychological violence against persons who support victims of sexual harassment'[1706] and 'the violence, attacks, and retaliation exerted by harassers against people who offer support to gender violence victims.'[1707] Such secondary violence is (sub) consciously used to (further) isolate survivors/victims, limit their support,

1700 NA016_1990_F_Albania_RSA_VGNT_DV_NL_NANSEN_[00:32:36].
1701 Park, Woo and Kim (n 1694) 1999–2000.
1702 Richard M Tolman and others, 'A Global Exploratory Analysis of Men Participating in Gender-Based Violence Prevention' (2019) 34 Journal of Interpersonal Violence 3438, 3439.
1703 DSu147_CGRS 1 (refusal)_F_Suriname_RSA_VGNT_FM_DV_9/5/2023_301 074_NL_Database_p. 2.
1704 NA001_A_B_2006_F_Albania_RSA_VGNT_FM_DV_NL_NANSEN_MINOR_[01:20:21].
1705 Park, Woo and Kim (n 1694) 2000.
1706 Flecha (n 1663) 1982.
1707 Elias Nazareno and others, 'Men Tackling Isolating Gender Violence to Fight against Sexual Harassment' (2022) 19 International Journal of Environmental Research and Public Health 1924, 1.

and/or smother future discussion of the violence.[1708] As such, next to the primary SGBV survivor/victim, their support network is exposing itself to real danger too.[1709]

In fact, threats against support networks are often as 'effective' as direct threats to survivors'/victims' themselves and are therefore common, as confirmed by Herman.[1710] In bystanders' cost-benefit analysis of whether or not to intervene, fear of these negative repercussions typically stands out in SGBV cases.[1711] The cases of Diana and Carmen, whose families both suffered violence from their ex-husbands too, illustrate this risk of second-order sexual harassment or isolating gender violence:

> '**It's not easy for my family either**. I had a very difficult time with [them] and then we stopped talking [...]. **They're tired**, tired, tired[...] There was a time when they said "it's all because of you". Now they're **too old to [...] have [these] problems** [...]. **They've experienced what I've been through, the violence** and all that.'[1712] | CASE OF DIANA

> (As described by her lawyer) '[S]he did not dare to use the protection order as she was afraid, psychologically exhausted and feared **reprisals from her ex-husband towards her, but also towards her children or her mother**.'[1713] | CASE OF CARMEN

Other applicants demonstrated anticipating to such secondary violence by not even disclosing the violence to their private support networks, such Aya to her partner. To the question if she ever told him, she replied:

> 'No, especially not to him. **If I ever tell him** such a thing, he'll never be able to keep his mouth shut and put up with it. So in the end, **I would have killed him myself**. [...] Because [...] this [colonel] is capable of anything.'[1714]

Zeynep did not disclose the rape to her friends either, explaining:

> 'Because of him, [...] my friends didn't want to have contact with me because **they knew he was in my life and harassing me and they were afraid**. Two close friends, [...] at the university, I spoke to them about it [not the rape, but my fear of him], **they were also very afraid of him**. [Now] it's been two or three years since I had any

1708 Flecha (n 1663) 1994; Nazareno and others (n 1707) 1.
1709 Flecha (n 1663) 1994; Nazareno and others (n 1707) 1.
1710 Herman (n 713) 77.
1711 Flecha (n 1663) 1984.
1712 NA001_A_B_2006_F_Albania_RSA_VGNT_FM_DV_NL_NANSEN_MINOR_[01:19:01].
1713 DEc120_CALL 1 (refusal)_lawyers' argumentation_1981_F_Ecuador_RSA_DV_29/4/2024_305 805_NL_Database_p. 10.
1714 NSy019 CGRS interview_1997_F_Syria_RSA_FR_NANSEN_p. 13.

> friends, [...] until I arrived here, **I didn't talk to anyone [about the rape]**.'[1715] | CASE OF ZEYNEP

Lastly, the private sphere cannot be qualified as a literal safe space either, since SGBV prevalence statistics (e.g. from the WHO and UN Women) have long established that 'violence by a husband or male intimate partner (or other male family member) is the most pervasive form of violence against women globally.'[1716] This is clearly illustrated by the many cases used throughout this research, where the perpetrators are members from applicants' own private networks. Zeynep articulated the fear of her own family, who forced her to marry her cousin, as follows:

> I am [...] afraid of [...] **my family's manipulation**, [...] they say I'm a [...] horrible person, they reject me. I've tried to commit suicide several times and I'm afraid of [doing it] again. [...] I was no longer in direct contact with **my father**, but he gave this mission to **my mother and my aunt**, he came several times to talk to me about it and when I replied that I did not want this marriage, **he grabbed me by the throat and hit me**, saying "you, **you do not have the right to speak, you cannot choose, you will do what is decided for you**".'[1717] | CASE OF ZEYNEP

Since asylum officials, as described above, remarkably often point to parents as decision makers in and therefore protectors of their children from female GMC in particular, it is important to highlight research on the actors involved in this decision-making processes. For female GMC, they vary from one region to another[1718] and argumentation on these actors in asylum decisions should therefore strictly rely on SGBV- and region-specific COI. Across these varying practices, the decision-making process generally involves multiple individuals with different power, including members of the nuclear family, extended family, and acquaintances.[1719]

In the Somali GMC case mentioned above, the CGRS stated that the applicant's family could not be a threat since she 'lived with [them] [...] after her first delivery.' The applicant's lawyer counterargued (according to her statements)

1715 NT015_CGRS interview 1_2_3_1996_F_Turkey_RSA_FM_DV_FR_p. 8–9 (memo).

1716 World Health Organization (WHO) and United Nations Inter-Agency Working Group on Violence Against Women Estimation and Data (VAW-IAWGED) (n 29) 1; UN Women, 'Facts and Figures: Ending Violence against Women' (*UN Women*), /www.unwomen.org/en/what-we-do/ending-violence-against-women/facts-and-figures; Breen and Boyce (n 401) 5233; Jones and others (n 29) 454.

1717 NT015_CGRS interview 1_2_3_1996_F_Turkey_RSA_FM_DV_FR_p. 3–4 (memo).

1718 Angi Alradie-Mohamed, Russell Kabir and SM Yasir Arafat, 'Decision-Making Process in Female Genital Mutilation: A Systematic Review' (2020) 17 International Journal of Environmental Research and Public Health 3362, 3362.

1719 E.g. mothers, co-wives, grandmothers, aunts, fathers, professional or anti-FGM/C activists, sons, daughters, uncles, grandfathers, guardians, sisters, or other adult members of the family, extended family, and members of the social circle. *Ibid.* 3378.

that '[she was circumcised] again after [this, which was undone due to] her second pregnancy, and [...] she was re-infibulated[1720] after her second delivery[, by a female nurse who] assisted [her] at home.'[1721] In Clarisse's case, concerning the risk of female GMC for her daughter coming from within their private sphere, her lawyer argued (based on COI):

> '[**Female GMC** is] often **carried out without the parents' consent** [...] [since female GMC] is **a matter of custom, religion and social perception** [...]. [H]er husband's support in her opposition to excision has no bearing since it is ineffective in the face of her mother-in-law's determination.'[1722] | CASE OF CLARISSE

In sum, I set out the evidence in health and social sciences rebutting the non-state protection myth, stressing the possible unwillingness and inability of both applicants to rely on non-state actors, and non-state actors to protect them from SGBV (and sometimes even committing the SGBV themselves). Therefore, non-state actor support is in no way guaranteed, let alone legally enforceable, which I will discuss below.

2.2.2. REBUTTAL IN LAW & LEGAL SCIENCES

According to (inter)national refugee law, it is state actors, controlling (substantial parts of) the state territory, who must offer protection against persecution to applicants.[1723] According to the EU Qualification Directive/Regulation, such protection must be accessible, effective, and non-temporary, for instance 'by operating an effective legal system for the detection, prosecution and punishment of acts constituting persecution.'[1724] The intent of the European legislator to dismiss 'non-state actors of protection' was already clear from the drafting stage of the EU Qualification Directive.

1720 '[T]he narrowing of the vaginal opening through the creation of a covering seal. The seal is formed by cutting and repositioning the labia minora, or labia majora, sometimes through stitching, with or without removal of the clitoral prepuce/clitoral hood and glans' World Health Organization (WHO), 'Female Genital Mutilation' (n 607).

1721 This argument, that her family *de facto* could not protect her against female GMC (re) victimisation, was accepted by the CALL, who recognised the applicant as a refugee. (DSo069_CALL 1 (recognition)_lawyers' argumentation_F_Somalia_GMC_VGNT_FM_DV_8/3/2024_302 889_NL_Case law selection by CALL_p. 11.).

1722 DIC074_CALL 1 (annulment)_lawyers' argumentation_F_Ivory Coast_GMC_VGNT_11/3/2024_302 979_FR_Case law selection by CALL_p. 5.

1723 Art. 1(A)2 UN Refugee Convention; UNHCR, 'Guidelines on International Protection No. 1' (n 35) para 19; UNHCR, *Handbook on Procedures and Criteria for Determining Refugee Status under the 1951 Convention and the 1967 Protocol Relating to the Status of Refugees* (n 254) paras 97–100.

1724 Art. 7(2) EU Qualification Directive; Art. 7(2) EU Qualification Regulation.

One of its proposals explicitly criticises asylum authorities' practice to qualify NGOs as actors of protection in female GMC and honour killing cases, 'despite the fact that such organisations can only provide temporary safety or even only shelter to victims of persecution.'[1725] More than ten years later, the CJEU in the *O.A. case* very clearly dismissed the idea of non-state actors as actors of protection and as facilitators to obtaining state protection. It explicitly judged that any support by private actors (e.g. families or clans), falls short of what is required to constitute protection and is 'of no relevance either to the assessment of the effectiveness or availability of the protection provided by the State.'[1726]

The ECtHR too has already ruled on the protection of non-state actors against SGBV. While this case is not directly relevant to the asylum context as it was not migration-related, it is nevertheless interesting to note how the Court specifically addressed the *de facto* protective qualities of SGBV shelters. In the *Opuz v. Turkey* case, it judged: '[E]ven assuming that the applicant had been admitted to one of the [domestic violence shelters], as suggested by the Government, [...] this would only be a temporary solution. Furthermore, it has not been suggested that there was any official arrangement to provide for the security of the victims staying in those houses.'[1727]

Several (socio-)legal scholars have echoed this principled concern that 'non-state actors cannot be held accountable under international law for a lack of protection.'[1728] In doing so, they label acceptance of the non-state protection myth an inadequate application of international (refugee) law.[1729] Querton also highlights that, from a human rights perspective, the obligation to seek non-state actor protection as such might violate applicants' freedom of movement, association and self-expression.[1730]

Furthermore, asking (potential) SGBV survivors/victims to seek support/ protection from male non-state actors specifically, also reinforces the idea

1725 Proposal for a Directive of the European Parliament and of the Council on minimum standards for the qualification and status of third country nationals or stateless persons as beneficiaries of international protection and the content of the protection granted 2009 [{SEC(2009) 1373} {SEC(2009) 1374}] 6.

1726 *Secretary of State for the Home Department v. O.A.* (n 742) para ruling 2.

1727 *Opuz v Turkey* [2009] ECtHR 33401/02 [172].

1728 Querton in *Women in Refugee Law (WiRL) Conference – Panel 1 on Protection & Credibility* (Directed by Women in Refugee Law (WiRL) UWE Bristol, 2021), www.youtube.com/watch?v=INFfNw5e34I.

1729 James C Hathaway and Michelle Foster, *The Law of Refugee Status* (Cambridge University Press 2014) 291–292; Christel Querton, 'Non-State Actors of Protection and the Sliding Scale of Protection for Refugee Women' (2022) 41 Refugee Survey Quarterly 1, 12–13 and 23; Spijkerboer, 'European Sexual Nationalism' (n 664) 4; Thomas Spijkerboer, 'Gender, Sexuality, Asylum and European Human Rights' (2018) 29 Law and Critique 221, 226.

1730 Querton, 'Non-State Actors of Protection and the Sliding Scale of Protection for Refugee Women' (n 1729) 25.

of (female) dependency on male family members,[1731] and ties in with the fundamentally patriarchal idea that 'men (should) be heads of households' and 'have ultimate power in interpersonal and family relationships.'[1732] It stems from the gender stereotype that men are the protectors of women,[1733] perpetuates the idea that state protection can be replaced by (patriarchal forms of) private protection,[1734] and turns a blind eye to state apparatuses that perpetuate gender inequality.[1735]

To summarise this (case) law and scholarship, as evident from the UN refugee definition, the presence of non-state actor support is entirely incidental to the main assessment of whether the state can offer accessible, effective, and non-temporary protection. As Middelburg and Balta confirm: '[T]he primary responsibility for protection against [SGBV] lies with the state, not with [non-state actors like] NGOs, however effective they may be.'[1736] Where such state protection is absent, the presence of non-state actors cannot compensate for this deficit. If applicants cannot make use of alleged pathways to state protection without the possibly benevolent but always unenforceable support from non-state actors, these cannot qualify as 'accessible, effective and non-temporary' state protection. On top of this, such reasoning may violate applicants' freedom of movement, association, and self-expression and may contribute to the inscription of patriarchal power structures in asylum jurisprudence.

Next to these principled arguments, legal scholars also recognise the barriers to disclosing SGBV to private support networks embedded in a broader patriarchal society[1737] and the limitations of private resistance to SGBV rooted in wider socio-cultural and institutional structures (e.g. ancestral customs, community pressure or discrimination by law).[1738] They also uncover asylum authorities' expectation of applicants to seek non-state actor support without necessarily verifying their *de facto* protective qualities.[1739] Further, this scholarship addresses decision makers' tendency to ignore the risk of SGBV

1731 Spijkerboer, 'European Sexual Nationalism' (n 664) 4; Spijkerboer, 'Gender, Sexuality, Asylum and European Human Rights' (n 1729) 227; Kneebone (n 5) 8.

1732 Simone Cusack, 'Eliminating Judicial Stereotyping: Equal Access to Justice for Women in Gender-Based Violence Cases' (OHCHR 2014) 21–22.

1733 Peroni (n 33) 364; Benslama-Dabdoub (n 20) 69.

1734 Peroni (n 33) 365.

1735 Middelburg and Balta (n 8) 446.

1736 *Ibid.* 450.

1737 M Jacqui Alexander, 'Not Just (Any) Body Can Be a Citizen: The Politics of Law, Sexuality and Postcoloniality in Trinidad and Tobago and the Bahamas' (1994) 48 Feminist Review 5, 19; Peroni (n 33) 365; Kneebone (n 5) 41.

1738 Peroni (n 33) 361; Middelburg and Balta (n 8) 446; Querton, 'Non-State Actors of Protection and the Sliding Scale of Protection for Refugee Women' (n 1729) 23.

1739 Wessels (n 94) 345 and 353.

revictimisation that such forms of forced dependence may entail (e.g. social exclusion and stigmatisation,[1740] forced marriage, domestic violence, or sexual violence[1741]).

This risk of revictimisation might occur when applicants return to an IFA. As mentioned earlier, suggesting such solutions not only risks to rely on the non-state protection myth, but also the resourcefulness (see Part III, Chapter 2.2.2), survival (see Part III, Chapter 4.2.2), and state protection myths (indirectly) (see Chapter 3 below). In short, such reasoning might come down to the idea that '(resourceful) applicants can (with support of non-state actors) reasonably and safely find protection against SGBV at an IFA (instead of fleeing the country as a survival reaction)'. It should first be noted that, according to the EU Qualification Directive/Regulation and the Belgian Aliens Act, both aspects (safety and reasonability) are cumulative conditions for an IFA.[1742]

The safety condition requires the absence of any fear/risk of persecution or access to effective and non-temporary state protection in this alternative location. The Council of Europe has already explicitly recommended states to 'restrict the use of IFAs for [applicants] who invoke gender-related claims, taking carefully into account the availability of state protection in the area [...] [and] the safety of the route.'[1743] The UN Special Rapporteur on Torture has urged similar vigilance, stating that, for SGBV cases in particular, 'the lack of State protection in one part of the country is often an indication that the State is also not able or willing to protect the [applicant] in any other part of the country.'[1744]

In addition, upon return, an IFA has to provide safety from the same perpetrator(s), but also from new ones. When this perpetrator is a non-state actor, as is often the case with SGBV, UNHCR emphasises: '[T]he main inquiries should include an assessment of the motivation of the persecutor, the ability of the persecutor to pursue the claimant in the proposed area, and the protection available to the claimant in that area from State authorities.'[1745] By analogy with the UNHCR guidelines on persecution by state actors, it can be argued that 'the ability to move internally can only be relevant if there are clear indications that the persecuting [actor] has no reach beyond its own region.'[1746] This 'reach' should be interpreted in its geographical and contemporary context, taking into

1740 Kiconco and Nthakomwa (n 805) 665.

1741 Querton, 'Non-State Actors of Protection and the Sliding Scale of Protection for Refugee Women' (n 1729) 25; Wessels (n 94) 345.

1742 Art. 8(1) EU Qualification Directive; Art. 8(1) EU Qualification Regulation. Both mentioning 'and' between the safety and reasonability conditions. Art. 48/5, §3 Belgian Aliens Act.

1743 Council of Europe Parliamentary Assembly, 'Resolution 1765: Gender-Related Claims for Asylum' (2010) para 10.5.

1744 UN Special Rapporteur on torture and other cruel, inhuman or degrading treatment or punishment, 'Promotion and Protection of All Human Rights, Civil, Political, Economic, Social and Cultural Rights, Including the Right to Development A/HRC/7/3' (2008) 21.

1745 UNHCR, 'Guidelines on International Protection No. 4' (n 428) para 15.

1746 *Ibid.* 14; Ali, Querton and Soulard (n 8) 72.

account the local level of social cohesion and the fact that social interactions nowadays are tracked through digital communication and online networks.[1747]

The EU Qualification Directive/Regulation and Belgian Aliens Act also prescribe that IFA assessments should take into account applicants' personal circumstances, general circumstances, and their ability to cater for their own basic needs.[1748] In the same Resolution as mentioned above, the Council of Europe specifies that authorities should carefully consider the prevailing socio-cultural conditions and applicants' possibilities to earn a living.[1749] When it comes to the reasonability condition for IFAs, serious questions can be raised about the 'solution' to return to a life dependent on private support networks or SGBV shelters. The question whether such discretion,[1750] avoiding one's own persecution by hiding, can be expected from applicants has already been answered negatively by the CJEU, for example when it comes to applicants' SOGI (*X, Y, and Z case*)[1751] or belief in gender equality *(K.L. case)*.[1752] Scholars like Querton defend the idea that this reasoning should be extended to applicants who fear other forms of SGBV.[1753]

Indeed, this form of discretion seems incompatible with CEDAW's recommendations to strictly screen IFAs on 'restrictions [...] on women travelling or living alone, [...] problems of securing accommodation, childcare and economic survival [...] and risk of harassment and exploitation.'[1754] To what extent could these aspects be guaranteed for applicants like Carmen, Diana, or Mary, who had to stop working and/or take their children out of school due to the threats from their perpetrators?

The UN Special Rapporteur on Violence Against Women has addressed both the safety and reasonability concerns for shelters and protection orders

---

1747 A good practice example of such a traceability assessment was given by a US Court of Appeals, as cited by Hathaway and Foster. It rejected an internal flight alternative in Mexico for a woman fleeing domestic violence, arguing that 'because of her age and vulnerability, she would most likely have to rely on relatives or friends for help, which would not make it difficult for her father (the source of violence) to find her.' Hathaway and Foster (n 1729) 345; An example of a gender-sensitive 'route safety' assessment was provided by the Federal Court of Canada, as cited by Kelley, which held that: 'the tribunal failed to consider how it could be objectively reasonable for the claimant to travel [...] with his wife and daughter in light of the [...] widespread rape and women and children in [the area]. 'Ninette Kelley, 'Internal Flight/Relocation/Protection Alternative: Is It Reasonable' (2002) 14 International Journal of Refugee Law 4, 14.

1748 Art. 8(2) EU Qualification Directive; Art. 8(5)a-c EU Qualification Regulation; Art. 48/5, §3 Belgian Aliens Act.

1749 Council of Europe Parliamentary Assembly (n 1743) para 10.5.

1750 Wessels (n 81) viii.

1751 *X, Y and Z v. The Netherlands* (n 67) paras 10, 71, 74 & 75.

1752 *K.L. v. Staatssecretaris van Justitie en Veiligheid* (n 78) para 63.

1753 Querton, 'Non-State Actors of Protection and the Sliding Scale of Protection for Refugee Women' (n 1729) 23.

1754 CEDAW, 'General Recommendation No. 32: The Gender-Related Dimensions of Refugee Status, Asylum, Nationality and Statelessness of Women' (n 34) 10.

specifically. The report highlights that many states consistently fail to establish holistic services that protect survivors/victims from SGBV, an obligation that is often considered facultative. Where such organisations do exist, they are often inaccessible (e.g. due to uneven territorial distribution, especially in rural areas) or provide inadequate services. For example, technical security of the premises often cannot be guaranteed and accessibility might be hindered by: requirements of formal recognition as a victim (when women are unable to refer themselves to a shelter), gender requirements (separating boys from their mothers or excluding male survivors/victims), the temporary nature, and the lack of/limited (mental) health care. Furthermore, the survival and functioning of such shelters often depend on irregular and unpredictable government funding.[1755]

To illustrate these limited safety guarantees with a concrete example, doctors running shelters for SGBV survivors/victims, such as the example cited by the attaché above about a doctor in Bukavu,[1756] have proven at risk of becoming targets themselves. For example, Amnesty International reports on an assassination attempt on activist Dr Mukwege, working for survivors of sexual violence in Bukavu, South Kivu. Not only do such centres gain visibility over time, but also the survivors/victims who they shelter. This may both constitute a risk factor for attacks and an access barrier for survivors/victims seeking help.[1757]

Legal scholars too point at the importance of taking into account applicants' individual circumstances when assessing IFAs (instead of treating all SGBV survivors/victims as a homogeneous group[1758]), including 'age, gender, health, disability, family situation and relationships, social or other vulnerabilities, ethnic, cultural or religious considerations, political and social affiliations and compatibility, language skills, educational, vocational and employment background and opportunities, and any past persecution and its psychological consequences.'[1759] In addition, they highlight the important role of general circumstances in assessing IFAs, such as: restrictions regarding travel, access to employment and housing, financial survival[1760] without help from family,[1761] stigmatisation and discrimination,[1762] or 'the general position in which

---

1755 UN Special Rapporteur on violence against women, its causes and consequences, 'Report A/HRC/35/30 of the Special Rapporteur on Violence against Women, Its Causes and Consequences with a Focus on Shelters and Protection Orders' (2017) paras 68, 71–72, 74, 76–77 and 79–80.

1756 RB007_CALL_Attaché_[00:44:52].

1757 'DR Congo Must Investigate Assassination Attempt on Activist Dr Denis Mukwege' (*Amnesty International*, 26 October 2012), www.amnesty.org/en/latest/news/2012/10/dr-congo/.

1758 Middelburg and Balta (n 8) 449.

1759 Ali, Querton and Soulard (n 8) 73.

1760 Peroni (n 33) 358.

1761 Hathaway and Foster (n 1729) 350.

1762 Council of Europe (CoE) and Hooper (n 1049) 28.

[survivors/victims] using [SGBV shelters] will find themselves [in the longer term].'[1763]

To conclude, acceptance of the non-state protection myth cannot be legally defended either. Such actors' support cannot constitute protection in the sense of the UN refugee definition and is irrelevant to assess the effectivity and accessibility of state protection, as confirmed by the CJEU. While its relevance for the reasonability assessment of IFAs is debatable (but highly questionable), unless any risk/fear of SGBV at this location can be completely ruled out, state protection must in any case also be guaranteed there.

2.2.3. REBUTTAL BY BELGIAN ASYLUM AUTHORITIES

The rebuttal in law and health/social/legal sciences of the non-state protection myth is at times taken up by the Belgian asylum officials. Some of them presented this rebuttal as uniformly applied throughout the CGRS or the CALL, by claiming: 'According to the CGRS' position, we can't […] say "you could have been protected by an NGO"',[1764] 'The Belgian asylum authorities […] systematically recognise girls [fleeing GMC] as refugees, even when the parents [are opposed to this practice]. […] There was a time when […] the CGRS distinguished between […] parents [protecting] the child or not, [but they] no longer do that',[1765] or '[If protection by NGOs is mentioned in CGRS decisions] […] they are reformed, as far as I know. I don't know if all judges do it, but I think so.'[1766] However, others recognised the ongoing debate about these arguments, both within themselves[1767] and within their institutions.[1768]

1763 Hathaway and Foster (n 1729) 344.

1764 CB001_CGRS_PO_[00:20:37].

1765 RB008_CALL_Judge_[00:29:51]. Interestingly, this statement clearly contrasts with another judge's statement on page 318, stating that in Guinean cases, where parents oppose female GMC, the children's fears are usually not substantiated. In internal communication, the CALL added that this contradiction might originate from a change in CGRS policy or a difference between the procedural languages (and countries of origin these treat). In any case, at the time of writing, the CALL and CGRS internally communicated being of the position that, for Guinea specifically, 'the principle is that the CGRS systematically recognises Guinean girls who have not been circumcised. It is only in very exceptional cases that it does not recognise them, particularly when it considers that the parents' profile suggests that their daughter(s) will not be exposed to this practice (educated parents, relatively high socio-economic status, mother herself not circumcised, etc.).' It is important to note the combination of the resourcefulness and non-state actor myth at play in the latter reasoning, as elaborated on in Part III, Chapter 2.2. Commissioner General for Refugees and Stateless Persons (CGRS), 'Internal Communication CGRS (Part V)' (n 331); Council for Alien Law Litigation (CALL), 'Internal Communication CALL' (n 168).

1766 RB008_CALL_Judge_[00:30:50].

1767 'I am personally undecided about that' (CB009_CGRS_PO_GENDER_[00:33:25]).

1768 'That's the hardest thing I think about these gender cases. I must say that we often disagree among ourselves on that too, about what to expect from someone'(CB002_CGRS_Supervisor + PO_[00:39:32]).

In rebutting the idea of non-state protection replacing or compensating for a lack of state protection, some asylum officials explicitly[1769] referred to the abovementioned CJEU case law.[1770] One judge also made a point of explicitly rebutting this myth in judgements: 'As soon as I see this [argument] in a [CGRS] decision, even if in the end I confirm it, I will remind them "no, [family or NGOs] are not actors of protection, we have rulings from the [CJEU] that state this very clearly".'[1771] Interestingly, the *O.A. case* of 2021 is only mentioned by interviewees at the CALL, where – according to an attaché – '[it] has clearly been communicated within the Chambers,'[1772] but not in the interviews at the CGRS. One PO did implicitly rebut the myth by stating: 'If someone cannot call on the police if [they] are personally threatened, [...] then, you cannot send them back because then there is a risk of persecution I think, [regardless of their social network].'[1773]

On the facilitating role of non-state actors to access state protection, two judges confirmed that this can only be relevant if effective state protection against SGBV is available in the country of origin[1774] or if NGOs for example 'work in conjunction with state actors.'[1775] One KAP respondent rebutted the relevance of non-state actors for the safety assessment of an IFA, by stating that 'private individuals and their (financial) support are generally irrelevant, except when the authorities provide protection in another region of the country and it is necessary to assess whether fleeing to that region constitutes a reasonable [IFA],'[1776] which was confirmed by another judge.[1777]

Some asylum officials also recognised the limited relevance of applicants' (ability to articulate their) non-state actor support-seeking behaviour as a credibility indicator. In doing so, they acknowledged the possible unwillingness or inability of both applicants to seek or obtain such support, as well as non-state actors to offer it. One PO considered seeking protection from NGOs 'a big step',[1778] and others took into account possible disclosure barriers to non-state actors, such as: the seriousness of violence,[1779] psychological issues (incl. denial, suppression, ...),[1780] shame,[1781] or societal norms.[1782]

1769 RB008_CALL_Judge_[00:29:33], RB002_CALL_Attaché_[00:37:59].
1770 Ruling 2. *Secretary of State for the Home Department v. O.A.* (n 742).
1771 RB006_CALL_Judge_[00:33:04].
1772 RB004_CALL_Attaché_[00:11:14].
1773 CB011_CGRS_Supervisor + PO_GENDER_[00:32:28].
1774 RB001_CALL_Judge_[00:25:51].
1775 RB008_CALL_Judge_[00:31:31].
1776 R_2PooXckHVX9GAU0_CGRS_PO/supervisor/gender coordinator/CEDOCA member.
1777 '[A shelter or] social network can play a role in the reasonableness, but not in the safety of an internal flight alternative' (RB001_CALL_Judge_[00:25:51]).
1778 CB003_CGRS_PO_[00:36:49].
1779 CB002_CGRS_Supervisor + PO_[00:42:31].
1780 CB002_CGRS_Supervisor + PO_[00:42:31], CB003_CGRS_PO_[00:39:24].
1781 CB011_CGRS_Supervisor + PO_GENDER_[00:49:54], CB003_CGRS_PO_[00:39:24].
1782 CB007_CGRS_PO_[00:29:48].

One PO for example stated: 'Not talking about it and being able to repress it [...] this doesn't mean you don't want to leave and live safely somewhere else. The risk of rejection [...], not being believed, [...] there are so many reasons why someone cannot disclose.'[1783]

Other asylum officials accepted that survivors/victims may deal with SGBV in avoidant (see Part III, Chapter 4.2.1) instead of active (e.g. by seeking non-state actor support) ways. They brought up justifying circumstances for such avoidance coping, like the fact that child custody is automatically assigned to the father, constituting a huge threshold for women to leave their husband (e.g. in Chechnya), even if she has her family, [...] who might still want to support her'[1784] or the fact that parents are very strictly religious and that divorce is out of the question, '[which might justify] that you are not going to ask your parents [for help].'[1785]

Moreover, asylum authorities also recognised the possible unwillingness or inability of non-state actors to offer support. One judge firmly argued that, in situations where a certain SGBV form is criminalised but its prevalence rates are very high, asylum authorities ought to know that the lack of state protection is obvious. 'When [decision makers do use the non-state protection myth], [they] don't know who the actors of protection are. There is simply no protection.'[1786] Others stressed the possible ineffectiveness[1787] of or lack of access[1788] to non-state actors *sensu stricto*, by pointing at: their primary capacity 'to raise awareness [...] but not [...] to protect victims,'[1789] their risk of being corrupted,[1790] or the fact that not every (potential) survivor/victim contacting them gets effective help.[1791] One attaché only specifically rebutted the effectiveness of legal support (as opposed to physical protection), arguing: 'If [...] NGOs [could] hide people [...] throughout the whole problem, yes, but [...] If you only have legal protection against an abusive husband, [he can keep hitting you or kill you] [...] it's not enough.'[1792]

As for private support networks, some asylum officials also confirmed the limitations to their support,[1793] such as: 'We can never be sure that [applicants]

1783 CB003_CGRS_PO_[00:39:24].
1784 CB002_CGRS_Supervisor + PO_[00:26:22].
1785 CB011_CGRS_Supervisor + PO_GENDER_[00:49:54].
1786 RB008_CALL_Judge_[00:38:29].
1787 CB011_CGRS_Supervisor + PO_GENDER_[00:19:15], CB001_CGRS_PO_[00:21:14], CB010_CGRS_Supervisor + PO_[00:24:23], RB005_CALL_Judge_[00:30:17], RB006_CALL_Judge_[00:32:08].
1788 CB011_CGRS_Supervisor + PO_GENDER_[00:49:54].
1789 CB010_CGRS_Supervisor + PO_[00:26:59].
1790 CB014_CGRS_PO_[00:56:55].
1791 CB003_CGRS_PO_[00:36:49].
1792 RB007_CALL_Attaché_[00:43:30].
1793 'A mother may support [her] child, but cannot take away [the risk of] persecution' (CB009_CGRS_PO_GENDER_[00:31:30].), 'if there is no state structure that can protect, why would

will actually be protected [by their family].'[1794] In reaction[1795] to the private support network argument in Sofia's (later withdrawn[1796]) decision, one PO found it very hard to imagine that 'if someone really mentions sexual violence within the family, [...] that [asylum authorities] would say "you still have family there [to protect you]".'[1797] Specifically in female GMC cases, one PO thought 'that [the CGRS] [...] looks at [...] the extent to which a community [...] influences [...] that decision [...] and whether one risks harsh discrimination [when going against it]. [...] [I]t is not [...] because [...] your family is opposed to it, that [...] [their] protection is effective.'[1798] A judge added that, for countries with high female GMC rates, 'there is a presumption that protection from social networks is not sufficient.'[1799]

Interestingly, the only cases in the case law sample explicitly rebutting the non-state protection myth are three female GMC cases. In one of these, the CALL explicitly referred to the CJEU's *O.A. case*[1800] to conclude that 'it cannot agree [...] that the applicant would be able to protect her daughter from female [GMC].'[1801] The second case is the abovementioned Somali case, where the CGRS had concluded that the applicant did not risk persecution from her family since she had stayed with them after giving birth 'without having [...] been circumcised [...] again.'[1802] In its judgement (marked as important by the CALL), the Council recognised the applicant as a refugee, relying on (among other elements) the fact 'that she was re-infibulated [after giving birth] under socio-familial pressure.'[1803]

The third is Clarisse's case (equally marked as important), in which the judge rejected the father's protective qualities, even though he was opposed to female

an aunt be able to offer effective protection?' (RB003_CALL_Attaché_[00:49:37].), 'If you can [...] take shelter with your family, but you are also abused there, then that is [...] not a safe option either' (CB008_CGRS_Supervisor + PO_GENDER_[00:42:13].).

1794 CB001_CGRS_PO_[00:22:48].

1795 Which I brought up during some of the interviews with asylum authorities.

1796 Upon refusal of her application by the CGRS, Sofia's appeal with the CALL was not registered, since her insufficient bank balance had caused an error in the payment of the registration fee. Despite a letter from her lawyer explaining this, the situation could not be rectified and she could not appeal against her refusal decision by the CGRS. Eventually, the CGRS decided to withdraw the initial refusal of Sofia's application and, after reconsidering her case (the reasoning of which is not made public), to recognise her as a refugee.

1797 CB003_CGRS_PO_[00:38:31].

1798 CB006_CGRS_PO_[00:33:02].

1799 RB008_CALL_Judge_[00:38:04].

1800 Ruling 2. *Secretary of State for the Home Department v. O.A.* (n 742).

1801 DS103_CALL 1 (annulment)_F_Senegal_GMC_FM_DV_30/4/2024_305 927_FR_Database_ p. 11.

1802 DSo069_CGRS 1 (refusal)_F_Somalia_GMC_VGNT_FM_DV_23/8/2023_302 889_NL_ Case law selection by CALL_p. 6.

1803 DSo069_CALL 1 (recognition)_F_Somalia_GMC_VGNT_FM_DV_8/3/2024_302 889_NL_ Case law selection by CALL_p. 15.

GMC and could visit his daughter at her hiding place a few minutes away.[1804] In annulling the CGRS' decision, the CALL demonstrated the importance of gender- and region-specific COI, criticising the CGRS' selective use thereof:

> 'Some [COI] reports indicate that the **father of the girl concerned has the final say.** However, other sources indicate that **only women, in particular grandmothers and GMC practitioners, decide on the matter.** Another source [...] states that **GMC is a woman's matter and that the father's formal authorisation is not necessary.**'[1805] | CASE OF CLARISSE

2.3. OCCURRENCE OF THE NON-STATE PROTECTION MYTHS

Below, the levels of acceptance (CGRS and CALL) vs. rebuttal (CALL) of the non-state protection myth in the analysed case law sample is visualised, according to asylum authority and procedural language (Figure 24 for non-state actors *sensu stricto*, Figure 25 for private support networks).

Figure 24: % of decisions in the case law sample including at least one non-state actor (sensu stricto) myth acceptance/rebuttal argument, according to asylum authority & language

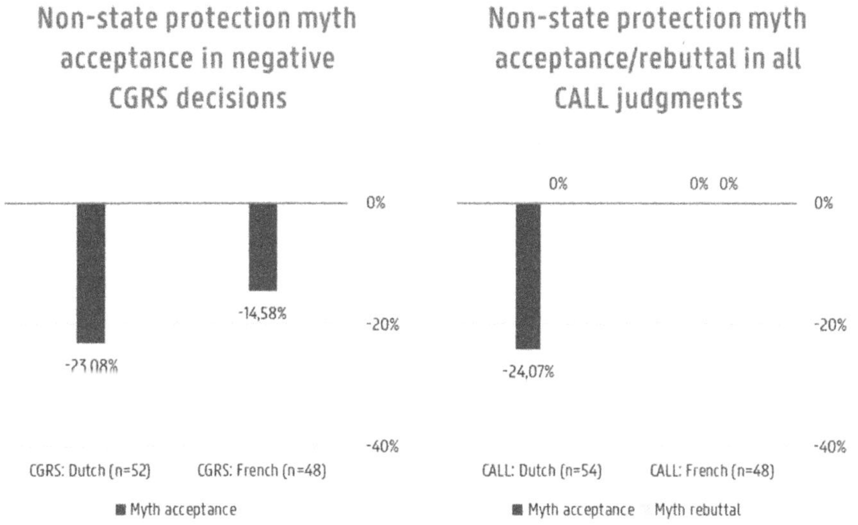

1804 DIC074_CGRS 1 (refusal)_F_Ivory Coast_GMC_VGNT_13/6/2023_302 979_FR_Case law selection by CALL_p. 3.

1805 DIC074_CALL 1 (annulment)_F_Ivory Coast_GMC_VGNT_11/03/2024_302 979_FR_Case law selection by CALL_p. 8.

Figure 25: % of decisions in the case law sample including at least one private support network myth acceptance/rebuttal argument, according to asylum authority & language

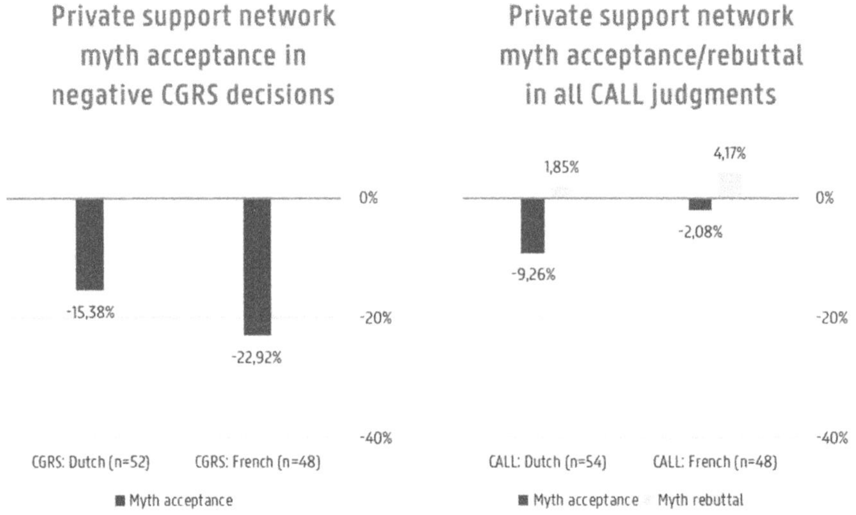

In the total case law sample, 15,84% of the 202 decisions and judgements included at least one argument accepting the non-state actor *sensu stricto* myth and 12,38% accepting the private support network myth. It is important to emphasise that this percentage is reduced considerably by the remarkably low acceptance in the French-language CALL judgements (0% for the non-state actor *sensu stricto* myth and 2,08% for the private support network myth). In contrast, almost a quarter of the Dutch-language decisions (both CGRS: 23,08% and CALL: 24,07%) accept the non-state actor sensu stricto myth. For the private support network myth, it is the French-language CGRS decisions that contain the highest level of myth acceptance, namely more than one fifth of the decisions (22,92%). It is also striking how little explicit rebuttal of the non-state protection myth can be found in the analysed CALL judgements (0% for the non-state actor *sensu stricto* myth and 1,85% in Dutch and 4,17% in French for the private support network myth). Remarkably, the CALL judgements in French contain virtually no engagement with both non-state protection myths.

3. THE MYTH THAT NON-EXHAUSTION OF STATE PROTECTION IMPLIES NON-CREDIBILITY OR ILL-FOUNDEDNESS OF SGBV FLIGHT STORIES

3.1. ACCEPTANCE OF THE STATE PROTECTION MYTH

3.1.1. FROM CRIMINAL JUSTICE TO ASYLUM CONTEXT

In contrast to the non-state actors described above, state actors of protection are, according to refugee law, the ones expected to protect applicants from persecution, such as SGBV. More precisely, the UN Refugee Convention qualifies refugees as persons who are, owing to their fear of persecution, 'unable or [...] unwilling to avail [themselves] of the protection of [their country of origin].'[1806] In the EU context, the concept of state protection has been further defined as cumulatively requiring accessible, effective, and non-temporary protection from persecution.[1807] Since unavailable state protection is a requirement to be recognised as a refugee, states' ability and willingness to protect applicants, as well as applicants' help-seeking behaviour from state actors, play a central role in refugee status determination. Specifically, it plays out in the assessment of both the credibility and well-foundedness of SGBV survivors'/victims' applications.

First, applicants' failure to report SGBV to local authorities before fleeing is regularly seen as an indication of non-credibility. This reasoning resonates with the established rape myths that 'any delay in reporting rape is suspicious'[1808] or '"real" victims of sexual violence will report [...] quickly.'[1809] In the criminal justice context, this tendency has been identified as 'the doctrine of recent/prompt complaint',[1810] referring to the ideas that SGBV survivors/victims will 'at

1806 Art. 1(A)2 UN Refugee Convention.

1807 Art. 7(1)–(2) EU Qualification Directive; Art. 7(1)–(2) EU Qualification Regulation.

1808 Leverick (n 139) 257.

1809 International Commission of Jurists (ICJ) (n 1049) 12; United Nations Office on Drugs and Crime (UNODC) and Skinnider (n 161) 36; Craig (n 1051) 3; Lochhead and Tan (n 397) 51.

1810 Craig (n 1051) 4; United Nations Office on Drugs and Crime (UNODC) and Skinnider (n 161) 89.

first opportunity, raise a hue and cry' and that 'silence on the part of witnesses, when it would be natural for them to speak, can give rise to an adverse inference as to their credibility.'[1811]

Second, failure to report SGBV to state actors is often equated with non-exhaustion of (reasonable) state protection. Asylum authorities therefore conclude that applicants did not demonstrate the unavailability of such protection and that the application for international protection is therefore ill-founded. This thinking pattern has also been identified through the preliminary case law analysis in the ECtHR's non-refoulement case law.[1812] Underlying this reasoning is the assumption that effective state protection against SGBV was accessible in the country of origin, often emphasising formal or *de jure* protection over the *de facto* barriers to obtaining it.[1813] This fundamental trust in the accessibility and effectiveness of state mechanisms to protect survivors/victims from SGBV has been described in rape mythology as: 'Nowadays, [those] who really sexually assault [others] are punished justly.'[1814] Both lines of reasoning, that survivors/victims normally report SGBV and that when they do, authorities respond adequately, might also result in the idea that statistics on lower SGBV prevalence, reporting, and condemnations (e.g. in COI) are accurate, since '[SGBV] is a deviant event.'[1815]

In the asylum context, the second type of the state protection myth (resulting in ill-foundedness) may take two specific forms. First, in some cases, exhausting state protection in the country of origin is seen as a condition for refugee status or for its determination, regardless of the reasonableness or success rate of such steps. Asylum authorities tend to reason here that state actors' protection pathways cannot be assessed, unless applicants have actually attempted to exhaust them in practice. Second, in other cases, this concrete exhaustion of state protection in practice is not required as such. However, it is argued that, regardless of applicants' attempts before fleeing, they could have relied on reasonable pathways to protection in the past and will be able to do so upon return.

All three forms of the state protection myth, focusing on credibility (1) and focusing on well-foundedness, requiring concrete exhaustion of state protection (no matter its reasonableness or effectivity) (2) or not (3), were accepted by the CGRS and the CALL in Aster's case.

1811 Craig (n 1051) 5–6.

1812 Roels, 'Rape Myths in the European Court of Human Rights' Non-Refoulement Case Law on Sexual and Gender-Based Violence' (n 33) 83.

1813 Heaven Crawley and Trine Lester, 'Comparative Analysis of Gender-Related Persecution in National Asylum Legislation and Practice in Europe' (UNHCR 2004) 55; Singer (n 8); Peroni (n 33) 353.

1814 Gerger and others (n 150) 440.

1815 Payne, Lonsway and Fitzgerald (n 134) 36.

CASE OF ASTER			
• Country of origin:	Ethiopia	• SGBV types:	Rape/sexual assault & sex trafficking/ forced prostitution
• Gender identity:	Woman	• Decisions in file:	CGRS 1 (inadmissible) – 17/3/2022
• Birth year:	1988		CALL 1 (refusal) – 6/4/2022 – n° 270 994
• Interview by:	CGRS		

According to Aster's statements, she was born in Ethiopia in 1988. She left the country in 2016, because of her husband's political problems. She arrived in Greece in September 2017, where she applied for and was granted international protection in June 2019. While she could rely on UNHCR support at first, this was no longer the case once she received her status. Aster was unable to find work and lacked the financial means to rent accommodation. As a result, she ended up on the streets and often spent the night in a bus station. As this precarious situation attracted people taking advantage of her, she was **raped** on multiple occasions. She never reported this to the police. She stated it was difficult to identify perpetrators and found it pointless, since she would have to sleep on the streets again the next day, risking the same violence. After two years, she received a job offer to work at a guesthouse, cleaning and making beds. She initially agreed and was made to sign a contract in Greek she could not read. After two weeks, she was taken to another location, where she was **forced into prostitution** together with other women. She was told they were being **recorded** and that their video tapes would be made public if they tried to escape or go to the police. The trafficker **threatened** them **with physical violence and death**, which he demonstrated by cutting off the ear of one of the women, whom they never saw again. After a few months, Aster managed to disclose the situation to one of her clients. He showed compassion, helped her escape the guesthouse, told her to flee, and that he would take care of reporting the trafficker. Fearing for her life, she did not go to the police herself, but fled the country.

Aster was intercepted by the Belgian authorities in November 2021, while attempting to reach the United Kingdom. She was questioned and ordered to leave the territory, but did not do so. One month later, she was placed in a closed centre to be repatriated to Greece, where she eventually applied for international protection. She submitted a handwritten testimony and two certificates by the centre's psychologist and doctor, reporting nightmares, during which she had grabbed her roommate's throat, and issues with accessing her memory and concentrating.

Having travelled with false identity documents, Aster's application was processed in an accelerated procedure[1816] and was found inadmissible because she already enjoyed international protection in another EU member state, Greece.[1817] The CGRS explained that such applications may be found inadmissible because of the principle of mutual trust between EU member states.[1818] However, this principle

1816 Art. 57/6/1, §1, c] Belgian Aliens Act.

1817 Art. 57/6, §3, 3° *Ibid.*

1818 'According to this principle, all Member States should be considered as compliant with EU law and fundamental rights, and thus as safe countries [to transfer applicants back to]. [...]. However, inter-state trust and the presumption of conformity with human rights is not

is not absolute. When applicants' foreseeable living conditions in this member state put them at serious risk of inhuman or degrading treatment, regardless of their international protection status, this prevents their applications from being found inadmissible.[1819] Both the CGRS and the CALL found this was not the case for Aster.

They argued, among other elements, that her failure to report her SGBV to the Greek authorities undermined the credibility and well-foundedness of her application. They argued that: 1) her sex trafficking/forced prostitution was not credible, and even if it was considered credible, that 2) her failure to report it to the Greek authorities prevented the CALL to assess their willingness/ability to protect her, and that 3) she did not demonstrate that their protection was insufficient in the past or would be in the future.

> 'You even state that you **did not go to the police** after you were able to escape, giving the reason "that you were afraid and you did not know where you were being held or the real name of [your trafficker]". [...] This places a **substantial question mark on the credibility**, at least the seriousness of the facts you invoke.'[1820]

> '[T]he applicant [...] did manage to escape but **did not go to the police** after[wards] either. However, if [she] does not report the forced prostitution she allegedly suffered to the police, she **makes it impossible [...], through her own attitude, to catch the perpetrators.** As she did not file a complaint, [the Court can] **hardly conclude that the police would be unwilling or unable to help her**.'[1821]

> '[I]f **there is any truth in her statements at all**, [...] [the applicant has not made] it plausible that [...] she could not [...] turn to the Greek authorities for protection [in the past or future]. [...] [T]herefore, no need for protection can be established in [...] Greece, where she enjoys international protection, and **she does not demonstrate that the protection granted to her in Greece would be insufficient**.'[1822] | CASE OF ASTER

---

absolute. Notably, Article 4 of the Charter (and the corresponding Article 3 of the ECHR) has been recognised by the CJEU to act as a barrier to a Dublin transfer or to a rejection of the application for IP as inadmissible, in both systemic deficiencies and individual violations cases.' EASO (European Asylum Support Office), 'Balancing Mutual Trust and Fundamental Rights in Inadmissibility Cases: An Increasing Challenge for International Protection Judges?' (2021).

1819 NE002_CGRS 1 (inadmissible)_1988_F_Ethiopia_RSA_STFP_17/3/2022_270 994_NL_NANSEN_p. 3., *ibid.* 2; Art. 4 Charter of Fundamental Rights of the European Union 2000 (Official Journal of the European Communities C 364/3); Art. 3 ECHR; The ECtHR has already found in 2011 that an applicant's transfer by Belgium to Greece gave rise to a violation of Article 3 of the Convention. *MSS v Belgium and Greece* [2011] ECtHR 30696/09 [359–360].

1820 NE002_CGRS 1 (inadmissible)_1988_F_Ethiopia_RSA_STFP_17/3/2022_270 994_NL_NANSEN_p. 5., NE002_CALL 1 (refusal)_1988_F_Ethiopia_RSA_STFP_6/4/2022_270 994_NL_NANSEN_p. 13.

1821 NE002_CALL 1 (refusal)_1988_F_Ethiopia_RSA_STFP_6/4/2022_270 994_NL_NANSEN_p. 14.

1822 NE002_CALL 1 (refusal)_1988_F_Ethiopia_RSA_STFP_6/4/2022_270 994_NL_NANSEN_p. 15.

As I have set out above and will further illustrate below, these state protection myths may co-occur with the disclosure, resourcefulness, or non-state protection myths, where asylum authorities argue that applicants did not appropriately/ timely disclose to state actors or could have been expected to report, given their resourcefulness, including social networks, for support. Below, I will primarily focus on the role of exhaustion of state protection in SGBV-related refugee status determination. In doing so, I will first distinguish between the impact on the credibility and well-foundedness of applications for international protection. Next, I will specifically focus on asylum authorities' interpretation of the legal requirements of reasonable state protection, namely: accessibility, effectiveness, and non-temporariness.

3.1.2. ROLE OF EXHAUSTION OF STATE PROTECTION IN REFUGEE STATUS DETERMINATION

As already introduced above, the role of applicants' (non-)exhaustion of state protection in refugee status determination is twofold. In order to be recognised as a refugee, survivors/victims have to demonstrate that they are both credibly and well-foundedly unable/unwilling, owing to their fear of SGBV, to avail themselves of the state protection in their country of origin.[1823] Below, I will demonstrate how asylum authorities may deny applicants refugee status, arguing that their fear of persecution is either non-credible (due to their failure to report SGBV, or the inappropriate ways in which they did report it) or ill-founded.

Concerning the credibility stage, asylum officials qualify 'the act of turning to or not turning to the authorities' as a key aspect of refugee status determination.[1824] As important factors in conducting this credibility assessment, they for example name applicants' resourcefulness,[1825] by explaining: 'I understand that an 18-year-old girl with little education, who is completely dependent on her family, cannot [seek state protection].'[1826] In the abovementioned Senegalese case of a woman forcibly married to a man carrying out human sacrifices, the CGRS also argued that her failure to seek state protection was not credible, given the contrasting initiative taking and resourcefulness she demonstrated by organising her flight out of the country (meeting a smuggler, selling goods to collect money for her journey ...).[1827]

1823 Art. 1(A)2 UN Refugee Convention.

1824 CB013_CGRS_PO_[00:28:01].

1825 RB008_CALL_Judge_[00:19:23].

1826 CB013_CGRS_PO_[00:28:03].

1827 NS005_CGRS 1 (refusal)_2002_F_Senegal_RSA_DV_FM_13/05/2022_274 056_FR_NANSEN_ p. 5–6.

Other asylum officials found that the credibility of applicants' help-seeking behaviour from state actors rather depends on how serious the SGBV was[1828] or how well the state apparatus in the country of origin functions.[1829] One attaché at the CALL for example mentioned Rwanda as an example of a country 'where rapists are prosecuted.' They concluded: 'If someone [...] from Rwanda [did not] file a complaint [...], while I know that the Rwandan authorities are trying to combat violence against women, I won't find that credible.'[1830]

In most cases, it is applicants' failure to seek state protection that is considered non-credible.[1831] Two judges at the CALL for example explained always expecting (potential) survivors/victims of domestic violence to file a complaint. The first stated being 'very doubtful' if they did not[1832] and the second required applicants to seek protection against SGBV before leaving the country in order to be found credible.[1833] In Qawtar's case, the CGRS and the CALL both argued in a similar way, regardless of her past steps to contact an NGO working on domestic violence and filing for divorce:

> '[Y]ou **did not make any concrete attempt to effectively seek help** in Morocco. [...] Given the precarious situation you outlined, your manifest and total **lack of initiative** to get out of your predicament appears so implausible that it further undermines the credibility of your statements.'[1834] | CASE OF QAWTAR

In other cases, applicants did seek contact with state actors of protection, but the ways in which they did or recounted it afterwards were considered inappropriate or insufficient and therefore non-credible. In the abovementioned Nigerian forced marriage case, the state protection myth overlapped with the detail myth and the resourcefulness myth. The CGRS expected a higher level of precision of the applicant, considering her higher education, and found it implausible that she was only able to describe the person to whom she had filed a complaint as '"the commissioner", whose rank [she had] identified solely on the basis that "it's the one we found at the police station"'.[1835]

As mentioned before, Lejla and her husband reported their daughter's abduction to the police, but were placed in the same room as her kidnappers, one of them giving Lejla 'greetings' from the mafia leader who had forced her

1828 CB002_CGRS_Supervisor + PO_[00:23:45].
1829 R_2vcXK3qiYvk544g_CGRS_PO/supervisor/gender coordinator/CEDOCA member.
1830 RB007_CALL_Attaché_[00:24:19].
1831 CB013_CGRS_PO_[01:05:10]., RB005_CALL_Judge_[00:22:52].
1832 RB005_CALL_Judge_[00:23:58].
1833 RB008_CALL_Judge_[00:19:48].
1834 DM116_CALL 1 (refusal)_1999_F_Morocco_VGNT_FM_DV_24/04/2024_305 429_NL_Database_p. 16, DM116_CGRS 1 (refusal)_1999_F_Morocco_VGNT_FM_DV_3/4/2024_305 429_NL_Database_p. 5.
1835 DN100_CGRS 1 (refusal)_1993_F_Nigeria _VGNT_FM_DV_6/10/2022_304 410_FR_Database_p. 8.

into prostitution, were questioned for five minutes, waited for the chief inspector who never came, and were advised by another police officer to file a complaint. Not wanting to fight these people again, they decided not to, and the perpetrators were released. These steps towards state actors of protection were not considered 'serious and credible precautions' by the CGRS.[1836]

In the abovementioned Bolivian domestic violence case, the applicant had filed a complaint, but her lack of following up on it was surprising and showed her lack of interest, according to the CGRS.[1837] Similarly, Carmen's failure to make continued use of a protection order against her ex-partner led the CGRS and the CALL to label all incidents that occurred after her first and only use of it non-credible. While her perpetrator was detained for eight days instead of sixty as provided, upon which his threats and her fear intensified, the authorities argued:

> '[It is **not**] **plausible that any incidents occurred after this protection order** [...] [during] the following years[, in which] [...] you, someone who **already had a protection order** since 2008 **and already appealed to the legal system** in Ecuador, **would not have used** [it] **following other attacks.** [...] Given your past history with your ex-partner and the severity of the alleged attack you faced, **some action could be expected.**'[1838] | CASE OF CARMEN

When it comes to the well-foundedness of applications for international protection, as stated above, the UN Refugee Convention qualifies refugees as persons who are unable/unwilling to avail themselves of the protection of their country of origin.[1839] While the Convention does not explicitly define 'state protection', the EU Qualification Directive and Regulation do. According to these instruments, such protection can only be provided by the state or an organisation controlling (a substantial part of) the state, must be effective, of a non-temporary nature, and is generally provided when reasonable steps are taken to prevent persecution, '*inter alia*, by operating an effective legal system for the detection, prosecution and punishment of acts constituting persecution [...] and when the applicant has access to [it].'[1840] This provision was literally incorporated into the Belgian Aliens Act.[1841] The fact that this

1836 DBH121_CGRS 1 (manifestly ill-founded)_F_Bosnia and Herzegovina_RSA_STFP_23/5/2023_305 882_NL_Database_p. 5–6.

1837 DB068_CGRS 1 (refusal)_1975_F_Bolivia_RSA_DV_25/1/2024_302 134_NL_Case law selection by CALL_p. 7.

1838 DEc120_CGRS 1 (refusal)_1981_F_Ecuador_RSA_DV_ 8/12/2023_NL_Database_p. 2–3., Dec120_ CALL 1 (refusal)_1981_F_Ecuador_RSA_DV_ 29/4/2024_ 305 805_NL_Database_p. 7.

1839 Art. 1(A)2 UN Refugee Convention; Art. 2(d) EU Qualification Directive; Art. 3(5) EU Qualification Regulation; Art. 48/3, §1 Belgian Aliens Act.

1840 Art. 7(1)–(2) EU Qualification Directive; Art. 7(1)–(2) EU Qualification Regulation.

1841 Art. 48/5, §2, part 2 Belgian Aliens Act.

definition is not thoroughly implemented or understood by all asylum officials was evident from a KAP survey respondent reporting not having understood the statement: 'To assess the potential protection against SGBV, I find it relevant to know whether the actor of protection controls (a substantial part of) the State.'[1842]

In short, the reasonable pathways towards state protection that applicants are expected to exhaust must cumulatively provide accessible, effective, and non-temporary protection. Applicants may provide justifications, owing to their well-founded fear of persecution, for being unable or unwilling to avail themselves of this protection, according to the refugee definition. Importantly, asylum authorities must base their assessment of whether reasonable pathways of state protection exist on 'any guidance which may be provided in relevant Union acts'[1843] (EU Qualification Directive) and 'precise and up-to-date [COI] from relevant and available [EU and (inter)national] sources and [EUAA country analyses and guidance notes]'[1844] (EU Qualification Regulation). Therefore, it is not a legal requirement to be recognised a refugee that applicants did in fact exhaust all possible avenues of state protection in practice before fleeing, while possibly putting themselves at further risk by doing so.

While the applicants' concrete testimonies about protection-seeking attempts may be relevant to their refugee status determination, their failure to take such steps does not prevent asylum authorities to assess their application. Nonetheless, some asylum officials do *contra legem* seem to add this practical exhaustion of state protection as a condition for refugee status/its determination, regardless of the reasonableness or success rate of such steps. One PO and one attaché for example reasoned: '[If] no attempt has been made to seek protection, then it cannot be assessed whether effective protection is available'[1845] and 'You didn't ask [for protection] so we don't know whether you could have gotten help at home.'[1846]

This reasoning can also be found in several CGRS decisions and CALL judgements, where the authorities argued that, if local authorities are not aware of SGBV, they cannot take action to protect survivors/victims and that the purpose of filing a complaint is precisely to obtain protection against perpetrators in the future.[1847] In Elene's case, this reasoning was reinforced by the resourcefulness myth:

1842 R_29b8m4TU9YfbAeT_CGRS_PO/supervisor/gender coordinator/CEDOCA member.

1843 Art. 7(3) EU Qualification Directive.

1844 Art. 7(3) EU Qualification Regulation.

1845 CB006_CGRS_PO_[00:41:44].

1846 RB003_CALL_Attaché_[00:32:31]., RB007_CALL_Attaché_[00:45:13].

1847 Dec120_CALL 1 (refusal)_1981_F_Ecuador_RSA_DV_ 29/4/2024_ 305 805_NL_Database_ p. 10.

> 'Even more than the average citizen in Georgia, as a law student, you should understand that **if you do not report threats, the authorities can hardly be expected to take action**.'[1848] | CASE OF ELENE

In Nino's case, it was confirmed, regardless of her previous failed attempts to seek state protection:

> '[S]he had already been told repeatedly that no protection was possible against mere threats [from her ex-husband], but that she would have to catch the perpetrator red-handed. The Council emphasises that **the very purpose of filing a complaint is to obtain protection** against the perpetrator(s) [...]. **If the authorities are not informed of the facts, they cannot, of course, take action against them. The fact that she previously sought help without success does not alter this.**'[1849] | CASE OF NINO

This leads some decision makers to argue that applicants are per definition legally obliged to have exhausted *all* pathways to state protection in the country of origin in order to be recognised as a refugee.[1850] One PO at the CGRS even confirmed that, although they understand that survivors/victims might not dare to seek state protection against SGBV, 'the [CGRS] policy says "you must have tried everything", which of course sometimes feels uncomfortable.'[1851]

This results in general expectations from applicants to exhaust state protection, leaving out the reasonability condition (i.e. the protection must be accessible, effective, and non-temporary) completely: 'An applicant for international protection may be expected to have made extensive efforts to obtain protection in the country of origin before applying for international protection.'[1852] This argument was used in Sofia's case, where the CGRS (in a later withdrawn decision[1853]) simply argued:

> 'You **did not take any steps to report your father or seek protection from him in Honduras**. It is **not** apparent from the above that you would **run a real risk of serious**

1848 DGe151_CALL 1 (refusal)_2003_F_Georgia_VGNT_DV_27/03/2024_303 891_NL_Database_ p. 15., DGe151_CGRS 1_(refusal)_2003_F_Georgia_VGNT_DV_27/7/2023_303 891_NL_Database_ p. 5.

1849 NGe014_CALL 1 (manifestly ill-founded)_1975_F_Georgia_RSA_DV_16/3/2022_269 856_ NL_NANSEN_p.17–18.

1850 CB015_CGRS_Supervisor + PO_GENDER_[00:38:28]., RB003_CALL_Attaché_[00:31:42].

1851 CB014_CGRS_PO_[00:34:57].

1852 DGe138_CGRS 1 (refusal)_1998_F_Georgia_RSA_DV_27/12/2023_307 108_NL_Database_ p. 5.

1853 Upon refusal of her application by the CGRS, Sofia's appeal with the CALL was not registered, since her insufficient bank balance had caused an error in the payment of the registration fee. Despite a letter from her lawyer explaining this, the situation could not be rectified and she could not appeal against her refusal decision by the CGRS. Eventually, the CGRS decided to withdraw the initial refusal of Sofia's application and, after reconsidering her case (the reasoning of which is not made public), to recognise her as a refugee.

harm if you returned to Honduras because of the abuse you suffered at the hands of your father.'[1854] | CASE OF SOFIA

Other asylum officials do not require exhaustion of state protection in practice, regardless of its reasonableness, as a condition for refugee status/its determination. However, they do consider applications ill-founded because, regardless of the steps taken by applicants before fleeing, they find that there was reasonable state protection against SGBV available, that applicants could have relied on in the past and will be able to rely on upon return. This reasoning is generally formulated as in Ana's case:

> 'It is up to applicant[s] themselves to demonstrate in [their] individual [...] situation that they have exhausted all **reasonable and useful possibilities for protection** or [...] that there are valid reasons in [their] individual circumstances why they cannot be expected to [do so].'[1855] | CASE OF ANA

Others phrased the same line of thought alternatively, arguing that applicants did not exhaust 'all reasonable and realistic possibilities of protection',[1856] 'which could nevertheless be expected of [them]'[1857] and the fact that they were unwilling or unable to do so 'does not mean [...] that the [...] authorities would be unwilling or unable to protect [them].'[1858] However, what these 'reasonable and realistic possibilities of protection' concretely entail, is interpreted in a variety of ways in the Belgian asylum procedure. One judge explained these internal differences in interpretation. If applicants had no chance of success, they stated, they cannot be blamed for not trying to seek state protection. However, '[t]his assessment may vary depending on [...] the strictness of the judges. We are quite strict [...], if there is even the slightest possibility of protection, we will still ask the person to have tried.'[1859]

In decision making practice, the original cumulative conditions for reasonable state protection (i.e. accessibility, effectiveness, and non-temporariness) seem to

1854 NH003_CGRS 1 (refusal)_1991_F_Honduras_RSA_DV_12/8/2021_NL_NANSEN_p. 2.

1855 DGe144_CALL 1 (refusal)_1985_F_Georgia_RSA_DV_29/05/2024_307 462_NL_Database_p. 10., Idem in: DGe110_CALL 1 (refusal)_1986_M_Georgia_VGNT_FM_27/3/2024_303 889_NL_Database_p.1.

1856 NA001_A_CALL 2 (refusal)_2006_F_Albania_RSA_VGNT_FM_DV_8/5/2024_306 251_NL_NANSEN_MINOR_p. 10.

1857 DGe139_CGRS 1 (refusal)_2005_F_Georgia_DV_21/11/2023_307 109_NL_Database_p. 2.

1858 DGe151_CALL 1 (refusal)_2003_F_Georgia_VGNT_DV_27/03/2024_303 891_NL_Database_p. 15., DGe151_CGRS 1_(refusal)_2003_F_Georgia_VGNT_DV_27/7/2023_303 891_NL_Database_p. 5.

1859 RB008_CALL_Judge_[00:16:12].

shift. As such, decision makers often rephrase these conditions in a standardised manner,[1860] as in Carmen's case:

> 'The protection offered by the national authorities must be **"real"**.[1861] **However, it does not have to be absolute** and offer protection against every act committed by third parties. The authorities have a **duty to protect** citizens, but this duty **does not imply an obligation to achieve a result.**'
>
> '[T]he measures taken [in this case] [...] against domestic violence are **not perfect, but neither are they purely theoretical.** It is therefore up to the applicant to demonstrate that she has exhausted all **reasonable and useful possibilities** of protection, which is not the case here.'[1862] | CASE OF CARMEN

Asylum officials replicated this shift in focus 'from result to intent' in the interviews and survey, stating that state protection is 'a commitment of means and of result',[1863] 'because [...] [if not,] we would have to grant everyone [refugee] status'[1864] and that '[in] a country where [...] the police and courts deal with complaints to the best of their ability, you will probably have to conclude that this person has not exhausted all possibilities [...] and is therefore not entitled to international protection.'[1865] A judge added that a protection measure might be considered unreasonable if 'it is never complied with [and] there is an extremely

1860 NGe014_CALL 1 (manifestly ill-founded)_1975_F_Georgia_RSA_DV_16/3/2022_269 856_NL_NANSEN_p. 16., DA118_CALL 1 (refusal)_F_Albania_STFP_DV_24/4/2024_305 447_NL_Database_p. 13., DGe109_CALL 1 (refusal)_F_Georgia_RSA_FM_DV_19/12/2023_303 313_NL_Database_p.4., DGe109_CALL 2 (refusal)_F_Georgia_RSA_FM_DV_15/3/2024_303 313_NL_Database_p. 11., DGe144_CALL 1_refusal)_1985_F_Georgia_RSA_DV_29/05/2024_307 462_NL_Database_p. 10., DGe151_CALL 1 (refusal)_2003_F_Georgia_VGNT_DV_27/03/2024_303 891_NL_Database_p. 14., DSu147_CGRS 1 (refusal)_F_Suriname_RSA_VGNT_FM_DV_9/5/2023_301 074_NL_Database_p. 3, DSu147_CALL 1 (refusal)_F_Suriname_RSA_VGNT_FM_DV_5/2/2024_301 074_NL_Database_p. 9., NA001_B_CALL 1 (refusal)_1973_F_Albania_RSA_VGNT_FM_DV_7/4/2020_234950_NL_NANSEN_p.3, NA001_B_CGRS 1 (manifestly ill-founded)_1973_F_Albania_RSA_VGNT_FM_DV_29/5/2019_234 950_NL_NANSEN_p. 3.

1861 The Dutch word used is 'daadwerkelijk', literally translating as 'real'. In alternative phrasings of this argument, other decision makers use the term 'doeltreffend', in line with the Dutch translation in the Belgian Aliens Act of the EU Qualification Directive and Regulation provisions on state protection, literally translating as 'effective'. 'Van Dale meaning of "daadwerkelijk"' (*Van Dale NEDERLANDS*), www.vandale.nl/gratis-woordenboek/nederlands/betekenis/daadwerkelijk.

1862 DEc120_CGRS 1 (refusal)_1981_F_Ecuador_RSA_DV_ 8/12/2023_NL_Database_p. 3, Dec120_CALL 1 (refusal)_1981_F_Ecuador_RSA_DV_ 29/4/2024_ 305 805_NL_Database_p. 9–10.

1863 In Dutch "Het is een middelenverbintenis en geen resultaatsverbintenis". CB002_CGRS_Supervisor + PO_[00:45:44].

1864 CB015_CGRS_Supervisor + PO_GENDER_[00:33:06].

1865 R_3KZba7RYvtc7NX5_CGRS_PO/supervisor/gender coordinator/CEDOCA member.

high rate of femicide. […] But […] the fact that it is being violated in some cases doesn't differ that much from […] Belgium.'[1866]

Alternatively, decision makers have argued in case law that applicants can rely on certain pathways to state protection, because they did not demonstrate their 'systematic failure or total absence',[1867] as in Marjorie's case:

> 'The applicant argues that the Surinamese authorities are unable to offer her protection and that gender-related violence remains a serious problem for which the laws are not adequately enforced, quoting from various reports and articles […]. The Council points out, however, that the [COI] **does not demonstrate that there is a systematic failure or structural inadequacy of government protection in Suriname, let alone that any government protection is totally absent** in cases of gender-based violence.'[1868] | CASE OF MARJORIE

In Nino's case, the CALL upheld that state actors offering 'some form of protection', regardless of their failure to prevent irreparable damage in the past, may nonetheless constitute a reasonable pathway to be exhausted by the applicant:

> 'That the **protection order only applied for one month**, would **not provide effective protection**, that **no criminal investigation** was opened and that **the police and the court had repeatedly told her that nothing could be done** against her ex-husband as long as he was not caught in the act, does not alter the finding that [she] did indeed turn to the authorities for domestic violence and **enjoyed some form of protection**. Furthermore, […] it was **not for the [CGRS] to examine whether the protection provided by the police was timely and sufficient to ensure that no irreparable damage was caused**.'[1869] | CASE OF NINO

To sum up, the descriptions of reasonable state protection that applicants are expected to exhaust seem to move from the pathways that are 'accessible, effective, and non-temporary' to all pathways that are: 'real' but not necessarily absolute; taking measures intended to protect, but not necessarily guaranteeing this result; dealing with complaints to the best of authorities' ability; offering 'some form of protection' (regardless of their failure to prevent irreparable damage in the past) or protection that is complied with at least in some cases; not systematically failing, structurally insufficient or completely absent; or not merely theoretical.

1866 RB001_CALL_Judge_[00:33:14].

1867 DA118_CALL 1 (refusal)_F_Albania_STFP_DV_24/4/2024_305 447_NL_Database_p. 13., DGe109_CALL 2 (refusal)_F_Georgia_RSA_FM_DV_15/3/2024_303 313_NL_Database_p. 11.

1868 DSu147_CALL 1 (refusal)_F_Suriname_RSA_VGNT_FM_DV_5/2/2024_301 074_NL_Database_p. 9.

1869 NGe014_CALL 1 (manifestly ill-founded)_1975_F_Georgia_RSA_DV_16/3/2022_269 856_NL_NANSEN_p. 16.

This *contra legem* interpretational shift can be visualised in Figure 26. As the interpretations of 'reasonable pathways to state protection' are expanding (left triangle), inversely, those pathways considered unreasonable and therefore not required to exhaust by applicants (right triangle) are shrinking. As a result, the steps applicants are expected to take before fleeing, and with these the conditions to being recognised as a refugee, are becoming more and more demanding.

Figure 26: Interpretation of state protection considered 'reasonable' to exhaust in refugee status determination, as articulated in analysed case law

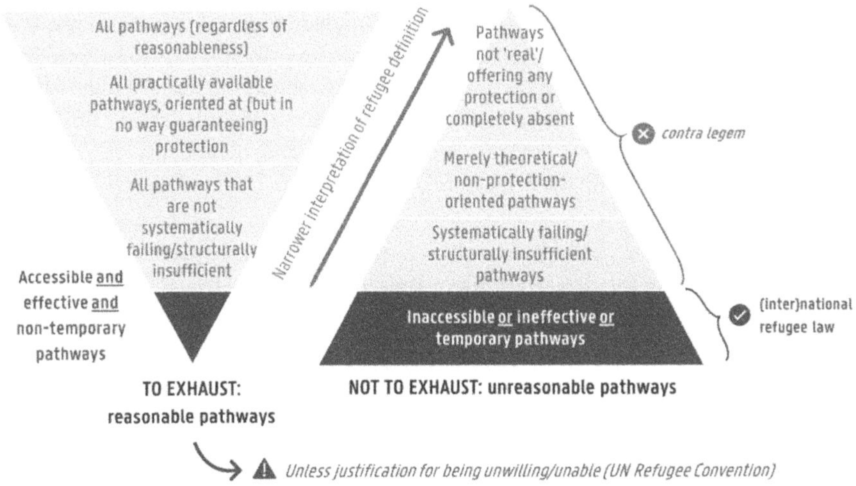

When applicants fear returning to countries designated as 'safe countries of origin' or to other EU Member States, it becomes even more difficult to meet the conditions of the refugee definition. In such cases, the interpretation of 'reasonable pathways' often boils down to virtually all pathways (the top of the left pyramid in Figure 26). In such cases, it is presumed that all avenues for state protection can and should be exhausted, regardless of applicants' individual justifications for not doing so. One of the attachés at the CALL (who had an overview of multiple cases) explained that judgements on Eastern European countries like Albania, North-Macedonia[...], being safe countries of origin, 'are often very standardised [...], establishing [that there are protection options left unexhausted], but there is rarely any discussion [...] on valid reasons for not invoking those [...] options for domestic violence.'[1870]

While applicants in theory may justify why a safe country of origin is not 'safe' in their specific circumstances[1871] or why the living conditions in an EU

1870 RB004_CALL_Attaché_[00:08:29].

1871 Art. 57/6/1, §3 Belgian Aliens Act.

member state put them at risk of inhuman or degrading treatment,[1872] decisions/judgements in practice tend to dismiss such justifications. Dismissal might be based on the circular argument that the country of origin is considered safe,[1873] or applicants may not even be asked for their justifications. In Vera's case for example, her CGRS decision was taken without even hearing her about the state protection against domestic violence in Albania, as it was based on her IO interview, where the subject was never raised.[1874] In the case of Aster, who feared being returned to Greece where she was sleeping on the streets, raped, and forced into prostitution, the CGRS argued:

> '[I]n light of the […] **presumption that your fundamental rights […] are respected in Greece** [and given] that **the authorities there are in principle capable of providing effective and equivalent protection**, you can reasonably be **expected to exhaust all possible means available to you under Greek law** and to document this […] at length. However, you have not submitted any supporting documents […] regarding any serious initiatives you have taken to obtain protection.'[1875] | CASE OF ASTER

Below, I will discuss how Belgian asylum authorities do interpret and implement the three conditions for reasonability of state protection pathways, as prescribed in the EU Qualification Directive/Regulation and Belgian Aliens Act, namely: 1) access to, 2) effectiveness of, and 3) non-temporariness of state protection.[1876] For each of these aspects, I will go into how applicants' justifications for considering the state protection unreasonable are assessed by the asylum authorities.

3.1.3. ACCESS TO STATE PROTECTION

When it comes to access to state protection against SGBV, Belgian asylum officials seem to base their assessments that accessible pathways were and will be available to survivors/victims primarily on three elements: 1) applicants'

1872 EASO (European Asylum Support Office), 'Balancing Mutual Trust and Fundamental Rights in Inadmissibility Cases: An Increasing Challenge for International Protection Judges?' (n 1818) 2; Art. 4 Charter of Fundamental Rights of the European Union; Art. 3 ECHR; The ECtHR has already found in 2011 that an applicant's transfer by Belgium to Greece gave rise to a violation of Article 3 of the Convention. *M.S.S. v. Belgium and Greece* (n 1819) paras 359–360.

1873 DA118_CALL 1 (refusal)_F_Albania_STFP_DV_24/4/2024_305 447_NL_Database_p. 13.

1874 NA016_CALL 1 (refusal)_lawyers' argumentation_1990_F_Albania_RSA_VGNT_DV_27/2/2023_285 363_NL_NANSEN_p. 7.

1875 NE002_CGRS 1 (inadmissible)_1988_F_Ethiopia_RSA_STFP_17/3/2022_270 994_NL_NANSEN_p. 5., NE002_CALL 1 (refusal)_1988_F_Ethiopia_RSA_STFP_6/4/2022_270 994_NL_NANSEN_p. 13.

1876 Art. 7(1)–(2) EU Qualification Directive; Art. 7(1)–(2) EU Qualification Regulation; Art. 48/5, §2, part 2 Belgian Aliens Act.

previous experiences, 2) applicants' resourcefulness, and 3) COI. I will discuss each of these elements below.

a) Applicants' Previous Experiences with Access to State Protection

The first element was demonstrated in both Diana's/Erina's and Nino's cases. In Diana and Erina's flight story, it is worth reminding that the state actors of protection they allegedly had access to continuously dismissed their complaints, refused to document evidence, failed to arrest the perpetrator, urged Diana into abandoning her divorce proceedings, and actively encouraged Erina to visit her abusive father, which led to a (failed) abduction. Both the CGRS and CALL argued:

> '[W]hen she did report [...], the Albanian authorities did take action, as evidenced by the **protection orders** imposed on her ex-husband and his Albanian **criminal record.** [...] [Therefore], **the applicant cannot seriously claim that she had no access to [...] the Albanian police and authorities for protection against her aggressive and violent ex-husband,** whose domestic violence she and their family were victims of.'[1877] | CASE OF DIANA & ERINA

For Nino, the Georgian authorities had issued three one-month protection orders (two of which were violated by her ex-husband, causing her to flee to Turkey), but never initiated a criminal investigation, repeatedly telling her that nothing could be done as long as he had not been caught in the act. The CGRS argued (in an identical decision as her husband's):

> 'Given that your wife has already been **able to seek protection from the Georgian authorities in the past** (*cf.* the **protection order** issued by the court and the fact that the **police regularly visited her** [upon its violation]), there are logically **no reasons to assume that you would not be able to [do so] again** if necessary.'[1878] | CASE OF NINO

b) Applicants' Resourcefulness & Access to State Protection

The second element underlying positive assessments of access to state protection against SGBV is applicants' resourcefulness. As already mentioned earlier, the resourcefulness myth often overlaps with the state protection myth, where decision

[1877] NA001_A_CALL 2 (refusal)_2006_F_Albania_RSA_VGNT_FM_DV_8/5/2024_306 251_NL_NANSEN_MINOR_p. 10–11., NA001_B_CALL 1 (refusal)_1973_F_Albania_RSA_VGNT_FM_DV_7/4/2020_234 950_NL_NANSEN_p. 8, NA001_B_CGRS 1 (manifestly ill-founded)_1973_F_Albania_RSA_VGNT_FM_DV_29/5/2019_234 950_NL_NANSEN_p. 5.

[1878] NGe014_CALL 1 (manifestly ill-founded)_1975_F_Georgia_RSA_DV_16/3/2022_269 856_NL_NANSEN_p. 18., NGe014_CGRS 1 (manifestly ill-founded)_1975_F_Georgia_RSA_DV_31/08/2021_269 856_NL_NANSEN_p. 4.

makers argue that 'someone with a network, money, opportunities, etc, will find it easier to turn to the authorities.'[1879] Several asylum officials elaborated that state protection against SGBV is considered more accessible to survivors/victims who are more: educated,[1880] independent,[1881] socially connected,[1882] wealthy,[1883] professionally experienced,[1884] assertive,[1885] talkative towards friends,[1886] or who are located in bigger cities.[1887] One CGRS supervisor explicitly recognised that a highly educated woman, living in Dakar, who therefore potentially has access to the police and is able to file a complaint, is still at increased risk of SGBV if she has no family support. At the same time, they admitted that this is not taken into account by some colleagues, who 'tend to jump to conclusions where [...] they shouldn't.'[1888]

In the case law, applicants' resourcefulness demonstrating their access to state protection against SGBV has for example been deducted from the fact that they managed to escape SGBV as such[1889] or their legal education (as already mentioned above in Elene's case).

> '[W]e can expect that you, as a law student, who yourself stated that **you chose to study law in order to be able to protect yourself, surely know what steps you can take to protect yourself.**'[1890] | CASE OF ELENE

In Carmen's and Vera's cases, their access to state protection was derived from past attempts to seek protection against SGBV (but which could not prevent Carmen from fleeing), higher education, and professional experience (regardless of Vera's diagnosed PTSD):

1879 CB013_CGRS_PO_[00:54:54].

1880 CB002_CGRS_Supervisor + PO_[00:30:21]., CB004_CGRS_PO_[00:10:47]., CB005_CGRS_Supervisor + PO_GENDER_[00:52:10]., CB008_CGRS_Supervisor + PO_GENDER_[00:38:47]., CB010_CGRS_Supervisor + PO_[00:21:03]., CB013_CGRS_PO_[00:56:07]., RB001_CALL_Judge_[00:17:52]., RB003_CALL_Attaché_[00:41:35].

1881 CB004_CGRS_PO_[00:10:47]., CB013_CGRS_PO_[00:56:07]., RB001_CALL_Judge_[00:17:52].

1882 CB005_CGRS_Supervisor + PO_GENDER_[00:52:10]., CB008_CGRS_Supervisor + PO_GENDER_[00:38:47]., CB013_CGRS_PO_[00:56:07].

1883 CB005_CGRS_Supervisor + PO_GENDER_[00:52:10]., CB013_CGRS_PO_[00:56:07].

1884 CB008_CGRS_Supervisor + PO_GENDER_[00:38:47].

1885 RB001_CALL_Judge_[00:17:52].

1886 CB009_CGRS_PO_GENDER_[00:27:08].

1887 RB003_CALL_Attaché_[00:41:35].

1888 CB010_CGRS_Supervisor + PO_[00:21:03].

1889 DIC105_CGRS 1 (refusal)_1999_F_Ivory Coast_RSA_VGNT_DV_26/10/2023_306 239_FR_Database_p. 6.

1890 DGe151_CALL 1 (refusal)_2003_F_Georgia_VGNT_DV_27/03/2024_303 891_NL_Database_p. 15., DGe151_CGRS 1_(refusal)_2003_F_Georgia_VGNT_DV_27/7/2023_303 891_NL_Database_p. 5.

'[You] clearly showed your **independence and resourcefulness**, as well as your **ability to assert your rights through the Ecuadorian legal system**. Nothing shows that you would not be able to **do so again** upon return.'[1891] | CASE OF CARMEN

'[I]t cannot be denied that **the applicant, highly educated and with work experience, should be able to access the protection opportunities available in Albania.** While [...] the applicant suffers from **serious mental health problems**, [...] the Council notes that [...] she had already been receiving treatment in Albania [...], and nothing indicates that she would not have access to healthcare [upon return].'[1892] | CASE OF VERA

c) COI on Access to State Protection

Thirdly, asylum authorities base arguments on access to state protection against SGBV on COI in a standardised manner, especially in Albanian and Georgian cases. In an Albanian sex trafficking/forced prostitution and domestic violence case, the CALL brought up COI that mentioned an increase in the free legal aid provision, especially in domestic violence cases, and that the police generally responds quickly and in the interest of its citizens.[1893] While the applicant cited other COI showing that women still face substantial barriers to accessing state protection, the CALL labelled this a selective and incorrect COI reading. The Council responded: 'That obstacles remain for women and domestic violence victims specifically [...] is not denied, but in no way alters the fact that women, as much as men, can access protection once they (dare to) take the necessary steps to do so.'[1894] A similar formalistic emphasis on access to state protection through free legal aid was noticeable in the (identical) CGRS and CALL arguments for Diana and Vera:

'[P]rovisions for **free legal aid** exist [...] and the Albanian government is committed to improving its effective functioning. Four **municipal 'legal aid clinics'** were also set up [...]. **[A]lthough further reforms are needed, there is strong political will to fight corruption** [...] [and] various **measures** and successful steps in recent years to combat corruption [...] **[have been taken]**.'[1895] | CASES OF DIANA & VERA

[1891] DEc120_CGRS 1 (refusal)_1981_F_Ecuador_RSA_DV_ 8/12/2023_NL_Database_p. 4.
[1892] NA016_CALL 1 (refusal)_1990_F_Albania_RSA_VGNT_DV_27/2/2023_285 363_NL_NANSEN_p. 15.
[1893] DA118_CALL 1 (refusal)_F_Albania_STFP_DV_24/4/2024_305 447_NL_Database_p. 12.
[1894] DA118_CALL 1 (refusal)_F_Albania_STFP_DV_24/4/2024_305 447_NL_Database_p. 13.
[1895] NA001_B_CALL 1 (refusal)_1973_F_Albania_RSA_VGNT_FM_DV_7/4/2020_234 950_NL_NANSEN_p. 3-4., NA016_CGRS 1 (manifestly ill-founded)_1990_F_Albania_RSA_VGNT_DV_10/10/2022_285 363_NL_NANSEN_p.5.

In three Georgian cases, including those of Elene and Ana, the CGRS and CALL (identically) argued:

> '[D]espite **information campaigns**, particularly vulnerable **victims** [...] still often **fail to find** their way to [...] **protection** mechanisms. [...] While certain **shortcomings** certainly still remain [...], the available information does **not** suggest that Georgian **authorities** in general are **unwilling or unable to provide protection to victims of domestic violence.** It can therefore reasonably be expected that you demonstrate the non-availability of protection in your individual case. However, you have not succeeded to do so.'[1896] | CASES OF ELENE & ANA

d) Assessment of Justifications for not Accessing State Protection

Even though state protection against SGBV is considered accessible to survivors/victims, the latter might still provide justifications for being unable or unwilling to access it.[1897] However, such justifications are often dismissed by decision makers, based on a variety of reasons, which I will discuss below. In the analysed case law, applicants have mentioned several factors obstructing their access, such as: perpetrators being state actors or having close connections with them; detention by and/or dependence on perpetrators; threats not to report; the fact that applicants themselves (forcibly) committed acts (they perceived as) criminalised; fear of reprisals/escalation or shame; lacking the necessary support to report; and discrimination by state actors. I will go into asylum authorities' position towards each of these justifications.

Several asylum officials in principle found that perpetrators who are or have links with state actors (such as police officers, military officials ...) might constitute a justification for not seeking state protection against SGBV.[1898] However, they added that this depends on the extent to which applicants can 'explain their role/connections and [...] go into detail [...], if they can, this may lead to recognition, but if they cannot, then we are back to square one.'[1899] In the case of Zeynep, who was stalked and raped by a police officer, the PO nevertheless asked her during the personal interview whether she had filed a complaint against him.[1900]

1896 DGe144_CALL 1 (refusal)_1985_F_Georgia_RSA_DV_29/05/2024_307 462_NL_Database_p. 10., DGe151_CALL 1 (refusal)_2003_F_Georgia_VGNT_DV_27/03/2024_303 891_NL_Database_p. 14., DGe151_CGRS 1_(refusal)_2003_F_Georgia_VGNT_DV_27/7/2023_303 891_NL_Database_p. 5., DGe109_CALL 1 (refusal)_F_Georgia_RSA_FM_DV_19/12/2023_303 313_NL_Database_p.4.

1897 Art. 1(A)2 UN Refugee Convention; Art. 2(d) EU Qualification Directive; Art. 3(5) EU Qualification Regulation; Art. 48/3, §1 Belgian Aliens Act.

1898 RB008_CALL_Judge_[00:33:32].

1899 CB014_CGRS_PO_[00:33:41].

1900 NT015_CGRS interview 1_2_3_1996_F_Turkey_RSA_FM_DV_FR_p. 8 (memo).

In the abovementioned Georgian case of a bisexual man forced to marry a woman by her family, he explained that his stepfather held a high position in the Georgian Security Service, was very influential, and had connections in the police force. However, in contrast to the more lenient position alleged above, both the CGRS and the CALL judged: '[A]cts of individual security force officers cannot be equated with organised persecution […] at the State level. Such an individual does not represent the entire power apparatus of Georgia and therefore your explanation is not sufficient to justify the failure to invoke protection from the authorities.'[1901]

One judge explicitly stated that, in domestic violence cases, if applicants make it plausible that their perpetrator('s family) had ties with the police, this would justify them not reporting to the authorities.[1902] In the case law, Marjorie did not manage to make such ties plausible, since she failed to explain her ex-husband's exact contacts with the police and relied on neighbours' testimonies that the police could be bribed.[1903] While the ties of Erina's paternal family to the police were credible, their influence was considered minimal, given the police's formal response to past complaints, regardless of their failure to prevent further violence. The CALL argued:

> '[While] **relatives of her father are members of the Albanian law enforcement services** […], their **power should be seriously nuanced**, since […] **the police nevertheless acted decisively every time her mother called on them** in the context of the problems with her ex-husband and furthermore, her complaints to the police continued to be followed up and were also **treated seriously by the courts**.'[1904] | CASE OF DIANA & ERINA

Similarly, for the justification that applicants were isolated by and/or dependent on perpetrators, one PO explained in principle accepting that 'if someone […] rarely leaves the house, then […] we can hardly expect [them to go to the police].'[1905] However, in Marjorie's case, the CALL argued:

> 'The applicant emphasises […] that she **had to stay at home** from day one of her marriage […], that she is **uneducated** and has **never worked**, which made her

1901 DGe110_CALL 1 (refusal)_1986_M_Georgia_VGNT_FM_27/3/2024_303 889_NL_Database_p.18, DGe110_CGRS 1 (refusal)_1986_M_Georgia_VGNT_FM_28/9/2023_303 889_NL_Database_p. 6.

1902 RB001_CALL_Judge_[00:21:04].

1903 DSu147_CALL 1 (refusal)_F_Suriname_RSA_VGNT_FM_DV_5/2/2024_301 074_NL_Database_p. 8–9., DSu147_CGRS 1 (refusal)_F_Suriname_RSA_VGNT_FM_DV_9/5/2023_301 074_NL_Database_p. 3.

1904 NA001_A_CALL 1 (refusal)_2006_F_Albania_RSA_VGNT_FM_DV_7/9/2022_276 951_NL_NANSEN_MINOR_p. 6.

1905 CB002_CGRS_Supervisor + PO_[00:30:30].

> **financially dependent** [...]. [However], this argument **does not explain why the applicant failed to turn to the Surinamese authorities.** Moreover, [...] if the authorities are not informed, they cannot, of course, take action.'[1906] | CASE OF MARJORIE

In cases where applicants are actively being threatened by their perpetrators, one judge did not necessarily consider this a justification not to report the SGBV: 'The government can only protect you if you report the threats, right? [...] In itself, a general threat doesn't seem convincing to me as a reason why [...] you couldn't invoke [protection].'[1907] This reasoning was reflected in case law[1908] like Nino's[1909] or Carmen's. While Carmen explained that she did not dare to use her protection order as she was afraid, psychologically exhausted, and feared reprisals from her ex-husband towards her and her children or mother, the authorities argued:

> '**Your defence that you stopped reporting because your husband threatened you not to do so cannot explain your failure** to [seek protection]. Indeed, the authorities can only act if you effectively report.'[1910] | CASE OF CARMEN

The same line of reasoning was used in the case of Uyi.

CASE OF UYI			
• Country of origin:	Nigeria	• SGBV types:	Sex trafficking/forced prostitution
• Gender identity:	Woman	• Decisions in file:	CGRS 1 (refusal) – 14/11/2023
• Birth year:	1993		CALL 1 (refusal) – 31/5/2024 – n° 307 592
• Interview by:	/		

According to her statements, Uyi was born in Nigeria in 1993. Until around the age of ten, she lived with her family, where she constantly had to work in the fields instead of attending school. As the eldest child, Uyi had to go and learn how to sew in Benin City, where she rented accommodation with money from the harvest. She lived there for about four years, but one day, her mother told her that a neighbour's daughter had

(continued)

1906 DSu147_CALL 1 (refusal)_F_Suriname_RSA_VGNT_FM_DV_5/2/2024_301 074_NL_Database_p. 9.

1907 RB001_CALL_Judge_[00:21:52].

1908 DK152_CALL 2 (refusal)_1997_F_Kenya_RSA_VGNT_FM_DV_4/4/2024_304 367_NL_Database_p. 20.

1909 NGe014_CALL 1 (manifestly ill-founded)_1975_F_Georgia_RSA_DV_16/3/2022_269 856_NL_NANSEN_p. 16., NGe014_CGRS 1 (manifestly ill-founded)_1975_F_Georgia_RSA_DV_31/08/2021_269 856_NL_NANSEN_p. 4.

1910 DEc120_CGRS 1 (refusal)_1981_F_Ecuador_RSA_DV_ 8/12/2023_NL_Database_p. 3., DEc120_CALL 1 (refusal)_1981_F_Ecuador_RSA_DV_ 29/4/2024_ 305 805_NL_Database_p. 9–10.

a large shop in Europe and was looking for someone trustworthy to help her. After the daughter came from Italy to their town to explain her everything, Uyi agreed to take the job. However, she would have to repay €25 000 for her travel costs to Italy. Unaware of the consequences, she accepted to swear a voodoo oath in case she could not repay the debt. Uyi left Nigeria in 2015, but upon arrival in Italy, the agreement changed. Uyi was **forced into prostitution**. When she refused, her 'madam' **threatened that the voodoo priest would kill her and her family**. Seeing no other option, she sold her body and lived with this madam. At one point, she was checked by the Italian police, asking for her documents, which she did not have. Her madam told her to apply for international protection in Italy but warned her not to tell the truth. Being forced to lie that her father was a member of a cult, her flight story was found non-credible and her application was rejected. One day, Uyi found her madam lifeless in the house. When the police arrived, Uyi finally told them the real story. A sister of the madam came to the funeral and told Uyi she **still had to repay the remaining debt** of €15 000. An unknown man called her with the same demand. Uyi threw away her SIM card, after which the threats stopped.

In January 2022, she left Italy and travelled to Belgium, where she applied for international protection. One evening, her sister called her to tell her that their father's leg had become swollen. Uyi had no money to send for medical care, and in July 2023, he died, leading her to suspect that voodoo may have been used to kill him.

The CGRS and CALL in Uyi's case rejected her justification that she was threatened to lie and not report to the Italian authorities, by arguing:

> 'Not only did [she] **lie to the Italian asylum authorities**, [she] also **failed to seek protection from the Italian police. When [her madam] was alive, she did not allow [her]. She would kill [her] family if [she] did** and call the voodoo priest in Nigeria. […] By merely repeating her statements, the applicant **does not alter the pertinent motives of the [CGRS] decision**.'[1911] | CASE OF UYI

Uyi's reluctance to report the crime because she was working in forced prostitution was not accepted as a valid justification either by the CALL:

> 'While the applicant claims that, **in view of her precarious circumstances and prostitution activities, she did not seek protection from the Italian authorities**, the Council notes that [she] at some point did inform [them] […]. In response, [they] stated that they could indeed protect her, making it **entirely incomprehensible why she did not [seek protection] again after […] new threats**.'[1912] | CASE OF UYI

Fear of escalation or reprisals (towards themselves or others) and shame as an explanation for not reporting SGBV are being dismissed too. While one PO

[1911] DN146_CALL 1 (refusal)_1993_F_Nigeria_STFP_31/5/2024_307 592_NL_Database_p. 11., DN146_CGRS 1 (refusal)_1993_F_Nigeria_STFP_14/11/2023_307 592_NL_Database_p. 4.

[1912] DN146_CALL 1 (refusal)_1993_F_Nigeria_STFP_31/5/2024_307 592_NL_Database_p. 11.

admitted 'as an individual' understanding why this would prevent survivors/victims from reporting, 'as a PO, I know my hands […] are tied. If it concerns a country where they can get protection, I already know it's over.'[1913] A judge nuanced that the relevance of such justifications depends on 'how it's presented, [it has to be given substance, it has to be made credible], because otherwise it becomes an easy justification to claim.'[1914] An attaché would only take shame into account if it appears from COI that this plays an enormous role in the country of origin's culture, as they believed is the case in Japan.[1915] Regardless of the culture in the country of origin, another judge simply argued: 'If you feel ashamed, you wouldn't dare to tell it here either […], so I find that a rather unconvincing argument.'[1916]

Fear was rejected as an explanation for non-reporting in several cases analysed, among which Elene's and Aster's.[1917] As mentioned above, Aster was threatened with physical violence, death (demonstrated by her trafficker cutting off the ear of another woman), and spreading video recordings of her forced prostitution if she would escape or go to the police. During her personal CGRS interview, she explained not having contacted the police out of fear for her trafficker, not knowing anything about him, not having any proof, and only thinking about saving her own life.[1918] Nonetheless, the CGRS argued, confirmed by the CALL:[1919]

> '[T]hat **you were afraid and did not know where you were being held or the real name of [your trafficker]** […] [does] not show why the authorities would not want to help or protect you for this reason. This substantially **discredits […] the seriousness of the facts you invoke.** […] You gave **no explanation as to why you could not appeal to the Greek government.**'[1920] | CASE OF ASTER

As mentioned earlier, the justification that survivors/victims were lacking support to report SGBV to the police, for example from male chaperones, was only imaginable in one country according to a judge: Afghanistan.[1921] The

1913 CB014_CGRS_PO_[00:34:57].
1914 RB006_CALL_Judge_[00:49:27].
1915 RB003_CALL_Attaché_[00:33:40].
1916 RB001_CALL_Judge_[00:21:52].
1917 DGe139_CALL1(refusal)_2005_F_Georgia_DV_23/5/2024_307109_NL_Database_p.9.,DGe151_CALL 1 (refusal)_2003_F_Georgia_VGNT_DV_27/03/2024_303 891_NL_Database_p. 16., DMol 140_CGRS 1 (refusal)_1971_F_Moldavia_DV_30/11/2023_307 172_NL_Database_p. 3.
1918 NE002_CGRS interview_1988_F_Ethiopia_RSA_STFP_NL_NANSEN_p. 13–14.
1919 NE002_CALL 1 (refusal)_1988_F_Ethiopia_RSA_STFP_6/4/2022_270 994_NL_NANSEN_p. 13.
1920 NE002_CGRS 1 (inadmissible)_1988_F_Ethiopia_RSA_STFP_17/3/2022_270 994_NL_NANSEN_p. 5–6.
1921 RB001_CALL_Judge_[00:24:47].

analysed case law indeed showed that this argument is dismissed for other countries of origin, such as Georgia[1922] or Suriname. The CALL for example argued in Marjorie's case:

> '[S]he had **no one to support her and did not dare to go to the police** [...] all the more so because she knew [her **ex-husband**] had the financial means and connections to [...] **the police**. The Council finds that the applicant's argument does not go beyond **repeating statements made earlier** [**which were rejected**].'[1923] | CASE OF MARJORIE

Lastly, discriminatory attitudes of state actors might impede access to protection for survivors/victims from ethnic and other minorities. One CGRS supervisor recognised that ethnic minorities, who are often 'less educated, professionally inactive, [...] [and] less empowered,' might face discrimination substantially complicating their access to state protection.[1924] However, Esmeralda's case illustrates how this sensitivity is not necessarily reflected in the Belgian asylum authorities' case law.

CASE OF ESMERALDA			
• Country of origin:	Moldova	• SGBV types:	Domestic violence
• Gender identity:	Woman	• Decisions in file:	CGRS 1 (refusal) – 30/11/2023
• Birth year:	1971		CALL 1 (refusal) – 24/05/2024 – n° 307 172
• Interview by:	/		

According to Esmeralda's statements, she was born in 1971 in Moldova, is of Romani ethnic origin, and is a Christian. She attended school up to the fourth grade but never worked. In Moldova, she was married. After her husband's father had passed away (two or three years before fleeing), he started **insulting and physically assaulting** her on a daily basis. The last time, he **hit her on the head** so hard she lost consciousness. The neighbours heard the commotion and alerted the emergency services. Esmeralda was hospitalised and afterwards went to stay with her sister until she eventually decided to flee the country. Esmeralda left Moldova in 2018 and travelled through Europe. Over a period of four years, she halted in France, the Netherlands, and Germany. In each of these countries, she applied for international protection but received a negative decision. Since her departure in 2018, Esmeralda heard that her husband was **still looking for her and threatening to kill her**. While in Germany, her sister and nephew joined her, seeking medical assistance for his schizophrenia. Together, they went back to France, where their application was again rejected.

(continued)

[1922] DGe138_CGRS 1 (refusal)_1998_F_Georgia_RSA_DV_27/12/2023_307 108_NL_Database_p. 5.

[1923] DSu147_CALL 1 (refusal)_F_Suriname_RSA_VGNT_FM_DV_5/2/2024_301 074_NL_Database_p. 9.

[1924] CB008_CGRS_Supervisor + PO_GENDER_[00:18:25].

In June 2022, they travelled to Belgium, where they applied for international protection. Since that day, she heard nothing concrete from her ex-husband, but her fear remained, especially since she has remarried in Belgium to a Macedonian Rom. In support of her application, she submitted a medical certificate attesting to her serious sleep problems, anxiety, loss of impulse control, increased stress, and impaired cognitive functions.

In Esmeralda's case, the CGRS, confirmed by the CALL, rejected her explanation for not reporting the domestic violence due to the Moldovan authorities' discriminatory attitude against the Roma community:

> 'You stated that you did not know whether the police [...] would protect you if you reported [...] [, since] they would **tell you to resolve the matter yourselves and that they know how Roma are**. You based this on the [...] **many similar incidents where the police do nothing.** [...] Such **general** [...] **statements can obviously not suffice [and] remain mere allegations.** [...] In contrast, the above information shows that in cases of discrimination or violence, a complaint can be filed with the police. Research [...] shows that **Roma (and other vulnerable groups) do have a certain degree of trust in the police and are more likely to call on the police than other groups in the population.**'[1925] | CASE OF ESMERALDA

3.1.4. EFFECTIVENESS OF STATE PROTECTION

The second condition for reasonable state protection, next to accessibility, is effectiveness to protect survivors/victims against SGBV.[1926] Asylum authorities often, but not always, base effectiveness assessments of state protection on COI. This COI mostly focuses on *de jure* protection (e.g. laws and policies), rather than their *de facto* impact in practice (e.g. SGBV prevalence rates, number of actual convictions, ...). Importantly, the COI used is not always comprehensively interpreted, nor is it consistently SGBV- and region-specific. Some decisions/judgements do not rely on any SGBV-specific COI at all. In addition, effectiveness assessments of state protection tend to rely on applicants' previous protection-seeking attempts (e.g. applicants' past complaints and perpetrators' criminal records) and exceptionally on their resourcefulness or the comparison with state protection against SGBV in Belgium. Below, I will discuss how each

1925 DMol140_CGRS 1 (refusal)_1971_F_Moldavia_DV_30/11/2023_307 172_NL_Database_ p. 3., DMol140_CALL 1 (refusal)_1971_F_Moldavia_DV_24/05/2024_307 172_NL_Database_ p. 9.

1926 Art. 7(1)–(2) EU Qualification Directive; Art. 7(1)–(2) EU Qualification Regulation; Art. 48/5, §2, part 2 Belgian Aliens Act.

of these types of argumentation play out in Belgian SGBV-related asylum procedures, and elaborate on asylum authorities' position towards justifications for being unable/unwilling to seek state protection due to (perceived) ineffectiveness.

a) COI on Effectiveness of State Protection

Firstly, the COI used to establish effectiveness of state protection against SGBV tends to mention a variety of legal and policy measures in a standardised manner.[1927] As legal measures, this COI for example stresses the formal criminalisation of: domestic violence,[1928] intimate partner violence,[1929] the

1927 In the Georgian and Albanian cases analysed, the COI -based argument on effective state protection is almost identical. DGe144_CALL 1 (refusal)_1985_F_Georgia_RSA_DV_29/05/2024_307 462_NL_Database., DGe151_CALL 1 (refusal)_2003_F_Georgia_VGNT_DV_27/03/2024_303 891_NL_Database., DGe151_CGRS 1_(refusal)_2003_F_Georgia_VGNT_DV_27/7/2023_303 891_NL_Database., NGe014_CALL 1 (manifestly ill-founded)_1975_F_Georgia_RSA_DV_16/3/2022_269 856_NL_NANSEN., NGe014_CGRS 1 (manifestly ill-founded)_1975_F_Georgia_RSA_DV_31/08/2021_269856_NL_NANSEN.,DA099_A_CGRS1(manifestly ill-founded)_M_Albania_DV_6/7/2023_303 553_FR_Database., NA001_A_CALL 2 (refusal)_2006_F_Albania_RSA_VGNT_FM_DV_8/5/2024_306 251_NL_NANSEN_MINOR., NA001_B_CALL 1 (refusal)_1973_F_Albania_RSA_VGNT_FM_DV_7/4/2020_234 950_NL_NANSEN., NA001_B_CGRS1(manifestlyill-founded)_1973_F_Albania_RSA_VGNT_FM_DV_29/5/2019_234 950_NL_NANSEN., NA001_B_CGRS 2 (inadmissible)_1973_F_Albania_RSA_VGNT_FM_DV_21/10/2021_270 155_NL_NANSEN., NA016_CGRS 1 (manifestly ill-founded)_1990_F_Albania_RSA_VGNT_DV_10/10/2022_285 363_NL_NANSEN., NA016_CALL 1 (refusal)_1990_F_Albania_RSA_VGNT_DV_27/2/2023_285 363_NL_NANSEN.

1928 DGe144_CALL 1 (refusal)_1985_F_Georgia_RSA_DV_29/05/2024_307 462_NL_Database_p. 9., DGe151_CALL 1 (refusal)_2003_F_Georgia_VGNT_DV_27/03/2024_303 891_NL_Database_p. 13., DA099_A_CGRS 1 (manifestly ill-founded)_M_Albania_DV_6/7/2023_303 553_FR_Database_p. 3., NA001_A_CALL 2 (refusal)_2006_F_Albania_RSA_VGNT_FM_DV_8/5/2024_306 251_NL_NANSEN_MINOR_p. 14., NA001_B_CALL 1 (refusal)_1973_F_Albania_RSA_VGNT_FM_DV_7/4/2020_234 950_NL_NANSEN_p. 4., NA001_B_CGRS 1 (manifestly ill-founded)_1973_F_Albania_RSA_VGNT_FM_DV_29/5/2019_234 950_NL_NANSEN_p. 4., NA001_B_CGRS 2 (inadmissible)_1973_F_Albania_RSA_VGNT_FM_DV_21/10/2021_270 155_NL_NANSEN_p. 5., NA016_CGRS 1 (manifestly ill-founded)_1990_F_Albania_RSA_VGNT_DV_10/10/2022_285 363_NL_NANSEN_p. 4., NA016_CALL 1 (refusal)_1990_F_Albania_RSA_VGNT_DV_27/2/2023_285 363_NL_NANSEN_p. 13., DSe093_CGRS 3 (manifestly ill-founded)_F_Serbia_DV_12/2/2022_301 311_FR_Database_p. 5., DEc120_CGRS 1 (refusal)_1981_F_Ecuador_RSA_DV_ 8/12/2023_NL_Database_p. 3, Dec120_CALL 1 (refusal)_1981_F_Ecuador_RSA_DV_ 29/4/2024_ 305 805_NL_Database_p. 10.

1929 NGe014_CALL 1 (manifestly ill-founded)_1975_F_Georgia_RSA_DV_16/3/2022_269 856_NL_NANSEN_p. 18., NGe014_CGRS 1 (manifestly ill-founded)_1975_F_Georgia_RSA_DV_31/08/2021_269 856_NL_NANSEN_p. 4., DGe151_CALL 1 (refusal)_2003_F_Georgia_VGNT_DV_27/03/2024_303 891_NL_Database_p. 15., DGe151_CGRS 1_(refusal)_2003_F_Georgia_VGNT_DV_27/7/2023_303 891_NL_Database_p. 6.

violation of protection orders,[1930] human trafficking,[1931] or rape[1932] in Eastern European countries like Albania (e.g. for Diana, Erina, and Vera), Georgia (e.g. for Nino, Ana, and Elene), and Serbia, but also in other countries, like in Ecuador (e.g. for Carmen), Nigeria (e.g. for Uyi), or Suriname (e.g. for Marjorie).

Importantly, these COI-based arguments often at the same time explicitly nuance the effectiveness of state protection. They for example mention that: 'domestic violence [...] is still a widespread problem in Albania [and] [...] there is considerable room for improvement, including in terms of prosecution';[1933] 'domestic violence is still a widespread problem in Serbia and much remains to be done to improve the situation';[1934] 'victims [in Ecuador] are sometimes hesitant to report because of social stigma, reprisals or other reasons';[1935] or 'gender-based violence still remains a significant problem [in Suriname] and [...] there is still room for improvement-.'[1936] In Nino's and Elene's cases, both the CGRS and the CALL for example added:

> 'As **victims reported that law enforcement officers do not respond enough to violations of protection orders, since August 2018, such violations were considered a crime from the first offence onwards,** and fewer protection order violations were already recorded in 2019.'[1937] | CASES OF ELENE & CASE OF NINO

[1930] NGe014_CALL 1 (manifestly ill-founded)_1975_F_Georgia_RSA_DV_16/3/2022_269 856_NL_NANSEN_p. 18., NGe014_CGRS 1 (manifestly ill-founded)_1975_F_Georgia_RSA_DV_31/08/2021_269 856_NL_NANSEN_p. 4., DGe151_CALL 1 (refusal)_2003_F_Georgia_VGNT_DV_27/03/2024_303 891_NL_Database_p. 15., DGe151_CGRS 1_(refusal)_2003_F_Georgia_VGNT_DV_27/7/2023_303 891_NL_Database_p. 6.

[1931] DN146_CALL 1 (refusal)_1993_F_Nigeria_STFP_31/5/2024_307 592_NL_Database_p. 9 & 11., DN146_CGRS 1 (refusal)_1993_F_Nigeria_STFP_14/11/2023_307 592_NL_Database_p. 5.

[1932] DSu147_CGRS 1 (refusal)_F_Suriname_RSA_VGNT_FM_DV_9/5/2023_301 074_NL_Database_p. 3, DSu147_CALL 1 (refusal)_F_Suriname_RSA_VGNT_FM_DV_5/2/2024_301 074_NL_Database_p. 9.

[1933] NA016_CGRS 1 (manifestly ill-founded)_1990_F_Albania_RSA_VGNT_DV_10/10/2022_285 363_NL_NANSEN_p. 4., NA016_CALL 1 (refusal)_1990_F_Albania_RSA_VGNT_DV_27/2/2023_285 363_NL_NANSEN_p. 13.

[1934] DSe093_CGRS 3 (manifestly ill-founded)_F_Serbia_DV_12/2/2022_301 311_FR_Database_p. 5.

[1935] DEc120_CGRS 1 (refusal)_1981_F_Ecuador_RSA_DV_ 8/12/2023_NL_Database_p. 3, Dec120_CALL 1 (refusal)_1981_F_Ecuador_RSA_DV_ 29/4/2024_ 305 805_NL_Database_p. 10.

[1936] DSu147_CGRS 1 (refusal)_F_Suriname_RSA_VGNT_FM_DV_9/5/2023_301 074_NL_Database_p. 3, DSu147_CALL 1 (refusal)_F_Suriname_RSA_VGNT_FM_DV_5/2/2024_301 074_NL_Database_p. 9.

[1937] NGe014_CALL 1 (manifestly ill-founded)_1975_F_Georgia_RSA_DV_16/3/2022_269 856_NL_NANSEN_p. 18., NGe014_CGRS 1 (manifestly ill-founded)_1975_F_Georgia_RSA_DV_31/08/2021_269 856_NL_NANSEN_p. 4., DGe151_CALL 1 (refusal)_2003_F_Georgia_VGNT_DV_27/03/2024_303 891_NL_Database_p. 15., DGe151_CGRS 1_(refusal)_2003_F_Georgia_VGNT_DV_27/7/2023_303 891_NL_Database_p. 6.

Interestingly, while the provisions on gender-sensitive refugee status determination in the Istanbul Convention are practically never cited in SGBV-related cases, the CGRS and the CALL do regularly refer to this Convention in arguments concerning effective state protection. In such reasoning, countries of origin's ratification of the Istanbul Convention is used to establish their intent to combat SGBV through action plans or new legislation. In the analysed case law, this argument has been used in Albanian,[1938] Georgian,[1939] and Serbian[1940] cases.

Next to legislative measures like formal criminalisation, COI also mentions states' policy efforts against SGBV. Interviewed asylum officials for example mentioned awareness raising campaigns[1941] or 'steps towards positive change'[1942] as relevant to assess the effectiveness of state protection. However, the need for such policy efforts often at the same time indicates that SGBV is deeply rooted in society and must therefore still be actively tackled. As one CGRS supervisor explained for Georgia: 'In principle, protection is available, but we also know that sexual and certainly domestic violence are a huge taboo [...] [and] a private matter [...]. Steps have been taken in Georgia to improve this, there are government-run [awareness raising] campaigns.'[1943]

In the analysed case law, decision makers often included a general finding along the lines of: '[A]uthorities, although much remains to be done to improve the situation [...] are paying increasing attention to [SGBV] and are making serious efforts to combat it.'[1944] In these effectiveness assessments, they for example mentioned the following concrete policy efforts as relevant: trainings on SGBV for police/other state actors; awareness raising campaigns; questionnaires for police officers to improve SGBV risk assessments; referral/coordination mechanisms to streamline state actors' response to SGBV; helplines; shelters; centres for healthcare and legal aid; mapping feminicide prevalence; creating databases of SGBV cases; monitoring SGBV research; action plans to combat SGBV; units and lawyers specialising in SGBV in police stations; 'victim rooms'

1938 DA099_A_CGRS 1 (manifestly ill-founded)_M_Albania_DV_6/7/2023_303 553_FR_Database_p. 3., NA001_A_CALL 2 (refusal)_2006_F_Albania_RSA_VGNT_FM_DV_8/5/2024_306 251_NL_NANSEN_MINOR_p. 14., NA001_B_CALL 1 (refusal)_1973_F_Albania_RSA_VGNT_FM_DV_7/4/2020_234 950_NL_NANSEN_p. 5., NA001_B_CGRS 2 (inadmissible)_1973_F_Albania_RSA_VGNT_FM_DV_21/10/2021_270 155_NL_NANSEN_p. 5.

1939 DGe144_CALL 1 (refusal)_1985_F_Georgia_RSA_DV_29/05/2024_307 462_NL_Database_p. 9., DGe151_CALL 1 (refusal)_2003_F_Georgia_VGNT_DV_27/03/2024_303 891_NL_Database_p. 13., DGe151_CGRS 1_(refusal)_2003_F_Georgia_VGNT_DV_27/7/2023_303 891_NL_Database_p. 4.

1940 DSe093_CGRS 3 (manifestly ill-founded)_F_Serbia_DV_12/2/2022_301 311_FR_Database_p. 5.

1941 CB001_CGRS_PO_[00:24:14].

1942 CB009_CGRS_PO_GENDER_[00:34:14].

1943 CB002_CGRS_Supervisor + PO_[00:16:38].

1944 DA099_A_CGRS 1 (manifestly ill-founded)_M_Albania_DV_6/7/2023_303 553_FR_Database_p.3.

and agencies; and disciplinary proceedings against police officers who fail to adequately respond to SGBV.[1945]

While such policy efforts may contribute to bring about change in attitudes and behaviour in the long run, they do not necessarily mean that applicants can/will already enjoy effective protection at the time of fleeing, applying for international protection, or upon return. However, in Uyi's case, the awareness raising campaigns on sex trafficking/forced prostitution in Benin City, Nigeria were considered so effective to protect (potential) survivors/victims, that her victimhood in itself was questioned:

> 'When [...] informed [...] that Benin City (the city where you were born and raised [...]) [...] is known for trafficking to/forced prostitution in Europe [...], you had not heard of it. However, [COI] **shows that the image of a young woman living in Benin City knowing nothing about migration and prostitution is not correct, as almost 100% of women do know what jobs they will do in Europe, due to** [...] **the many sensitisation campaigns.** [...] Moreover, [...] it can be assumed that [your parents] too would be aware of what you were facing in Europe, which was not the case.'[1946] | CASE OF UYI

In contrast to this COI on *de jure* protection (laws and policy efforts), some effectiveness assessments are based on COI on these laws' and policies' *de facto* impact in practice (e.g. SGBV prevalence rates, number of convictions ...). However, one CGRS supervisor admitted that such statistics are sometimes used to support effectiveness assessments in a selective and therefore deceptive manner. They stated that an often-used argument on Ivory Coast is that there have

---

1945 DA099_A_CGRS 1 (manifestly ill-founded)_M_Albania_DV_6/7/2023_303 553_FR_Database_p.3 DEc120_CGRS 1 (refusal)_1981_F_Ecuador_RSA_DV_ 8/12/2023_NL_Database_p. 4, Dec120_CALL 1 (refusal)_1981_F_Ecuador_RSA_DV_ 29/4/2024_ 305 805_NL_Database_p. 10., DGe144_CALL 1 (refusal)_1985_F_Georgia_RSA_DV_29/05/2024_307 462_NL_Database_p. 9., DGe151_CALL 1 (refusal)_2003_F_Georgia_VGNT_DV_27/03/2024_303 891_NL_Database_p. 13., DGe151_CGRS 1_(refusal)_2003_F_Georgia_VGNT_DV_27/7/2023_303 891_NL_Database_p. 5., DK152_CALL 2 (refusal)_1997_F_Kenya_RSA_VGNT_FM_DV_4/4/2024_304 367_NL_Database_p. 20, DK152_CGRS 2 (refusal)_1997_Kenya_RSA_VGNT_FM_DV_7/3/2024_304367_NL_Database_p.8.,DSe093_CGRS3 (manifestly ill-founded)_F_Serbia_DV_12/2/2022_301 311_FR_Database_p. 5., DSu147_CGRS 1 (refusal)_F_Suriname_RSA_VGNT_FM_DV_9/5/2023_301 074_NL_Database_p. 3, DSu147_CALL 1 (refusal)_F_Suriname_RSA_VGNT_FM_DV_5/2/2024_301 074_NL_Database_p. 9., NA001_A_CALL 2 (refusal)_2006_F_Albania_RSA_VGNT_FM_DV_8/5/2024_306251_NL_NANSEN_MINOR_p.14.,NA001_B_CGRS1(manifestlyill-founded)_1973_F_Albania_RSA_VGNT_FM_DV_29/5/2019_234 950_NL_NANSEN_p. 4., NA016_CGRS 1 (manifestly ill-founded)_1990_F_Albania_RSA_VGNT_DV_10/10/2022_285 363_NL_NANSEN_p.4.,NA016_CALL1(refusal)_1990_F_Albania_RSA_VGNT_DV_27/2/2023_285 363_NL_NANSEN_p. 13.

1946 DN146_CALL 1 (refusal)_1993_F_Nigeria_STFP_31/5/2024_307 592_NL_Database_p. 10., DN146_CGRS 1 (refusal)_1993_F_Nigeria_STFP_14/11/2023_307 592_NL_Database_p. 3.

been a few convictions of female GMC practitioners. However, these are always the same cases, which do not give 'an overall picture because we don't know how many complaints have been lodged. In my opinion, this is not representative of the situation and it's a bit hypocritical to use this as an argument.'[1947]

This selective interpretation of prevalence and complaint statistics on SGBV[1948] is also illustrated in several Eastern European cases (on Albania, Georgia, and Moldova). In both the Albanian and Georgian cases, the authorities linked the increased number of domestic violence complaints to 'greater confidence in the system, [...] more effective monitoring [...] by the courts'[1949] and 'the increased number of protection measures for victims and [...] awareness around legal solutions.'[1950] Neither the CGRS nor the CALL mentioned or rebutted the possibility that complaints are increasing because domestic violence is simply becoming more prevalent or its survivors/victims more resistant. In the Georgian[1951] and Moldovan cases, among whom Ana, Elene, and Esmeralda, the COI appeared to suggest that state protection against domestic violence is not effective, but the authorities nevertheless drew the opposite conclusion:

> 'The texts quoted show that **domestic violence is considered a private matter within the Roma community, making it difficult for victims to talk about it out of shame,**

1947 CB010_CGRS_Supervisor + PO_[00:35:24].

1948 Femke Vogelaar, 'Analyse landeninformatie inzake het individueel dossier van X' (NANSEN 2021) 11.

1949 DA099_A_CGRS 1 (manifestly ill-founded)_M_Albania_DV_6/7/2023_303 553_FR_Database_p. 3., NA001_A_CALL 2 (refusal)_2006_F_Albania_RSA_VGNT_FM_DV_8/5/2024_306 251_NL_NANSEN_MINOR_p. 14., NA001_B_CALL 1 (refusal)_1973_F_Albania_RSA_VGNT_FM_DV_7/4/2020_234 950_NL_NANSEN_p. 5., NA001_B_CGRS 2 (inadmissible)_1973_F_Albania_RSA_VGNT_FM_DV_21/10/2021_270 155_NL_NANSEN_p. 5., NA016_CGRS 1 (manifestly ill-founded)_1990_F_Albania_RSA_VGNT_DV_10/10/2022_285 363_NL_NANSEN_p. 4., NA016_CALL 1 (refusal)_1990_F_Albania_RSA_VGNT_DV_27/2/2023_285 363_NL_NANSEN_p. 14.

1950 DGe144_CALL 1 (refusal)_1985_F_Georgia_RSA_DV_29/05/2024_307 462_NL_Database_p. 9., DGe151_CALL 1 (refusal)_2003_F_Georgia_VGNT_DV_27/03/2024_303 891_NL_Database_p. 13., DGe151_CGRS 1_(refusal)_2003_F_Georgia_VGNT_DV_27/7/2023_303 891_NL_Database_p. 5., DGe109_CALL 1 (refusal)_F_Georgia_RSA_FM_DV_19/12/2023_303 313_NL_Database_p. 4.

1951 'The response of law enforcement agencies to situations of domestic violence has also improved considerably, although effective protection of victims against secondary victimisation and repeated violence remains problematic, as does the provision of information and insensitivity of the state actors involved and the selective approach when influential persons are the perpetrators of violence. There is also considerable room for improvement in the handling of sexual violence cases. [...] Consequently, while there are certainly still certain shortcomings in the Georgian authorities' response to victims of domestic violence, the available information does not suggest that Georgian authorities are generally unwilling or unable to provide protection to victims of domestic violence.'(DGe144_CALL 1 (refusal)_1985_F_Georgia_RSA_DV_29/05/2024_307 462_NL_Database_p. 9., DGe151_CALL 1 (refusal)_2003_F_Georgia_VGNT_DV_27/03/2024_303 891_NL_Database_p. 13., DGe151_CGRS 1_(refusal)_2003_F_Georgia_VGNT_DV_27/7/2023_303 891_NL_Database_p. 5., DGe109_CALL 1 (refusal)_F_Georgia_RSA_FM_DV_19/12/2023_303 313_NL_Database_p. 4.).

> **that there is a need for training of police forces to deal with domestic violence complaints and that courts often do not impose protection measures because of misconceptions about victims. From the above information,** [...] together with the personal interview notes, it **cannot be concluded that** in the event of any (serious) problems [...] with her ex-husband [...], if she were to make the necessary, serious and persistent efforts to do so, **she would risk being deprived of the necessary protection.**'[1952] | CASE OF ESMERALDA

In other cases, asylum authorities did not base their effectiveness assessments on any SGBV-specific COI at all. In the case of Lejla for example, the COI mentioned by the CGRS only generally concerned corruption, organised crime, and citizens' rights to a fair trial, but did not at any point focus on Bosnia-Herzegovina's effective protection against SGBV, such as the forced prostitution or rape she invoked. The CGRS simply concluded:

> '[T]he CGRS' information shows that **the functioning of the police is undoubtedly aimed at creating a safe environment for the entire population.**'[1953] | CASE OF LEJLA

In the abovementioned Georgian case of a male applicant who feared GMC by his family in order to convert him to Islam, no information on male GMC in Georgia was cited. The CALL simply stated that 'in general, protection is provided by the Georgian authorities, except in specific [...] situations [...][, mainly such as] high-profile cases, in which high-ranking opponents of the [...] regime [...] are persecuted.'[1954] In the interviews with asylum officials, two POs also bluntly stated: '[Senegal, Ivory Coast, Ghana, or Tanzania,] these are operational states [...] where [in response to] gender-based violence [...] state actors [...] function relatively well'[1955] and in Afghanistan, 'in theory the Taliban Courts [can provide protection for] personal problems [like domestic violence].'[1956] Both statements have been firmly contradicted, the latter by the CJEU in the *A.H. and F.N. case* (see Part I, Chapter 1.1),[1957] the former, for example for Ivory Coast, by the CALL itself in two judgements marked as important (one mentioned above and one of Clarisse, further discussed in chapter 3.2.3).[1958]

1952 DMol140_CALL 1 (refusal)_1971_F_Moldavia_DV_24/05/2024_307 172_NL_Database_p. 9. Emphasis added.

1953 DBH121_CGRS 1 (manifestly ill-founded)_F_Bosnia and Herzegovina_RSA_STFP_23/5/2023_305 882_NL_Database_p. 8.

1954 DGe112_CALL 1 (refusal)_M_Georgia_GMC_28/11/2023_304 208_NL_Database_p. 4.

1955 CB013_CGRS_PO_[00:54:01].

1956 CB014_CGRS_PO_[00:45:03].

1957 Ruling 1. *AH & FN v. Bundesamt für Fremdenwesen und Asyl* (n 82).

1958 "[A]ny effective protection by the Ivorian authorities ... [is] illusory". (DIC153_CALL 2 (recognition)_1979_F_Ivory Coast_RSA_GMC_VGNT_FM_DV_29/5/2024_307 471_FR_Case law selection by CALL_p. 14.); 'Although Ivorian law criminalises [...] female [GMC] [...], and victim support structures have been set up, access to the law remains problematic for many Ivorians. While significant progress has been made in terms of *de jure* equality, *de facto*

While asylum authorities seem to use this general COI to override applicants' individual experiences with ineffective state protection, SGBV-specific COI provided by applicants themselves tends to be rejected because it is insufficiently individualised or specific. Applicants in the analysed cases for example provided information on: the patriarchal society and high number of rejected complaints and feminicides in Ecuador;[1959] the government's passivity on SGBV, the recent rise in femicides, and the recent ECtHR condemnations due to ineffective protection of SGBV survivors/victims in Georgia;[1960] violence related to extra-marital relations and children in Iran;[1961] human traffickers' strategies to control survivors/victims and their risk of retaliation and revictimisation;[1962] the authorities' inadequate response to domestic violence complaints in Moldova;[1963] the government's inadequate enforcement of SGBV laws in Suriname;[1964] and feminicide rates and a UN Human Rights Committee case finding the authorities unable to protect an applicant from SGBV in Albania.[1965]

All of the above listed information was found insufficient to establish the ineffectiveness of state protection against SGBV in these individual cases. The reasons given boiled down to the fact that such information: does not rely on or relate to applicants' concrete and personal experiences; does not show a systematic failure or total absence of state protection; or does not demonstrate applicants' fear of persecution in concrete terms.[1966] As mentioned above, although authorities' arguments on COI demonstrating effective state protection are sometimes identically copy-pasted, especially across Albanian and Georgian

equality remains a challenge.' (DIC074_CALL 1 (annulment)_lawyers' argumentation_F_Ivory Coast_GMC_VGNT_11/3/2024_302 979_FR_Case law selection by CALL_p. 8.).

1959 Dec120_CALL 1 (refusal)_1981_F_Ecuador_RSA_DV_ 29/4/2024_ 305 805_NL_Database_p. 10.

1960 DGe151_CALL 1 (refusal)_2003_F_Georgia_VGNT_DV_27/03/2024_303 891_NL_Database_p. 14., DGe109_CALL 2 (refusal)_F_Georgia_RSA_FM_DV_15/3/2024_303 313_NL_Database_p. 11.

1961 DI131_CALL 1 (refusal)_F_Iran_VGNT_FM_DV_14/5/2024_306 520_NL_Database_p. 11.

1962 NE002_CALL 1 (refusal)_1988_F_Ethiopia_RSA_STFP_6/4/2022_270 994_NL_NANSEN_p. 14.

1963 DMol140_CALL 1 (refusal)_1971_F_Moldavia_DV_24/05/2024_307 172_NL_Database_p. 9.

1964 DSu147_CALL 1 (refusal)_F_Suriname_RSA_VGNT_FM_DV_5/2/2024_301 074_NL_Database_p. 9.

1965 NA001_A_CALL 2 (refusal)_2006_F_Albania_RSA_VGNT_FM_DV_8/5/2024_306 251_NL_NANSEN_MINOR_p. 14.

1966 E.g. DGe112_CALL 1 (refusal)_M_Georgia_GMC_28/11/2023_304 208_NL_Database_p. 5–6., Dec120_CALL 1 (refusal)_1981_F_Ecuador_RSA_DV_ 29/4/2024_ 305 805_NL_Database_p. 10., DGe109_CALL 2 (refusal)_F_Georgia_RSA_FM_DV_15/3/2024_303 313_NL_Database_p. 11., DI131_CALL 1 (refusal)_F_Iran_VGNT_FM_DV_14/5/2024_306 520_NL_Database_p. 11., NE002_CALL 1 (refusal)_1988_F_Ethiopia_RSA_STFP_6/4/2022_270 994_NL_NANSEN_p. 14., DA118_CALL 1 (refusal)_F_Albania_STFP_DV_24/4/2024_305 447_NL_Database_p. 13., DSu147_CALL 1 (refusal)_F_Suriname_RSA_VGNT_FM_DV_5/2/2024_301 074_NL_Database_p. 9.

SGBV cases,[1967] the CALL dismissed Elene's and Erina's SGBV-specific information through UN Human Rights Committee and ECtHR case law with the following words:

> 'The two **ECHR judgments** [...] **condemning the Georgian State** [...] for failing to provide effective protection to [SGBV] victims, **do not** necessarily **mean** that the applicant has a **well-founded fear of persecution** [...]. Indeed, **each application** [...] **must be assessed individually**.'[1968] | CASE OF ELENE

> '**Every application** [...] **must be examined on its own merits**, and by [referencing a **UN Human Rights Committee case** finding **Albania's protection against SGBV insufficient**] the applicant does **not** in any way **demonstrate** in **concrete** terms that she and her mother would **not be able to rely on** the protection of **the Albanian authorities**.'[1969] | CASE OF ERINA

It is true that the assessment of whether acts feared by applicants amount to persecution must be based on their individual circumstances,[1970] making the reasoning in Elene's case in principle legally accurate. On the contrary, assessments on state protection may take into account 'information on countries of origin obtained from relevant and available [EU and (inter)national] sources' that are not (necessarily) individualised.[1971] As such, the broader conclusions on states' (in)effective protection against SGBV in international case law, or in the other abovementioned information sources, are in fact of relevance for the (effectiveness) assessment of state protection in refugee status determination.

1967 E.g. DGe144_CALL 1 (refusal)_1985_F_Georgia_RSA_DV_29/05/2024_307 462_NL_Database., DGe151_CALL 1 (refusal)_2003_F_Georgia_VGNT_DV_27/03/2024_303 891_NL_Database., DGe151_CGRS 1_(refusal)_2003_F_Georgia_VGNT_DV_27/7/2023_303 891_NL_Database., NGe014_CALL 1 (manifestly ill-founded)_1975_F_Georgia_RSA_DV_16/3/2022_269 856_NL_NANSEN., NGe014_CGRS 1 (manifestly ill-founded)_1975_F_Georgia_RSA_DV_31/08/2021_269 856_NL_NANSEN., DA099_A_CGRS 1 (manifestly ill-founded)_M_Albania_DV_6/7/2023_303 553_FR_Database., NA001_A_CALL 2 (refusal)_2006_F_Albania_RSA_VGNT_FM_DV_8/5/2024_306 251_NL_NANSEN_MINOR., NA001_B_CALL 1 (refusal)_1973_F_Albania_RSA_VGNT_FM_DV_7/4/2020_234 950_NL_NANSEN., NA001_B_CGRS 1 (manifestly ill-founded)_1973_F_Albania_RSA_VGNT_FM_DV_29/5/2019_234 950_NL_NANSEN., NA001_B_CGRS 2 (inadmissible)_1973_F_Albania_RSA_VGNT_FM_DV_21/10/2021_270 155_NL_NANSEN., NA016_CGRS 1 (manifestly ill-founded)_1990_F_Albania_RSA_VGNT_DV_10/10/2022_285 363_NL_NANSEN., NA016_CALL 1 (refusal)_1990_F_Albania_RSA_VGNT_DV_27/2/2023_285 363_NL_NANSEN.

1968 DGe151_CALL 1 (refusal)_2003_F_Georgia_VGNT_DV_27/03/2024_303 891_NL_Database_p. 14.

1969 NA001_A_CALL 2 (refusal)_2006_F_Albania_RSA_VGNT_FM_DV_8/5/2024_306 251_NL_NANSEN_MINOR_p. 14.

1970 Art. 4(3)c EU Qualification Directive; Art. 4(3) EU Qualification Regulation; Art. 34(2)d EU Asylum Procedures Regulation; Art. 48/6, §5, c] Belgian Aliens Act.

1971 Art. 7(3) EU Qualification Directive; Art. 7(3) EU Qualification Regulation.

b) *Applicants' Previous Experiences with Effectiveness of State Protection*

In addition, asylum authorities at times base their conclusion that effective state protection against SGBV is available on applicants' 'successful' experiences with (seeking) state protection. What successfully seeking state protection means seems to vary from (potential) survivors/victims registering a complaint, to obtaining protection orders or a divorce, to perpetrators being convicted. One judge explained that if applicants manage to submit credible evidence of their steps towards the authorities (e.g. complaints), this usually demonstrates that they could obtain state protection in their country of origin.[1972] As such, applicants' failure to report SGBV may be considered an indication of non-credibility or that they could and should have done so. If they did report it, this is considered as evidence that state protection was and is available in the future. Either way, applicants' state protection-seeking behaviour will result in denial of international protection.

In the analysed case law, this conclusion has been drawn when: applicants had filed complaints,[1973] obtained protection orders,[1974] or initiated court procedures (e.g. divorce).[1975] In Nino's case, her court proceedings, protection orders, and police visits when the latter were repeatedly violated, led the CGRS and the CALL to establish the Georgian authorities' effective protection against SGBV, instead of her increased risk of future violence:

1972 RB005_CALL_Judge_[00:18:18].

1973 DB068_CGRS 1 (refusal)_1975_F_Bolivia_RSA_DV_25/1/2024_302 134_NL_Case law selection by CALL_p. 8., NA001_A_CALL 1 (refusal)_2006_F_Albania_RSA_VGNT_FM_DV_7/9/2022_276 951_NL_NANSEN_MINOR_p. 6., NA001_B_CALL 1 (refusal)_1973_F_Albania_RSA_VGNT_FM_DV_7/4/2020_234 950_NL_NANSEN_p. 4–5., NA016_CGRS 1 (manifestly ill-founded)_1990_F_Albania_RSA_VGNT_DV_10/10/2022_285 363_NL_NANSEN_p.3.

1974 DEc120_CGRS 1 (refusal)_1981_F_Ecuador_RSA_DV_ 8/12/2023_NL_Database_p. 2–3, Dec120_CALL 1 (refusal)_1981_F_Ecuador_RSA_DV_ 29/4/2024_ 305 805_NL_Database_p. 9., DGe151_CALL 1 (refusal)_2003_F_Georgia_VGNT_DV_27/03/2024_303 891_NL_Database_p. 15., DGe151_CGRS 1_(refusal)_2003_F_Georgia_VGNT_DV_27/7/2023_303 891_NL_Database_p. 6., NA001_A_CALL 2 (refusal)_2006_F_Albania_RSA_VGNT_FM_DV_8/5/2024_306 251_NL_NANSEN_MINOR_p. 10., NA001_B_CALL 1 (refusal)_1973_F_Albania_RSA_VGNT_FM_DV_7/4/2020_234 950_NL_NANSEN_p. 5., NA001_B_CGRS 1 (manifestly ill-founded)_1973_F_Albania_RSA_VGNT_FM_DV_29/5/2019_234 950_NL_NANSEN_p. 3.

1975 DM116_CALL 1 (refusal)_1999_F_Morocco_VGNT_FM_DV_24/04/2024_305 429_NL_Database_p. 16, DM116_CGRS 1 (refusal)_1999_F_Morocco_VGNT_FM_DV_3/4/2024_305 429_NL_Database_p. 5., NA001_A_CALL 2 (refusal)_2006_F_Albania_RSA_VGNT_FM_DV_8/5/2024_306 251_NL_NANSEN_MINOR_p. 10., NA001_B_CALL 1 (refusal)_1973_F_Albania_RSA_VGNT_FM_DV_7/4/2020_234 950_NL_NANSEN_p. 4., NA001_B_CGRS 1 (manifestly ill-founded)_1973_F_Albania_RSA_VGNT_FM_DV_29/5/2019_234 950_NL_NANSEN_p. 3.

> '[Y]our wife['s] problems with her ex-husband [are not disputed] [...], as evidenced by [her] **statements and the [...] protection order she submitted** [...]. However, **in doing so, your wife also demonstrates that she did receive protection from the authorities** [...]. Specifically, [...] a total of **four trials** were held and a **protection order** was issued on **three occasions** [...]. In addition, [she] indicates that during this period **the police visited her home every 2-3 days when problems with her ex-husband occurred.**'[1976] | CASE OF NINO

The same goes for perpetrators' past arrests[1977] or criminal records,[1978] often without considering that perpetrators will at some point be released again,[1979] sometimes prematurely or through bribery. In Carmen's case, the CGRS and the CALL argued:

> 'Your defence that you stopped reporting because your husband threatened you not to cannot explain your failure to do so [...] [, e]specially since [**he**] **has a criminal record, which once again confirms that the Ecuadorian authorities can and do take criminal action against him.**'[1980] | CASE OF CARMEN

c) *Applicants' Resourcefulness & Effectiveness of State Protection*

Exceptionally, one PO found that whether state actors can provide effective protection against SGBV depends on applicants' resourcefulness, such as geographical and socio-economic factors. They explained: 'It's obvious that for a poorly educated woman living in the countryside, it will be much more difficult, if not completely impossible, but for an educated woman in [a big city], there will be effective protection.'[1981]

d) *Effectiveness of State Protection in Comparison to Belgium*

Lastly, asylum officials also seem to take into account SGBV prevalence statistics in Belgium when making effectiveness assessments of protection in countries of

1976 NGe014_CALL 1 (manifestly ill-founded)_1975_F_Georgia_RSA_DV_16/3/2022_269 856_NL_NANSEN_p. 16., NGe014_CGRS 1 (manifestly ill-founded)_1975_F_Georgia_RSA_DV_31/08/2021_269 856_NL_NANSEN_p. 3.

1977 DEc120_CGRS 1 (refusal)_1981_F_Ecuador_RSA_DV_ 8/12/2023_NL_Database_p. 3, Dec120_CALL 1 (refusal)_1981_F_Ecuador_RSA_DV_ 29/4/2024_ 305 805_NL_Database_p. 9.

1978 NA001_A_CALL2(refusal)_2006_F_Albania_RSA_VGNT_FM_DV_8/5/2024_306251_NL_NANSEN_MINOR_p. 10., NA001_B_CGRS 1 (manifestly ill-founded)_1973_F_Albania_RSA_VGNT_FM_DV_29/5/2019_234 950_NL_NANSEN_p. 3 & 5.

1979 DA118_CGRS 1 (manifestly ill-founded)_F_Albania_STFP_DV_22/12/2022_305 447_NL_Database_p. 3, DA118_CALL 1 (refusal)_F_Albania_STFP_DV_24/4/2024_305 447_NL_Database_p. 14.

1980 DEc120_CGRS 1 (refusal)_1981_F_Ecuador_RSA_DV_ 8/12/2023_NL_Database_p. 3, Dec120_CALL 1 (refusal)_1981_F_Ecuador_RSA_DV_ 29/4/2024_ 305 805_NL_Database_p. 9.

1981 CB013_CGRS_PO_[00:54:54].

origin. One judge for example wondered: 'Adequate protection is never 100%, neither is it in Belgium, right?' Observing that in Belgium, women are being raped or killed by ex-partners under protection orders too, without them daring to report or perpetrators' being convicted, they rhetorically asked: 'So does that mean we do not have a good legal protection system [...] [or] that [...] [applicants] need protection in another country?'[1982] A CGRS supervisor added: 'The question is whether international protection is the solution in [SGBV] cases [...], because in the long run, you can have problems here in Belgium as well.'[1983]

Another PO more concretely mentioned that applicants for example claim that the legal system in Ivory Coast is dysfunctional. They replied: 'Well, do you want to lodge a complaint here in Belgium to see if the justice system in Belgium isn't crap? It's [...] expensive, it's complicated. I had a difficult divorce, I can guarantee you. [...] My [partner] earned [a lot more than me] at the CGRS. It was easier for [them].'[1984] This excerpt is a reminder of how SGBV-related refugee status determination is logically influenced by the positionality and emotionality of the persons conducting it (see Part III, 3.4.2).

While these observations that the Belgian government does not offer absolute protection against SGBV either are correct and understandable, they do not alter the legal conditions of the UN refugee definition as such. The definition does not contain any requirement that the host country granting refugee protection must be able to offer absolute protection against the type of violence from which applicants are fleeing, regardless of which actor is inflicting it. Instead, the purpose of refugee status is to protect applicants from specific actors of persecution who threaten to commit such violence in their country of origin.

e) Assessment of Justification for not Relying on State Protection

Even when state protection against SGBV is found to be effective, applicants might still provide justifications for being unable or unwilling to avail themselves of it.[1985] As the CALL put it: '[I]t is [...] up to [applicants] [...] to make a plausible case that [they have] exhausted all reasonable and useful possibilities for protection or, if not, that there are well-founded reasons in [their] individual circumstances such that [they] cannot be expected to [do so].'[1986] In practice, however, authorities' position that state protection should be 'effective, but not absolute' appears to serve as a pass to reject the individual justifications for not

1982 RB001_CALL_Judge_[00:32:47] & [00:56:16].

1983 CB002_CGRS_Supervisor + PO_[00:45:44].

1984 CB013_CGRS_PO_[00:22:36], [00:54:35] & [01:05:32].

1985 Art. 1(A)2 UN Refugee Convention; Art. 2(d) EU Qualification Directive; Art. 3(5) EU Qualification Regulation; Art. 48/3, §1 Belgian Aliens Act.

1986 DGe144_CALL 1 (refusal)_1985_F_Georgia_RSA_DV_29/05/2024_307 462_NL_Database_ p. 10.

(or no longer) resorting to state actors for protection.[1987] This was illustrated in Diana's case:

> 'Although you claim that the police did nothing when your ex-husband kept harassing you, there was an arrest warrant pending against him. As mentioned above, police protection need not be absolute and cannot be expected to be able to protect against every act.'[1988] | CASE OF DIANA

One supervisor at the CGRS stated: '[If] there is protection according to the COI, [applicants] should just seek protection, regardless of their personal problems.' While this supervisor claimed this to be a strict but correct interpretation of the refugee definition, since 'the Convention [...] only [grants] international protection if there is no national protection available,'[1989] it leaves no room for applicants' justifications for, owing to their fear of persecution, being unable/unwilling to seek state protection, as provided in the UN Refugee Convention.[1990] More concretely, another supervisor for example admitted that the CGRS' gender guidelines do not go beyond prescribing that protection orders suggest state protection, without necessarily taking into account applicants' testimonies that these were violated and offered no protection in practice.[1991]

Another gender-specialised supervisor did claim that it is relevant whether or not, 'after the violation of a protection order, the government takes action.'[1992] However, the analysed cases, such as Elene's, showed a different practice. Knowing that her mother had obtained a protection order against Elene's father, and that this was violated by him and could not prevent her from fleeing Georgia, the CGRS and CALL argued:

> '[T]he fact that your father violated the protection order, does not alter [the criminalisation of and therefore protection against such violations]. If the perpetrator seeks contact again after a protection order was imposed, the authorities must be addressed again so that additional measures can be taken.'[1993] | CASE OF ELENE

1987 NA001_B_CALL 2 (refusal)_1973_F_Albania_RSA_VGNT_FM_DV_21/3/2022_270 155_NL_NANSEN_p. 10., NGe014_CALL 1 (manifestly ill-founded)_1975_F_Georgia_RSA_DV_16/3/2022_269 856_NL_NANSEN_p. 16.

1988 NA001_B_CALL 1 (refusal)_1973_F_Albania_RSA_VGNT_FM_DV_7/4/2020_234 950_NL_NANSEN_p. 4.

1989 CB002_CGRS_Supervisor + PO_[00:43:15].

1990 Art. 1(A)2 UN Refugee Convention; Art. 2(d) EU Qualification Directive; Art. 3(5) EU Qualification Regulation; Art. 48/3, §1 Belgian Aliens Act.

1991 CB010_CGRS_Supervisor + PO_[00:33:31].

1992 CB015_CGRS_Supervisor + PO_GENDER_[00:32:37].

1993 DGe151_CALL1(refusal)_2003_F_Georgia_VGNT_DV_27/03/2024_303891_NL_Database_p.15., DGe151_CGRS 1_(refusal)_2003_F_Georgia_VGNT_DV_27/7/2023_303 891_NL_Database_p. 6.

Like for Elene, many SGBV survivors'/victims' inability/unwillingness to turn to state actors of protection stems from their own or others' negative experiences with such help-seeking behaviour, resulting in mistrust. In other cases, applicants' beliefs that state actors cannot effectively protect them against SGBV may originate from societal norms or authorities' general passivity towards SGBV. Next to this passivity, some applicants even fear authorities' active role in putting them at risk of (further) SGBV. This may for example happen when perpetrators have custody/visitation rights towards their children or filed a complaint for international child abduction against their (ex-)partners. I will go into asylum authorities' position towards each of these justifications below.

First, applicants often bring up their own or others' negative experiences with past state protection-seeking as justifications for their inability/unwillingness to do so (again). Instead of accepting such justifications or even considering these as indications of heightened future risk of SGBV, asylum authorities tend to dismiss them as insufficient to establish a lack of effective state protection. In the analysed case law, such negative experiences for example concerned: receiving insufficient or no protection at all after filing complaints;[1994] being attacked although a protection order[1995] or arrest warrant[1996] was in force; or perpetrators being released prematurely from prison after violating a protection order.[1997] In Lejla's case, despite what she experienced after testifying against the mafia that forced her into prostitution (i.e. physical violence, stalking, threats, rape, and the abduction of her daughter in 2022), the CGRS simply countered:

> '[Y]ou have no confidence in the authorities [...] and consider them corrupt. You refer to your experiences [...] and indicate that you did not receive sufficient help. **Leaving aside the shortcomings of the authorities' actions [...] in the 1990s and early 2000s,** it should be emphasised that [they] have **evolved since then** [...] [and a] significant part of the Bosnian population has a **certain to high level of trust in the police**.'[1998]
> | CASE OF LEJLA

[1994] DC079_C_CGRS 1 (refusal)_2006_F_Gabon_RSA_20/2/2023_303 320_FR_Database MINOR_ p. 9., DT071_CGRS 1 (refusal)_1999_F_Turkey_RSA_23/3/2023_300 506_FR_Case law selection by CALL_p. 4–5., NGe014_CALL 1 (manifestly ill-founded)_1975_F_Georgia_RSA_DV_ 16/3/2022_269 856_NL_NANSEN_p. 17.

[1995] DEc120_CGRS 1 (refusal)_1981_F_Ecuador_RSA_DV_8/12/2023_NL_Database_p. 3, DEc120_ CALL 1 (refusal)_1981_F_Ecuador_RSA_DV_ 29/4/2024_ 305 805_NL_Database_p. 9.

[1996] NA001_B_CALL 1 (refusal)_1973_F_Albania_RSA_VGNT_FM_DV_7/4/2020_234 950_ NL_NANSEN_p. 4.

[1997] DEc120_CALL 1 (refusal)_1981_F_Ecuador_RSA_DV_ 29/4/2024_ 305 805_NL_Database_ p. 10.

[1998] DBH121_CGRS 1 (manifestly ill-founded)_F_Bosnia and Herzegovina_RSA_STFP_23/5/2023_ 305 882_NL_Database_p. 8.

In an abovementioned Georgian rape and domestic violence case, the applicant explained that she had no trust in the authorities, based on stories about '[survivors/victims] being beaten [...] [and] "victimised" by the police after reporting family members [...] [, and] [...] an incident in which [her] father wanted to beat [her] and a friend of his, also an ex-policeman, urged [her] not to talk about this.'[1999] The CGRS and CALL replied that the stories about unsafe reporting did not apply to her case since she never filed a complaint in the first place and that she failed to establish why the Georgian government would target her.[2000] This reasoning conflicts with the future-oriented nature of refugee status determination[2001] and the fact that applicants should not necessarily be targeted by the state, but their lack of protection from persecution by private actors is sufficient to qualify as refugees.[2002]

Next to being dismissed as indicators of ineffective state protection, negative past experiences might even lead asylum authorities to argue that applicants should have reported this malfunctioning as such in order to have exhausted all reasonable protection pathways. In an Albanian sex trafficking/forced prostitution and domestic violence case, the CGRS for example reasoned: '[Y] ou did not report [the] inadequate police actions anywhere. Your explanation that [...] the police did not do anything and you wondered where you had to go other than to the police, cannot excuse your negligence.'[2003] Similarly, Lejla, Erina, Diana, Vera, and Marjorie were reproached for not denouncing the police's abuse of power or malfunctioning to: internal complaint mechanisms within police forces, the Ministries of Home Affairs, or Ombuds Services.[2004]

1999 DGe138_CALL 1 (refusal)_1998_F_Georgia_RSA_DV_23/5/2024_307 108_NL_Database_p.13–14., DGe138_CGRS 1 (refusal)_1998_F_Georgia_RSA_DV_27/12/2023_307 108_NL_Database_p. 3 & 5.

2000 DGe138_CALL 1 (refusal)_1998_F_Georgia_RSA_DV_23/5/2024_307 108_NL_Database_p.13–14., DGe138_CGRS 1 (refusal)_1998_F_Georgia_RSA_DV_27/12/2023_307 108_NL_Database_p. 3 & 5.

2001 Art. 1(A)2 UN Refugee Convention; UNHCR, 'Guidelines on International Protection No. 12' (n 681) para 24.

2002 UNHCR, 'Guidelines on International Protection No. 1' (n 35) para 19.

2003 DA118_CGRS 1 (manifestly ill-founded)_F_Albania_STFP_DV_22/12/2022_305 447_NL_Database_p. 4, DA118_CALL 1 (refusal)_F_Albania_STFP_DV_24/4/2024_305 447_NL_Database_p. 14.

2004 DBH121_CGRS 1 (manifestly ill-founded)_F_Bosnia and Herzegovina_RSA_STFP_23/5/2023_305 882_NL_Database_p. 9., NA001_A_CALL 2 (refusal)_2006_F_Albania_RSA_VGNT_FM_DV_8/5/2024_306 251_NL_NANSEN_MINOR_p. 14., NA001_B_CALL 1 (refusal)_1973_F_Albania_RSA_VGNT_FM_DV_7/4/2020_234 950_NL_NANSEN_p. 5., NA001_B_CGRS 1 (manifestly ill-founded)_1973_F_Albania_RSA_VGNT_FM_DV_29/5/2019_234 950_NL_NANSEN_p. 5., NA016_CGRS 1 (manifestly ill-founded)_1990_F_Albania_RSA_VGNT_DV_10/10/2022_285 363_NL_NANSEN_p.4–5., NA016_CALL 1 (refusal)_1990_F_Albania_RSA_VGNT_DV_27/2/2023_285 363_NL_NANSEN_p. 14., DA118_CGRS 1 (manifestly ill-founded)_F_Albania_STFP_DV_22/12/2022_305 447_NL_Database_p. 4, DA118_CALL 1 (refusal)_F_Albania_STFP_DV_24/4/2024_305 447_NL_Database_p. 12., DSu147_CGRS 1

Second, apart from negative past experiences with state protection, other applicants do not believe that state actors will be able to protect them effectively against SGBV due to societal norms (e.g. 'SGBV is a family matter')[2005] or authorities' general passivity towards SGBV (e.g. due to corruption, harmful gender stereotyping, lack of knowledge or sensitivity on SGBV, ...).[2006] Several interviewed asylum officials considered it insufficient when applicants for example mentioned: the Salvadoran police's corrupt response to gang violence;[2007] the fact that women cannot report their husbands in Guinea;[2008] or authorities' refusal to interfere with SGBV considered a family matter, such as forced marriage.[2009] In one Nigerian female GMC case, the CALL itself confirmed that 'the decision to have a girl circumcised is a family matter.'[2010] However, this observation does not prompt discussion on the effectiveness of state protection, but is used to argue that parents should therefore be able to protect their own children (non-state protection myth, see Chapter 2.1.3. of this Part).[2011]

One PO expressed incomprehension of this explanation for not filing a complaint that 'SGBV is considered a family matter'. They compared it to a personal experience with reporting a stolen work phone in Mumbai. The PO recounted having to insist for four hours at the station before the police would accept a complaint, but they eventually did. They hereby implied that filing a police complaint is a matter of persistence, whether its subject is a stolen phone or SGBV. When applicants justify their non-reporting of SGBV because of authorities' non-interference with family matters, this PO reasoned: 'Maybe we're too Western to say that [...], [but] if my father ever forcibly aborts [a woman] [...], beats me to death [...], at some point, I wouldn't give a damn [...] that he's my father' and would tell applicants: 'She wants to cut off your little girl's clitoris, madam! I would lodge a complaint, I wouldn't care that she's

(refusal)_F_Suriname_RSA_VGNT_FM_DV_9/5/2023_301 074_NL_Database_p. 3, DSu147_CALL 1 (refusal)_F_Suriname_RSA_VGNT_FM_DV_5/2/2024_301 074_NL_Database_p. 8.

2005 DA118_CGRS 1 (manifestly ill-founded)_F_Albania_STFP_DV_22/12/2022_305 447_NL_Database_p. 3., DA118_CALL 1 (refusal)_F_Albania_STFP_DV_24/4/2024_305 447_NL_Database_p. 14., DMol140_CGRS 1 (refusal)_1971_F_Moldavia_DV_30/11/2023_307 172_NL_Database_p. 3., DMol140_CALL 1 (refusal)_1971_F_Moldavia_DV_24/05/2024_307 172_NL_Database_p. 9.

2006 DGe144_CALL 1 (refusal)_1985_F_Georgia_RSA_DV_29/05/2024_307 462_NL_Database_p. 7 & 10., DIC153_CGRS 2 (refusal)_1979_F_Ivory Coast_RSA_GMC_VGNT_FM_DV_3/8/2023_307 471_FR_Case law selection by CALL_p. 8.

2007 RB005_CALL_Judge_[00:18:04].

2008 CB004_CGRS_PO_[00:16:24].

2009 CB010_CGRS_Supervisor + PO_[00:21:03].

2010 DN154_CALL 1 (refusal)_1988_F_Nigeria_GMC_VGNT_14/3/2024_303239_NL_Database_p. 11.

2011 DN154_CGRS 1 (refusal)_1988_F_Nigeria_GMC_VGNT_16/10/2023_303239_NL_Database_p. 5, DN154_CALL 1 (refusal)_1988_F_Nigeria_GMC_VGNT_14/3/2024_303 239_NL_Database_p. 9–10.

my mum!'[2012] In doing so, this PO interpreted this justification as an individual choice of applicants, rather than a structural social norm not to resolve private matters such as SGBV in public.

Third, in cases where perpetrators have custody/visitation rights towards their children and/or filed a complaint for international child abduction against their (ex-)partners-applicants, authorities might find themselves in a conflict of interest upon applicants' return. In such situations, state actors would both have to protect applicants from SGBV persecution, prosecute them for international child abduction, and enforce perpetrators' visitation rights towards applicants and/or their children. This justification for not wanting/being able to seek protection from state actors (again) was not recognised or dismissed in both Vera's[2013] and Diana and Erina's cases.

As described above, in Diana and her ex-husband's divorce proceedings, visitation rights with Erina were granted to him and he retained part of the custody over her.[2014] Despite Erina's explicit opposition throughout the procedure and his extensive criminal record, from that moment on, she was legally obliged to spend every weekend and certain holiday periods with her father, unsupervised.[2015] Before they fled Albania, the police's active enforcement of his visitation right even led to the father's (unsuccessful) attempt to kidnap Erina to marry her off at age 13.[2016] Although the Albanian police claimed to have an arrest warrant against the father, he was never actually arrested and, after their departure, was able to file a complaint for international child abduction against Diana, who had violated his custody/visitation rights by fleeing.[2017] Diana was subsequently questioned by the police in Namur, Belgium. Her parents were also interrogated by the police in Albania, who asked them where Erina was and warned them that Diana was wanted and could face a prison sentence.[2018]

These circumstances raise complex questions of private international law that are beyond the scope of this research.[2019] Knowing that international child abduction (defined as unlawfully taking or retaining a child in violation of custody or visitation rights) is a criminal offense under the Albanian Penal Code, punishable by up to six months of imprisonment,[2020] the CGRS and the CALL approached the matter in Diana and Erina's case as follows:

2012 CB013_CGRS_PO_[00:19:41], [00:23:20] & [01:20:29].

2013 NA016_1990_F_Albania_RSA_VGNT_DV_NL_NANSEN_[00:13:22].

2014 NA001_A_B_2006_F_Albania_RSA_VGNT_FM_DV_NL_NANSEN_MINOR_[00:34:17] & [01:05:44].

2015 NA001_A_B_2006_F_Albania_RSA_VGNT_FM_DV_NL_NANSEN_MINOR_[00:45:34].

2016 NA001_A_B_2006_F_Albania_RSA_VGNT_FM_DV_NL_NANSEN_MINOR_[01:05:33].

2017 NA001_A_B_2006_F_Albania_RSA_VGNT_FM_DV_NL_NANSEN_MINOR_[01:02:03].

2018 NA001_A_B_2006_F_Albania_RSA_VGNT_FM_DV_NL_NANSEN_MINOR_[01:03:20].

2019 However, see a recent judgment of the CALL that deals with a similar situation in Spain: (n 1453).

2020 Art. 127 Criminal Code of the Republic of Albania (Kodi Penal i Republikës së Shqipërisë) 1995 (Fletorja zyrtare, No 2).

> 'Although you claim that the police did nothing when your ex-husband continued to harass you, there was an **arrest warrant pending** against him. [...] **Even when your ex-husband tried to use the police to abduct your daughter [...], [they] responded correctly by telling him that he was only allowed to see his daughter one day a week as stipulated in the divorce ruling.**'[2021]
>
> '[T]**he mere fact that her father was able to lodge a complaint with the police in no way demonstrates that the Albanian authorities would (no longer) be willing to take steps against her father** if (again) necessary.'[2022]
>
> '[A]lthough [...] her mother was **heard by the Belgian authorities concerning the complaint [for international child abduction] lodged by her father, there is no evidence that the Albanian authorities are actually prosecuting [her]. The fear that her mother would be imprisoned as a result is therefore entirely hypothetical.**'[2023] | CASE OF DIANA & ERINA

3.1.5. NON-TEMPORARINESS OF STATE PROTECTION

Unlike the accessibility and effectiveness conditions for reasonable state protection, asylum authorities pay remarkably little attention to the requirement that this protection must be durable and non-temporary.[2024] On the contrary, they regularly mention temporary forms of state protection to establish states' ability and willingness to protect applicants against SGBV themselves, such as (temporary) protection orders or SGBV shelters.[2025] At times, the authorities

---

2021 NA001_B_CALL 1 (refusal)_1973_F_Albania_RSA_VGNT_FM_DV_7/4/2020_234 950_NL_NANSEN_p. 7., NA001_B_CGRS 1 (manifestly ill-founded)_1973_F_Albania_RSA_VGNT_FM_DV_29/5/2019_234 950_NL_NANSEN_p. 4.

2022 NA001_A_CALL 2 (refusal)_2006_F_Albania_RSA_VGNT_FM_DV_8/5/2024_306 251_NL_NANSEN_MINOR_p. 13.

2023 NA001_A_CALL 1 (refusal)_2006_F_Albania_RSA_VGNT_FM_DV_7/9/2022_276 951_NL_NANSEN_MINOR_p. 6., NA001_B_CALL 2 (refusal)_1973_F_Albania_RSA_VGNT_FM_DV_21/3/2022_270 155_NL_NANSEN_p. 7 & 10.

2024 Art. 7(1)–(2) EU Qualification Directive; Art. 7(1)–(2) EU Qualification Regulation; Art. 48/5, §2, part 2 Belgian Aliens Act.

2025 CB008_CGRS_Supervisor + PO_GENDER [00:18:25]. NA001_A_CALL 2 (refusal)_2006_F_Albania_RSA_VGNT_FM_DV_8/5/2024_306 251_NL_NANSEN_MINOR_p. 14., NA001_B_CALL 1 (refusal)_1973_F_Albania_RSA_VGNT_FM_DV_7/4/2020_234 950_NL_NANSEN_p. 7., NA001_B_CGRS 1 (manifestly ill-founded)_1973_F_Albania_RSA_VGNT_FM_DV_29/5/2019_234 950_NL_NANSEN_p. 3–4., NGe014_CALL 1 (manifestly ill-founded)_1975_F_Georgia_RSA_DV_16/3/2022_269 856_NL_NANSEN_p. 16., NGe014_CGRS 1 (manifestly ill-founded)_1975_F_Georgia_RSA_DV_31/08/2021_269 856_NL_NANSEN_p. 3 & 5., DGe109_CALL 1 (refusal)_F_Georgia_RSA_FM_DV_19/12/2023_303 313_NL_Database_p. 4., DGe151_CALL 1 (refusal)_2003_F_Georgia_VGNT_DV_27/03/2024_303 891_NL_Database_p. 13., DGe151_CGRS 1_(refusal)_2003_F_Georgia_VGNT_DV_27/7/2023_303 891_NL_Database_p.5., DGe138_CGRS 1 (refusal)_1998_F_Georgia_RSA_DV_27/12/2023_307 108_NL_Database_p.5., DGe144_CALL 1 (refusal)_1985_F_Georgia_RSA_DV_29/05/2024_307 462_NL_Database_p.9., DN146_CALL 1 (refusal)_1993_F_Nigeria_STFP_31/5/2024_307 592_NL_Database_p. 9 & 11.,

hereby recognised that 'support [...] for victims of domestic violence after leaving a shelter remains a stumbling block.'[2026]

In Nino's case, the CALL even explicitly dismissed her justification that the protection orders mentioned as forms of state protection were only temporary measures:

> '**The fact that the protection order is only valid for one month** [and] would not provide effective protection [...] **does not alter the finding that the applicant actually** turned to the authorities in the context of domestic violence and **enjoyed some form of protection**.'[2027] | CASE OF NINO

3.2. REBUTTAL OF THE STATE PROTECTION MYTH

3.2.1. REBUTTAL IN HEALTH & SOCIAL SCIENCES

a) *Empirical Evidence on Help-Seeking Behaviour from State Actors of Protection*

The state protection myth cannot find support in health and social sciences expertise on the nature and consequences of SGBV. First, the belief that 'true' survivors/victims will report SGBV, and that their failure to (appropriately) do so undermines their credibility, must be firmly rebutted. Specifically, the idea that, the more operational a state apparatus is perceived, the more readily applicants will report SGBV experiences/fears, must be fundamentally nuanced.

Loraine M. Mponela, a migrant rights campaigner with lived refugee experience testifies: '[I]t takes time to be comfortable talking about things you have suffered, especially of a sexual nature.'[2028] That her experience stands, regardless of the state apparatus in which such disclosure takes place, is supported by the fact that survivors'/victims' reporting barriers are equally restraining in the Belgian and European context itself. For example, the EU-wide survey on

---

DN146_CGRS 1 (refusal)_1993_F_Nigeria_STFP_14/11/2023_307 592_NL_Database_p. 6., DSe093_CGRS 3 (manifestly ill-founded)_F_Serbia_DV_12/2/2022_301 311_FR_Database_p. 5., DA099_A_CGRS 1 (manifestly ill-founded)_M_Albania_DV_6/7/2023_303 553_FR_Database_p. 3., DSu147_CGRS 1 (refusal)_F_Suriname_RSA_VGNT_FM_DV_9/5/2023_301 074_NL_Database_p. 3, DSu147_CALL 1 (refusal)_F_Suriname_RSA_VGNT_FM_DV_5/2/2024_301074_NL_Database_p. 9.

2026 DGe109_CALL 1 (refusal)_F_Georgia_RSA_FM_DV_19/12/2023_303 313_NL_Database_p. 4., DGe151_CALL 1 (refusal)_2003_F_Georgia_VGNT_DV_27/03/2024_303891_NL_Database_p. 13., DGe151_CGRS 1_(refusal)_2003_F_Georgia_VGNT_DV_27/7/2023_303 891_NL_Database_p. 5., DGe138_CGRS 1 (refusal)_1998_F_Georgia_RSA_DV_27/12/2023_307 108_NL_Database_p. 5., DGe144_CALL 1 (refusal)_1985_F_Georgia_RSA_DV_29/05/2024_307 462_NL_Database_p.9. Emphasis added.

2027 NGe014_CALL 1 (manifestly ill-founded)_1975_F_Georgia_RSA_DV_16/3/2022_269 856_NL_NANSEN_p. 16.

2028 Masiya Mponela (n 267) 385.

violence against women mentioned above shows that 35% of survivors/victims have never spoken to anyone[2029] and: 'Of those women who [did] or reported the most serious incident to some authority, [...] 4% of victims contacted the police.'[2030] For Belgian citizens, the figures are similar: 'Only [...] 4% reported the incident to the police or know someone else did.'[2031] For applicants of international protection in Belgium specifically, 0% of the participants in the latter study contacted the police.[2032]

These barriers remain just as strong in so-called 'safe countries of origin' (based on their legal situation, rule of law, democratic system, and general political circumstances[2033]), let alone in countries that are not considered safe by the authorities. Specifically for the Balkan region, where most of Belgium's safe countries of origin are located,[2034] it has been reported that: 'Prevalence of domestic violence [...] is high across the [entire] region, while rates of reporting violence to institutions are very low, especially, in cases of sexual violence.'[2035] The statistics for reporting SGBV to state actors of protection for example count: 4,4% (police) and 2,8% (court/judges) of the 8,4% who sought help for domestic violence and 8,3% (police) and 4,7% (court/judges) of the 4,6% who sought help for non-partner SGBV in Albania;[2036] 5,5% (institutional support) of women subjected to SGBV in Bosnia-Herzegovina;[2037] or 10% (institutional help) of women facing domestic violence, of whom only ca. 20% assessed that these institutions helped them significantly, in Serbia.[2038]

Because help-seeking from state actors of protection is necessarily preceded by SGBV disclosure, the barriers to doing so mentioned earlier (see Part III, Chapter 3.3.2) are relevant here as well. SGBV survivors'/victims' prompt disclosure might be hampered by factors related to the memory (effects of trauma, such as recall deficit, avoidance, suppression, or minimisation of the facts[2039]), as well as external factors (fear, stigma, shame, distrust in the authorities,

2029 European Union Agency for Fundamental Rights (FRA) (n 1109) 115.
2030 *Ibid.* 116.
2031 Keygnaert and others (n 713) 40.
2032 *Ibid.* 74; De Schrijver and others (n 1110) 13.
2033 Art. 57/6/1, §3, part 2 Belgian Aliens Act.
2034 At the time of writing, consisting of: Albania, Bosnia-Herzegovina, India, Kosovo, Moldova, Montenegro, North-Macedonia, and Serbia. Art. 1 Koninklijk besluit tot uitvoering van het artikel 57/6/1, §3, vierde lid, van de wet van 15 december 1980 betreffende de toegang tot het grondgebied, het verblijf, de vestiging en de verwijdering van vreemdelingen, houdende de vastlegging van de lijst van veilige landen van herkomst.
2035 Dasa Duhacek and others, 'Women's Rights in Western Balkans' (European Parliament's Committee on Women's Rights and Gender Equality 2019) 51.
2036 *Ibid.* 46; UN Women and others, 'National Population Survey: Violence Against Women and Girls in Albania' (2019) 19–21.
2037 Duhacek and others (n 2035) 50.
2038 *Ibid.* 50–51.
2039 Herlihy (n 731) 116; Keygnaert and Linthout (n 177) 22; Rousseau and others (n 7) 50.

(self-)blame, lack of self-identification as a survivor/victim (especially for men), mental health problems, ...[2040]).

Similar barriers have been described in research on reporting SGBV to state actors specifically. Failure to report may be prompted by fear of the consequences, such as: getting (others) in trouble/danger, losing someone, mistreatment or disbelief by actors in the justice system, not achieving legal accountability for perpetrators, stigmatisation, and humiliation. Emotions or thoughts like (self-)blame, shame, guilt, minimisation, denial, or mistrust in how others will react (incl. friends, family, or the criminal justice system at large) might also inhibit SGBV reporting. The same goes for practical barriers, such as a lack of knowledge on how/where to report or evidence on the SGBV. Lastly, the circumstances of the SGBV itself might block state protection-seeking, such as: having some form of prior relationship to the perpetrator; a smaller age difference between survivor/victim and perpetrator; SGBV that was not physically violent; and SGBV occurring in the survivor's/victim's/perpetrator's home and/or under influence of alcohol/drugs.[2041]

Many of these factors were reflected in applicants' testimonies or argumentation. Mistrust in how the criminal justice system would react was for example reinforced by the (perceived) ties between perpetrators and state actors of protection in several testimonies,[2042] including those of Vera and Zeynep:

> 'I'm very afraid of him [...], he knows everyone [...]. It's a very well-known family in our town, [...] **the chief of police is the first cousin of [my ex-husband]. If you call the police, he'll know everything.** [...] They're always one step ahead of the state.'[2043] | CASE OF VERA

> '**The person who raped me was a police officer, so it wasn't possible for me to lodge a complaint.** [...] [H]e told me I could never file a complaint against him. [...] [H]e said that he has a lot of connections, [...] that he can destroy my life.'[2044] | CASE OF ZEYNEP

Others explained not being able to seek state protection due to: their physical and/or psychological isolation, hardly ever leaving the house/their room;[2045]

2040 Herlihy (n 731) 116; Keygnaert and Linthout (n 177) 22; Rousseau and others (n 7) 50.

2041 Michelle Wieberneit and others, 'Silenced Survivors: A Systematic Review of the Barriers to Reporting, Investigating, Prosecuting, and Sentencing of Adult Female Rape and Sexual Assault' (2024) 25 Trauma, Violence, & Abuse 3742, 9; Maria Hansen, Kari Stefansen and May-Len Skilbrei, 'Non-Reporting of Sexual Violence as Action: Acts, Selves, Futures in the Making' (2021) 22 Nordic Journal of Criminology 42, 44.

2042 NEr018_1985_F_Eritrea_RSA_NL_NANSEN_[00:46:36]., DGe110_CALL 1 (refusal)_lawyers' argumentation_1986_M_Georgia_VGNT_FM_27/3/2024_303 889_NL_Database_p. 7.

2043 NA016_1990_F_Albania_RSA_VGNT_DV_NL_NANSEN_[00:25:36], [00:44:12] & [00:55:15].

2044 NT015_CGRS interview 1_2_3_1996_F_Turkey_RSA_FM_DV_FR_p. 1 & 8 (memo).

2045 NS005_CGRS interview_2002_F_Senegal_RSA_DV_FM_FR_NANSEN_p. 12.

being financially dependent on parents (in a society where 'children should not interfere in their parents' fights [...] [and] are usually blamed'[2046]) or on partners;[2047] and being controlled and manipulated not to escape forced prostitution.[2048] Some applicants were explicitly threatened by their perpetrators not to report or after reporting,[2049] such as Amani's stepfather who said he would kill her if she told anyone about his sexual abuse[2050] and both Aster's and Lejla's perpetrators who had forced them into prostitution:

> 'One day, [the trafficker] [...] called us [...] and told [one of us to come closer]. When she [did], **he cut off her ear** and put it into her hand. [...] We [...] cried and screamed. He became even more aggressive. He said, 'I have **videos** of everyone [...] I will **put [them] on the internet and bring shame** on your family'. **He warned us: 'If anyone tries to escape or tell the police, this is going to happen'.** [...] The next day, **[she] disappeared.** I don't know where she was taken to.'[2051] | CASE OF ASTER

> '**I testified in court,** I could no longer speak because [he had knocked my teeth out] but answered all questions in writing. [...] **[He] threatened me and said I was safe as long as he was in prison but if he was released he would know where to find me. He said he would do much worse things to me [...]. He wanted to kill me.** I sent him and all his men to prison through my testimony.'[2052] | CASE OF LEJLA

Some applicants were reluctant to report their SGBV because it occurred in a context where they themselves were (forcibly) involved in criminal acts (or acts perceived as such), such as: giving birth to an extramarital child 'which is punishable by 100 lashes' in Iran;[2053] participating in sexual practices, as a woman, with other women in Kenya;[2054] or being active in prostitution in Italy.[2055]

2046 DGe139_CALL 1 (refusal)_lawyers' argumentation_2005_F_Georgia_DV_23/5/2024_307 109_NL_Database_p.4.

2047 DSu147_CALL 1 (refusal)_lawyers' argumentation_F_Suriname_RSA_VGNT_FM_DV_5/2/2024_301 074_NL_Database_p. 9.

2048 NE002_CALL 1 (refusal)_lawyers' argumentation_1988_F_Ethiopia_RSA_STFP_6/4/2022_270 994_NL_NANSEN_p. 7.

2049 DK152_CALL 2 (refusal)_lawyers' argumentation_1997_F_Kenya_RSA_VGNT_FM_DV_4/4/2024_304 367_NL_Database_p. 9., DN146_CALL 1 (refusal)_lawyers' argumentation_1993_F_Nigeria_STFP_31/5/2024_307 592_NL_Database_p. 9.

2050 NC004_CGRS interview 2_1991_F_DRC_RSA_DV_FR_NANSEN_p. 5.

2051 NE002_CGRS interview_1988_F_Ethiopia_RSA_STFP_NL_NANSEN_p. 7–8.

2052 DBH121_CALL 1 (annulment)_lawyers' argumentation_F_Bosnia and Herzegovina_RSA_STFP_30/4/2024_305 882_NL_Database_p. 22.

2053 DI131_CALL 1 (refusal)_lawyers' argumentation_F_Iran_VGNT_FM_DV_14/5/2024_306 520_NL_Database_p. 7.

2054 DK152_CALL 2 (refusal)_lawyers' argumentation_1997_F_Kenya_RSA_VGNT_FM_DV_4/4/2024_304 367_NL_Database_p. 11.

2055 DN146_CALL 1 (refusal)_lawyers' argumentation 1993_F_Nigeria_STFP_31/5/2024_307 592_NL_Database_p. 9.

Fear,[2056] guilt,[2057] or (self-)blame[2058] were the main reasons for applicants like Erina, Sofia, Aya, Zeynep, and Angele not to take steps towards state protection. Angele even framed police reporting as an additional problem instead of a solution:

> '[**I did not take any legal steps**], **we already had a problem** with my missing husband. [And] what was I going to tell them?'[2059] | CASE OF ANGELE

Sofia explained why she feared reporting her father as follows:

> 'I did not press charges because I was **scared, my dad was a respectable man**, it was **his word against mine**, he also knew very well what he was doing because there was **no penetration so no evidence** either.'[2060] | CASE OF SOFIA

Others stated lacking the necessary financial means[2061] or support figures (e.g. male chaperones)[2062] to access actors of state protection in the first place or feared being discriminated by them. The latter formed a barrier to seeking state protection for a trans woman of Romani ethnicity in a North-Macedonian rape/sexual assault and domestic violence case,[2063] as well as for a lesbian woman in a Kenyan rape/sexual assault, forced marriage, and domestic violence case.[2064]

The temporariness of some state protection measures has also proven to be a reporting barrier for the applicants in this research, increasingly weighing on their help-seeking efforts over time.[2065] Diana for example managed to obtain a temporary protection order for six months for herself, but not for her children or parents, who were equally threatened by her ex-husband. She testified:

> '[**The protection order had to be renewed every**] **six months**. [...] The first [time] he breached it, I told the police. [...] He broke [...] the windows, he threw

2056 NA001_B_1973_F_Albania_RSA_VGNT_FM_DV_NL_NANSEN_[00:34:17].,NS005_CGRS interview_2002_F_Senegal_RSA_DV_FM_FR_NANSEN_p.13., NSy019_CGRS interview_1997_F_Syria_RSA_FR_NANSEN_p. 13.

2057 NT015_CGRS interview 1_2_3_1996_F_Turkey_RSA_FM_DV_FR_p. 1–2 (memo).

2058 DGe139_CALL 1 (refusal)_lawyers' argumentation_2005_F_Georgia_DV_23/5/2024_307 109_NL_Database_p. 3–4.

2059 NC006_CGRS interview 3_1984_F_DRC_RSA_FR_NANSEN_p. 16.

2060 NH003_1991_F_Honduras_RSA_DV_NL_NANSEN_p. 3.

2061 NG012_1987_F_Guinea_RSA_GMC_FM_FR_NANSEN_[01:12:07].

2062 NG012_1987_F_Guinea_RSA_GMC_FM_FR_NANSEN_[01:10:12]., DGe138_CALL 1 (refusal)_lawyers' argumentation_1998_F_Georgia_RSA_DV_23/5/2024_307 108_NL_Database_p. 7.

2063 DNM117_CALL 1 (annulment)_lawyers' argumentation_1974_F (trans)_North-Macedonia_RSA_VGNT_DV_24/4/2024_305 445_NL_Database_p. 5.

2064 DK152_CALL 2 (refusal)_lawyers' argumentation_1997_F_Kenya_RSA_VGNT_FM_DV_4/4/2024_304 367_NL_Database_p. 11.

2065 NGe014_CALL 1 (manifestly ill-founded)_lawyers' argumentation_1975_F_Georgia_RSA_DV_16/3/2022_269 856_NL_NANSEN_p. 9.

> things, […] glass. […] So I wanted to renew the protection order […] [but] when I went to **court […] they told me: "You have to go to the police." […] And the police, they told me: You have to go to a judge," back and forth, two, three times.'**[2066] | CASE OF DIANA

In addition, applicants' general mistrust in the effectiveness of state actors' response, due to: social norms considering SGBV a family/community matter, corruption, or passivity/insensitivity towards such violence, were often reflected in applicants' testimonies too.[2067] In a Guinean forced marriage case, the applicant explained: 'We'll sort it out within the family or we'll turn to God. […] Because my father can say "I'm the one who […] raised [my child] and […] will decide what to do".'[2068] Mary, who was forced to take over from her mother as a female GMC practitioner in Liberia, explained:

> '**The government** […] **will say it's family business** […]. **Tradition is tradition** […] [and **politicians who**] **want to be in power** […] [**and**] **want people to vote** […] **won't go against the traditional leaders in Liberia.** […] [**Going to the police**] […] **is useless,** […] you just waste your time.'[2069] | CASE OF MARY

Such mistrust might also originate specifically from applicants' or others' negative experiences, equally constituting a barrier to do so (again) in the future. Literature on optimism bias[2070] (see chapter 8.2), through which potential survivors/victims 'in general perceive themselves as less likely than their peers to be sexually assaulted,' stresses that this bias significantly decreases with negative experiences of SGBV itself and of disclosing/reporting it.[2071]

Because those with a SGBV history and negative help-seeking experiences afterwards tend to 'perceive a decreased sense of control and increased sense of vulnerability,'[2072] even minor negative events may 'undermine a person's

---

2066 NA001_B_1973_F_Albania_RSA_VGNT_FM_DV_NL_NANSEN_[00:47:26].

2067 NT015_CGRS interview 1_2_3_1996_F_Turkey_RSA_FM_DV_FR_p. 10 (memo)., NA016_1990_F_Albania_RSA_VGNT_DV_NL_NANSEN_[00:33:59]., NG012_1987_F_Guinea_RSA_GMC_FM_FR_NANSEN_[01:14:17]., NGe014_1975_F_Georgia_RSA_DV_NL_NANSEN_[00:21:38]., NC004_CGRS interview 2 1991_F_DRC_RSA_DV_FR_NANSEN_p. 10., DGe139_CALL 1 (refusal)_lawyers' argumentation_2005_F_Georgia_DV_23/5/2024_307 109_NL_Database_p. 3., DGe151_CALL 1 (refusal)_lawyers' argumentation_2003_F_Georgia_VGNT_DV_27/3/2024_303 891_NL_Database_p. 7–8., DSo069_CALL 1 (recognition)_lawyers' argumentation_F_Somalia_GMC_VGNT_FM_DV_8/3/2024_302 889_NL_Case law selection by CALL_p.13., NE002_CGRS interview_1988_F_Ethiopia_RSA_STFP_NL_NANSEN_p. 15.

2068 NG012_1987_F_Guinea_RSA_GMC_FM_FR_NANSEN_[01:14:17].

2069 NL017_1980_F_Liberia_STFP_GMC_VGNT_FM_NL_NANSEN_[01:04:19], [01:13:26] & [01:22:58].

2070 Gidycz, McNamara and Edwards (n 1355) 452; Evans Cameron, 'Risk Theory and "Subjective Fear"' (n 1366) 573.

2071 Gidycz, McNamara and Edwards (n 1355) 450.

2072 *Ibid.* 444.

"protection motivation" and lead to "precaution abandonment".[2073] This knowledge is of utmost importance when assessing the credibility of SGBV survivors'/victims' help-seeking behaviour. As Evans Cameron notes, the fact that they might 'come to believe that [they] simply cannot affect the risks [they face]' might contrast sharply with the kinds of risk-reducing measures, such as seeking state protection before fleeing, expected by asylum authorities.[2074]

Applicants in this research based their sense of helplessness towards perpetrators and loss of trust in authorities on previous experiences such as: early release of perpetrators from prison;[2075] forced withdrawal of complaints against them;[2076] merely formal registration of complaints without concrete consequences;[2077] refusal to register complaints as such,[2078] to collect evidence,[2079] to issue protection orders,[2080] to start an investigation or prosecute,[2081] or to arrest perpetrators;[2082] ignoring survivors'/victims' wishes to avoid any contact with perpetrators;[2083] revictimisation due to sexually transgressive behaviour by police;[2084] and persistent threats or revictimisation despite moving to an SGBV shelter[2085] or protection orders.[2086] The impact of the latter experience was aptly described by Diana and Nino:

> '**He wanted to beat me up and he started breaking everything, everything, everywhere, everything. It wasn't a house anymore.** [...] I called the police and while I was talking to [them], he started talking [...] *speaks in an agitated manner* [...] **He wanted to ... *makes the gesture of strangulation*, he tried to ... to ...** and like a miracle I ... And then he was gone [...]. **When the police came, I [...] [asked**

2073 Evans Cameron, 'Risk Theory and "Subjective Fear"' (n 1366) 580.

2074 *Ibid.*

2075 DEc120_CALL 1 (refusal)_lawyers' argumentation_1981_F_Ecuador_RSA_DV_29/4/2024_305 805_NL_Database_p. 10.

2076 DG092_CALL 1 (refusal)_lawyers' argumentation_F_Guinea_RSA_VGNT_FM_DV_4/1/2024_299 471_FR_Database_p. 6., DB068_CALL 1 (annulment)_lawyers' argumentation_1975_F_Bolivia_RSA_DV_23/2/2024_302 134_NL_Case law selection by CALL_p. 4.

2077 NA001_A_B_2006_F_Albania_RSA_VGNT_FM_DV_NL_NANSEN_MINOR_[00:28:57]., NEr018_1985_F_Eritrea_RSA_NL_NANSEN_[00:51:47].

2078 NC006_CGRSinterview3_1984_F_DRC_RSA_FR_NANSEN_p.14.,DA118_CALL1 (refusal)_lawyers' argumentation_F_Albania_STFP_DV_24/4/2024_305 447_NL_Database_p. 7.

2079 NA001_A_B_2006_F_Albania_RSA_VGNT_FM_DV_NL_NANSEN_MINOR_[00:18:41].

2080 NA001_A_B_2006_F_Albania_RSA_VGNT_FM_DV_NL_NANSEN_MINOR_[00:44:14].

2081 DBH121_CALL 1 (annulment)_lawyers' argumentation_F_Bosnia and Herzegovina_RSA_STFP_30/4/2024_305 882_NL_Database_p. 17.

2082 NA001_A_B_2006_F_Albania_RSA_VGNT_FM_DV_NL_NANSEN_MINOR_[00:51:17] & [00:06:24].

2083 NA001_A_B_2006_F_Albania_RSA_VGNT_FM_DV_NL_NANSEN_MINOR_[01:10:20].

2084 NT015_CGRS interview 1_2_3_1996_F_Turkey_RSA_FM_DV_FR_p. 7 (memo).

2085 DBH121_CALL 1 (annulment)_lawyers' argumentation_F_Bosnia and Herzegovina_RSA_STFP_30/4/2024_305 882_NL_Database_p. 17.

2086 NA001_A_B_2006_F_Albania_RSA_VGNT_FM_DV_NL_NANSEN_MINOR_[00:06:24]., DEc120_CALL 1 (refusal)_lawyers' argumentation_1981_F_Ecuador_RSA_DV_29/4/2024_305 805_NL_Database_p. 10.

them] to come [...] and see, to take photos ... they told me: "No, you're coming downstairs"'.[2087] | CASE OF DIANA

'**[All the police] gave [me] was [an order] that he couldn't [...] get within 50 metres [of me], but he didn't care**, he came, he burnt cigarettes [on me], put [my] hand in the oven [and] threatened his daughter that "if she doesn't come back, your mother, I'm going to behead her" [...]. He really has to [...] shoot or strangle you. **He has to kill you before [they] can do something. [...] The judge told me I was making up stories,** [...] 'Why should I believe you?"'[2088] | CASE OF NINO

Instead of establishing the availability of formal state protection (as often argued by asylum authorities, see Chapter 3.1.3 above), such experiences may also serve as proof of the severity of past persecution and non-effectiveness of state responses to it. Such proof is essential when applying the abovementioned burden of proof reversal, where asylum authorities have to establish good reasons that such persecution will not recur (see Part III, Chapter 2.2.3).[2089] The same counts for perpetrators' criminal records, which are often selectively used to argue for effective state protection, while they may also prove perpetrators' history of violence and therefore applicants' future risk. In addition, as in Diana and Erina's case, while their ex-husband/father did have an extensive criminal record, none of his convictions concerned the rape, domestic violence, stalking, and breaching of protection orders suffered by the applicants.[2090]

b) The Use of COI on Effectiveness of State Protection against SGBV

Whether state protection is in fact accessible, effective, and non-temporary, depends on each country of origin's specific context. When certain contexts do allow for *de facto* protection against SGBV, it must be recognised that the state protection myth is not necessarily or always untrue. Like with the resourcefulness myth (Part III, Chapter 2.2), this nuance is reflected in the indication of the state protection myth with an asterisk/* in the figures of this research. As such, state protection myth-based argumentation may be used, under the strict condition that it is supported by accurate, up-to-date, SGBV-, and region-specific COI confirming the state's accessible, effective, and non-temporary protection against SGBV.

2087 NA001_B_1973_F_Albania_RSA_VGNT_FM_DV_NL_NANSEN_[00:53:23].

2088 NGe014_1975_F_Georgia_RSA_DV_NL_NANSEN_[00:07:23].

2089 This provision reverses the burden of proof where applicants have experienced or feared persecution in the past. In such cases, previous threats with or acts of persecution or serious harm directly aimed at applicants clearly indicate the well-foundedness of their fear, unless the asylum authorities substantiate that there are good reasons to believe that such persecution or serious harm will not recur. Art. 48/7 Belgian Aliens Act; Art. 4(4) EU Qualification Directive; Art. 4(4) EU Qualification Regulation; Denys (n 43) 626.

2090 NA001_A_B_2006_F_Albania_RSA_VGNT_FM_DV_NL_NANSEN_MINOR_[00:26:42].

As mentioned earlier, it should again be stressed that such information is not always available. If it is, authorities must take into account the abovementioned barriers to SGBV disclosure and reporting, which substantially obstruct truthful documentation of SGBV prevalence, complaints, and condemnations. This means that existing SGBV statistics and figures are most likely underestimates.[2091] Therefore, COI reports may be useful for observing public and/or widespread events. However, they are often neither designed nor suitable for assessing private, intangible, or sensitive phenomena, such as the prevalence of SGBV (complaints/condemnations), gender norms, or power relations.[2092]

The risk that refugee status determination is based on an inaccurate representation of reality is all the greater when the COI used focuses solely on *de jure* protection (e.g. laws or policies) without any nuance on the *de facto* barriers to obtaining it. Such access barriers were highlighted, for example, by the empirical evidence in COI used by lawyers in an Albanian and Senegalese case. They stated: '[I]t is even more difficult for women to access protection from national authorities' in Albania[2093] or '[Women] face numerous difficulties to access justice due to illiteracy, the lack of knowledge of their rights [...], the poor geographical distribution of institutions throughout the country, the high costs of legal proceedings and the delays in the Senegalese justice system.'[2094]

Other applicants(' lawyers) provided empirical information showing that, while the laws in their countries offer theoretical protection from SGBV, their implementation in practice is ineffective[2095] (due to a lack of resources, capacity, awareness, and knowledge about SGBV among state actors[2096]), SGBV prevalence rates remain high,[2097] or survivors'/victims' situation after transgressing gender norms remains precarious.[2098] Regarding legislation that in theory criminalises acts of SGBV, Zeynep stated:

> 'I firmly believe that in Turkey, the laws are made [...] and are on the side of men. [...] In this country, you can abuse women [...] and get away with it. These are things

2091 Herlihy (n 731) 128.

2092 *College 3 Rechtspsychologie: Wie is het? Het toetsen van levensverhalen in asielzaken* (n 166).

2093 DA118_CALL 1 (refusal)_lawyers' argumentation_F_Albania_STFP_DV_24/4/2024_305447_NL_Database_p. 7.

2094 DS088_CALL 1 (refusal)_lawyers' argumentation_F_Senegal_RSA_GMC_VGNT_FM_DV_28/5/2024_307 398_FR_Database_p. 14.

2095 DSu147_CALL 1 (refusal)_lawyers' argumentation_F_Suriname_RSA_VGNT_FM_DV_5/2/2024_301 074_NL_Database_p. 9.

2096 DGe139_CALL 1 (refusal)_lawyers' argumentation_2005_F_Georgia_DV_23/5/2024_307 109_NL_Database_p. 5.

2097 DIC074_CALL 1 (annulment)_lawyers' argumentation_F_Ivory Coast_GMC_VGNT_11/3/2024_302 979_FR_Case law selection by CALL_p. 5.

2098 DM116_CALL 1 (refusal)_lawyers' argumentation_1999_F_Morocco_VGNT_FM_DV_24/4/2024_305 429_NL_Database_p. 7.

we hear every day. **When that policeman raped me, he knew that the laws** [...] **and people's attitudes would be on his side.**'[2099] | CASE OF ZEYNEP

In some cases, the authorities were even explicitly called out for their incomplete reading or selective use of empirical evidence in COI.[2100] Lawyers for example countered authorities' assessments that state protection would be effective with elaborate information to the contrary, sometimes from the CGRS' own COI reports.[2101] In Elene's case, her lawyer for example argued:

> '[The CGRS'] **"optimistic" reports** are **contradicted** by [...] recent rulings by the [**ECtHR and CEDAW,**] [...] finding that **the police in Georgia systematically failed to provide protection against gender-related violence** [...] and "**a generalised and discriminatory legal inaction** that creates an environment in which **domestic violence thrives**" [...]. Furthermore, even the Georgian **authorities themselves** recently had to **admit** that there is still **much work** [...] to protect women victims of domestic violence.'[2102] | CASE OF ELENE

In other cases, the authorities are being criticised for not using any SGBV-specific empirical evidence in COI at all.[2103] In Erina's case for example, her lawyer argued:

> '[T]he [CGRS] has **not provided any information on the situation and protection of** persons like her, namely **women/girls who are victims of domestic violence in Albania**, and the information submitted by her is not effectively contradicted.'[2104] | CASE OF ERINA

3.2.2. REBUTTAL IN LAW & LEGAL SCIENCES

As illustrated above in Figure 26, by expanding the concept of 'reasonable state protection' to be exhausted by survivors/victims, the Belgian authorities seem to move away from the notion of 'protection as result' towards 'protection as intent'. The *contra legem* nature of this interpretational shift is demonstrated by the

2099 NT015_CGRS interview 1_2_3_1996_F_Turkey_RSA_FM_DV_FR_p. 1 (memo).

2100 DA118_CALL 1 (refusal)_lawyers' argumentation_F_Albania_STFP_DV_24/4/2024_305 447_NL_Database_p. 7.

2101 DGe139_CALL 1 (refusal)_lawyers' argumentation_2005_F_Georgia_DV_23/5/2024_307 109_NL_Database_p. 3.

2102 DGe151_CALL 1 (refusal)_lawyers' argumentation_2003_F_Georgia_VGNT_DV_27/3/2024_303 891_NL_Database_p. 7.

2103 DS088_CALL 1 (refusal)_lawyers' argumentation_F_Senegal_RSA_GMC_VGNT_FM_DV_28/5/2024_307 398_FR_Database_p. 14.

2104 NA001_A_CALL 2 (refusal)_lawyers' argumentation_2006_F_Albania_RSA_VGNT_FM_DV_8/5/2024_306 251_NL_NANSEN_MINOR_p. 5.

preparatory works of the EU Qualification Directive defining 'state protection'.[2105] These clearly explain that 'mere "willingness to protect" is not sufficient [...]. Moreover, even actors who are willing and able in principle to provide protection but not providing it in reality or [...] only on a [...] temporary basis are excluded from the scope of the concept.'[2106]

Another *contra legem* practice lies in adding conditions for refugee recognition to the existing definition, such as requiring that the host country, such as Belgium, can offer absolute protection against the type of violence feared (regardless of the actor of persecution) or that applicants exhaust all possible pathways to state protection before fleeing (regardless of their reasonableness or applicants' justification for not wanting/being able to do so). The latter requirement specifically conflicts with the future-oriented nature of state protection assessments, based on general '[COI] obtained from relevant and available [EU and (inter)national] sources,' regardless of whether individual applicants' have tested these *in concreto*.[2107]

Furthermore, state protection is described in EU and Belgian law as 'operating an effective legal system for the detection, prosecution and punishment of acts constituting persecution.'[2108] Knowing this, the direct legal relevance of mere policy efforts, such as trainings, awareness raising, healthcare/legal aid centres, databases, research monitoring, action plans, ... for refugee status determination can be seriously questioned. Moreover, the Belgian authorities' interpretation that state protection should be 'effective but not absolute' cannot serve as a free pass for authorities to dismiss any of applicants' personal experiences suggesting the ineffectiveness of state protection or justifications for not wanting/being able to avail themselves to it. This would lead to a purely formalistic implementation of the concept of state protection, which goes against authorities' obligation to individually assess applications for international protection,[2109] obliging decision makers to take into account applicants' personal circumstances (i.e. their background, gender, and age).

This formalistic approach to state protection, rejecting gendered justifications for not seeking state protection against SGBV, has been addressed in a Council of Europe report on articles 60 and 61 of the Istanbul Convention. It explicitly confirms: 'Where the state has a law prohibiting a persecutory practice it will

2105 Art. 7(1)–(2) EU Qualification Directive; Art. 7(1)–(2) EU Qualification Regulation.

2106 Proposal for a Directive of the European Parliament and of the Council on minimum standards for the qualification and status of third country nationals or stateless persons as beneficiaries of international protection and the content of the protection granted (n 1725) 7. Emphasis added.

2107 Art. 7(3) EU Qualification Directive; Art. 7(3) EU Qualification Regulation.

2108 Art. 7(1)–(2) EU Qualification Directive; Art. 7(1)–(2) EU Qualification Regulation; Art. 48/5, §2, part 2 Belgian Aliens Act.

2109 Art. 4(3)c EU Qualification Directive; Art. 4(3) EU Qualification Regulation; Art. 34(2)d EU Asylum Procedures Regulation; Art. 48/6, §5, c] Belgian Aliens Act.

not constitute "effective protection" [...] unless it is enforced effectively.'[2110] The report proposes measures to ensure such effective enforcement, such as: prompt and effective investigations, risk assessment and management to ensure survivors'/victims' safety (e.g. through enforced protection orders), continuation of proceedings even if the complaint is withdrawn ...[2111] This assessment should also consider the impact of any custody/visitation rights and/or complaints for international child abduction on local authorities' willingness/ability to protect applicants. While this is beyond the scope of current research, asylum authorities should correctly apply private international law to assess the potential conflict of interest in such situations.

As illustrated above, while COI on effective state protection against SGBV often seems to overrule applicants' individual experiences/justifications suggesting the opposite, COI brought up by applicants on ineffective state protection is conversely dismissed because it is insufficiently individualised and therefore irrelevant. As mentioned earlier, this double standard conflicts with the provision in EU refugee law that state protection assessments should take into account general '[COI] obtained from relevant and available [EU and (inter) national] sources.'[2112]

Also mentioned earlier, in both the *A.H. & F.N.* and *K.L. cases*, the CJEU has already pronounced itself on the types of COI to be considered by decision makers in SGBV-related procedures for international protection, namely 'precise and up-to-date information'[2113] with 'relevance for the examination of women's applications for refugee status.' It specifically names information relevant to state protection assessments, such as: women's position before the law; their political, social, and economic rights; the cultural and social mores and consequences for transgressing these; prevalence and forms of SGBV reported; protection available to survivors/victims; penalties imposed on perpetrators; and risks that (potential) survivors/victims might face upon return after fleeing and applying for international protection.[2114]

Lastly, concerning the worryingly high SGBV prevalence and low reporting rates in so-called 'safe countries of origin' as demonstrated above, it is relevant to name another CJEU ruling. In the *C.V. case*, the Court explicitly and clearly ruled that 'a third country [is precluded] from being designated as a safe country of origin where certain parts of its territory do not satisfy the material conditions for such designation,'[2115] i.e. are not considered 'safe', based on their legal

2110 Council of Europe (CoE) and Hooper (n 1049) 24.

2111 *Ibid.* 25.

2112 Art. 7(3) EU Qualification Directive; Art. 7(3) EU Qualification Regulation.

2113 *AH & FN v. Bundesamt für Fremdenwesen und Asyl* (n 82) para 52; *K.L. v. Staatssecretaris van Justitie en Veiligheid* (n 78) para 60.

2114 UNHCR, 'Guidelines on International Protection No. 1' (n 35) para 36; *WS v. Intervyuirasht organ na Darzhavna agentsia za bezhantsite pri Ministerskia savet* (n 44) para 61.

2115 *CV v. Ministerstvo vnitra České republiky, Odbor azylové a migrační politiky* (n 559) [Ruling 2].

situation, rule of law, democratic system, and general political circumstances.[2116] In other words, if one part of a country is not safe (e.g. from persecution, such as SGBV), its entire territory cannot be labelled a 'safe country of origin' either.

The above-described expertise on barriers to help-seeking from state actors has been reflected in guidelines and recommendations of for example UNHCR, the International Commission of Jurists (ICJ), or CEDAW. The ICJ confirms that it is not inherently 'natural' for survivors/victims to immediately disclose/report SGBV, '[i]nstead survivors are often afraid of reporting the crime because of stigma and shame. If the perpetrator is someone the survivor knows personally, as is often the case, it can be even more difficult to report the crime.'[2117] CEDAW goes on that it is often unrealistic to expect SGBV survivors/victims to seek state protection before fleeing, especially as they might 'lack confidence in the justice system and access to justice or fear abuse, harassment or retaliation for making such complaints.'[2118] Not reporting SGBV before fleeing should therefore 'not prejudice [their] asylum claim, especially where [SGBV] is tolerated or there is a pattern of failure in responding to women's complaints.'[2119]

UNHCR then draws the link between these barriers to seeking state protection and underreporting in COI: 'Stigma attached to [SGBV] contributes to incidents going unreported. People may not report [...] to the authorities, or the authorities in certain countries may be unwilling to issue documentation about what they consider taboo.'[2120] As mentioned earlier, the assumption that SGBV is a rare or deviant event[2121] may hinder a critical attitude towards lower statistics of such violence in COI. As such, UNHCR and the UN Inter-Agency Standing Committee (IASC) have reminded that SGBV is underreported worldwide and that it is virtually impossible to get an accurate view on the magnitude of the problem. Therefore, SGBV should be assumed to take place and should be recognised as 'a serious and life-threatening protection issue, regardless of the presence or absence of concrete and reliable evidence.'[2122]

Consequently, UNHCR urges asylum authorities in SGBV-related procedures to resort to alternative types of evidence, such as similarly situated survivors'/victims' testimonies, as the usual information (e.g. COI) is less/not accurate or available due to under-reporting and/or lack of prosecution.[2123] For the Belgian context specifically, UNHCR confirmed that an absence or lack of COI on SGBV

2116 Art. 57/6/1, §3, part 2 Belgian Aliens Act.
2117 International Commission of Jurists (ICJ) (n 1049) 14.
2118 CEDAW, 'General Recommendation No. 32: The Gender-Related Dimensions of Refugee Status, Asylum, Nationality and Statelessness of Women' (n 34) para 29.
2119 *Ibid.*
2120 UNHCR, 'Beyond Proof. Credibility Assessment in EU Asylum Systems (Full Report)' (n 19) 73.
2121 Payne, Lonsway and Fitzgerald (n 134) 36.
2122 UNHCR and Inter-Agency Standing Committee (IASC) (n 753) 12.
2123 UNHCR, 'Guidelines on International Protection No. 1' (n 35) para 37.

does not imply a lack of persecution, nor effective state protection against it, requiring to take into account the application's individual and contextual circumstances.[2124]

CEDAW confirms that effective state protection requires, next to formal criminalisation of SGBV, effective prevention, punishment and compensation for SGBV. Its General Recommendation No. 35 confirms that states' failure to take appropriate preventive measures against, to investigate, to prosecute, to punish, and to provide reparations for SGBV equals tacit permission or even encouragement to perpetrate such violence.[2125] As summarised by UNHCR: 'Even though a [...] State may have prohibited a persecutory practice [...], [it] may nevertheless continue to condone or tolerate the practice, or may not be able to stop the practice effectively. In such cases, the practice would still amount to persecution.'[2126]

The above outlined barriers to (timely) accessing and reporting SGBV to state actors of protection have made their way into international legal guidelines/recommendations and scholarship too.[2127] These for example mention: shame, stigmatisation,[2128] fear of rejection or reprisals,[2129] distrust in institutions[2130] (due to systematic lack of response to SGBV[2131]), social isolation,[2132] self-blame, lack of self-identification as a survivor/victim,[2133] mental health issues,[2134] and family pressure not to report.[2135]

2124 UNHCR, 'Note Du Haut Commissariat Des Nations Unies Pour Les Réfugiés Relative à l'évaluation Des Demandes d'asile Introduites Par Des Femmes' (n 751) 2.

2125 CEDAW, 'CEDAW General Recommendation No. 35: Gender-Based Violence against Women, Updating General Recommendation No. 19' (2017) 9.

2126 UNHCR, 'Guidelines on International Protection No. 1' (n 35) 4.

2127 United Nations Office on Drugs and Crime (UNODC) and Skinnider (n 161) 25; Crawley and Lester (n 1813) 55; Peroni (n 33) 355.

2128 European Union Agency for Fundamental Rights (FRA) (n 1109) 114; Council of Europe (CoE) and Hooper (n 1049) 37; CEDAW, 'General Recommendation No. 32: The Gender-Related Dimensions of Refugee Status, Asylum, Nationality and Statelessness of Women' (n 34) para 25; United Nations Office on Drugs and Crime (UNODC) and Skinnider (n 161) 17 and 25; International Commission of Jurists (ICJ) (n 1049) 12; Craig (n 1051) 7; Middelburg and Balta (n 8) 443; Lamonaca and others (n 280) 13–14.

2129 Singer (n 8) 109; Bloemen and Mellink (n 932) 891; UNHCR, 'Beyond Proof. Credibility Assessment in EU Asylum Systems (Full Report)' (n 19) 72.

2130 Middelburg and Balta (n 8) 443; Baillot, Cowan and Munro, '"Hearing the Right Gaps"' (n 92) 281; Bloemen and Mellink (n 932) 891; Keygnaert and others (n 969) 13–14; Bogner, Herlihy and Brewin (n 934) 75; Lamonaca and others (n 280) 13–14; Pertek, Phillimore and Goodson (n 997) 18; Magugliani (n 93) 5 and 11.

2131 Peroni (n 33) 355; United Nations Office on Drugs and Crime (UNODC) and Skinnider (n 161) 17; Lamonaca and others (n 280) 14.

2132 Saroléa, Raimondo and Crine (n 93) 80–81; Josse (n 936) 177–186; GAMS België vzw (n 937) 4.

2133 Magugliani (n 93) 11.

2134 Craig (n 1051) 7; Council of Europe (CoE) and Hooper (n 1049) 38–39; Keygnaert and Linthout (n 177) 22; Rousseau and others (n 7) 50; UN Voluntary Fund for Victims of Torture (n 731) 9.

2135 United Nations Office on Drugs and Crime (UNODC) and Skinnider (n 161) 17; Singer (n 8) 105; Lamonaca and others (n 280) 13.

These barriers do not simply disappear through legislative and policy efforts to combat SGBV, '*On ne change pas la société par décret*,' as Brems puts it.[2136] For example, laws criminalising culturally embedded SGBV, such as female GMC, exist in most countries where the practice is still widespread, due to their limited implementation and effectiveness.[2137] Hathaway and Foster highlight a good practice example from the Federal Court of Canada, ruling: 'It cannot be said that a state is making "serious efforts" to protect women merely by making due diligence preparations to do so,' such as creating ombudspersons to investigate police malfunctioning in response to SGBV, initiating commissions of inquiry on the reality of SGBV, or organise trainings on gender equality for police, which 'are not evidence of effective state protection.'[2138]

As such, the critique on asylum authorities' 'formalistic due diligence standard', particularly in SGBV cases, has been voiced in legal scholarship too.[2139] Where legislative/policy efforts appear to be yielding (slow and gradual) progress, the state's willingness and ability to protect survivors/victims is too quickly considered proven. However, such efforts can only signal willingness, not ability to protect.[2140] In fact, 'a variety of factors, entirely unconnected to willingness, can explain a state's inability in practice to protect, including entrenched cultural, social, or religious mores which are difficult to change.'[2141]

Furthermore, rather than the state apparatus' level of functioning, survivors'/victims' help-seeking behaviour from state actors will depend on the sensitivity, severity, and other individual circumstances of the SGBV feared/experienced.[2142] This idea that the more functional their country of origin is (perceived) (e.g. safe countries of origin), the more applicants can be expected to have reported SGBV, has been criticised by Amnesty International too. Concretely, in the context of the Dutch asylum procedure, it has warned that qualifying countries as 'safe', where SGBV prevalence is nevertheless high and reporting rates are low, might risk 'fundamentally undermining access to a fair, effective and individual asylum procedure.'[2143] More generally, Vogelaar also points at the risks of selective use of COI in national designation of safe countries of origin.[2144]

2136 Translated: 'You can't change society by decree'. Eva Brems, '"Strong Women Don't Need Asylum" (the European Court on FGM)' (*Strasbourg Observers*, 19 August 2010), https://strasbourgobservers.com/2010/08/19/strong-women-dont-need-asylum-the-european-court-on-fgm/.

2137 *Ibid.*

2138 Hathaway and Foster (n 1729) 317.

2139 *Ibid.* 311; Peroni (n 33) 353.

2140 Peroni (n 33) 354.

2141 Hathaway and Foster (n 1729) 311–312.

2142 Roels, 'How Protecting Your Daughter Can Lead You to Being Denied International Protection in Belgium' (n 1048).

2143 Amnesty International Nederalnd and instituut voor Mensenrechten en Medisch Onderzoek (iMMO) (n 993) 60–61.

2144 Vogelaar (n 88) 110.

Legal scholarship has also recognised the problems arising when having to rely on SGBV-specific COI in asylum procedures. These scholars identify a first challenge in the private nature of many SGBV forms. Reports used as COI tend to focus on public forms of persecution to demonstrate the general human rights situation in a country. A study by Asylum Aid points out that 'information on women's human rights in country reports often constitutes only a paragraph unless the report is specifically focused on women.'[2145] The reason for this is not necessarily a disinterest in gender issues, but also the fact that 'the forms of persecution women suffer from are often hidden and take place in private. There is simply less public information [...] and it is therefore more difficult to access.'[2146] Vogelaar confirmed that the lack of COI 'seems to be a particular problem with regard to gender issues.'[2147]

As a second issue, analyses of phenomena such as social norms, gender roles[2148] and gendered power relations[2149] are less available in mainstream COI because they are less tangible and measurable. This lack of information can hinder asylum authorities in making informed refugee status determinations. Third, the particularly sensitive nature of SGBV experiences may lead to deep-rooted social or self-stigma and taboo, preventing disclosure, reporting, and eventually documentation of the issue.[2150] In sum, instead of relying on the state protection myth, asylum authorities should base their assessments of such protection on applicants' individual experiences with/access to such protection, on SGBV prevalence/conviction rates, and on other up-to-date, region-, and SGBV-specific COI on its *de facto* effectiveness, while assuming that the available information underestimates the problem in reality.

3.2.3. REBUTTAL BY BELGIAN ASYLUM AUTHORITIES

The above set out rebuttal in law and health/social/legal sciences of the state protection myth has to some extent trickled down into the Belgian asylum authorities' thinking patterns and practices. Below, I will first discuss how asylum officials rebut the different state protection myth forms, by 1) unlinking non-reporting and non-credibility ('non-exhaustion of state protection does not imply non-credibility' and 2) unlinking non-reporting and ill-foundedness ('exhaustion of all state protection is not a condition for refugee status determination/recognition' and 'non-exhaustion of state protection does

2145 Collier (n 88) 11.
2146 Ali, Querton and Soulard (n 8) 69.
2147 Vogelaar (n 88) 110.
2148 Collier (n 88) 11.
2149 Crawley, 'Gender, "Refugee Women" and the Politics of Protection' (n 89) 364.
2150 UNHCR, 'Beyond Proof. Credibility Assessment in EU Asylum Systems (Full Report)' (n 19) 73.

not imply ill-foundedness'). Then, I will specifically describe 3) the Belgian asylum authorities' tolerance towards applicants' justifications for not wanting/being able to access state protection or to rely on it due to its ineffectiveness or temporariness.

a) Non-Reporting of SGBV and Credibility

On the link between non-reporting of SGBV and credibility, some interviewed asylum officials,[2151] such as this gender-specialised supervisor at the CGRS, stated: 'It is [...] not because no complaint has been lodged that it would not be credible.'[2152] One attaché at the CALL said: 'I never saw the magistrate I was working for using this argument in the credibility analysis.'[2153] Some based this rebuttal on what they know about the help-seeking behaviour of SGBV survivors/victims in Belgium or Europe.[2154]

One attaché at the CALL for example admitted that they used to label non-rporting as 'abnormal'. However, 'when you listen to rape victims here in Europe, where there's a lot of freedom, women know how to make a complaint, [...] you still hear [them] saying "I didn't dare [to]" or "I [only did so] later"', which made them and colleagues more sensitive.[2155] One CGRS PO only showed such sensitivity towards survivors/victims in Europe. When explicitly asked whether they would extend this conclusion to, for example, a woman in Ivory Coast who had experienced domestic violence but did not file a complaint, they replied negatively: 'I don't find it very credible to cross the Mediterranean [...] before going to the police in your own country.'[2156]

b) Non-Reporting of SGBV and Well-Foundedness

On the link between non-reporting of SGBV and well-foundedness, others explicitly disagreed with the idea that applicants have to exhaust all possible state protection in order to be assessed and/or recognised as a refugee, regardless of the reasonability or success rate of such protection.[2157] One judge firmly stated: 'It makes no sense to [...] criticise someone for not going to the authorities, if you know [...] that [this protection] doesn't work.'[2158] There were two cases (a Guinean and Iraqi case above), in which the CALL recognised the applicants as refugees, and generally established that applicants' help-seeking behaviour from

2151 RB002_CALL_Attaché_[00:32:43].
2152 CB008_CGRS_Supervisor + PO_GENDER_[00:16:41].
2153 RB002_CALL_Attaché_[00:36:46].
2154 CB008_CGRS_Supervisor + PO_GENDER_[00:16:41].
2155 RB007_CALL_Attaché_[00:27:06].
2156 CB013_CGRS_PO_[01:04:58].
2157 CB006_CGRS_PO_[00:41:44]., RB001_CALL_Judge_[00:20:32].
2158 RB006_CALL_Judge_[00:46:28].

authorities should be taken into account, as well as the authorities' response (when applicable), but that this is not the only relevant factor to assess state protection. The Council continued: '[W]here […] individual circumstances […] or general information […] show that any procedure would have been futile or ineffective or that there was no protection available offering reasonable prospects of success and capable of providing […] redress […], [the applicant] cannot be required to have turned to [the] authorities.'[2159]

Some asylum officials explicitly recognised that non-exhaustion of state protection does not necessarily imply ill-foundedness in SGBV-related cases. One judge confirmed that 'there may be situations where it is justified […] to have fled directly without going to the authorities, even if they are functioning well.'[2160] Exceptionally, this reasoning is extended to safe countries of origin, for example by two judges stating: 'Albanian society is […] even more than […] patriarchal […]. It [is] illusory to obtain protection from the authorities [against SGBV] […]. It is […] common sense, really'[2161] or: '[In] Albania […] the state functions, but there are still a lot of documented failures [to offer protection against SGBV].'[2162] Below, I will discuss rebuttal of the state protection myth on well-foundedness in relation to each of the legal conditions for reasonable state protection: 1) accessibility, 2) effectiveness, and 3) non-temporariness.

c) *Acceptance of Justifications on Inaccessibility, Ineffectiveness & Temporariness of State Protection*

First, focusing on the accessibility of state protection against SGBV specifically, the CALL's argumentation in Clarisse's case serves as a good practice for taking into account *de facto* barriers to access state protection, despite formal legislation intended to protect survivors/victims:

> 'Although **Ivorian law criminalises […] female [GMC] […]**, and **victim support structures** have been set up, **access to the law remains problematic** for many Ivorians. While significant progress has been made in terms of *de jure* equality, ***de facto* equality remains a challenge**.'[2163] | CASE OF CLARISSE

Only one of the analysed cases specifically mentioned financial barriers or lack of knowledge as valid justifications for not being able/willing to access

---

2159 DG072_CALL 2 (recognition)_F_Guinea_STFP_GMC_VGNT_FM_DV_12/2/2024_301 330_FR_Database_p. 17., DIq095_CALL 1 (recognition)_M_Iraq_RSA_DV_29/2/2024_302 595_FR_Database_p. 12.

2160 RB006_CALL_Judge_[00:46:28].

2161 RB006_CALL_Judge_[00:31:12].

2162 RB008_CALL_Judge_[00:18:29].

2163 DIC074_CALL 1 (annulment)_F_Ivory Coast_GMC_VGNT_11/03/2024_302 979_FR_Case law selection by CALL_p. 8.

state protection: the same Guinean case as mentioned above. There, the CALL recognised the applicant as a refugee, arguing: '[A]lthough the law allows forced marriage to be refused, women in Guinea have difficulty obtaining legal assistance because they have little knowledge of [their] rights, illiteracy rates are very high[,] legal fees are unaffordable for most women […] [, and] the length of trial[s] is likely to deter […] young girl[s] considering taking [their] case to court.'[2164]

Another access barrier considered acceptable was the fact that applicants experienced/(forcibly) engaged in acts that were punishable in itself, such as 'a woman complaining of rape [in Mauritania, where] she herself can be imprisoned because it's sex outside marriage.'[2165] In the same Iraqi case as mentioned above, of the applicant who had been sexually abused by his aunt under the threat that she would spread that he raped her, the CALL also took into account that 'the applicant fears violence from his own family because of the sexual relations he has had with his aunt, [which qualify as] adultery, punishable under Iraqi law.'[2166]

Applicants' justifications of shame,[2167] denial, suppression, fear of rejection[2168] or escalation,[2169] or the fact that it is painful to disclose[2170] have also been accepted by certain asylum officials in the interviews. One judge added that their tolerance for such justifications has grown after the pilot module organised by NANSEN NGO (see Part II, Chapter 2.3) on gender sensitivity in asylum procedures.[2171] In the analysed case law, two cases explicitly accepted fear of rejection or stigmatisation as justifications for not seeking state protection against SGBV, one of them the same Guinean case as mentioned above,[2172] the other the case of Clarisse:

> '[COI indicates] that recourse to the courts is a **public procedure** and can mean that victims expose themselves to **stigmatisation and exclusion from their family and**

2164 DG072_CALL 2 (recognition)_F_Guinea_STFP_GMC_VGNT_FM_DV_12/2/2024_301 330_FR_Database_p. 17.
2165 CB007_CGRS_PO_[00:24:16].
2166 DIq095_CALL 1 (recognition)_M_Iraq_RSA_DV_29/2/2024_302 595_FR_Database_p. 12.
2167 RB007_CALL_Attaché_[00:24:33]., CB003_CGRS_PO_[00:39:24]., RB005_CALL_Judge_[00:24:24].
2168 CB003_CGRS_PO_[00:39:24].
2169 RB005_CALL_Judge_[00:24:24].
2170 CB008_CGRS_Supervisor + PO_GENDER_[00:19:27].
2171 RB005_CALL_Judge_[00:24:24].
2172 'Victims are often held back by the fear of lodging a complaint against their family. In doing so, they run the risk of being rejected by their parents and stigmatised by society. […] The [COI] goes in the same direction, stating that […] "The fear of being rejected by […] family most often dissuades [girls] from persisting in her opposition".' (DG072_CALL 2 (recognition)_F_Guinea_STFP_GMC_VGNT_FM_DV_12/2/2024_301 330_FR_Database_p. 17–18.).

community [and] that, moreover, survivors or witnesses of [SGBV] **do not benefit from any legal protection.**'[2173] | CASE OF CLARISSE

On discrimination by authorities as a barrier to access state protection, one gender-specialised supervisor indirectly accepted this justification as follows: 'From someone who […] does not belong to an ethnic minority, […] you can surely expect them to take a step towards protection.'[2174] Again in the same Guinean case as mentioned above, gender discrimination was accepted as an explanation,[2175] as well as in a Turkish case. In the latter, the applicant had experienced intersectional[2176] discrimination on the grounds of her Kurdish ethnicity and gender, being harassed by her internship supervisor. In her recognition judgement, the CALL criticised the CGRS on reproaching 'the applicant for not having [sought state] protection […] after the harassment […]: her particular profile – none of which is called into question – constitutes a concrete element […] demonstrating that the Turkish authorities are not prepared to [adequately protect her].'[2177]

Interviewed asylum officials have also accepted psychological instability as a valid reason for not accessing state protection, although one of them mentioned that there is internal disagreement about this at the CGRS.[2178] One CGRS supervisor also accepted detention by and/or dependence on perpetrators as a justification, such as the fact that 'a woman lives completely isolated, […] is a housewife […] who always stays at home […] or someone […] [who] hardly ever goes outside.'[2179] Both justifications were reflected in one recognition judgement of the abovementioned Ivorian case of the applicant accused of sorcery, where the CALL argued: '[A]ny effective protection by the Ivorian authorities […] [is] illusory, especially in this case, given the particular psychological vulnerability of the applicant and her social isolation.'[2180]

Other justifications were brought up in the interviews but did not appear in any of the case law. For example, some interviewees accepted that reporting

2173 DIC074_CALL 1 (annulment)_F_Ivory Coast_GMC_VGNT_11/03/2024_302 979_FR_Case law selection by CALL_p. 8.

2174 CB008_CGRS_Supervisor + PO_GENDER_[00:38:47].

2175 '[T]he testimony of women carries less weight than that of men. [COI] also notes that women face pervasive gender discrimination and are disadvantaged in both formal and traditional justice systems.' (DG072_CALL 2 (recognition)_F_Guinea_STFP_GMC_VGNT_FM_DV_12/2/2024_301 330_FR_Database_p. 17.).

2176 Crenshaw (n 178) 140.

2177 DT071_CALL 1 (recognition)_1999_F_Turkey_RSA_23/1/2024_300 506_FR_Case law selection by CALL_p. 6.

2178 CB002_CGRS_Supervisor + PO_[00:42:31]., RB006_CALL_Judge_[00:48:41].

2179 CB002_CGRS_Supervisor + PO_[00:12:44] & [00:30:30].

2180 DIC153_CALL 2 (recognition)_1979_F_Ivory Coast_RSA_GMC_VGNT_FM_DV_29/5/2024_307 471_FR_Case law selection by CALL_p. 14.

SGBV was not possible when perpetrators were influential figures,[2181] military officials,[2182] or had connections with the police. Lastly, one PO at the CGRS explicitly mentioned threats by perpetrators as a justification for not accessing state protection, out of 'fear of what might happen [...] when you go to the police [...] [or because] you want to put it behind you.'[2183] Neither of these explanations were explicitly accepted in the analysed case law.

Second, moving on to the effectiveness assessment, in contrast to the above demonstrated tendency to rely on COI about formal legislative/policy efforts to combat SGBV, some asylum officials do explicitly focus on *de facto* SGBV prevalence rates and whether authorities' responses offer protection in practice. As one gender-specialised supervisor stated: 'If the COI says that the law remains a dead letter [...], you cannot use it.'[2184] Others for example take into account the fact that, in reality: authorities are insensitive to,[2185] are untrained on, or lack the resources to adequately respond to SGBV (despite political will to tackle the issue);[2186] legal provisions and practice are not aligned;[2187] laws still have no practical effect after years;[2188] laws or protection orders are poorly implemented;[2189] or perpetrators are not convicted/punished.[2190]

In the same Guinean, Iraqi, and Ivorian cases, as respectively mentioned on p. 250, 144 and 227, the CALL used SGBV-specific COI focusing on *de facto* effectiveness of state protection to recognise the applicants as refugees. The judges respectively argued: 'Guinean society is an unequal one in which a single woman with a modest education level risks being placed in a very precarious situation and cannot hope to find adequate state protection';[2191] '[M]en may also be targeted because of [...] perceived [gender norm transgression] [...] [and] there are no shelters [for men] in the Iraqi Kurdistan region and few actors protect them [...]. [A]ccording to COI, "The protection of the [Iraqi] State is generally not considered available to victims of domestic or honour-related violence"';[2192] and '[According to COI on Ivory Coast,] persons accused of witchcraft may be subjected to various cruel, inhuman or degrading treatment [or] torture, including ordeals, stoning, beatings and immolation by fire, and the

2181 R_3KZrj8buCVQx8y1_CGRS_PO/supervisor/gender coordinator/CEDOCA member.
2182 RB007_CALL_Attaché_[00:24:19].
2183 CB006_CGRS_PO_[00:39:01].
2184 CB015_CGRS_Supervisor + PO_GENDER_[00:39:28].
2185 CB005_CGRS_Supervisor + PO_GENDER_[00:32:53].
2186 CB010_CGRS_Supervisor + PO_[00:28:07].
2187 RB001_CALL_Judge_[00:30:04].
2188 RB003_CALL_Attaché_[00:37:33]., RB008_CALL_Judge_[00:38:29].
2189 RB004_CALL_Attaché_[additional e-mail after interview]., CB004_CGRS_PO_[00:08:41].
2190 CB007_CGRS_PO_[00:37:11]., CB009_CGRS_PO_GENDER_[00:35:42].
2191 DG072_CALL2(recognition)_F_Guinea_STFP_GMC_VGNT_FM_DV_12/2/2024_301 330_FR_Database_p. 17.
2192 DIq095_CALL 1 (recognition)_M_Iraq_RSA_DV_29/2/2024_302 595_FR_Database_p. 11.

violence […] sometimes extends to family members.'[2193] In Clarisse's case, the CALL annulled the CGRS' decision, arguing (among other elements):

> '[T]he **gender inequality level** in Ivory Coast is […] at a level of four out of five. […] [W]hile **some prosecutions for [female GMC] have taken place**, details of the cases are limited and **information on the execution of sentences is not publicly available.** The report also shows that **convictions are rare.** […] [T]o date, **only twelve cases of imprisonment have been recorded in the whole** [country]. […] [O]n the basis of the [COI] provided […] **despite the fairly low prevalence rate** […] in Abidjan **and the authorities' legislation against the practice,** [female GMC] **continues to be practised,** which tends to **demonstrate *de facto* and *a contrario* that the authorities' efforts to eradicate such practices are not having the desired effect.** […] [T]he […] mechanisms put in place […] [for] people exposed to the risk of [female GMC **do not]** **currently offer them sufficient and effective protection.**'[2194] | CASE OF CLARISSE

In two cases mentioned in a Guinean (p. 250) and Iraqi case above (p. 144), the CALL also specifically commented on the insufficient protection of mere legislative measures: '[T]he [legal progress] is not always perceptible in practice. In fact, cultural and societal constraints are deeply entrenched, […] explaining why few young girls or women take legal action for forced marriage [in Guinea]'[2195] and '[A]lthough Iraq criminalises honour-related violence, in practice the authorities intervene very little.'[2196] Other asylum officials then focused on policy efforts in particular, stating: '[When] dealing with unstable regimes, […] the policy of the authorities on the ground doesn't have any impact, especially on gender issues.'[2197] This particular form of rebuttal of the state protection myth was reflected in another abovementioned case from Ivory Coast.[2198]

Importantly, several asylum officials recognised that SGBV-specific COI on *de facto* protection (instead of formal legislative/policy efforts) is not always available (to the CGRS) or submitted (to the CALL). One CGRS supervisor called the lack of precise COI on *de facto* protection an important point of action for the CGRS, since this gives POs/supervisors the impression that they have substantial discretionary power, which would not be the case if they had access

---

2193 DIC153_CALL 2 (recognition)_1979_F_Ivory Coast_RSA_GMC_VGNT_FM_DV_29/5/2024_307 471_FR_Case law selection by CALL_p. 14.

2194 DIC074_CALL 1 (annulment)_F_Ivory Coast_GMC_VGNT_11/03/2024_302 979_FR_Case law selection by CALL_p. 8.

2195 DG072_CALL 2 (recognition)_F_Guinea_STFP_GMC_VGNT_FM_DV_12/2/2024_301 330_FR_Database_p. 17.

2196 DIq095_CALL 1 (recognition)_M_Iraq_RSA_DV_29/2/2024_302 595_FR_Database_p. 12.

2197 CB001_CGRS_PO_[00:30:20].

2198 DIC153_CALL 2 (recognition)_1979_F_Ivory Coast_RSA_GMC_VGNT_FM_DV_29/5/2024_307 471_FR_Case law selection by CALL_p. 15.

to very precise statistics.[2199] One judge confirmed that the COI on *de facto* protection sometimes is poor in quality and unsatisfactory.[2200]

In contrast to the Belgian asylum authorities' tendency to overrule applicants' individual experiences/justifications with general COI establishing (formally) effective state protection, one attaché at the CALL explained that 'effectiveness [should] be deduced from relevant COI and case file documents, including the [applicant's] statements [...] [and] an individual assessment is always appropriate.'[2201] As explained by one PO: 'It's possible that, according to COI, there is protection in theory and [...] in practice, but if the person can show that in [their] specific case there was [none], that can also be accepted.'[2202]

Asylum officials for example confirmed that such individual assessments may take into account whether: 'the person has already had problems with the authorities [...] before, if so [...] it's more normal if they don't want to turn to the authorities [again]'[2203] out of mistrust;[2204] whether survivors/victims were offered a safe haven, protecting them from the consequences of their complaint;[2205] or whether applicants' protection orders were violated in the past.[2206] However, an attaché nuanced that the latter would probably only be credible if supported with documentational evidence of complaints reporting such breaches.[2207] A CGRS supervisor added that this consideration on violated protection orders is not instructed in the gender guidelines as such, but is taken into account on POs'/supervisors' own initiative.[2208]

A lack of individual assessment is what led the judge to annul the CGRS decision in Lejla's case, instructing:

> 'a **further and thorough investigation into** the alleged **abduction** of the applicants' daughter and [...] **whether the protection [...] in Bosnia-Herzegovina is sufficiently effective, given what happened to [her]** at the time – including [her] **residence in the "safe house" of which the location was revealed by a corrupt agent and [the mafia] found her there and left her for dead** – and their current specific **personal situation.**'[2209] | CASE OF LEJLA

2199 CB010_CGRS_Supervisor + PO_[00:30:52].
2200 RB001_CALL_Judge_[00:30:32].
2201 RB004_CALL_Attaché_[additional e-mail after interview].
2202 CB004_CGRS_PO_[00:21:37].
2203 CB004_CGRS_PO_[00:17:09].
2204 RB006_CALL_Judge_[00:48:41].
2205 RB008_CALL_Judge_[00:31:31].
2206 RB005_CALL_Judge_[00:35:41].
2207 RB007_CALL_Attaché_[00:47:36].
2208 CB010_CGRS_Supervisor + PO_[00:33:31].
2209 DBH121_CALL 1 (annulment)_lawyers' argumentation_F_Bosnia and Herzegovina_RSA_STFP_30/4/2024_305 882_NL_Database_p. 24.

In the same Guinean case mentioned above, the CALL did recognise the applicant as a refugee based on the individual assessment that: 'In light of [...] the applicant's objectively vulnerable profile as an isolated woman with no resources and showing great psychological fragility, [...] [she] has no effective remedy upon return to Guinea.'[2210]

Apart from applicants' past experiences suggesting a lack of effective state protection against SGBV, their general mistrust in the system at times is also accepted as a justification. As accepted by some asylum authorities, such mistrust might originate from: corruption;[2211] the taboo surrounding SGBV;[2212] or its treatment as a private matter to be solved within the home.[2213] The latter justification was considered valid by the CALL, again in the same above case already mentioned repeatedly,[2214] as well as in Clarisse's case:

> '[COI] indicates that **[SGBV] cases are often [...] considered as private** [...] [, resulting in] a preference for recourse to **traditional mechanisms [...] rather than state institutions.** People affected by [female GMC for example] **rarely go to court, and family mediation is preferred.**'[2215] | CASE OF CLARISSE

Thirdly and importantly, no rebuttal on the non-temporariness condition of state protection was found, neither in the interviews nor in the analysed case law.

3.3. OCCURRENCE OF THE STATE PROTECTION MYTH

How the level of acceptance (CGRS and CALL) vs. rebuttal (CALL) of the state protection myth in the analysed case law sample is divided, between the asylum authorities, according to the procedural language, can be visualised as follows (Figure 27).

2210 DG072_CALL2(recognition)_F_Guinea_STFP_GMC_VGNT_FM_DV_12/2/2024_301330_FR_Database_p. 18.

2211 RB005_CALL_Judge_[00:23:22].

2212 CB002_CGRS_Supervisor + PO_[00:16:38].

2213 CB010_CGRS_Supervisor + PO_[00:28:07] & [00:31:00]., CB002_CGRS_Supervisor + PO_[00:16:38]., RB002_CALL_Attaché_[00:36:14]., RB008_CALL_Judge_[00:14:26].

2214 DG072_CALL 2 (recognition)_F_Guinea_STFP_GMC_VGNT_FM_DV_12/2/2024_301 330_FR_Database_p. 14 & 17.

2215 DIC074_CALL 1 (annulment)_F_Ivory Coast_GMC_VGNT_11/03/2024_302 979_FR_Case law selection by CALL_p. 8.

Figure 27: % of decisions in the case law sample including at least one state protection myth acceptance/rebuttal argument, according to asylum authority & language

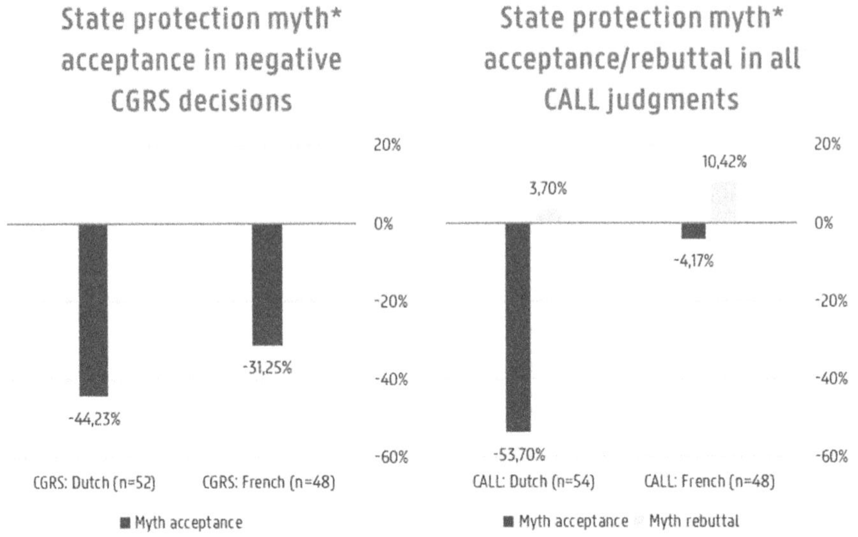

In the total case law sample, 34,16% of the 202 decisions and judgements included at least one argument based on acceptance of the state protection myth. It is important to emphasise that this percentage is reduced considerably by the remarkably low acceptance in the French-language CALL judgements (4,17%). In contrast, **ca. half of the Dutch-language decisions** (both CGRS: 44,23% and CALL: 53,70%) and **ca. one third of the French-language CGRS decisions** (31,25%) contain an argument **accepting** the **state protection myth**. The rebuttal level of this myth at the CALL counts 3,70%, for the judgments in Dutch and 10,42% for those in French.

Figure 28 below visualises how the two SGBV myths on the meso/exo level may be accepted in argumentation across the stages of refugee status determination in SGBV cases, namely: the assessment of credibility, well-foundedness, and IFAs. It summarises the most important reasons for the rebuttal of these myths in health and social sciences, as well as in international refugee (case) law.

Figure 28: Visual of most important rebuttal reasons of the meso/exo myths

	MYTH-BASED ARGUMENTATION	REBUTTAL in health & social sciences	REBUTTAL in international refugee (case) law
	→ APPLICANTS FLEEING SGBV DO **NOT QUALIFY FOR REFUGEE PROTECTION** BECAUSE: [not applicable]		
	→ SGBV QUALIFIES FOR REFUGEE PROTECTION, BUT IS **NOT CREDIBLE** BECAUSE:		
CREDIBILITY	'Inappropriate' help-seeking from non-state actors undermines SGBV flight stories' credibility	- SGBV disclosure barriers - **Very low help-seeking rate** from non-state actors *sensu stricto*	
CREDIBILITY	'Inappropriate' help-seeking from state actors undermines SGBV flight stories' credibility	- SGBV disclosure & reporting barriers - **Precaution abandonment** after negative help-seeking experiences - **Very low help-seeking rate** from state actors	
	→ SGBV QUALIFIES FOR REFUGEE PROTECTION, IS CREDIBLE, BUT THE FEAR IS **ILL-FOUNDED** BECAUSE:		
WELL-FOUNDEDNESS	Applicants with (facilitating) non-state actor support do not need protection against SGBV	- Underestimation of SGBV & **overestimation of non-state protection** in COI (country of origin information) - **Bystander intervention barriers**	- **Actors of protection** must **control the state territory** (art. 7 EU QualDir/Reg)
WELL-FOUNDEDNESS	→ Non-state actors *sensu stricto*	- **Limited** accessibility, capacity, services, duration, safety guarantees… and instable funding of **protection** from non-state actors *sensu strico*	
WELL-FOUNDEDNESS	→ Private support networks	- **SGBV is most prevalent** within **private** support networks	- **Private actor support** is **irrelevant** to effectiveness & availability of **state protection** (*O.A.*, CJEU)
WELL-FOUNDEDNESS	Non-exhaustion of state protection implies ill-foundedness of SGBV flight stories (or prevents their assessment)*	- Underestimation of SGBV & **overestimation of state protection** in COI - *De jure* measures alone are **inaccurate indicators** for *de facto* protection against SGBV	- Only **accessible, effective & non-temporary** state protection must be exhausted, unless applicants are justifiably unable/unwilling to do so (art. 7 EU QualDir/Reg & art. 1 RefConv) - **Inability/unwillingness to seek state protection** must be assessed individually (art. 1 RefConv & art. 4 EU QualDir/Reg) - **State protection** must be assessed via **up-to-date, region-, SGBV-specific & *de facto* COI** (*A.H. & F.N.* and *K.L.*, CJEU) - **Safe countries of origin** must be 'safe' across their **entire territory** (*C.V.*, CJEU)
	→ SGBV QUALIFIES FOR REFUGEE PROTECTION, IS CREDIBLE, THE FEAR IS WELL-FOUNDED, BUT THERE IS AN **IFA** (internal flight alternative):		
IFA	Applicants' (facilitating) non-state actor support renders an IFA safe and/or reasonable	See ↑	- See ↑ - Applicants should **not seek non-state support** (*O.A.*, CJEU) or behave discreetly (e.g. by **hiding**) (*X, Y & Z* and *K.L.*, CJEU) - IFAs must be **accessible, reasonable & exclude** any **fear** of or provide **state protection** against persecution (art. 8 EU QualDir/Reg)
IFA	State protection renders an IFA safe*	See ↑	

EU QualDir/Reg: EU Qualification Directive/Regulation, RefConv: UN Refugee Convention & CJEU: Court of Justice of the EU

4. CONCLUSION

To sum up, as visualised in Figure 28, the above illustrated myth acceptance/rebuttal forms and levels on the meso/exo level uncover asylum authorities' tendency to negatively assess applicants' credibility and/or need of international protection against SGBV, based on their help-seeking behaviour from both non-state and state actors of protection. Since the refugee definition is built around states' ability and willingness to protect applicants from persecution, non-state actors may only play a peripheral role in refugee status determination, if in the first place reasonable (i.e. accessible, effective, and non-temporary) state protection is available and applicants are individually willing and able to avail themselves of this protection.

On acceptance of the non-state protection myth, I discussed: the roles both non-state actors *sensu stricto* and private support networks play in refugee status determination (as actors of/facilitators to obtaining protection and indicators of safety/reasonability of an IFA, applicants' credibility, or their risk/fear of SGBV); the types of actors and protection deemed relevant (e.g. NGOs, lawyers, doctors, teachers, family, friends ... and physical, psychological, financial, legal, ... support); and the authorities' rejection of justifications for not relying on non-state protection (applicants' or non-state actors' unwillingness or inability to seek or provide protection). Importantly, assessing the effective protective qualities of these non-state actors does not seem standardly included in the refugee status determination of Belgian asylum authorities.

For the state protection myth, I distinguished between the roles that exhaustion of state protection plays in refugee status determination, namely as: a credibility indicator, a *contra legem* condition for refugee status determination and/or recognition, and in the well-foundedness assessment of SGBV-related applications for international protection. For the latter, asylum authorities' practice tends to move away from the legal conditions for 'reasonable state protection' (i.e. accessibility, effectiveness, and non-temporariness) towards broader descriptions, raising the hurdles for applicants before they are 'allowed' to flee. This *contra legem* shift, from result-based to formalistic intent-based notions of state protection, also risks overlooking applicants' individual negative experiences with state protection and/or justifications for not wanting/being able to avail themselves to it (again).

I demonstrated how asylum authorities base accessibility and effectiveness assessments of state protection on applicants' previous experiences, their resourcefulness, the level of protection in Belgium, or COI. However, this COI is not always SGBV- and region-specific, nor comprehensively interpreted. Often, it focuses on states' legislative/policy efforts to combat SGBV, rather than their effect on SGBV prevalence, reporting, and convictions in practice. Such COI, formalistically establishing effective state protection, tends to overrule applicants' individual experiences/justifications for not relying on state protection suggesting the opposite. At the same time, applicants' COI on the ineffectiveness of state protection against SGBV is at times dismissed because it is considered insufficiently individualised and therefore irrelevant.

Both concerning the accessibility and effectiveness of state protection against SGBV, I illustrated the authorities' tendency to discard justifications for not accessing state protection (e.g. perpetrators' role as/connections with authorities, detention by/dependence on/threats from perpetrators, criminalisation of applicants' behaviour, fear, shame, lack of support, and discrimination) or not relying on state protection due to its (perceived) ineffectiveness (e.g. through negative past experiences, mistrust in the system, and authorities' conflict of interest in the case of custody/visitation rights and/or complaints for international child abduction). Alarmingly, the non-temporariness requirement for reasonable state protection does not seem to play a role in asylum authorities' refugee status determination in SGBV-related cases at all.

In rebutting the non-state protection myths, I emphasised long-established (inter)national refugee (case) law that protection against persecution must be provided by actors controlling the state, not by non-state actors, and that the latter are irrelevant to assess the effectiveness or availability of such state protection. I also demonstrated, relying on (case) law and health/social/legal sciences, how non-state actors are possibly unwilling or unable and never obliged (by international law) to protect applicants from SGBV, neither can the latter be expected to become dependent on such non-state actor support. This would not only violate (inter)national refugee law and applicants' freedom of movement, association, and self-expression, but also inscribe patriarchal power structures in asylum jurisprudence.

I also explained that SGBV survivors/victims very rarely seek help from non-state actors *sensu stricto* or state actors, regardless of how well the state apparatus functions, making such protection-seeking behaviour a very poor credibility indicator. Legally, I established that reasonability of state protection should be assessed, in line with its definition in (inter)national refugee law, CJEU case law, as well as private international law, relying on up-to-date, region- and SGBV-specific COI on protection against SGBV in practice. Where such COI is not available due to underreporting, instead of concluding that SGBV is rare or that state protection is available, decision makers should take into account alternative forms of evidence, such as testimonies of (other) survivors/victims. Applicants' justifications for not wanting/being unable to avail themselves of state protection are therefore all the more important.

Such justifications should be assessed in line with existing expertise on barriers to (obtaining) effective protection against SGBV and COI on gender norms in the country of origin that perpetuate SGBV. Such barriers might be equally present in safe countries of origin, a qualification that cannot serve as a free pass to disregard applicants' individual experiences. When establishing the list of safe countries of origin, particular attention must be paid to gender-related forms of persecution, as well as to the CJEU's case law, ruling that countries cannot be considered 'safe' when a certain part of their territory is not.

Lastly, across the micro- and meso/exo levels, I rebutted the reasoning that, instead of fleeing the country, (resourceful) applicants should move to an IFA, rendered safe and/or reasonable through their (facilitating) non-state actor support and/or state protection. The health, social, and legal expertise mentioned throughout all three levels are relevant for refugee status determination, regardless of whether it concerns the location from where applicants fled or the IFA to where they might return. For such alternative locations specifically, I emphasised the established EU refugee case law that applicants are not expected to take avoiding action by turning to non-state actors or by behaving discreetly (e.g. going into hiding). EU refugee law adds that IFAs must, considering applicants' personal circumstances, general circumstances, and their ability to cater for their own basic needs, be accessible, provide reasonable resettlement, and exclude fear of persecution or provide state protection against it.

Only when any fear of (new) SGBV is excluded or such state protection is available and applicants are willing and able to avail themselves to it, IFAs can exceptionally be considered. This consideration depends on thorough verification of: the protective qualities of non-state actors supporting the reasonability of this solution; the safety of the return route; applicants' ability to build a life with respect to their freedom of movement, association, and self-expression; the absence of gender norms sustaining/increasing their SGBV risk upon return; and their non-traceability by perpetrators.

For the Belgian asylum procedure, acceptance of the meso/exo level myths amounted to **15,84%** for the **non-state actor *sensu stricto* myth, 12,38%** for the **private support network myth** and **34,16%** for the **state protection myth**. In order for the available expertise in law and health/social/legal sciences rebutting these SGBV myths to be taken into account in refugee status determination, asylum authorities should move away from relying on these SGBV myth-like thinking patterns. Instead, their reasoning should in the first place focus on the availability of *de facto* accessible, effective, and non-temporary state protection, assessed through up-to-date, SGBV- and region-specific COI. Training/awareness raising on disclosure/reporting barriers to and limitations of reliance on (non-) state actors to protect survivors/victims from SGBV may contribute to reducing these levels of SGBV myth acceptance at the meso and exo level.

PART V

THE PRIVATE ISSUE MYTH ON THE MACRO LEVEL

1. INTRODUCTION

As mentioned in the previous chapter, survivors/victims might be unwilling or unable to report SGBV to state actors of protection due to deep-rooted social norms that such violence is a private matter in which state actors should not and cannot intervene (see Part IV Chapter 3.1.4). This belief appears to be endorsed not only by local authorities in countries of origin, but at times also by (asylum) authorities in host countries such as Belgium. In this chapter on SGBV myths operating on the macro level (encompassing broader socio-cultural attitudes), I will go into the origins of this belief in rape mythology in the criminal justice context, relying on ideas such as 'SGBV is a private matter, outsiders should not interfere, nor should it be solved publicly'.

I will demonstrate how this construction of SGBV as a private matter plays out in refugee status determination for persons fleeing SGBV (Chapter 2.1 below). In some cases, the asylum authorities' reasoning directly reflects the idea that SGBV is considered a private issue and therefore falling outside the scope of the Refugee Convention. In others, the argumentation indirectly results in the same conclusion, by focusing on the lacking link between the SGBV and one of the UN Refugee Convention grounds (i.e. race, religion, nationality, membership of a particular social group, or political opinion) or on the fact that the SGBV does not meet the severity threshold to qualify as persecution. Although I discuss this myth last, it is the first step asylum authorities take in determining refugee status. If an SGBV-related flight story is excluded from the Convention scope for these reasons, the determination ends there and all other myths identified above become irrelevant.

I will rebut the macro level myth that SGBV is a private issue excluded from the UN Refugee Convention scope both from the health/social sciences and law/legal sciences perspective (Chapter 2.2). I will first and foremost establish the statistical omnipresence of SGBV and its public health, safety, and economic costs at societal level. Next, I will highlight the relevant authoritative and good practice (case) law, guidelines, and scholarship on why the private setting of the violence cannot as such exclude it from the Convention scope, how particular social groups should be defined, how SGBV can be qualified as persecution, and why asylum authorities must consider *all* Convention grounds, including those of political opinion, religion or nationality/ethnicity, in SGBV cases.

In discussing the rebuttal of the macro level myth excluding SGBV from the Convention scope, I will specifically go into the significant discrepancy between the Dutch- and French-language decision making (both at the CGRS and CALL). These conflicting interpretations of the UN Refugee Convention scope and grounds substantially undermine the unity of decision making in SGBV cases and applicants' legal certainty in the Belgian asylum procedure. This difference is reflected in the overview of the acceptance (CGRS and CALL) and rebuttal (CALL) levels of this macro level myth across all analysed case law (n=202), according to language and asylum authority in Belgium, at the end of the chapter (2.3).

2. THE MYTH THAT SGBV IS A PRIVATE ISSUE EXCLUDED FROM THE CONVENTION SCOPE

2.1. ACCEPTANCE OF THE MYTH EXCLUDING SGBV FROM THE CONVENTION SCOPE

2.1.1. FROM CRIMINAL JUSTICE TO ASYLUM CONTEXT

In the criminal justice context, the belief that SGBV is a private matter in which state actors should not and cannot intervene has been linked to rape myths such as: 'Family and intra-familial relationships are private, even when characterized by violence';[2216] 'Domestic violence [is] a private matter[, e.g. because it] happened at the home and [...] the offender was not a danger to the public';[2217] and 'Violence against women is a private matter and should not be discussed publicly [and] outsiders should not interfere.'[2218] These beliefs underlie the idea that 'if the harm is inflicted privately, then it suffices that the women find help privately as well.'[2219]

Operating on the macro level, encompassing broader socio-cultural attitudes,[2220] this myth fails to conceive SGBV as a 'global health problem of epidemic proportions', as widely established by the WHO and the UN.[2221] It disregards the impact of such violence, both for individual survivors/victims and for society at large, as a widespread economic, safety, and health concern

---

2216 United Nations Office on Drugs and Crime (UNODC) and Skinnider (n 161) 9.

2217 *Ibid.* 122.

2218 World Health Organization (WHO), 'Caring for Women Subjected to Violence' (n 402) 8.

2219 Wessels (n 94) 355.

2220 Bronfenbrenner (n 390) 513–515; Heise (n 391) 262–265.

2221 World Health Organization (WHO), 'Violence against Women: A "Global Health Problem of Epidemic Proportions"' (20 June 2013), www.who.int/news/item/20-06-2013-violence-against-women-a-global-health-problem-of-epidemic-proportions-; United Nations Academic Impact, 'The Preventable Pandemic: Sexual and Gender-Based Violence' (*United Nations*), www.un.org/en/academic-impact/preventable-pandemic-sexual-and-gender-based-violence; World Health Organization (n 561) 1–3; World Health Organization (WHO) and United Nations Inter-Agency Working Group on Violence Against Women Estimation and Data (VAW-IAWGED) (n 29) xix&1.

(see Chapter 2.2.1).[2222] Instead, it reduces the phenomenon to a 'deviant event',[2223] being 'the problem of certain neighbourhoods [...] and certain types of people.'[2224] In the asylum context, this might lead decision makers to conceive SGBV as a private (law) problem, falling outside the scope of the UN Refugee Convention.

As already pointed out in the introduction (see Part I, Chapter 1.1), early criticism on this public/private divide[2225] gradually shifted (inter)national refugee law's blindness for private forms of persecution towards inclusion of SGBV as a refugee status-worthy form of persecution.[2226] Albeit initially only in soft law instruments,[2227] hard (inter[2228]) national[2229] refugee law too has now abandoned the idea that SGBV cannot be attributed to the state or that it cannot be linked to the Convention grounds.[2230] Instead, EU as well as international

---

2222 World Health Organization (WHO) and United Nations Inter-Agency Working Group on Violence Against Women Estimation and Data (VAW-IAWGED) (n 29) 1; United Nations Economic and Social Commission for Western Asia, UNFPA, and UN Women, 'Estimating the Economic Cost of Domestic Violence' (*United Nations Economic and Social Commission for Western Asia*, 21 June 2019), https://archive.unescwa.org/sub-site/costing-vaw; European Institute for Gender Equality (EIGE), 'Estimating the Costs of Gender-Based Violence in the European Union: Report' (2014) 12–16; National Center for Injury Prevention and Control, 'Costs of Intimate Partner Violence against Women in the United States' (Centers for Disease Control and Prevention 2003) 1–2; Institute for Womens Policy Research (IWPR), 'The Economic Cost of Intimate Partner Violence, Sexual Assault, and Stalking (Fact Sheet)' (2017) 1–4.

2223 Payne, Lonsway and Fitzgerald (n 134) 36.

2224 Ticktin, 'In the Name of Violence against Women' (n 396) 156.

2225 Oxford (n 11) 157–158; UNHCR Executive Committee, 'General Conclusion on Refugee Women and International Protection No. 39 (XXXVI)' (n 34) para k; UNHCR Executive Committee, 'General Conclusion on International Protection No. 77 (XLVI)' (n 34) para g; CEDAW, 'General Recommendation No. 32: The Gender-Related Dimensions of Refugee Status, Asylum, Nationality and Statelessness of Women' (n 34) para 25.

2226 World Health Organization (WHO) and United Nations Inter-Agency Working Group on Violence Against Women Estimation and Data (VAW-IAWGED) (n 29) 1; Jones and others (n 29) 454.

2227 UNHCR Executive Committee, 'General Conclusion on International Protection No. 77 (XLVI)' (1995) para k; UNHCR Executive Committee, 'General Conclusion on Refugee Women and International Protection No. 39 (XXXVI)' (1985) para k; CEDAW, 'General Recommendation No. 32: The Gender-Related Dimensions of Refugee Status, Asylum, Nationality and Statelessness of Women' (2014) para 25; UNHCR, 'Guidelines on International Protection No. 1: Gender-Related Persecution within the Context of Article 1A(2) of the 1951 Convention and/or Its 1967 Protocol Relating to the Status of Refugees (HCR/GIP/02/01)' (2002) para 9.

2228 Art. 60 & 61 Istanbul Convention; Art. 10(3)d, 15(3)a & 24(3) EU Procedures Directive; Art. 13(7)a, 13(9), 15(3)b-c, 20(4-5), 21(2) & 34(2)d-(3) EU Asylum Procedures Regulation; Art. 4(3)c, 6(c), 9(2)a & f & 10(1)d EU Qualification Directive; Art. 4(3), 6(c), 9(2)a & f & 10(1)d EU Qualification Regulation.

2229 Art. 48/3, §2, a] & f); §4, d]; art. 48/5, §1, c); art. 48/6, §5, c] Belgian Aliens Act.

2230 Dadhania (n 33) 3; Sullivan (n 33) 126; Goodwin-Gill and McAdam (n 33) 81 & 351; Roels, 'Rape Myths in the European Court of Human Rights' Non-Refoulement Case Law on Sexual and Gender-Based Violence' (n 33) 4; Pearce (n 33) 538; Middelburg and Balta (n 8) 445; Smith (n 33) 57; Firth and Mauthe (n 25) 472; Peroni (n 33) 351.

refugee law[2231] have established that a state may be responsible for SGBV by non-state actors 'if such acts are knowingly tolerated by the authorities, or if the authorities refuse or are unable to provide effective protection.'[2232] In addition, refugee status determination on SGBV should consider the link of such persecution to all Convention grounds[2233] and interpret these gender-sensitively.[2234]

Nevertheless, these legislative steps to centralise gender sensitivity in (inter) national refugee law are still not fully implemented in the practice of asylum authorities.[2235] As such, they still at times appear to exclude SGBV from the scope of the UN Refugee Convention due to its private nature, and thus also (potential) survivors/victims from international protection.[2236] In the case of Sofia for example, who fled Honduras after being sexually abused by her father since she was 12, the CGRS (in a later withdrawn decision[2237]) argued:

> 'First of all, you claim to have left El Salvador *[sic]* because you were **sexually abused by your father** from the age of [12] to [17]. However, **private law problems are not related to the criteria as set out in the Refugee Convention.**'[2238] | CASE OF SOFIA

As explained above, the decision maker here interpreted international protection as applying only to persecution arising from an applicant's public status or persecution experiences/fears.[2239] This public/private divide[2240] was challenged by Sofia herself, who did not consider SGBV in the private sphere as separate from, but as an indicator of SGBV in the public sphere:

> 'Ever since I was little and living with my father, I saw and knew abuse, older men who came there always looked at me […] [and] said things to me that you don't say to a child. […] **If I was already experiencing such violence inside the house, can you imagine what it was like outside?** *Cries* […] In Honduras, women are constantly

---

2231 Art. 6(c) EU Qualification Directive; Art. 6(c) EU Qualification Regulation; Peroni (n 33) 351.

2232 UNHCR, 'Guidelines on International Protection No. 1' (n 35) para 19.

2233 *Ibid*, 22–34; Council of Europe (CoE) and Hooper (n 1049) 28–31.

2234 Art. 60 Istanbul Convention.

2235 Arbel, Dauvergne and Millbank (n 12) 14; Querton, 'Gender and the Boundaries of International Refugee Law' (n 13) 379–381.

2236 Crawley, 'Gender, "Refugee Women" and the Politics of Protection' (n 89) 359; Firth and Mauthe (n 25) 472; Goodwin-Gill and McAdam (n 33) 81; Anderson and Foster (n 17) 64.

2237 Upon refusal of her application by the CGRS, Sofia's appeal with the CALL was not registered, since her insufficient bank balance had caused an error in the payment of the registration fee. Despite a letter from her lawyer explaining this, the situation could not be rectified and she could not appeal against her refusal decision by the CGRS. Eventually, the CGRS decided to withdraw the initial refusal of Sofia's application and, after reconsidering her case (the reasoning of which is not made public), to recognise her as a refugee.

2238 NH003_CGRS 1 (refusal)_1991_F_Honduras_RSA_DV_12/8/2021_NL_NANSEN_p. 2.

2239 Kneebone (n 5) 26.

2240 Pearce (n 33) 538; Middelburg and Balta (n 8) 445.

murdered and raped. I don't know how the CGRS reasons, but I experienced that in my own home, [...] **my home is no different from the situation in the rest of Honduras.**'[2241] | CASE OF SOFIA

The macro level myth excluding SGBV from the Convention scope plays out in three different forms. In cases like the one of Sofia, the asylum authorities' reasoning literally reflects the idea that SGBV is considered a private issue falling outside the Convention scope (1). In others, their argumentation indirectly results in the same conclusion. The latter happens when authorities argue that the SGBV cannot be linked to one of the five Convention grounds (2). As hinted at above, this reasoning aligns with the existing rape myth that 'rape is a deviant event',[2242] rather than a structural public issue, where survivors/victims are often particularly targeted at the intersection of their gender as such and another Convention ground.[2243]

The other form of the myth indirectly excluding SGBV from the Convention scope occurs when it is not considered sufficiently serious to meet the qualification of 'persecution' (3). This belief that the severity of SGBV is frequently overestimated also traces back to existing rape myths, such as: 'Many [individuals] tend to exaggerate the problem of [SGBV]'[2244] or '[Survivors/victims] tend to exaggerate how much rape affects them.'[2245] Below, I will go into the ways in which Belgian asylum authorities accept each of these three forms of the macro level myth.

2.1.2. SGBV AS A PRIVATE ISSUE WITH PRIVATE SOLUTIONS

Some asylum officials, among whom a gender-specialised supervisor, confirmed the reasoning in Sofia's (later withdrawn[2246]) decision as legally correct argumentation.[2247] One PO however stressed that this reasoning is mainly used by the Dutch-speaking POs/supervisors and that it is, albeit legally correct, 'a bit silly and mean.'[2248] Indeed, a Dutch-speaking gender-specialised supervisor

2241 NH003_1991_F_Honduras_RSA_DV_NL_NANSEN_p. 2.
2242 Payne, Lonsway and Fitzgerald (n 134) 36.
2243 Querton, 'Gender and the Boundaries of International Refugee Law' (n 13) 394.
2244 Gerger and others (n 150) 439.
2245 Payne, Lonsway and Fitzgerald (n 134) 49.
2246 Upon refusal of her application by the CGRS, Sofia's appeal with the CALL was not registered, since her insufficient bank balance had caused an error in the payment of the registration fee. Despite a letter from her lawyer explaining this, the situation could not be rectified and she could not appeal against her refusal decision by the CGRS. Eventually, the CGRS decided to withdraw the initial refusal of Sofia's application and, after reconsidering her case (the reasoning of which is not made public), to recognise her as a refugee.
2247 CB011_CGRS_Supervisor + PO_GENDER_[00:44:53]., CB001_CGRS_PO_[00:35:19]., RB005_CALL_Judge_[00:26:11]., CB007_CGRS_PO_[00:40:34].
2248 CB001_CGRS_PO_[00:35:55].

did explain: 'There are few people who would seek asylum purely because of domestic violence. [...] Does that fit the Convention? I would rather say no.'[2249] A Dutch-speaking judge added that domestic violence as such or rape as gang violence in Latin American countries 'is criminal violence, criminal law [...] is not covered by the Refugee Convention.'[2250]

The same judge nuanced that such violence may enter the scope of the UN Refugee Convention if applicants are personally targeted, such as 'in [a] neighbourhood where [...] really young girls are specifically targeted [...] [by] gang-related violence.'[2251] By contrast, a PO stated this is the case 'when there is a cultural practice behind [the violence, such as forced marriage,] and [it is] not [...] specific to the family and the individual.'[2252] Others assessed whether an SGBV-related flight story falls within the Convention scope according to the duration since the incident, and whether violence has occurred since then,[2253] or to what extent survivors/victims are stigmatised and/or can be accommodated at home.[2254] In this last consideration, the myth excluding SGBV from the Convention scope overlaps with the myth about non-state protection (private support networks in particular).

In the case of Qawtar, she had been forced to marry a man who was physically and sexually abusive and forbade her to work. While she managed to divorce him, she had to move from one violent setting to another, namely her parental home, because she had never been able to become financially independent and did not receive sufficient maintenance money for her and her daughter. The CGRS and CALL ruled:

> '[Y]our lawsuit about the maintenance money is still pending and [...] you yourself have lodged an appeal against the first judgment of the family court [...]. Consequently, you have not at all made it plausible that you could not assert your rights as a result, quite the contrary. [...] **The fact that you disagree with the content of a private law judgment in your country of origin clearly also falls outside the scope of international protection.**'[2255] | CASE OF QAWTAR

Here, the Moroccan legal system is not seen as a structure that perpetuates gender inequality and facilitates SGBV, but as a private solution to a private problem. Both asylum authorities disregarded the fact that gender norm transgression

[2249] CB011_CGRS_Supervisor + PO_GENDER_[00:04:26].
[2250] RB005_CALL_Judge_[00:26:49].
[2251] RB005_CALL_Judge_[00:04:17], [00:09:29] & [00:10:37].
[2252] CB007_CGRS_PO_[00:39:18].
[2253] CB005_CGRS_Supervisor + PO_GENDER_[00:11:09].
[2254] CB008_CGRS_Supervisor + PO_GENDER_[00:50:39].
[2255] DM116_CALL 1 (refusal)_1999_F_Morocco_VGNT_FM_DV_24/04/2024_305 429_NL_Database_p. 16, DM116_CGRS 1 (refusal)_1999_F_Morocco_VGNT_FM_DV_3/4/2024_305 429_NL_Database_p. 5.

(e.g. by filing for divorce) in Morocco affects the family/community honour, which by definition transcends the individual.[2256] Dishonour through SGBV victimisation is a social construction of reality going beyond the individual survivor's/victim's actual experience,[2257] rendering a purely private law analysis senseless.

The same line of reasoning, albeit less explicitly phrased, was found in the CGRS decision of a Guinean applicant who gave birth to an extramarital child after being raped. The decision maker argued that by only disclosing the rape to her brother, who had not reacted negatively, she had kept her 'secret' private, rendering her fear of persecution purely hypothetical.[2258] In another Russian case, the sexual abuse disclosed by the applicant was not even identified as a potential form of persecution, nor did it give rise to any COI on state protection for sexual violence survivors/victims (from the queer community). Instead, the CGRS treated it as a private matter and suggested: 'You stayed in Poland with your aunt […], something you would prefer to avoid upon your return given the sexual abuse that took place in the past. It can reasonably be assumed that you are able to find another place of residence.'[2259]

2.1.3. SGBV LACKING A LINK TO THE CONVENTION GROUNDS

In other cases, the SGBV disclosed is excluded from the UN Refugee Convention scope because it cannot be linked to one of the five Convention grounds (i.e. race, religion, nationality, membership of a particular social group, or political opinion). Most asylum officials who excluded SGBV for this reason did so in relation to the particular social group-ground. As mentioned before (see Part I, Chapter 1.1), in EU and Belgian refugee law, individuals may form a particular social group when two cumulative conditions are met.[2260] Firstly, its members should share a common characteristic, belief, or background that is innate, unchangeable, or so fundamental that they cannot be forced to renounce it. Secondly, the group should be perceived as different by society due to its distinct identity. In determining membership of such particular social groups, asylum authorities should especially take into account gender-related aspects,

2256 Fatima Sadiqi, 'Morocco' in Sanja Kelly and Julia Breslin (eds), *Women's Rights in the Middle East and North Africa: Progress Amid Resistance* (Freedom House/Rowman & Littlefield Publishers 2010) 6.

2257 Herman (n 713) 67.

2258 DG092_CGRS 1 (refusal)_F_Guinea_RSA_VGNT_FM_DV_27/4/2023_299 471_FR_Database_p. 4, DG092_CALL 1 (refusal)_F_Guinea_RSA_VGNT_FM_DV_4/1/2024_299 471_FR_Database_p. 17.

2259 DR145_CGRS 1 (inadmissible)_2003_F_Russia_RSA_VGNT_30/3/2023_307 559_NL_Database_p. 3.

2260 EASO (European Asylum Support Office), 'EASO Guidance on Membership of a Particular Social Group' (n 66) 11.

according to the EU Qualification Directive/Regulation and the Belgian Aliens Act.[2261]

On the one hand, some asylum officials explained that sexual violence survivors/victims might in principle form a social group, 'but not if [the violence] remains within the private sphere'[2262] (PO) or only if they are being stigmatised or rejected for example[2263] (gender-specialised supervisor). On the other hand, a PO considered sexual violence as principally excluded from the Convention scope and its survivors/victims from the particular social group-ground, except for forced marriage and GMC, as these are cultural practices.[2264] They nuanced that this exception concerns an 'invented' extension of the social group-ground in practice and that 'it goes without saying that there is no such thing as a social group of all women in any country.'[2265] This position was confirmed by another PO, claiming: 'We make [SGBV] fit into a social group, [...] of what? We invent [one].'[2266]

Other POs' objection to social groups encompassing all women in a country mainly concerned their size.[2267] As such, a gender-specialised supervisor at the CGRS considered incest towards children 'foreign to the Convention', since a particular social 'group of women [...] would be too broad [...]. Otherwise, we could include all women in the world.'[2268] A Dutch-speaking attaché at the CALL (who had an overview of multiple cases) had the impression that the CALL has never, except for Afghanistan, identified all women in a country as a social group and observed a general reluctance to define such groups in broad terms.[2269]

While some interviewees considered sexual violence usually unrelated to political, religious, ethnic, or nationality grounds,[2270] one judge conversely found sexual violence possibly linked to a political opinion or religious belief, but hardly ever to a particular social group.[2271] A gender-specialised supervisor at the CGRS only considered domestic violence included in the Convention scope when there is an underlying 'motivation' such as political or religious beliefs (e.g. in a mixed religious marriage).[2272] The latter further reflected on the discrepancy between having to apply legal rules and wanting to make humane decisions. Acknowledging they find the link to the Convention in SGBV cases sometimes 'very vague', they

---

2261 Art. 10(1)d EU Qualification Directive; Art. 10(1)d EU Qualification Regulation; Art. 48/3, §4(d) Belgian Aliens Act.

2262 CB014_CGRS_PO_[00:46:47].

2263 CB015_CGRS_Supervisor + PO_GENDER_[00:47:57].

2264 CB007_CGRS_PO_[00:39:18].

2265 CB007_CGRS_PO_[00:38:04] & [00:40:28].

2266 CB013_CGRS_PO_[00:59:40] & [00:59:58].

2267 CB007_CGRS_PO_[00:40:32].

2268 CB005_CGRS_Supervisor + PO_GENDER_[00:13:03].

2269 RB004_CALL_Attaché_[00:07:37] & [00:33:12].

2270 CB015_CGRS_Supervisor + PO_GENDER_[00:47:57].

2271 RB001_CALL_Judge_[00:34:47] & [00:36:41].

2272 CB011_CGRS_Supervisor + PO_GENDER_[00:05:05].

reckoned that the CGRS often is 'very humane, [...] it's not black and white, it's not because [...] there's no link with the Convention, [that we'll] reject [someone], I [...] wouldn't be able to do something like that.'[2273]

Interestingly, two Dutch-speaking judges did remember recognising applicants who fled SGBV as refugees or annulling the CGRS' refusal decisions, but not necessarily on which Convention grounds. They described the cases of an Afghan boy whose rape in Belgium had been filmed and most likely spread in his hometown and the case of a Kurdish girl who feared female GMC in Iraq. They respectively commented: 'I did not cite social group [as the ground], [...] it was individual because he was also at risk on return, then what was the problem ...? *Leaves this question hanging*'[2274] and '"Not all women in Iraq [face this risk], [...] yet she was recognised as a refugee, I wouldn't know on what [...] ground. She is still too young to talk about a political [or] religious belief, well, I don't know'[2275]

In the analysed case law, asylum authorities appear to exclude SGBV from the Convention scope both by naming a specific ground that is inapplicable, or by concluding the violence does not relate to any of the grounds. The first type of reasoning occurred in an abovementioned Turkish case of a Kurdish applicant who experienced transgressive behaviour from her internship supervisor. She stated seeking international protection against this and other discriminatory violence, in line with her family's repeated targeting by the authorities (e.g. through legal proceedings and police raids at the family home, even leading to her sister's death). Failing to acknowledge the intersectionally[2276] discriminatory persecution she risked by being Kurdish and a woman, the CGRS argued that, since not all Kurds risk ethnicity-based persecution, the applicant should have demonstrated why she was individually targeted, which she did not do.[2277]

In Carmen's case, the CGRS and the CALL argued, in assessing the medical documents she submitted to establish the mental/physical/sexual abuse and death threats from her ex-husband (e.g. photographs and medical reports attesting her injuries and need of long-term psychological support):

> 'Should you wish to assert your mental health problems in your application, it should be noted that the **medical problems [...] are not related to the criteria set out in** Article 1, A (2) of **the Geneva Convention**.'[2278] | CASE OF CARMEN

[2273] CB011_CGRS_Supervisor + PO_GENDER_[00:08:30].
[2274] RB005_CALL_Judge_[00:14:04].
[2275] RB001_CALL_Judge_[00:37:30].
[2276] Crenshaw (n 178) 140.
[2277] DT071_CGRS 1 (refusal)_1999_F_Turkey_RSA_23/3/2023_300 506_FR_Case law selection by CALL_p. 4.
[2278] DEc120_CGRS 1 (refusal)_1981_F_Ecuador_RSA_DV_ 8/12/2023_NL_Database_p. 4, DEc120_ CALL 1 (refusal)_1981_F_Ecuador_RSA_DV_ 29/4/2024_ 305 805_NL_Database_p. 9.

The CGRS and the CALL hereby completely disregarded the gender-based nature of her experiences and fears, which may be linked to Convention grounds such as particular social group or political opinion (e.g. resisting patriarchal gender norms by leaving her marriage) (see Chapter 2.2.2 below).

The second type of reasoning, not relating the SGBV to any Convention ground, was used in the abovementioned Ghanese case of an applicant whose forced marriage was not considered 'forced' due to her lack of resistance against it. Consequently, the CGRS and the CALL agreed that her flight motives merely concerned 'socio-economic reasons not related to any of the criteria in the Refugee Convention.'[2279] In Aster's[2280] and Lejla's cases, the CALL similarly argued:

> 'The applicants' […] **problems, including [those] because of [the mafia, who had forced her into prostitution] […] concern facts of a private law (criminal) nature and do not show a nexus with any of the [Convention] grounds** […]. For this reason, the applicants do not qualify for refugee status.'[2281] | CASE OF LEJLA

In some cases, applicants do not (immediately) describe their own experiences as a form of SGBV-related persecution (constituting a form of hermeneutical injustice, see Part III, Chapter 3.3.1[2282]). This increases the risk that authorities will fail to establish a link between their flight story and one of the Convention grounds. In her CGRS personal interview, Qawtar for example emphasised the fact that her violent forced husband and father had forbidden her to work and that she risked being stigmatised as a divorced woman, curtailing her chances of building an independent life. The CALL concluded:

> 'In essence, the applicant [fled for] socio-economic reasons […], [concretely fearing] upon return to Morocco that it would be **impossible for her to find work and support herself and her two-year-old daughter**. The Council points out that **purely socio-economic considerations and concerns are not related to the criteria of the Geneva Convention.**'[2283] | CASE OF QAWTAR

2279 DGh115_CALL 1 (refusal)_1999_F_Ghana_RSA_FM_DV_19/4//2024_305 147_NL_Database_p. 9, DGh115_CGRS 1 (refusal)_1999_F_Ghana_RSA_FM_DV_26/3/2024_305 147_NL_Database_p. 5.

2280 NE002_CALL 1 (refusal)_1988_F_Ethiopia_RSA_STFP_6/4/2022_270 994_NL_NANSEN_p. 15.

2281 DBH121_CALL 1 (annulment)_lawyers' argumentation_F_Bosnia and Herzegovina_RSA_STFP_30/4/2024_305 882_NL_Database_p. 23.

2282 When a marginalised position deprives a person of cognitive interpretive resources to give dominantly accepted words to their own experiences. Fricker (n 226) 1.

2283 DM116_CALL 1 (refusal)_1999_F_Morocco_VGNT_FM_DV_24/04/2024_305 429_NL_Database_p. 14, DM116_CGRS 1 (refusal)_1999_F_Morocco_VGNT_FM_DV_3/4/2024_305 429_NL_Database_p. 4.

A similar argument appeared in Uyi's case, who did in fact initially leave Nigeria for socio-economic reasons, being told she would move to Italy to work there as a tailor. It was only after arriving in Italy, that it became clear she would be forced into prostitution there, and that she feared returning to Nigeria because of the voodoo oath she had sworn. Uyi could qualify as what is called a 'refugee *sur place*'[2284]: a person who did not leave their country out of fear of persecution, but whose fear only originated later, once they had already left. Nonetheless, both the CGRS and the CALL failed to recognise her as such, arguing:

> 'You explicitly stated that **you only left the country / travelled to Europe because you accepted an offer to work** in Italy in a shop [...]. However, **this economic motive [...] is not related to any of the criteria set out in the Refugee Convention.**'[2285] | CASE OF UYI

2.1.4. SGBV NOT QUALIFYING AS PERSECUTION

Lastly, applicants' SGBV experiences might also be excluded from the scope of the UN Refugee Convention because they are not considered sufficiently severe to qualify as persecution. According to the EU Qualification Directive/ Regulation and the Belgian Aliens Act, an act may qualify as such if it is 'sufficiently serious by its nature or repetition as to constitute a severe violation of basic human rights' or 'an accumulation of various measures, including violations of human rights, [...] sufficiently severe as to [result in a similar effect].' These instruments specifically mention as examples: acts of physical or mental violence, including sexual violence, and acts of a gender-specific or child-specific nature.[2286]

As this assessment is subject to the discretion of asylum authorities, different interpretations on qualifying SGBV as persecution exist in practice. One gender-specialised supervisor at the CGRS, illustrating the case of a boy who performed self-mutilation and was abused in Afghanistan, confirmed that he could be considered member of a particular social group, but only 'in the context of

2284 'The requirement that a person must be outside [the] country to be a refugee does not mean that [they] must necessarily have left that country illegally, or even that [they] must have left it on account of well-founded fear. [...] [P]erson[s] who [were] not a refugee when [they] left [their] country, but who [become] a refugee at a later date, [are] called a refugee "sur place".' UNHCR, *Handbook on Procedures and Criteria for Determining Refugee Status under the 1951 Convention and the 1967 Protocol Relating to the Status of Refugees* (n 254) 26.

2285 DN146_CALL 1 (refusal)_1993_F_Nigeria_STFP_31/5/2024_307 592_NL_Database_p. 12., DN146_CGRS 1 (refusal)_1993_F_Nigeria_STFP_14/11/2023_307 592_NL_Database_ p. 2–3.

2286 Art. 9(1) & (2)a & f EU Qualification Directive; Art. 9(1) & (2)a & f EU Qualification Regulation; Art. 48/3, §2 Belgian Aliens Act.

bacha bazi[2287] etc., [...] talking about really serious abuse.'[2288] Another interviewed judge reflected on SGBV along migration routes and whether the stigma surrounding survivors/victims upon return could qualify as persecution. While admitting they did 'not know how to assess this at all,' they also stated: 'The mere fact that [an applicant] was raped during her migration, I [...] would tend to say that [...] the fear of stigmatisation [...] is not enough for her to get refugee status, it's too hypothetical.'[2289]

In the analysed case law, the CALL specifically assessed whether stigmatisation of parents who refuse to (let someone) perform female GMC on their children and of girls/women who did not undergo it would amount to persecution. In a Nigerian case, this assessment was preceded by the non-state protection myth-based argument that 'the parents of an uncircumcised minor girl should be able to protect their daughter from the practice.' This then led the authorities to accept the myth excluding SGBV from the Convention scope, by arguing that the social consequences for parents and their daughters may include loss of status or social exclusion, but never violence or denial of essential services (e.g. healthcare, education, ...). According to the CALL, such community rejection cannot be equated to persecution and as 'it is an intimate subject that is considered taboo[, m]any women do not [even] know about themselves or each other whether they have been circumcised or not.'[2290]

In the same Turkish case as mentioned above, where a Kurdish applicant was assaulted at her internship, the CGRS did not consider these experiences severe enough to qualify as persecution either, especially since it happened in a specific context not likely to recur, as '[she had] since completed [her] university studies and [...] had no further contact with this person.'[2291] This view of SGBV as a one-off event, specific to a certain private setting rather than a structural public issue, was also observed in a Kenyan case. The applicant recounted having experienced rejection, domestic violence, rape, and (threats of) forced marriage because of her lesbian orientation before fleeing. In their decisions, the CGRS and the CALL isolated one incident at the market where a saleswoman had called her 'a homosexual' and had torn her T-shirt apart. They qualified this as 'a one-off incident of purely interpersonal (between private individuals) nature, difficult to be seen as systematic persecution because of [her] sexual orientation.'[2292]

2287 Misra (n 676) 350.

2288 CB011_CGRS_Supervisor + PO_GENDER_[00:08:30].

2289 RB008_CALL_Judge_[00:23:02] & [00:24:36].

2290 DN154_CGRS1(refusal)__F_Nigeria_GMC_VGNT_16/10/2023_303239_NL_Database_p.5, DN154_CALL1(refusal)_1988_F_Nigeria_GMC_VGNT_14/3/2024_303239_NL_Database_p. 9–10.

2291 DT071_CGRS 1 (refusal)_1999_F_Turkey_RSA_23/3/2023_300 506_FR_Case law selection by CALL_p. 4.

2292 DK152_CALL 2 (refusal)_1997_F_Kenya_RSA_VGNT_FM_DV_4/4/2024_304 367_NL_Database_p. 20, DK152_CGRS 2 (refusal)_1997_Kenya_RSA_VGNT_FM_DV_7/3/2024_304 367_NL_Database_p. 8.

Similarly, in the abovementioned Georgian case of a bisexual man forced to marry a woman by her family, the CGRS and the CALL did not consider the forced marriage an act of persecution as such. The CALL further argued that, apart from two 'incidents' with his family-in-law (in which they abducted, scolded, and physically assaulted him by stabbing a knife into his leg, leading to his hospitalisation), he 'did not mention any [...] problems [...] because of his sexual orientation. [...] [D]iscriminatory treatment does not in itself constitute persecution in the refugee law sense.'[2293] Similarly, in the (what should be a future-oriented) assessment of Elene's case, the domestic violence she suffered and the fear that her violent father and brothers would find out about her sexual orientation were not considered as sufficiently serious:

> '[Y]**ou have not been persecuted because of your sexual orientation** [...] despite the fact that your father and brothers [...] may not have known that you are a lesbian but they suspected it. You indicated that they asked you questions when you played football with boys or asked you questions about your clothing.'[2294] | CASE OF ELENE

In Lejla's case, the CGRS argued that the fact that she was stigmatised was not sufficiently serious either, regardless of the fact that this had also led to their house being set on fire and their possessions being stolen. In Nino's case, the same was concluded for the continuous stalking and threats from her ex-husband and son, even when these had led to concrete, repeated, and severe violence in the past.

> '[T]**hat it was said about your wife that she was "a prostitute" and "a dirty woman"** [...] [are] mere verbal allegations [which], however reprehensible they may be, are in themselves **insufficiently serious to amount to persecution**.'[2295] | CASE OF LEJLA

> '[T]he facts in which **her ex-husband and her son [...] continued to harass her** are bare allegations that are **not sufficiently serious to give rise to an actual well-founded fear of prosecution**.'[2296] | CASE OF NINO

Similar to the example of hermeneutical injustice cited above, when applicants cannot (immediately) frame their SGBV experiences as persecution, authorities might fail to do so too. For example, as mentioned above, a Georgian applicant disclosed only incidentally at the end of her personal interview that she experienced attempted sexual assault several times, both by a family friend and

---

2293 DGe110_CALL1(refusal)_1986_M_Georgia_VGNT_FM_27/3/2024_303889_NL_Database_p. 16.

2294 DGe151_CGRS 1_(refusal)_2003_F_Georgia_VGNT_DV_27/7/2023_303 891_NL_Database_p. 3.

2295 DBH121_CGRS 1 (manifestly ill-founded)_F_Bosnia and Herzegovina_RSA_STFP_23/5/2023_305 882_NL_Database_p. 9.

2296 NGe014_CALL 1 (manifestly ill-founded)_1975_F_Georgia_RSA_DV_16/3/2022_269 856_NL_NANSEN_p. 19.

on the metro. The CGRS and the CALL both failed to qualify this as persecution potentially warranting refugee status and concluded: as 'it appears that these were always attempts, which could apparently be avoided by you moving to another room, [...] [you do not state having] any future fears as a result of this.'[2297]

In line with Uyi's case mentioned above, the authorities also failed to recognise Ana as a 'refugee *sur place*' by excluding her experiences from the Convention scope. While it became clear throughout her procedure that she had suffered domestic violence both in Georgia and in Belgium at the hands of her husband, with whom she had fled (initially for other reasons) and with whom she would be returned if both their applications were rejected, the CALL nevertheless decided:

> '[T]he fact that the applicant was the victim of domestic violence in Belgium **does not give rise to a fear of persecution [...]. The applicant states [...] that she is terrified of returning to Georgia in view of recent events, but does not explain why these events would cause her problems if she were to return.**'[2298] | CASE OF ANA

2.2. REBUTTAL OF THE MYTH EXCLUDING SGBV FROM THE CONVENTION SCOPE

2.2.1. REBUTTAL IN HEALTH & SOCIAL SCIENCES

The reasons for perpetrators to commit SGBV (and thus the link to Convention grounds), as well as the severity of the (feared) violence (and thus its qualification as persecution), depend on the individual circumstances in each case and thus cannot be empirically generalised. What is certain, however, is that SGBV is a global public health, safety, and economic problem.[2299] The WHO's latest Global, Regional and National Prevalence Estimates for Violence Against Women, based on data from 161 countries/areas (for intimate partner violence) and 137 countries/areas (for non-partner sexual violence), confirm that globally, 'almost

2297 DGe138_CALL 1 (refusal)_1998_F_Georgia_RSA_DV_23/5/2024_307 108_NL_Database_ p. 15.; DGe138_CGRS 1 (refusal)_1998_F_Georgia_RSA_DV_27/12/2023_307 108_NL_Database_ p. 4.

2298 DGe144_CALL 1 (refusal)_1985_F_Georgia_RSA_DV_29/05/2024_307 462_NL_Database_ p. 8.

2299 World Health Organization (WHO), 'Violence against Women' (n 2221); United Nations Academic Impact (n 2221); World Health Organization (n 561) 1–3; World Health Organization (WHO) and United Nations Inter-Agency Working Group on Violence Against Women Estimation and Data (VAW-IAWGED) (n 29) xix&1; United Nations Economic and Social Commission for Western Asia, UNFPA, and UN Women (n 2222); European Institute for Gender Equality (EIGE) (n 2222) 12–16; National Center for Injury Prevention and Control (n 2222) 1–2; Institute for Womens Policy Research (IWPR) (n 2222) 1–4.

1 in 3 women [...] have experienced one or both of these forms of violence at least once in their lifetime.'[2300]

This makes SGBV in the private sphere the most common cause of post-traumatic disorders, as confirmed in psychological literature. As such, Herman describes how SGBV is hidden in the personal sphere, with its privacy creating 'a powerful barrier to consciousness[,] render[ing survivors'/victims'] reality practically invisible.'[2301] Not only does this 'tyranny of private life' prevent them from finding the words to describe their SGBV experiences. When they do, speaking about it may generate humiliation, ridicule, and disbelief. So, survivors/victims keep silent, due to their fear and shame, perpetuating this very public/private divide rendering them invisible in the first place.[2302]

Globally, the cost of SGBV has been estimated 1,5 trillion US dollar, equivalent to approximately 2% of the global gross domestic product (GDP).[2303] Health and social sciences research identifies the origins of this cost as: health-related (e.g. urgent treatment of injuries and long-term psychological/medical care), social (e.g. housing aid, financial assistance, child protection, family support, ...), criminal justice-related (e.g. costs for police services, courts/trials, prosecution, forensic services, prisons, conditional sentencing and probation, offender programmes, second-generation crime, ...), policy-related (e.g. setting up shelters, helplines, victim support centres, advocacy, awareness raising, trainings, ...), economic (e.g. damage to property, lost earnings, costs for security measures, moving expenses, legal costs, ...), and professional/educational (e.g. absence from work, job instability, school dropout, ...) in nature.[2304]

Therefore, the WHO firmly rebuts the macro level myth considering SGBV as a private issue with private solutions, by concluding: 'Violence against women [...] is not a small problem that only occurs in some pockets of society; rather, it is a global public health problem of pandemic proportions, affecting hundreds of millions of women and requiring urgent action.'[2305] For the asylum context, UNHCR and the UN Inter-Agency Standing Committee (IASC) have

2300 World Health Organization (WHO) and United Nations Inter-Agency Working Group on Violence Against Women Estimation and Data (VAW-IAWGED) (n 29) xvi.

2301 Herman (n 713) 28.

2302 *Ibid.*

2303 The World Bank, 'COVID-19 and Violence Against Women in Lowand Middle-Income Countries' (2022) 5; David Stenzel and Rasmane Ouedraogo, 'The Heavy Economic Toll of Gender-Based Violence: Evidence from Sub-Saharan Africa' (International Monetary Fund 2021) 3; UN Assistant Secretary-General and Deputy Executive Director of UN Women Lakshmi Puri, 'The Economic Costs of Violence against Women' (*UN Women – Headquarters*, 21 September 2016), www.unwomen.org/en/news/stories/2016/9/speech-by-lakshmi-puri-on-economic-costs-of-violence-against-women.

2304 European Institute for Gender Equality (EIGE) (n 2222) 12–16; National Center for Injury Prevention and Control (n 2222) 7–8; Institute for Womens Policy Research (IWPR) (n 2222) 1–4; The World Bank (n 2303) 5.

2305 World Health Organization (WHO) and United Nations Inter-Agency Working Group on Violence Against Women Estimation and Data (VAW-IAWGED) (n 29) xix.

reminded that SGBV is underreported worldwide and almost impossible to accurately measure and that it should therefore be assumed to take place and be acknowledged as 'a serious and life-threatening protection issue.'[2306]

2.2.2. REBUTTAL IN LAW & LEGAL SCIENCES

It is also legally rebutted that SGBV occurring in the private sphere should be resolved there. This is precisely why (inter)national refugee law[2307] has long established that a state may be responsible for SGBV by non-state actors 'if such acts are knowingly tolerated by the authorities, or if the authorities refuse or are unable to provide effective protection.'[2308] Therefore, contrary to what some asylum officials claimed above, it is not relevant whether the SGBV occurred in the private sphere or not, but rather whether state actors can protect (potential) survivors/victims against it. This again leads to the conclusion that refugee status determination should move away from myth-based arguments such as excluding private forms of SGBV from the Convention scope, but refocus on the availability of accessible, effective, and non-temporary state protection.

With regard to the discrepancy in acceptance/rebuttal of this myth between Dutch- and French-speaking asylum officials, it should be reminded that the Belgian Aliens Act prescribes to safeguard the unity of jurisprudence to take the necessary measures to this end.[2309] Therefore, the First President, the President, and the Chamber Presidents at the CALL must take responsibility for ensuring that (inter)national refugee law is uniformly implemented across both procedural languages. This goes for the macro level myth that SGBV is a private issue, as well as for the other micro (see Part III, Chapters 2.3, 3.5 & 4.3), meso, and exo (see Part IV, Chapters 2.3 & 3.3) level myths for which differences between these languages were identified throughout this research.

When it comes to linking SGBV to one of the Convention grounds, authoritative case law and guidelines have mostly focused on membership of a particular social group. As such, UNHCR has clarified that, contrary to what was sometimes claimed by Belgian asylum officials above, neither the size of a group, nor the question whether every member of the group is at risk of persecution, are of relevance to its qualification as a 'particular social group' in the sense of the UN Refugee Convention. To this end, neither the group's cohesion nor the voluntary nature of its members' association is required.[2310]

2306 UNHCR and Inter-Agency Standing Committee (IASC) (n 753) 12.
2307 Art. 6(c) EU Qualification Directive; Art. 6(c) EU Qualification Regulation; Art. 48/5, §1(c) Belgian Aliens Act; Peroni (n 33) 351.
2308 UNHCR, 'Guidelines on International Protection No. 1' (n 35) para 19.
2309 Art. 39/6, §1 & 3 Belgian Aliens Act.
2310 UNHCR, 'Guidelines on International Protection No. 1' (n 35) para 31.

As mentioned earlier (see Part I, Chapter 1.1), the CJEU has finally addressed the much debated issue of how to demarcate such groups in the case of SGBV in a series of relevant judgments.

In the *W.S. case* of January 2024, the Court clarified how the two conditions for membership of a particular social group (i.e. sharing an innate characteristic and being perceived as different by society[2311]) should be interpreted in SGBV-related cases. It clarified that 'being female constitutes an innate characteristic and therefore suffices to satisfy [the first] condition.'[2312] As to the second condition, 'it is clear that women may be perceived as [...] different by the surrounding society [...], in particular because of social, moral or legal norms,' whereby 'society' may refer either to the entire country of origin or a select group within it.[2313] Both interpretations do not exclude the possibility that this social group of women may share an additional common characteristic or background, such as having left their home or marriage.[2314] The CJEU generally concluded that 'women, as a whole, may be regarded as belonging to a "particular social group" [...] where [...], in their country of origin, they are [...] exposed to [SGBV].'[2315]

In the *K.L. case* of June 2024, the Court confirmed that such an additional common characteristic might exist in the fact that 'women [...] genuinely come to identify with the fundamental value of [gender] equality during their stay in [an EU] Member State.'[2316] In a third case of October 2024, *A.H. and F.N.*, initiated by Afghan women fearing SGBV, the CJEU clarified that women subjected to cumulative discriminatory measures, such as those imposed by the Taliban regime, qualify as a particular social group, merely due to their nationality and gender, without further need to examine their individual circumstances.[2317]

While these are welcome clarifications for female SGBV survivors/victims, it is important to note that, in practice, male survivors/victims will far less likely meet the criteria to have their refugee status recognised under the particular social group-ground. However, it could be argued that fleeing forced recruitment into armed groups for example, besides being an expression of a political opinion, can also be linked to membership of the particular social group of young able-bodied men, as only they are targeted for this gendered practice. The point that such cases deserve more attention in case law and research has been made by

2311 Art. 10(d) EU Qualification Directive; Art. 10(d) EU Qualification Regulation; Art. 48/3, §4(d) Belgian Aliens Act.

2312 *WS v. Intervyuirasht organ na Darzhavna agentsia za bezhantsite pri Ministerskia savet* (n 44) para 49.

2313 *Ibid.* 52 & 54.

2314 *Ibid.* 50–51 & 53.

2315 *Ibid.* 57 & ruling 1.

2316 *K.L. v. Staatssecretaris van Justitie en Veiligheid* (n 78) paras 45 & (Ruling) 1.

2317 *AH & FN v. Bundesamt für Fremdenwesen und Asyl* (n 82) paras 47–58 & (Ruling) 1-2.

scholars, such as Anderson and Foster,[2318] Querton,[2319] and Magugliani, who for example stated: '"[T]rafficked" women and girls are more likely to be recognised as members of a [particular social group] than adult men.'[2320]

Next to the particular social group-ground, as stipulated in the Istanbul Convention, all Convention grounds must be interpreted in a gender-sensitive manner.[2321] In UNHCR's Guidelines on Gender-Related Persecution and a Council of Europe report on the topic, SGBV is explicitly linked to other grounds, like political opinion, race, nationality, and religion.[2322] While the particular social group-ground in SGBV cases received the necessary attention in the above listed judgments, the same cannot be said for the other grounds. This lack of attention is also evident in the EU Qualification Directive and the new Regulation,[2323] in which 'there is still no mention of gender in relation to the four other grounds.'[2324] This is despite explicit calls to do so, for example by the CJEU's Advocate General Collins stating that this omission 'does not prevent gender-related aspects from being considered within the context of the other reasons for persecution,'[2325] and in wider scholarship.

As such, several (socio-)legal scholars, like Ali, Soulard, and Querton;[2326] Anderson and Foster;[2327] Benslama-Dabdoub;[2328] Crawley;[2329] Dadhania;[2330] Firth and Mauthe;[2331] Kneebone;[2332] Spijkerboer[2333] [...], have made an elaborate and firm case problematising how applicants' (resistance to) SGBV is rarely considered a political/religious/ethnicity-related, but rather a cultural, emotional, and above all private struggle/experience, 'and as such is placed outside refugee law.'[2334] In doing so, SGBV survivors/victims are not only made invisible to refugee law, but their opposition is also paternalistically treated as a mere private struggle, unworthy of refugee status. Other scholars have focused on the (dis)advantages of

2318 Anderson and Foster (n 17) 68–69.
2319 Querton, 'Gender and the Boundaries of International Refugee Law' (n 13) 384–385.
2320 Magugliani (n 89).
2321 Art. 60 Istanbul Convention.
2322 UNHCR, 'Guidelines on International Protection No. 1' (n 35) paras 22–34; Council of Europe (CoE) and Hooper (n 1049) 28–31.
2323 Querton, 'Session II: Implications of Recent Jurisprudence on Gender-Based Asylum Claims: Specific Focus on ECJ Ruling (AH & FN) on Afghan Women' (n 73).
2324 Warin (n 69) 99.
2325 *Opinion of Advocate General in K.L. v. Staatssecretaris van Justitie en Veiligheid* (n 70) Footnote 18.
2326 Ali, Querton and Soulard (n 8) 45.
2327 Anderson and Foster (n 17) 67.
2328 Benslama-Dabdoub (n 28) 69–70.
2329 Crawley, 'Gender, "Refugee Women" and the Politics of Protection' (n 89) 363–364.
2330 Dadhania (n 33) 1565–1566.
2331 Firth and Mauthe (n 25) 477.
2332 Kneebone (n 5) 39–41.
2333 Spijkerboer, 'Stereotyping and Acceleration – Gender, Procedural Acceleration and Marginalised Judicial Review in the Dutch Asylum System' (n 1202) 72–88.
2334 Thomas Spijkerboer, 'Sheherazade En Haar Zusters' (1994) 4 Nemesis 95, 95.

adding 'gender' as such as an additional Convention ground.[2335] Given that this is not currently a legal reality and therefore cannot be considered in current refugee status determination, I will not discuss this scholarship here.

Concretely, the above listed authors point to examples of SGBV that could indeed be linked to applicants' political opinion, religion, or ethnicity, such as their opposition to (and flight from): dress codes for women, forced sterilisation/abortion (e.g. due to one-child policies), gendered cultural/religious practices (e.g. GMC), (forced and/or inter-ethnic) violent marriages/relationships, or patriarchal gender norms in general, as well as SGBV they experienced in the context of political/religious/anti-racist resistance by themselves or their relatives, even when such activism was merely attributed to them by actors of persecution.[2336]

While it remains the exception rather than the rule, certain asylum authorities do demonstrate a gender-sensitive interpretation of the Convention grounds beyond the particular social group.[2337] A good practice can for example be observed in the asylum case law of New Zealand, which already in 1996 established that SGBV-related flight stories can logically be linked to the Convention grounds of religion or political opinion. In the *Refugee Appeal No. 2039/93 Re MN* case, the New Zealand Refugee Status Appeals Authority linked the applicant's flight story to both grounds. The appellant was a single Iranian woman, who opposed the patriarchal power structures present both within her (extended) family and in Iranian society at large.

Two of her female family members had been murdered, one for marrying outside the family and the other for being found not to be a virgin on her wedding night. The applicant herself became pregnant outside of marriage and underwent an abortion out of fear for the consequences. In the broader society, she was forced (but failed) to disguise her views on the oppression of women in Iran, eventually driving her to mental exhaustion and causing her to flee.[2338] The asylum authority in this case ruled: '[T]he religious and political imperatives which operate at state level are intended to […] and in fact operate at the domestic or family level as well […]. [T]he persecution feared by [the applicant] is not only well-founded, it is also 'for reason of' the Convention grounds of religion and political opinion.'[2339]

2335 Querton, 'Gender and the Boundaries of International Refugee Law' (n 13) 383–384; Heaven Crawley, 'Gender, Persecution and the Concept of Politics in the Asylum Determination Process' (2000) 9 Forced Migration Review 17, 1; Jacqueline Greatbatch, 'The Gender Difference: Feminist Critiques of Refugee Discourse' (1989) 1 International Journal of Refugee Law 518, 518.

2336 'Attribution of the Convention ground to the claimant by the State or non-State actor of persecution is sufficient to establish the required causal connection.' UNHCR, 'Guidelines on International Protection No. 1' (n 35) para 20.

2337 Aitchison (n 1358) 80.

2338 Rodger Haines, 'Gender-Based Persecution: New Zealand Jurisprudence' (1996) paras 58–60.

2339 'Title: Religion and Political Opinion' [1996] Refugee Status Appeals Authority New Zealand 2039/93.

Considering the inclusion of SGBV as persecution in (inter)national refugee law, it should be reminded that the relevant instruments, when describing acts of persecution, explicitly mention sexual violence and 'acts of a gender-specific nature' as examples.[2340] The Istanbul Convention specifically obliges its parties to take measures ensuring that gender-based violence against women may be recognised as a form of persecution.[2341] This Convention explicitly defines SGBV as (threats of) violence that (will likely) result in physical/sexual/psychological/economic suffering, 'whether occurring in public or in private life' (e.g. psychological violence, physical violence, sexual violence/harassment, domestic violence, stalking, forced marriage, female GMC, or forced abortion and sterilisation[2342]).[2343] UNHCR has also clearly confirmed: 'There is no doubt that rape and other forms of [SGBV], such as dowry-related violence, [female GMC], domestic violence, and trafficking, are acts which [...] have been used as [...] persecution, whether perpetrated by State or private actors.'[2344]

In the same *A.H. and F.N. case* mentioned above, on SGBV in Afghanistan, the CJEU ruled that an accumulation of discriminatory measures against women (e.g. deprivation of legal protection against SGBV, domestic violence, and forced marriage; requirements to cover one's body and face; restrictions on or prohibition of access to healthcare, education, sports, employment, political life, and freedom of movement, ...), adopted or tolerated by actors of persecution, qualifies as persecution.[2345]

In the context of non-refoulement procedures before the ECtHR, it is also worth mentioning the *A.A. and Others v. Sweden case*, where a Yemeni applicant, forced into marriage at the age of fourteen, who experienced severe domestic violence, tried to file for divorce, but was told to resolve her marital problems with her husband.[2346] The ECtHR did not question the SGBV as such, but relied on several SGBV myths[2347] to conclude that she did not risk refoulement, such as the argument that her private support network could protect her (incl. her brother and sons),[2348] disregarding that the latter had applied for protection themselves and that the former's previous help led him to risk his own life.[2349] While the ECtHR did not find a violation of the

2340 Art. 9(1) & (2)a & f EU Qualification Directive; Art. 9(1) & (2)a & f EU Qualification Regulation; Art. 48/3, §2 Belgian Aliens Act.

2341 Art. 60(1) Istanbul Convention.

2342 Art. 3(b) & 33-40 *ibid.*

2343 Art. 3(a) *ibid.*

2344 UNHCR, 'Guidelines on International Protection No. 1' (n 35) para 9.

2345 Ruling 1. *AH & FN v. Bundesamt für Fremdenwesen und Asyl* (n 82).

2346 *A.A. and Others v. Sweden* (n 700) para 10; Spijkerboer, 'Gender, Sexuality, Asylum and European Human Rights' (n 1729) 228; Querton, 'Non-State Actors of Protection and the Sliding Scale of Protection for Refugee Women' (n 1729) 22.

2347 *A.A. and Others v. Sweden* (n 700). (Resoucefulness myth [83], disclosure myths on detail and delayed disclosure [81–82], non-state protection sensu stricto myth [83].).

2348 *Ibid.* 83 & 85.

2349 Roels, 'Rape Myths in the European Court of Human Rights' Non-Refoulement Case Law on Sexual and Gender-Based Violence' (n 33) 86.

non-refoulement principle in this case, judge Power-Forde argued in a dissenting opinion: 'The applicants' problems "within the personal sphere" [...] are [...] sufficiently serious as to amount to a violation of Article 3.'[2350]

2.2.3. REBUTTAL BY BELGIAN ASYLUM AUTHORITIES

In the practice of the Belgian asylum authorities, the macro level myth excluding SGBV from the Convention scope is certainly not accepted by all asylum officials. There appears to be a marked difference between Dutch-speaking and French-speaking POs/supervisors/attachés/judges on this topic. Firstly, while some Dutch-speaking asylum officials, as described above, firmly qualified SGBV such as domestic violence as a private (criminal) law issue falling outside the Convention scope,[2351] others take a more nuanced stance. Three Dutch-speaking interviewees at the CGRS, all gender-specialised, did place SGBV within the Convention scope, specifically under the particular social group-ground.[2352]

A Dutch-speaking attaché at the CALL[2353] did recognise that the argument qualifying certain violence as merely interpersonal is sometimes used but was surprised by its occurrence in SGBV-related cases. They did not find this a sufficient argument for denying someone protection, 'because it is precisely in those gender-specific cases that [...] interpersonal problems do get linked to a convention ground.'[2354] When confronted with the argumentation in Sofia's (later withdrawn[2355]) decision, they considered this an isolated example and in any case not a good practice.[2356]

Among the French-speaking interviewees at the CGRS, several readily categorised SGBV under the particular social group-ground.[2357] A gender-specialised PO admitted: 'Ten ..., twenty years ago, [...] we'd have said "that's the private sphere", that was a long time ago.'[2358] Another supervisor more clearly

2350 Dissenting opinon judge Power-Forde in *A.A. and Others v. Sweden* (n 700) 29 (EN).

2351 E.g. "Domestic violence is criminal violence, criminal law, it is not covered by the refugee convention". (RB005_CALL_Judge_[00:26:49].)

2352 CB008_CGRS_Supervisor + PO_GENDER_[00:47:27]., CB009_CGRS_PO_GENDER_[00:49:07]., CB015_CGRS_Supervisor + PO_GENDER_[00:43:56].

2353 Who reads and summarises judgments. Council for Alien Law Litigation (CALL), 'Activiteitenverslag RvV 2012' (2012) 2.

2354 RB004_CALL_Attaché_[00:36:36].

2355 Upon refusal of her application by the CGRS, Sofia's appeal with the CALL was not registered, since her insufficient bank balance had caused an error in the payment of the registration fee. Despite a letter from her lawyer explaining this, the situation could not be rectified and she could not appeal against her refusal decision by the CGRS. Eventually, the CGRS decided to withdraw the initial refusal of Sofia's application and, after reconsidering her case (the reasoning of which is not made public), to recognise her as a refugee.

2356 RB004_CALL_Attaché_[00:38:08].

2357 CB001_CGRS_PO_[00:32:53]., CB004_CGRS_PO_[00:27:43].

2358 CB005_CGRS_Supervisor + PO_GENDER_[00:09:12].

stated: 'As soon as there is a gender element [...], it falls under the Geneva Convention [as membership of] a social group.'[2359] This supervisor was trained at the CGRS during the COVID-19 pandemic, exceptionally enabling more intensive training for new POs. When confronted with examples of argumentation accepting the myth excluding SGBV from the Convention scope, they attributed these to a possible lack of training of decision makers outside this period.[2360]

At the CALL, one French-speaking attaché opened their response by saying: 'You are perfectly aware that, in Belgium, women are considered [...] a [particular] social group,' continued that there are no real limits to the particular social group of women, that a public/private divide as such does not exist, and even reported never having seen a case where the legal qualification of SGBV as persecution posed a problem. Confronted with a judgement including an argument excluding private SGBV from the Convention scope, they explicitly pointed at the 'significant difference in case law between the Dutch- and French-speaking chambers' and considered it unlikely that similar examples would exist for the DRC or Guinea (countries assigned to the French chambers).[2361] While there is also a noticeable difference in acceptance/rebuttal for other SGBV myths according to decision makers' language, this is the only one where this difference was so explicitly emphasised by interviewed asylum officials themselves.

The fact that inclusion of SGBV in the Convention scope is mainly seen as the exception in the CALL's Dutch-speaking chambers is evident from a Dutch-speaking judge finding it 'interesting' that a colleague once wrote a recognition judgment on domestic violence in Latin America.[2362] By contrast, a French-speaking judge clearly stated: 'From the moment we're dealing with [gender, like female GMC, forced marriage, or] domestic violence [...], we're in the social group [or maybe political opinion for honour crimes], we're in Geneva, there's no discussion. I think [excluding it] is pretty crazy.'[2363] In response to cited argumentation excluding SGBV from the Convention scope, they responded in disbelief, calling this practice extremely alarming and concerning.[2364]

A French-speaking attaché added that it must be a copy-paste error: 'We're also overworked [...] it must be that, people don't [always] reread ...'[2365] This hypothesis was for example confirmed in Sofia's case, whose (later withdrawn[2366])

2359 CB010_CGRS_Supervisor + PO_[00:42:08].
2360 CB010_CGRS_Supervisor + PO_[00:44:14].
2361 RB002_CALL_Attaché_[00:09:41], [00:12:32], [00:14:05], [00:15:08] & [00:58:16].
2362 RB005_CALL_Judge_[00:27:41].
2363 RB006_CALL_Judge_[00:51:51] & [00:56:14].
2364 RB006_CALL_Judge_[00:54:13].
2365 RB007_CALL_Attaché_[00:49:48].
2366 Upon refusal of her application by the CGRS, Sofia's appeal with the CALL was not registered, since her insufficient bank balance had caused an error in the payment of the registration fee. Despite a letter from her lawyer explaining this, the situation could not be rectified and she

CGRS decision mentioned: '[Y]ou claim to have left El Salvador,'[2367] while her country of origin is Honduras. This attaché continued: 'Everything to do with gender-based violence, we don't even question whether it falls within [the] Convention or not, because it always does.'[2368] Another judge in the French chambers, confirming this reasoning, did recognise that gender-related cases are extra complex, both for applicants 'to establish [...] persecution by private perpetrators [...] and [...] the lack of protection [...] by state agents [...] because they have to provide negative evidence,' and for asylum authorities to access COI on stigma surrounding SGBV, which they themselves has never seen.[2369]

In the case law, three judgements explicitly rebutted the myth excluding SGBV from the Convention scope. In the first, similar to the abovementioned Guinean case on extramarital childbirth, the CALL rejected the CGRS' suggestion that keeping the situation secret could suffice as a private solution. Instead, it argued: '[T]he fact that the applicant's family was unaware of such a birth [...] should not prevent a concrete examination of the fears invoked by the applicant as the single mother of a child born out of wedlock in the event of her return to Guinea.'[2370]

The second case concerned an Algerian applicant, born as an extramarital child, who was abducted and raped repeatedly by his father and uncles. They made footage of this abuse, which they threatened to release if he contacted them. At the same time, he needed his father's permission to be able to do his military service. In appeal, the CALL annulled the CGRS' refusal decision and specifically instructed to further examine the applicant's 'unambiguously establishe[d] link between [the SGBV] [...] on account of his extramarital birth and his inability to perform his military service.'[2371]

The third judgement (marked as important by the CALL) concerned the abovementioned Kurdish applicant who experienced transgressive behaviour from her internship supervisor in Turkey. In rebutting the CGRS' argument that these experiences did not meet the severity level required for persecution, the CALL clarified: '[T]he question is not whether each of these experiences taken in isolation is likely to give rise to a well-founded fear of persecution [...], but whether the totality of these circumstances is,' and proceeded to recognise her as a refugee.[2372]

---

could not appeal against her refusal decision by the CGRS. Eventually, the CGRS decided to withdraw the initial refusal of Sofia's application and, after reconsidering her case (the reasoning of which is not made public), to recognise her as a refugee.

2367 NH003_CGRS 1 (refusal)_1991_F_Honduras_RSA_DV_12/8/2021_NL_NANSEN_p. 2.

2368 RB007_CALL_Attaché_[00:48:34].

2369 RB008_CALL_Judge_[00:08:46] & [00:22:36].

2370 DG072_CALL 2 (recognition)_F_Guinea_STFP_GMC_VGNT_FM_DV_12/2/2024_301 330_FR_Database_p. 14.

2371 DAlg076_CALL 1 (annulment)_M_Algeria_RSA_VGNT_30/4/2024_305 949_FR_Database_p. 9–10.

2372 DT071_CALL 1 (recognition)_1999_F_Turkey_RSA_23/1/2024_300 506_FR_Case law selection by CALL_p. 6.

2.3. OCCURRENCE OF THE MYTH EXCLUDING SGBV FROM THE CONVENTION SCOPE

How the level of acceptance (CGRS and CALL) vs. rebuttal (CALL) of 'the myth that SGBV is a private issue excluded from the UN Refugee Convention scope' in the analysed case law sample is divided, between the CGRS and the CALL, according to the procedural language, can be visualised as follows (Figure 29).

Figure 29: % of decisions in the case law sample including at least one private issue myth acceptance/rebuttal argument, according to asylum authority & language

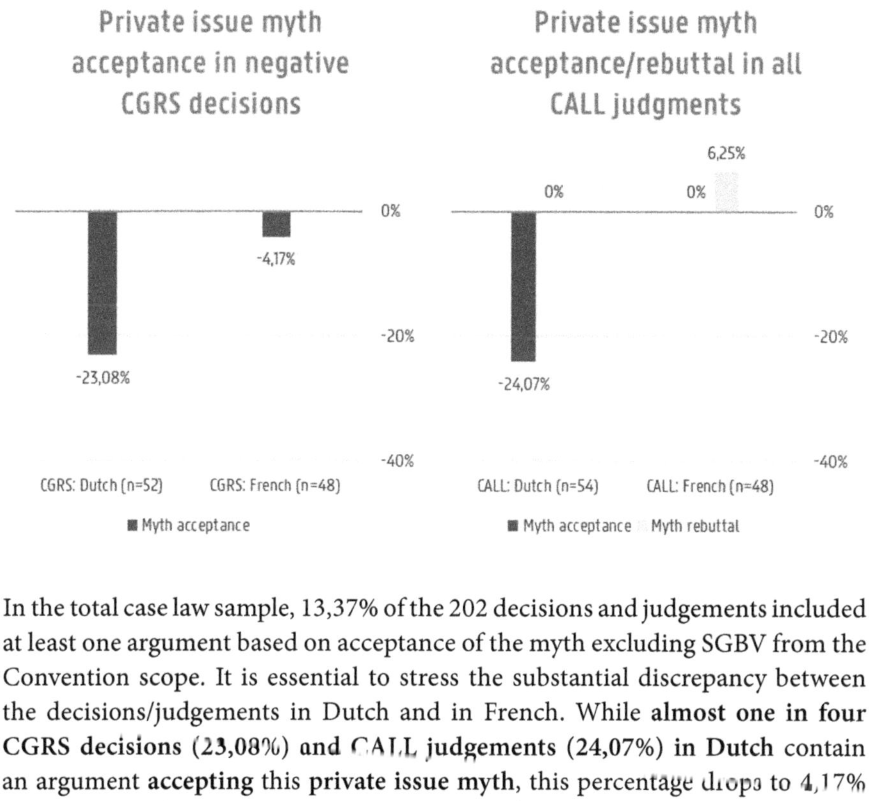

In the total case law sample, 13,37% of the 202 decisions and judgements included at least one argument based on acceptance of the myth excluding SGBV from the Convention scope. It is essential to stress the substantial discrepancy between the decisions/judgements in Dutch and in French. While **almost one in four CGRS decisions (23,08%) and CALL judgements (24,07%) in Dutch** contain an argument **accepting** this **private issue myth**, this percentage drops to 4,17% for the CGRS decisions and 0% for the CALL judgements in French. All of the judgements rebutting the private issue myth originate from the French-speaking chambers at the CALL (6,25%).

Figure 30 below visualises how this macro level SGBV myth may be accepted in the first stage of refugee status determination in SGBV cases, namely determining whether the SGBV falls within the UN Refugee Convention scope and therefore qualifies for refugee protection. It summarises the most important reasons for the rebuttal of this myth in health and social sciences, as well as in international refugee (case) law.

Figure 30: Visual of most important rebuttal reasons of the macro myth

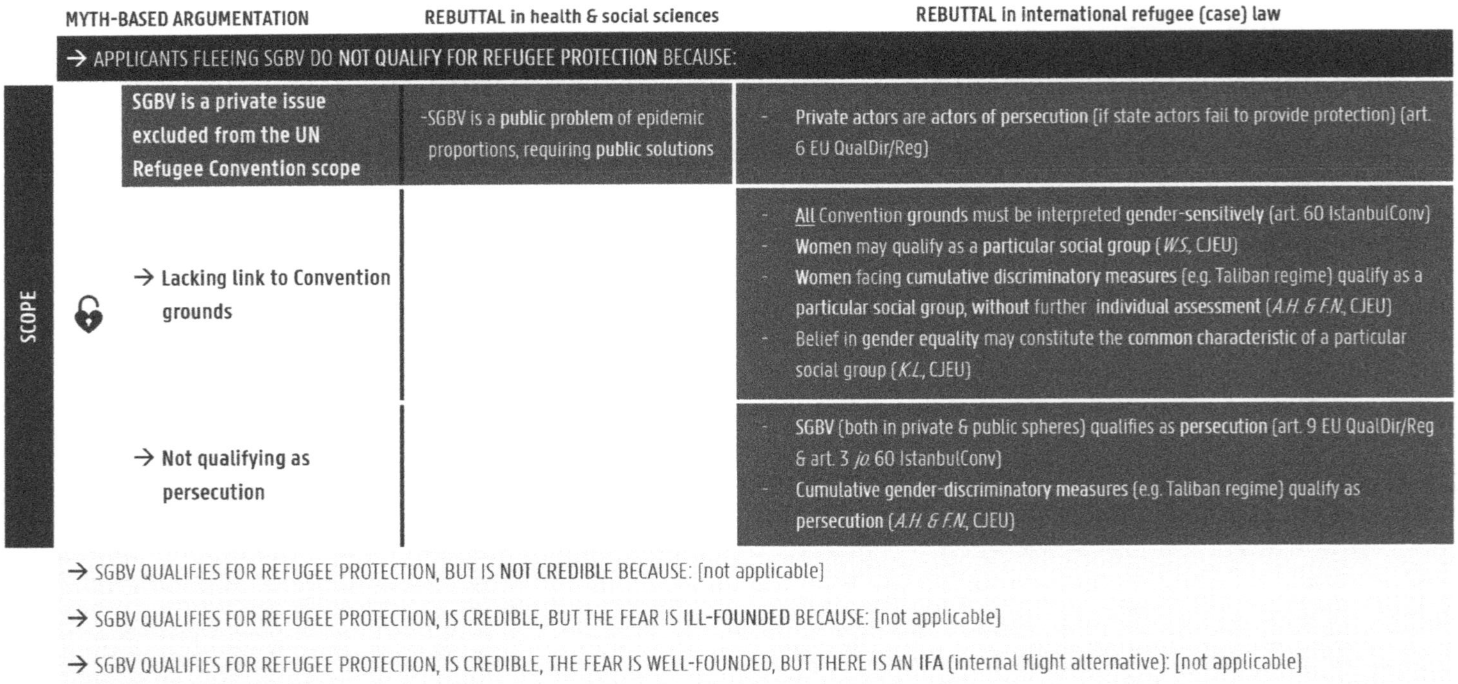

3. CONCLUSION

As visualised above (Figure 30), this chapter discussed the acceptance/rebuttal of the myth that 'SGBV is a private issue requiring private solutions' in the asylum context, resulting in exclusion of SGBV from the UN Refugee Convention scope. I first demonstrated how the acceptance of this myth in the Belgian asylum procedure takes both direct and indirect forms. At times, asylum authorities' reasoning directly reflects the idea that SGBV is considered a private issue falling outside the Convention scope. Other times, the argumentation indirectly results in the same conclusion, by concluding that there is no link between the SGBV and the Convention grounds or that the (feared) SGBV does not meet the severity threshold required to qualify as persecution. Importantly, as this myth plays a role at the start of refugee status determination, exclusion of SGBV-related flight stories from the Convention scope because of it renders all other micro, meso, and exo level myths irrelevant.

By rebutting this myth in health and social sciences literature, I illustrated how its acceptance disregards the statistical evidence that SGBV is an omnipresent public health, safety, and economic concern. The price we as a society pay for it is health-related, social, criminal justice-related, policy-related, economic, and professional in nature. In addition, it is more often than not structurally instigated (e.g. by patriarchal gender norms and political, religious, or ethnic motives), rather than a one-off event solely driven by interpersonal dynamics.

Citing relevant (case) law and legal guidelines/scholarship on the topic, I illustrated how decision makers at times show incorrect understanding and implementation in SGBV cases of: the relevant factors to determine the Convention scope, particular social groups, or persecution as such; the relevance of the other Convention grounds (both for male and female applicants); the concept of 'refugees *sur place*'; and the authorities' duty to collaborate when hermeneutical injustice prevents applicants to present their (fear of) SGBV as persecution linked to the Convention grounds.

Instead, asylum authorities should correctly and uniformly apply (inter) national refugee law and move away from myth-based arguments placing SGBV outside of the Convention scope due to its 'merely' private nature. They should qualify it as persecution linked to the Convention grounds and refocus on the availability of accessible, effective, and non-temporary state protection against it. This especially counts for the Dutch-speaking decision makers in the Belgian asylum procedure, where significantly higher myth acceptance levels are counted. Communication across the procedural languages and training/awareness raising on both the structural dimension of SGBV and the relevant legal concepts on the UN Refugee Convention scope and grounds in SGBV cases may reduce this acceptance level and enhance legal certainty for applicants and unity of jurisprudence at the CALL.

In sum, although (inter)national refugee law is gender-neutral in theory, practice shows how the public/private divide can lead to SGBV becoming invisible in refugee status determination. The macro level myth excluding SGBV from the Convention scope is not only rooted in an underestimation of the structural (as opposed to individual) nature of SGBV but also stems from inaccurate implementation of (inter)national refugee law as such. The impact of the acceptance of this myth in the Belgian asylum procedure (mainly in the Duch-language procedures) is visualised at the end of this chapter, showing how almost **one in four** CGRS decisions (23,08%) and CALL judgements (24,07%) **in Dutch** contain an argument accepting the macro level **private issue myth**, versus 4,17% of the CGRS decisions and 0% of the CALL judgements in French.

PART VI

CONCLUSION: TOWARDS GENDER-SENSITIVE ASYLUM PROCEDURES & DECISIONS

In this research, I examined how sexual and gender-based violence (SGBV) myths permeate asylum procedures and decisions (RQ). Now, I will draw conclusions and recommendations (SQ5) on gender sensitivity in asylum procedures and decisions on SGBV, studied through the lens of rape mythology, using Belgium as a case study. In this concluding chapter, I will provide: methodological conclusions on the research process (1); theoretical conclusions on the applicability of rape mythology from the criminal justice to the asylum context (2); legal conclusions on the gender sensitivity of the Belgian asylum procedure and its decisions (3); and recommendations on how to challenge the acceptance and support the rebuttal of SGBV myths in this asylum context (4).

Figure 31: Overview of research questions

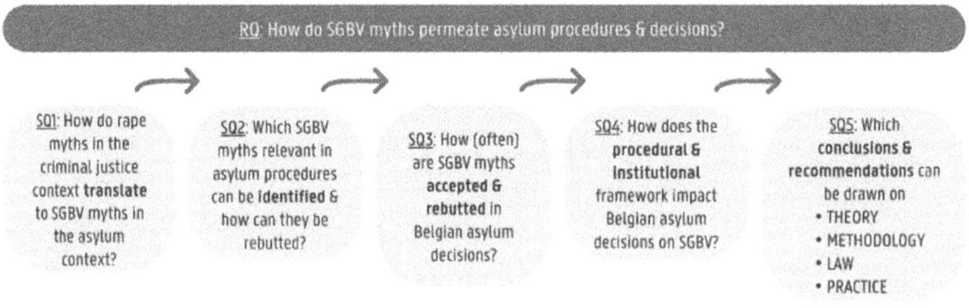

I will first go into the methodological lessons that can be learnt from the process of answering the above visualised research questions. The second theoretical part will summarise the answer to the following sub-questions (SQ) that structured this research (Figure 31 and see Part I, Chapter 2): 'How do rape myths in the criminal justice context translate to SGBV myths in the asylum context?' (SQ1) and 'Which SGBV myths relevant in asylum procedures can be identified & how can they be rebutted?' (SQ2). In doing so, I will discuss this research's substantive and conceptual contributions to the field. Third, the legal conclusions answer the question: 'How (often) are SGBV myths accepted & rebutted in Belgian asylum decisions?' (SQ3). They discuss the distribution (across asylum authorities, procedural languages, countries of origin, types of SGBV, …) and the cumulative use of SGBV myth-accepting argumentation within individual decisions (3.1). As a result, I argue how such deep-rooted SGBV myth acceptance risks to violate (inter)national refugee and human rights law provisions on gender-sensitive refugee status determination (3.2).

The fourth part provides recommendations on how to challenge SGBV myth acceptance and support SGBV myth rebuttal, tailored to the Belgian asylum procedure, but with relevance beyond it in other national asylum contexts. Hereby, I provide an answer to the analysis of how the Belgian procedural and institutional framework impacts asylum decisions on SGBV (SQ4). These recommendations will concern the content of asylum decisions (substantive recommendations, 4.1), the asylum procedure (procedural recommendations, 4.2), and suggestions on how to move forward in research on this topic (recommendations for further research, 4.3). I will conclude by summarising the main takeaways on gender sensitivity in asylum procedures and decisions on SGBV, studied through the lens of rape mythology, using Belgium as a case study (5).

1. METHODOLOGICAL CONCLUSIONS

Researching SGBV Mythology in the Asylum Context

This research relied on data source triangulation by consulting different standpoints (i.e. interviews with asylum applicants, KAP survey and interviews with asylum authorities, case law analysis, and law/literature analysis) in order to get a nuanced understanding of the phenomenon. Some methods to gather this data proved more suitable as preparatory steps to shape further data collection, such as the KAP survey. The survey was not designed to capture all complexity and nuance in SGBV-related asylum decision making, but served to outline a large-scale (n=209) and institution-wide context, within which the topic guide for the subsequent interviews could be framed.

It is important to note that the survey did aim to preliminarily capture the essence of respondents' knowledge, attitudes, and practices on the topic (to be explored further in the interviews). However, several of them indicated that they were unable to answer the questions (properly) at all, even concisely, as they did not allow for nuance or as the answer would be different in each specific asylum procedure. It therefore appears that, contrary to what the common practice of KAP surveys and rape myth acceptance scales would suggest, this method was less appropriate for a subject as complex and a target audience as specialised as (decision makers in) SGBV-related asylum procedures.

I drew up the survey before I had a complete view of how rape myth acceptance/rebuttal exactly played out in the Belgian asylum procedure (i.e. before the interviews with asylum officials and the case law analysis). Although a reverse methodological chronology would have allowed the questions to be tailored more specifically to the (Belgian) asylum context, in that scenario, the survey could not have been used as preparation for the in-depth interviews. Thus, there are advantages and disadvantages to both approaches. In any case, the choice made in this research does not preclude the development of an adapted KAP survey/SGBV myth acceptance scale in the future, based on the research results, which could be conducted with asylum authorities in and outside Belgium in future research (see Chapter 4.3). What this survey did unambiguously reveal, were respondents' level of vicarious trauma, using

Vrklevski and Franklin's validated Vicarious Trauma Scale.[2373] I will come back to these results in the recommendations on mental health support (see Chapter 4.2) and the recommendations for further research (see Chapter 4.3).

Other methods did appear successful in capturing the nuance in this complex issue, namely the in-depth interviews with asylum officials and applicants (facilitated through the KAP survey and participatory fieldwork respectively). The interviews with asylum officials at the Office of the Commissioner General for Refugees and Stateless Persons (CGRS) in first instance and Council for Alien Law Litigation (CALL) in appeal were fruitful not only thanks to the openness of the interviewees and the richness of their answers, but also because they served to validate findings from the case law analysis, which necessarily concerned a selection of cases (n=202). These interviews also provided a necessary insight into the human thinking patterns behind the written decisions I analysed. After having conducted fieldwork at an NGO and interviews from the perspectives of applicants, it was essential to complement these with the experiences and reflections of decision makers. Planning the interviews with asylum officials after the fieldwork with the NGO had the advantage that the case files I analysed beforehand could serve to illustrate and concretise (in a pseudonymised manner) the questions of the interview with the decision makers. This allowed for more in-depth, rather than formal or institutionally desirable answers sometimes given in 'elite interviews' (i.e. with experts in their professional context).[2374]

On interviewing applicants about their SGBV-related asylum procedures, I previously discussed the ethical challenges this entailed and the methodological measures I took to mitigate these to the extent possible (see Part I, Chapter 3). Provided the strict application of these ethical safeguards, in particular ensuring trauma-sensitive interviewing and reciprocal research design, these interviews with experts by experience were absolutely crucial to the depth and comprehensiveness of the research findings. In fact, it turned out that without this direct reliance on their expertise, certain SGBV myths would have remained silenced. While most of the SGBV myths have been touched upon (to some extent) in existing scholarship on gender and asylum, this was for example not the case for the micro level myth about survival reactions. I could only identify the latter through the interviewed applicants' reflections on feeling misunderstood

---

2373 Vicarious trauma is described as 'the negative effects that result from working with trauma survivors. These include compassion fatigue or secondary traumatic stress, countertransference, and burnout.' Vrklevski and Franklin developed a 8 question Vicarious Trauma Scale (VTS) in order to assess subjective levels of distress associated with working with traumatised persons. The VTS items are rated on a 7-point Likert-type scale, ranging from 1 (strongly disagree) to 7 (strongly agree). Vrklevski and Franklin (n 371) 106, 110 & 115.

2374 Olga Petintseva, Rita Faria and Yarin Eski, *Interviewing Elites, Experts and the Powerful in Criminology* (Palgrave 2019) 32.

in the Belgian asylum procedure regarding their help-seeking behaviour and risk mitigation in response to SGBV (fears).

The setting in which these interviews took place, the fieldwork at NANSEN NGO, ensured that applicants did not have to be actively recruited and tell their flight stories (again) purely 'for the sake of' research data collection. Instead, the primary purpose of the interview was to enable their legal support by the NGO, and only subordinately and optionally to inform the research as data. The risk remains that applicants felt obliged to participate in the research in order to receive legal support, despite my explicit attempts to contradict this fear in the explanation beforehand to obtain informed consent. This tension, between respecting participants' autonomy and shielding them from pressure to participate, is a dilemma that remains unresolved, but that I recognise as an ethical challenge inherent in research that aims to be reciprocally designed.

Lastly, NANSEN NGO offered a warm, mutually enriching collaboration and colleagues with whom I could share the mental load of the interviews. The psychological support I found with them, as well as with my university colleagues, supervisors, and personal network, somewhat reduced the emotional impact of the SGBV-related flight stories and thus contributed to reducing the risk of my own vicarious traumatisation. This experience gives rise to another suggestion for further research (see Chapter 4.3). In my opinion, some form of psychological support, preferably both informally and formally offered within universities, should be standardly included in research on SGBV and/or forced migration dealing with personal stories, in order to prevent, follow-up, and/or respond to vicarious trauma among researchers.

A final methodological contribution of this research is its case-based approach, rooted in lived experience and in line with the feminist standpoint theories shaping it (see Part I, Chapter 3.1.1). The in-depth qualitative analysis of SGBV-related flight stories in the case law analysis and interviews with applicants allowed me to construct and present this research bottom-up around applicants' own standpoints. It was a deliberate choice to take the reader by the hand and introduce them via the individual case studies one by one throughout the research. This approach aimed to emphasise the diversity in and reality of their experiences. Instead of pursuing representative generalisability, I considered the standpoints of these individual applicants essential for demonstrating the power structures within their asylum procedures. They leave room for future research to enrich these with new standpoints of others' lived experiences with fleeing SGBV and applying for international protection. In addition, the case-based approach consciously intended to confront the reader with the real people behind and impact of these procedures, in an attempt to appeal to the potential of storytelling as a catalyst for social change.[2375]

[2375] Van Impe (n 245) 99.

I started this research by reflecting on the ethical challenges the design and methodology entailed. At the end, I conclude, in line with Gardî,[2376] that the methodological hurdles coming with directly including applicants' expertise by experience should not prevent us from ensuring meaningful survivor/victim/applicant participation in research. Above all, this work is an invitation to conduct further research directly building on applicants' experiences, complemented by asylum authorities' perspectives, doing so in a reciprocally enriching manner, with particular attention to avoiding re- and vicarious traumatisation of participants and researchers, and eventually aiming at social change in the power dynamics researched.

[2376] Gardî (n 221) viii.

2. THEORETICAL CONCLUSIONS

Expanding Rape Mythology to the Asylum Context

In order to translate 'rape myths in the criminal justice context' to 'SGBV myths in the asylum context', this research took into account the 1) evidentiary, 2) temporal, 3) personal, and 4) substantive differences between the two settings (see Part I, Chapter 1.4). As visualised in Figure 1, this led me to coin the term 'SGBV myths', expanding the original rape myths to other SGBV forms relevant to the asylum context and reorienting them towards the credibility/well-foundedness of survivors'/victims' fear of future persecution (instead of perpetrators' guilt for past offences). Since, to my knowledge, this is the first research to explicitly apply rape mythology to asylum procedures and decisions in order to examine their gender sensitivity, this constitutes its main conceptual contribution. The concrete SGBV myths that were identified throughout this research can be visualised as follows (Figure 32):

Figure 32: SGBV myths identified throughout the research

Level	Existing rape myths (illustrative)[2377]	SGBV myths identified in asylum context:
MICRO	'[SGBV] is [...] the problem of certain neighbourhoods ... and certain types of people' or 'Men cannot be raped; they can resist'	**Resourcefulness myth*** (resourceful applicants do not need protection against SGBV)
	A real survivor/victim 'is absolutely certain about the details', 'does not change [the] account of what happened', 'will disclose [the] violation at the first reasonable opportunity', or is 'visibly upset'	**Disclosure myths** ('inappropriate' disclosure undermines SGBV flight stories' credibility)
	'Survivors never remain in contact with offenders following an assault' or 'will finally be safe when [they leave] [a violent] relationship'	**Survival myths** ('inappropriate' survival reactions undermine SGBV flight stories' credibility)

(continued)

[2377] See Part I, Chapter 4.5 for references.

MESO/EXO	'Rape is unlikely to happen in the [person]'s own familiar neighbourhood' or 'Nowadays, sexual violence [victims] receive sufficient help in the form of [...] shelters, therapy [...], and support groups'	**Non-state protection myths** (applicants with non-state actor support do not need protection against SGBV)
	'[A real] victim would promptly seek help and report' or 'Nowadays, [those] who really sexually assault [others] are punished justly'	**State protection myth*** (non-exhaustion of state protection implies non-credibility/ ill-foundedness of SGBV flight stories)
MACRO	'Domestic violence [is] a private matter[, as] the attack happened at the home and [...] the offender was not a danger to the public'	**Private issue myth** (SGBV is a private issue excluded from the Convention scope)

While this translation allowed for many parallels to be drawn between existing rape mythology and myths in the asylum context, it also uncovered differences. One prominent example concerned the survival myths on the micro level, whereby asylum authorities seem to qualify both applicants' active and passive reactions to SGBV as non-credible. In contrast, such rape myths in the criminal justice context still tend to consider active reactions as 'normal' and credible in certain circumstances. The same counts for the demeanour myth, where asylum authorities seem to qualify both disclosures that are 'lacking emotions' or 'are too emotional' as non-credible, whereas the rape myth in the criminal justice context only discredits the former. Consequently, the SGBV myths accepted in the asylum context may set the barrier for survivors/victims to be believed and recognised even higher than is already the case in the criminal justice context.

It is important to stress that the contribution of this research to the fields of gender and asylum studies is therefore primarily a conceptual one. From a substantive perspective, the contribution differs. On the one hand, the rebuttal of most myths is not new in legal research. For example, case law and scholarship before me have criticised the use of resourcefulness arguments (see Part II, Chapter 2.2.1), reliance on 'inappropriate' disclosure as a credibility indicator (see Part III, Chapters 3.2.2, 3.3.2 & 3.4.2), or the designation of non-state actors to provide protection (see Part IV, Chapter 2.2.2.). Other myths, on the other hand, are still largely unexplored in legal scholarship. For the survival myths for example (see Part III, Chapter 4.2), this research does make a substantive contribution, thanks to direct input from experts by experience. Consequently, the nature of the rebuttals in this research differs depending on how extensively the myths have already been addressed in legal sources. Especially for arguments on which the Court of Justice of the European Union (CJEU) has already ruled or the law is clear, such as the resourcefulness (Part II, Chapter 2.2.), (non-)state protection

(Part III, Chapters 2.2.2. & 4.2.2.), and private issue myths (), the rebuttal was more legally oriented. Where this was less so, for the disclosure (Part III, Chapters 3.2.2, 3.3.2 & 3.4.2) and survival myths (Part III, Chapter 4.2.1), the rebuttal relied more on health and social sciences.

I also sought to substantively contribute to existing legal analyses on gender and asylum by demonstrating the need to inform asylum decision making with expertise outside the law (echoing UNHCR's recommendation[2378]), in particular from health and social sciences. As such, I pointed out the relevance of knowledge on: SGBV survivors'/victims' survival reactions, help-seeking behaviour, risk management, disclosure/reporting barriers, risk factors for (re)victimisation; SGBV prevalence in the private sphere and across socio-economic backgrounds/ gender identities; bystander theory; the cycle of violence; the impact of trauma and other mental health issues on memory and disclosure; … Only in this way can we uncover myth-based thinking patterns in refugee status determination that lack grounds in available evidence-based research on the causes, nature, and consequences of SGBV.

It is important to stress that this research, while focusing on SGBV as its subject, does not seek to single out applicants fleeing this violence as exceptional in comparison to other applicants. I do not mean to contribute to an exclusionary asylum rationale that categorises only the 'most vulnerable' cases, like those of SGBV survivors'/victims' 'morally legitimate suffering' in Ticktin's words,[2379] as worthy of protection. In fact, not all SGBV myths identified in this research are unique to SGBV-related asylum procedures; some impact other cases just as strongly. For example, non-state actors are also suggested as actors of protection in other cases and disclosure myths are relevant to all flight stories (especially those causing mental health issues, which most are). For that matter, all applications for international protection deserve a trauma- and gender-sensitive assessment, to which the conclusions in this research may contribute.

Other aspects however, such as: shame and the other specific survival reactions after SGBV, the paralysing effect of the cycle of violence, the inaccuracy of resourcefulness as a predictor of SGBV, the private nature of SGBV leading to exclusion from the Convention scope, or underreporting of SGBV and therefore underestimation in country of origin information (COI), do specifically characterise gender-related asylum procedures.

Therefore, the main conceptual contribution of this research does not concern the individual myths per se, some of which have already been described elsewhere and are relevant outside SGBV cases, but in the identification of a comprehensive set of myths and their impact on the outcome of SGBV-related asylum procedures specifically. More precisely, this contribution of applying

2378 UNHCR, 'Beyond Proof. Credibility Assessment in EU Asylum Systems (Full Report)' (n 19) 56.

2379 Ticktin, 'In the Name of Violence against Women' (n 396) 130.

the rape mythology framework to SGBV-related asylum decision making is threefold, in that it allows for 1) comprehensive analysis, 2) interdisciplinary rebuttal, and 3) practice-oriented implementation.

Comprehensively, the combined set of SGBV myths focuses on multiple substantive aspects of refugee status determination. This enables the assessment of asylum decisions as a whole on their gender-sensitivity and anticipates on the fact that decision makers might 'hide' behind the minor impact of individual arguments on eventual decisions or the particularity of individual cases. In addition, it requires decision makers to look beyond improving special procedural guarantees or credibility assessments alone, but to recognise that the decision-making process from beginning (e.g. determining the Convention scope) to end (e.g. consideration of an internal flight alternative or IFA) can be permeated with SGBV myth-based argumentation. Below, I will discuss how this 'SGBV mythology framework' allows analysis of both the widespread use of SGBV myths across decisions with different types of SGBV, countries of origin, gender identities/ages of applicants, and their factual circumstances, as well as their cumulative use within a single decision (see Chapter 3.1 below).

On the interdisciplinary level, by applying the theoretical framework of rape mythology to the asylum context, this research 'borrowed' expertise on SGBV from multiple disciplines, established through more than 50 years of research on rape myths in the criminal justice context. The authoritative value of this body of knowledge is especially relevant in SGBV-related asylum procedures, where two cultures of disbelief intersect, namely surrounding applicants seeking asylum[2380] and survivors/victims seeking justice after SGBV.[2381] This approach not only demonstrates the importance of relying on expertise outside the law in SGBV-related refugee status determination. It also leads to procedural recommendations, such as involving non-legal experts (e.g. in health and social sciences) in this decision-making process, as suggested by Nino during her interview,[2382] which I will elaborate on below (see Chapter 4.2).

Thirdly, this research envisioned practically implementable results tailored to the asylum context. In practice, the mist obscuring the term 'gender sensitivity'[2383] risks to violate the rights of (potential) SGBV survivors/victims as applicants for international protection.[2384] Therefore, it is essential to clarify the concept by rendering occurrences of gender insensitivity concrete, identifiable and therefore remediable. Rape myths allow for specific gender-stereotypical thinking patterns to be uncovered and for levels of rape

2380 Rousseau and others (n 7) 50; Millbank (n 7) 16; Jubany (n 7) 74.

2381 Edwards and others (n 9) 768.

2382 NGe014_1975_F_Georgia_RSA_DV_NL_[00:42:09].

2383 Anderson and Foster (n 17) 60.

2384 Middelburg and Balta (n 8) 436; Baillot, Cowan and Munro, '"Hearing the Right Gaps"' (n 92) 292; Wessels (n 94) 348.

myth acceptance to be quantified. Since these myths are time- and culture-bound,[2385] the underlying (legal) context should be taken into account. This is why research on the prevalence and possible remediation of acceptance of these myths must focus specifically on the asylum context, rather than simply replicating conclusions already drawn in the criminal justice context. Following Breen and Boyce, this research seeks to both identify and deconstruct biases toward SGBV survivors/victims, as well as examine the (lack of) knowledge and attitudes driving their acceptance. Such knowledge 'can be used to inform the development of effective interventions to target and dismantle biases, improve legal decision making, and foster ethical and supportive interactions with survivors,'[2386] such as training, awareness raising, and guidelines, which I will elaborate on below (see Chapter 4.2).

As explained above, since applicants were not actively recruited for interviews and the case sampling was not driven by data saturation for ethical reasons, these research results are not exhaustive. Instead, the six SGBV myths (incl. their sub-myths) identified may be complemented by new SGBV myths in future research, from legal or other disciplinary perspectives. This might broaden the range of identifiable myths and expertise necessary to rebut them.[2387] Just like the work of moving gender from the margins to the centre of refugee law,[2388] the work of identifying SGBV myths in the asylum context is unfinished and invites future research to continue it from other disciplines, in other asylum contexts, and relying on other applicants' standpoints (see Chapter 4.3).

In sum, this research provides the substantive and mainly conceptual contribution of translating the framework of rape mythology from the criminal justice context to the asylum context. Not all myths identified are unique to SGBV-related cases, rendering some of them more broadly relevant to other asylum procedures. The combined set of SGBV myths allowed for a comprehensive, multidisciplinary, and practice-oriented analysis of gender sensitivity in SGBV-related asylum decisions and procedures, of which I will discuss the implications as 'legal conclusions' and 'recommendations' below.

2385 Schlegel and Courtois (n 146) 24–25.

2386 Breen and Boyce (n 401) 5244–5245.

2387 For example, the data collected in this research suggested another parallel with the existing rape myth that 'real' sexual assault involves physical force/injury and will be easily substantiated by medical evidence. However, the issue of assessing medical certificates for refugee status determination has already been the subject of extensive debate, scholarship and case law (both within and outside of Belgium). As my legal expertise limits a substantive contribution to these in-depth analyses, I chose not to include it in this research.

2388 Arbel, Dauvergne and Millbank (n 12) 14.

3. LEGAL CONCLUSIONS

Uncovering Gender Insensitivity in Asylum Procedures & Decisions

In each chapter throughout this research, I have provided a quantitative representation of the SGBV myth acceptance levels in the Belgian asylum procedure, according to asylum authority (negative CGRS decisions and all CALL decisions) and procedural language (Dutch and French). Below, I will give an overview, allowing to compare these levels across first instance (CGRS) and appeal (CALL) decision making. I will proceed to present how this SGBV myth acceptance is distributed across countries of origin, types of SGBV, gender identities, and ages of applicants. Next to this pervasiveness across decision makers and cases, I will also illustrate how SGBV myths are employed cumulatively within the same decision. Finally, I will discuss the legal conclusions that can be drawn from this widespread and cumulative use of SGBV myth acceptance in relation to (inter)national law obligations on gender-sensitive refugee status determination.

3.1. PERVASIVENESS OF SGBV MYTH ACCEPTANCE IN THE BELGIAN ASYLUM CONTEXT

3.1.1. DISTRIBUTION OF SGBV MYTH ACCEPTANCE ACROSS ASYLUM AUTHORITIES AND LANGUAGES

Figure 33 and Figure 34 below demonstrate how the myth acceptance (MA) of each SGBV myth (incl. their sub-myths) is spread across the procedural languages at the CGRS and the CALL. Generally stated, the identified SGBV myths are accepted more frequently at the CGRS than at the CALL. For both asylum authorities, the most accepted SGBV myth is the one on SGBV disclosure, with acceptance levels rising to 77% of the French-language/71% of the Dutch-language CGRS decisions and 57% of the Dutch-language CALL judgements. At the CGRS, there are no substantial differences in myth acceptance between the procedural languages, except for the private issue myth, which is substantially more accepted in decisions in Dutch (23%) than in French (4%). Interestingly, at the CALL, the latter trend applies to all SGBV myths. The acceptance levels in judgments in French at the CALL are strikingly lower than those in

Dutch. For the non-state protection (2%), state protection (4%), and private issue myths (0%), they are even (practically) non-existent in French-language judgments.

Figure 33: % of decisions in the CGRS case law sample in Dutch (n=52) and French (n=48) accepting (at least 1 sub-myth of) a SGBV myth

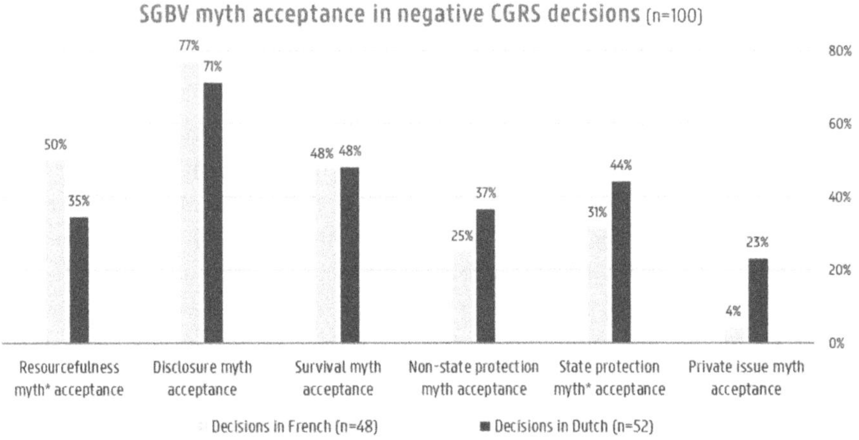

Figure 34: % of judgements in the CALL case law sample in Dutch (n=54) and French (n=48) accepting (at least 1 sub-myth of) a SGBV myth

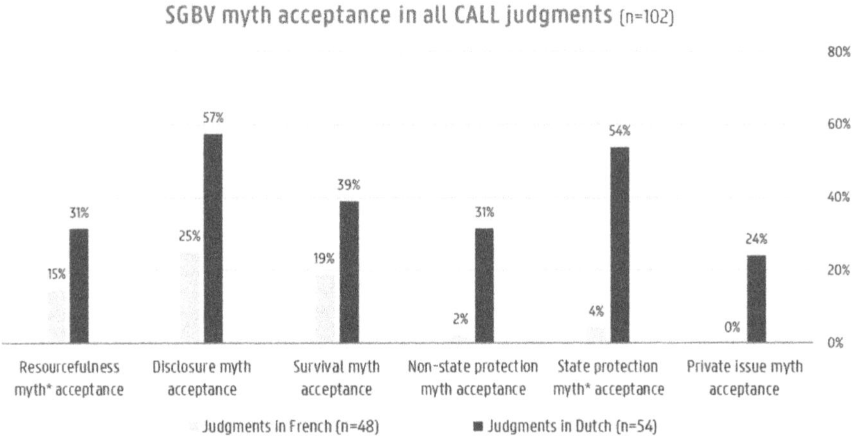

These conclusions are in line with previous research by Desmet, pointing at the divergence (at the time) between the CALL jurisprudence on minors in Dutch (more strict) and in French (more lenient).[2389] As described throughout

2389 Desmet, 'Appellate Asylum and Migration Proceedings in Belgium' (n 106) 214–215.

the research, this imbalance was also confirmed by POs/supervisors and attachés/judges during the interviews, when they explicitly named the gap between French- and Dutch-language decision making tradition or implicitly expressed their dissenting opinion with arguments I used as illustrations in the interviews, that were drafted in the other procedural language.[2390] It is important to remind that the Belgian Aliens Act specifically obliges the CALL to safeguard the unity of jurisprudence[2391] and ensure that (inter)national refugee law is uniformly implemented across both procedural languages. If not, applicants' legal certainty is fundamentally undermined by the fact that the outcome of their asylum procedure depends on the procedural language to which their case is assigned.

Overall, the most important conclusion to be drawn from this quantitative representation of SGBV myth acceptance is that it is no marginal phenomenon. On the contrary, each identified myth is accepted to some extent, both in first instance and in appeal, both in Dutch and in French decisions, with several acceptance levels exceeding 50% of the case law sample analysed.

3.1.2. DISTRIBUTION OF SGBV MYTH ACCEPTANCE ACROSS COUNTRIES OF ORIGIN, TYPES OF VIOLENCE & APPLICANTS

Figure 35 and Figure 36 visualise the distribution of SGBV myth acceptance per geographical region (according to WHO classification)[2392] and per type of SGBV. While the number of decisions/judgements is not equally spread across both variables, these distributions do confirm that <u>all</u> SGBV myths identified are accepted in asylum decision making on <u>all</u> regions and on <u>all</u> SGBV types. In addition, SGBV myth acceptance is prevalent across all applicants' gender identities included in the case sample (i.e. 84 cisgender women, 1 transgender

---

2390 E.g. RB002_CALL_Attaché_[00:09:41], [00:12:32], [00:14:05], [00:15:08] & [00:58:16]., CB001_CGRS_PO_[00:35:55]., CB004_CGRS_PO [00:27:43].

2391 Art. 39/6, §1 & 3 Belgian Aliens Act.

2392 World Health Organization (WHO) and Human Reproduction Programme (HRP), 'Global Database on the Prevalence of Violence Against Women', https://vaw-data.srhr.org/map. With EUROPE including: Albania (n=14), Bosnia and Herzegovina (n=2), Georgia (n=18), Moldavia (n=2), North-Macedonia (n=2), Russia (n=2), Serbia (n=2), Turkey (n=6); EASTERN MEDITERRANEAN including: Afghanistan (n=6), Iran (n=2), Iraq (n=2), Morocco (n=4), Palestine (n=2), Syria (n=2); AMERICAS including Honduras (n=1), Bolivia (n=2), Ecuador (n=2), Suriname (n=2); and AFRICA including: Algeria (n=2), Angola (n=2), Benin (n=2), Burkina Faso (n=2), Burundi (n=4), DRC (n=12), Gabon (n=6), Ethiopia (n=4), Eritrea (n=7), Guinea (n=34), The Gambia (n=2), Ghana (n=2), Ivory Coast (n=6), Kenya (n=2), Liberia (n=4), Mauritania (n=2), Nigeria (n=12), Senegal (n=6), Somalia (n=16), and Uganda (n=2).

woman, and 12 cisgender men) and across all applicants' ages[2393] (i.e. years of birth ranging from 1971 until 2014), with the case sample including at least three minors at the time of the first CGRS decision analysed.

Figure 35: Distribution (in %) of SGBV myths accepted in case law sample per geographical region, according to WHO classification

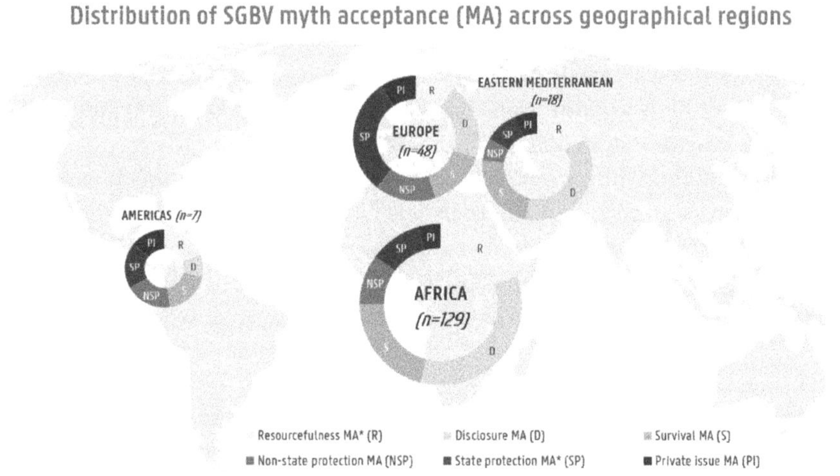

Figure 36: % of all decisions/judgments concerning the SGBV type accepting (at least 1 sub-myth of) a SGBV myth, with rape/sexual assault or RSA (n=138), sex trafficking/forced prostitution or STFP (n=19), genital mutilation/cutting or GMC (n=60), violence related to gender norm transgression or VGNT (n=84), forced marriage or FM (n=102) & domestic violence or DV (n=118)

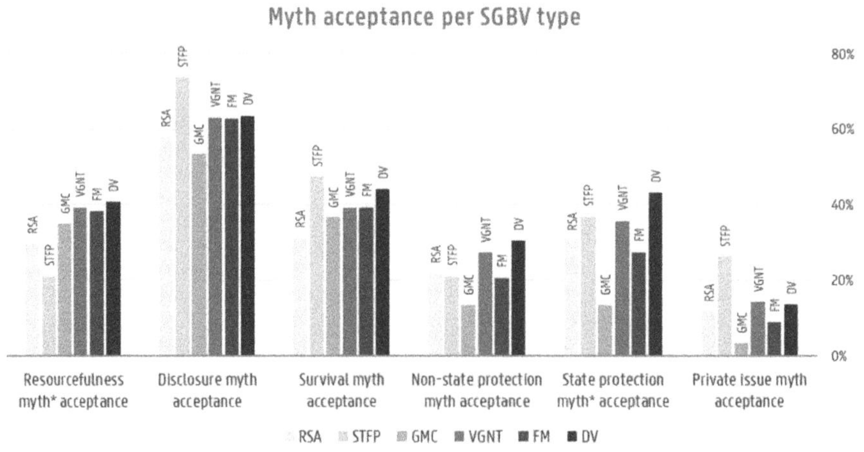

[2393] The age distribution cannot be accurately described, since not all decisions and judgements analysed mention the applicants' year of birth and in some cases their age is subject to discussion. This info concerns those applicants whose age is mentioned.

It is essential to stress that each applicant included in this research has a unique experience and their individual circumstances may give rise to different forms of oppression.[2394] These quantitative representations of the data do not aim to erase this uniqueness. Instead, rather than focusing on the differences between the cases, this research intended to uncover how these widely diverse experiences are repeatedly assessed in similar ways in the asylum procedure, relying on the same myth-based arguments. As such, in line with feminist standpoint theorists, with this research I attempted to recognise both difference and commonality,[2395] to not let the divisive power of the former overshadow the transformative potential of the latter and 'not [to] hide behind the [...] separations that have been imposed upon us.'[2396]

However, the figures above do pave the way for further research into the differences between applicants' experiences and their assessment in asylum procedures. For example, the regional distribution of SGBV myth acceptance seems to suggest that decision making on African and Eastern-Mediterranean countries makes greater use of micro level arguments about applicants' personal characteristics and credibility (resourcefulness, disclosure, and survival myths). In turn, decisions/judgments on Europe seem to rely more on argumentation based on (non-)state protection myths. The type of argumentation matters, since several applicants testified struggling most with the feeling of not being believed as such. Mary for example could not understand how the authorities, after she explained what happened to her, simply said:

> '"No, [...] that's not what happened". [...] The second **negative [decision]** they gave me, **it really broke me**, I just got weak, **[I lost] every strength I was using to push through** [...] there's no use. But what am I supposed to tell myself? I said [to myself:] "You can't just give up, you have a child that is depending on you".'[2397] | CASE OF MARY

From this distribution of SGBV myth across regions, it might be suggested that the more 'operative' the state apparatus in a country of origin is perceived to be (e.g. Europe where many 'safe' countries of origin are located), the less applicants' credibility is/has to be questioned. What the underlying reasons might be for this difference in argumentation and how it may or may not lead to differential treatment of SGBV cases according to applicants' origins is beyond the scope of this research. However, it does provide a suggestion for

2394 Crenshaw (n 178) 140.

2395 D Lynn O'Brien Hallstein, 'Where Standpoint Stands Now: An Introduction and Commentary' (2000) 23 Women's Studies in Communication 1, 3–4.

2396 Lorde (n 1) 32.

2397 NL017_1980_F_Liberia_STFP_GMC_VGNT_FM_NL_[00:11:55] & [01:51:23].

further intersectional analyses of SGBV-related refugee status determination (see Chapter 4.3 below).

3.1.3. CUMULATIVE USE OF SGBV MYTH-ACCEPTING ARGUMENTATION

When the asylum officials interviewed were confronted with reasoning based on SGBV myths, some objected that 'it is not a decisive argument, it is just an argument'[2398] or that they 'would never use it as the only argument.'[2399] They explained that asylum decisions are cumulatively composed of multiple 'building blocks' or 'puzzle pieces', but that these do not all carry the same weight. Therefore, some arguments, as several interviewees stated, only serve as 'additional weight' or to prevent a decision from being annulled by the CALL for lack of argumentation, otherwise 'the [asylum crisis] will never be fixed,' as one protection officer (PO) at the CGRS put it.[2400] One gender-specialised PO explicitly stated: 'The mindset of some supervisors is to use as many elements as possible, and then you start adding the stupidest element, when really these shouldn't be there.'[2401]

When introducing rape myth acceptance (see Part I, Chapter 1.3), I mentioned how the phenomenon may on the one hand originate from subconscious cultural stereotypes and/or well-intended self-protection mechanisms like the 'just world hypothesis'.[2402] On the other hand, this research and the latter quote illustrate how SGBV myths are also consciously instrumentalised to foster a politics of exhaustion. The latter term was coined by Welander as 'the ways in which exhaustion is employed as a tool of [migration] governance and control.'[2403] As such, asylum officials' strategy of trying out as many arguments as possible and 'seeing what sticks', risks causing applicants' procedural exhaustion, both

---

2398 RB008_CALL_Judge_[00:21:48].

2399 CB005_CGRS_Supervisor+PO_GENDER_[00:21:06]., CB008_CGRS_Supervisor + PO_GENDER_[00:35:09]., CB011_CGRS_Supervisor + PO_GENDER_[00:43:51]., CB013_CGRS_PO_[00:22:19].

2400 CB014_CGRS_PO_[00:31:07], [00:50:36], [00:53:52] & [01:02:37]., CB002_CGRS_PO_[00:33:58]., CB004_CGRS_PO_[00:21:01]., CB005_CGRS_Supervisor+PO_GENDER_[00:36:07]., CB009_CGRS_PO_GENDER_[00:32:03] & [00:35:21]., CB010_CGRS_Supervisor + PO_[00:29:51]., CB013_CGRS_PO_[01:13:36]., & RB004_CALL_Attaché_[00:50:04]., RB006_CALL_Judge_[01:21:39].

2401 CB009_CGRS_PO_GENDER_[01:03:24].

2402 Bohner and others (n 132) 27; Rich (n 137) 21–22.

2403 Leonie Ansems de Vries and Marta Welander, 'Refugees, Displacement, and the European "Politics of Exhaustion"' (*Mediterranean Journeys in Hope*, 30 September 2016), www.opendemocracy.net/en/mediterranean-journeys-in-hope/refugees-displacement-and-europ/.

by not being believed[2404] and facing victim-blaming argumentation,[2405] as well as by having to consistently appeal their decisions.

A cumulative approach to asylum decision making is not objected to as such, given the complexity of refugee status determination and the numerous elements that must be taken into account. However, this does not alter the fact that every argument used must hold its ground independently. If an asylum decision is largely or even entirely built on SGBV myth-based arguments, chances are very real that its final outcome also lacks foundation. Therefore, asylum authorities must first ensure that their decisions are not based on SGBV myths, and secondly, if this turns out to be the case, verify whether their final conclusion still holds its ground once the argumentation has been stripped of these myths. The CALL in Qawtar's case did not seem to agree:

> '[T]he **reasoning as a whole** must be taken into account and **not the various parts of the reasoning in isolation**, since **one part may not be sufficiently robust to support the decision** but may be so in conjunction with the other grounds.'[2406] | CASE OF QAWTAR

However, both Qawtar's CGRS decision and CALL judgement relied on <u>all</u> six SGBV myths identified in this research. The same counts for the (later withdrawn[2407]) CGRS decision of Sofia, of which the full argumentation (concerning the child sexual abuse by her father) reads as follows (Figure 37).

It is worth reiterating that, after this refusal decision, Sofia failed to appeal at the CALL due to her insufficient bank balance to pay the registration fee, a situation that could not be rectified. Eventually, the CGRS decided to withdraw the initial refusal decision and to recognise her as a refugee after all. As the reasons for this withdrawal are not made public, there is no way of knowing whether or not this was based on any form of SGBV myth rebuttal by the CGRS.

2404 As demonstrated by Mary above. (NL017_1980_F_Liberia_STFP_GMC_VGNT_FM_NL_ [00:11:55] & [01:51:23].)

2405 Roels, 'The Use of Rape Myths and Resulting Victim-Blaming Mechanisms in Asylum Interviews and Decisions on the Grounds of Sexual and Gender-Based Violence (SGBV)' (n 500).

2406 DM116_CALL 1 (refusal)_1999_F_Morocco_VGNT_FM_DV_24/04/2024_305 429_NL_ Database_p. 14.

2407 Upon refusal of her application by the CGRS, Sofia's appeal with the CALL was not registered, since her insufficient bank balance had caused an error in the payment of the registration fee. Despite a letter from her lawyer explaining this, the situation could not be rectified and she could not appeal against her refusal decision by the CGRS. Eventually, the CGRS decided to withdraw the initial refusal of Sofia's application and, after reconsidering her case (the reasoning of which is not made public), to recognise her as a refugee.

Figure 37: Excerpt from a CGRS refusal decision (later withdrawn) concerning child sexual abuse in Honduras, visualising the cumulative use of six SGBV myth-accepting arguments at the same time

CASE OF SOFIA

You [...] submitted a certificate from your psychologist [...] stating that you show signs of post-traumatic stress as a result of the sexual abuse you suffered in your country of origin and that you have a deep sense of sadness and distrust. However, **this report is not sufficient to demonstrate that you would be unable to make statements**. You state that you feel able to attend the interview and you are given the opportunity to request additional breaks. Furthermore, the personal interview notes do not indicate anywhere that you were unable to make coherent statements. In view of the above, it can reasonably be assumed [...] that your rights in the present procedure are being respected and that you are able to fulfil your obligations. — **Disclosure MA**

However, after your personal interview [...], **you have not been able to demonstrate having a well-founded fear of persecution** [...].

Firstly, you claim to have left El Salvador [sic] because you were sexually abused by your father from the age of 12 to 17. However, **private law problems are not related to the Refugee Convention criteria.** — **Private issue MA**

[...] You state that the sexual abuse stopped when you were 17. You then stayed in Honduras for several years. You add that he continued to seek contact afterwards by asking for hugs or telling you to sit on his lap, but [...] when he came home [...], you tried to spend as little time with him as possible. However serious and reprehensible the acts of which you were a victim [...] may be, **you do not demonstrate that you had problems in Honduras in the three years prior to your departure** that would have led to serious harm. — Survival MA

It should also be noted that after your arrival in Belgium, **you waited more than seven years before submitting an application for protection.** You simply state that you did not know that you could apply for asylum and that you were waiting for regularisation. [...] This is not a convincing justification for the late [...] application, especially since your statements show that **you were sufficiently resourceful** and that you also sought information about the procedures in Belgium through a lawyer. — **Resourcefulness MA***

In this regard, the CGRS emphasises that a person who claims to be persecuted in their country of origin and who invokes Geneva Convention protection [...] may reasonably be expected, if they are in need of actual protection, to apply [...] upon arrival or as soon as possible thereafter [...]. The fact that you only submitted an application [...] more than seven years after your arrival in Belgium is **a counter-indication to the seriousness and credibility of your need for international protection and the problems and fears you have outlined.** This shows that you did not consider international protection to be (urgently) necessary, which completely relativises the seriousness of the persecution you invoked. — Disclosure MA

Furthermore, the CGRS notes that you told your mother about this abuse after your arrival in Belgium. Your mother believed you immediately and apologised. You also have a good relationship with your sister [...] who no longer lives with your parents. You state that you cannot go and live with her because she lives with her husband. When asked why she would not be able to help you, you vaguely state that it would not change much because she lives only 10 minutes away. Your statements therefore show that **you have family members in Honduras with whom you have a good relationship and there is no indication whatsoever that they would not support you.** — **Non-state protection MA**

In this regard, it should be noted that you did not seek protection from your father in Honduras in any way. You refer to the general behaviour of men towards women in Honduras. **You have not taken any steps to report your father or seek protection from him [...].** — **State protection MA***

[...] Based on the elements in your file, I conclude that **you cannot be recognised as a refugee in the meaning of [...] the Aliens Act.**

with MA: myth acceptance

As visualised in Figure 38, across the entire case law sample analysed, 76% of the decisions/judgements rely at least on one SGBV myth and 20% are based on all six (3%), five (9%), or four (8%) SGBV myths combined.

Figure 38: % of decisions/judgements in the total case law sample (n=202) accepting 0, 1, 2, 3, 4, 5, and 6 SGBV myths

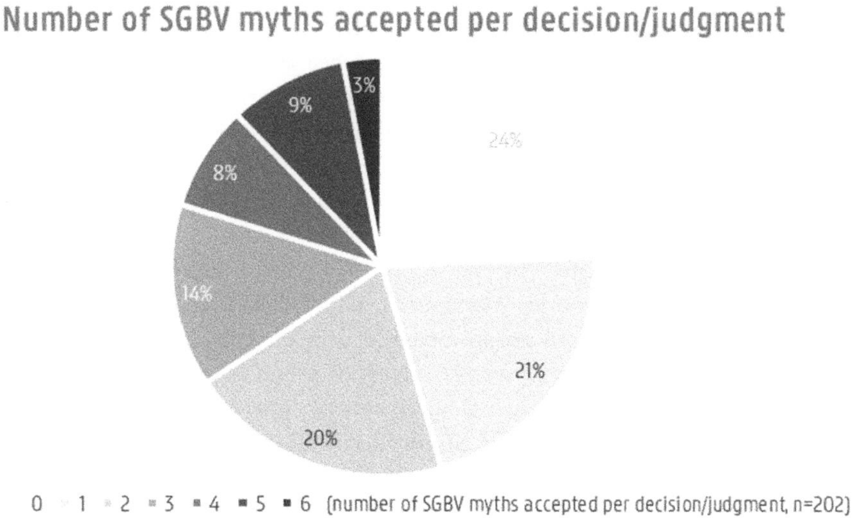

Categories: resourcefulness myth*, disclosure myths, survival myths, non-state protection myths, state protection myth* & private issue myth

Based on the above summarised institutional, geographical, factual, and demographic distribution and cumulative use of SGBV myths in asylum procedures, this research shows that SGBV myth acceptance is not a phenomenon limited to a few cases with specific features. On the contrary, it is a practice that is widespread throughout decision making practice, regardless of the stage/language of the procedure, the country of origin/gender identity/age of the applicant, or the type of SGBV feared. The SGBV myth-based arguments are not merely subordinate or insignificant 'extra weight' in decisions, but often largely (or completely) substantiate their reasoning. This inevitably leads this research to conclude that refugee status determination for applicants fleeing SGBV is permeated to an alarming degree by acceptance of SGBV myths in the Belgian asylum procedure.

3.2. THE VIOLATION OF (INTER)NATIONAL LAW PROVISIONS ON GENDER-SENSITIVE REFUGEE STATUS DETERMINATION

As I have argued throughout the previous chapters, acceptance of SGBV myths often coincides with the (risk of) misinterpreting or misapplying rules of (inter) national refugee (case) law. This risk arises at four different stages of refugee status determination, namely in determining whether: 1) the flight story falls within the Convention scope, 2) it is credible, 3) the fear of persecution is well-founded, and 4) whether an IFA is available.

In the first phase, acceptance of the idea that 'SGBV is a private issue excluded from the Convention scope' risks to violate refugee law provisions and case law prescribing to: include private SGBV in the Convention scope (when authorities are unable/unwilling to provide protection against it);[2408] take into account gender when determining membership of a particular social group;[2409] qualify women facing SGBV as a particular social group[2410] and leaving one's marriage (*W.S. case*)[2411] or believing in gender equality (*K.L. case*)[2412] as an additional common characteristic; qualify SGBV as persecution[2413] (incl. cumulatively gender-discriminatory measures as in Afghanistan under the Taliban,[2414] and those facing it as a particular social group merely due to their nationality and gender (*A.H. & F.N. case*)[2415]); and interpret <u>all</u> Convention grounds gender-sensitively.[2416]

In the second phase, assessing applicants as non-credible due to their 'inappropriate' ways or timing of SGBV disclosure, asylum authorities risk to disregard the international refugee (case) law that denial of international protection cannot solely rely on delayed application[2417] and that a certain lack of detail/consistency or an initial false statement is accepted, as long as the former does not jeopardise applicants' overall credibility (*R.C. v. Sweden, A.A. v. France & A.F. v. France*)[2418] and the latter is clarified and withdrawn as soon as possible (*Attentat au Pakistan case*).[2419] When asylum authorities base non-credibility assessments on (potential) survivors'/victims' 'inappropriate' survival reactions, such reasoning might conflict with the CJEU case law that applicants are not expected to avoid their own persecution by behaving discreetly (e.g. by going into hiding) (*X, Y, Z & K.L. cases*)[2420] or seeking protection from non-state actors (*O.A. case*).[2421]

2408 Art. 6(c) EU Qualification Directive; Art. 6(c) EU Qualification Regulation; Art. 48/5, §1(c) Belgian Aliens Act.

2409 Art. 10(1)d EU Qualification Directive; Art. 10(1)d EU Qualification Regulation; Art. 48/3, §4(d) Belgian Aliens Act.

2410 *WS v. Intervyuirasht organ na Darzhavna agentsia za bezhantsite pri Ministerskia savet* (n 44) paras 49, 52, 54 57 & ruling 1.

2411 *Ibid.* 50–51 & 53.

2412 *K.L. v. Staatssecretaris van Justitie en Veiligheid* (n 78) paras 45 & (Ruling) 1.

2413 Art. 60(1) Istanbul Convention; Art. 9(1) & (2)a & f EU Qualification Directive; Art. 9(1) & (2)a & f EU Qualification Regulation; Art. 48/3, §2 Belgian Aliens Act.

2414 Ruling 1. *AH & FN v. Bundesamt für Fremdenwesen und Asyl* (n 82).

2415 *Ibid.* 47–58 & ruling 1-2.

2416 Art. 60 Istanbul Convention.

2417 Art. 10 (1) EU Procedures Directive.

2418 *R.C. v. Sweden* (n 989) para 52; *A.A. v. France* (n 990) para 54; *A.F. v. France* (n 991) para 56.

2419 *International Protection Appeals Tribunal and Others (Attentat au Pakistan)* (n 1107) para 96.

2420 *X, Y and Z v. The Netherlands* (n 67) paras 10, 71, 74 & 75; *K.L. v. Staatssecretaris van Justitie en Veiligheid* (n 78) para 63.

2421 *Secretary of State for the Home Department v. O.A.* (n 742) para ruling 2.

Thirdly, in the well-foundedness stage of refugee status determination, when relying on the idea that 'resourceful applicants do not need protection against SGBV', asylum authorities risk to violate the CJEU's refugee case law that applicants' social or financial support is irrelevant for refugee status determination (*O.A. case*).[2422] In addition, defending the same reasoning for applicants with non-state actor support (non-state actor myths) constitutes an incorrect implementation of (inter)national refugee law prescribing that protection can only be offered by actors controlling (substantial parts of) the state territory[2423] and CJEU case law that applicants' private actor support is irrelevant to assess the effectiveness or availability of protection against persecution (*O.A. case*).[2424]

By accepting the myth that 'non-exhaustion of state protection implies ill-foundedness of SGBV flight stories' (the state protection myth), asylum authorities risk to violate the (inter)national refugee law provisions prescribing that state protection should only be exhausted when it is (cumulatively) accessible, effective, and non-temporary, for example by 'operating an effective legal system for the detection, prosecution and punishment of [...] persecution.'[2425] When hereby disregarding the applicants' justifications for being unable or unwilling to avail themselves to such protection or expecting them to exhaust it regardless of its reasonableness, they risk to incorrectly implement the UN refugee definition[2426] and fail to assess asylum applications individually, as prescribed by the EU Qualification Directive/Regulation.[2427] Also, states' designation of countries of origin as 'safe' without verifying that reasonable state protection against SGBV is available across the entire territory goes against established CJEU case law (*C.V. case*).[2428]

In the fourth stage, asylum authorities, relying on a combination of the survival, resourcefulness, non-state, and state protection myths, could suggest that, instead of fleeing the country, (resourceful) applicants' should return to an IFA, rendered safe and/or reasonable through their (facilitating) non-state actor support and/or state protection. In doing so, such 'solutions' might disregard (inter)national refugee law when the IFA suggested is not accessible, does not provide reasonable resettlement, or does not exclude any (other) fear of or does not provide state protection against persecution.[2429] Here too, according to the CJEU, applicants cannot be expected to return to an IFA that is only safe when

2422 *Ibid.* 48.
2423 Art. 7(2) EU Qualification Directive; Art. 7(2) EU Qualification Regulation; Art. 48/5, §2 Belgian Aliens Act.
2424 *Secretary of State for the Home Department v. O.A.* (n 742) para ruling 2.
2425 Art. 7(1)-(2) EU Qualification Directive; Art. 7(1)-(2) EU Qualification Regulation; Art. 48/5, § 2, part 2 Belgian Aliens Act.
2426 Art. 1(A)2 UN Refugee Convention.
2427 Art. 4(3)c EU Qualification Directive; Art. 4(3) EU Qualification Regulation; Art. 34(2)d EU Asylum Procedures Regulation; Art. 48/6, § 5, c] Belgian Aliens Act.
2428 *CV v. Ministerstvo vnitra České republiky, Odbor azylové a migrační politiky* (n 559) [Ruling 2].
2429 Art. 8(2) EU Qualification Directive; Art. 8(5)a-c EU Qualification Regulation; Art. 48/5, §3 Belgian Aliens Act.

applicants avoid their own persecution by behaving discreetly an/or going into hiding (*X, Y, Z & K.L. cases*)[2430] or when they have to become dependent on non-state actors (*O.A. case*).[2431] On top of this, the new EU Qualification Regulation adds that, specifically in determining the safety/reasonability of an IFA, asylum authorities should take applicants' gender into account.[2432]

It is also worth noting that expecting applicants to return to an IFA where their safety requires discretion, going underground, or even full dependence on others, risks to violate international human rights law (i.e. the freedom of movement, association, self-expression, …). Suggesting an IFA that prevents contact between applicants' children and parent-perpetrators risks violating the latter's visitation/custody rights. Expecting state authorities to unequivocally protect parent-applicants from parent-perpetrators upon return might also conflict with the rules of private international law. Concretely in the case where a parent-perpetrator has filed a complaint for international child abduction against the parent-applicant, local authorities might face a conflict of interest upon return, forcing them both to protect the parent-applicant against the parent-perpetrator (the actor of persecution) and to prosecute the parent-applicant for fleeing with their child (international child abduction). If such prosecution results in a prison sentence for example, children might not have any parental support left upon return. Although outside the direct scope of this research, the interplay between refugee, human rights and private international law in SGBV-related asylum procedures is largely unexplored territory that deserves attention in future research (see Chapter 4.3 below).

Finally, it is essential that the entire process of refugee status determination is based on precise and up-to-date information, in line with CJEU case law (*A.H. and F.N. & K.L. cases*).[2433] SGBV-related asylum decisions might violate CJEU refugee case law in particular, when they are not supported by COI relevant to gender-related applications, including information on: SGBV prevalence and forms reported; women's position before the law and their political, social, and economic rights; gender norms and consequences for transgressing these; protection available to survivors/victims; penalties imposed on perpetrators; and risks that (potential) survivors/victims might face upon return after fleeing and applying for international protection (*W.S. case*).[2434]

Across all the abovementioned stages, parties to the Istanbul Convention, including Belgium and the EU itself,[2435] are bound to 'take the necessary

2430 *X, Y and Z v. The Netherlands* (n 67) paras 10, 71, 74 & 75; *K.L. v. Staatssecretaris van Justitie en Veiligheid* (n 78) para 63.

2431 *Secretary of State for the Home Department v. O.A.* (n 742) para ruling 2.

2432 Art. 8(5)b EU Qualification Regulation.

2433 *AH & FN v. Bundesamt für Fremdenwesen und Asyl* (n 82) para 52; *K.L. v. Staatssecretaris van Justitie en Veiligheid* (n 78) para 60.

2434 *WS v. Intervyuirasht organ na Darzhavna agentsia za bezhantsite pri Ministerskia savet* (n 44) para 61.

2435 Council of Europe Treaty Office (n 43).

legislative or other measures to develop [...] gender-sensitive asylum procedures, including refugee status determination.'[2436] This research cannot and did not aim to give an exact meaning to 'gender sensitivity', nor does it definitively answer the question of how gender sensitivity should be implemented, as the Istanbul Convention does not define the term itself. However, with this research, I have provided a framework to operationalise gender sensitivity and assess the level of gender sensitivity in asylum procedures.

As mentioned in the beginning (see Part I, Chapter 2), gender sensitivity may concern multiple aspects of asylum decision making, including procedural gender sensitivity. With this research, I propose one substantive way of many to interpret and implement gender sensitivity in the asylum context, inspired by the concept of rape mythology. In doing so, I was able to identify concrete thinking patterns that are based on 'prejudicial, stereotyped, or false beliefs'[2437] about SGBV (what I call SGBV myths), rather than grounded in evidence-based expertise.

Although 'gender-sensitive refugee status determination' remains undefined, in my opinion, it cannot allow asylum authorities to base asylum decisions on SGBV myths, regardless of how heavily they weigh on the argumentation and eventual decision. If a final conclusion not to recognise applicants as refugees does not hold its ground when stripped of such myth-based arguments, it must be labelled gender-insensitive and therefore in violation of the international legal obligation in Article 60 of the Istanbul Convention.

The pervasiveness of the phenomenon, across countries of origin/ SGBV types/gender identities/ages, and its impact on individual decisions, as demonstrated above (see Chapter 3.1 below), make the risk of such a violation alarmingly pressing. When, on top of that, national asylum authorities' decisions vary substantially depending on individual decision makers' SGBV myth acceptance, for example between procedural languages as is the case in Belgium, they also risk failing to ensure unity of jurisprudence and to leave applicants at the mercy of arbitrariness.[2438]

Since SGBV myth acceptance often stems from a lack of empirical knowledge about the risk factors, nature, consequences, and prevalence of SGBV, it is all the more crucial to consult recent, SGBV- and region-specific COI, as well as relevant expertise in health and social sciences. The legal and empirical expertise necessary for gender-sensitive refugee status determination on persons fleeing SGBV, as elaborately described throughout this research, is summarised and visualised below in Figure 39. These types of expertise should be considered in conjunction with each case's individual circumstances and are non-exhaustive (as they might be expanded through further research on SGBV mythology in the asylum context).

2436 Art. 60(3) Istanbul Convention.
2437 Burt (n 131) 217.
2438 Art. 39/6, §1 & 3 Belgian Aliens Act.

Figure 39: Visualisation of necessary empirical & legal expertise for gender-sensitive refugee status determination rebutting SGBV myths

	ARGUMENTATION		NECESSARY EMPIRICAL EXPERTISE: Expertise in health & social sciences on …	NECESSARY EMPIRICAL EXPERTISE: Recent, SGBV- & region-specific country of origin information (COI) on …	NECESSARY LEGAL EXPERTISE on …
→ APPLICANTS FLEEING SGBV **DO NOT QUALIFY FOR REFUGEE PROTECTION** BECAUSE:					
SCOP	Private issue myth	SGBV is a **private issue** excluded from the UN Refugee Convention scope	SGBV as a global **public health, safety & economic problem**	The **scale** of SGBV prevalence, **public nature** of **its consequences**…	Refugee (case) law **including SGBV** in the Convention **scope**
→ SGBV QUALIFIES FOR REFUGEE PROTECTION, BUT IS **NOT CREDIBLE** BECAUSE:					
CREDIBILITY	Disclosure myths	'Inappropriate' **disclosure** undermines SGBV flight stories' credibility	The human **memory, barriers** to & the impact of **trauma/culture** on content/manner/timing of SGBV disclosure…		Refugee (case) law prescribing **not** to refuse international protection solely due to **delayed application** & the **subordinate role of credibility arguments** in refugee status determination
CREDIBILITY	Survival myths	'Inappropriate' **survival reactions** undermine SGBV flight stories' credibility	SGBV survivors'/victims' (subconscious) **survival reactions, risk management**…		
CREDIBILITY	(Non-) state protection myths	'Inappropriate' **help-seeking from (non-) state actors** undermines SGBV flight stories' credibility	SGBV survivors'/victims' **disclosure/reporting barriers, help-seeking behaviour, risk management**…		
→ SGBV QUALIFIES FOR REFUGEE PROTECTION, IS CREDIBLE, BUT THE FEAR IS **ILL-FOUNDED** BECAUSE:					
WELL-FOUNDEDNESS	Resource-fulness myth*	**Resourceful** applicants do not need protection against SGBV	SGBV prevalence across **all socio-economic backgrounds/gender identities, inaccuracy of resourcefulness** as an SGBV predictor…	**Risk factors/groups** related to **SGBV prevalence**	Refugee (case) law on the **irrelevance** of individual resourcefulness (e.g. **social/financial support**…) in refugee status determination
WELL-FOUNDEDNESS	Non-state protection myths	Applicants with (facilitating) **non-state actor support** do not need protection against SGBV	**Overestimates** of **(non-) state protection** against SGBV due to underreporting, **barriers to bystander intervention, SGBV** prevalence in the **private sphere**…		Refugee (case) law on **actors of protection** & the **irrelevance of private actor support** in refugee status determination
WELL-FOUNDEDNESS	State protection myth*	Non-exhaustion of **state protection** implies ill-foundedness of SGBV flight stories (or prevents their assessment)		*De facto* **state protection** related to patriarchal gender norms & SGBV prevalence/prosecution	Refugee (case) law on the **refugee definition**, the qualification of reasonable **state protection & safe countries of origin**…
→ SGBV QUALIFIES FOR REFUGEE PROTECTION, IS CREDIBLE, THE FEAR IS WELL-FOUNDED, BUT THERE IS AN **IFA** (internal flight alternative):					
IFA	Resource-fulness* & survival myths; (Non-) state* protection myths	Instead of fleeing the country, (resourceful) applicants' should **return to an IFA**, rendered safe and/or reasonable through their (facilitating) non-state actor support and/or state protection	-See ↑ - Lasting impact of **(traumatic) SGBV** on survivors'/victims' **health**, risk of **revictimisation**, the **cycle of violence**, **dependency** on perpetrators/others… upon return	-See ↑ - Risk of violence due to **gender norm transgression, social cohesion & traceability** by perpetrators, **route safety**, applicants' **legal, political, social, and cultural status & risks**… upon return	-See ↑ - **Refugee (case) law** on the conditions for IFAs, their limited role in SGBV cases, discretion/taking avoiding action… upon return - **Human rights (case) law** on the freedom of movement, association, self-expression… upon return - **Private international (case) law** on international child abduction, visitation/custody rights… upon return
→ **ACROSS ALL REFUGEE STATUS DETERMINATION STAGES**					**Gender-sensitive refugee status determination**

As a researcher examining international law, I and many others experience the tension between 'working beyond the constraints of [the international legal system] to reimagine international law' versus 'working within [that system], seeking change from within'[2439] and therefore the tension between 'resistance and obedience.'[2440] Walking the first principled path, the above conclusions necessarily raise the question of whether it is possible at all for asylum officials, some of whom are not trained legally and/or on gender-related persecution specifically, to master all the expertise mentioned in Figure 39. If we allow ourselves to think beyond the constraints of international refugee law, the conclusion may be that mastering all this expertise as an individual decision maker is simply impossible. This would also mean that trying to accurately assess, in a trauma- and gender-sensitive manner, SGBV-related flight stories on credibility and well-foundedness, inside the time frame and walls of a personal interview or asylum hearing, is in itself a Sisyphean task.

For me, this fundamental reflection exists alongside the second pragmatic path of working towards change within the existing asylum system. As such, the above conclusions can lead to concrete recommendations, that specifically focus on sharing the necessary legal and empirical expertise and thereby urge decision makers to actively rebut SGBV myths. Below, I will go into both substantive and procedural recommendations to enable such rebuttal.

2439 Emily Jones, 'Theory as Practice in International Law' (*Völkerrechtsblog*, 25 May 2023), https://voelkerrechtsblog.org/theory-as-practice-in-international-law/.

2440 Irene Manganini, 'Refugee Law between Resistance and Compliance: A Reparative Reading of a Classic Feminist Struggle' (*Refugee Law Initiative Blog*, 15 October 2024), https://rli.blogs.sas.ac.uk/2024/10/15/refugee-law-between-resistance-and-compliance-a-reparative-reading-of-a-classic-feminist-struggle/.

4. RECOMMENDATIONS

Challenging SGBV Myth Acceptance in Asylum Procedures & Decisions

4.1. SUBSTANTIVE RECOMMENDATIONS

Below, the substantive recommendations following from the research findings can be visualised (Figure 40). These constitute practical directives for challenging SGBV myth acceptance in refugee status determination on applicants fleeing SGBV. They are informed and shaped by the various rebuttals of SGBV myths identified throughout this research in relevant (case) law and health, social, and legal sciences. The overall substantive recommendation urges asylum officials not to rely on SGBV myths to (cumulatively) substantiate decisions and to actively rebut them when reconsidering previous decisions. Hereby, it should be reminded that for two of the six myths, this recommendation is nuanced, as indicated by the asterisk/* in the figure.

What is true for all myths, is that they concern assumptions that lack confirmation in legal and/or empirical (i.e. social/health sciences and COI) expertise. Where these myths differ, is in the chance that these assumptions might in fact be confirmed by such expertise. As such, the SGBV myths are situated along a continuum of their 'myth-like character', with the chance of confirmation through empirical/legal expertise ranging from 'never' to 'exceptionally'.

Four of the SGBV myths will never be confirmed: the disclosure, survival, non-state protection, and private issue myths. For example, it will never be confirmed that delayed SGBV disclosure indicates untruthfulness (delayed disclosure myth), because this is simply not how the human memory and body reacts to and copes with such violence (see Part III, Chapter 3.3.2) or it will never be confirmed that SGBV as such falls outside the scope of the UN Refugee Convention (private issue myth), because this is legally incorrect (see Part V, Chapter 3). However, the resourcefulness and state protection myths might exceptionally be confirmed through COI that respectively: excludes a specific type of resourcefulness as a risk factor to experience specific forms of SGBV (Part III, Chapter 2.2.1) or confirms the accessibility, effectiveness, and non-temporariness of state protection against SGBV in a specific region (Part V, Chapter 2.2.1).

Nonetheless, such exceptional use of resourcefulness and state protection myth-based argumentation requires extreme caution for two important reasons. Firstly, COI on certain forms of resourcefulness lowering one's risk to SGBV does not make such violence impossible. Also, COI on generally accessible, effective, and non-temporary state protection does not exclude specific situations where the system failed individual (potential) SGBV survivors/victims.

Figure 40: Substantive recommendations

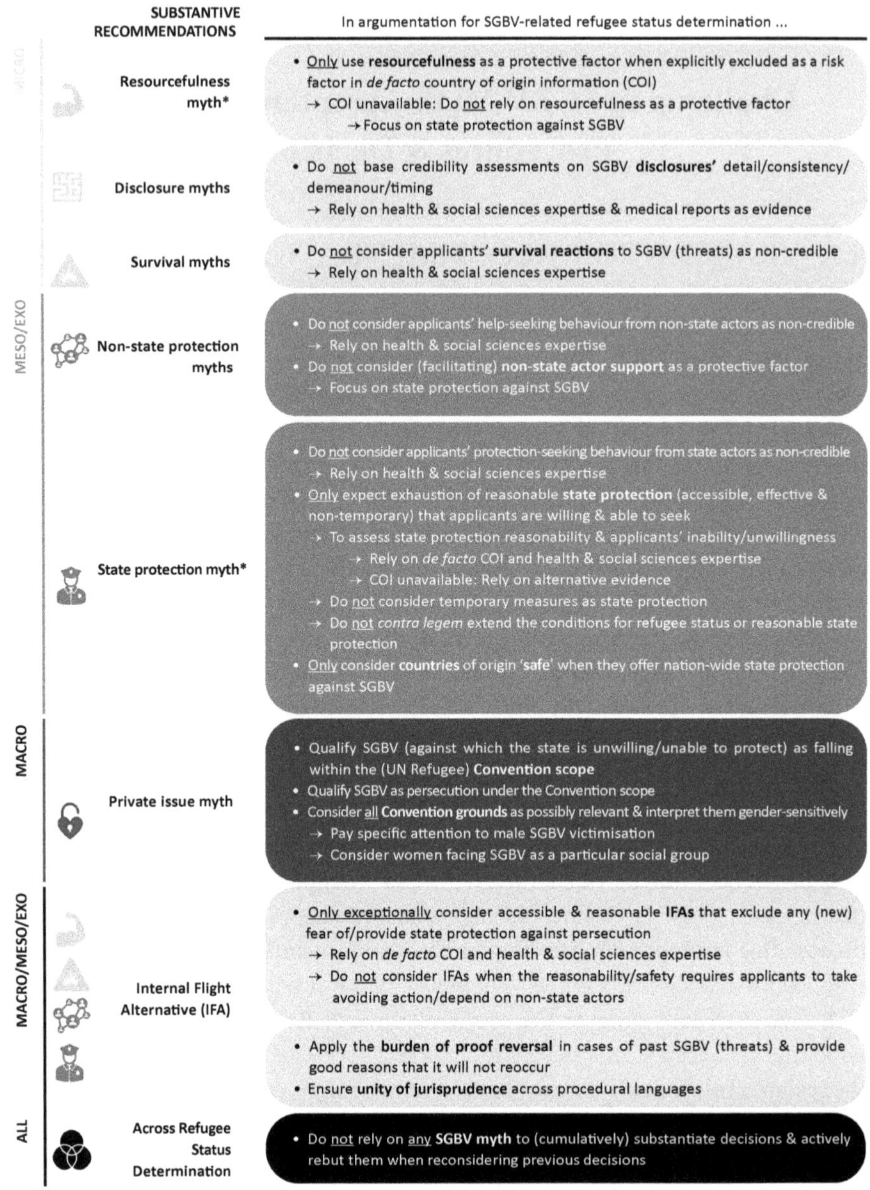

Secondly, the confirmation of these assumptions in empirical expertise, like COI, requires such COI to be available in the first place. Knowing that SGBV is a structurally underreported, under-researched, and therefore underestimated phenomenon (see Part V, Chapter 2.2), asylum authorities should acknowledge that the accurate, factual, up-to-date, SGBV-, and region-specific COI necessary to rely on the resourcefulness and state protection myths are extremely rare and difficult to find. When no such empirical expertise to confirm the assumptions underlying these myths can be found, they cannot be accepted in asylum decision making.

4.1.1. ARGUMENTATION ON RESOURCEFULNESS, DISCLOSURE & SURVIVAL REACTIONS (MICRO LEVEL)

When assessing the well-foundedness of SGBV-related applications for international protection, decision makers should only consider applicants' material and non-material resourcefulness as a protective factor when accurate, recent, SGBV-, and region-specific COI explicitly excludes these as SGBV risk factors. The fact that the resourcefulness myth is therefore not necessarily or always untrue, allowing for its exceptional use when supported by such COI, is reflected in the asterisk/* indication in Figure 40. Importantly, when such COI is unavailable, resourcefulness should not be considered as a protective factor at all. Instead of accepting the resourcefulness myth, the argumentation should focus on state protection against SGBV.

When assessing the credibility of applicants' SGBV experiences/fears, decision makers should not consider applicants' level of detail or consistency in, delay of, or demeanour during SGBV disclosure (whether on traumatic or broader autobiographical events) as non-credible. When registration interviews (preceding the actual personal asylum interview) do not allow legal assistance from a lawyer and the interviewers are not gender-trained under the conditions recommended by this research (as is the case for the Belgian Immigration Office or IO), decision makers should not rely on inconsistencies with the information collected during such a registration interview.

This recommendation specifically aligns with an abovementioned CALL judgment in a Burundian rape case, confirming that 'the purpose of the hearings at the IO is not to obtain a full and detailed account of the applicant's story, but rather to provide an opportunity for the applicant to present their case.'[2441] Instead of accepting the disclosure myths, argumentation should rely on health and social sciences expertise (e.g. on the memory, disclosure barriers, the impact of trauma/culture on content/manner/timing of disclosure, ...) and medical (incl. psychological) reports in the same way asylum authorities now rely on COI: as evidence.

Also, in SGBV-related refugee status determination, decision makers should not consider applicants' survival reactions to SGBV experiences/fears, whether short or long-term, whether active or passive, as non-credible. Instead of accepting the survival reactions myths, argumentation should rely on health and social sciences expertise, proving that any reaction (whether active, passive, or a combination evolving over time) may constitute 'normal' survivor/victim behaviour.

2441 DBu089_CALL 1 (recognition)_F_Burundi_RSA_30/5/2024_307 576_FR_Database_p. 16.

4.1.2. ARGUMENTATION ON NON-STATE & STATE PROTECTION (MESO/EXO LEVEL)

Decision makers should not consider applicants' help-seeking behaviour from non-state actors, both *sensu stricto* and private support networks, in response to SGBV experiences/fears as non-credible. Instead of accepting the non-state protection myth, argumentation should rely on health and social sciences expertise (e.g. on disclosure barriers, help-seeking behaviour, risk management, ...). When assessing the well-foundedness of SGBV-related applications, decision makers should not consider (facilitating) support from non-state actors as protective factors. Instead of accepting the non-state protection myth, their argumentation should focus on state protection against SGBV.

Further, applicants' protection-seeking behaviour from state actors should not be considered non-credible. Instead of accepting the state protection myth, argumentation should rely on health and social sciences expertise (e.g. on reporting barriers, protection-seeking behaviour, risk management, ...). When assessing the well-foundedness of SGBV-related applications, asylum authorities should only expect applicants to exhaust reasonable state protection (i.e. accessible, effective, and non-temporary), to which they were willing and able to avail themselves.

In doing so, assessments of the reasonability of state protection and applicants' inability/unwillingness to avail themselves to it should rely on health and social sciences expertise on barriers to (obtaining) effective protection against SGBV and on accurate, recent, SGBV-, and region-specific COI on *de facto* prevalence and protection. Here too, the asterisk/* in Figure 40 indicates the fact that the state protection myth is therefore not necessarily or always untrue, allowing for its exceptional use when supported by COI meeting these conditions.

When such COI is unavailable, the refugee status determination should rely on alternative forms of evidence (e.g. testimonies of (other) survivors/victims). Temporary measures should never be considered as reasonable state protection against SGBV. The conditions for refugee status or reasonable state protection should not be extended beyond what is *de jure* required. This means that SGBV-related applications can be assessed, regardless of whether its applicants concretely exhausted (all) pathways to state protection in practice (no matter their reasonableness). In addition, asylum authorities should only qualify countries of origin as 'safe' when state protection against SGBV is available across its entire territory.

4.1.3. ARGUMENTATION ON THE CONVENTION SCOPE (MACRO LEVEL)

Asylum authorities should consider SGBV inflicted by private perpetrators (against which the state is unwilling/unable to protect) as falling within the UN Refugee Convention scope and SGBV in itself as persecution. In linking such violence to the

Convention grounds, decision makers should consider all five Convention grounds as possibly relevant, pay specific attention to linking male SGBV victimisation, and interpret all grounds gender-sensitively. On the particular social group-ground, they should consider women facing SGBV as a particular social group, regardless of its size/cohesion, the risk level of each separate member, or the voluntariness of their association. In line with asylum authorities' duty to collaborate, they should qualify SGBV in flight stories as persecution related to a Convention ground (if applicable), regardless of whether/when applicants present it as such themselves (e.g. due to hermeneutical injustice).

4.1.4. ARGUMENTATION ON INTERNAL FLIGHT ALTERNATIVES (MICRO & MESO/EXO LEVEL)

Decision makers should only consider IFAs when they are accessible, provide reasonable resettlement, and exclude any (other) fear of or provides state protection against persecution. As absence of state protection against SGBV generally applies to the entire state territory, IFAs should only be suggested exceptionally. IFA assessments should rely on health and social sciences expertise, as well as on *de facto* SGBV- and region-specific COI.

Such expertise and COI should focus on: applicants' heightened risk of SGBV upon return (by the same or new perpetrators), e.g. due to past SGBV as such, applicants' traceability, and perpetrators' motivation/means to do so (considering past stalking/abduction/threats, international child abduction complaints, custody/visitation rights, ...); patriarchal and honour-related gender norms; social cohesion; route safety; socio-cultural conditions determining applicants' possibility of rebuilding a safe life without renewed fear of persecution and with respect to their freedom of movement/association/self-expression/... Importantly, decision makers should not consider IFAs when these are only reasonable and/or safe when applicants have to avoid their own persecution (e.g. through discretion and/or going into hiding) or become dependent on non-state actors.

4.1.5. ARGUMENTATION ACROSS REFUGEE STATUS DETERMINATION

Across SGBV-related refugee status determination, asylum authorities should consistently apply the burden of proof reversal when applicants experienced SGBV (threats) in the past, in which case decision makers should provide good reasons that such violence will not occur again.[2442] Further, asylum authorities should ensure unity of jurisprudence across procedural languages. Finally, asylum decisions and judgments should not rely on any SGBV myth in order

2442 Art. 48/7 Belgian Aliens Act; Denys (n 43) 626.

to (cumulatively) substantiate their conclusion and should actively rebut SGBV myth acceptance upon reconsideration of previous decisions.

On the one hand, this last substantive recommendation calls for caution and restraint in SGBV-related refugee status determination, to ensure that asylum decisions are not based on SGBV myths, as any unjustified refusal of international protection would entail a real risk of (re)victimisation upon return. On the other hand, they call on asylum authorities to (pro)actively and explicitly rebut SGBV myth acceptance in decisions that they have to (re)assess. This good practice is already adopted by some, such as an abovementioned judge who systematically and explicitly rebuts the non-state protection myth when it is used by the CGRS, even if they ultimately confirm the CGRS' decision.[2443]

While many judgments implicitly omit arguments considered irrelevant or non-decisive,[2444] others follow the practice of the judge above. In the case of Amani for example, with which this research opened, the CGRS' refusal decision was annulled by a CALL judgement explicitly rebutting the disclosure and resourcefulness myths:

> 'The Council is **not convinced by** the grounds for the contested decision **questioning the reality of the sexual abuse** by the applicant's stepfather over a period of years. It notes that [she] was able to **provide information** about this person and details of their life under the same roof. [Her] level of **independence and resourcefulness** [...] **cannot lead to the conclusion** that it is **not credible** that she was at the mercy of a violent stepfather.'[2445] | CASE OF AMANI

After this annulment judgment, Amani was heard again by the CGRS and NANSEN NGO intervened in her case twice, once before and once after this new personal interview. Upon reassessment of her case, Amani was eventually recognised as a refugee.

In recommending active and explicit rebuttal of SGBV myths in asylum decisions/judgments, this research aligns with the position of Navi Pillay, former UN High Commissioner for Human Rights, that '[e]xplicit action is required to ensure that government officials, especially those working in the justice system, do not deliver decisions based on harmful stereotypes [...]. Rather, officials should be identifying and challenging such negative beliefs, to help create environments that more fully respect [...] human rights.'[2446]

4.2. PROCEDURAL RECOMMENDATIONS

Figure 41 below, listing the procedural recommendations, visualises what it may mean to 'develop [...] gender-sensitive asylum procedures' for persons fleeing SGBV,

---

2443 RB006_CALL_Judge_[00:32:10] &[00:33:04].
2444 RB001_CALL_Judge_[00:41:22].
2445 NC004_CALL 1 (annulment)_1991_F_DRC_RSA_DV_17/1/2022_266 712_FR_NANSEN_p. 7.
2446 Pillay (n 140).

as the Istanbul Convention obliges state parties to do.[2447] Specifically, they address the following aspects of SGBV-related asylum procedures: 1) SGBV training and guidelines, 2) gender specialisation, 3) unity of decision making, 4) interdisciplinary decision making, 5) special procedural guarantees and accelerated procedures, and 6) mental health support. These too are informed and shaped by relevant (case) law and health, social, and legal sciences, as well as by existing rules/practices in other legal fields and by applicants' standpoints mentioned throughout this research.

Figure 41: Procedural recommendations

	PROCEDURAL RECOMMENDATIONS	LEGISLATOR	CGRS	CALL
SGBV TRAINING & GUIDELINES	• Provide **training** & practice-oriented **guidelines**: → **On** all SGBV types relevant in asylum procedures o Focusing on specificities in all regions where prevalent o Incl. the necessary empirical (health/social sciences & country of origin information or COI) & legal expertise allowing for gender-sensitive refugee status determination & SGBV myth rebuttal → **On** gender-, trauma- & culture- sensitive interviewing of SGBV survivors/victims → **For** all decision makers handling SGBV cases • Generally **monitor** their implementation & individually **follow-up** on decision makers' knowledge, attitudes & practices → **Refresh & adjust** trainings/guidelines according to the results	✓	✓	✓
GENDER SPECIALISATION	• Only assign SGBV cases (no matter the n° of SGBV types involved) to **decision makers** who followed the **training** above & adjust their n° to the amount of SGBV cases • Allow decision makers to opt out from handling (a specific n°/type/any) SGBV cases (confidentially & without giving a reason)	✓	✓	✓
UNITY OF DECISION MAKING	• Provide regular opportunities for **dialogue** on SGBV decision making across geographical sections & procedural languages • Apply/reinforce mechanisms to **monitor** the unity of decision making	✓	✓	✓
INTER-DISCIPLINARY DECISION MAKING	• Provide *de facto*, up-to-date, SGBV- and region-specific COI & (if applicable) alert decision makers of its unavailability/incompleteness and the importance of alternative forms of evidence on SGBV		✓	
	• Provide & make use of the option for decision makers to seek **expert advice** from other disciplines & to request medical/psychological reports	✓	✓	✓
SPECIAL PROCEDURAL GUARANTEES & ACCELERATED PROCEDURES	• Standardly grant applicants with SGBV-related flight stories **special procedural guarantees** & lower the standard of proof according to relevant health/social sciences expertise on disclosure of, reactions to, and protection against SGBV • Do not handle SGBV cases in **accelerated procedures** • Do not rely on the **registration interview** to deny special procedural guarantees	✓	✓	
	• Ensure that decisions/judgments are only shared with applicants themselves		✓	✓
	• Remove countries without nation-wide protection against SGBV from the **safe countries of origin** list	✓		
MENTAL HEALTH SUPPORT	• Provide mandatory & periodic in-house psychological follow-up for all decision-makers handling SGBV cases (to monitor the impact & potential vicarious trauma)	✓	✓	✓

[2447] Art. 60(3) Istanbul Convention.

4.2.1. SGBV TRAINING & GUIDELINES

The EU Procedures Directive/Regulation oblige member states to ensure that asylum officials interviewing applicants and making asylum decisions are properly trained to conduct refugee status determinations 'individually, objectively and impartially', and in particular have knowledge of problems that might prevent applicants from being interviewed, such as indications of past torture (e.g. SGBV).[2448] In addition, they should provide 'conditions which allow applicants to present the grounds for their applications in a comprehensive manner'[2449] and should be competent to take their personal circumstances into account, specifically mentioning their gender and vulnerability.[2450] The Istanbul Convention further explicitly obliges its state parties to develop gender-sensitive SGBV guidelines (for refugee status determination specifically)[2451] and 'provide [...] appropriate training for [...] professionals dealing with victims [...] of [SGBV]' (in general).[2452]

As mentioned earlier, Belgium has implemented the latter provision for all Belgian judges in criminal, family and juvenile law, but not for those in migration law. The former must undergo in-depth training on SGBV within one year of their appointment, according to the Judicial Code.[2453] Whether SGBV is assessed under private (criminal, family, juvenile) or under public (migration) law, their survivors/victims, whether born in or migrated to Belgium, deserve the same standards of expertise from (judicial and administrative) decision makers.

This conclusion is confirmed in the preparatory works and law introducing the abovementioned SGBV trainings. These stress that the trainings are essential 'for those whose role involves dealing concretely with cases of sexual and intra-family violence'[2454] and that the legislative change 'aims to provide a general framework for the control and prevention of feminicides and gender-based killings [...] [for] all persons in the public sector, including government agencies, and all <u>administrative and judicial</u> authorities.'[2455] A judge explicitly applauded this research and, while admitting that 'it is not always

2448 Art. 4(3) *jo.* 10(3) EU Procedures Directive; Art. 4(8) *jo.* 13(7-8) *jo.* 34(2-3) EU Asylum Procedures Regulation.

2449 Art. 15(3) EU Procedures Directive; Art. 13(9) EU Asylum Procedures Regulation.

2450 Art. 15(3)a EU Procedures Directive; Art. 13(7)a EU Asylum Procedures Regulation.

2451 Art. 60(3) Istanbul Convention.

2452 Art. 15 *ibid.*

2453 Art. 78, part 10 Judicial Code.

2454 Belgische Kamer van Volksvertegenwoordigers Wetsvoorstel houdende diverse bepalingen inzake justitie, onder meer in het kader van de strijd tegen de verspreiding van het coronavirus: Amendementen (n 595) 7.

2455 Art. 3 *jo.* 5 Wet voor de preventie en de bestrijding van feminicides en gendergerelateerde dodingen. Emphasis added.

comfortable for the court in question,' stated: 'We have to face that [...] where improvement is needed, [...] it is [...] a matter of [...] getting the necessary training and [...] skills.'[2456] Therefore, I firmly recommend SGBV trainings for decision makers in asylum (and migration) law, specifically tailored to this context, both in first instance and in appeal.

Importantly, such trainings should aim to transfer the above-listed empirical and legal expertise (Figure 39), necessary for effective rebuttal of SGBV myths in asylum decision making, in a practical[2457] and practice-oriented manner that is tailored to the asylum context. To this end, it is essential that such courses are developed and given by/with the help of a combination of and/or collaboration between experts from the various disciplines involved (health/social sciences and law). The importance of such training and awareness raising on SGBV was stressed by several asylum officials interviewed in this research themselves.

One attaché for example admitted not believing highly-educated SGBV survivors/victims before taking the pilot module on gender and asylum organised by NANSEN NGO and learning that 'victims of sexual violence are not always ready to change their lives, to speak out or to rebel [and] they can even be [...] highly educated people.'[2458] A judge pointed out that this same module was confronting, especially because decision makers often look for and find contradictions, while the module completely dismissed such reasoning, showing that 'it is very normal that these people do not remember correctly. So [...] we will have to take that into account.'[2459]

An attaché also described the evolution in the CALL's jurisprudence on delayed disclosure, especially after awareness-raising on how survivors/victims may react after SGBV. This attaché explained how applicants not being able or willing to talk about SGBV used to be considered 'abnormal' and non-credible. This trend changed 'when [they] heard that rape victims here in Europe, where there is a lot of freedom, [...] still say "I didn't dare to file a complaint" or "I filed a complaint later" or "I was incoherent, they didn't believe me" [...]. It made us much more attentive.'[2460] Another judge, who is well-informed about gender issues by taking courses on their own initiative, stated thinking that knowledge

2456 RB001_CALL_Judge_[00:49:20].

2457 At the occasion of presenting the preliminary results and recommendations to the ICAB in the final phase of the research, members of this Advisory Board stressed the importance of organising the part on gender-, trauma-, and culture-sensitive interviewing of such trainings in a practice-oriented manner (e.g. through role play and opportunity to practice), in order to actively train these skills. Implementation & Community Advisory Board (ICAB) (n 334).

2458 RB007_CALL_Attaché_[00:33:53].

2459 RB005_CALL_Judge_[00:07:56].

2460 RB007_CALL_Attaché_[00:27:15].

on the distancing effects of trauma were common sense. However, when reading certain decisions, they admitted that 'it might be good to set some guidelines.'[2461]

The CGRS already developed and offers such trainings and guidelines to some extent. However, there is no standardised training on any form of gender-based violence (i.e. violence related to gender norm transgression, forced marriage, or domestic violence). For sex trafficking/forced prostitution, domestic violence, and violence related to gender norm transgression (other than honour killings), there are neither trainings nor guidelines available (Figure 13, see Part II, Chapter 2.2.2). On the guidelines that are in place at the CGRS, a gender-specialised supervisor pointed out their inconsistent implementation, both among POs and supervisors, and the need to repeat them often,[2462] since they are generally introduced to POs at the beginning of their career, but never updated or refreshed after that.[2463] The same supervisor and another PO admitted that the knowledge and implementation of both training content and gender guidelines depend on individual POs, supervisors, and their personal interest.[2464] For (administrative) courts that rule on appeal, such guidelines exist, for example in Canada[2465] and in New Zealand,[2466] but not in Belgium.

It is important to reiterate that, as mentioned above (see Chapter 3.1 of this part), rape and SGBV myths are accepted in both subconscious/well-intended and conscious/ill-intended ways. In the latter case, even though the information to rebut these myths is available in long-established health/social/legal sciences expertise, (case) law, and applicants own testimonies, dominant actors like decision makers in asylum procedures may still choose not to apply it. They hereby deliberately ignore (parts of) SGBV survivors'/victims' reality.[2467] 'If we do not recognise the SGBV as credible or well-founded, we do not have to protect survivors/victims', seems to be the rationale. Such thinking patterns were reflected in asylum officials' individual coping mechanisms to distance themselves from the cases they were assessing.[2468]

2461 RB008_CALL_Judge_[00:48:52].

2462 CB015_CGRS_Supervisor+PO_GENDER_[01:03:26].

2463 Commissioner General for Refugees and Stateless Persons (CGRS), 'Internal Communication CGRS (Part II)' (n 435).

2464 CB015_CGRS_Supervisor+PO_GENDER_[01:04:28]., CB003_CGRS_PO_[00:15:59].

2465 Immigration and Refugee Board of Canada, 'Chairperson Guideline 4: Gender Considerations in Proceedings Before the Immigration and Refugee Board' (2022).

2466 Rodger Haines, 'Advancing a Gendered Interpretation of the Refugee Convention (National Members' Conference of the Migration Review Tribunal and Refugee Review Tribunal)' (2009).

2467 Mason (n 232) 306.

2468 One attaché admitted comforting themselves with the thought that a forced marriage could always be made up 'to get papers'. For infibulation, proven by medical documents, this is not the case, making it the hardest cases to handle. RB007_CALL_Attaché_[01:04:50]. Infibulation refers to female GMC type 3: the narrowing of the vaginal opening through the creation of a covering seal. The seal is formed by cutting and repositioning the labia minora, or labia majora, sometimes through stitching, with or without removal of the clitoral prepuce/clitoral

As mentioned earlier (see Part I, Chapter 3.1.1), Pohlhaus Jr. termed this phenomenon 'wilful hermeneutical ignorance'.[2469] Such ignorance, through conscious rape and SGBV myth acceptance, can thereby even constitute a political strategy of state actors to turn a blind eye to the omnipresence of SGBV and avoid allocating resources to protect survivors/victims (both in the criminal justice and asylum context). When SGBV myth acceptance arises from such motives, trainings and guidelines alone are not enough to counteract it. Previous research on challenging rape myth acceptance has already shown that training does not always have the desired effect. If individuals do not want to rebut these myths, training/guidelines will not make them do so.[2470]

These findings advocate for installing mechanisms to both generally monitor the uniform implementation of and individually follow-up on decision makers' knowledge, attitudes, and practices on the SGBV trainings and guidelines. Such a general monitoring exercise was already organised for sexual orientation and gender identity (SOGI)-related cases by the CGRS in 2022, leading to the finding that 'things still need to be improved, otherwise POs do what they want.'[2471] In order for positive developments to be observed externally too, it is recommended that the CGRS make the reasoning behind positive decisions available for further research. If not, the level of SGBV myth rebuttal cannot be evaluated accurately, as constituted a limitation of this research.

Based on the results of such general monitoring, the SGBV trainings and guidelines should be repeated and adjusted accordingly. Based on the individual following-up of decision makers, they should be instructed to retake the trainings, refresh the guidelines, or opt out from handling SGBV cases (see below). To conclude, standardised, comprehensive, and practice-oriented training and guidelines on the causes, nature, and consequences of <u>all</u> forms of SGBV relevant to asylum procedures and monitoring/follow-up of their implementation may contribute to limiting SGBV myth acceptance in asylum decision making, both in first instance and appeal, and enhancing gender-sensitivity in refugee status determination more generally.

For the sake of completeness, albeit outside the direct scope of this research and its recommendations, both the ICAB and CALL internally communicated the importance of simultaneously informing and training lawyers on how to

---

hood and glans. World Health Organization (WHO), 'Female Genital Mutilation' (n 607). Another PO simply ignored the impact of negative decisions on applicants' lives altogether. They believed 'very few [applicants] are sent back to their country,' rendering their job 'very comfortable.' They continue: 'If [...] every time I refused, [...] a human being was put on a plane [...], I'd find it harder [...] but that's not the case, [...] in fact [...] I don't know, but I think [...] it's very rare.' CB013_CGRS_PO_[01:38:42].

2469 Pohlhaus Jr. (n 233) 715; McKinnon (n 217) 442.

2470 Smith and Skinner (n 135) 445 & 459.

2471 CB009_CGRS_PO_GENDER_[01:01:15].

identify and rebut SGBV myth acceptance in asylum procedures,[2472] as well as on how to gender- and trauma-sensitively approach clients fleeing such violence.[2473] Some of the practice-oriented forms of output developed during this research could serve as a starting point, such as the practice guide for lawyers on gender-related asylum procedures[2474] or the workshop series for practitioners on gender sensitivity and safe spaces in asylum interviewing.[2475]

4.2.2. GENDER SPECIALISATION

As mentioned earlier (see Part II, Chapter 2.2.1.), the CGRS assigns 'complex gender cases' (concerning at least four forms of SGBV[2476]) to a group of specialised 'gender POs'. As demonstrated throughout this research, this quantitative criterion is not necessarily accurate in determining the complexity of SGBV cases. Furthermore, the number of cases labelled as 'complex' by this selection process is far below the number of trained gender POs (in 2024, for example, only 7 cases were handled by 48 gender POs[2477]). All other 'non-complex' gender cases are handled by non-gender-specialised POs.[2478] At the CALL, there are no standard gender trainings for judges/attachés (only *ad hoc* courses that they follow on their own initiative) and SGBV cases are also handled by all judges/attachés.

As one PO concluded: 'All gender cases are complicated.'[2479] As such, all SGBV cases (no matter the number of SGBV types involved) should be exclusively

---

2472 This rebuttal can be both reactive (in appeal) and proactive (during the personal interview by anticipating possible SGBV myth acceptance in the first instance decision) and can be done both in the argumentation itself or by providing relevant expertise (e.g. scientific research) as evidence in the documents. Implementation & Community Advisory Board (ICAB) (n 334).

2473 Council for Alien Law Litigation (CALL), 'Internal Communication CALL' (n 168); Implementation & Community Advisory Board (ICAB) (n 334).

2474 Roels and Casteleyn, 'Praktijkgids voor advocaten' (n 323); Roels and Casteleyn, 'Guide pratique pour les avocat·es' (n 323); Lore Roels and Liselot Casteleyn, 'Presentatie voor praktijkwerkers: gendergerelateerde procedures om internationale bescherming (seksueel en gendergerelateerd geweld, seksuele oriëntatie en genderidentiteit)' (NANSEN Intervisie 'Gender en Asiel', 21 December 2022).

2475 Roels, 'The Use of Rape Myths and Resulting Victim-Blaming Mechanisms in Asylum Interviews and Decisions on the Grounds of Sexual and Gender-Based Violence (SGBV)' (n 500); Lore Roels, 'The Use of Rape Myths & Victim-Blaming Mechanisms in Asylum Interviews and Decisions on the Grounds of SGBV' (Women in Refugee Law (WiRL) Workshop: 'Safe Spaces in Gender Sensitive Interviews', 2024).

2476 Commissioner General for Refugees and Stateless Persons (CGRS), 'Internal Communication CGRS (Part I)' (n 128).

2477 In addition, 14 cases on gender identity (falling outside the scope of this research) were assigned to the gender POs over the course of this same year. *Ibid.*

2478 Except for those that 'randomly' (not through deliberate assignment) end up with gender POs.

2479 CB010_CGRS_Supervisor + PO_[00:44:46].

assigned to decision makers who followed SGBV training as described above. Such training can be provided either to a select group, opting in to gender specialisation, or to all decision makers, but with the option to opt out from handling (a specific number/type/… or any) SGBV cases. It is important that this choice to opt out does not require justification and can be communicated anonymously, as the reasons for this may be highly personal (e.g. one's own experiences, as pointed out by one PO[2480]).

In any case, the number of decision makers handling SGBV cases should be adjusted to the number of SGBV-related applications for international protection. This group must be large enough to enable the member-decision makers to handle a feasible number of SGBV cases without adverse impact on their mental health (see below for follow-up on this). Such an organisational adjustment could ensure that the resources allocated to gender specialisation within the asylum system and its added value are optimally utilised in cases where gender-sensitivity is most needed. In addition, it would address the concerns of some asylum officials that not everyone is equally suited to handle gender cases[2481] and that a lack of interest in the theme or inability to put applicants at ease 'can have a negative impact on the outcome of the procedure.'[2482] Lastly, in the case of multiple personal interviews, it is recommended to assign one gender-specialised PO per case and per (subsequent) procedure, to avoid situations like Angele's, who had to retell her flight story (and the SGBV in it) to three different interviewers at the CGRS, while, in her own words, 'It should have been just one.'[2483]

4.2.3. UNITY OF DECISION MAKING

At the CGRS, internal disagreement on decision making in SGBV cases is recognised, as this supervisor stated: 'That's the hardest part about gender cases […] that we often disagree among ourselves about what we expect from [applicants].'[2484] Two POs observed 'too many individual fluctuations,'[2485] both among supervisors and POs. They stated: 'Even within sections, […] [a case could be a recognition] to [one supervisor], [but] automatically a refusal to another'[2486] and 'We're all human beings and so, inevitably […] I've already retrieved [negative decisions] from my colleagues where […] in fact, to me,

2480 CB014_CGRS_PO_[01:26:31].
2481 CB002_CGRS_PO_[00:50:17].
2482 CB010_CGRS_PO_[00:16:23].
2483 NC006_CGRS interview 3_1984_F_DRC_RSA_FR_p. 19.
2484 CB002_CGRS_Supervisor + PO_[00:39:32].
2485 CB003_CGRS_PO_[00:54:41].
2486 CB003_CGRS_PO_[00:54:41].

it still seemed credible.'[2487] At the CALL, legally obliged to ensure unity of jurisprudence,[2488] a similar discrepancy in decision making tradition has been demonstrated between the procedural languages (see Chapter 3.1 of this part).

Guaranteeing the unity of decision making is all the more important when we know that applicants (who need an interpreter) have no say in the language in which their case is handled. In addition, the assigned language remains the same throughout the procedure[2489] and cannot be appealed.[2490] The CALL's yearly activity reports list initiatives already taken to ensure this unity, such as: sharing case law developments via an internal platform, appointing chamber lawyers to monitor this case law, joint training days, judgments by the united chambers[2491] or the general assembly[2492] (with an equal number of French-speaking and Dutch-speaking judges), ...[2493]

Nonetheless, this research shows that the work to harmonise SGBV case law across procedural languages is still incomplete. Therefore, it recommends organising regular and standard opportunities for dialogue on SGBV decision making across geographical sections and procedural languages, as well as mechanisms to follow-up the unity of decision making, both at the CGRS and the CALL. In doing so, both asylum authorities must watch over the fact that such harmonisation aligns with the relevant (inter)national (case) law and health, social, and legal science expertise mentioned throughout this research.

4.2.4. INTERDISCIPLINARY DECISION MAKING

The handling of SGBV cases should be supported by the provision of precise and up-to-date COI, as prescribed by the CJEU (*A.H. and F.N. & K.L. cases*).[2494] Such COI, if available/accessible, should be specifically relevant to SGBV-related applications and include factual information already mentioned above, in line with CJEU case law (*W.S. case*).[2495] This recommendation should, to the

2487 CB004_CGRS_PO_[00:58:52].

2488 Art. 39/6, §1 & 3 Belgian Aliens Act.

2489 Art. 51/4 *jo.* 39/9, §1, part 3 *ibid.*

2490 Agentschap Integratie en Inburgering (AGII) (n 100).

2491 Art. 39/11-12 *jo.* 57/23*bis* Belgian Aliens Act.

2492 Art. 39/11 *jo.* 39/4 *ibid.*

2493 Council for Alien Law Litigation (CALL), 'Activiteitenverslag RvV 2023' (n 356) 48; Council for Alien Law Litigation (CALL), 'Activiteitenverslag RvV 2022' (n 580) 11; Council for Alien Law Litigation (CALL), 'Activiteitenverslag RvV 2021' (n 581) 9; Council for Alien Law Litigation (CALL), 'Activiteitenverslag RvV 2020' (n 581) 10; Council for Alien Law Litigation (CALL), 'Activiteitenverslag RvV 2024' (2024) 28.

2494 *AH & FN v. Bundesamt für Fremdenwesen und Asyl* (n 82) para 52; *K.L. v. Staatssecretaris van Justitie en Veiligheid* (n 78) para 60.

2495 *WS v. Intervyuirasht organ na Darzhavna agentsia za bezhantsite pri Ministerskia savet* (n 44) para 61.

extent possible, address the gaps in COI identified by asylum officials throughout this research, such as on male SGBV victimisation, compliance with protection orders, or stigmatisation after SGBV upon return. However, it must be recognised, as already mentioned, that such (accurate) information is not always available and/or accessible due to underreporting and underestimation in statistics on certain countries of origin and/or types of SGBV. In this case, decision makers should be alerted of this knowledge gap, should refrain from basing decisions/judgements on the assumption that the violence does not/rarely take place, and should rely on alternative forms of evidence on SGBV (e.g. testimonies by (other) survivors/victims).[2496]

In addition to using precise and up-to-date COI, the EU Procedures Directive/Regulation oblige member states to provide the possibility for decision makers to seek advice from experts on issues encountered in their refugee status determination, such as 'medical, cultural, religious, child-related or gender issues.'[2497] This includes the possibility to, subject to applicants' consent, 'arrange for [their] medical examination [...] concerning [possible] signs [of] past persecution or serious harm.'[2498] This also applies in appeal proceedings, where the 'full and *ex nunc* examination of both facts and [...] law'[2499] means that the judge may order a medical examination, as ruled by the CJEU in the *B.F. case*.[2500] The new EU Procedures Regulation also adds a provision allowing authorities to refer applicants to trained medical/psychological/other professionals for particular advice on their special procedural needs and possible measures responding to these, prioritising cases where there are indications of SGBV.[2501]

These provisions encourage interdisciplinary decision making in asylum procedures, in line with the aforementioned recommendation of the UN Refugee Agency (UNHCR) to inform refugee status determination and credibility assessments by 'the substantial body of relevant empirical evidence that exists in' fields exceeding legal scholarship, such as 'neurobiology, psychology, gender and cultural studies, anthropology, and sociology.'[2502] Such interdisciplinary decision making would also respond to calls for support by asylum officials themselves. One PO for example found it 'outrageous [that] there isn't even a psychologist to help us with psychological documents, [...] especially in relation to traumas, [...] I didn't study that [...]. There's no one who can give us any concrete explanation about this.'[2503]

2496 UNHCR, 'Guidelines on International Protection No. 1' (n 35) para 37.
2497 Art. 10(3)d EU Procedures Directive; Art. 34(3) EU Asylum Procedures Regulation.
2498 Art. 18(1) EU Procedures Directive; Art. 24(1) EU Asylum Procedures Regulation.
2499 Art. 46(3) EU Procedures Directive; Art. 67(3) EU Asylum Procedures Regulation.
2500 *B.F. v. Kypriaki Dimokratia* (n 56) para ruling.
2501 Art. 20(4) & (5) EU Asylum Procedures Regulation.
2502 UNHCR, 'Beyond Proof. Credibility Assessment in EU Asylum Systems (Full Report)' (n 19) 56.
2503 CB014_CGRS_PO_[01:18:30].

This possibility to call on interdisciplinary expert advice in SGBV cases would also compensate for the limitations of the SGBV training mentioned above. In their restricted time frame, only a certain amount of relevant expertise from health and social sciences on SGBV can be passed on to decision makers who are (usually) not educated in these fields. Ideally, this possibility is made use of as the rule rather than the exception in decision making practice. Also, preference should be given to its structural and permanent (rather than *ad hoc*) integration into the functioning of the CGRS and the CALL. Finally, it is also recommended that asylum authorities initiate/continue projects that can facilitate such interdisciplinary decision-making, such as collaborations with experts and NGOs[2504] working in/on the above-mentioned disciplines.

4.2.5. SPECIAL PROCEDURAL GUARANTEES & ACCELERATED PROCEDURES

As demonstrated throughout this research, most SGBV cases involve some form of trauma and/or lasting mental health issues (e.g. post-traumatic stress disorder, depression, …) and there is a substantial risk that decision makers (partially or largely) base their decisions/judgments on SGBV myths. Therefore, it is recommended that applicants with SGBV-related flight stories are standardly granted special procedural guarantees, unless there are specific reasons not to.

Importantly, this standard assignment of special procedural guarantees in SGBV cases should prevent their processing in an accelerated procedure, in line with provisions in the EU Procedures Directive/Regulation[2505] and Belgian Aliens Act.[2506] As this research included several examples where this rule was not applied, it recommends strictly doing so for SGBV cases in the future. Given the complexity of most SGBV cases and to allow for the abovementioned pathways to interdisciplinary decision making to be utilised, it recommends not processing any SGBV case in an accelerated procedure, regardless of whether the applicant's country of origin is considered 'safe' or not.[2507]

2504 E.g. Minister van Asiel en Migratie Anneleen Van Bossuyt Beleidsnota Asiel en Migratie (n 123) 19; Julie Lejeune and NANSEN, 'Voor een interdisciplinaire benadering van asiel' (*NANSEN*, 24 April 2024), https://nansen-refugee.be/nl/2024/04/24/voor-een-interdisciplinaire-benadering-van-asiel/.

2505 Art. 24(3) EU Procedures Directive; Art. 21(2) EU Asylum Procedures Regulation.

2506 Art. 48/9, §5 Belgian Aliens Act; Commissioner General for Refugees and Stateless Persons (CGRS), 'Special Procedural Needs' (n 532).

2507 Art. 57/6/1, §1–2 Belgian Aliens Act.

For that matter, this research recommends updating Belgium's 'safe countries of origin'-list[2508] in accordance with the CJEU *C.V. case*,[2509] by removing those countries that cannot provide territory-wide state protection against SGBV. Which countries these are exactly depends on the actual situation on the ground (and how it evolves), but in any case, the determination must be based on *de facto*, up-to-date, region-, and SGBV-specific COI.

As mentioned above, decision makers should be trained to identify and appropriately respond to applicants' special procedural needs. This includes identifying possible interview barriers (e.g. indications of past SGBV),[2510] taking into account applicants' vulnerability,[2511] and providing conditions allowing them to present the grounds for their applications.[2512] The new EU Procedures Regulation adds the possibility to call on expert advice concerning applicants' special procedural needs and possible measures accommodating these (especially in SGBV cases).[2513] Both decision makers and the latter experts should be trained on detecting signs of vulnerability and addressing them.[2514]

When responding to the detected special procedural needs, asylum authorities should strictly follow the advice in medical certificates, provided by the applicant or upon request of the decision maker. The guarantees should be implemented in line with the trainings on gender-, trauma-, and culture- sensitive hearing of SGBV survivors/victims mentioned above (Figure 41). Some asylum officials already reported applying specific guarantees in SGBV cases, such as: avoiding direct questions on SGBV details, explaining the purpose of questions around SGBV (after verifying their necessity and non-victim-blaming formulation),[2515] installing an empathic climate, encouraging free narrative, mirroring applicants' words while describing SGBV, ... (see Part II, Chapter 2.2.1).

For applicants whose (trauma-related) mental health issues prevent them from accepting the CGRS' interview invitation(s) (upon presentation of a medical certificate, for example), decisions should not be made solely on the basis of the registration interview at the IO. Instead, special procedural guarantees must be considered, that enable the person to set out their flight story in other ways/

2508 Art. 1 Koninklijk besluit tot uitvoering van het artikel 57/6/1, §3, vierde lid, van de wet van 15 december 1980 betreffende de toegang tot het grondgebied, het verblijf, de vestiging en de verwijdering van vreemdelingen, houdende de vastlegging van de lijst van veilige landen van herkomst.

2509 *CV v. Ministerstvo vnitra České republiky, Odbor azylové a migrační politiky* (n 559) Ruling 2.

2510 Art. 4(3) *jo.* 10(3) EU Procedures Directive; Art. 4(8) *jo.* 13(7-8) *jo.* 34(2-3) EU Asylum Procedures Regulation.

2511 Art. 15(3)a EU Procedures Directive; Art. 13(7)a EU Asylum Procedures Regulation.

2512 Art. 15(3) EU Procedures Directive; Art. 13(9) EU Asylum Procedures Regulation.

2513 Art. 20(4) & (5) EU Asylum Procedures Regulation.

2514 Art. 20(5) *ibid.*

2515 Roels, 'The Use of Rape Myths and Resulting Victim-Blaming Mechanisms in Asylum Interviews and Decisions on the Grounds of Sexual and Gender-Based Violence (SGBV)' (n 500).

later on. These might for example consist of: allowing the CGRS' questions to be answered in writing (possibly with the support of psychologists/psychiatrists), organising the interview in a familiar environment (in person or through videoconferencing, possibly in the presence of psychologists/psychiatrists and other trusted persons), and/or postpone the interview until the person is able to attend the interview.

In SGBV cases, special procedural guarantees should also move beyond practical measures that merely facilitate the course of the interview (e.g. glass of water, additional breaks, …). Instead, they should involve a lowering of the substantive standard of proof, according to the relevant health/social sciences expertise mentioned throughout this research. More concretely, this means that decision makers should adjust their expectations on applicants': level of detail, consistency, timeliness, and demeanour of disclosure; survival reactions; (evidence of) help/protection-seeking attempts, information on SGBV prevalence; ….

Further, asylum authorities should ensure that case files/decisions are not shared with applicants' relatives, but only with applicants themselves (and their lawyers), to avoid situations like Angele's. She did not want her husband and children to know about her rape experience, but her decision, containing a description of the facts, had been sent to her husband directly nonetheless.[2516] Also, since applicants do not enjoy legal assistance from a lawyer during their IO interview and the IO interviewers are not gender-trained under the conditions recommended above, decision makers should not rely on information from the IO registration interview to deny applicants special procedural guarantees.

Lastly, I observed the variety of special procedural needs and guarantees that were (not) assigned to applicants with SGBV-related flight stories. As a thorough examination of these practices and their impact on individual cases goes beyond the scope of this research, which mainly focused on the content of SGBV-related refugee status determination, it suggests further research into this matter (see Chapter 4.3 below).

4.2.6. MENTAL HEALTH SUPPORT

As mentioned earlier, it is important to be attentive to the psychological impact of hearing and assessing SGBV-related flight stories. Decision makers' coping with such exposure may result in attitudes ranging from very empathic to

2516 NC006_CGRS interview 3_1984_F_DRC_RSA_FR_p. 7, 10 & 20.

non-empathic ones[2517] and may naturally originate from compassion fatigue[2518] and/or vicarious traumatisation.[2519] This psychological impact was recognised by several asylum officials themselves, for example feeling insufficiently equipped to hear severe SGBV stories[2520] or feeling exhausted due to regular exposure to them.[2521] Some actively identified their need for mental health support, such as a PO who reported not finding a clear pathway to psychological counselling within the CGRS' internal structure.[2522] Others never do, which leads them to coping with this mental load individually, by 'put[ting] up a shield [...] [or] succumb[ing] to it,' as testified by a gender-specialised supervisor.[2523] Where the former group risks developing non-empathic attitudes (and decision making) over time, the latter group 'letting the stories in' may eventually drop out.[2524]

At the moment, neither the CGRS nor the CALL provide standard and periodic internal psychological follow-up for decision makers. In contrast, one judge explicitly referred to a legal setting where this is the case: '[W]e don't have any psychological support at the CALL and I think there should be (as is the case, for example, at the Brussels Public Prosecutor's Office).'[2525] Other professionals in the legal system for whom such psychological support is provided, and even made obligatory, are police inspectors working on sexual violence cases in Belgium's Sexual Assault Care Centres. For them, annual individual supervision by an external psychologist is mandatory.[2526] Voluntary follow-up carries the risk that only those who out of self-reflection identify their own need for it are supported, but also that their visibility and possible stigmatisation increases due to the taboo surrounding psychological support. A standardised trajectory, by contrast, offers equal treatment for all decision makers.

The need for mental health support was also confirmed by the KAP survey results (i.e. through the validated vicarious trauma scale included[2527]). It measured an average vicarious trauma level of 4,5 (CGRS, Dutch-speaking); 4,7 (CGRS, French-speaking); 3,9 (CALL, Dutch-speaking); and 4,7 (CALL,

2517 E.g. avoidance, denial, trivialisation of horror, cynicism, lack of empathy, anger ..., as demonstrated in Angele's case (see Part II, Chapter 2.2). Rousseau and others (n 7) 49 & 58–59.

2518 Rauvola, Vega and Lavigne (n 501) 303–304.

2519 Rousseau and others (n 7) 49 & 58–59.

2520 CB013_CGRS_PO_[00:04:42].

2521 CB005_CGRS_Supervisor+PO_GENDER_[00:56:49]., RB007_CALL_Attaché_[01:04:33]., RB005_CALL_Judge_[00:56:08].

2522 R_215mekDbAHvOGHc_CGRS_ PO/supervisor/gender coordinator/CEDOCA member.

2523 CB011_CGRS_Supervisor+PO_GENDER_[00:51:29].

2524 CB014_CGRS_PO_[01:19:53].

2525 R_3LXa1xWZookEix6_CALL_Judge_1976.

2526 Keygnaert and Baert (n 520) 20; Instituut voor de gelijkheid van vrouwen en mannen (n 520); Art. 2, 10° *jo.* Chapter 3 Sexual Assault Care Centres (SACC) Act.

2527 Vrklevski and Franklin (n 371) 115.

French-speaking) out of 7 (where 1 indicates no vicarious trauma at all and 7 indicates a very high degree[2528]). Therefore, this research recommends providing standard and periodic in-house psychological follow-up for all decision makers at the CGRS and the CALL (individually and possibly complemented by group sessions) to monitor the impact of SGBV case handling and potential vicarious trauma. In addition, as a thorough analysis of the prevalence and impact of vicarious trauma in SGBV-related asylum decision making goes beyond the scope of this research and is practically unexplored terrain, further research into this matter is suggested (see the next Chapter).

4.3. RECOMMENDATIONS FOR FURTHER RESEARCH

Lastly, as mentioned throughout this chapter, the findings suggest further research into the following topics and in the following ways (Figure 42). First, the research opens pathways for broadening studies into other SGBV myths (relying on other applicants' standpoints/from other disciplines) and/or in other asylum contexts. Second, within the Belgian asylum context, it encourages an in-depth examination into the myth acceptance concerning SGBV on which the Belgian asylum system provides least training and guidance (i.e. domestic violence, forced marriage, violence related to gender norm transgression, and sex trafficking/forced prostitution). Third, learning from the KAP survey experiences, an adapted SGBV myth acceptance scale/KAP survey could be developed, tailored to the nuanced understanding of SGBV myth acceptance/rebuttal in asylum contexts revealed by this research. It could be conducted with Belgian/other authorities deciding on international (and non-refoulement) protection in order to get an understanding of their levels of gender-sensitivity.

Fourth, this research suggests intersectional studies into the distribution of SGBV myth acceptance across applicants' regions of origin/other characteristics and their impact on SGBV-related refugee status determination. Fifth, it highlighted the relatively unexplored terrain of research on the interplay between refugee, human rights, and private international law in SGBV-related asylum procedures. Sixth, the impact of the types of special procedural needs and guarantees (not) assigned to applicants on SGBV-related refugee status determination should be studied further. Seventh, the recommendation to provide support to asylum officials in SGBV cases raises new research questions into the types of tools useful (e.g. training, guidelines, risk assessment tools, ...), as well as their implementation and impact on asylum decisions (both positive and negative ones).

[2528] *Ibid.*

Eighth, as the scale[2529] conducted in this research revealed concerning levels of vicarious trauma among Belgian asylum officials, further examination into the prevalence and impact of vicarious trauma in/on (SGBV-related) asylum decision making/makers is required. Lastly, not only asylum officials risk such vicarious traumatisation; researchers do too. Next to suggestions on research content above, I also suggest that the design of future research, on SGBV and/or forced migration dealing with personal stories, standardly includes informal and formal mental health support to prevent, monitor, and/or respond to vicarious traumatisation of researchers.

Figure 42: Recommendations for further research

RECOMMENDATIONS FOR FURTHER RESEARCH into ...

RESEARCH CONTENT

- **Other SGBV myths** & SGBV myth acceptance in **other asylum contexts**
- Myth acceptance on **SGBV** for which the **Belgian asylum system** provides **least guidance**
- SGBV myth acceptance distribution across applicants' regions of origin/other characteristics & the **intersectional** impact on refugee status determination
- The interplay between **refugee, human rights & private international law** in SGBV-related asylum procedures
- The impact of **special procedural needs & guarantees** (not) assigned to applicants on SGBV-related refugee status determination
- Developing an **SGBV myth acceptance scale** tailored to the research results & conducting it with Belgian/other asylum officials
- Developing **support tools** for asylum officials in SGBV cases (e.g. training, guidelines, risk assessment tools...) & analysing their implementation/impact on decision making practice
- The prevalence & impact of **vicarious trauma** in/on (SGBV-related) asylum decision making

RESEARCH DESIGN

- Research on personal SGBV/forced migration stories should include (in)formal **mental health support** to prevent, monitor & respond to vicarious trauma among **researchers**

2529 Vicarious trauma is described as 'the negative effects that result from working with trauma survivors. These include compassion fatigue or secondary traumatic stress, countertransference, and burnout.' Vrklevski and Franklin developed a 8 question Vicarious Trauma Scale (VTS) in order to assess subjective levels of distress associated with working with traumatised persons. The VTS items are rated on a 7-point Likert-type scale, ranging from 1 (strongly disagree) to 7 (strongly agree). *Ibid.* 106, 110 & 115.

5. CONCLUDING THOUGHTS

This research revealed the pervasiveness of SGBV myth acceptance in the asylum context, by establishing that 76% of the analysed decisions in the Belgian asylum procedure (n=202) were based on at least one SGBV myth and 20% on four or more cumulatively. SGBV myth acceptance occurred in decisions on all types of SGBV and all regions of origin, regardless of applicants' age or gender identity, making it evident that it is not a marginal phenomenon in a handful of cases with specific circumstances. It is neither a practice among a few decision makers or authorities, as it widely occurs in first instance (at the CGRS) as well as in appeal (at the CALL). The SGBV myths are used across both procedural languages, but at the CALL clearly more frequently on the Dutch-speaking than on the French-speaking side. Concretely, six SGBV myths were identified, situated at four ecological levels, which play a role in four phases of refugee status determination.

The macro level myth that 'SGBV is a private issue excluded from the UN Refugee Convention scope' comes into play when assessing whether SGBV qualifies for refugee status protection in the first place. If so, the micro level disclosure and survival myths and meso/exo level non-state and state protection myths may impact the credibility assessment, when applicants' (content/timing/manner of) disclosure, (active/passive) survival reactions, or help-seeking behaviour from (non-)state actors are seen as inappropriate and therefore non-credible.

If the fear of SGBV is considered credible, both the micro level resourcefulness myth and the meso/exo level (non-)state protection myths can affect the assessment of the application's well-foundedness. In this stage, authorities may argue that 'resourceful applicants' and/or 'applicants with (facilitating) non-state actor support do not need protection against SGBV' and/or that 'non-exhaustion of state protection implies ill-foundedness of SGBV flight stories (or prevents their assessment)'. Finally, if the fear of SGBV is declared well-founded, decision makers may still conclude (based on the micro level resourcefulness and survival myths and the meso/exo level (non-)state protection myths) that 'instead of fleeing the country, (resourceful) applicants should return to an IFA, rendered safe and/or reasonable through their (facilitating) non-state actor support and/or state protection.'

Although 'gender-sensitive refugee status determination' remains undefined in law and literature, this research argues that it must imply that asylum decisions cannot rely on any SGBV myths, regardless of their decisiveness for the outcome.

Decisions that do, especially those of which the final conclusion does not hold its ground when stripped of such myth-based arguments, must be considered gender-insensitive and therefore violating the legal obligation of gender-sensitive refugee status determination for state parties to the Istanbul Convention, like Belgium.

Next to the forms and levels of SGBV myth acceptance described above, asylum officials in this research also demonstrated (a degree of) SGBV myth rebuttal. Some even proved to actively rebut SGBV myths in their decision making. SGBV myth acceptance may constitute a self-protection response as part of the just world hypothesis and vicarious trauma may cause decision makers to distance themselves from the stories they assess. This knowledge and the observation of SGBV myth rebuttal nonetheless present in the Belgian asylum system both point to a potential for change, to which recommendations may be tailored.

This research described the reasons for rebutting each identified SGBV myth in health and social sciences, as well as in law and legal sciences. It compiled these into a body of empirical and legal expertise necessary to avoid SGBV myth acceptance in asylum decision making. Fundamentally, this compilation leads to the inevitable question of whether, within the constraints of the current asylum procedure, it is possible for decision makers to master all this expertise needed for interdisciplinary, trauma-, gender-sensitive, and evidence-based assessments of SGBV in survivors'/victims' flight stories.

Pragmatically aiming at change within these constraints, this research formulates substantive and procedural recommendations to facilitate gender-sensitive decision making. Substantially, I recommend to strictly base SGBV-related refugee status determination on the above-listed empirical and legal expertise. Procedurally, I recommend working towards more gender-sensitive asylum procedures, focusing on: SGBV training/guidelines, gender specialisation, unity of decision making, interdisciplinary decision making, special procedural guarantees/accelerated procedures, and mental health support for decision makers.

The concluding chapter also highlighted issues that fell outside the scope of this research, but deserve attention in further research, namely into: other SGBV myths and/or other asylum contexts; the forms of myth acceptance on SGBV for which the Belgian asylum system provides least support; the distribution of SGBV myth acceptance across applicants' regions of origin/other characteristics; the interplay between refugee, human rights, and private international law in SGBV-related cases; the assignment of special procedural needs/guarantees in SGBV-related cases; vicarious trauma among decision makers; and the development and impact of support tools for asylum officials in SGBV cases as recommended in this research.

Lastly, this concluding chapter drew methodological and theoretical conclusions on the process and contributions of the research. Methodologically, it mainly serves as an invitation to conduct further research directly building on applicants' standpoints and expertise yet including asylum authorities' perspectives, upholding ethical standards that aim for reciprocally enriching experiences and minimising re- and vicarious traumatisation, and eventually advocating for social change. Conceptually, applying the rape mythology framework to the asylum context, and hereby coining the term 'SGBV mythology', resulted in the identification of six main SGBV myths. This combined set allowed for a comprehensive, multidisciplinary, and practice-oriented analysis of gender (in)sensitivity in SGBV-related asylum decision making.

Uncovering the level of gender (in)sensitivity of asylum decisions is not merely of theoretical relevance. On the contrary, the impact on individual applicants' lives is very real. Of the 26 applicants whose SGBV flight stories served as a case study, (to my knowledge[2530]) seven were ultimately recognised as refugees: Angele, Amani, Zeynep, Nella, Fatou, Sofia, and Clarisse. Lejla's case is still pending at the CGRS at the time of writing, after the previous negative CGRS decision was annulled by the CALL. 18 of them were denied refugee protection: Mary, Vera, Carmen, Yusuf, Binta, Nyakato, Ana, Diana, Erina, Marjorie, Rahel, Elene, Nino, Aya, Qawtar, Aster, Uyi, and Esmeralda. After having gotten two negative decisions (in first instance and in appeal), Rahel expressed this impact by testifying:

> 'Sometimes, I feel bad, […] I say 'Why I live in here? Why I am here? Why [is this] my life?' […] I, I fight with my mind. I will say "[Rahel], be strong" *says this with a firm voice* […] because now I don't have a future […]. **My future *points at turned off tv screen in the room*, it's black** for me, it's like that *cries*.'[2531] | CASE OF RAHEL

This research showed how an enormous variety of SGBV experiences are continuously subjected to the same set of expectations based on SGBV myths. Audre Lorde wrote that, regardless of the separations between individuals' gender-based experiences, 'we must each of us recognize our responsibility to seek [their] words out, to read them and share them and examine them in their pertinence to our lives'[2532] and, for this research, in their pertinence to how our asylum procedures scrutinise survivors/victims seeking to navigate from (SGBV) survival to (refugee) recognition.

[2530] Current state of these cases was communicated to me by the CGRS in: Commissioner General for Refugees and Stateless Persons (CGRS), 'Internal Communication CGRS (Part III)' (n 469).

[2531] NEr018_1985_F_Eritrea_RSA_NL_NANSEN_[00:07:35] & [00:09:06].

[2532] Lorde (n 1) 32.

BIBLIOGRAPHY

BOOKS & BOOK CHAPTERS

American Psychiatric Association, Diagnostic and Statistical Manual of Mental Disorders, Fifth Edition (APA Publishing 2013)

Anderson A and Foster M, 'A Feminist Appraisal of International Refugee Law' in Cathryn Costello, Michelle Foster and Jane McAdam (eds), The Oxford Handbook of International Refugee Law (Oxford University Press 2021)

Anker DE, 'Legal Change from the Bottom up: The Development of Gender Asylum Jurisprudence in the United States' in Efrat Arbel, Catherine Dauvergne and Jenni Millbank (eds), Gender in Refugee Law: From the Margins to the Centre (Routledge 2014)

Arbel E, Dauvergne C and Millbank J, 'Introduction: Gender in Refugee Law: From the Margins to the Centre' in Efrat Arbel, Catherine Dauvergne and Jenni Millbank (eds), Gender in Refugee Law: From the Margins to the Centre (Routledge 2014)

Barsky RF, Constructing a Productive Other: Discourse Theory and the Convention Refugee Hearing (John Benjamins Publishing Company 1994)

Bassel L, 'Why a Politics of Listening?' in Leah Bassel, The Politics of Listening: Possibilities and Challenges for Democratic Life (Palgrave Macmillan UK 2017)

Bohner G and others, 'Rape Myth Acceptance: Cognitive, Affective and Behavioural Effects of Beliefs That Blame the Victim and Exonerate the Perpetrator' in Miranda Horvath and Jennifer Brown (eds), Rape: Challenging contemporary thinking (Willan Publishing 2011)

Brownmiller S, Against Our Will: Men, Women and Rape (Open Road Integrated Media, Inc 1975)

Charmaz K, Constructing Grounded Theory: A Practical Guide through Qualitative Analysis (Sage 2012)

Christie N, 'The Ideal Victim' in Ezzat A Fattah (ed), From Crime Policy to Victim Policy: Reorienting the Justice System (Palgrave Macmillan UK 1986)

Collins PH, Black Feminist Thought: Knowledge, Consciousness, and the Politics of Empowerment (Routledge 1990)

Crawley H, Refugees and Gender: Law and Process (Jordan Publishing Limited 2001)

——, 'Gender, "Refugee Women" and the Politics of Protection' in Claudia Mora and Nicola Piper (eds), The Palgrave Handbook of Gender and Migration (Palgrave Macmillan UK 2021)

Crine Z, Flamand C and Raimondo F, 'Time(S), Space(S) and Shapes of Vulnerabilities in the Belgian Asylum System' in Luc Leboeuf and others (eds), Between Protection and Harm: Negotiated Vulnerabilities in Asylum Laws and Bureaucracies (Springer Nature Switzerland 2025)

Denys L, Overzicht van het migratierecht (Die Keure 2025)

Desmet E, 'Appellate Asylum and Migration Proceedings in Belgium: Challenges for the Best Interests of the Child Principle and Unity of Jurisprudence' in Mark Klaassen and others (eds), Safeguarding children's rights in immigration law (Intersentia 2020)

——, 'Gender en migratierecht in België: een decennium in vogelvlucht' in Eva Brems, Pieter Cannoot and Liesbet Stevens (eds), Recht en gender in België : 10 jaar later (die Keure 2021)

Fricker M, Epistemic Injustice: Power and the Ethics of Knowing (Oxford University Press 2007)

Gardî R, 'Foreword' in Cathryn Costello, Michelle Foster and Jane McAdam (eds), The Oxford Handbook of International Refugee Law (Oxford University Press 2021)

Goodwin-Gill GS and McAdam J, The Refugee in International Law (Oxford University Press 2007)

Haines R, 'Gender-Related Persecution' in Erika Feller, Frances Nicholson and Volker Türk (eds), Refugee Protection in International Law: UNHCR's Global Consultations on International Protection (Cambridge University Press 2003)

Harding S, 'Introduction: Is There a Feminist Method?' in Sandra Harding, Feminism and Methodology: Social Science Issues (Highlighting edition, Indiana University Press 1988)

——, Whose Science? Whose Knowledge?: Thinking from Women's Lives (Cornell University Press 1991)

Hathaway JC and Foster M, The Law of Refugee Status (Cambridge University Press 2014)

Herlihy J, 'Psychological Barriers to Fair Refugee Status Determination Related to Our Understanding and Expression of Gender' in Efrat Arbel, Catherine Dauvergne and Jenni Millbank (eds), Gender in Refugee Law (Routledge 2014)

Herman JL, Trauma and Recovery: The Aftermath of Violence – from Domestic Abuse to Political Terror (Basic Books/Hachette Book Group 1992)

Jaji R, '"Aberrant" Masculinity: Men, Culture and Forced Migration' in Claudia Mora and Nicola Piper (eds), The Palgrave Handbook of Gender and Migration (Palgrave Macmillan UK 2021)

Kolankiewicz M, 'The Ethics of Renaming: On Challenges and Dilemmas of Anonymization in a Study of Anti-Muslim Racism' in The Critical Methodologies Collective (ed), The Politics and Ethics of Representation in Qualitative Research: Addressing Moments of Discomfort (Routledge 2022)

Lewis C, 'Systemic Silencing: Addressing Sexual Violence against Men and Boys in Armed Conflict and Its Aftermath' in Gina Heathcote and Dianne Otto (eds), Rethinking Peacekeeping, Gender Equality and Collective Security (Palgrave Macmillan UK 2014)

Lorde A, 'The Transformation of Silence into Language and Action', Sister outsider: essays and speeches (Crossing Press 1984)

Malkki LH, Purity and Exile: Violence, Memory, and National Cosmology among Hutu Refugees in Tanzania (University of Chicago Press 1995)

Noll G, 'Credibility, Reliability, and Evidential Assessment' in Cathryn Costello, Michelle Foster and Jane McAdam (eds), The Oxford Handbook of International Refugee Law (Oxford University Press 2021)

Oxford C, 'Where Are the Women?' in Efrat Arbel, Catherine Dauvergne and Jenni Millbank, Gender in Refugee Law: From the Margins to the Centre (Routledge 2014)

Petintseva O, Faria R and Eski Y, Interviewing Elites, Experts and the Powerful in Criminology (Palgrave 2019)

Picozza F, The Coloniality of Asylum: Mobility, Autonomy and Solidarity in the Wake of Europe's Refugee Crisis (Rowman & Littlefield Publishers 202145)

Pittaway E and Bartolomei LA, Only Rape! Human Rights and Gender Equality for Refugee Women: From Refugee Camps to the United Nations (Springer Nature 2023)

Rich K, Interviewing Rape Victims: Practice and Policy Issues in an International Context (Palgrave Pivot 2014)

Roels L, 'Het Cassandracomplex in Gendergerelateerde Asielprocedures: Luisteren als feministische methode in onderzoek over verkrachtingsmythologie' in Pieter Cannoot, Elise Goossens and Marie Spinoy (eds), Feministische en queer onderzoeksmethoden in het recht (Intersentia 2025)

Sadiqi F, 'Morocco' in Sanja Kelly and Julia Breslin (eds), Women's Rights in the Middle East and North Africa: Progress Amid Resistance (Freedom House/Rowman & Littlefield Publishers 2010)

Singer D, 'Falling at Each Hurdle: Assessing the Credibility of Women's Asylum Claims in Europe' in Efrat Arbel, Catherine Dauvergne and Jenni Millbank (eds), Gender in Refugee Law: From the Margins to the Centre (Routledge 2014)

Spijkerboer T, 'Gender and Refugee Status' (Routledge 2000)

——, 'Stereotyping and Acceleration – Gender, Procedural Acceleration and Marginalised Judicial Review in the Dutch Asylum System' in Gregor Noll (ed), Proof, Evidentiary Assessment and Credibility in Asylum Procedures (Brill Nijhoff 2005)

——, 'Asylum Decision-Making, Gender and Sexuality' in Evangelia Tsourdi and De Bruycker (eds), Research Handbook on EU Migration and Asylum Law (Edward Elgar Publishing 2022)

Spivak GC, 'Can the Subaltern Speak?' in Cary Nelson and Lawrence Grossberg (eds), Marxism and the interpretation of culture (University of Illinois Press 1988)

Stringer R, Knowing Victims: Feminism, Agency and Victim Politics in Neoliberal Times (Routledge 2014)

Sullivan D, 'The Public/Private Distinction in International Human Rights Law' in JS Peters and Andrea Wolper (eds), Women's Rights, Human Rights (Routledge 1995)

Ticktin M, Casualties of Care: Immigration and the Politics of Humanitarianism in France (University of California Press 2011)

——, 'In the Name of Violence against Women' in Miriam Ticktin, Casualties of Care: Immigration and the Politics of Humanitarianism in France (University of California Press 2011)

——, 'Innocence: Shaping the Concept and Practice of Humanity' in Michael N Barnett (ed), Humanitarianism and Human Rights: A World of Differences? (Cambridge University Press 2020)

Vande Lanotte J, Goedertier G and Haeck Y, Handboek Belgisch Publiekrecht. Deel 2: Basiskenmerken van de Belgische Staatstructuur (die Keure 2015)

JOURNAL ARTICLES

Aitchison S, 'The Temporality of Intimate Partner Violence – How an Understanding of Time and Gendered Threats Can Foster Protection-Positive Outcomes' (2024) 43 Refugee Survey Quarterly 73

Alaggia R, Collin-Vézina D and Lateef R, 'Facilitators and Barriers to Child Sexual Abuse (CSA) Disclosures: A Research Update (2000–2016)' (2019) 20 Trauma, Violence & Abuse 260

Alcoff L, 'The Problem of Speaking for Others' (1991) 20 Cultural Critique 5

Alcoff L and Gray L, 'Survivor Discourse: Transgression or Recuperation?' (1993) 18 Signs 260

Alexander MJ, 'Not Just (Any) Body Can Be a Citizen: The Politics of Law, Sexuality and Postcoloniality in Trinidad and Tobago and the Bahamas' (1994) 48 Feminist Review 5

Alradie-Mohamed A, Kabir R and Arafat SMY, 'Decision-Making Process in Female Genital Mutilation: A Systematic Review' (2020) 17 International Journal of Environmental Research and Public Health 3362

Ask K, 'A Survey of Police Officers' and Prosecutors' Beliefs About Crime Victim Behaviors' (2010) 25 Journal of Interpersonal Violence 1132

Babacan Gümüş A, Şıpkın S and Erdem Ö, 'The Prevalence of Intimate Partner Violence against Women and Women's Methods of Coping with Partner Violence*' (2020) 11 Journal of Psychiatric Nursing 79

Badenes-Sastre M and others, 'Cognitive Distortions and Decision-Making in Women Victims of Intimate Partner Violence: A Scoping Review' (2025) 34 Psychosocial Intervention 23

Baert S and others, 'Factors Related to Police Reporting in Sexual Assault Care Centers: Are We Underestimating the Role of Support Persons?' (2024) 30 Violence Against Women 3943

Baillot H, Cowan S and Munro VE, 'Seen but Not Heard? Parallels and Dissonances in the Treatment of Rape Narratives across the Asylum and Criminal Justice Contexts' (2009) 36 Journal of Law and Society 195

——, '"Hearing the Right Gaps": Enabling and Responding to Disclosures of Sexual Violence within the UK Asylum Process' (2012) 21 Social & Legal Studies 269

——, 'Reason to Disbelieve: Evaluating the Rape Claims of Women Seeking Asylum in the UK' (2014) 10 International Journal of Law in Context 105

Bellew K, 'Silent Suffering: Uncovering and Understanding Domestic Violence in Affluent Communities Note' (2005) 26 Women's Rights Law Reporter 39

Ben-David S and Schneider O, 'Rape Perceptions, Gender Role Attitudes, and Victim-Perpetrator Acquaintance' (2005) 53 Sex Roles 385

Benslama-Dabdoub M, 'Epistemic Violence and Colonial Legacies in the Representation of Refugee Women: Contesting Narratives of Vulnerability and Victimhood' (2024) 20 International Journal of Law in Context 54

Benson ML and others, 'Neighborhood Disadvantage, Individual Economic Distress and Violence Against Women in Intimate Relationships' (2003) 19 Journal of Quantitative Criminology 207

Bingham AJ, 'From Data Management to Actionable Findings: A Five-Phase Process of Qualitative Data Analysis' (2023) 22 International Journal of Qualitative Methods 1

Bloemen E and Mellink R, '"Ik Kan Niet Alles Vertellen …" Asielzoekers Met Psychische Problemen in de Asielprocedure' (2008) 11 Maandblad geestelijke volksgezondheid 890

Bögner D, Herlihy J and Brewin CR, 'Impact of Sexual Violence on Disclosure during Home Office Interviews' (2007) 191 The British Journal of Psychiatry 75

Bohner G and others, 'Rape Myths as Neutralizing Cognitions: Evidence for a Causal Impact of Anti-Victim Attitudes on Men's Self-Reported Likelihood of Raping' (1998) 28 European Journal of Social Psychology 257

Breen LH and Boyce MA, '"Why Did She Talk to Him Again?" The Effects of the Justice Motive, Relationship Type, and Degree of Postassault Contact on Perceptions of Sexual Assault' (2021) 36 Journal of Interpersonal Violence 5229

Briddick C, 'Unprincipled and Unrealised: CEDAW and Discrimination Experienced in the Context of Migration Control' (2022) 22 International Journal of Discrimination and the Law 224

Bronfenbrenner U, 'Toward an Experimental Ecology of Human Development' (1977) 32 American Psychologist 513

Burt MR, 'Cultural Myths and Supports for Rape' (1980) 38 Journal of Personality and Social Psychology 217

Calton JM, Cattaneo LB and Gebhard KT, 'Barriers to Help Seeking for Lesbian, Gay, Bisexual, Transgender, and Queer Survivors of Intimate Partner Violence' (2016) 17 Trauma, Violence, & Abuse 585

Campbell JC and others, 'Risk Factors for Femicide in Abusive Relationships: Results From a Multisite Case Control Study' (2003) 93 American Journal of Public Health 1089

Campbell R and others, 'Training Interviewers for Research on Sexual Violence A Qualitative Study of Rape Survivors' Recommendations for Interview Practice' (2009) 15 Violence Against Women 594

Candel I and Merckelbach H, 'Het Geheugen Voor Negatieve Gebeurtenissen' (2002) 57 Nederlands Tijdschrift voor de Psychologie en haar Grensgebieden 1

Carter N and others, 'The Use of Triangulation in Qualitative Research' (2014) 5 Methods & Meanings (Oncology Nursing Forum) 545

Chynoweth SK and others, 'A Social Ecological Approach to Understanding Service Utilization Barriers among Male Survivors of Sexual Violence in Three Refugee Settings: A Qualitative Exploratory Study' (2020) 14 Conflict and Health 1

——, 'Characteristics and Impacts of Sexual Violence Against Men and Boys in Conflict and Displacement: A Multicountry Exploratory Study' (2020) 37(9–10) Journal of Interpersonal Violence 1

Clark-Kazak C, 'Ethical Considerations: Research with People in Situations of Forced Migration' (2017) 33 Refuge: Canada's Journal on Refugees / Refuge : revue canadienne sur les réfugiés 11

Comack E and Peter T, 'How the Criminal Justice System Responds to Sexual Assault Survivors: The Slippage between "Responsibilization" and "Blaming the Victim."' (2005) 17 Canadian Journal of Women & the Law 283

Craig E, 'The Relevance of Delayed Disclosure to Complainant Credibility in Cases of Sexual Offence' (2011) 36 Queen's Law Journal 1

Crawley H, 'Gender, Persecution and the Concept of Politics in the Asylum Determination Process' (2000) 9 Forced Migration Review 17

Crenshaw K, 'Demarginalizing the Intersection of Race and Sex: A Black Feminist Critique of Antidiscrimination Doctrine, Feminist Theory and Antiracist Politics' (1989) 1989 University of Chicago Legal Forum 139

Cullen MM and Brennan NM, 'Grounded Theory: Description, Divergences and Application' (2021) 27 Accounting, Finance & Governance Review 1

Dadhania PR, 'Gender-Based Religious Persecution' (2023) 4 Minnesota Law Review 1563
Das PK and Roy T, 'Women Refugees and Their Unrecognised Plights in International Refugee Law Regime: A Critical Analysis' (2022) 1 Indian Journal of Law and Justice 78
Davies M, Gilston J and Rogers P, 'Examining the Relationship Between Male Rape Myth Acceptance, Female Rape Myth Acceptance, Victim Blame, Homophobia, Gender Roles, and Ambivalent Sexism' (2012) 27 Journal of Interpersonal Violence 2807
De Schrijver L and others, 'Prevalence of Sexual Violence in Migrants, Applicants for International Protection, and Refugees in Europe: A Critical Interpretive Synthesis of the Evidence' (2018) 15 International Journal of Environmental Research and Public Health 1979
——, 'Victimization of Applicants for International Protection Residing in Belgium: Sexual Violence and Help-Seeking Behavior' (2022) 19 International Journal of Environmental Research and Public Health 12889
Della Torre J, 'Taking the Evolution of the Standards of Proof for a Criminal Conviction Seriously' (2024) 8 Quaestio facti. Revista internacional sobre razonamiento probatorio 155
Depraetere J and others, 'Big Boys Don't Cry: A Critical Interpretive Synthesis of Male Sexual Victimization' (2020) 21 Trauma, Violence, & Abuse 991
Depraetere J, Decrock C and Vandeviver C, 'Een factorieel survey experiment naar de aanvaarding van verkrachtingsmythes binnen de politie in België' (2020) 4 Panopticon 373
Desmet E, 'Analysing Users' Trajectories in Human Rights: A Conceptual Exploration and Research Agenda' (2014) 8 Human Rights & International Legal Discourse 121
Diab JL and Al-Azzeh D, 'Inclusive Inquiry: A Compassionate Journey in Trauma-Informed Qualitative Research with GBV Survivors from Displaced Communities' (2024) 15 Frontiers in Psychology 1
Dunn JL, '"Victims" and "Survivors": Emerging Vocabularies of Motive for "Battered Women Who Stay"*' (2005) 75 Sociological Inquiry 1
Ebren G, Demircioğlu M and Çırakoğlu OC, 'A Neglected Aspect of Refugee Relief Works: Secondary and Vicarious Traumatic Stress' (2022) 35 Journal of Traumatic Stress 891
Edwards KM and others, 'Rape Myths: History, Individual and Institutional-Level Presence, and Implications for Change' (2011) 65 Sex Roles 761
Ermer AE and others, 'Deconstructing Attitudes About Intimate Partner Violence and Bystander Intervention: The Roles of Perpetrator Gender and Severity of Aggression' (2021) 36 Journal of Interpersonal Violence NP896
Evans Cameron H, 'Risk Theory and "Subjective Fear": The Role of Risk Perception, Assessment, and Management in Refugee Status Determinations' (2008) 20 International Journal of Refugee Law 567
——, 'Risk and the Reasonable Refugee: Exploring a Key Credibility Inference in Canadian Refugee Status Rejections' (2023) 35 International Journal of Refugee Law 10
——, 'Refugee Status Determinations and the Limits of Memory' (2010) 22 International Journal of Refugee Law 469
Feild HS, 'Attitudes toward Rape: A Comparative Analysis of Police, Rapists, Crisis Counselors, and Citizens' (1978) 36 Journal of Personality and Social Psychology 156
Fereday J and Muir-Cochrane E, 'Demonstrating Rigor Using Thematic Analysis: A Hybrid Approach of Inductive and Deductive Coding and Theme Development' (2006) 5 International Journal of Qualitative Methods 80

Firth G and Mauthe B, 'Refugee Law, Gender and the Concept of Personhood' (2013) 25 International Journal of Refugee Law 470

Flecha R, 'Second-Order Sexual Harassment: Violence Against the Silence Breakers Who Support the Victims' (2021) 27 Violence Against Women 1980

Foster EL and others, 'Coping with Intimate Partner Violence: Qualitative Findings from the Study of Dynamics of Husband to Wife Abuse' (2015) 33 Families, Systems, & Health 285

Fynn Bruey V and others, 'Rewriting Refugee Law: Centring Refugee Knowledges and Lived Experience' (2024) 43 Refugee Survey Quarterly 115

Galván-Álvarez E, 'Epistemic Violence and Retaliation: The Issue of Knowledges in "Mother India" / Violencia y Venganza Epistemológica: La Cuestión de Las Formas de Conocimiento En Mother India' (2010) 32 Atlantis 11

Garcia-Moreno C and others, 'Prevalence of Intimate Partner Violence: Findings from the WHO Multi-Country Study on Women's Health and Domestic Violence' (2006) 368 The Lancet 1260

Gavey N, 'Feminist Poststructuralism and Discourse Analysis: Contributions to Feminist Psychology' (1989) 13 Psychology of Women Quarterly 459

Gerger H and others, 'The Acceptance of Modern Myths about Sexual Aggression Scale: Development and Validation in German and English' (2007) 33 Aggressive Behavior 422

Gevorgyan M and Matevosyan A, 'Bacha Bazi: Unraveling Debate between Crime Against Humanity and Regional Tradition' (2023) 2 European Journal of Law and Political Science 38

Ghorashi H, 'Giving Silence a Chance: The Importance of Life Stories for Research on Refugees' (2008) 21 Journal of Refugee Studies 117

Gidycz CA, McNamara JR and Edwards KM, 'Women's Risk Perception and Sexual Victimization: A Review of the Literature' (2006) 11 Aggression and Violent Behavior 441

Gill A, 'Patriarchal Violence in the Name of "Honour"' (2006) 1 International Journal of Criminal Justice Sciences 1

Given-Wilson Z, Herlihy J and Hodes M, 'Telling the Story: A Psychological Review on Assessing Adolescents' Asylum Claims.' (2016) 57 Canadian Psychology / Psychologie canadienne 265

Graffin N, 'The Emotional Impacts of Working as an Asylum Lawyer' (2019) 38 Refugee Survey Quarterly 30

Graham B, Herlihy J and Brewin CR, 'Overgeneral Memory in Asylum Seekers and Refugees' (2014) 45 Journal of Behavior Therapy and Experimental Psychiatry 375

Granhag PA and Strömwall LA, 'Repeated Interrogations – Stretching the Deception Detection Paradigm' (1999) 7 Expert Evidence 163

Greatbatch J, 'The Gender Difference: Feminist Critiques of Refugee Discourse' (1989) 1 International Journal of Refugee Law 518

Guest G, Bunce A and Johnson L, 'How Many Interviews Are Enough?: An Experiment with Data Saturation and Variability' (2006) 18 Field Methods 59

Hansen M, Stefansen K and Skilbrei M-L, 'Non-Reporting of Sexual Violence as Action: Acts, Selves, Futures in the Making' (2021) 22 Nordic Journal of Criminology 42

Haselschwerdt ML and Hardesty JL, 'Managing Secrecy and Disclosure of Domestic Violence in Affluent Communities' (2017) 79 Journal of Marriage and Family 556

Hathaway J and Hicks W, 'Is There a Subjective Element in the Refugee Convention's Requirement of "Well-Founded Fear"?' (2005) 26 Michigan Journal of International Law 505

Heise L, 'Violence Against Women: An Integrated, Ecological Framework' (1998) 4 Violence against women 262

Herlihy J, Jobson L and Turner S, 'Just Tell Us What Happened to You: Autobiographical Memory and Seeking Asylum' (2012) 26 Applied Cognitive Psychology 661

Herlihy J, Scragg P and Turner S, 'Discrepancies in Autobiographical Memories – Implications for the Assessment of Asylum Seekers: Repeated Interviews Study' (2002) 324 the British Medical Journal 324

Herlihy J and Turner S, 'Should Discrepant Accounts given by Asylum Seekers Be Taken as Proof of Deceit' (2006) 16 Torture 81

——, 'Untested Assumptions: Psychological Research and Credibility Assessment in Legal Decision-Making' (2015) 6 European Journal of Psychotraumatology 1

Hershkowitz I, Lanes O and Lamb ME, 'Exploring the Disclosure of Child Sexual Abuse with Alleged Victims and Their Parents' (2007) 31 Child Abuse & Neglect 111

Hill Collins P, 'It's All In the Family: Intersections of Gender, Race, and Nation' (1998) 13 Hypatia 62

Hugman R, Pittaway E and Bartolomei L, 'When "Do No Harm" Is Not Enough: The Ethics of Research with Refugees and Other Vulnerable Groups' (2011) 41 The British Journal of Social Work 1271

Jacobs M and Maryns K, 'Managing Narratives, Managing Identities: Language and Credibility in Legal Consultations with Asylum Seekers' (2022) 51 Language In Society 1

Jami H and Kamal A, 'Measuring Attitudes toward Hijras in Pakistan: Gender and Religiosity in Perspective' (2015) 1 Pakistan Journal of Psychological Research 151

Johnson NL, Walker RV and Rojas-Ashe EE, 'A Social Justice Approach to Measuring Bystander Behavior: Introducing the Critically Conscious Bystander Scale' (2019) 81 Sex Roles 731

Johnsson AB, 'The International Protection of Women Refugees: A Summary of Principal Problems and Issues' (1989) 1 International Journal of Refugee Law 221

Jones JS and others, 'Comparison of Sexual Assaults by Strangers versus Known Assailants in a Community-Based Population' (2004) 22 The American Journal of Emergency Medicine 454

Josse E, '"They Came with Two Guns": The Consequences of Sexual Violence for the Mental Health of Women in Armed Conflicts' (2010) 92 International Review of the Red Cross 177

Jubany O, 'Constructing Truths in a Culture of Disbelief: Understanding Asylum Screening from Within' (2011) 26 International Sociology 74

Kakhnovets R and Holohan DR, 'Initial Steps in Treating the Male Patient' (2007) 24 Federal Practitioner 16

Kaviani Johnson A, 'Grooming and Child Sexual Abuse in Organizational Settings – an Expanded Role for International Human Rights Law' (2024) 16 Journal of Human Rights Practice 355

Kelley N, 'Internal Flight/Relocation/Protection Alternative: Is It Reasonable' (2002) 14 International Journal of Refugee Law 4

Keygnaert I and others, 'Sexual Violence and Sub-Saharan Migrants in Morocco: A Community-Based Participatory Assessment Using Respondent Driven Sampling' (2014) 10 Globalization and Health 1

Keygnaert I, Vettenburg N and Temmerman M, 'Hidden Violence Is Silent Rape: Sexual and Gender-Based Violence in Refugees, Asylum Seekers and Undocumented Migrants in Belgium and the Netherlands' (2012) 14 Culture, Health & Sexuality 505

Kiconco A and Nthakomwa M, 'Wartime Captivity and Homecoming: Culture, Stigma, and Coping Strategies of Formerly Abducted Women in Post-Conflict Northern Uganda' (2022) 46 Disasters 654

Kneebone S, 'Women within the Refugee Construct: Exclusionary Inclusion in Policy and Practice – the Australian Experience' (2005) 17 International Journal of Refugee Law 7

Krahé B, 'Cognitive Coping With the Threat of Rape: Vigilance and Cognitive Avoidance' (2005) 73 Journal of Personality 609

——, 'Prospective Lawyers' Rape Stereotypes and Schematic Decision Making about Rape Cases' (2008) 14 Psychology, Crime & Law 461

Krause U, 'Invisibilization of the Unwanted Others? Feminist, Queer, and Postcolonial Perspectives on the 1951 Refugee Convention's Drafting' (2024) 107 Women's Studies International Forum 1

Kritzman-Amir T, 'Not in My Backyard: On the Morality of Responsibility Sharing in Refugee Law' (2009) 34 Brooklyn Journal of International Law 355

Leverick F, 'What Do We Know about Rape Myths and Juror Decision Making?' (2020) 24 The International Journal of Evidence & Proof 255

Lodrick Z, 'Psychological Trauma – What Every Trauma Worker Should Know.' (2007) 2 The British Journal of Psychotherapy Integration 1

Lokot M, 'The Space between Us: Feminist Values and Humanitarian Power Dynamics in Research with Refugees' (2019) 27 Gender & Development 467

Lonsway KA and Fitzgerald LF, 'Rape Myths: In Review' (1994) 18 Psychology of Women Quarterly 133

Magugliani N, '(In)Vulnerable Masculinities and Human Trafficking: Men, Victimhood, and Access to Protection in the United Kingdom' (2022) 14 Journal of Human Rights Practice 1

Mainwaring C, Gabbert F and Scott AJ, 'A Systematic Review Exploring Variables Related to Bystander Intervention in Sexual Violence Contexts' (2023) 24 Trauma, Violence & Abuse 1727

Marcantonio TL and others, 'Sexual and Gender Minority Men's Bystander Behaviors and Barriers in Response to Witnessing Minor Sexual Aggression' (2023) 13 Psychology of violence 319

Maryns K, 'Disclosure and (Re)Performance of Gender-Based Evidence in an Interpreter-Mediated Asylum Interview' (2013) 17 Journal of Sociolinguistics 661

Masiya Mponela L, '"Our Wish Is To Be Human Again": Refugee Women Speaking Up and Taking Space' (2022) 41 Refugee Survey Quarterly 381

Mason R, 'Two Kinds of Unknowing' (2011) 26 Hypatia 294

McGee H and others, 'Rape and Child Sexual Abuse: What Beliefs Persist About Motives, Perpetrators, and Survivors?' (2011) 26 Journal of Interpersonal Violence 3580

McKinnon R, 'Epistemic Injustice' (2016) 11 Philosophy Compass 437

McKinnon SL, 'Citizenship and the Performance of Credibility: Audiencing Gender-Based Asylum Seekers in U.S. Immigration Courts' (2009) 29 Text & Performance Quarterly 205

McLeod DA and others, 'The Model of Systemic Relational Violence: Conceptualizing IPV as a Method of Continual and Enforced Domination' (2021) 1 Trauma Care 87

McMahon S and others, 'Predicting Bystander Behavior to Prevent Sexual Assault on College Campuses: The Role of Self-Efficacy and Intent' (2015) 56 American Journal of Community Psychology 46

McMahon S and Banyard VL, 'When Can I Help? A Conceptual Framework for the Prevention of Sexual Violence Through Bystander Intervention' (2012) 13 Trauma, Violence, & Abuse 3

McMahon S and Farmer GL, 'An Updated Measure for Assessing Subtle Rape Myths' (2011) 35 Social Work Research 71

Middelburg A and Balta A, 'Female Genital Mutilation/Cutting as a Ground for Asylum in Europe' (2016) 3 International Journal of Refugee Law 416

Millbank J, '"The Ring of Truth": A Case Study of Credibility Assessment in Particular Social Group Refugee Determinations' (2009) 21 International Journal of Refugee Law 1

Misra A, 'Men on Top: Sexual Economy of Bacha Bazi in Afghanistan' (2023) 60 International Politics 350

Mohanty CT, 'Under Western Eyes: Feminist Scholarship and Colonial Discourses' (1988) 30 Feminist Review 61

Moore SA and Zoellner LA, 'Overgeneral Autobiographical Memory and Traumatic Events' (2007) 133 Psychological bulletin 419

Nazareno E and others, 'Men Tackling Isolating Gender Violence to Fight against Sexual Harassment' (2022) 19 International Journal of Environmental Research and Public Health 1924

Nijenhuis E, van der Hart O and Steele K, 'Trauma-Related Structural Dissociation of the Personality' (2010) 52 Activitas Nervosa Superior 1

O'Brien Hallstein DL, 'Where Standpoint Stands Now: An Introduction and Commentary' (2000) 23 Women's Studies in Communication 1

Olwan DM, 'Gendered Violence, Cultural Otherness, and Honour Crimes in Canadian National Logics' (2013) 38 The Canadian Journal of Sociology 533

Papoutsi A and others, 'Geographies of Shame: Diachronic and Transnational Shame in Forced Migrants with Experiences of Sexual and Gender-Based Violence' (2022) 35 Journal of Refugee Studies 1221

Park S, Woo H and Kim S-H, 'A Systematic Review and Meta-Analysis of Bystander's Barriers to Intervene in Gender-Based Violence and the Role of Failed Prior Attempts' (2024) 25 Trauma, Violence, & Abuse 1998

Parsons A and Mojtahedi D, 'Can Jurors Be Biased in Their Evaluation of Third-Party Evidence within Cases of Rape?' (2022) 85 International Journal of Law and Psychiatry 1

Parsons JR and Riva S, 'Innocence and Danger at the Border: Migrants, "Bad" Mothers, and the Nation's Protectors' (2024) 12 Comparative Migration Studies 1

Payne DL, Lonsway KA and Fitzgerald LF, 'Rape Myth Acceptance: Exploration of Its Structure and Its Measurement Using the Illinois Rape Myth Acceptance Scale' (1999) 33 Journal of Research in Personality 27

Pearce H, 'An Examination of the International Understanding of Political Rape and the Significance of Labeling It Torture' (2002) 14 International Journal of Refugee Law 534

Peroni L, 'The Protection of Women Asylum Seekers under the European Convention on Human Rights: Unearthing the Gendered Roots of Harm' (2018) 18 Human Rights Law Review 347

Pijlman V and others, '"Sometimes It Seems Easier to Push It Away": A Study Into the Barriers to Help-Seeking for Victims of Sexual Violence' (2023) 38 Journal of Interpersonal Violence 7530

Pohlhaus Jr. G, 'Relational Knowing and Epistemic Injustice: Toward a Theory of "Willful Hermeneutical Ignorance"' (2012) 27 Hypatia 715

Powell KM and Takayoshi P, 'Accepting Roles Created for Us: The Ethics of Reciprocity' (2003) 54 College Composition and Communication 394

Querton C, 'Gender and the Boundaries of International Refugee Law: Beyond the Category of "Gender-Related Asylum Claims"' (2019) 37 Netherlands Quarterly of Human Rights 379

——, 'Non-State Actors of Protection and the Sliding Scale of Protection for Refugee Women' (2022) 41 Refugee Survey Quarterly 1

Randall M, 'Sexual Assault Law, Credibility, and "Ideal Victims": Consent, Resistance, and Victim Blaming' (2010) 22 Canadian Journal of Women and the Law/Revue Femmes et Droit 397

Rauvola RS, Vega DM and Lavigne KN, 'Compassion Fatigue, Secondary Traumatic Stress, and Vicarious Traumatization: A Qualitative Review and Research Agenda' (2019) 3 Occupational Health Science 297

Razack S, 'Domestic Violence as Gender Persecution: Policing the Borders of Nation, Race, and Gender' (1995) 8 Canadian Journal of Women and the Law 45

Roels L, 'Socialemedia- en smartphonescreenings tegen misbruik in Belgische verzoekprocedures om internationale bescherming : een doel dat de middelen niet wettigt' (2020) 4 Tijdschrift voor Vreemdelingenrecht 329

——, 'Rape Myths in the European Court of Human Rights' Non-Refoulement Case Law on Sexual and Gender-Based Violence' (2024) 36 International Journal of Refugee Law 77

Rønning L, Blumberg J and Dammeyer J, 'Vicarious Traumatisation in Lawyers Working with Traumatised Asylum Seekers: A Pilot Study' (2020) 27 Psychiatry, Psychology and Law 665

Rousseau C and others, 'The Complexity of Determining Refugeehood: A Multidisciplinary Analysis of the Decision-Making Process of the Canadian Immigration and Refugee Board' (2002) 15 Journal of Refugee Studies 43

Schilt K and Westbrook L, 'Doing Gender, Doing Heteronormativity: "Gender Normals," Transgender People, and the Social Maintenance of Heterosexuality' (2009) 23 Gender & Society 440

Schlegel A and Courtois R, 'Scales for Evaluating the Acceptance of the Rape Myth: Benefits and Limitations' (2019) 2 International Journal of Risk and Recovery 23

Schwendinger JR and Schwendinger H, 'Rape Myths: In Legal, Theoretical, and Everyday Practice' (1974) 1 Crime and Social Justice 18

Shepp V, O'Callaghan E and Ullman SE, 'Interactions with Offenders Post-Assault and Their Impacts on Recovery: A Qualitative Study of Sexual Assault Survivors and Support Providers' (2020) 29 Journal of aggression, maltreatment & trauma 725
Skrifvars J and others, 'Psychological Assumptions Underlying Credibility Assessments in Finnish Asylum Determinations' (2022) 76 Nordic Psychology 1
Smith K, 'Telling Stories of Resistance and Ruination: Women Seeking Asylum' (2016) 2 Journal of Resistance Studies 33
Smith MD, 'Rethinking Gender in the International Refugee Regime' (2016) 53 Forced Migration Review 65
Smith O and Skinner T, 'How Rape Myths Are Used and Challenged in Rape and Sexual Assault Trials' (2017) 26 Social & Legal Studies 441
Sorvatzioti DF and Manson A, 'Burden of Proof and L'intime Conviction: Is the Continental Criminal Trial Moving to the Common Law?' (2018) 23 Canadian Criminal Law Review 107
Spijkerboer T, 'Sheherazade En Haar Zusters' (1994) 4 Nemesis 95
——, 'Gender, Sexuality, Asylum and European Human Rights' (2018) 29 Law and Critique 221
Stepnitz A, 'Believing Asylum-Seeking Women: Doing Gender in Legal Narratives of Sexual and Gender-Based Violence' (2023) (forthcoming) Social & Legal Studies 1
Struckman-Johnson C and Struckman-Johnson D, 'Acceptance of Male Rape Myths Among College Men and Women' (1992) 27 Sex Roles 85
Testa M, VanZile-Tamsen C and Livingston JA, 'Prospective Prediction of Women's Sexual Victimization by Intimate and Nonintimate Male Perpetrators' (2007) 75 Journal of Consulting and Clinical Psychology 52
Theunissen TPM and others, 'Adult Eyewitness Memory for Single Versus Repeated Traumatic Events' (2017) 31 Applied Cognitive Psychology 164
Tolman RM and others, 'A Global Exploratory Analysis of Men Participating in Gender-Based Violence Prevention' (2019) 34 Journal of Interpersonal Violence 3438
Tong A, Sainsbury P and Craig J, 'Consolidated Criteria for Reporting Qualitative Research (COREQ): A 32-Item Checklist for Interviews and Focus Groups' (2007) 19 International Journal for Quality in Health Care 349
van der Bruggen M and Grubb A, 'A Review of the Literature Relating to Rape Victim Blaming: An Analysis of the Impact of Observer and Victim Characteristics on Attribution of Blame in Rape Cases' (2014) 19 Aggression and Violent Behavior 523
van der Kolk BA and van der Hart O, 'Het Binnendringend Verleden: De Flexibiliteit van Het Geheugen En de Inprenting van Trauma's' (1992) 8 ICODO–INFO 1
Van Eekert N and others, 'Rethinking the Definition of Medicalized Female Genital Mutilation/Cutting' (2024) 53 Archives of Sexual Behavior 441
Van Impe M, 'Narratieve criminologie meets participatief actieonderzoek' (2020) 10 Tijdschrift over Cultuur & Criminaliteit 97
Van Veldhuizen T, 'Effectief Horen in Asielzaken: Niet Inperken Maar Uit Laten Weiden' (2017) 16 Journaal Vreemdelingenrecht 48
Vermetten E, Raaijmakers W and Gersons B, 'Trauma, dissociatie en het geheugen: neurobiologische aspecten' (1998) 18 Directieve therapie 275
Viejo C, Linde Valenzuela G and Ortega Ruiz R, 'Adult Partner Violence and Previous Violence Experiences: Retrospective Study with Women Victims of Gender-Based

Violence' (2018) 18 International journal of psychology and psychological therapy 179
Vogelaar F, 'The Presumption of Safety Tested: The Use of Country of Origin Information in the National Designation of Safe Countries of Origin' (2021) 40 Refugee Survey Quarterly 106
Vrklevski LP and Franklin J, 'Vicarious Trauma: The Impact on Solicitors of Exposure to Traumatic Material' (2008) 14 Traumatology 106
Waldron JC and others, 'Sexual Victimization History, Depression, and Task Physiology as Predictors of Sexual Revictimization: Results From a 6-Month Prospective Pilot Study' (2015) 30 Journal of Interpersonal Violence 622
Waldrop AE and Resick PA, 'Coping Among Adult Female Victims of Domestic Violence' (2004) 19 Journal of Family Violence 291
Walsh K and others, 'A Preliminary Examination of Sexual and Physical Victimization 6 Months after Recent Rape' (2023) 26 Archives of women's mental health 495
Warin C, 'Gender in European Union Asylum Law: The Istanbul Convention as a Game Changer?' (2024) 36 International Journal of Refugee Law 93
Weare S, '"Oh You're a Guy, How Could You Be Raped by a Woman, That Makes No Sense": Towards a Case for Legally Recognising and Labelling "Forced-to-Penetrate" Cases as Rape' (2018) 14 International Journal of Law in Context 110
Wessel E and others, 'Credibility of the Emotional Witness: A Study of Ratings by Court Judges' (2006) 30 Law and Human Behavior 221
Wessels J, 'The Boundaries of Universality – Migrant Women and Domestic Violence before the Strasbourg Court' (2019) 37 Netherlands Quarterly of Human Rights 336
Wieberneit M and others, 'Silenced Survivors: A Systematic Review of the Barriers to Reporting, Investigating, Prosecuting, and Sentencing of Adult Female Rape and Sexual Assault' (2024) 25 Trauma, Violence, & Abuse 3742
Young SL and Maguire KC, 'Talking about Sexual Violence' (2003) 26 Women and Language 40
Zadhy-Çepoğlu AN, 'Reflexive Reciprocity under an Ethics of Care: Reflections from the Field for Refugee Studies' (2023) 12 Migration Studies 1
Zonp Z and others, 'Coping Strategies among Women Exposed to Gender-Based Violence in Turkey' (2022) 78 Journal of Advanced Nursing 4236

REPORTS, PAPERS & PRESENTATIONS

Ali HC, Querton C and Soulard E, 'Gender Related Asylum Claims in Europe: A Comparative Analysis of Law Policies and Practice Focusing on Women in Nine EU Member States' (EU Directorate-General for International Policies 2012)
Amnesty International, 'Eastern Europe and Central Asia: Protect Women from Violence in Crises and Beyond' (2022)
——, 'Amnesty International Report 2022/2: The State of the World's Human Rights: India 2022' (2023)
Amnesty International and International Commission of Jurists (ICJ), 'Afghanistan: The Taliban's War on Women: The Crime against Humanity of Gender Persecution in Afghanistan' (2023)

Amnesty International Nederalnd and instituut voor Mensenrechten en Medisch Onderzoek (iMMO), 'Slachtoffers seksueel geweld: blinde vlek in asielprocedure?' (2023)

Antonioni Luftensteiner (Judge at the Federal Administrative Court in Switzerland) E, 'Les enjeux actuels du régime d'asile européen commun à travers la pratique des juridictions et magistrats francophones des pays membres et associés de l'Union européenne – 3ème table ronde : L'évaluation de la crédibilité et des éléments de preuve sur les questions liées au genre et échange avec l'auditoire' (Conférence de Agence de l'Union européenne pour l'asile et de la Cour nationale du droit d'asile, en collaboration avec le Conseil d'Etat, Paris, 2022)

Baker L and others, 'Trauma- and Violence-Informed Interview Strategies in Work with Survivors of Gender-Based Violence' (Learning Network 2020)

Belgian Women's Council, 'Vrouwenraad-Memorandum Gendergerelateerd Geweld: Aanbevelingen Voor de Vlaamse En Federale Regering' (2019)

British Red Cross and the VOICES Network, 'We Want to Be Strong, but We Don't Have the Chance: Women's Experiences of Seeking Asylum in the UK' (2022)

Browne E, 'Gender Norms, LGBTQI Issues and Development: A Topic Guide' (ALiGN (Advancing Learning and Innovation on Gender Norms) 2019)

Collier B, 'Country of Origin Information and Women: Researching Gender and Persecution in the Context of Asylum and Human Rights Claims' (Asylum Aid 2007)

Crawley H and Lester T, 'Comparative Analysis of Gender-Related Persecution in National Asylum Legislation and Practice in Europe' (UNHCR 2004)

Cusack S, 'Eliminating Judicial Stereotyping: Equal Access to Justice for Women in Gender-Based Violence Cases' (OHCHR 2014)

Dozois E and Germann K, 'No One Deserves To Be Abused: An Inquiry to Inform the Development of Supports for Affluent Survivors: Highlights from a Literature Review, Environmental Scan & Qualitative Research' (Sagesse 2017)

Duhacek D and others, 'Women's Rights in Western Balkans' (European Parliament's Committee on Women's Rights and Gender Equality 2019)

Equality Now, 'Sexual Violence in South Asia: Legal and Other Barriers to Justice for Survivors' (2021)

Fanflik PL, Office on Violence Against Women, and National District Attorneys Association, 'Victim Responses to Sexual Assault: Counterintuitive or Simply Adaptive' (American Prosecutors Research Institute 2007)

Fenix Humanitarian Legal aid and others, 'A Gendered Gaze On Migration: Report on Sexual and Gender-Based Violence in the Context of the Greek Asylum Policy on Lesvos' (2024)

GAMS België vzw, 'Impact van gendergerelateerd geweld op de gezondheid (Transversale fiche 3)' (2019)

Graham A and others, Ethical Research Involving Children (UNICEF Office of Research – Innocenti 2013)

Gumucio S, 'The Kap Survey Model – Knowledge Attitude and Practices' (Médecins du Monde 2011)

Haines R, 'Gender-Based Persecution: New Zealand Jurisprudence' (1996)

——, 'Advancing a Gendered Interpretation of the Refugee Convention (National Members' Conference of the Migration Review Tribunal and Refugee Review Tribunal)' (2009)

Her Majesty's Inspectorate of Constabulary (HMIC), 'The Depths of Dishonour: An Inspection of the Police Response to Honour-Based Violence, Forced Marriage and Female Genital Mutilation' (2015)
Hugo J and Pertl L, 'Intersex Refugees & Asylum Seekers Toolkit' (Organisation Intersex International Europe (OII Europe) 2023)
Human Rights Watch, 'Fast-Tracked Unfairness: Detention and Denial of Women Asylum Seekers in the UK' (2010)
Immigration and Refugee Board of Canada, 'Chairperson Guideline 4: Gender Considerations in Proceedings Before the Immigration and Refugee Board' (2022)
Institute for Womens Policy Research (IWPR), 'The Economic Cost of Intimate Partner Violence, Sexual Assault, and Stalking (Fact Sheet)' (2017)
International Association of Chiefs of Police (IACP), 'Successful Trauma Informed Victim Interviewing' (2020)
International Commission of Jurists (ICJ), 'Sexual Violence Against Women: Eradicating Harmful Gender Stereotypes and Assumptions in Laws and Practice' (2015)
Keygnaert I and Linthout L, 'Triage Tool for Identification, Care and Referral of Victims of Sexual Violence at European Asylum Reception and Accommodation Initiatives' (ICRH, Ghent University 2020)
Keygnaert I and others, 'UN-MENAMAIS: Understanding the Mechanisms, Nature, Magnitude and Impact of Sexual Violence in Belgium, Final Report' (Belgian Science Policy 2021)
Krause U, Zanker F and Fröhlich C, 'Ethics Guidelines of the German Network for Forced Migration Studies' (German Network for Forced Migration Studies 2024)
Lamonaca S and others, 'Good Practice Tool for Police Hearings with Migrant, Applicant for International Protection, Refugee (MAR), Trafficked, and LGBT+ Victims of Sexual Violence' (Payoke & ICRH, Ghent University 2021)
Leboeuf L, 'Lived Vulnerabilities in Asylum and Migration: Confronting the "Vulnerability" Label with Migrants' Experiences' (VULNER 2023)
Lochhead J and Tan PL, Seeking Justice for Victims of Sexual Crime (Women's Centre for Change (WCC) Penang 2009)
Lonsway KA and others, 'False Reports: Moving Beyond the Issue to Successfully Investigate and Prosecute Non-Stranger Sexual Assault' (End Violence Against Women International (EVAWI) 2009)
Mahieu R, Vanheule D and Timmerman C, 'De genderdimensie in het Belgische en Europese asiel- en migratiebeleid' (Instituut Voor de Gelijkheid van Vrouwen En Mannen (IGVM) 2010)
Médicins du Monde, 'The Kap Survey Model (Knowledge, Attitudes, & Practices) (Tool Summary)' (USAID 2011)
Mudge L and Human Rights Watch, '"We Will Beat You to Correct You": Abuses Ahead of Burundi's Constitutional Referendum' (Human Rights Watch 2018)
Muggeridge H and Maman C, 'Unsustainable: The Quality of Initial Decision-Making in Women's Asylum Claims' (Asylum Aid 2011)
National Center for Injury Prevention and Control, 'Costs of Intimate Partner Violence against Women in the United States' (Centers for Disease Control and Prevention 2003)

Obe ED and 28 Too Many, 'Country Profile: FGM in Liberia' (FGM/C Research Initiative 2019)
Pertek S, Phillimore J and Goodson L, 'Forced Migration and Sexual and Gender-Based Violence: Findings from the SEREDA Project in the UK' (University of Birmingham 2021)
Querton C, '"I Feel like as a Woman I'm Not Welcome": A Gender Analysis of UK Asylum Law, Policy and Practice' (Asylum Aid 2012)
——, 'Session II: Implications of Recent Jurisprudence on Gender-Based Asylum Claims: Specific Focus on ECJ Ruling (AH & FN) on Afghan Women' (ECRE Webinar on women & girls' access to international protection, 2024)
Roels L, 'The Use of Rape Myths & Victim-Blaming Mechanisms in Asylum Interviews and Decisions on the Grounds of SGBV' (Women in Refugee Law (WiRL) Workshop: 'Safe Spaces in Gender Sensitive Interviews', 2024)
——, 'The Use of Rape Myths and Resulting Victim-Blaming Mechanisms in Asylum Interviews and Decisions on the Grounds of Sexual and Gender-Based Violence (SGBV)' (WiRL Workshop: Gender sensitivity in asylum interviews, 2025)
Roels L and Casteleyn L, 'Presentatie voor praktijkwerkers: gendergerelateerde procedures om internationale bescherming (seksueel en gendergerelateerd geweld, seksuele oriëntatie en genderidentiteit)' (NANSEN Intervisie 'Gender en Asiel', 21 December 2022)
——, 'Guide pratique pour les avocat·es : procédures de protection internationale liées au genre : violences sexuelles ou basées sur le genre, orientation sexuelle et identité de genre' (Université de Gand 2023)
——, 'Praktijkgids voor advocaten : gendergerelateerde procedures om internationale bescherming (seksueel en gendergerelateerd geweld, seksuele oriëntatie en genderidentiteit)' (Universiteit Gent 2023)
Saroléa S, Raimondo F and Crine Z, 'Exploring Vulnerability's Challenges and Pitfalls in Belgian Ayslum System' (Université catholique de Louvain 2021)
——, 'Through the Eyes of the "Vulnerable": Exploring Vulnerabilities in the Belgian Asylum System' (Zenodo 2022)
Shankley W, Ramanov M and Jaber Y, 'Exploring the Significance of the Kanun in Young Albanian People's Asylum Journeys in the UK' (University of Liverpool, Shpresa Programme & University of Nottingham 2024)
Spiegel D and others, 'Dissociation, Hypnotizability and Trauma' (Annual meeting of the American Psychiatric Association, San Francisco 1989)
Spijkerboer T, 'European Sexual Nationalism: Refugee Law after the Gender & Sexuality Critiques.' (Social Science Research Network 2015)
Stenzel D and Ouedraogo R, 'The Heavy Economic Toll of Gender-Based Violence: Evidence from Sub-Saharan Africa' (International Monetary Fund 2021)
The World Bank, 'COVID-19 and Violence Against Women in Lowand Middle-Income Countries' (2022)
Vluchtelingenwerk Vlaanderen (Flemish Refugee Action), 'Country Report: Belgium' (The Asylum Information Database (AIDA) 2023)
Vogelaar F, 'Analyse landeninformatie inzake het individueel dossier van X' (NANSEN 2021)
UK Home Office, 'Asylum Policy Instruction: Assessing Credibility and Refugee Status' (2015)

DISSERTATIONS

Hawkinberry JC, 'Examining the Perceived Role of Empathy and Self-Efficacy among College Students That Have Completed Bystander Training and Intervened to Prevent a Potential Sexual Assault Situation: A Phenomenological Study' (Liberty University 2022)

Melanson PSK, 'Belief in Male Rape Myths: A Test of Two Competing Theories' (Queen's University 1998)

Verhaeghe L, 'To be or not to be believed: discoursanalyse van het geloofwaardigheidsonderzoek tijdens asielprocedures van lesbische, biseksuele en transgender vrouwen' (Ghent University 2018)

Wessels JM, 'The Concealment Controversy : Sexual Orientation, "Discretion" Reasoning and the Scope of Refugee Protection' (University of Technology Sydney 2017)

POLICY DOCUMENTS & DOCUMENTS OF INTERNATIONAL ORGANISATIONS

Belgian Federal Government, 'Nationaal Actieplan in De Strijd Tegen Gendergerelateerd Geweld 2021–2025: Strategische Pijlers En Belangrijkste Maatregelen' (2021)

CEDAW, 'General Recommendation No. 25, on Article 4, Paragraph 1, of the Convention on the Elimination of All Forms of Discrimination against Women, on Temporary Special Measures' (2004)

——, 'General Recommendation No. 32: The Gender-Related Dimensions of Refugee Status, Asylum, Nationality and Statelessness of Women' (2014)

——, 'CEDAW General Recommendation No. 35: Gender-Based Violence against Women, Updating General Recommendation No. 19' (2017)

Commissioner General for Refugees and Stateless Persons (CGRS), 'The Asylum Procedure at the CGRS' (2019)

——, 'Women, Girls and Asylum in Belgium Brochure' (2020)

——, 'Jaarverslag 2023' (2024)

——, 'Asielstatistieken 2024: Overzicht' (2025)

Council for Alien Law Litigation (CALL), 'Activiteitenverslag RvV 2012' (2012)

——, 'Activiteitenverslag RvV 2020' (2020)

——, 'Activiteitenverslag RvV 2021' (2021)

——, 'Activiteitenverslag RvV 2022' (2022)

——, 'Activiteitenverslag RvV 2023' (2023)

——, 'Activiteitenverslag RvV 2024' (2024)

Council of Europe (CoE), 'Explanatory Report to the Council of Europe Convention on Preventing and Combating Violence against Women and Domestic Violence' (2011)

Council of Europe Parliamentary Assembly, 'Recommendation 1325: Traffic in Women and Forced Prostitution in Council of Europe Member States' (1997)

——, 'Resolution 1765: Gender-Related Claims for Asylum' (2010)

Council of Europe (CoE) and Hooper L, 'Gender-Based Asylum Claims and Non-Refoulement: Articles 60 and 61 of the Istanbul Convention: A Collection of Papers on the Council of Europe Convention on Preventing and Combating Violence against Women and Domestic Violence' (2019)

EUAA (European Union Asylum Agency), 'Evidence and Credibility Assessment in the Context of the Common European Asylum System, Judicial Analysis, Second Edition' (2023)

——, 'Jurisprudence Related to Gender-Based Violence against Women: Analysis of Case Law from 2020–2024' (2025)

EUAA (European Union Asylum Agency) and IGC (Intergovernmental Consultations on migration, asylum and refugees), 'Practical Guide on Interpretation in the Asylum Procedure' (2024)

EASO (European Asylum Support Office), 'EASO Practical Guide: Evidence Assessment' (2015)

——, 'EASO Guidance on Membership of a Particular Social Group' (2020)

——, 'Balancing Mutual Trust and Fundamental Rights in Inadmissibility Cases: An Increasing Challenge for International Protection Judges?' (2021)

European Institute for Gender Equality (EIGE), 'Estimating the Costs of Gender-Based Violence in the European Union: Report' (2014)

European Parliamentary Research Service and Orav A, 'The Gender Dimension of Asylum Claims' (2025)

European Union Agency for Fundamental Rights (FRA), 'Violence against Women: An EU-Wide Survey. Main Results Report' (2014)

Group of Experts on Action against Violence against Women and Domestic Violence (GREVIO), 'GREVIO's (Baseline) Evaluation Report on Legislative and Other Measures Giving Effect to the Provisions of the Council of Europe Convention on Preventing and Combating Violence against Women and Domestic Violence (Istanbul Convention) Albania' (2017)

——, 'GREVIO's (Baseline) Evaluation Report on Legislative and Other Measures Giving Effect to the Provisions of the Council of Europe Convention on Preventing and Combating Violence against Women and Domestic Violence (Istanbul Convention) Belgium' (2020)

Immigration Office (IO), 'Internal Communication IO' (20 February 2025)

Instituut Voor de Gelijkheid van Vrouwen En Mannen (IGVM), 'Tussentijds verslag over de tenuitvoerlegging van het nationaal actieplan ter bestrijding van gendergerelateerd geweld 2021–2025' (2024)

Keygnaert I and Baert S, 'Zorgcentra Na Seksueel Geweld in België: Het ZSG-Model – Nationale Criteria En Standaardprocedures' (Instituut Voor de Gelijkheid van Vrouwen En Mannen (IGVM) 2024)

Minister van Asiel en Migratie Anneleen Van Bossuyt, Beleidsnota Asiel en Migratie 2025 DOC 56 0856/038

Staatssecretaris voor Asiel en Migratie Nicole De Moor, Algemene beleidsnota Asiel en Migratie 2022 DOC 55 2934/006

Staatssecretaris voor Asiel en Migratie Sammy Mahdi, Beleidsnota Asiel en Migratie 2021 DOC 55 2294/022

UN Special Rapporteur on the independence of judges and lawyers, 'Report of the Special Rapporteur on the Independence of Judges and Lawyers (UN Doc. A/66/289)' (2011)
UN Special Rapporteur on the situation of human rights in Burundi, 'Report of the Special Rapporteur on the Situation of Human Rights in Burundi (A/HRC/57/58)' (2024)
UN Special Rapporteur on torture and other cruel, inhuman or degrading treatment or punishment, 'Promotion and Protection of All Human Rights, Civil, Political, Economic, Social and Cultural Rights, Including the Right to Development A/HRC/7/3' (2008)
UN Special Rapporteur on violence against women, its causes and consequences, 'Report A/HRC/35/30 of the Special Rapporteur on Violence against Women, Its Causes and Consequences with a Focus on Shelters and Protection Orders' (2017)
UN Voluntary Fund for Victims of Torture, 'Report on Expert Panel & Workshop – Surviving Torture and Fighting Stigma: The Road to Recovery for Victims of Sexual and Gender-Based Torture' (2019)
UN Women, 'National Population Survey: Violence Against Women and Girls in Albania' (2019)
UNAIDS, 'UNAIDS Guidance Note on HIV and Sex Work' (2012)
UNHCR, 'Note on Burden and Standard of Proof in Refugee Claims' (1998)
——, 'Guidelines on International Protection No. 1: Gender-Related Persecution within the Context of Article 1A(2) of the 1951 Convention and/or Its 1967 Protocol Relating to the Status of Refugees (HCR/GIP/02/01)' (2002)
——, 'Guidelines on International Protection No. 2: "Membership of a Particular Social Group" within the Context of Article 1A(2) of the 1951 Convention and/or Its 1967 Protocol Relating to the Status of Refugees (HCR/GIP/02/02)' (2002)
——, 'Guidelines on International Protection No. 4: "Internal Flight or Relocation Alternative" within the Context of Article 1A(2) of the 1951 Convention and/or 1967 Protocol Relating to the Status of Refugees (HCR/GIP/03/04)' (2003)
——, 'Working with Men and Boy Survivors of Sexual and Gender-Based Violence in Forced Displacement' (2012)
——, 'Avis Du HCR Relatif à l'évaluation Des Demandes d'asile de Personnes Ayant Des Besoins Particuliers et En Particulier de Personnes Qui Ont Subi Des Tortures, Des Viols Ou d'autres Formes Graves de Violence Psychologique, Physique Ou Sexuelle' (2012)
——, 'Note Du Haut Commissariat Des Nations Unies Pour Les Réfugiés Relative à l'évaluation Des Demandes d'asile Introduites Par Des Femmes' (2012)
——, 'Beyond Proof. Credibility Assessment in EU Asylum Systems (Full Report)' (2013)
——, 'Guidelines on International Protection No. 12: Claims for Refugee Status Related to Situations of Armed Conflict and Violence under Article 1A(2) of the 1951 Convention and/or 1967 Protocol Relating to the Status of Refugees and the Regional Refugee Definitions (HCR/GIP/16/12)' (2016)
——, Handbook on Procedures and Criteria for Determining Refugee Status under the 1951 Convention and the 1967 Protocol Relating to the Status of Refugees (2019)
UNHCR and Inter-Agency Standing Committee (IASC), 'Guidelines for Gender-Based Violence Interventions in Humanitarian Settings: Focusing on Prevention of and Response to Sexual Violence in Emergencies' (2005)

UNHCR Executive Committee, 'General Conclusion on Refugee Women and International Protection No. 39 (XXXVI)' (1985)
——, 'General Conclusion on International Protection No. 77 (XLVI)' (1995)
United Nations Office on Drugs and Crime (UNODC), 'Resource Book for Trainers on Effective Prosecution Responses to Violence against Women and Girls' (2017)
United Nations Office on Drugs and Crime (UNODC) and Skinnider E, 'Handbook for the Judiciary on Effective Criminal Justice Responses to Gender-Based Violence Against Women and Girls' (2019)
Women's Refugee Commission and UNICEF Europe & Central Asia, 'Supporting Young Male Refugees and Migrants Who Are Survivors or at Risk of Sexual Violence: A Field Guide for Frontline Workers in Europe' (2021)
World Health Organization (WHO), London School of Hygiene & Tropical Medicine, and South African Medical Research Council, 'Global and Regional Estimates of Violence against Women: Prevalence and Health Effects of Intimate Partner Violence and Non-Partner Sexual Violence' (2013)
World Health Organization (WHO), 'World Report on Violence and Health' (2002)
——, 'Guidelines for Medico-Legal Care of Victims of Sexual Violence' (2003)
——, 'Ethical and Safety Recommendations for Researching, Documenting and Monitoring Sexual Violence in Emergencies' (2007)
——, 'Caring for Women Subjected to Violence: A WHO Training Curriculum for Health Care Providers' (2021)
World Health Organization (WHO) and United Nations Inter-Agency Working Group on Violence Against Women Estimation and Data (VAW-IAWGED), 'Violence Against Women Prevalence Estimates, 2018: Global, Regional and National Prevalence Estimates for Intimate Partner Violence against Women and Global and Regional Prevalence Estimates for Non-Partner Sexual Violence against Women' (2021)

WEB PAGES & BLOG POSTS

Agentschap Integratie en Inburgering (AGII), 'Opstart verzoek om internationale bescherming' (Vreemdelingenrecht.be, 29 January 2025), www.vreemdelingenrecht.be/verblijfsrecht/bescherming/internationale-bescherming-asiel/standaardprocedure-internationale-bescherming-0/standaardprocedure-asiel-fase-bij-dvz/opstart-verzoek-om-internationale-bescherming
Amnesty International, 'DR Congo Must Investigate Assassination Attempt on Activist Dr Denis Mukwege' (26 October 2012), www.amnesty.org/en/latest/news/2012/10/dr-congo/
Bowell T, 'Feminist Standpoint Theory' (Internet Encyclopedia of Philosophy: A Peer-Reviewed Academic Resource, 2022), https://iep.utm.edu/fem-stan/
Brems E, 'Strong Women Don't Need Asylum (the European Court on FGM)' (Strasbourg Observers, 19 August 2010), https://strasbourgobservers.com/2010/08/19/%e2%80%98strong-women-don%e2%80%99t-need-asylum%e2%80%99-the-european-court-on-fgm/
Centre for the Study of Emotion and Law, 'Centre for the Study of Emotion and Law' https://csel.psychologyresearch.co.uk/

Commissioner General for Refugees and Stateless Persons (CGRS), 'Gender' (22 January 2015), www.cgvs.be/nl/gender
——, 'Omzetting Asielprocedurerichtlijn in Belgisch recht' (21 March 2018), www.cgvs.be/nl/actueel/omzetting-asielprocedurerichtlijn-belgisch-recht
——, 'Special Procedural Needs' (1 October 2019), www.cgrs.be/en/asylum/special-procedural-needs
——, 'About the CGRS', www.cgrs.be/en/about-the-cgrs
——, 'CEDOCA', www.cgvs.be/nl/landeninfo/over-cedoca
Council for Alien Law Litigation (CALL), 'FAQ' (29 October 2014), www.rvv-cce.be/nl/faq
——, 'Organogram RvV/CCE/CALL' (29 October 2014), www.rvv-cce.be/nl/rvv/organogram
——, 'Over de Raad' (29 October 2014), www.rvv-cce.be/nl/rvv/over-de-raad
——, 'Abortus in Senegal' (25 November 2021) https://www.rw-cce.be/nl/actua/abortus-senegal
——, 'Arresten', www.rvv-cce.be/nl/arr
——, 'Maandelijkse selectie van arresten van de Raad', www.rvv-cce.be/nl/select-arr
——, 'Nieuws', www.rw-cce.be/nl/actua
Council of Europe Treaty Office, 'Chart of Signatures and Ratifications of Treaty 210 (Council of Europe Convention on Preventing and Combating Violence against Women and Domestic Violence, CETS No. 210)' (Treaty Office, 21 February 2025), www.coe.int/en/web/conventions/full-list
de Vries LA and Welander M, 'Refugees, Displacement, and the European "Politics of Exhaustion"' (Mediterranean Journeys in Hope, 30 September 2016), www.opendemocracy.net/en/mediterranean-journeys-in-hope/refugees-displacement-and-europ/
Department of Justice of the Government of Canada, 'The Impact of Trauma on Adult Sexual Assault Victims: PART II – The Neurobiological Impact of Trauma on the Brain' (10 January 2017), www.justice.gc.ca/eng/rp-pr/jr/trauma/p3.html
European Commission and EU Directorate-General for Migration and Home Affairs, 'Common Implementation Plan to Turn the Pact on Migration and Asylum into a Reality' (12 June 2024), https://home-affairs.ec.europa.eu/news/common-implementation-plan-turn-pact-migration-and-asylum-reality-2024-06-12_en
European Institute for Gender Equality, 'Crimes Committed in the Name of So-Called Honour' (10 December 2024), https://eige.europa.eu/publications-resources/thesaurus/terms/1194?language_content_entity=en
——, 'Forced Marriage' (10 December 2024), https://eige.europa.eu/publications-resources/thesaurus/terms/1171?language_content_entity=en
——, 'Heteronormativity' (10 December 2024), https://eige.europa.eu/publications-resources/thesaurus/terms/1384?language_content_entity=en
Girls Not Brides, 'Albania' (1 January 2014), www.girlsnotbrides.org/learning-resources/child-marriage-atlas/regions-and-countries/albania/
Gorman J, 'Beyond Extractivism in Research with Communities and Movements' (The Commons: Social Change Library, 23 January 2024), https://commonslibrary.org/beyond-extractivism-in-research-with-communities-and-movements/
Harding S, 'The Feminist Standpoint Theory Reader : Intellectual and Political Controversies', http://catdir.loc.gov/catdir/toc/ecip043/2003009900.html

Human Rights Watch, 'World Report 2024: Türkiye' (11 January 2024), www.hrw.org/world-report/2024/country-chapters/turkey

Institute for War and Peace Reporting (IWPR) and European Country of Origin Information Network, 'Draft Law on Foreign Agents Sparks Outcry in Georgia and Abroad' (3 March 2023), www.ecoi.net/en/document/2088225.html

Instituut Voor de Gelijkheid van Vrouwen En Mannen (IGVM), 'Zorgcentra Na Seksueel Geweld (ZSG)', https://igvm-iefh.belgium.be/nl/themas/geweld/seksueel-geweld/zsg

International Centre for Reproductive Health Belgium, 'ICRH', www.icrhb.org/en

Jaji R, 'Ethics and Intellectual Harm in Research with Refugees' (Kujenga Amani, 21 February 2024), https://kujenga-amani.ssrc.org/2024/02/21/ethics-and-intellectual-harm-in-research-with-refugees/

Jones E, 'Theory as Practice in International Law' (Völkerrechtsblog, 25 May 2023), https://voelkerrechtsblog.org/theory-as-practice-in-international-law/

Kuschminder K, 'We Interviewed 150 Women Migrants – Revealing How Their Journeys Involve Peril at Every Turn (Women and Migration: Stories of Resilience Project)' (The Conversation, 26 November 2021), http://theconversation.com/we-interviewed-150-women-migrants-revealing-how-their-journeys-involve-peril-at-every-turn-171238

Lejeune J and NANSEN, 'Voor een interdisciplinaire benadering van asiel' (24 April 2024), https://nansen-refugee.be/nl/2024/04/24/voor-een-interdisciplinaire-benadering-van-asiel/

Linthout L and others, 'INHeRE E-Learning Course on Sexual Violence & Migration (International Centre for Reproductive Health at Ghent University)' (Inclusive Holistic Care for Migrant victims of sexual violence (INHeRE), 2021), www.icrhb.org/storage/attachments/attachment/72.pdf?t=1633358005

——, 'Hoe het migratiebeleid van Nicole de Moor discrimineert: "Eerst vrouwen en kinderen, dan de honden. Pas daarna de mannen"' (MO* Magazine, 2023), www.mo.be/opinie/eerst-vrouwen-en-kinderen-dan-de-honden-pas-daarna-de-mannen

Magugliani N, 'Trafficked Adult Males and Their Recognition as Members of a Particular Social Group in the United Kingdom's Upper Tribunal' (Refugee Law Initiative Blog, 9 November 2020), https://rli.blogs.sas.ac.uk/2020/11/09/trafficked-adult-males-and-their-recognition-as-members-of-a-particular-social-group-in-the-united-kingdoms-upper-tribunal/

Manganini I, 'Refugee Law between Resistance and Compliance: A Reparative Reading of a Classic Feminist Struggle' (Refugee Law Initiative Blog, 15 October 2024), https://rli.blogs.sas.ac.uk/2024/10/15/refugee-law-between-resistance-and-compliance-a-reparative-reading-of-a-classic-feminist-struggle/

Masiya Mponela L, 'Women for Refugee Women : Loraine's Story' (Women for Refugee Women, 22 February 2024), www.refugeewomen.co.uk/loraines-story/

Migration Law Research Group Universiteit Gent, 'Migration Law Research Group', www.ugent.be/re/epir/en/researchgroups/public-law/research/migration-law

NANSEN, 'NANSEN – Assistance and Legal Aid for Refugees – Belgium', https://nansen-refugee.be/en/

Ogg K, 'Feminism as Method: How Do We Do Gender in International Refugee Law?' (Refugee Law Initiative Blog, 25 January 2023), https://rli.blogs.sas.ac.uk/2023/01/25/feminism-as-method-how-do-we-do-gender-in-international-refugee-law/

Organisation Intersex International Europe, 'What Is Intersex Genital Mutilation (IGM)?' (4 February 2021), www.oiieurope.org/igm/

Oxford English Dictionary, 'Cisgender', www.oed.com/dictionary/cisgender_adj

Phillimore J and Pertek S, 'The Interests and Vulnerabilities of Female Forced Migrants Need to Be Recognised and Integrated within the National Strategy for Tackling Violence against Women and Girls' (British Politics and Policy at LSE, 30 November 2021), https://blogs.lse.ac.uk/politicsandpolicy/forced-migrants-sgbv/

Pillay N, 'Equality and Justice in the Courtroom' (Display News OHCHR (Office of the UN High Commissioner for Human Rights), 5 March 2014), www.ohchr.org/en/NewsEvents/Pages/DisplayNews.aspx?NewsID=14721&LangID=E

Radboud universitair medisch centrum, 'Scholing Huiselijk en seksueel geweld: Over de cursus' (2022), www.radboudumc.nl/onderwijs/scholingen/huiselijk-en-seksueel-geweld/over-de-cursus

Roels L, 'Hoe lid worden van de majorettes ertoe kan leiden dat je verzoek om internationale bescherming wordt geweigerd' (Tijd voor Mensenrechten, 8 March 2023), https://tijd.mensenrechten.be/2023/03/08/hoe-lid-worden-van-de-majorettes-ertoe-kan-leiden-dat-je-verzoek-om-internationale-bescherming-wordt-geweigerd/

——, 'How Protecting Your Daughter Can Lead You to Being Denied International Protection in Belgium: On Rape Mythology, Delayed Disclosure, and Asylum' (Refugee Law Initiative Blog, 11 May 2023), https://rli.blogs.sas.ac.uk/2023/05/11/how-protecting-your-daughter-can-lead-you-to-being-denied-international-protection-in-belgium/

——, 'How Joining a Majorette Group Can Lead You to Being Denied International Protection: On Rape Mythology in Asylum/Non-Refoulement Procedures' (Völkerrechtsblog, 7 March 2023), https://voelkerrechtsblog.org/how-joining-a-majorette-group-can-lead-you-to-being-denied-international-protection/

Thomas More Hogeschool, 'Postgraduaat Forensische Psychodiagnostiek en Counseling (module 8: slachtofferschap in forensische context)' (2022), https://thomasmore.be/nl/opleidingen/postgraduaat/forensische-psychodiagnostiek-en-counseling/antwerpen/basistraject

UN Assistant Secretary-General and Deputy Executive Director of UN Women Lakshmi Puri, 'The Economic Costs of Violence against Women' (UN Women – Headquarters, 21 September 2016), www.unwomen.org/en/news/stories/2016/9/speech-by-lakshmi-puri-on-economic-costs-of-violence-against-women

UN Population Fund (UNFPA), 'Female Genital Mutilation Dashboard (FGM) – Guinea', www.unfpa.org/data/fgm/GN

UN Women, 'Facts and Figures: Ending Violence against Women', www.unwomen.org/en/what-we-do/ending-violence-against-women/facts-and-figures

UNICEF, 'What Is Female Genital Mutilation?', www.unicef.org/protection/female-genital-mutilation

United Nations Academic Impact, 'The Preventable Pandemic: Sexual and Gender-Based Violence', www.un.org/en/academic-impact/preventable-pandemic-sexual-and-gender-based-violence

United Nations Economic and Social Commission for Western Asia, 'Corrective Rape', www.unescwa.org/sd-glossary/corrective-rape

United Nations Economic and Social Commission for Western Asia, UNFPA, and UN Women, 'Estimating the Economic Cost of Domestic Violence' (21 June 2019), https://archive.unescwa.org/sub-site/costing-vaw

University of Strathclyde, 'Developing a Trauma-Informed Response' (FutureLearn, 2022), www.futurelearn.com/courses/understanding-violence-against-women/6/steps/1415956

——, 'Understanding Violence Against Women: Myths and Realities' (FutureLearn, 2022), www.futurelearn.com/courses/understanding-violence-against-women/6

Van Bossuyt A, 'Anneleen Van Bossuyt | Belgium.Be', www.belgium.be/nl/anneleen_van_bossuyt

Van Dale, 'Van Dale meaning of "daadwerkelijk"', www.vandale.nl/gratis-woordenboek/nederlands/betekenis/daadwerkelijk

Van Veldhuizen T, 'College 3 Rechtspsychologie: Wie is het? Het toetsen van levensverhalen in asielzaken (Directed by Tanja van Veldhuizen, 2021)', www.youtube.com/watch?v=q_-t7M9rGlM

Warin C and Ilareva V, 'Vulnerability in the New Pact: An Empty Promise to Protect, or an Operational Concept? – EU Immigration and Asylum Law and Policy' (11 October 2024), https://eumigrationlawblog.eu/vulnerability-in-the-new-pact-an-empty-promise-to-protect-or-an-operational-concept/

Woman'Dō, 'Woman'Dō', https://womando.be/nl/

Women in Refugee Law (WiRL) Conference – Panel 1 on Protection & Credibility (Directed by Women in Refugee Law (WiRL) UWE Bristol, 2021), www.youtube.com/watch?v=INFfNw5e34I

World Health Organization (WHO), 'Female Genital Mutilation', www.who.int/news-room/fact-sheets/detail/female-genital-mutilation

——, 'Violence against Women: A "Global Health Problem of Epidemic Proportions"' (20 June 2013), www.who.int/news/item/20-06-2013-violence-against-women-a-global-health-problem-of-epidemic-proportions-

World Health Organization (WHO) and Human Reproduction Programme (HRP), 'Global Database on the Prevalence of Violence Against Women', https://vaw-data.srhr.org/map

INTERNATIONAL LAW & PREPARATORY WORKS

European Union

Proposal for a Directive of the European Parliament and of the Council on minimum standards for the qualification and status of third country nationals or stateless persons as beneficiaries of international protection and the content of the protection granted 2009 [{SEC(2009) 1373} {SEC(2009) 1374}]

Charter of Fundamental Rights of the European Union 2000 (Official Journal of the European Communities C 364/3)

Directive on common procedures for granting and withdrawing international protection (EU Procedures Directive) 2013 (Official Journal of the European Union L 180/60)

Directive on standards for the qualification of third-country nationals or stateless persons as beneficiaries of international protection, for a uniform status for refugees or for persons eligible for subsidiary protection, and for the content of the protection granted (EU Qualification Directive) 2011 (Official Journal of the European Union L 337/9)

Regulation establishing a common procedure for international protection in the Union and repealing Directive 2013/32/EU (EU Procedures Regulation) 2024 (Official Journal of the European Union L 2024/1348)

Regulation establishing the criteria and mechanisms for determining the Member State responsible for examining an application for international protection lodged in one of the Member States by a third-country national or a stateless person (Dublin Regulation) 2013 (Official Journal of the European Union L 180/31)

Regulation on standards for the qualification of third-country nationals or stateless persons as beneficiaries of international protection, for a uniform status for refugees or for persons eligible for subsidiary protection and for the content of the protection granted, amending Council Directive 2003/109/EC and repealing Directive 2011/95/EU of the European Parliament and of the Council (EU Qualification Regulation) 2024 (Official Journal of the European Union L 2024/1347)

Regulation on the protection of natural persons with regard to the processing of personal data and on the free movement of such data, and repealing Directive 95/46/EC (GDPR) 2016 (Official Journal of the European Union L 119/1)

Treaty on the Functioning of the European Union 2012 (Official Journal of the European Union C 326/47)

Council of Europe

Convention for the Protection of Human Rights and Fundamental Freedoms (ECHR) 1950 (CETS, no 005)

Council of Europe Convention on Preventing and Combating Violence against Women and Domestic Violence (Istanbul Convention) 2011 (CETS, no 210)

United Nations

Convention and Protocol Relating to the Status of Refugees (UN Refugee Convention) 1951 (UNTS, vol 189, p 137)

INTERNATIONAL CASE LAW

ECtHR

AA and Others v Sweden [2012] ECtHR 14499/09

AA v France [2015] ECtHR 18039/11

AF v France [2015] ECtHR 80086/13

Izevbekhai and Others v Ireland [2011] ECtHR 43408/08

MH v Finland [2020] ECtHR 42255/18

MSS v Belgium and Greece [2011] ECtHR 30696/09

Opuz v Turkey [2009] ECtHR 33401/02
RC v Sweden [2010] ECtHR 41827/07
Soering v The United Kingdom [1989] ECtHR 14038/88

CJEU

AH & FN v Bundesamt für Fremdenwesen und Asyl [2024] Court of Justice of the European Union C-608/22 & C-609/22
BF v Kypriaki Dimokratia [2025] Court of Justice of the European Union C-283/24
CV v Ministerstvo vnitra České republiky, Odbor azylové a migrační politiky [2024] Court of Justice of the European Union C-406/22
International Protection Appeals Tribunal and Others (Attentat au Pakistan) [2023] Court of Justice of the European Union C-756/21
KL v Staatssecretaris van Justitie en Veiligheid [2024] Court of Justice of the European Union C-646/21
Opinion of Advocate General in KL v Staatssecretaris van Justitie en Veiligheid [2023] Court of Justice of the European Union C-646/21
Secretary of State for the Home Department v OA [2021] Court of Justice of the European Union C-255/19
WS v Intervyuirasht organ na Darzhavna agentsia za bezhantsite pri Ministerskia savet [2024] Court of Justice of the European Union C-621/21
X, Y and Z v The Netherlands [2013] Court of Justice of the European Union C-199/12, C 200/12, C 201/12

Other

IAM (on behalf of KYM) v Denmark [2018] UN Committee on the Rights of the Child 3/2016

BELGIAN NATIONAL LAW & PREPARATORY WORKS

Belgische Kamer van Volksvertegenwoordigers, Wetsvoorstel houdende diverse bepalingen inzake justitie, onder meer in het kader van de strijd tegen de verspreiding van het coronavirus: Amendementen 2020 [DOC 55 1295/007]
——, Wetsvoorstel houdende diverse bepalingen inzake justitie, onder meer in het kader van de strijd tegen de verspreiding van het coronavirus: Verslag van de tweede lezing 2020 [DOC 55 1295/008]
——, Wetsontwerp inzake de preventie en de bestrijding van feminicides, gendergerelateerde dodingen en het geweld dat daar aan voorafgaat: Voorstel van resolutie betreffende de officiële telling van het aantal vrouwenmoorden en de oprichting van een observatorium voor vrouwenmoorden in België: Verslag 2023 [DOC 55 3400/004]
Gecoördineerde wetten op de Raad van State 1973 (Belgisch Staatsblad of 21 March 1973, p 3461)
Gerechtelijk Wetboek 1967 (Belgisch Staatsblad of 31 October 1967, p 11360)

Koninklijk besluit betreffende de toegang tot het grondgebied, het verblijf, de vestiging en de verwijdering van vreemdelingen (Belgian Aliens Royal Decree) 1981 (Belgisch staatsblad of 27 October 1981, p 13740)
Koninklijk besluit houdende vaststelling van bepaalde elementen van de procedure die dienen gevolgd te worden door de dienst van de Dienst Vreemdelingenzaken die belast is met het onderzoek van de asielaanvragen op basis van de wet van 15 december 1980 betreffende de toegang tot het grondgebied, het verblijf, de vestiging en de verwijdering van vreemdelingen (Belgian Royal Decree on the IO) 2003 (Belgisch staatsblad of 27 January 2004, p 4645)
Koninklijk besluit tot regeling van de werking van en de rechtspleging voor het Commissariaat-generaal voor de Vluchtelingen en de Staatlozen (Belgian Royal Decree on the CGRS) 2003 (Belgisch Staatsblad of 27 January 2004, p 4638)
Koninklijk besluit tot uitvoering van het artikel 57/6/1, §3, vierde lid, van de wet van 15 december 1980 betreffende de toegang tot het grondgebied, het verblijf, de vestiging en de verwijdering van vreemdelingen, houdende de vastlegging van de lijst van veilige landen van herkomst 2024 (Belgisch Staatsblad of 27 May 2024, p 65231)
Strafwetboek 1867 (Belgisch Staatsblad of 9 June 1867, p 3133)
Wet betreffende de toegang tot het grondgebied, het verblijf, de vestiging en de verwijdering van vreemdelingen (Belgian Aliens Act) 1980 (Belgisch Staatsblad of 31 December 1980, p 14584)
Wet betreffende de Zorgcentra na Seksueel Geweld 2024 (Belgisch Staatsblad of 31 May 2024, p 68926)
Wet houdende diverse dringende bepalingen inzake justitie 2020 (Belgisch Staatsblad of 7 August 2020, p. 58048)
Wet voor de preventie en de bestrijding van feminicides en gendergerelateerde dodingen 2023 (Belgisch Staatsblad of 31 August 2023, p. 70960)

BELGIAN NATIONAL CASE LAW[2533]

Not included in case law analysis

[2023] RvV 294 383
[2024] RvV 309 148

Included in case law analysis

[2020] RvV 234 950
[2020] CCE 243 679
[2021] CCE 255 907
[2022] CCE 266 712
[2022] RvV 269 856
[2023] CCE 283 107
[2023] CCE 285 279
[2023] RvV 285 363
[2023] CCE 293 489
[2023] RvV 304 208
[2024] RvV 301 914
[2024] CCE 302 063
[2024] RvV 302 134
[2024] CCE 302 595
[2024] RvV 302 605

2533 RvV for 'Raad voor Vreemdelingenbetwistingen' (CALL judgments in Dutch), CCE for 'Conseil du Contentieux des Etrangers' (CALL judgments in French).

[2022] RvV 270 155
[2022] RvV 270 994
[2022] CCE 274 056
[2022] RvV 275 866
[2022] CCE 275 955
[2022] RvV 276 951
[2022] RvV 280 827
[2024] RvV 303 213
[2024] RvV 303 239
[2024] RvV 303 313
[2024] CCE 303 320
[2024] CCE 303 553
[2024] CCE 303 543
[2024] RvV 303 889
[2024] RvV 303 891
[2024] RvV 304 208
[2024] RvV 304 367
[2024] CCE 304 393
[2024] RvV 304 388
[2024] CCE 304 410
[2024] CCE 304 646
[2024] CCE 304 652
[2024] RvV 305 003
[2024] RvV 305 147
[2024] CCE 305 334
[2024] RvV 305 429
[2024] RvV 305 445
[2024] RvV 305 447
[2024] RvV 307 173
[2024] RvV 305 790
[2024] CCE 305 436
[2023] RvV 303 313
[2024] CCE 299 471
[2024] CCE 300 255
[2024] CCE 300 506
[2024] RvV 301 074
[2024] CCE 301 330
[2024] CCE 301 311
[2024] RvV 305 805
[2024] CCE 305 819
[2024] CCE 305 949
[2024] RvV 305 882
[2024] CCE 305 941
[2024] CCE 305 927
[2024] RvV 305 966
[2024] RvV 306 071
[2024] CCE 306 239
[2024] RvV 306 251
[2024] RvV 306 520
[2024] RvV 306 550
[2024] RvV 306 755
[2024] CCE 306 929
[2024] RvV 307 106
[2024] RvV 307 108
[2024] RvV 307 109
[2024] RvV 307 172
[2024] RvV 307 178
[2024] CCE 307 398
[2024] RvV 307 462
[2024] CCE 307 471
[2024] CCE 307 565
[2024] CCE 307 576
[2024] RvV 302 900
[2024] RvV 302 889
[2024] CCE 302 979
[2024] CCE 302 961
[2024] CCE 302 978
[2024] CCE 303 273
[2024] CCE 303 242
[2024] RvV 307 559
[2024] RvV 307 592

OTHER NATIONAL LAW

Criminal Code of the Republic of Albania (Kodi Penal i Republikës së Shqipërisë) 1995 (Fletorja zyrtare, No 2)

OTHER NATIONAL CASE LAW

[1996] Refugee Status Appeals Authority New Zealand 2039/93

OTHER

Commissioner General for Refugees and Stateless Persons (CGRS), 'Internal Communication on KAP Participants CGRS' (January 2023)
——, 'Internal Communication CGRS (Part I)' (7 January 2025)
——, 'Internal Communication CGRS (Part II)' (24 January 2025)
——, 'Internal Communication CGRS (Part III)' (28 May 2025)
——, 'Internal Communication CGRS (Part IV)' (2 June 2025)
——, 'Internal Communication CGRS (Part V)' (25 August 2025)
Council for Alien Law Litigation (CALL), 'Internal Communication CALL' (21 August 2025)
De Schrijver L, International Centre for Reproductive Health (ICRH), and Universiteit Gent, 'Training Voor Interviews Rond Seksueel Geweld' (2022)
Ghidoni E, 'The Nexus between Gender Stereotypes and Evidence: Insights from the CEDAW Committee' (Unpublished 2023)
Implementation & Community Advisory Board (ICAB), "Internal Communication ICAB" (19 August 2025)
Interview with Emilie Berghmans and Woman'Dō, 'Expert interview during fieldwork at NANSEN NGO (Brussels, Belgium)' (19 October 2022)
Interview with Jane Herlihy, 'Expert Interview during Fieldwork at NANSEN NGO (Brussels, Belgium)' (17 October 2022)

RESEARCH OUTPUT & VALORISATION

JOURNAL ARTICLES

Roels L, 'Rape Myths in the European Court of Human Rights' Non-Refoulement Case Law on Sexual and Gender-Based Violence' (2024) 36 **International Journal of Refugee Law** 77

Roels L, 'Het ontkrachten van verkrachtingsmythes in asielprocedures over seksueel en gendergerelateerd geweld' (2026) 1 Tijdschrift voor Vreemdelingenrecht (forthcoming 2026)

Roels L, 'Démystifier les mythes de viol dans les procédures d'asile sur la violence sexuelle et sexiste' (2026) Revue du Droit des Etrangers (forthcoming 2026)

BOOKS AND BOOK CHAPTERS

Roels L, 'Het Cassandracomplex in Gendergerelateerde Asielprocedures: Luisteren als feministische methode in onderzoek over verkrachtingsmythologie' in Pieter Cannoot, Elise Goossens and Marie Spinoy (eds), **Feministische en queer onderzoeksmethoden in het recht** (Intersentia 2025)

Roels L, Challenging Myths on Sexual & Gender-Based Violence in Asylum Procedures (Larcier Intersentia 2026)

BLOG POSTS

Roels L, 'How Joining a Majorette Group Can Lead You to Being Denied International Protection: On Rape Mythology in Asylum/Non-Refoulement Procedures' (**Völkerrechtsblog**, 7 March 2023), https://voelkerrechtsblog.org/how-joining-a-majorette-group-can-lead-you-to-being-denied-international-protection/

——, 'Hoe lid worden van de majorettes ertoe kan leiden dat je verzoek om internationale bescherming wordt geweigerd' (**Tijd voor Mensenrechten**, 8 March 2023), https://tijd.mensenrechten.be/2023/03/08/hoe-lid-worden-van-de-majorettes-ertoe-kan-leiden-dat-je-verzoek-om-internationale-bescherming-wordt-geweigerd/

——, 'How Protecting Your Daughter Can Lead You to Being Denied International Protection in Belgium: On Rape Mythology, Delayed Disclosure, and Asylum' (Refugee Law Initiative (**RLI**) **Blog**, 11 May 2023), https://rli.blogs.sas.ac.uk/2023/05/11/how-protecting-your-daughter-can-lead-you-to-being-denied-international-protection-in-belgium/

ACADEMIC PRESENTATIONS

Roels L, 'Rape mythology In credibility assessments of asylum applications based on sexual or gender-based violence' (Centre for the Social Study of Migration and Refugees (**CESSMIR**) Present your own work PhD meeting, Online, 25 November 2021)

——, 'Knowledge, Attitudes & Practices (KAP) Surveys in Legal Research' (Migration Law Research Group (**MigrLaw**) monthly meeting presentation, Ghent, 21 April 2022)

——, 'Rape mythology applied to credibility assessments of applications based on sexual or gender-based violence (SGBV) in the European asylum procedure' (Workshop on Research Methods in Fundamental Rights **Hertie School**, Berlin, 9 June 2022)

——, 'Rape myths in the European Court of Human Rights' asylum case law: the harsh reality' (Centre for the Social Study of Migration and Refugees (**CESSMIR**) **PhD Pre-Conference** 'Contemporary forms of racism and discrimination', Ghent, 19 September 2022)

——, 'Draft article presentation: Rape myths in the European Court of Human Rights' non-refoulement case law on sexual and gender-based violence: the reality' (Migration Law Research Group (**MigrLaw**) monthly meeting presentation, Ghent, 6 October 2022)

——, 'Draft article presentation: Rape myths in the European Court of Human Rights' non-refoulement case law on sexual and gender-based violence: the reality' (Human Rights Centre (**HRC**) meeting, Ghent, 13 December 2022)

——, L, 'Rape myths in asylum procedures of persons fleeing sexual and gender-based violence' (International Centre for Reproductive Health (**ICRH**) Scientific Lunch Meeting, Ghent, 9 May 2023)

Roels L, Ghidoni E and Dembour M-B, 'Thinking about How to Counteract the Polluting Effect of Stereotypes on Evidence' (Talking Evidence Series: Episode 5 (**DISSECT**), Online, 26 June 2023)

Roels L, 'Rape Myths in Asylum Procedures of Persons fleeing Sexual and Gender-Based Violence' (Migration Law Research Group (**MigrLaw**) research day presentation, Ghent, 28 June 2023)

——, 'Rape Mythology in Research on SGBV-related Refugee Status Determination' (Refugee Law Initiative (**RLI**) **Feminist Theory Working Group** Presentation, 20 September 2023)

——, 'Rape myths in the European Court of Human Rights' Non-Refoulement Case Law on Sexual and Gender-Based Violence' (Human Rights Research Network (**HRRN**) **Conference**, Ghent, 7 December 2023)

——, 'Rape Myth Acceptance in Refugee Status Determination for Persons Fleeing Sexual and Gender-Based Violence: A Case Study on Belgium' (Refugee Law Initiative (**RLI**) **Conference**, London, 3 June 2024)

——, 'Luisteren als feministische methode in onderzoek over verkrachtingsmythologie in gendergerelateerde asielprocedures' (Book Project Feministische en queer onderzoeksmethoden in het recht (**FemQ**) Introductory workshop, Antwerp, 16 September 2024)

——, 'Listening as a feminist method in research on rape mythology in asylum procedures related to sexual and gender-based violence (SGBV)' (Migration Law Research Group (**MigrLaw**) monthly meeting presentation, Ghent, 23 January 2025)
——, 'The Cassandra Complex in Gender-Based Asylum Procedures: Listening as a Feminist Method in Research on Rape Mythology' (Refugee Law Initiative (**RLI**) **Conference** (15th Anniversary), London, 2 June 2025)

PRACTICE-ORIENTED LECTURES, TRAININGS & WORKSHOPS

Roels L and Casteleyn L, 'Presentatie voor praktijkwerkers: gendergerelateerde procedures om internationale bescherming (seksueel en gendergerelateerd geweld, seksuele oriëntatie en genderidentiteit)' (**NANSEN** Intervisie 'Gender en Asiel', Online, 21 December 2022)
Roels L, 'The use of rape myths & victim-blaming mechanisms in asylum interviews and decisions on the grounds of SGBV' (Women in Refugee Law (**WiRL**) Workshop for practitioners: Safe Spaces in Gender-Sensitive Interviews Online, 8 April 2024)
——, 'Gender & International Refugee Law: Gender sensitivity in refugee status determination for persons fleeing SGBV' (Refugee and Protection Training Workshop for the **New Zealand Immigration and Protection Tribunal**, Online, 20 September 2024)
——, 'Gender & asiel: Gendersensitiviteit in asiel- en nonrefoulementprocedures over seksueel en gendergerelateerd geweld (SGG)' (**Leerstoel Migratie- en migrantenrecht**, Antwerp, 5 December 2024)
——, 'The Use of Rape Myths and Resulting Victim-Blaming Mechanisms in Asylum Interviews and Decisions on the Grounds of Sexual and Gender-Based Violence (SGBV)' (Women in Refugee Law (**WiRL**) Workshop for practitioners: Gender sensitivity in asylum interviews, Online, 30 April 2025)
——, 'From survival to recognition: het Ontkrachten van Mythes over Seksueel en Gendergerelateerd Geweld (SGG) in Procedures om Internationale Bescherming' (Mid-info session celebrating 20 years of Gender Coordination at the **CGRS**, Brussels, 18 September 2025)

PRACTICE-ORIENTED REPORTS

Roels L and Casteleyn L, 'Praktijkgids voor advocaten : gendergerelateerde procedures om internationale bescherming (seksueel en gendergerelateerd geweld, seksuele oriëntatie en genderidentiteit)' (Universiteit Gent 2023)
——, 'Guide pratique pour les avocat·es : procédures de protection internationale liées au genre : violences sexuelles ou basées sur le genre, orientation sexuelle et identité de genre' (Université de Gand 2023)

POSTER PRESENTATIONS

Roels L, 'Poster presentation valorisation project: Rape Mythology in Asylum Procedures' (**Faculty Research Day**, Ghent, 17 May 2022)

——, 'Talking to a brick wall: Over gendergerelateerd geweld in de asielprocedure' (**Colloquium 'Diversiteit en Justitie'**, Ghent, 17 March 2023)

——, 'Expo: Talking To A Brick Wall' (**BELMUNDO** Festival 'Recht op actievoeren', Ghent, 24-26 March 2023)

——, 'Equity and fairness for survivors/victims of sexual and gender-based violence navigating the asylum procedure in Belgium: Towards gender-sensitive asylum justice' (Refugee Law Initiative (**RLI**) **Conference**, London, 21 June 2023)

——, 'Visual exhibition/poster series: Talking to a Brick Wall, On Sexual and Gender based Violence in the Asylum Procedure' (Human Rights Research Network (**HRRN**) **Conference**, Ghent, 6-8 December 2023)

OPINION PIECES

Linthout L and others, 'Hoe het migratiebeleid van Nicole de Moor discrimineert: "Eerst vrouwen en kinderen, dan de honden. Pas daarna de mannen"' (**MO* Magazine**, 4 September 2023), www.mo.be/opinie/eerst-vrouwen-en-kinderen-dan-de-honden-pas-daarna-de-mannen

——, 'Ook Mannelijke Asielzoekers Zijn Kwetsbaar' (**De Tijd**, 4 September 2023), www.tijd.be/opinie/algemeen/ook-mannelijke-asielzoekers-zijn-kwetsbaar/10490331.html

AWARDS

Roels L, 'Best Presentation Award at Ghent University's Law & Criminology Faculty Research Day 2022' (**Ghent University's Law & Criminology Faculty**, Ghent, 17 May 2022)

ANNEX

A. LIST OF CASE STUDIES

CASE OF AMANI			
• Country of origin:	DRC	• SGBV types:	Rape/sexual assault & domestic violence
• Gender identity:	Woman	• Decisions in file:	CGRS 1 (refusal) – 21/12/2021
• Birth year:	1991		CALL 1 (annulment) – 17/01/2022 – n° 266 712
• Interview by:	CGRS		

According to Amani's statements, after her father had died, her mother remarried her stepfather, a teacher involved in local politics. From the age of 14, her stepfather started **raping** her when her mother was away for work. He made her drop out of school, wanting to prioritise his own children's education first. She never returned, explaining she had lost all self-confidence and the few friends she had, because the abuse had isolated her. She did work as a braider and sold goods, and found a religious community, the only place she really felt safe. When she was not out for these activities, she avoided her stepfather by staying in her room, since she could not bear facing him. In 2016, Amani fell ill, leading her to discover that she was **pregnant as a result of the sexual abuse**. As her stepfather threatened to kill her if she told anyone, she lied to her mother that she was no longer in contact with the child's father. From her son's birth onwards, fearful that her stepfather would come back to rape her at night, Amani avoided spending the night at home. When her son fell ill and had to go to hospital, Amani felt compelled to tell someone the truth and confided in her cousin. To protect her, the latter wanted to take the baby away from Amani's mother and stepfather. When her mother asked why, the cousin told her about the abuse. The next day, Amani was **abducted** and **raped** by 2 men dressed as policemen and a third. They left her in a graveyard. Upon returning home, her stepfather threatened her with a gun for bringing out the truth and locked her in the house. Finding the door open in the morning, she fled to her maternal cousin in Congo-Brazzaville. After receiving anonymous phone calls there, she travelled on to Turkey, where she collected money to travel to Belgium by working in a night club.

She was apprehended at the airport for travelling with false identity documents, applied for international protection and was detained in a closed centre. In support of her application, Amani submitted two psychological reports, attesting her difficulties in recounting her experiences and her wish to be heard by a female PO and interpreter.

CASE OF ANA			
• Country of origin:	Georgia	• SGBV types:	Rape/sexual assault & domestic violence
• Gender identity:	Woman	• Decisions in file:	CGRS 1 (refusal) – 27/10/2023
• Birth year:	1985		CALL 1 (refusal) – 29/05/2024 – n° 307 462
• Interview by:	/		

According to her statements, Ana met her husband in 2003 and aspired to open a household goods store in the same year, leading them to borrow money from an acquainted prosecutor. Her business suffered financially and was ultimately destroyed in a fire caused by faulty electrical wiring. When they were unable to repay the loan, the prosecutor began threatening them. In 2006, her husband was first sentenced to three years in prison under false charges of theft by the prosecutor and afterwards, in 2009, again to another six years. Although he was granted amnesty in 2012 following a political shift, the prosecutor lost his position but never ceased his threats against them. Fearing for their safety, Ana and her husband left Georgia for Turkey, where they lived for seven years, but the threats persisted. In 2021, her husband returned to Georgia briefly, hiding with family before fleeing to Poland and then Belgium, where his application for international protection was rejected twice. Meanwhile, Ana was left behind in Georgia to secure travelling documents for their daughter.

She finally managed to flee with her daughter, arriving in Belgium in December 2022, where she filed her own asylum application. Despite mentioning she was **raped** by the prosecutor in Georgia in the questionnaire (to be read by the CGRS) at the IO, the CGRS copied her husband's refusal decision in her procedure, stating that their flight stories rested on identical grounds and making no mention of the sexual violence in the argumentation. In the appeal procedure before the CALL, Ana disclosed that she had continuously suffered **domestic violence** from her husband, both in Georgia and Belgium. Her husband was arrested and imprisoned in Belgium, but the violence started over upon his release. While she never filed a complaint in Georgia, having no trust in the Georgian authorities' response to gender-based violence, she did do so in Belgium. At the time of the appeal, she learnt through others that he was back in prison. At the hearing, she confirmed fearing for herself and for her child should they be forced, along with her husband, to return to Georgia.

CASE OF ANGELE			
• Country of origin:	DRC	• SGBV types:	Rape/sexual assault
• Gender identity:	Woman	• Decisions in file:	CGRS 1 (refusal) – 30/03/2020
• Birth year:	1984		CALL 1 (annulment) – 5/11/2020 – n° 243 679
• Interview by:	CGRS		CGRS 2 (refusal) – 30/08/2021
			CALL 2 (recognition) – 11/08/2022 – n° 275 955

(continued)

According to her statements, Angele was born in the DRC, where she lived with her husband, a lawyer, and their two children. While she was abroad for work, her husband had participated in a political march where he went missing. During her absence, her maid reported that armed men had come to the home to steal documents and jewellery. After Angele's return, several men, dressed in civilian clothes (she recalled trainers, no military shoes) and carrying weapons, came back looking for documents allegedly in possession of her husband. They beat up her brother-in-law, chased the maid away, and **raped** Angele while her children were hiding in the house. The neighbours called the police but were told that they were understaffed and could not get there. No investigation was ever launched afterwards. From then on, she recounted fearing the return of these men, since the home had now become 'their battlefield'. The day after the rape, she went to live at her parents' house with the children. There, she took medication used for abortions and when the pain in her genital area had not stopped after two days, she went to the hospital. She did not dare to go to her gynaecologist, who was a family friend, but visited another doctor. The doctor wanted to know what happened, seeing her injuries, but Angele did not disclose the rape to her, nor to anyone else. Afterwards, she was contacted by a man who confirmed that her husband was safe and she agreed for him to organise the whole family's flight out of the country.

In Belgium, they applied for international protection. In support of her application, she submitted (among other elements) medical documents from the hospital in the DRC, as well as from her psychologist in Belgium, stating that she shows symptoms corresponding to those of sexual violence survivors/victims and of PTSD.

CASE OF ASTER

• Country of origin:	Ethiopia	• SGBV types:	Rape/sexual assault & sex trafficking/forced prostitution
• Gender identity:	Woman	• Decisions in file:	CGRS 1 (inadmissible) – 17/3/2022
• Birth year:	1988		CALL 1 (refusal) – 6/4/2022 – n° 270 994
• Interview by:	CGRS		

According to Aster's statements, she was born in Ethiopia in 1988. She left the country in 2016, because of her husband's political problems. She arrived in Greece in September 2017, where she applied for and was granted international protection in June 2019. While she could rely on UNHCR support at first, this was no longer the case once she received her status. Aster was unable to find work and lacked the financial means to rent accommodation. As a result, she ended up on the streets and often spent the night in a bus station. As this precarious situation attracted people taking advantage of her, she was **raped** on multiple occasions. She never reported this to the police. She stated it was difficult to identify perpetrators and found it pointless, since she would have to sleep on the streets again the next day, risking the same violence. After two years, she received a job offer to work at a guesthouse, cleaning and making beds. She initially agreed and was made to sign a contract in Greek she could not read. After two weeks, she was taken to another location, where she was **forced into prostitution** together with other women. She was told they were being **recorded** and that their video tapes would be made public if they tried to escape or go to the police. The trafficker **threatened** them **with physical violence and death**, which he demonstrated by cutting off the ear of one of the women,

(continued)

whom they never saw again. After a few months, Aster managed to disclose the situation to one of her clients. He showed compassion, helped her escape the guesthouse, told her to flee, and that he would take care of reporting the trafficker. Fearing for her life, she did not go to the police herself, but fled the country.

Aster was intercepted by the Belgian authorities in November 2021, while attempting to reach the United Kingdom. She was questioned and ordered to leave the territory, but did not do so. One month later, she was placed in a closed centre to be repatriated to Greece, where she eventually applied for international protection. She submitted a handwritten testimony and two certificates by the centre's psychologist and doctor, reporting nightmares, during which she had grabbed her roommate's throat, and issues with accessing her memory and concentrating.

CASE OF AYA

• Country of origin:	Syria	• SGBV types:	Rape/sexual assault
• Gender identity:	Woman	• Decisions in file:	CGRS 1 (refusal) – 8/8/2023
• Birth year:	1997		CALL 1 (annulment) – 31/8/2023 – n° 293 489
• Interview by:	CGRS		

According to her statements, Aya was born in 1997 in Syria. Her husband was forced to do military service, where she visited him in March 2023. Upon arriving, she noticed an officer stepping out of his office to look at the queue of visitors. He spoke to a guard while pointing at her. After meeting her husband, the same guard ordered Aya to follow him to his superior. She found herself alone with the officer (who turned out to be a colonel) in his office, upon which he began making **sexual advances** towards her. She categorically refused these, but he became more insistent and **grabbed her** by the arm to **prevent her from leaving**. She tried to intimidate him by lying that she knew a general in the army. The colonel appeared to be deterred by this, which allowed her to leave, though he warned her that he would find a way to make her return. Two months later, Aya received a phone call from her husband's phone. The caller said that her husband had been injured and that she needed to come to sign documents for his hospital treatment. She went there again, but this time, the guard took her firmly by the arm and led her directly to the colonel's office. Before he could force her inside, she resisted and loudly warned that if he touched her again, she would scream. The colonel then asked if she had been mocking him by lying about the general and **threatened** that he would harm her daughter, her husband, her family, and Aya herself for not obeying him. He then pushed her and ordered her to leave. One to two weeks later, her husband was transferred to another region, which Aya saw as a retaliation from the colonel. She lived in constant fear that something would happen to her or her family.

In May 2023, she saw an opportunity to leave while she was in Lebanon with family, using her sister's passport. She arrived in Belgium without legal travel documents and submitted an application for international protection, upon which she was placed in a detention centre.

CASE OF BINTA			
• Country of origin:	Guinea	• SGBV types:	Rape/sexual assault, GMC, violence related to gender norm transgression, forced marriage & domestic violence
• Gender identity:	Woman	• Decisions in file:	CGRS 1 (refusal) – 20/6/2023
• Birth year:	/		CALL 1 (refusal) – 11/4/2024 – n° 304 652
• Interview by:	/		

According to her statements, after Binta's father had died, her mother remarried her paternal uncle. She was circumcised at the age of eight, **forced** by her uncle **to marry** at the age of 14, and therefore never got any higher education. During this marriage, she was **verbally, physically and sexually abused** by her husband regularly, and gave birth to a daughter. She shared the house with her husband's mother and three sisters, who had started accusing her of bringing bad luck, and **attacking her**. She suspected them of having **attempted to poison her**. When her husband left for Mozambique in 2018, her sisters-in-law blamed her for having chased him out of the house. Their attacks intensified by **threatening to kill her**. Out of fear they might succeed, Binta eventually fled the country in 2021, travelling via Morocco, Spain and France before arriving in Belgium.

She applied for international protection, fearing for herself to be sent back to her husband's house and to be killed by her family-in-law, and for her **daughter to be circumcised**. In support of her applications, she submitted medical reports on her own circumcision and her injuries following the abuse. She also provided proof of her registration/treatment with an organisation specialising in female GMC and with a psychologist, since she had difficulties accessing her memory of the experiences.

CASE OF CARMEN			
• Country of origin:	Ecuador	• SGBV types:	Rape/sexual assault & domestic violence
• Gender identity:	Woman	• Decisions in file:	CGRS 1 (refusal) – 8/12/2023
• Birth year:	1981		CALL 1 (refusal) – 28/04/2024 – n° 305 805
• Interview by:	/		

According to her statements, Carmen is a pharmacist who owned and afterwards worked for a pharmaceutical business in Ecuador. She had to quit her job in 2019 after her ex-husband had attacked her with a knife over an alimony dispute. She got married to him in 2007, but his **mental, physical, and sexual abuse** started one year earlier, after their daughter was born. The next child, her son, was the result of **intramarital rape**. She sought help from a foundation supporting domestic violence survivors/victims, filed a complaint with the police, and obtained a protection order. She reported his first violation of the order, upon which he was detained for 8 days instead of 60 as provided. After being released, his threats got worse. After this, she dared not report the violations

(continued)

again. She managed to divorce him, but alimony for her children was denied. Unable to accept the divorce, her husband **hit Carmen with a car** in 2010, **attacked her with a knife in the chest** in 2018, and **poured burning liquid in her face** in 2020, forcing her to quit her job again. In 2021, he **threatened to kill her** on the phone, whereupon she fled the country fearing he would succeed.

With the help of a friend, she flew to Turkey and then to Brussels, where she applied for international protection. She supported her application with legal documents, such as the protection order, the divorce petition, and her ex-husband's criminal record, as well as medical documents, such as photographs and medical attestations of her injuries, and a psychological report confirming her need of long-term psychological support.

CASE OF CLARISSE

• Country of origin:	Ivory Coast	• SGBV types:	GMC & violence related to gender norm transgression
• Gender identity:	Woman	• Decisions in file:	CGRS 1 (refusal) – 13/6/2023
• Birth year:	/		CALL 1 (annulment) – 11/03/2024 – n° 302 979
• Interview by:	/		

According to her statements, Clarisse was born in Ivory Coast and was subjected to female GMC at the age of six. In her family, all young girls endured this practice. In 2002, her family relocated to Abidjan. Clarisse started a job in financial services, but had to abandon this when a marriage was arranged for her with her current husband. She moved into his family's compound and gave birth to three children, but the effects of her GMC made childbirth incredibly painful. Her husband, having already realised the distress she suffered during intimate relations, gradually came to understand the unjust nature of this practice. Over time, their shared opposition to GMC (among other factors) transformed their forced union into a genuine partnership. As their daughter's sixth birthday approached, Clarisse's mother-in-law announced she would **subject the child to female GMC,** in the name of tradition, despite both parents' clear disapproval. In 2020, Clarisse learnt that the excision was planned for August. Clarisse and her husband made urgent arrangements, placing their youngest child in the care of a childhood friend, and organising the escape of Clarisse and her oldest daughter (at immediate risk of GMC). Clarisse's husband would stay behind, regularly visiting their other daughter in secret.

In August 2020, Clarisse and her almost six-year-old daughter fled Ivory Coast by plane to Tunisia. Shortly thereafter, her mother-in-law filed a complaint against Clarisse. They undertook a sea journey to Italy and after transiting through France, they reached Belgium in May 2021. Five days later, they submitted an application for international protection. Clarisse feared for her daughters' GMC and for the consequences of her own opposition to this practice. In support of her demand, Clarisse provided several documents, including medical certificates attesting Clarisse's GMC and her daughter's lack thereof, as well as a police letter following her mother-in-law's complaint, dated 29 August 2020.

CASE OF DIANA & ERINA			
• Country of origin:	Albania	• SGBV types:	Rape/sexual assault, violence related to gender norm transgression, forced marriage & domestic violence
• Gender identity:	Women	• Decisions for Diana:	CGRS 1 (manifestly ill-founded) – 29/05/2019
• Birth year:	1973 (D)		CALL 1 (refusal) – 7/04/2020 – n° 234 950
	2006 (E)		CGRS 2 (inadmissible) – 21/10/2021
• Interview by:	Researcher		CALL 2 (refusal) – 21/03/2022 – n° 270 155
		• Decisions for Erina:	CGRS 1 (inadmissible) – 2/12/2021
			CALL 1 (refusal) – 7/09/2022 – n° 276 951
			CGRS 2 (inadmissible) – 14/9/2023
			CALL 2 (refusal) – 8/5/2024 – n° 306 251

According to their statements, Diana and Erina, a mother and her 14-year-old daughter at the time, fled Albania in 2019 to escape severe **verbal, psychological, physical, and sexual violence** inflicted by their ex-husband/father. During her parents' forced marriage, Erina was born out of **marital rape**. Apart from Erina and her brother, Diana's ex-husband had prevented previous pregnancies through **forced abortion** and physical violence, leading to miscarriages. He was a convicted criminal for fraud, assault, and attempted murder, but never for the violence towards his family. Upon his release from prison, he returned home, once again abusing Diana while pregnant. When Erina was five months old, he abandoned the family and left for the UK, only to be extradited back to Albania twice, in 2011 and 2012. Upon his return, their home became a site of constant violence and psychological terror. Erina and her brother faced daily **beatings, death threats** – including threats with a **knife** – and exposure to their father's **exhibitionism**. They witnessed their mother being **raped, strangled, and threatened with firearms**. Meanwhile, their father refused to work, drank a lot, engaged in human trafficking, stole from Diana, and accumulated significant debt. As a result, their family home was repeatedly targeted by criminal associates seeking retribution. Desperate for protection, Diana and Erina sought help from authorities at least 16 times, filing complaints and requesting protection orders. Diana only managed to secure temporary protection orders for herself, but never for her children and parents, who also suffered violence. Nonetheless, the Albanian authorities consistently failed to enforce these orders, allowing the abuse to continue. Police on several occasions dismissed their complaints, refusing to document property damage or collect evidence.

After years of **legal battles sabotaged** by her husband, Diana was finally granted a divorce in 2015. However, the ruling allowed Erina's father **unsupervised visitation rights** with her every weekend and during school holidays. In 2018, while Diana was

(continued)

briefly away in Switzerland, Erina stayed with her maternal grandparents. During this time, her father violently broke into their home, changed the locks, and repeatedly threatened them. He even filed a police report accusing the grandparents of kidnapping Erina, prompting law enforcement to actively pressure her into meeting him. This led to an attempted **abduction**, during which the father and his sisters tried to take Erina to his hometown, where he planned to hide and **force her into marriage** at age 13. With the help of her maternal aunt, Erina managed to escape. Despite multiple **kidnapping attempts** afterwards, including at her school, the authorities failed to act. A month before fleeing Albania, Diana encountered her ex-husband in court while another temporary protection order was still in place. He openly threatened her, but despite an alleged arrest warrant and her contacting the police, he remained free. The police advised Diana to change the locks and stay indoors. Having been forced to **quit her job** due to the ex-husband's threats at her workplace and to eventually **take Erina out of school** for safety, Diana saw no choice but to flee.

In March 2019, Diana and Erina left Albania for Belgium, where Diana initially applied for international protection alone. After her case was found manifestly ill-founded in an accelerated procedure due to Albania being a safe country of origin (which was confirmed in appeal), Diana applied a second time, and Erina a first time in her own name in 2021. In between these procedures, Belgian police questioned Diana following an **international child abduction complaint** filed by Erina's father from Albania. He continued to harass their relatives in Albania, demanding to know their whereabouts. In support of their applications, Erina and Diana submitted multiple documents, such as the divorce certificate including visitation rights, multiple medical and psychological certificates, the invitation letter from the Belgian police, and an official document stating the ex-husband's convictions.

CASE OF ELENE

• Country of origin:	Georgia	• SGBV types:	Violence related to gender norm transgression & domestic violence
• Gender identity:	Woman	• Decisions in file:	CGRS 1 (refusal) – 27/07/2023
• Birth year:	2003		CALL 1 (refusal) – 27/03/2024 – n° 303 891
• Interview by:	/		

According to her statements, Elene was born in Georgia in 2003, studied law, and lived with her parents. She described the domestic violence taking place by her father and brothers, both **threatening and abusing her and her mother**. Her parents got divorced, but her father kept stalking and abusing her mother. As a result, her mother fled the country. From then on, Elene was left living with her father, sister, and two brothers. While her father had forbidden her to contact her mother in an attempt to manipulate her and turn them against each other, they kept in touch in secret. Elene had always identified as lesbian, but never dared to tell anyone. She had a few brief relationships in secret and eventually told a few friends about her sexual orientation. While in Georgia, Elene never dared to tell her family, including her mother, because she feared they would reject her. Elene explained thinking that her father and brothers suspected her **sexual orientation**, because they asked questions about her playing football with boys or her clothes. Eventually, she fled Georgia in 2022, fearing that her father and brothers might kill her if they found out about her sexual orientation or her contact with her mother.

(continued)

After fleeing the country seven years earlier, Elene's mother applied for international protection in Belgium, stating that she feared her ex-husband and son, because of her marriage to another man and her ex-husband's continuous stalking and abuse. The Belgian asylum authorities refused her international protection in March 2022. A cassation appeal against the appeal judgement was pending at the time of Elene's own procedure. Elene's mother and maternal uncle helped her travel to Belgium, where she too applied for international protection in December 2022. Meanwhile, her father and brothers believe she was in Sweden for an Erasmus exchange program and she was still in contact with them so as not to cause suspicion. In support of her application, she submitted a psychological report attesting that she had to grow up in an extremely unsafe and violent environment.

CASE OF ESMERALDA

• Country of origin:	Moldova	• SGBV types:	Domestic violence
• Gender identity:	Woman	• Decisions in file:	CGRS 1 (refusal) – 30/11/2023
• Birth year:	1971		CALL 1 (refusal) – 24/05/2024 – n° 307 172
• Interview by:	/		

According to Esmeralda's statements, she was born in 1971 in Moldova, is of Romani ethnic origin, and is a Christian. She attended school up to the fourth grade, but never worked. In Moldova, she was married. After her husband's father had passed away (two or three years before fleeing), he started **insulting and physically assaulting** her on a daily basis. The last time, he **hit her on the head** so hard she lost consciousness. The neighbours heard the commotion and alerted the emergency services. Esmeralda was hospitalised and afterwards went to stay with her sister until she eventually decided to flee the country. Esmeralda left Moldova in 2018 and travelled through Europe. Over a period of four years, she halted in France, the Netherlands, and Germany. In each of these countries, she applied for international protection but received a negative decision. Since her departure in 2018, Esmeralda heard that her husband was **still looking for her and threatening to kill her**. While in Germany, her sister and nephew joined her, seeking medical assistance for his schizophrenia. Together, they went back to France, where their application was again rejected.

In June 2022, they travelled to Belgium, where they applied for international protection. Since that day, she heard nothing concrete from her ex-husband, but her fear remained, especially since she has remarried in Belgium to a Macedonian Rom. In support of her application, she submitted a medical certificate attesting to her serious sleep problems, anxiety, loss of impulse control, increased stress, and impaired cognitive functions.

CASE OF FATOU

• Country of origin:	Guinea	• SGBV types:	Rape/sexual assault, forced marriage & domestic violence
• Gender identity:	Woman	• Decisions in file:	CGRS 1 (refusal) – 30/3/2023
• Birth year:	/		CALL 1 (recognition) – 18/1/2024 – n° 300 255
• Interview by:	/		

(continued)

According to her statements, Fatou was born in Conakry and never knew her father, who had passed away. At the age of four, her mother abandoned her with a neighbour. Later, her paternal aunt took her in. At five years old, she was subjected to female GMC, an experience that took the life of one of her friends. That same year, her aunt died, leaving her to live with her cousin, where she faced **domestic violence**. The husband of her cousin, an influential man involved in drug trafficking, never accepted her presence. One night, while she was sleeping, he **poured hot water on her leg**. At age 11, Fatou began experiencing severe pain in her leg, but she only received painkillers, **never proper medical care**. In sixth grade, her cousin took her out of school to take care of her children. At age 12, her cousin's husband **sexually abused** her, resulting in pregnancy, which was terminated by a befriended doctor. Later that year, she became pregnant again and underwent another **forced abortion**. While being forced to sell clothes and water in markets, Fatou met a man in whom she confided and they started a relationship. When she became pregnant of him, her cousin's husband forced her again to take abortion pills and **confined her at home**. In 2013, her cousin, also pregnant, was beaten severely by her husband, leading to her death. Fearing for her life, Fatou escaped during the mourning period and sought refuge with her boyfriend, whom she later married in 2014. Their son was born with health issues. At a certain point, her husband decided to leave Guinea and travel to Europe. Although he initially contacted her from Italy, their communication became scarce after he moved to Belgium. After this, Fatou was **forced** by her cousin's husband into **marriage** with a wealthy and influential gold miner. Since she had no other means of support and was financially dependent on her cousin's husband, Fatou was pressured into accepting the marriage despite her strong objections.

In 2019, she eventually managed to flee Guinea and reached Belgium, where she reunited with the father of her daughter and applied for international protection. Fatou submitted, among other documents, several psychological and psychiatric reports to support her application. In 2021, she received the news that her son had died in unknown circumstances.

CASE OF LEJLA

• Country of origin:	Bosnia-Herzegovina	• SGBV types:	Rape/sexual assault & sex trafficking/forced prostitution
• Gender id:	Woman	• Decisions in file:	CGRS 1 (manifestly ill-founded) – 23/5/2023
• Birth year:	/		CALL 1 (annulment) – 30/4/2024 – n° 305 882
• Interview by:	/		

According to her statements, Lejla was born in Transnistria (part of the Soviet Union at the time), where she was **abducted and forced into prostitution** by the mafia and was repeatedly **sexually abused** in this context. When two undercover police officers came to a club where she was forced to work, the mafia leader ordered to attack them. One of them died and Lejla helped the other escape, for which she was severely punished (e.g. with **beatings** that **broke her teeth**). Eventually, the police arrived and she was taken to the hospital first and to a safe house later. However, the mafia leader found her and **attacked** her again, including **with a glass bottle**, marking her with scars that remain to

(continued)

this day. She was moved to another safe house and eventually testified at a trial in 2002. The mafia leader was sentenced to 20 years in prison and **threatened** Lejla that he would come back for her upon his release.

In 2001, Lejla met her current husband, with whom she moved to Bosnia-Herzegovina. They both obtained international protection, got married and raised five children (three boys and two girls). They spent much of their lives in reception centres, only moving to private accommodation in 2019. Shortly after the mafia trial, a YouTube video was published in which Lejla shared her life story, revealing how she had been abducted and who had abused her. While they immediately reported it and it was removed, they began receiving **threats** from the convicted mafia leader and his associates, continuing until 2007. In 2018 or 2019, while still living in a reception centre, Lejla was **raped and beaten** by a man who had locked her in a barrack. She kept this a secret from her husband until 2022.

In 2021 or 2022, while having coffee with her husband in Sarajevo, Lejla suddenly saw the mafia leader again. Shortly after, her **daughter was abducted** 50 metres from their home. They heard screams and her husband saw their daughter being dragged into a car. After informing the police, the kidnappers were intercepted. At the police station, they were placed in the same room as the four kidnappers, with one of them giving Lejla **'greetings' from the mafia leader**. Lejla, her husband, and her daughter were eventually questioned for five minutes and told to wait for the chief inspector, who never came. A police officer advised them to file a complaint, which they did not do, not wanting to fight these people again. The perpetrators were released. The day after the abduction, in April 2022, her husband brought both their daughters into safety with family in Poland.

Right before they fled, the whole family obtained Bosnian citizenship. They eventually travelled together to Belgium in June 2022, where they applied for international protection. In support of her application, Lejla submitted various legal and medical documents, attesting her forced prostitution, her PTSD, the abduction of her daughter, her hospitalisation after the rape in the reception centre, and other proof of the threats they received. Lejla could not be interviewed by or provide written information to the CGRS, as her psychiatrist declared her unfit to do so. After several declined interview invitations (supported by a medical certificate) for that reason, the CGRS made a decision identical to her husband's, since their applications were deemed to rely on the same facts. As Bosnia-Herzegovina is listed as a 'safe country of origin', her husband's application was assessed via the accelerated procedure. Lejla herself had indicated at the IO that 'her husband and children were not aware of everything and that she wished to keep it that way'.

CASE OF MARJORIE			
• Country of origin:	Suriname	• SGBV types:	Rape/sexual assault, violence related to gender norm transgression, forced marriage & domestic violence
• Gender identity:	Woman	• Decisions in file:	CGRS 1 (refusal) – 9/5/2023
• Birth year:	/		CALL 1 (refusal) – 5/2/2024 – n° 301 074
• Interview by:	/		

(continued)

According to her statements, Marjorie was forcibly married off by her parents to a man who repeatedly **physically and sexually abused** her, including through **death threats**. He was also physically violent towards her daughter and son. She could not find support with her family, since they felt that once married, she had to stay with her husband. In January 2019, Marjorie took her children and secretly fled the home to move in with acquaintances, to whom she had explained the situation and who wanted to help. She managed to divorce her husband in April 2019. Because of this, her family cut off all contact, except for her brother, who called and threatened her for **disgracing the family**. She received similar **death threats** from her ex-husband's family. Fearing retaliations, she left Suriname with her daughter in October 2019.

After arriving in Belgium, she met someone, with whom she started a relationship and gave birth to another daughter in January 2021. However, the father did not want to take care of this child and left Marjorie. After a failed attempt at family reunification with her brother, who lives in the Netherlands, Marjorie applied for international protection in August 2022. Upon return to Suriname, she feared being killed by her ex-husband, his family, or her brother, and that her youngest daughter would be at risk of ostracism as an extramarital child. Due to this delayed application, for which her reasons were not considered a justification, her case was assessed in an accelerated procedure.

CASE OF MARY			
• Country of origin:	Liberia	• SGBV types:	Sex trafficking/forced prostitution, GMC, violence related to gender norm transgression & forced marriage
• Gender identity:	Woman	• Decisions in file:	CGRS 1 (refusal) – 17/02/2022
• Birth year:	1980		CALL 1 (refusal) – 10/08/2022 – n° 275 866
• Interview by:	Researcher		

According to her statements, Mary did not grow up with her parents but was raised in Liberia by guardians from the United States. When she asked why her parents left her, her guardians first replied that she wouldn't understand, and at an older age that her mother wanted to save her from GMC, but nothing more. She finished high school, left her guardians and moved to Ghana to take courses to become a tailor. She married her partner and they had a son. Later on, back in Liberia, Mary met her biological father and relatives, who invited her to a family meeting without disclosing its purpose. At the gathering, they insisted she **take on her role as a GMC practitioner**, **forcibly marry** an older man, and **undergo GMC** herself. She had to replace her mother, who had recently passed away, as a 'Zoe'. Opposed to the practice, she refused and left, but her relatives came back to remind her of her duties. She went into hiding at a friend's house, together with her son. However, she spotted her family around the house several times, pointing at her. Fearing for her safety but also for the dangerous migration journey, Mary left Liberia with assistance from a smuggler, leaving her son in the care of her friend. Since the Liberian government, overruled by traditional leaders, dismisses GMC as 'family business', she fled to a country that is against the practice, like Belgium. After she left, her friend sent Mary a letter reporting how her family visited her son at school to ask about her, upon which she unenrolled him.

(continued)

Upon arriving in Belgium, Mary was **forced into prostitution** and repeatedly **sexually abused**. She submitted psychological certificates that describe her post-traumatic stress disorder (PTSD), resulting in memory issues, confusion, and difficulty discussing her past.

CASE OF NELLA			
• Country of origin:	Burundi	• SGBV types:	Rape/sexual assault
• Gender identity:	Woman	• Decisions in file:	CGRS 1 (refusal) – 29/6/2023
• Birth year:	/		CALL 1 (recognition) – 11/4/2024 – n° 304 646
• Interview by:	/		

According to her statements, Nella is engaged to a taxi driver who is also involved in a political Movement for Solidarity and Democracy. She supported this movement upon request of her fiancé, but was never a party member. He regularly invited taxi passengers and friends over to spend one or more nights at their house, but the names of the latter were never registered. When Nella asked about the reason for this or their identities, he refused to answer. In October 2021, several visitors spent the night and left the next day. Five days later, at around 9pm, three men in uniforms and five Imbonerakure members (the youth league of Burundi's ruling party) came to the house. They arrested her fiancé and questioned him on his membership of a rebel party fighting for the rule of law in Burundi (RED Tabara), given his incorrect visitor registrations and involvement in demonstrations. Two of the men **raped** Nella. After they left, she managed to get to her neighbour's house, who took her to the hospital. There, she received medication and care. The next day, her neighbour noticed two individuals loitering near their homes. Fearing for her safety and that of her family, she suggested that Nella moved in with a widow further away. Her parents' house was searched the same day. After staying with the widow for one month, her uncle helped her to flee the country via a smuggler.

She arrived in Belgium in December 2021 and immediately applied for international protection, supported by a medical report attesting the rape and care she received at the hospital.

CASE OF NINO			
• Country of origin:	Georgia	• SGBV types:	Rape/sexual assault & domestic violence
• Gender identity:	Woman	• Decisions in file:	CGRS 1 (manifestly ill-founded) – 31/08/2021
• Birth year:	1975		CALL 1 (refusal) – 16/3/2022 – n° 269 856
• Interview by:	Researcher		

According to her statements, Nino was born in 1975 and was initially married to a man with whom she had four children and lived in Georgia. During this marriage, he **abused her both physically, psychologically and sexually**. She managed to divorce him in 2013, but he continued to **stalk and physically assault** her afterwards. Between 2013 and 2016, she changed her address seven times, but was tracked down by him

(continued)

each time. She obtained three temporary protection orders (each for one month) against him, but these offered no effective protection. No criminal investigation was ever opened and the police and courts repeatedly told her that nothing could be done against her ex-husband as long as he had not been caught red-handed. Having obtained the last one-month protection order in November 2015, she eventually felt forced to flee to Turkey in order to find safety. She lived in Istanbul from 2016 to 2019 without legal residence status or protection. In January 2019, she met her current husband and decided to return to Georgia, where she could go into hiding with him. They stayed there for nine months, but ultimately fled to France, when this situation was no longer tenable. While in France, Nino's eldest son found out about her remarrying and her current location. Being warned by her daughter that he was **on his way to France to kill them**, they left the country and travelled on.

Nino arrived in Belgium and applied for international protection in September 2020. While in Belgium, she learnt from acquaintances at the French reception centre that unknown men had been asking about her. To support her asylum application, Nino submitted several legal and medical documents attesting her divorce, protection order rulings, and her scars caused by physical abuse.

CASE OF NYAKATO

• Country of origin:	Uganda	• SGBV types:	Rape/sexual assault
• Gender identity:	Woman	• Decisions in file:	CGRS 1 (refusal) – 22/6/2023
• Birth year:	/		CALL 1 (refusal) – 5/4/2024 – n° 304 388
• Interview by:	/		

According to her statements, Nyakato was sent to live with her mother's stepsister at the age of 12. This aunt **forced her to marry** a man from Dubai, by whom she was repeatedly **raped**. She managed to escape and ended up on the streets, where she was found by a nun. The nun offered her shelter, education, and work at an Italian orphanage. It was there that she met her husband, an Italian businessman operating in Uganda. Around the age of sixteen, in 2017, she obtained her mother's approval to marry him. Two years in, her husband became involved in financial disputes with business partners, though he did not disclose the details to her. In September 2019, Nyakato fell pregnant and discovered that her husband had been arrested. She managed to bail him out, upon which he went into hiding. His business associates started searching for him. During this period, she felt increasingly unsafe in their marital home, but because she had dogs that had to be fed, she still went there a few times a week. On those visits, she first noticed that someone had tried to break-in, and later that her large dog had been killed and her small dog had been hanged. She filed a complaint with the police and, following the advice of a friend, paid three men working as police officers to protect her home. While taking a shower, Nyakato was **raped** by one of the officers. Being pregnant at the time and losing a lot of blood, she went to the hospital, where they confirmed that she had lost the baby and that the remains had to be removed. Her sister drove her to another clinic so that the procedure could be performed by her family doctor, the only person to whom she confided the rape.

Fearing for her safety, she left Uganda and applied for international protection in Belgium in April 2020.

CASE OF QAWTAR			
• Country of origin:	Morocco	• SGBV types:	Violence related to gender norm transgression, forced marriage & domestic violence
• Gender identity:	Woman	• Decisions in file:	CGRS 1 (refusal) – 3/04/2024
• Birth year:	1999		CALL 1 (refusal) – 24/04/2024 – n° 305 429
• Interview by:	/		

According to Qawtar's statements, she was born in Morocco in 1999. She grew up under the authority of her father, who **forbade his daughter to study, work, or own a phone, and obliged her to wear a hijab**. Without him knowing and with the help of a teacher, she obtained a baccalaureate. When she turned 20, Qawtar was **forced to marry** a wealthy man, eleven years older. He too **forbade her to work** and was **physically violent**. She **gave birth** to a daughter, in whom her husband had never shown any interest. She sought support from an organisation helping domestic violence survivors/victims, but gave up out of fear that they would pass on information to her husband. With the help of a lawyer, she managed to divorce him in 2022, but ended up in a legal battle over child support. Without any work experience, money, or a place to live with her daughter, Qawtar was forced to go back to her parents' home. Her father **blamed her for causing the divorce** and **hit her** for leaving the house without a hijab. She received **death threats** from her ex-husband's brother, and was almost **hit by a car**, presumably by her ex-husband. Two years before fleeing the country, Qawtar met her current fiancé, who has a Dutch nationality.

She travelled to Belgium with a short-stay visa to get married to him. In December 2023, the Belgian authorities found Qawtar to be residing irregularly in the territory and therefore detained her in a closed centre. A first repatriation was postponed since she refused to return to Morocco. A second attempt was cancelled because she eventually applied for international protection in February 2024. She submitted fearing to be abused by her father and ex-husband and being stigmatised in Moroccan society because of her divorce. In support of her application, she submitted, among other documents, a certificate attesting her divorce and two photos of her with a black eye.

CASE OF RAHEL			
• Country of origin:	Eritrea	• SGBV types:	Rape/sexual assault
• Gender identity:	Woman	• Decisions in file:	CGRS 1 (refusal) – 30/5/2022
• Birth year:	1985		CALL 1 (refusal) – 25/11/2022 – n° 280 827
• Interview by:	Researcher		

According to her statements, Rahel was born in 1985 in Eritrea, where she worked in a beauty salon. Rahel met a man, who she said was a spy for the Eritrean government and who asked to marry her multiple times, but she refused. Unable to accept this, he warned her that she would 'face the consequences'. One day, Rahel was attacked on her way home from work and was **raped** by a masked man, who later turned out to be him. After her mother found her, she was hospitalised because of her injuries, turned out to be pregnant, and gave birth to a daughter. She initially wanted to confront him after

(continued)

her police complaint was left without consequences, but could not find him. For a long time, Rahel heard nothing from this man, but in 2018, he resurfaced. He demanded that she hand over his daughter to him, or he would kill her. He threatened her both verbally on the phone and physically by **stalking** her along her commuting route. Rahel's initial anger made room for fear of escalation, eventually leading her to go into hiding at her aunt's house, quitting her job and taking her daughter out of school. Having stayed hidden and having blocked her phone, she heard nothing more from him during this period. After a year in hiding, realising that they could not go on living like this, she saw no other way out than to flee the country, a journey she considered so dangerous that she left her daughter in the care of her mother, to later rescue her through legal migration pathways. She left Eritrea with a smuggler in January 2020.

She arrived in Belgium in August 2020 and submitted an application for international protection in November 2020. While she was already in Belgium, she learnt that someone had seen her rapist in a shop in her neighbourhood. Aside from her fear of him, she also stated that she feared the Eritrean government, as she had left the country irregularly.

CASE OF SOFIA

• Country of origin:	Honduras	• SGBV types:	Rape/sexual assault & domestic violence
• Gender identity:	Woman	• Decisions in file:	CGRS 1 (refusal) – 12/8/2021 (withdrawn)
• Birth year:	1991		/ (error in paying registration fee prevented an appeal)
• Interview by:	Researcher		CGRS 2 (recognition) – 15/03/2023

According to Sofia's statements, she was born in 1991 in Honduras, where she lived with her family. Her father was only home every two weeks, but when he was, he **sexually abused** her when he came in at night, often drunk. This happened the first time when she was 12 years old and continued for five years. When she was 17, she found the courage to tell her cousin. The latter confronted Sofia's father and threatened to contact the police if the abuse did not stop. While her father thereupon blamed Sofia and told her he would have stopped if she had asked him, the **assault continued** in more subtle forms. He asked her to sit on his lap or touched her 'as a woman and not as his daughter'. She coped with the abuse by feeling angry and sad all the time, but not knowing where else to seek help. She never thought of contacting the police herself, as she was young, she dared not talk to anyone about this (not even to her mother), there was no proof, and she normalised her father's behaviour as 'consistent with how men approach girls in Honduras'. While she used to avoid her home by visiting her grandmother, the latter eventually died. Sofia's aunt, who was living in Belgium, arranged her flight on the pretext that she would learn French and then return.

She left Honduras in 2012 for Belgium, where she took French courses and found work through the church. In Belgium, Sofia started having nightmares and feeling guilty that her silence might put her sisters (still in Honduras) at risk of the same violence. Supported by someone in church, she eventually told her mother about the abuse on the phone. While her mother believed Sofia, she kept protecting her husband and

(continued)

stayed with him. Only years later, after receiving psychological support in Belgium, Sofia realised the gravity of the child sexual abuse she had suffered, and that this could be a reason to obtain international protection. In 2019, she applied and supported her demand with (among other documents) a psychological certificate attesting her PTSD and news articles/reports on the widespread violence against women in Honduras.

CASE OF UYI

• Country of origin:	Nigeria	• SGBV types:	Sex trafficking/forced prostitution
• Gender identity:	Woman	• Decisions in file:	CGRS 1 (refusal) – 14/11/2023
• Birth year:	1993		CALL 1 (refusal) – 31/5/2024 – n° 307 592
• Interview by:	/		

According to her statements, Uyi was born in Nigeria in 1993. Until around the age of ten, she lived with her family, where she constantly had to work in the fields instead of attending school. As the eldest child, Uyi had to go and learn how to sew in Benin City, where she rented accommodation with money from the harvest. She lived there for about four years, but one day, her mother told her that a neighbour's daughter had a large shop in Europe and was looking for someone trustworthy to help her. After the daughter came from Italy to their town to explain her everything, Uyi agreed to take the job. However, she would have to repay €25 000 for her travel costs to Italy. Unaware of the consequences, she accepted to swear a voodoo oath in case she could not repay the debt. Uyi left Nigeria in 2015, but upon arrival in Italy, the agreement changed. Uyi was **forced into prostitution**. When she refused, her 'madam' **threatened that the voodoo priest would kill her and her family**. Seeing no other option, she sold her body and lived with this madam. At one point, she was checked by the Italian police, asking for her documents, which she did not have. Her madam told her to apply for international protection in Italy, but warned her not to tell the truth. Being forced to lie that her father was a member of a cult, her flight story was found non-credible and her application was rejected. One day, Uyi found her madam lifeless in the house. When the police arrived, Uyi finally told them the real story. A sister of the madam came to the funeral and told Uyi she **still had to repay the remaining debt** of €15 000. An unknown man called her with the same demand. Uyi threw away her SIM card, after which the threats stopped.

In January 2022, she left Italy and travelled to Belgium, where she applied for international protection. One evening, her sister called her to tell her that their father's leg had become swollen. Uyi had no money to send for medical care, and in July 2023, he died, leading her to suspect that voodoo may have been used to kill him.

CASE OF VERA

• Country of origin:	Albania	• SGBV types:	Rape/sexual assault, violence related to gender norm transgression & domestic violence
• Gender identity:	Woman	• Decisions in file:	CGRS 1 (manifestly ill-founded) – 10/10/2022
• Birth year:	1990		CALL 1 (refusal) – 27/02/2023 – n° 285 363
• Interview by:	Researcher		

(continued)

According to her statements, Vera was born in Shkodër (Albania), where she worked as a secondary school teacher. She met her husband at university, gave birth to a son, and married him two months later. During the five years of this marriage, her husband used constant **psychological, physical and sexual violence** against her and was addicted to alcohol and drugs. Her husband and family-in-law carried a firearm at all times due to their involvement in a blood feud and problems with the mafia. Because of this, her son was kidnapped once, leading her to not let him go to school or outside anymore. She herself was not allowed to leave the house either. With the property surrounded by surveillance cameras, she could only leave for work or when accompanied by her husband. She did not dare to report the violence, fearing her husband's threats and family-in-law's ties with the police. She sought support through a few therapy sessions on the phone when her husband, who could not know, was out of the house. She eventually fled the country with her son and filed for divorce. In these proceedings, her husband was awarded full custody and consequently filed a complaint for international child abduction, upon which she was questioned by the Belgian police. Especially in Northern-Albanian areas like Shkodër, patriarchal cultural norms are upheld by the Kanun: a book containing traditional customary laws, for example prohibiting a woman to leave her husband. Since she **violated her family's honour** by doing so, they do not support her and she fears for her life upon return.

In her asylum procedure, she submitted: news items and police reports on her son's abduction; video recordings of the domestic violence by a surveillance camera outside their house; and medical certificates by both Albanian and Belgian psychologists and psychiatrists, documenting her PTSD, treatment with medication, insomnia, anxiety, and inability to talk about her experiences.

CASE OF YUSUF

• Country of origin:	Afghanistan	• SGBV types:	Rape/sexual assault
• Gender identity:	Man	• Decisions in file:	CGRS 1 (refusal) – 5/10/2023
• Birth year:	/		CALL 1 (refusal) – 8/03/2024 – n° 302 900
• Interview by:	/		

According to his statements, Yusuf grew up in Afghanistan, where he was educated up to sixth grade and lived with his parents, four sisters, and four brothers. His father was approached several times by a known Taliban member (or *talib*), asking that Yusuf join the Taliban. His father refused this request, arguing that he was too young and still needed to study. Without his father knowing, the same *talib* had also repeatedly approached Yusuf directly with **unwanted sexual advances, by trying to touch him, telling him he loved him, and asking him to have sexual intercourse**. Yusuf managed to escape these, but was ashamed and dared not tell his father anything, as he feared he would bring shame to the family and be rejected by them. Yusuf understood from the *talib's* advances that his request to join the Taliban to his father was only a false motive. The last time the *talib* approached Yusuf's father, he informed him that he would come and get Yusuf the next day, upon which his father decided it was safer to send Yusuf away.

He eventually fled Afghanistan with his uncle and arrived in Belgium, where he applied for international protection.

CASE OF ZEYNEP			
• Country of origin:	Turkey	• SGBV types:	Rape/sexual assault, forced marriage & domestic violence
• Gender identity:	Woman	• Decisions in file:	CGRS 1 (refusal) – 22/12/2022
• Birth year:	1996		CALL 1 (annulment) – 12/1/2023 – n° 283 107
• Interview by:	CGRS		CGRS 2 (refusal) – 1/2/2023
			CALL 2 (annulment) – 23/2/2023 – n° 285 279

According to her statements, Zeynep is of Kurdish ethnicity and was born in Turkey, where she obtained a university degree in web design, against the wishes of her conservative father. During her studies, she attended Gülen study centres, inspired by the religious teachings of a political opponent of president Erdoğan. The Gülen movement is deemed a terrorist organisation by the government, with many of its member persecuted through unfair trials. In 2017, Zeynep's university residence was searched, she was detained at the police station for four days, and she was questioned again two months later. One of the police officers involved (in his fifties) also worked as a security guard on her university campus and contacted her afterwards. This contact gradually evolved into a friendship, but in 2018, he confessed romantic feelings to her, which she rejected. He began **stalking and harassing** her, forcing Zeynep to move to another city. He tracked down her address and contacted her again in 2020. Hoping he would leave her alone after rejecting him one last time, she got into his car, where he **raped** her. He kept threatening her afterwards, upon which she stayed inside and isolated herself. She tried to take her own life at the end of 2020. In 2021, she learnt about a legal procedure running against her, aggravated by her previous police custody. Next to this, Zeynep's family had started pressuring her into a **forced marriage** with her cousin. She refused, as she considered this incest, but was **beaten** several times by her father when doing so. Knowing the value of a woman's virginity in Kurdish culture and that rape survivors/victims risk being blamed for having provoked the violence, she never told anyone about the rape. She feared that her experience would be revealed by this marriage due to the fact that she was no longer a virgin. She eventually fled the country in 2022.

Once arrived in Belgium, she applied for international protection and was detained in a closed centre. She submitted documents on several doctors' and psychologists' consultations in Belgium and Turkey (e.g. attesting her suicide attempt in 2020 and current medication prescriptions).

B. SAMPLING STRATEGY FOR SYSTEMATIC CASE LAW ANALYSIS

Figure 43: Visualisation of sampling strategy for systematic search in the online CALL database as first pathway of case law analysis

SGBV type	Search in French Search round 1	Search in Dutch Search round 1	Search round 2
RSA	Term: 'genre+sex+viol' Most recent case: 31/05/2024 No. of results: 89 No. included: 16 No. excluded: 73	Term: 'gender+seks+verkracht' Most recent case: 16/04/2024 No. of results: 8 No. included: 3 No. excluded: 5	Term: 'seksueel' Most recent case: 31/05/2024 No. of results: 155 (1–20 checked) No. included: 7 No. excluded: 148
STFP	Term: 'genre+prostitution' Most recent case: 30/05/2024 No. of results: 9 No. included: 1 No. excluded: 8	Term: 'gender+prostitutie' Most recent case: 15/04/2024 No. of results: 2 No. included: 0 No. excluded: 2	Term: 'prostitutie' Most recent case: 31/05/2024 No. of results: 22 (1–11 checked) No. included: 5 No. excluded: 17
GMC	Term: 'genre+mutil' Most recent case: 30/05/2024 No. of results: 99 No. included: 18 No. excluded: 81	Term: 'gender+vermink' Most recent case: 06/05/2024 No. of results: 7 No. included: 2 No. excluded: 5	Search term: 'besnijdenis' Most recent case: 17/05/2024 No. of results: 38 (1–19 checked) No. included: 8 No. excluded: 30
DV	Term: 'genre+violence domestique' Most recent case: 30/05/2024 No. of results: 23 No. included: 16 No. excluded: 7	Term: 'gender+huiselijk geweld' Most recent case: 29/05/2024 No. of results: 38 No. included: 8 No. excluded: 30	/ (enough results for this type of violence in search round 1)
FM	Term: 'genre+mariage forcé' Most recent case: 30/05/2024 No. of results: 134 No. included: 21 No. excluded: 113	Term: 'gender+gedwongen huwelijk' Most recent case: 23/05/2024 No. of results: 15 No. included: 4 No. excluded: 11	Term: 'gedwongen+huwelijk' Most recent case: 23/05/2024 No. of results: 31 (1–15 checked) No. included: 12 No. excluded: 19

(continued)

VGNT	Term: 'genre+honte' Most recent case: 28/05/2024 No. of results: 59 No. included: 12 No. excluded: 47	Term: 'gender+schaamte' Most recent case: 14/05/2024 No. of results: 25 No. included: 3 No. excluded: 22	Search term: 'schaamte' Most recent case: 31/05/2024 No. of results: 152 (1–20 checked) No. included: 3 No. excluded: 149
SGBV in general	/	/	Term: 'gender' Most recent case: 31/05/2024 No. of results: 154 (1–20 checked) No. included: 4 No. excluded: 150
TOTAL CASES INCL.	(84 of which 49 overlapping) **35**	(20 of which 9 overlapping) 11	(39 of which 11 overlapping) 28
		(59 of which 23 overlapping) **39**	

C. CODE BOOK

Figure 44: Coding tree used for integrative analysis with NVivo

CODING category	Level	Scope	Myth	MA/MR
1. SGBV Mythology	1.1. Micro level	Disclosure myths	Delayed (disclosure in) asylum procedure	MA
				MR
			Inappropriate demeanour	MA
				MR
			Inconsistency	MA
				MR
			Level of detail	MA
				MR
			Other disclosure aspects	
		Resourceful-ness myths	Male SGBV victimisation	MA
				MR
			Resourcefulness	MA
				MR
			Other resourcefulness types	

(continued)

		Survival myths	Appease	MA
				MR
			Fight	MA
				MR
			Flight	MA
				MR
			Freeze	MA
				MR
			Other survival reactions	
	1.2. Meso & exo level	Non-state protection myths	Private support networks	MA
				MR
			Non-state actors of protection *sensu stricto*	MA
				MR
			Other non-state protection	
		State protection myth	(Reporting to actors of) state protection	MA
				MR
			Other state protection aspects	
	1.3. Macro level	Private issue myth	Qualifying SGBV as a private issue	MA
				MR
			Other macro level aspects	
2. SGBV type	GBV			DV
				FM
				VGNT
				Other GBV
	SV			GMC
				RSA
				STFP
				Other SV
	Male SGBV victimisation			
	SGBV along migration route			
3. Decision making attitudes	Empathic attitudes			
	Non-empathic attitudes			
	Other attitudes			
4. Decision making process	Asylum interview & hearing			
	Benefit of the doubt			
	Conflicting opinions & attitudes			
	Cumulative argumentation			
	Fast-track procedures			
	Gender POs at the CGRS			

(continued)

	Impact on applicants
	Istanbul Convention
	Opt-out option for gender cases
	Particular social group & other Convention grounds
	Previous persecution (incl. reversal of the burden of proof)
	Qualification of SGBV as a (separate) asylum motive
	Special procedural needs
	Uniform opinions & attitudes
	Other procedural aspects
5. Decision-making support	Gender guidelines
	Gender training and awareness raising
	Individual coping mechanisms
	Peer support
	Psychological support
	Quality control mechanisms
	Other support mechanisms

D. GEOGRAPHICAL CASE LAW SAMPLE DISTRIBUTION ACCORDING TO PROCEDURAL LANGUAGE AND SGBV TYPE

Figure 45: Geographical case law sample distribution according to procedural language and type of SGBV

Countries of origin	in Dutch	in French	RSA	STFP	GMC	VGNT	FM	DV
Afghanistan	6		6					2
Albania	12	2	10	2		10	8	14
Algeria		2	2			2		
Angola	2		2	2				
Benin		2			2		2	
Bolivia	2		2					2
Bosnia & Herzegovina	2		2	2				
Burkina Faso		2	2		2	2	2	2
Burundi		4	4					
The DRC		12	12			2	2	4
Ecuador	2		2					2
Eritrea	7		7	3			2	
Ethiopia	4		2	2			2	

(continued)

Gabon		6	6			2		
Georgia	18		10		2	4	4	13
Ghana	2		2				2	2
Guinea		34	24	4	24	18	32	26
Honduras	1		1					1
Iran	2					2	2	2
Iraq		2	2					2
Ivory Coast		6	4		4	6	2	4
Kenya	2		2			2	2	2
Liberia	4			2	2	2	4	2
Mauritania		2	2		2	2	2	2
Moldavia	2							2
Morocco	2	2	2			4	2	4
Nigeria	10	2	4	2	6	8	4	4
North-Macedonia	2		2			2		2
Palestine	2		2					
Russia	2		2			2		
Senegal		6	4		4	2	4	6
Serbia		2						2
Somalia	16		2		12	10	14	8
Suriname	2		2			2	2	2
Syria		2	2					
The Gambia		2					2	2
Turkey		6	6				4	
Uganda	2		2					
TOTAL	106	96	136	19	60	84	100	114

E. KAP SURVEYS (CALL IN DUTCH & FRENCH, CGRS IN DUTCH & FRENCH)[2534]

KAP Survey RvV (NL)

Deel	Vraag/mededeling
INLEIDING	Beste deelnemer,
Informed consent	Gelieve het document via onderstaande link grondig te lezen alvorens op volgende te klikken. *(link naar informatiefiche)*

(continued)

[2534] RvV & CGVS: CALL & CGRS in Dutch (NL), CCE & CGRA: CALL & CGRS in French (FR).

Informed consent	Deze enquête wordt **anoniem** afgenomen, waardoor uw antwoorden op geen enkele manier aan uw persoon kunnen worden gelinkt. U kunt ten allen tijde uw **deelname beëindigen**, door het invullen van de enquête (definitief) te onderbreken zonder opgave van enige reden. Indien u tijdens het invullen van de enquête **vragen** heeft over de inhoud ervan of het onderzoek in het algemeen, kunt u de enquête steeds (tijdelijk) onderbreken en contact opnemen via [Lore.Roels@UGent.be]. Gelieve onderstaande tekst aan te klikken om akkoord te gaan met deelname aan deze enquête.
	KNOP (verplicht vooraleer verder te gaan): Ik verklaar de informatiefiche doorgenomen en begrepen te hebben en stem op geïnformeerde wijze toe met deelname aan deze enquête
Structuur	Deze enquête bevat de volgende onderdelen: I. PERSOONLIJK PROFIEL II. KENNIS- EN ATTITUDEVRAGEN III. PRAKTIJKVRAGEN IV. DEELNAME INTERVIEWS (optioneel) Indien relevant, vindt u bovenaan elk onderdeel toelichting bij het soort vragen en hoe u hierop kunt antwoorden. Gebruikte afkortingen: – **SGG**: seksueel en gendergerelateerd geweld – **IB**: internationale bescherming – **VGV**: vrouwelijke genitale verminking – **RvV**: Raad voor Vreemdelingenbetwistingen In dit onderzoek verwijst de term "**SGG**" naar: 1) **seksueel geweld**: geweld van seksuele aard gericht naar een persoon om redenen die al dan niet verband houden met gender Bv. verkrachting, ongewenste seksuele toenadering, gedwongen verrichten van seksuele handelingen bij zichzelf of anderen, huiselijk geweld (seksueel), (mannelijke/vrouwelijke/intersekse) genitale verminking/besnijdenis, (mensenhandel met het oog op) seksuele uitbuiting, gedwongen gezinsplanning (gedwongen sterilisatie, gedwongen abortus, ontzegging van het recht op het gebruik van anticonceptie …), verplichte controles op maagdelijkheid … EN 2) **gendergerelateerd geweld**: geweld in welke vorm dan ook (behalve seksueel) gericht naar een persoon om redenen die verband houden met gender Bv. huiselijk geweld (niet-seksueel), gedwongen huwelijken (inclusief kindhuwelijken) of samenwonen (voorafgegaan door bruidsontvoering), geweld in verband met eer en gendernormen, femi(ni)cide …
I. PERSOONLIJK PROFIEL	I.0 Werkt u bij de RvV als rechter of als attaché? □ Rechter □ Attaché □ Anders, namelijk: […]
	I.1 In welk jaar bent u geboren? […]

(continued)

I.2 Hoe identificeert u zich? Als: (meerdere antwoordmogelijkheden)

- □ (Cis)* vrouw
- □ (Cis)* Man
- □ Non-binair** persoon
- □ Trans*** vrouw
- □ Trans*** man
- □ Inter(sekse)**** persoon
- □ Anders, namelijk: […]
- □ Zeg ik liever niet

* De term cis(gender) wil zeggen dat het geslacht dat je toegewezen krijgt bij je geboorte (op basis van je geslachtsdelen) overeenkomt met je genderidentiteit. Als je bij je geboorte het vrouwelijk geslacht krijgt toegewezen en je voelt je ook vrouw, dan noemt men dit cisgender.

** De term non-binair wil zeggen dat iemand zich niet herkent in de binaire opdeling van gender, de klassiek westerse tweedeling in man en vrouw, en alle verwachtingen en rollen die de binaire gendernormen daaraan koppelen.

*** De term trans(gender) wil zeggen dat het geslacht dat je toegewezen kreeg bij de geboorte niet overeenkomt met je genderidentiteit. Als je bij de geboorte het vrouwelijk geslacht krijgt toegewezen maar je voelt je een man, dan ben je een trans man.

**** De term inter(sekse) wil zeggen dat iemands fysieke geslachtskenmerken niet binnen de klassieke tweedeling M/V vallen.

Bron: www.cavaria.be/woordenlijst

I.3 Hoe lang werkt u reeds bij de RvV?

- □ 0–2 jaar
- □ 3–5 jaar
- □ 6–10 jaar
- □ 11–15 jaar
- □ 16–20 jaar
- □ 21–25 jaar
- □ 26–30 jaar
- □ 31–35 jaar
- □ 36–40 jaar
- □ 41– … jaar

I.4 Wat is uw hoogste opleidingsniveau?

- □ Middelbare school
- □ Hogeschool
- □ Universiteit
- □ Anders, namelijk: […]

I.5 In welke categorie plaatst u uw opleiding(en)? (meerdere antwoordmogelijkheden)

- □ **Recht en Criminologie** (incl. Rechten, Criminologie, Rechtspraktijk …)
- □ **Psychologie en Pedagogische Wetenschappen** (incl. Psychologie, (Ortho)pedagogie, Toegepaste psychologie, Sociaal(-Cultureel) werk, Maatschappelijk werk, Educatieve bachelor/master …)
- □ **Politieke en Sociale Wetenschappen** (incl. Politieke wetenschappen, Sociologie, EU-studies, Conflict & Development, Gender & Diversiteit, Communicatie(wetenschappen), Journalistiek …)

(continued)

	□ **Letteren en wijsbegeerte** (incl. Taal- en letterkunde, Toegepaste taalkunde, Tolk, Geschiedenis, Wijsbegeerte, Kunstwetenschappen, Afrikaanse/Oost-Europese/Oosterse talen en culturen ...) □ Anders, namelijk: [...]
	I.6 Hoe vaak komt u in aanraking met verzoeken om IB op grond van SGG? □ < 1 × per jaar □ Ca. 1 × per jaar □ Ca. 1 × per 6 maanden □ Ca. 1 × per 3 maanden □ Ca. 1 × per maand □ Ca. 1 × per week □ > 1 × per week
	I.7 Heeft u reeds opleidingen, trainings, workshops ... over gender (intern en/of extern) gevolgd in de afgelopen 5 jaar? Gelieve zowel de opleidingen in het kader van uw werk bij de RvV, als die in een eerdere beroepsactiviteit of andere context te vermelden. □ Ja, namelijk: [...] □ Nee
Identificatie-code	**I.8 Identificatiecode** Deze studie wil mogelijks verandering doorheen de tijd bestuderen. Daarom is het belangrijk dat we de antwoorden in de toekomst (vb. in een volgende vragenlijst) kunnen koppelen aan dezelfde persoon. We vragen u om enkele vragen te beantwoorden, waarmee we een **persoonlijke code** aanmaken. Deze code is uniek en laat ons toe om uw antwoorden aan elkaar te koppelen. We willen hierbij benadrukken dat **enkel de onderzoekers** deze code zullen kunnen raadplagen en dat het hierbij **onmogelijk** blijft om uw **identiteit** te achterhalen.
	Duid de EERSTE LETTER van je moeders VOORNAAM aan. Met moeder bedoelen we diegene die je 'moeder' noemt. Dit hoeft dus niet per definitie je biologische moeder te zijn. Duid XX aan indien je je moeder niet kent.
	Duid de EERSTE LETTER van je vaders VOORNAAM aan. Met vader bedoelen we diegene die je 'vader' noemt. Dit hoeft dus niet per definitie je biologische vader te zijn. Duid XX aan indien je je vader niet kent.
	Duid aan op welke DAG van de maand je GEBOREN bent. Duid XX aan indien je niet weet op welke dag van de maand je geboren bent.
	Duid de EERSTE LETTER van je VOORNAAM aan.
	Duid aan in welke MAAND je GEBOREN bent. Duid XX aan indien je niet weet in welke maand je bent geboren.
	Duid de EERSTE LETTER van je GEBOORTEPLAATS aan. Duid XX aan indien je je geboorteplaats niet kent.

(continued)

Mentaal welzijn	**I.9 Mentaal welzijn** In dit onderdeel peilen we naar mentaal welzijn in relatie tot uw werkinhoud en -omgeving. Gelieve aan te geven hoezeer u akkoord/niet akkoord gaat met volgende stellingen, waarbij de niveaus worden aangegeven als: **1 (helemaal niet akkoord)** tot 7 **(helemaal akkoord).**
	Mijn job houdt in dat ik word blootgesteld aan verontrustend materiaal en ervaringen.
	In mijn job word ik blootgesteld aan getraumatiseerde of verontruste verzoekers.
	Ik voel me verontrust als ik luister naar de verhalen en situaties van verzoekers.
	Ik vind het moeilijk om met de verhalen en situaties van verzoekers om te gaan.
	Ik denk thuis aan verontrustende verhalen en situaties waarmee ik tijdens mijn job in contact kwam.
	Soms voel ik me niet in staat om verzoekers bij te staan op de manier die ik zou willen.
	Soms voel ik me overweldigd door de werklast van mijn job.
	Het is moeilijk om positief en optimistisch te blijven, gezien sommige zaken waarmee ik in mijn job word geconfronteerd.
II. KENNIS- EN ATTITUDE-VRAGEN	In dit onderdeel peilen we naar kennis en attitudes over seksueel en gendergerelateerd geweld. Het is bij het invullen belangrijk dat u hier uw **persoonlijke mening** weergeeft. Gelieve aan te geven hoezeer u akkoord/niet akkoord gaat met volgende stellingen, waarbij de niveaus worden aangegeven als: **1 (helemaal niet akkoord)** tot 5 **(helemaal akkoord).**
II.1 Statistische gegevens met betrekking tot SGG	Wereldwijd **komt SGG** het meest **voor** in landen en regio's met lage en gemiddelde inkomens.
	Verzoekers om IB lopen een groter **risico op SGG** dan EU-burgers zonder nood aan IB.
	Seksueel geweld wordt meestal **gepleegd** door onbekenden.
II.2 Kwalificatie van (het risico op) SGG	Bij het beoordelen van de geloofwaardigheid van een vluchtverhaal over **seksueel geweld**, vind ik het relevant of het slachtoffer voordien vrijwillig **alcohol of drugs** had gebruikt.
	Bij het beoordelen van de geloofwaardigheid van een vluchtverhaal over **seksueel geweld**, vind ik het relevant of de dader **fysiek(e) bedreigingen of geweld** heeft gebruikt.
	Als er geen **lichamelijk letsel** kan worden vastgesteld, beoordeel ik een vluchtverhaal over **seksueel geweld** als <u>minder</u> geloofwaardig.
	Als er geen **beschadiging van het hymen*** kan worden vastgesteld, beoordeel ik een vluchtverhaal over **verkrachting** bij jonge vrouwen als <u>minder</u> geloofwaardig. * In de volksmond ook 'maagdenvlies' genoemd
	Bij het beoordelen van de geloofwaardigheid van een vrees voor **seksueel geweld**, vind ik het **geslacht van een verzoeker** relevant.

(continued)

	Bij het beoordelen van de geloofwaardigheid van een vrees voor **seksueel geweld**, vind ik het **geslacht van de potentiële dader** relevant.
	Bij het beoordelen van de geloofwaardigheid van een vrees voor **SGG** vind ik het **opleidingsniveau en de beroepservaring** van een verzoeker relevant.
	Bij het beoordelen van de geloofwaardigheid van een vrees voor **SGG** vind ik de **autonomie, maturiteit en assertiviteit** van een verzoeker relevant.
	Vormen van **SGG** die zich afspelen in de **privésfeer** vallen **buiten** het toepassingsgebied van de VN **Vluchtelingenconventie**.
II.3 Gedragingen van slachtoffers van SGG en hun omgeving	Als een verzoeker zich **emotieloos** gedraagt bij het terugdenken aan of praten over een vluchtverhaal over **SGG**, beoordeel ik dit als <u>minder</u> geloofwaardig.
	Als een verzoeker een vluchtverhaal over **SGG** niet **chronologisch** kan vertellen, beoordeel ik dit als <u>minder</u> geloofwaardig.
	Als een vluchtverhaal over **SGG inconsistenties** bevat, beoordeel ik dit als <u>minder</u> geloofwaardig.
	Als een verzoeker geen **contextuele details** kan geven bij een vluchtverhaal over **SGG**, beoordeel ik dit als <u>minder</u> geloofwaardig.
	Kinderen die niet aan **VGV** worden onderworpen in een gemeenschap waar dit de norm is, lopen het risico om **gestigmatiseerd en sociaal uitgesloten** te worden.
	Als een verzoeker met een vluchtverhaal over **seksueel geweld** niet heeft geprobeerd zich te **verweren of te vluchten**, beoordeel ik dit als <u>minder</u> geloofwaardig.
	Als een verzoeker met een vrees voor **SGG** dit niet zo snel mogelijk aan iemand heeft **verteld**, beoordeel ik dit als <u>minder</u> geloofwaardig.
	Als een verzoeker die beweert gerekruteerd te zijn door een **netwerk voor seksuele uitbuiting** nooit heeft geprobeerd te **ontsnappen**, beoordeel ik dit als <u>minder</u> geloofwaardig.
	Als een verzoeker met een vluchtverhaal over **huiselijk geweld** nooit hebben geprobeerd **tegen te spreken of terug te vechten**, beoordeel ik dit als <u>minder</u> geloofwaardig.
	Als een verzoeker met een vrees voor **SGG** dit niet zo snel mogelijk aan de lokale autoriteiten heeft **aangegeven**, beoordeel ik dit als <u>minder</u> geloofwaardig.
	Als een **mannelijke** verzoeker met een vrees voor **seksueel geweld** (door een man) in een land waar **homoseksualiteit strafbaar** is dit niet zo snel mogelijk aan de lokale autoriteiten heeft **aangegeven**, beoordeel ik dit als <u>minder</u> geloofwaardig.
	Als een verzoeker met een vrees voor **SGG** dit niet in het eerste **interview** met de (asiel)autoriteiten heeft **verteld**, beoordeel ik dit als <u>minder</u> geloofwaardig.
	Als een verzoeker met een vrees voor **SGG** niet zo snel mogelijk na aankomst een **verzoek om IB** heeft ingediend, beoordeel ik dit als <u>minder</u> geloofwaardig.
	Als ouders zich openlijk **tegen VGV** durven **uitspreken**, zouden zij de **druk** van de gemeenschap om hun kinderen aan VGV te onderwerpen ook moeten kunnen **weerstaan**.

(continued)

II.4 Bewijs-materiaal in de procedure om IB op grond van SGG	Bij een vrees voor **SGG** zijn de **soorten bewijs** die gebruikelijk zijn in verzoekprocedures om IB minder gemakkelijk beschikbaar dan bij andere vervolgingsvormen.
	Als het risico op **SGG** niet in de relevante **landeninformatie** terug te vinden is, beoordeel ik een vrees voor dit soort SGG als minder geloofwaardig.
II.5 Bescherming tegen SGG in het land van oorsprong	Als een verzoeker met vrees voor een **strafbare vorm van SGG** nooit ter plaatse **aangifte** heeft gedaan, kan deze geen beroep doen op een gebrek aan bescherming (in de zin van de VN Vluchtelingenconventie).
	Staatsbescherming tegen SGG moet worden gezien als een **resultaatsverbintenis**, eerder dan een middelenverbintenis.
	Als een verzoeker met vrees voor **SGG** nooit heeft geprobeerd om bij (mannelijke) **familieleden/kennissen bescherming** te zoeken, kan deze geen beroep doen op een gebrek aan bescherming (in de zin van de VN Vluchtelingenconventie).
	Als een verzoeker met vrees voor **SGG** nooit heeft geprobeerd om zichzelf te beschermen door bijvoorbeeld **publieke plaatsen te mijden**, kan deze geen beroep doen op een gebrek aan bescherming (in de zin van de VN Vluchtelingenconventie).
	Als een verzoeker met een vrees voor **huiselijk geweld** nooit heeft geprobeerd om de **relatie te verlaten** en te verhuizen, kan deze geen beroep doen op een gebrek aan bescherming (in de zin van de VN Vluchtelingenconventie).
	Bij het beoordelen van een intern beschermingsalternatief tegen **SGG** vind ik het relevant of de **beschermende actor** (een substantieel deel van) de **staat controleert**.
	Bij het beoordelen van een intern beschermingsalternatief tegen **SGG** vind ik het relevant of er plaatselijke SGG-gerelateerde **NGO's** zijn.
	Bij het beoordelen van een intern beschermingsalternatief tegen **SGG** vind ik de beschikbaarheid van (mannelijke) **private ondersteuningsnetwerken** van een verzoeker relevant.
	Bij het beoordelen van een intern beschermingsalternatief tegen **SGG** vind ik de **sociale en financiële ondersteuning** (door het persoonlijk netwerk) van een verzoeker relevant.
	Bescherming (in de zin van de VN Vluchtelingenconventie) tegen **SGG** kan enkel worden geboden door een **doeltreffend juridisch systeem** dat dergelijke daden cumulatief opspoort, vervolgt en bestraft.
II.6 Juridisch kader van de procedure om IB op grond van SGG	De Belgische asielautoriteiten zijn verplicht om ervoor te zorgen dat **SGG** kan worden **erkend** als een vorm van **vervolging**.
	De Belgische asielautoriteiten zijn verplicht om een verzoek om IB **gendersensitief** te **beoordelen**.
Feedback-optie	Bent u van mening dat de vraagstelling in dit onderdeel u verhinderde om bepaalde nuances mee te geven? U vindt hieronder ruimte om deze (of andere) feedback aan ons mee te delen. [...]

(continued)

III. PRAKTIJKVRAGEN	Dit onderdeel peilt naar praktijken tijdens de procedure om IB op grond van SGG. Het is bij het invullen belangrijk dat u hier uw **persoonlijke mening/ervaring** weergeeft.
III.1 Praktijken in de procedure om IB op grond van SGG	Gelieve aan te geven hoezeer u akkoord/niet akkoord gaat met volgende stellingen, waarbij de niveaus worden aangegeven als: **1 (helemaal niet akkoord)** tot **5 (helemaal akkoord).**
	Ik heb toegang tot voldoende gespecialiseerde **opleidingen** om accuraat **om te gaan met verklaringen** van SGG tijdens een zitting.
	Ik beschik over voldoende **vaardigheden** om accuraat te **reageren op verklaringen** van SGG.
	Ik beschik over voldoende **vaardigheden** om **gepaste vragen** te stellen die tot relevante verklaringen van SGG kunnen leiden.
	Ik beschik over voldoende **vaardigheden en mogelijkheden** om tegemoet te komen aan de **bijzondere procedurele noden** van verzoekers met SGG-gerelateerde vluchtverhalen.
	Ik heb toegang tot voldoende gespecialiseerde **opleidingen** om verzoeken om IB op grond van SGG accuraat te kunnen **beoordelen.**
	Ik heb voldoende **kennis** om verzoeken om IB op grond van SGG accuraat te kunnen **beoordelen.**
	Ik heb toegang tot **psychologische begeleiding** binnen mijn werkomgeving **als ik dit wens.**
	Ik ben **verplicht** om **psychologisch begeleid** te worden binnen mijn werkomgeving.
III.2 Betrokkenheid bij het thema van SGG (in de procedure om IB)	Hoe vaak **denkt u na** over de onderwerpen die in deze enquête aan bod komen, namelijk SGG in de procedure om IB? 1 **(helemaal niet vaak)** tot 5 **(zeer vaak)**
	Hoe snel komt uw **eigen mening** tegenover deze kwesties naar voren wanneer u dergelijke vragen moet beantwoorden? 1 **(helemaal niet snel)** tot 5 **(zeer snel)**
	Heeft u over deze onderwerpen een **uitgesproken mening?** 1 **(helemaal niet uitgesproken)** tot 5 **(zeer uitgesproken)**
	Hoe **belangrijk** is uw mening over deze onderwerpen voor u? 1 **(helemaal niet belangrijk)** tot 5 **(zeer belangrijk)**
	Hoe **zeker** bent u van uw mening over deze kwesties? 1 **(helemaal niet zeker)** tot 5 **(zeer zeker)**
	Voelt u zich over deze onderwerpen eerder goed of slecht **geïnformeerd?** 1 **(helemaal niet geïnformeerd)** tot 5 **(zeer geïnformeerd)**
	Hoeveel **weet** u over deze onderwerpen? 1 **(helemaal niet veel)** tot 5 **(zeer veel)**
	De onderwerpen die in deze enquête aan bod komen **belangen mij persoonlijk aan.** 1 **(helemaal niet akkoord)** tot 5 **(helemaal akkoord)**

(continued)

Feedback-optie	Bent u van mening dat de vraagstelling in dit onderdeel u verhinderde om bepaalde nuances mee te geven? U vindt hieronder ruimte om deze (of andere) feedback aan ons mee te delen. [...]
IV. DEELNAME INTERVIEWS (optioneel)	IV. DEELNAME INTERVIEWS (optioneel) Als u in een later stadium via een interview **uitgebreidere vragen over het thema** van deze studie wilt beantwoorden via een **interview**, kunt u uw **e-mailadres opgeven** door op de blauwe pijl onderaan te klikken. Deze enquête wordt dan afgesloten en u zal worden doorgestuurd naar een nieuwe pagina. De antwoorden in uw enquête blijven anoniem en zullen op geen enkele manier kunnen worden gelinkt aan dit e-mailadres. U zal hierover in een later stadium van het onderzoek worden gecontacteerd.
SLOT	U kunt steeds bijkomende vragen stellen via [Lore.Roels@UGent.be] over uw deelname. Als u specifieke vragen heeft over de bescherming van uw persoonsgegevens, kunt u altijd contact opnemen met de Functionaris Gegevensbescherming van de Universiteit Gent via [Privacy@UGent.be]. **Hartelijk bedankt voor het invullen van deze enquête!** Lore Roels (onderzoeker) Prof. Dr. Ellen Desmet (promotor) Prof. Dr. Ines Keygnaert (copromotor)
END OF SURVEY	[Link naar aparte survey voor contactgegevens] Dit onderzoek bevat in een latere fase de optie om uitgebreidere vragen over het thema van dit onderzoek te beantwoorden in de vorm van een **interview**. Het is belangrijk te vermelden dat een uitnodiging voor deze interviews **niet gegarandeerd** is. Na het analyseren van de enquêteresultaten zullen de onderzoekers samen met de RvV besluiten of en hoeveel gesprekken worden ingepland. Duid aan welke opties voor u van toepassing zijn. □ Ik wens mij kandidaat te stellen voor de vervolginterviews (zonder garantie tot uitnodiging) □ Ik wens mij geen kandidaat te stellen Om u te kunnen contacteren vragen we u hieronder **een e-mailadres** door te geven. Dit zal enkel gebruikt worden voor het plannen van de interviews en zal na afloop worden verwijderd. [ ] Het e-mailadres wordt **los van uw antwoorden** opgeslagen. Daarom werd u nu doorverwezen naar een aparte webpagina. Het is voor de onderzoekers dus niet mogelijk om uw antwoorden in de enquête te koppelen aan uw e-mailadres. Voor meer informatie over de bescherming van uw contactgegevens kan u contact opnemen met de Functionaris Gegevensbescherming van de Universiteit Gent via [Privacy@UGent.be]. **Hartelijk bedankt voor uw bereidwillige deelname!** Lore Roels (onderzoeker) Prof. Dr. Ellen Desmet (promotor) Prof. Dr. Ines Keygnaert (copromotor)

KAP Survey CCE (FR)

PARTIE	Question/information
INTRO Consentement informé	Cher·ère participant·e, Veuillez lire attentivement le document accessible via le lien ci-dessous avant de cliquer sur "Suivant". *(Lien vers la fiche d'information)*
Consentement informé	Cette enquête est **anonyme** : vos réponses ne peuvent en aucun cas être reliées à votre personne. Vous pouvez mettre **fin à votre participation** à tout moment, en interrompant (définitivement) l'enquête, sans donner de raison. Si, pendant que vous répondez à l'enquête, vous avez des **questions** sur son contenu ou sur l'enquête en général, vous pouvez toujours interrompre (temporairement) l'enquête et nous contacter à l'adresse électronique suivante : [Lore.Roels@UGent.be]. Veuillez cliquer sur le texte ci-dessous pour accepter de participer à cette enquête.
	BOUTON (requis avant de poursuivre) : Je déclare avoir lu et compris la fiche d'information et consens à participer à cette enquête de manière informée.
Structure	Cette enquête se divise comme suit : V. PROFIL PERSONNEL VI. QUESTIONS SUR LES CONNAISSANCES ET LES ATTITUDES VII. QUESTIONS SUR LES PRATIQUES VIII. PARTICIPATION AUX INTERVIEWS (facultatif) Le cas échéant, vous trouverez en haut de chaque section des explications sur le type de questions et la manière d'y répondre. Abréviations utilisées : – **VSS** : violence sexuelle et sexiste – **PI** : protection internationale – **MGF** : mutilation génitale féminine – **CCE** : Conseil du Contentieux des Etrangers Dans cette étude, le terme "VSS" fait référence à : 3) **violence sexuelle :** violence de nature sexuelle orientée vers une personne pour des raisons liées ou non au genre. Par exemple, le viol, les avances sexuelles non désirées, l'exécution forcée d'actes sexuels sur soi-même ou sur d'autres personnes, la violence domestique (sexuelle), les circoncisions/mutilations génitales (masculines/féminines/intersexuelles), (la traite des êtres humains à des fins d')exploitation sexuelle, la planification familiale forcée (stérilisation forcée, avortement forcé, déni du droit d'utiliser des moyens de contraception …), les contrôles de virginité obligatoires … ET 4) **violence sexiste :** toute forme de violence (autre que sexuelle) orientée vers une personne pour des raisons liées au genre. Par exemple, la violence domestique (non sexuelle), le mariage (y compris le mariage d'enfants) ou la cohabitation forcés (précédés d'enlèvement), la violence liée à l'honneur et aux normes de genre, le femi(ni)cide …

(continued)

I. PROFIL PERSONNEL	I.0 Travaillez-vous au CCE en tant que juge ou attaché ? □ Juge □ Attaché □ Autre, notamment : […]
	I.1 Quelle est votre année de naissance ? […]
	I.2 Comment vous identifiez-vous ? Comme : (possibilité de réponses multiples) □ Femme (cis)* □ Homme (cis)* □ Personne non-binaire** □ Femme trans*** □ Homme trans*** □ Personne inter(sexe)**** □ Autre, notamment : … □ Je préfère ne pas réponde à cette question * Le terme cis(genre) signifie que le sexe qui vous a été attribué à la naissance (en fonction de vos organes génitaux) correspond à votre identité de genre. Si l'on vous attribue le sexe féminin à la naissance et que vous vous sentez également de sexe féminin, on dira que vous êtes cisgenre. ** Le terme "non-binaire" signifie que quelqu'un ne se reconnaît pas dans la division binaire du genre (la division occidentale classique entre homme et femme), et toutes les attentes et rôles que les normes de genre binaires y attachent. *** Le terme trans(genre) signifie que le sexe qui vous a été attribué à la naissance ne correspond pas à votre identité de genre. Si l'on vous a assigné le sexe féminin à la naissance mais que vous vous sentez homme, vous êtes un homme trans. **** Le terme inter(sexe) signifie que les caractéristiques sexuelles physiques d'une personne ne correspondent pas à la dichotomie classique H/F. Source: https://www.cavaria.be/woordenlijst
	I.3 Depuis combien de temps travaillez-vous au CCE ? □ 0–2 ans □ 3–5 ans □ 6–10 ans □ 11–15 ans □ 16–20 ans □ 21–25 ans □ 26–30 ans □ 31–35 ans □ 36–40 ans □ 41– … ans
	I.4 Quel est votre plus haut niveau d'éducation ? □ École secondaire □ Haute école spécialisée □ Université □ Autre·s, notamment : […]

(continued)

	I.5 Dans laquelle de ces catégories situez-vous votre·vos formation·s ? (Possibilité de réponses multiples) □ **Droit et Criminologie** (y.c. Droit, Criminologie, Pratique juridique …) □ **Psychologie et Sciences de l'Education** (y.c. Psychologie, (Ortho) pédagogie, Psychologie appliquée, Travail Social (Culturel), Travail Communautaire, Licence/Master en sciences de l'Education …) □ **Sciences Politiques et Sociales** (y.c. Sciences Politiques, Sociologie, Etudes Européennes, Conflit et Développement, Genre et Diversité, (Sciences de) Communication, Journalisme …) □ **Littérature et Philosophie** (y.c. Langue et Littérature, Linguistique Appliquée, Interprète, Histoire, Philosophie, Etudes Artistiques, Langues et Cultures Africaines/Orientales/d'Europe de l'Est …) □ Autre·s, notamment:
	I.6 À quelle fréquence rencontrez-vous des demandes de PI fondées sur la VSS ? □ < 1 × par an □ Env. 1 × par an □ Env. 1 × par 6 mois □ Env. 1 × par 3 mois □ Env. 1 × par mois □ Env. 1 × par semaine □ > 1 × par semaine
	I.7 Avez-vous déjà participé à des cours, formations, ateliers … sur le genre (interne et/ou externe) lors des 5 dernières années ? Veuillez mentionner à la fois les formations dans le cadre de votre travail au CCE, et celles dans le cadre d'une activité professionnelle antérieure ou dans un autre contexte. □ Oui, notamment : […] □ Non
Code d'identification	**I.8 Code d'identification** Cette étude veut évaluer les éventuelles évolutions dans le temps. Il est donc important que nous puissions toujours relier les réponses à la même personne (par exemple, dans un éventuel futur questionnaire). Nous vous demandons de répondre à quelques questions, que nous utilisons pour créer un **code personnel**. Ce code est unique et nous permet de relier vos réponses. Nous tenons à souligner que seuls les chercheurs seront en mesure de consulter ce code et qu'il sera **impossible** de découvrir votre **identité**.
	Indiquez la PREMIÈRE LETTRE du prénom de votre mère. Par mère, nous entendons la personne que vous appelez "mère". Il ne s'agit pas nécessairement de votre mère biologique. Indiquez XX si vous ne connaissez pas votre mère.
	Indiquez la PREMIÈRE LETTRE du prénom de votre père. Par père, nous entendons la personne que vous appelez "père". Il ne s'agit pas nécessairement de votre père biologique. Indiquez XX si vous ne connaissez pas votre père.

(continued)

	Indiquez le JOUR du mois où vous êtes né·e (en chiffres). Indiquez XX si vous ne savez pas quel jour du mois vous êtes né.
	Indiquez la PREMIÈRE LETTRE de votre PRENOM.
	Indiquez le MOIS où vous êtes né·e. Indiquez XX si vous ne savez pas quel est le mois de votre naissance.
	Indiquez la PREMIÈRE LETTRE de votre LIEU DE NAISSANCE. Indiquez XX si vous ne connaissez pas votre lieu de naissance.
Bien-être mental	**I.9 Bien-être mental** Dans cette section, nous nous intéressons au bien-être mental en relation avec le contenu et l'environnement de votre travail. Veuillez indiquer dans quelle mesure vous êtes d'accord/en désaccord avec les déclarations suivantes, les niveaux étant indiqués comme suit : **1 (pas du tout d'accord) à 7 (tout à fait d'accord).**
	Mon travail implique une exposition à des **matériaux et des expériences perturbants.**
	Dans mon travail, je suis exposé·e à des **demandeurs·euses traumatisés·ées ou en détresse.**
	Je me **sens troublé·e** en écoutant les histoires et les situations des demandeurs·euses.
	Je **trouve difficile de faire face** aux histoires et situations des demandeurs·euses.
	A la maison, je repense à des histoires et des situations perturbantes auxquelles j'ai été en confronté·e pendant mon travail.
	Parfois, je me sens **incapable d'aider les demandeurs·euses** comme je le souhaiterais.
	Parfois, je me **sens dépassé·e** par la charge de travail de mon travail.
	Il est **difficile de rester positif·ve et optimiste**, étant donné certains des sujets auxquels je suis confronté·e dans mon travail.
II. QUESTIONS SUR LES CONNAIS-SANCES ET LES ATTITUDES	Dans cette section, nous évaluons les connaissances et les attitudes concernant la VSS. Il est important que vous reflétiez ici votre **opinion personnelle** lorsque vous remplissez le formulaire. Veuillez indiquer dans quelle mesure vous êtes d'accord/en désaccord avec les déclarations suivantes, les niveaux étant indiqués comme suit : **1 (pas du tout d'accord) à 5 (tout à fait d'accord).**
II.1 Statistiques en rapport ayant VSS	Au niveau mondial, la **VSS** est plus **fréquente** dans les pays et régions à revenu faible ou intermédiaire.
	Les demandeurs·euses de PI sont plus exposés·ées au **risque de VSS** que les citoyens de l'UE qui n'ont pas besoin de PI.
	La violence sexuelle est généralement **commise** par des inconnus
II.2 Qualification (du risque) de la VSS	Pour évaluer la crédibilité d'un récit de fuite fondé sur la **violence sexuelle**, je trouve pertinent de savoir si la victime avait déjà consommé de **l'alcool** ou de **la drogue** de façon volontaire auparavant.
	Pour évaluer la crédibilité d'un récit de fuite fondé sur la **violence sexuelle**, je trouve pertinent de savoir si l'auteur a recouru à des **menaces ou des violences physiques**.

(continued)

	Si aucune **blessure physique** ne peut être établie, je considère un récit de fuite fondé sur la **violence sexuelle** comme moins crédible.
	Si aucune blessure **à l'hymen** ne peut être identifiée, je considère un récit de fuite fondé sur le **viol** chez une jeune femme comme moins crédible.
	Pour évaluer la crédibilité d'une crainte fondée sur la **violence sexuelle**, je trouve que le **sexe du/de la demandeur·euse** est un élément pertinent.
	Pour évaluer la crédibilité d'une crainte fondée sur la **violence sexuelle**, je trouve que le **sexe de l'auteur potentiel** est un élément pertinent.
	Pour évaluer la crédibilité d'une crainte fondée sur la **VSS**, je trouve que le **niveau d'éducation et l'expérience professionnelle** du/de la demandeur·euse sont des éléments pertinents.
	Pour évaluer la crédibilité d'une crainte fondée sur la **VSS**, je trouve que **l'autonomie, la maturité et l'assertivité** du/de la demandeur·euse sont des éléments pertinents.
	Les formes de **VSS** qui ont lieu dans **la sphère privée** ne relèvent **pas** du champ d'application de la **Convention des Nations Unies sur les Réfugiés.**
II.3 Comporte-ments attendus des victimes de VSS et de leur environ-nement	Si un·e demandeur·euse se comporte **sans émotion** lorsqu'il/elle se rappelle ou parle d'un récit de fuite fondé sur la **VSS**, je considère le récit comme moins crédible.
	Si un·e demandeur·euse ne peuvent pas raconter un récit de fuite fondé sur la **VSS** de manière **chronologique**, je considère le récit comme moins crédible.
	Si un récit de fuite fondé sur la **VSS** contient des **incohérences**, je le considère comme moins crédible.
	Si un·e demandeur·euse ne peut pas donner des **détails contextuels** d'un récit de fuite fondé sur la **VSS**, je considère le récit comme moins crédible.
	Les enfants qui ne sont pas soumis aux **MGF** dans une communauté où cela est la norme risquent d'être **stigmatisés et exclus socialement.**
	Si un·e demandeur·euse présentant un récit de fuite fondé sur la **violence sexuelle** n'a pas essayé de **se défendre ou de fuir**, je considère le récit comme moins crédible.
	Si un·e demandeur·euse craignant la **VSS** ne l'a pas **dit** à quelqu'un dès que possible, je considère le récit comme moins crédible.
	Si un·e demandeur·euse déclarant avoir été recruté·e dans un **réseau d'exploitation sexuelle** n'a jamais essayé de **s'échapper**, je considère le récit comme moins crédible.
	Si un·e demandeur·euse présentant un récit de fuite fondé sur la **violence domestique** n'a jamais essayé de **contester le traitement subi** ou de se **défendre**, je considère le récit comme moins crédible.
	Si un·e demandeur·euse craignant la **VSS** ne l'a pas **signalé aux autorités locales** dès que possible, je considère le récit comme moins crédible.
	Si un demandeur craignant la **violence sexuelle** dans un pays où l'homosexualité est punissable ne l'a pas **signalé aux autorités locales** dès que possible, je considère le récit comme moins crédible.
	Si un·e demandeur·euse craignant la **VSS** n'a pas **signalé** les faits de VSS subis aux autorités (d'asile) lors du premier **entretien**, je considère le récit comme moins crédible.

(continued)

	Si un·e demandeur·euse craignant la **VSS** n'a pas **demandé de la PI** dès que possible après son arrivée, je considère le récit comme <u>moins</u> crédible.
	Si les parents osent **s'exprimer** ouvertement **contre les MGF**, ils devraient également être en mesure de résister aux **pressions** de la communauté pour que leurs enfants y soient soumis.
II.4 Preuves dans les procédures de PI fondées sur la VSS	En cas de crainte de **VSS**, les **types de preuves** qui sont couramment utilisés dans les procédures de PI sont <u>moins</u> faciles à obtenir que dans le cas d'autres formes de persécution.
	Si le risque de **VSS** n'est pas mentionné dans les **informations** pertinentes **sur les pays d'origine**, je considère le récit d'un·e demandeur·euse craignant ce type de VSS comme <u>moins</u> crédible.
II.5 Protection contre la VSS dans le pays d'origine	Si un·e demandeur·euse craignant **une forme punissable de VSS** n'a jamais déposé de **plainte** sur place, il/elle ne peut <u>pas</u> prétendre à un manque de protection (au sens de la Convention des Nations Unies sur les Réfugiés).
	La protection de l'État contre la VSS doit être considérée comme une **obligation de résultat** plutôt qu'une obligation de **moyens**.
	Si un·e demandeur·euse craignant la **VSS** n'a jamais essayé de déménager chez des **membres de la famille/connaissances** (masculins) pour se protéger, il/elle ne peut <u>pas</u> prétendre à un manque de protection (au sens de la Convention des Nations Unies sur les Réfugiés).
	Si un·e demandeur·euse craignant la **VSS** n'a jamais essayé de se protéger, par exemple en **évitant les lieux publics**, il/elle ne peut pas prétendre à un manque de protection (au sens de la Convention des Nations Unies sur les Réfugiés).
	Si un·e demandeur·euse craignant la **violence domestique** n'a jamais essayé de **quitter la relation** et de déménager, il/elle ne peut <u>pas</u> prétendre à un manque de protection (au sens de la Convention des Nations Unies sur les Réfugiés).
	Pour évaluer la protection potentielle (au sens de la Convention des Nations Unies sur les Réfugiés) contre la **VSS**, je trouve pertinent de savoir si **l'acteur de protection contrôle** (une partie substantielle de) **l'État**.
	Pour évaluer une possibilité de protection interne contre la **VSS**, je trouve que l'existence et la disponibilité des **ONG** locales actives en matière de VSS est un élément pertinent.
	Pour évaluer une possibilité de protection interne contre la **VSS**, je trouve que l'existence et la disponibilité de **réseaux de soutien privés** (masculins) d'un·e demandeur·euse est un élément pertinent.
	Pour évaluer une possibilité de protection interne contre la **VSS**, je trouve que le **soutien social et financier** (par le réseau privé) d'un·e demandeur·euse est un élément pertinent.
	La protection (au sens de la Convention des Nations Unies sur les Réfugiés) contre la **VSS** ne peut être assurée que par un **système juridique efficace** qui, de manière cumulative, détecte, poursuit et punit de tels actes.
II.6 Cadre juridique de la procédure de demande de PI fondée sur la VSS	Les autorités d'asile belges sont tenues de veiller à ce que la **VSS** puisse être **reconnue** comme une forme de persécution.
	Les autorités d'asile belges sont tenues **d'évaluer** une demande de PI en tenant compte de la **dimension de genre**.

(continued)

Option de feedback	Avez-vous l'impression que les questions de cette section vous ont empêché de fournir certaines nuances ? Vous trouverez ci-dessous un espace pour nous communiquer vos éventuelles remarques à cet égard. […]
III. QUESTIONS SUR LES PRATIQUES	Cette section examine les pratiques au cours de la procédure de PI fondée sur la VSS. En le complétant, il est important que vous reflétiez ici votre **opinion/expérience personnelle**.
III.1 Pratiques dans les procédures de PI fondées sur la VSS	Veuillez indiquer dans quelle mesure vous êtes d'accord/en désaccord avec les déclarations suivantes, les niveaux étant indiqués comme suit : **1 (pas du tout d'accord) à 5 (tout à fait d'accord).**
	J'ai accès à des **formations** spécialisées suffisantes pour **réagir** adéquatement **aux déclarations** de VSS lors d'une audition.
	Je dispose de **compétences** suffisantes pour **réagir** adéquatement **aux déclarations** de VSS lors d'une audition.
	Je dispose de **compétences** suffisantes pour poser des **questions appropriées** qui peuvent conduire à des déclarations pertinentes de VSS.
	Je dispose de **compétences** suffisantes pour répondre aux **besoins procéduraux spéciaux** des demandeurs·euses ayant des récits de fuite fondé sur la VSS.
	J'ai accès à des **formations** spécialisées suffisantes pour **évaluer** correctement les demandes de PI fondées sur la VSS.
	Je dispose de **connaissances** suffisantes pour **évaluer** correctement les demandes de PI fondées sur la VSS.
	J'ai accès à des **services de soutien psychologique** dans mon environnement de travail **si je le souhaite**.
	Je suis **tenu·e de** recevoir un **soutien psychologique** dans mon environnement de travail.
III.2 Engagement sur le thème de la VSS (dans les procédures de PI)	À quelle fréquence **pensez**-vous aux sujets abordés dans cette enquête, notamment la VSS dans la procédure de PI ? 1 **(pas du tout souvent)** à 5 **(très souvent)**
	À quelle vitesse votre **propre opinion** sur ces sujets émerge-t-elle lorsque vous devez répondre à de telles questions ? 1 **(pas du tout vite)** à 5 **(très vite)**
	Avez-vous des **opinions tranchées** sur ces sujets ? 1 **(pas du tout tranchées)** à 5 **(très tranchées)**
	Quelle est **l'importance** pour vous de vos opinions sur ces sujets ? 1 **(pas du tout important)** à 5 **(très important)**
	Dans quelle mesure êtes-vous **sûr·e** de votre opinion sur ces sujets ? 1 **(pas du tout sûr·e)** à 5 **(très sûr·e)**
	Êtes-vous plus susceptible de vous sentir bien ou mal **informé·e** sur ces sujets ? 1 **(pas du tout informé·e)** à 5 **(très informé·e)**
	Que **savez**-vous à propos de ces sujets ? 1 **(très peu)** à 5 **(beaucoup)**
	Les sujets soulevés ci-dessus **me touchent personnellement.** 1 **(pas du tout d'accord)** à 5 **(tout à fait d'accord)**

(continued)

Option de feedback	Avez-vous l'impression que les questions de cette section vous ont empêché de fournir certaines nuances ? Vous trouverez ci-dessous un espace pour nous communiquer vos éventuelles remarques à cet égard. [...]
IV. PARTICI-PATION AUX INTERVIEWS (facultatif)	IV. PARTICIPATION AUX ENTRETIENS (facultatif) Si vous souhaitez répondre à **des questions plus approfondies sur le sujet de cette étude,** à un stade ultérieur, dans le cadre **d'un entretien**, vous pouvez fournir votre **adresse électronique** en cliquant sur la flèche bleue en bas de la page. Cette enquête sera ensuite fermée et vous serez redirigé·e vers une nouvelle page. Les réponses à cette enquête resteront anonymes et ne pourront en aucun cas être reliées à votre adresse électronique. Vous serez contacté·e pour l'entretien à un stade ultérieur de la recherche.
FIN	Vous pouvez toujours poser des questions supplémentaires concernant votre participation à [Lore.Roels@UGent.be]. Si vous avez des questions spécifiques sur la protection de vos données personnelles, vous pouvez toujours contacter le délégué à la protection des données de l'Université de Gand à l'adresse électronique suivante : [Privacy@UGent.be]. **Merci beaucoup d'avoir répondu à cette enquête !** Lore Roels (chercheuse) Prof. Dr. Ellen Desmet (superviseure) Prof. Dr. Ines Keygnaert (co-superviseure)
FIN DE L'ENQUÊTE	[Lien vers une enquête séparée pour les coordonnées] Dans le cadre de cette enquête, nous offrons la possibilité de répondre à **des questions plus approfondies sur le thème de l'étude** à un stade ultérieur dans le cadre **d'un entretien.** Il est important de noter qu'une invitation à ces entretiens n'est **pas garantie**. Après avoir analysé les résultats de l'enquête, les chercheurs décideront, en collaboration avec le CCE, si et combien d'entretiens seront prévus. Veuillez indiquer les options qui vous concernent. □ Je souhaite participer aux entretiens de suivi (sans garantie d'invitation). □ Je ne souhaite pas participer aux entretiens de suivi Pour vous contacter, nous vous demandons de fournir **une adresse électronique** ci-dessous. Ces données ne seront utilisées que pour planifier les entretiens et seront supprimées par la suite. [ ] L'adresse électronique est conservée séparément de vos réponses. Par conséquent, vous avez été redirigé vers une page Web distincte. Il n'est donc pas possible pour les chercheurs d'établir un lien entre vos réponses à l'enquête et votre adresse électronique. Pour plus d'informations sur la protection de vos coordonnées, veuillez contacter le délégué à la protection des données de l'Université de Gand à l'adresse suivante : [Privacy@UGent.be]. **Merci beaucoup pour votre participation volontaire** ! Lore Roels (chercheuse) Prof. Dr. Ellen Desmet (superviseure) Prof. Dr. Ines Keygnaert (co-superviseure)

KAP Survey CGVS (NL)

<table>
<tr><th>Deel</th><th>Vraag/mededeling</th></tr>
<tr><td>INLEIDING

Informed consent</td><td>Beste deelnemer,

Gelieve het document via onderstaande link grondig te lezen alvorens op volgende te klikken.

(Link naar informatiefiche)</td></tr>
<tr><td>Informed consent</td><td>Deze enquête wordt anoniem afgenomen, waardoor uw antwoorden op geen enkele manier aan uw persoon kunnen worden gelinkt.

U kunt ten allen tijde uw deelname beëindigen, door het invullen van de enquête (definitief) te onderbreken zonder opgave van enige reden.

Indien u tijdens het invullen van de enquête vragen heeft over de inhoud ervan of het onderzoek in het algemeen, kunt u de enquête steeds (tijdelijk) onderbreken en contact opnemen via [Lore.Roels@UGent.be].

Gelieve onderstaande tekst aan te klikken om akkoord te gaan met deelname aan deze enquête.</td></tr>
<tr><td></td><td>KNOP (verplicht vooraleer verder te gaan): Ik verklaar de informatiefiche doorgenomen en begrepen te hebben en stem op geïnformeerde wijze toe met deelname aan deze enquête</td></tr>
<tr><td></td><td>Deze enquête bevat de volgende onderdelen:
IX. PERSOONLIJK PROFIEL
X. KENNIS- EN ATTITUDEVRAGEN
XI. PRAKTIJKVRAGEN
XII. DEELNAME INTERVIEWS (optioneel)

Indien relevant, vindt u bovenaan elk onderdeel toelichting bij het soort vragen en hoe u hierop kunt antwoorden.

Gebruikte afkortingen:
- SGG: seksueel en gendergerelateerd geweld
- IB: internationale bescherming
- VGV: vrouwelijke genitale verminking
- CGVS: Commissariaat-Generaal voor de Vluchtelingen en de Staatlozen

In dit onderzoek verwijst de term “SGG” naar:
5) seksueel geweld: geweld van seksuele aard gericht naar een persoon om redenen die al dan niet verband houden met gender
Bv. verkrachting, ongewenste seksuele toenadering, gedwongen verrichten van seksuele handelingen bij zichzelf of anderen, huiselijk geweld (seksueel), (mannelijke/vrouwelijke/intersekse) genitale verminking/besnijdenis, (mensenhandel met het oog op) seksuele uitbuiting, gedwongen gezinsplanning (gedwongen sterilisatie, gedwongen abortus, ontzegging van het recht op het gebruik van anticonceptie …), verplichte controles op maagdelijkheid …
EN</td></tr>
</table>

(continued)

Structuur	6) **gendergerelateerd geweld**: geweld in welke vorm dan ook (behalve seksueel) gericht naar een persoon om redenen die verband houden met gender Bv. huiselijk geweld (niet-seksueel), gedwongen huwelijken (inclusief kindhuwelijken) of samenwonen (voorafgegaan door bruidsontvoering), geweld in verband met eer en gendernormen, femi(ni)cide …
I. PERSOONLIJK PROFIEL	I.1 In welk jaar bent u geboren? […]
	I.2 Hoe identificeert u zich? Als: (meerdere antwoordmogelijkheden) □ (Cis)* vrouw □ (Cis)* Man □ Non-binair** persoon □ Trans*** vrouw □ Trans*** man □ Inter(sekse)**** persoon □ Anders, namelijk: […] □ Zeg ik liever niet * De term cis(gender) wil zeggen dat het geslacht dat je toegewezen krijgt bij je geboorte (op basis van je geslachtsdelen) overeenkomt met je genderidentiteit. Als je bij je geboorte het vrouwelijk geslacht krijgt toegewezen en je voelt je ook vrouw, dan noemt men dit cisgender. ** De term non-binair wil zeggen dat iemand zich niet herkent in de binaire opdeling van gender, de klassiek westerse tweedeling in man en vrouw, en alle verwachtingen en rollen die de binaire gendernormen daaraan koppelen. *** De term trans(gender) wil zeggen dat het geslacht dat je toegewezen kreeg bij de geboorte niet overeenkomt met je genderidentiteit. Als je bij de geboorte het vrouwelijk geslacht krijgt toegewezen maar je voelt je een man, dan ben je een trans man. **** De term inter(sekse) wil zeggen dat iemands fysieke geslachtskenmerken niet binnen de klassieke tweedeling M/V vallen. Bron: https://www.cavaria.be/woordenlijst
	I.3 Hoe lang werkt u reeds bij het CGVS? □ 0–2 jaar □ 3–5 jaar □ 6–10 jaar □ 11–15 jaar □ 16–20 jaar □ 21–25 jaar □ 26–30 jaar □ 31–35 jaar □ 36–40 jaar □ 41– … jaar
	I.4 Wat is uw hoogste opleidingsniveau? □ Middelbare school □ Hogeschool □ Universiteit □ Anders, namelijk: […]

(continued)

I.5 In welke categorie plaatst u uw opleiding(en)? (meerdere antwoordmogelijkheden)

- □ **Recht en Criminologie** (incl. Rechten, Criminologie, Rechtspraktijk …)
- □ **Psychologie en Pedagogische Wetenschappen** (incl. Psychologie, (Ortho)pedagogie, Toegepaste psychologie, Sociaal(-Cultureel) werk, Maatschappelijk werk, Educatieve bachelor/master …)
- □ **Politieke en Sociale Wetenschappen** (incl. Politieke wetenschappen, Sociologie, EU-studies, Conflict & Development, Gender & Diversiteit, Communicatie(wetenschappen), Journalistiek …)
- □ **Letteren en wijsbegeerte** (incl. Taal- en letterkunde, Toegepaste taalkunde, Tolk, Geschiedenis, Wijsbegeerte, Kunstwetenschappen, Afrikaanse/Oost-Europese/Oosterse talen en culturen …)
- □ Anders, namelijk: […]

I.6 Hoe vaak komt u in aanraking met verzoeken om IB op grond van SGG?

- □ < 1 × per jaar
- □ Ca. 1 × per jaar
- □ Ca. 1 × per 6 maanden
- □ Ca. 1 × per 3 maanden
- □ Ca. 1 × per maand
- □ Ca. 1 × per week
- □ > 1 × per week

I.7 Welke opleidingen, trainings, workshops … over gender (intern en/of extern) heeft u in de afgelopen 5 jaar gevolgd? (meerdere antwoordmogelijkheden)

- □ **Gender, Gender Identity & Sexual Orientation**
- □ **Gender, Gender Identity & Sexual orientation** – Train the trainers
- □ Rekening houden met **gender** in de procedure bij het CGVS
- □ **Terugkomdag** (specialisatietraject van Gender PO's)
- □ Behandeling van verzoeken om IB waarin **seksuele oriëntatie** wordt aangehaald
- □ Behandeling van verzoeken om IB waarin **seksueel geweld** wordt aangehaald
- □ Behandeling van verzoeken om IB waarin **Vrouwelijke Genitale Verminking** wordt aangehaald
- □ **Genderidentiteit**
- □ Vorming over **VGV** door artsen, verloskundigen, psychologen …
- □ Vorming over **trauma** en de gevolgen (neurologisch, psychologisch) van het geleden geweld, in het bijzonder seksueel geweld
- □ Anders, namelijk: […]
- □ Geen

(continued)

Identificatiecode	**I.8 Identificatiecode** Deze studie wil mogelijks verandering doorheen de tijd bestuderen. Daarom is het belangrijk dat we de antwoorden in de toekomst (vb. in een volgende vragenlijst) kunnen koppelen aan dezelfde persoon. We vragen u om enkele vragen te beantwoorden, waarmee we een **persoonlijke code** aanmaken. Deze code is uniek en laat ons toe om uw antwoorden aan elkaar te koppelen. We willen hierbij benadrukken dat **enkel de onderzoekers** deze code zullen kunnen raadplagen en dat het hierbij **onmogelijk** blijft om uw **identiteit** te achterhalen.
	Duid de EERSTE LETTER van je moeders VOORNAAM aan. Met moeder bedoelen we diegene die je 'moeder' noemt. Dit hoeft dus niet per definitie je biologische moeder te zijn. Duid XX aan indien je je moeder niet kent.
	Duid de EERSTE LETTER van je vaders VOORNAAM aan. Met vader bedoelen we diegene die je 'vader' noemt. Dit hoeft dus niet per definitie je biologische vader te zijn. Duid XX aan indien je je vader niet kent.
	Duid aan op welke DAG van de maand je GEBOREN bent. Duid XX aan indien je niet weet op welke dag van de maand je geboren bent.
	Duid de EERSTE LETTER van je VOORNAAM aan.
	Duid aan in welke MAAND je GEBOREN bent. Duid XX aan indien je niet weet in welke maand je bent geboren.
	Duid de EERSTE LETTER van je GEBOORTEPLAATS aan. Duid XX aan indien je je geboorteplaats niet kent.
Mentaal welzijn	**I.9 Mentaal welzijn** In dit onderdeel peilen we naar mentaal welzijn in relatie tot uw werkinhoud en -omgeving. Gelieve aan te geven hoezeer u akkoord/niet akkoord gaat met volgende stellingen, waarbij de niveaus worden aangegeven als: **1 (helemaal niet akkoord)** tot 7 **(helemaal akkoord).**
	Mijn job houdt in dat ik word blootgesteld aan **verontrustend materiaal en ervaringen.**
	In mijn job word ik blootgesteld aan **getraumatiseerde of verontruste verzoekers.**
	Ik **voel me verontrust** als ik luister naar de verhalen en situaties van verzoekers.
	Ik **vind het moeilijk** om met de verhalen en situaties van verzoekers **om te gaan.**
	Ik **denk thuis** aan verontrustende verhalen en situaties waarmee ik tijdens mijn job in contact kwam.
	Soms voel ik me **niet in staat om verzoekers bij te staan** op de manier die ik zou willen.
	Soms **voel ik me overweldigd** door de werklast van mijn job.

(continued)

	Het is **moeilijk om positief en optimistisch te blijven**, gezien sommige zaken waarmee ik in mijn job word geconfronteerd.
II. KENNIS- EN ATTITUDEVRAGEN	In dit onderdeel peilen we naar kennis en attitudes over seksueel en gendergerelateerd geweld. Het is bij het invullen belangrijk dat u hier uw **persoonlijke mening** weergeeft. Gelieve aan te geven hoezeer u akkoord/niet akkoord gaat met volgende stellingen, waarbij de niveaus worden aangegeven als: **1 (helemaal niet akkoord)** tot **5 (helemaal akkoord).**
II.1 Statistische gegevens met betrekking tot SGG	Wereldwijd **komt SGG** het meest **voor** in landen en regio's met lage en gemiddelde inkomens.
	Verzoekers om IB lopen een groter **risico op SGG** dan EU-burgers zonder nood aan IB.
	Seksueel geweld wordt meestal **gepleegd** door onbekenden.
II.2 Kwalificatie van (het risico op) SGG	Bij het beoordelen van de geloofwaardigheid van een vluchtverhaal over **seksueel geweld**, vind ik het relevant of het slachtoffer voordien vrijwillig **alcohol of drugs** had gebruikt.
	Bij het beoordelen van de geloofwaardigheid van een vluchtverhaal over **seksueel geweld**, vind ik het relevant of de dader **fysiek(e) bedreigingen of geweld** heeft gebruikt.
	Als er **geen lichamelijk letsel** kan worden vastgesteld, beoordeel ik een vluchtverhaal over **seksueel geweld** als minder geloofwaardig.
	Als er **geen beschadiging van het hymen*** kan worden vastgesteld, beoordeel ik een vluchtverhaal over **verkrachting** bij jonge vrouwen als minder geloofwaardig. * In de volksmond ook 'maagdenvlies' genoemd
	Bij het beoordelen van de geloofwaardigheid van een vrees voor **seksueel geweld**, vind ik het **geslacht van een verzoeker** relevant.
	Bij het beoordelen van de geloofwaardigheid van een vrees voor **seksueel geweld**, vind ik het **geslacht van de potentiële dader** relevant.
	Bij het beoordelen van de geloofwaardigheid van een vrees voor **SGG** vind ik het **opleidingsniveau en de beroepservaring** van een verzoeker relevant.
	Bij het beoordelen van de geloofwaardigheid van een vrees voor **SGG** vind ik de **autonomie, maturiteit en assertiviteit** van een verzoeker relevant.
	Vormen van **SGG** die zich afspelen in de **privésfeer** vallen **buiten** het toepassingsgebied van de VN **Vluchtelingenconventie**.
II.3 Gedragingen van slachtoffers van SGG en hun omgeving	Als een verzoeker zich **emotieloos** gedraagt bij het terugdenken aan of praten over een vluchtverhaal over **SGG**, beoordeel ik dit als minder geloofwaardig.
	Als een verzoeker een vluchtverhaal over **SGG niet chronologisch** kan vertellen, beoordeel ik dit als minder geloofwaardig.
	Als een vluchtverhaal over **SGG inconsistenties** bevat, beoordeel ik dit als minder geloofwaardig.
	Als een verzoeker **geen contextuele details** kan geven bij een vluchtverhaal over **SGG**, beoordeel ik dit als minder geloofwaardig.

(continued)

	Kinderen die **niet** aan **VGV** worden onderworpen in een gemeenschap waar dit de norm is, lopen het risico om **gestigmatiseerd en sociaal uitgesloten** te worden.
	Als een verzoeker met een vluchtverhaal over **seksueel geweld niet** heeft geprobeerd zich te **verweren of te vluchten**, beoordeel ik dit als minder geloofwaardig.
	Als een verzoeker met een vrees voor **SGG** dit **niet** zo snel mogelijk aan iemand heeft **verteld**, beoordeel ik dit als minder geloofwaardig.
	Als een verzoeker die beweert gerekruteerd te zijn door een **netwerk voor seksuele uitbuiting nooit** heeft geprobeerd te **ontsnappen**, beoordeel ik dit als minder geloofwaardig.
	Als een verzoeker met een vluchtverhaal over **huiselijk geweld nooit** hebben geprobeerd **tegen te spreken of terug te vechten**, beoordeel ik dit als minder geloofwaardig.
	Als een verzoeker met een vrees voor **SGG** dit **niet** zo snel mogelijk aan de lokale autoriteiten heeft **aangegeven**, beoordeel ik dit als minder geloofwaardig.
	Als een **mannelijke** verzoeker met een vrees voor **seksueel geweld** (door een man) in een land waar **homoseksualiteit strafbaar** is dit **niet** zo snel mogelijk aan de lokale autoriteiten heeft **aangegeven**, beoordeel ik dit als minder geloofwaardig.
	Als een verzoeker met een vrees voor **SGG** dit **niet** in het eerste **interview** met de (asiel)autoriteiten heeft **verteld**, beoordeel ik dit als minder geloofwaardig.
	Als een verzoeker met een vrees voor **SGG niet** zo snel mogelijk na aankomst een **verzoek om IB** heeft ingediend, beoordeel ik dit als minder geloofwaardig.
	Als ouders zich openlijk **tegen VGV** durven **uitspreken**, zouden zij de **druk** van de gemeenschap om hun kinderen aan VGV te onderwerpen ook moeten kunnen **weerstaan**.
II.4 Bewijsmateriaal in de procedure om IB op grond van SGG	Bij een vrees voor **SGG** zijn de **soorten bewijs** die gebruikelijk zijn in verzoekprocedures om IB minder gemakkelijk beschikbaar dan bij andere vervolgingsvormen.
	Als het risico op **SGG niet** in de relevante **landeninformatie** terug te vinden is, beoordeel ik een vrees voor dit soort SGG als minder geloofwaardig.
II.5 Bescherming tegen SGG in het land van oorsprong	Als een verzoeker met vrees voor een **strafbare vorm van SGG nooit** ter plaatse **aangifte** heeft gedaan, kan deze geen beroep doen op een gebrek aan bescherming (in de zin van de VN Vluchtelingenconventie).
	Staatsbescherming tegen SGG moet worden gezien als een **resultaatsverbintenis**, eerder dan een middelenverbintenis.
	Als een verzoeker met vrees voor **SGG nooit** heeft geprobeerd om bij (mannelijke) **familieleden/kennissen bescherming** te zoeken, kan deze geen beroep doen op een gebrek aan bescherming (in de zin van de VN Vluchtelingenconventie).
	Als een verzoeker met vrees voor **SGG nooit** heeft geprobeerd om zichzelf te beschermen door bijvoorbeeld **publieke plaatsen te mijden**, kan deze geen beroep doen op een gebrek aan bescherming (in de zin van de VN Vluchtelingenconventie).

(continued)

	Als een verzoeker met een vrees voor **huiselijk geweld nooit** heeft geprobeerd om de **relatie te verlaten** en te verhuizen, kan deze geen beroep doen op een gebrek aan bescherming (in de zin van de VN Vluchtelingenconventie).
	Bij het beoordelen van een intern beschermingsalternatief tegen **SGG** vind ik het relevant of de **beschermende actor** (een substantieel deel van) de **staat controleert**.
	Bij het beoordelen van een intern beschermingsalternatief tegen **SGG** vind ik het relevant of er plaatselijke SGG-gerelateerde **NGO's** zijn.
	Bij het beoordelen van een intern beschermingsalternatief tegen **SGG** vind ik de beschikbaarheid van (mannelijke) **private ondersteuningsnetwerken** van een verzoeker relevant.
	Bij het beoordelen van een intern beschermingsalternatief tegen **SGG** vind ik de **sociale en financiële ondersteuning** (door het persoonlijk netwerk) van een verzoeker relevant.
	Bescherming (in de zin van de VN Vluchtelingenconventie) tegen **SGG** kan enkel worden geboden door een **doeltreffend juridisch systeem** dat dergelijke daden cumulatief opspoort, vervolgt en bestraft.
II.6 Juridisch kader van de procedure om IB op grond van SGG	De Belgische asielautoriteiten zijn verplicht om ervoor te zorgen dat **SGG** kan worden **erkend** als een vorm van **vervolging**.
	De Belgische asielautoriteiten zijn verplicht om een verzoek om IB **gendersensitief** te **beoordelen**.
Feedbackoptie	Bent u van mening dat de vraagstelling in dit onderdeel u verhinderde om bepaalde nuances mee te geven? U vindt hieronder ruimte om deze (of andere) feedback aan ons mee te delen.
III. PRAKTIJKVRAGEN	Dit onderdeel peilt naar praktijken tijdens de procedure om IB op grond van SGG. Het is bij het invullen belangrijk dat u hier uw **persoonlijke mening/ervaring** weergeeft.
III.1 Praktijken in de procedure om IB op grond van SGG	Gelieve aan te geven hoezeer u akkoord/niet akkoord gaat met volgende stellingen, waarbij de niveaus worden aangegeven als: **1 (helemaal niet akkoord)** tot **5 (helemaal akkoord).**
	Ik heb toegang tot voldoende gespecialiseerde **opleidingen** om accuraat **om te gaan met verklaringen** van SGG tijdens het persoonlijk onderhoud.
	Ik beschik over voldoende **vaardigheden** om accuraat te **reageren op verklaringen** van SGG.
	Ik beschik over voldoende **vaardigheden** om **gepaste vragen** te stellen die tot relevante verklaringen van SGG kunnen leiden.
	Ik beschik over voldoende **vaardigheden en mogelijkheden** om tegemoet te komen aan de **bijzondere procedurele noden** van verzoekers met SGG-gerelateerde vluchtverhalen.
	Ik heb toegang tot voldoende gespecialiseerde **opleidingen** om verzoeken om IB op grond van SGG accuraat te kunnen **beoordelen.**
	Ik heb voldoende **kennis** om verzoeken om IB op grond van SGG accuraat te kunnen **beoordelen.**
	De interne richtlijnen laten voldoende **ruimte** om verzoeken om IB op grond van SGG accuraat te kunnen **beoordelen.**

(continued)

	Ik heb toegang tot **psychologische begeleiding** binnen mijn werkomgeving **als ik dit wens.**
	Ik ben **verplicht** om **psychologisch begeleid** te worden binnen mijn werkomgeving.
III.2 Betrokkenheid bij het thema van SGG (in de procedure om IB)	Hoe vaak **denkt u na** over de onderwerpen die in deze enquête aan bod komen, namelijk SGG in de procedure om IB? 1 **(helemaal niet vaak)** tot 5 **(zeer vaak)**
	Hoe snel komt uw **eigen mening** tegenover deze kwesties naar voren wanneer u dergelijke vragen moet beantwoorden? 1 **(helemaal niet snel)** tot 5 **(zeer snel)**
	Heeft u over deze onderwerpen een **uitgesproken mening**? 1 **(helemaal niet uitgesproken)** tot 5 **(zeer uitgesproken)**
	Hoe **belangrijk** is uw mening over deze onderwerpen voor u? 1 **(helemaal niet belangrijk)** tot 5 **(zeer belangrijk)**
	Hoe **zeker** bent u van uw mening over deze kwesties? 1 **(helemaal niet zeker)** tot 5 **(zeer zeker)**
	Voelt u zich over deze onderwerpen eerder goed of slecht **geïnformeerd**? 1 **(helemaal niet geïnformeerd)** tot 5 **(zeer geïnformeerd)**
	Hoeveel **weet** u over deze onderwerpen? 1 **(helemaal niet veel)** tot 5 **(zeer veel)**
	De onderwerpen die in deze enquête aan bod komen **belangen mij persoonlijk aan.** 1 **(helemaal niet akkoord)** tot 5 **(helemaal akkoord)**
Feedbackoptie	Bent u van mening dat de vraagstelling in dit onderdeel u verhinderde om bepaalde nuances mee te geven? U vindt hieronder ruimte om deze (of andere) feedback aan ons mee te delen.
IV. DEELNAME INTERVIEWS (optioneel)	IV. DEELNAME INTERVIEWS (optioneel) Als u in een later stadium via een interview **uitgebreidere vragen over het thema** van deze studie wilt beantwoorden via een **interview**, kunt u uw **e-mailadres opgeven** door op de blauwe pijl onderaan te klikken. Deze enquête wordt dan afgesloten en u zal worden doorgestuurd naar een nieuwe pagina. De antwoorden in uw enquête blijven anoniem en zullen op geen enkele manier kunnen worden gelinkt aan dit e-mailadres. U zal hierover in een later stadium van het onderzoek worden gecontacteerd.
SLOT	U kunt steeds bijkomende vragen stellen via [Lore.Roels@UGent.be] over uw deelname. Als u specifieke vragen heeft over de bescherming van uw persoonsgegevens, kunt u altijd contact opnemen met de Functionaris Gegevensbescherming van de Universiteit Gent via [Privacy@UGent.be]. **Hartelijk bedankt voor het invullen van deze enquête!** Lore Roels (onderzoeker) Prof. Dr. Ellen Desmet (promotor) Prof. Dr. Ines Keygnaert (copromotor)

(continued)

END OF SURVEY	[Link naar aparte survey voor contactgegevens] Dit onderzoek bevat in een latere fase de optie om uitgebreidere vragen over het thema van dit onderzoek te beantwoorden in de vorm van een **interview**. Het is belangrijk te vermelden dat een uitnodiging voor deze interviews **niet gegarandeerd** is. Na het analyseren van de enquêteresultaten zullen de onderzoekers samen met het CGVS besluiten of en hoeveel gesprekken worden ingepland. Duid aan welke opties voor u van toepassing zijn. □ Ik wens mij kandidaat te stellen voor de vervolginterviews (zonder garantie tot uitnodiging) □ Ik wens mij geen kandidaat te stellen Om u te kunnen contacteren vragen we u hieronder **een e-mailadres** door te geven. Dit zal enkel gebruikt worden voor het plannen van de interviews en zal na afloop worden verwijderd. Het e-mailadres wordt **los van uw antwoorden** opgeslagen. Daarom werd u nu doorverwezen naar een aparte webpagina. Het is voor de onderzoekers dus niet mogelijk om uw antwoorden in de enquête te koppelen aan uw e-mailadres. Voor meer informatie over de bescherming van uw contactgegevens kan u contact opnemen met de Functionaris Gegevensbescherming van de Universiteit Gent via [Privacy@UGent.be]. **Hartelijk bedankt voor uw bereidwillige deelname!** Lore Roels (onderzoeker) Prof. Dr. Ellen Desmet (promotor) Prof. Dr. Ines Keygnaert (copromotor)

KAP Survey CGRA (FR)

PARTIE	Question/information
INTRO Consentement informé	Cher·ère participant·e, Veuillez lire attentivement le document accessible via le lien ci-dessous avant de cliquer sur "Suivant". *(Lien vers la fiche d'information)*
Consentement informé	Cette enquête est **anonyme** : vos réponses ne peuvent en aucun cas être reliées à votre personne. Vous pouvez mettre **fin à votre participation** à tout moment, en interrompant (définitivement) l'enquête, sans donner de raison. Si, pendant que vous répondez à l'enquête, vous avez des **questions** sur son contenu ou sur l'enquête en général, vous pouvez toujours interrompre (temporairement) l'enquête et nous contacter à l'adresse électronique suivante : [Lore.Roels@UGent.be]. Veuillez cliquer sur le texte ci-dessous pour accepter de participer à cette enquête. *BOUTON (requis avant de poursuivre) : Je déclare avoir lu et compris la fiche d'information et consens à participer à cette enquête de manière informée.*

(continued)

Structure	Cette enquête se divise comme suit : XIII. PROFIL PERSONNEL XIV. QUESTIONS SUR LES CONNAISSANCES ET LES ATTITUDES XV. QUESTIONS SUR LES PRATIQUES XVI. PARTICIPATION AUX INTERVIEWS (facultatif) Le cas échéant, vous trouverez en haut de chaque section des explications sur le type de questions et la manière d'y répondre. Abréviations utilisées : – **VSS** : violence sexuelle et sexiste – **PI** : protection internationale – **MGF** : mutilation génitale féminine – **CGRA** : Commissaire général aux réfugiés et aux apatrides Dans cette étude, le terme "VSS" fait référence à : 7) **violence sexuelle :** violence de nature sexuelle orientée vers une personne pour des raisons liées ou non au genre. Par exemple, le viol, les avances sexuelles non désirées, l'exécution forcée d'actes sexuels sur soi-même ou sur d'autres personnes, la violence domestique (sexuelle), les circoncisions/mutilations génitales (masculines/féminines/intersexuelles), (la traite des êtres humains à des fins d')exploitation sexuelle, la planification familiale forcée (stérilisation forcée, avortement forcé, déni du droit d'utiliser des moyens de contraception …), les contrôles de virginité obligatoires … ET 8) **violence sexiste :** toute forme de violence (autre que sexuelle) orientée vers une personne pour des raisons liées au genre. Par exemple, la violence domestique (non sexuelle), le mariage (y compris le mariage d'enfants) ou la cohabitation forcés (précédés d'enlèvement), la violence liée à l'honneur et aux normes de genre, le femi(ni)cide …
I. PROFIL PERSONNEL	I.1 Quelle est votre année de naissance ? […]
	I.2 Comment vous identifiez-vous ? Comme : (possibilité de réponses multiples) □ Femme (cis)* □ Homme (cis)* □ Personne non-binaire** □ Femme trans*** □ Homme trans*** □ Personne inter(sexe)**** □ Autre, notamment : … □ Je préfère ne pas réponde à cette question * Le terme cis(genre) signifie que le sexe qui vous a été attribué à la naissance (en fonction de vos organes génitaux) correspond à votre identité de genre. Si l'on vous attribue le sexe féminin à la naissance et que vous vous sentez également de sexe féminin, on dira que vous êtes cisgenre.

(continued)

	** Le terme “non-binaire” signifie que quelqu’un ne se reconnaît pas dans la division binaire du genre (la division occidentale classique entre homme et femme), et toutes les attentes et rôles que les normes de genre binaires y attachent. *** Le terme trans(genre) signifie que le sexe qui vous a été attribué à la naissance ne correspond pas à votre identité de genre. Si l’on vous a assigné le sexe féminin à la naissance mais que vous vous sentez homme, vous êtes un homme trans. **** Le terme inter(sexe) signifie que les caractéristiques sexuelles physiques d’une personne ne correspondent pas à la dichotomie classique H/F. Source: https://www.cavaria.be/woordenlijst
	I.3 Depuis combien de temps travaillez-vous au CGRA ? □ 0–2 ans □ 3–5 ans □ 6–10 ans □ 11–15 ans □ 16–20 ans □ 21–25 ans □ 26–30 ans □ 31–35 ans □ 36–40 ans □ 41– … ans
	I.4 Quel est votre plus haut niveau d’éducation ? □ École secondaire □ Haute école spécialisée □ Université □ Autre·s, notamment : […]
	I.5 Dans laquelle de ces catégories situez-vous votre·vos formation·s ? (Possibilité de réponses multiples) □ **Droit et Criminologie** (y.c. Droit, Criminologie, Pratique juridique …) □ **Psychologie et Sciences de l’Education** (y.c. Psychologie, (Ortho) pédagogie, Psychologie appliquée, Travail Social (Culturel), Travail Communautaire, Licence/Master en sciences de l’Education …) □ **Sciences Politiques et Sociales** (y.c. Sciences Politiques, Sociologie, Etudes Européennes, Conflit et Développement, Genre et Diversité, (Sciences de) Communication, Journalisme …) □ **Littérature et Philosophie** (y.c. Langue et Littérature, Linguistique Appliquée, Interprète, Histoire, Philosophie, Etudes Artistiques, Langues et Cultures Africaines/Orientales/d’Europe de l’Est …) □ Autre·s, notamment :
	I.6 À quelle fréquence rencontrez-vous des demandes de PI fondées sur la VSS ? □ < 1 × par an □ Env. 1 × par an □ Env. 1 × par 6 mois □ Env. 1 × par 3 mois □ Env. 1 × par mois □ Env. 1 × par semaine □ > 1 × par semaine

(continued)

	I.7 Quels sont les cours, formations, ateliers … sur le genre (interne et/ou externe) que vous avez suivis dans le cadre de votre travail au CGRA lors des 5 dernières années ? □ **Gender, Gender Identity & Sexual Orientation** □ **Gender, Gender Identity & Sexual orientation** – Train the trainers □ La prise en compte du **genre** dans la procédure au CGRA □ **Journée d'approfondissement** (trajet de spécialisation des OPs Genre) □ Traitement des demandes de PI fondées sur **l'orientation sexuelle** □ Traitement des demandes de PI pour cause de **violence sexuelle** □ Traitement des demandes de PI pour cause de **MGF** □ **Identité de genre** □ Éducation sur les **MGF** par des médecins, des infirmiers ou des psychologues … □ Éducation sur la **mémoire traumatique** et les conséquences (neurologiques, psychologiques) des violences subies, notamment les violences sexuelles. □ Autre·s, notamment : […] □ Aucun
Code d'identification	**I.8 Code d'identification** Cette étude veut évaluer les éventuelles évolutions dans le temps. Il est donc important que nous puissions toujours relier les réponses à la même personne (par exemple, dans un éventuel futur questionnaire). Nous vous demandons de répondre à quelques questions, que nous utilisons pour créer un **code personnel**. Ce code est unique et nous permet de relier vos réponses. Nous tenons à souligner que **seuls les chercheurs** seront en mesure de consulter ce code et qu'il sera **impossible** de découvrir votre **identité**.
	Indiquez la PREMIÈRE LETTRE du prénom de votre mère. Par mère, nous entendons la personne que vous appelez "mère". Il ne s'agit pas nécessairement de votre mère biologique. Indiquez XX si vous ne connaissez pas votre mère.
	Indiquez la PREMIÈRE LETTRE du prénom de votre père. Par père, nous entendons la personne que vous appelez "père". Il ne s'agit pas nécessairement de votre père biologique. Indiquez XX si vous ne connaissez pas votre père.
	Indiquez le JOUR du mois où vous êtes né·e (en chiffres). Indiquez XX si vous ne savez pas quel jour du mois vous êtes né.
	Indiquez la PREMIÈRE LETTRE de votre PRENOM.
	Indiquez le MOIS où vous êtes né·e. Indiquez XX si vous ne savez pas quel est le mois de votre naissance.
	Indiquez la PREMIÈRE LETTRE de votre LIEU DE NAISSANCE. Indiquez XX si vous ne connaissez pas votre lieu de naissance.
Bien-être mental	**I.9 Bien-être mental** Dans cette section, nous nous intéressons au bien-être mental en relation avec le contenu et l'environnement de votre travail. Veuillez indiquer dans quelle mesure vous êtes d'accord/en désaccord avec les déclarations suivantes, les niveaux étant indiqués comme suit : **1 (pas du tout d'accord)** à **7 (tout à fait d'accord).**

(continued)

	Mon travail implique une exposition à des **matériaux et des expériences perturbants.**
	Dans mon travail, je suis exposé·e à des **demandeurs·euses traumatisés·ées ou en détresse.**
	Je me **sens troublé·e** en écoutant les histoires et les situations des demandeurs·euses.
	Je **trouve difficile** de **faire face** aux histoires et situations des demandeurs·euses.
	A la maison, je repense à des histoires et des situations perturbantes auxquelles j'ai été en confronté·e pendant mon travail.
	Parfois, je me sens **incapable d'aider les demandeurs·euses** comme je le souhaiterais.
	Parfois, je me **sens dépassé·e** par la charge de travail de mon travail.
	Il est **difficile de rester positif·ve et optimiste**, étant donné certains des sujets auxquels je suis confronté·e dans mon travail.
II. QUESTIONS SUR LES CONNAISSANCES ET LES ATTITUDES	Dans cette section, nous évaluons les connaissances et les attitudes concernant la VSS. Il est important que vous reflétiez ici votre **opinion personnelle** lorsque vous remplissez le formulaire. Veuillez indiquer dans quelle mesure vous êtes d'accord/en désaccord avec les déclarations suivantes, les niveaux étant indiqués comme suit : **1 (pas du tout d'accord) à 5 (tout à fait d'accord).**
II.1 Statistiques en rapport ayant VSS	Au niveau mondial, la **VSS** est plus **fréquente** dans les pays et régions à revenu faible ou intermédiaire.
	Les demandeurs·euses de PI sont plus exposés·ées au **risque de VSS** que les citoyens de l'UE qui n'ont pas besoin de PI.
	La violence sexuelle est généralement **commise** par des inconnus
II.2 Qualification (du risque) de la VSS	Pour évaluer la crédibilité d'un récit de fuite fondé sur la **violence sexuelle**, je trouve pertinent de savoir si la victime avait déjà consommé de **l'alcool** ou de **la drogue** de façon volontaire auparavant.
	Pour évaluer la crédibilité d'un récit de fuite fondé sur la **violence sexuelle**, je trouve pertinent de savoir si l'auteur a recouru à des **menaces ou des violences physiques.**
	Si **aucune blessure physique** ne peut être établie, je considère un récit de fuite fondé sur la **violence sexuelle** comme <u>moins</u> crédible.
	Si **aucune blessure à l'hymen** ne peut être identifiée, je considère un récit de fuite fondé sur le **viol** chez une jeune femme comme <u>moins</u> crédible.
	Pour évaluer la crédibilité d'une crainte fondée sur la **violence sexuelle**, je trouve que le **sexe du/de la demandeur·euse** est un élément pertinent.
	Pour évaluer la crédibilité d'une crainte fondée sur la **violence sexuelle**, je trouve que le **sexe de l'auteur potentiel** est un élément pertinent.
	Pour évaluer la crédibilité d'une crainte fondée sur la **VSS**, je trouve que le **niveau d'éducation et l'expérience professionnelle** du/de la demandeur·euse sont des éléments pertinents.
	Pour évaluer la crédibilité d'une crainte fondée sur la **VSS**, je trouve que **l'autonomie, la maturité et l'assertivité** du/de la demandeur·euse sont des éléments pertinents.

(continued)

	Les formes de **VSS** qui ont lieu dans **la sphère privée** ne relèvent **pas** du champ d'application de la **Convention des Nations Unies sur les Réfugiés**.
II.3 Comportements attendus des victimes de VSS et de leur environnement	Si un·e demandeur·euse se comporte **sans émotion** lorsqu'il/elle se rappelle ou parle d'un récit de fuite fondé sur la **VSS**, je considère le récit comme moins crédible.
	Si un·e demandeur·euse ne peuvent **pas** raconter un récit de fuite fondé sur la **VSS** de manière **chronologique**, je considère le récit comme moins crédible.
	Si un récit de fuite fondé sur la **VSS** contient des **incohérences**, je le considère comme moins crédible.
	Si un·e demandeur·euse ne peut **pas** donner des **détails contextuels** d'un récit de fuite fondé sur la **VSS**, je considère le récit comme moins crédible
	Les enfants qui ne sont **pas** soumis aux **MGF** dans une communauté où cela est la norme risquent d'être **stigmatisés et exclus socialement.**
	Si un·e demandeur·euse présentant un récit de fuite fondé sur la **violence sexuelle** n'a **pas** essayé de **se défendre ou de fuir**, je considère le récit comme moins crédible.
	Si un·e demandeur·euse craignant la **VSS** ne l'a **pas dit** à quelqu'un dès que possible, je considère le récit comme moins crédible.
	Si un·e demandeur·euse déclarant avoir été recruté·e dans un **réseau d'exploitation sexuelle** n'a **jamais** essayé de **s'échapper**, je considère le récit comme moins crédible.
	Si un·e demandeur·euse présentant un récit de fuite fondé sur la **violence domestique** n'a **jamais** essayé de **contester** le traitement subi ou de **se défendre**, je considère le récit comme moins crédible.
	Si un·e demandeur·euse craignant la **VSS** ne l'a **pas signalé aux autorités locales** dès que possible, je considère le récit comme moins crédible.
	Si un demandeur craignant la **violence sexuelle** dans un pays où l'homosexualité est punissable ne l'a **pas signalé aux autorités locales** dès que possible, je considère le récit comme moins crédible.
	Si un·e demandeur·euse craignant la **VSS** n'a **pas signalé** les faits de VSS subis aux autorités (d'asile) lors du premier **entretien**, je considère le récit comme moins crédible.
	Si un·e demandeur·euse craignant la **VSS** n'a **pas demandé de la PI** dès que possible après son arrivée, je considère le récit comme moins crédible.
	Si les parents osent **s'exprimer** ouvertement **contre les MGF**, ils devraient également être en mesure de **résister aux pressions** de la communauté pour que leurs enfants y soient soumis.
II.4 Preuves dans les procédures de PI fondées sur la VSS	En cas de crainte de **VSS**, les **types de preuves** qui sont couramment utilisés dans les procédures de PI sont moins faciles à obtenir que dans le cas d'autres formes de persécution.
	Si le risque de **VSS** n'est **pas** mentionné dans les **informations** pertinentes **sur les pays d'origine**, je considère le récit d'un·e demandeur·euse craignant ce type de VSS comme moins crédible.
II.5 Protection contre la VSS dans le pays d'origine	Si un·e demandeur·euse craignant **une forme punissable de VSS** n'a **jamais** déposé de **plainte** sur place, il/elle ne peut pas prétendre à un manque de protection (au sens de la Convention des Nations Unies sur les Réfugiés).

(continued)

	La protection de l'État contre la VSS doit être considérée comme une **obligation de résultat** plutôt qu'une obligation de moyens.
	Si un·e demandeur·euse craignant la **VSS** n'a **jamais** essayé de déménager chez des **membres de la famille/connaissances** (masculins) pour se protéger, il/elle ne peut pas prétendre à un manque de protection (au sens de la Convention des Nations Unies sur les Réfugiés).
	Si un·e demandeur·euse craignant la **VSS** n'a **jamais** essayé de se protéger, par exemple en **évitant les lieux publics**, il/elle ne peut pas prétendre à un manque de protection (au sens de la Convention des Nations Unies sur les Réfugiés).
	Si un·e demandeur·euse craignant la **violence domestique** n'a **jamais** essayé de **quitter la relation** et de déménager, il/elle ne peut pas prétendre à un manque de protection (au sens de la Convention des Nations Unies sur les Réfugiés).
	Pour évaluer la protection potentielle (au sens de la Convention des Nations Unies sur les Réfugiés) contre la **VSS**, je trouve pertinent de savoir si **l'acteur de protection contrôle** (une partie substantielle de) **l'État**.
	Pour évaluer une possibilité de protection interne contre la **VSS**, je trouve que l'existence et la disponibilité des **ONG** locales actives en matière de VSS est un élément pertinent.
	Pour évaluer une possibilité de protection interne contre la **VSS**, je trouve que l'existence et la disponibilité de **réseaux de soutien privés** (masculins) d'un·e demandeur·euse est un élément pertinent.
	Pour évaluer une possibilité de protection interne contre la **VSS**, je trouve que le **soutien social et financier** (par le réseau privé) d'un·e demandeur·euse est un élément pertinent.
	La protection (au sens de la Convention des Nations Unies sur les Réfugiés) contre la **VSS** ne peut être assurée que par un **système juridique efficace** qui, de manière cumulative, détecte, poursuit et punit de tels actes.
II.6 Cadre juridique de la procédure de demande de PI fondée sur la VSS	Les autorités d'asile belges sont tenues de veiller à ce que la **VSS** puisse être **reconnue** comme une forme de persécution.
	Les autorités d'asile belges sont tenues **d'évaluer** une demande de PI en tenant compte de la **dimension de genre**.
Option de feedback	Avez-vous l'impression que les questions de cette section vous ont empêché de fournir certaines nuances ? Vous trouverez ci-dessous un espace pour nous communiquer vos éventuelles remarques à cet égard. […]
III. QUESTIONS SUR LES PRATIQUES	Cette section examine les pratiques au cours de la procédure de PI fondée sur la VSS. En le complétant, il est important que vous reflétiez ici votre **opinion/expérience personnelle**.
III.1 Pratiques dans les procédures de PI fondées sur la VSS	Veuillez indiquer dans quelle mesure vous êtes d'accord/en désaccord avec les déclarations suivantes, les niveaux étant indiqués comme suit : **1 (pas du tout d'accord) à 5 (tout à fait d'accord).**

(continued)

	J'ai accès à des **formations** spécialisées suffisantes pour **réagir** adéquatement **aux déclarations** de VSS lors d'un entretien personnel.
	Je dispose de **compétences** suffisantes pour **réagir** adéquatement **aux déclarations** de VSS lors d'un entretien personnel.
	Je dispose de **compétences** suffisantes pour poser des **questions appropriées** qui peuvent conduire à des déclarations pertinentes de VSS.
	Je dispose de **compétences** suffisantes pour répondre aux **besoins procéduraux spéciaux** des demandeurs·euses ayant des récits de fuite fondé sur la VSS.
	J'ai accès à des **formations** spécialisées suffisantes pour **évaluer** correctement les demandes de PI fondées sur la VSS.
	Je dispose de **connaissances** suffisantes pour **évaluer** correctement les demandes de PI fondées sur la VSS.
	Les directives internes laissent suffisamment de **flexibilité** pour **évaluer** correctement les demandes de PI fondées sur la VSS.
	J'ai accès à des **services de soutien psychologique** dans mon environnement de travail **si je le souhaite**.
	Je suis **tenu·e de** recevoir un **soutien psychologique** dans mon environnement de travail.
III.2 Engagement sur le thème de la VSS (dans les procédures de PI)	À quelle fréquence **pensez**-vous aux sujets abordés dans cette enquête, notamment la VSS dans la procédure de PI ? 1 **(pas du tout souvent)** à 5 **(très souvent)**
	À quelle vitesse votre **propre opinion** sur ces sujets émerge-t-elle lorsque vous devez répondre à de telles questions ? 1 **(pas du tout vite)** à 5 **(très vite)**
	Avez-vous des **opinions tranchées** sur ces sujets ? 1 **(pas du tout tranchées)** à 5 **(très tranchées)**
	Quelle est **l'importance** pour vous de vos opinions sur ces sujets ? 1 **(pas du tout important)** à 5 **(très important)**
	Dans quelle mesure êtes-vous **sûr·e** de votre opinion sur ces sujets ? 1 **(pas du tout sûr·e)** à 5 **(très sûr·e)**
	Êtes-vous plus susceptible de vous sentir bien ou mal **informé·e** sur ces sujets ? 1 **(pas du tout informé·e)** à 5 **(très informé·e)**
	Que **savez**-vous à propos de ces sujets ? 1 **(très peu)** à 5 **(beaucoup)**
	Les sujets soulevés ci-dessus **me touchent personnellement.** 1 **(pas du tout d'accord)** à 5 **(tout à fait d'accord)**
Option de feedback	Avez-vous l'impression que les questions de cette section vous ont empêché de fournir certaines nuances ? Vous trouverez ci-dessous un espace pour nous communiquer vos éventuelles remarques à cet égard. [...]

(continued)

IV. PARTICIPATION AUX INTERVIEWS (facultatif)	IV. PARTICIPATION AUX ENTRETIENS (facultatif) Si vous souhaitez répondre à **des questions plus approfondies sur le sujet de cette étude,** à un stade ultérieur, dans le cadre **d'un entretien,** vous pouvez fournir votre **adresse électronique** en cliquant sur la flèche bleue en bas de la page. Cette enquête sera ensuite fermée et vous serez redirigé·e vers une nouvelle page. Les réponses à cette enquête resteront anonymes et ne pourront en aucun cas être reliées à votre adresse électronique. Vous serez contacté·e pour l'entretien à un stade ultérieur de la recherche.
FIN	Vous pouvez toujours poser des questions supplémentaires concernant votre participation à [Lore.Roels@UGent.be]. Si vous avez des questions spécifiques sur la protection de vos données personnelles, vous pouvez toujours contacter le délégué à la protection des données de l'Université de Gand à l'adresse électronique suivante : [Privacy@UGent.be]. **Merci beaucoup d'avoir répondu à cette enquête !** Lore Roels (chercheuse) Prof. Dr. Ellen Desmet (superviseure) Prof. Dr. Ines Keygnaert (co-superviseure)
FIN DE L'ENQUÊTE	[Lien vers une enquête séparée pour les coordonnées] Dans le cadre de cette enquête, nous offrons la possibilité de répondre à **des questions plus approfondies sur le thème de l'étude** à un stade ultérieur dans le cadre **d'un entretien.** Il est important de noter qu'une invitation à ces entretiens n'est pas garantie. Après avoir analysé les résultats de l'enquête, les chercheurs décideront, en collaboration avec le CGRA, si et combien d'entretiens seront prévus. Veuillez indiquer les options qui vous concernent. □ Je souhaite participer aux entretiens de suivi (sans garantie d'invitation). □ Je ne souhaite pas participer aux entretiens de suivi Pour vous contacter, nous vous demandons de fournir **une adresse électronique** ci-dessous. Ces données ne seront utilisées que pour planifier les entretiens et seront supprimées par la suite. [ ] L'adresse électronique est conservée **séparément de vos réponses**. Par conséquent, vous avez été redirigé vers une page Web distincte. Il n'est donc pas possible pour les chercheurs d'établir un lien entre vos réponses à l'enquête et votre adresse électronique. Pour plus d'informations sur la protection de vos coordonnées, veuillez contacter le délégué à la protection des données de l'Université de Gand à l'adresse suivante : [Privacy@UGent.be]. **Merci beaucoup pour votre participation volontaire** ! Lore Roels (chercheuse) Prof. Dr. Ellen Desmet (superviseure) Prof. Dr. Ines Keygnaert (co-superviseure)

F. VISUALS OF SUMMARISED RESEARCH RESULTS

Figure 46: Summarised visualisation for communication of research results to & gather feedback from applicant-interview participants

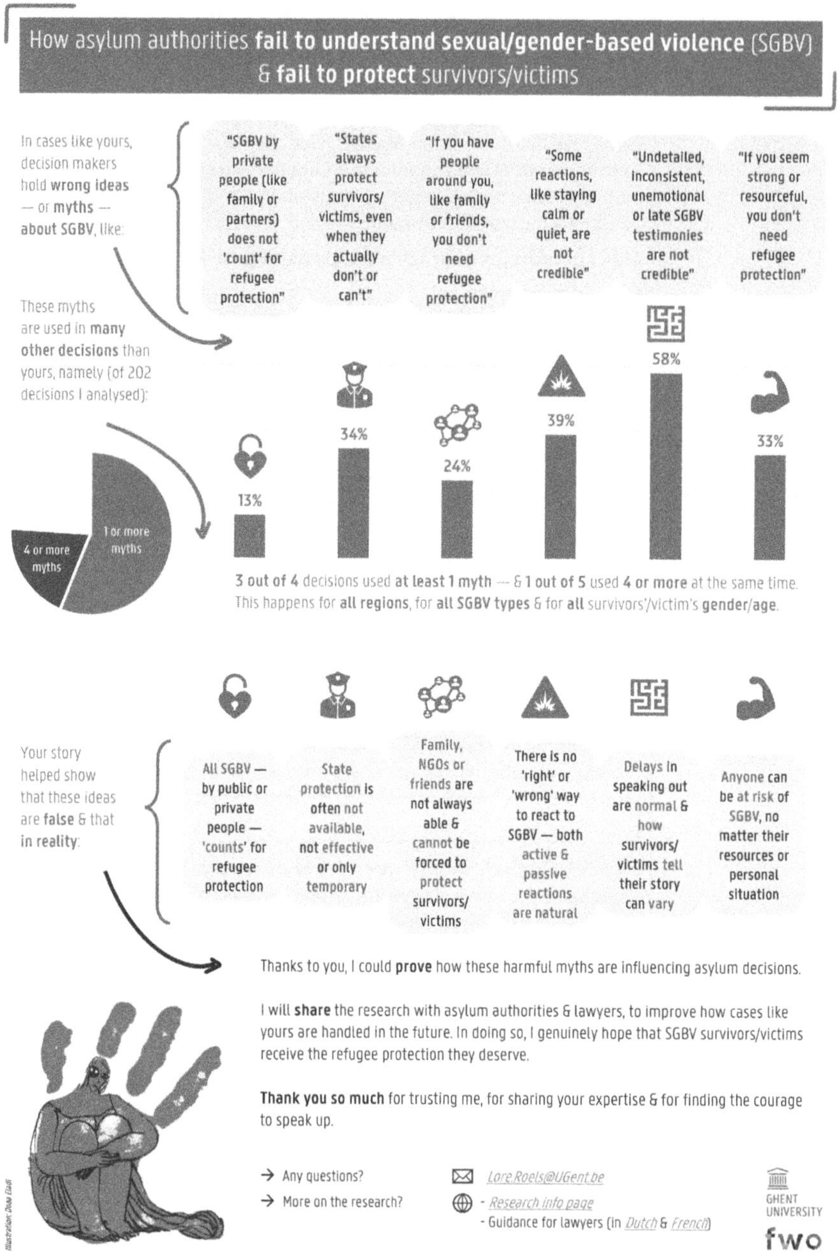

ACKNOWLEDGEMENTS

First and foremost, my gratitude goes out to those whom this research has always been for: the applicants I had the chance to meet and learn from. I will be forever in awe of your courage to flee, to keep fighting, and to share your stories, no matter the harshness with which they were met upon arrival in Belgium. It was a true privilege to listen.

It was a privilege to get to do this work in the first place. I never pictured myself starting a PhD, and still have difficulty believing that I am finishing one. It is no exaggeration to say that I would never have done so without others opening my eyes to the possibility. To my supervisors Ellen and Ines, thank you for seeing what you saw in me long before I did and continuing to do so until the very end. Thank you for demonstrating the importance of our work, the care with which it can be conducted, and the genuine human connection it can create. Ellen, it says enough that our last functioning talk ended in establishing that, after four years, 'we're definitely still in our honeymoon phase'. Ines, I cannot think of a better compliment than the fact that your choir songs about fighting for justice remind you of me, I learnt from the best.

It is truly invaluable to be surrounded by people who so generously uplift others, like yourselves and like the other members of my Doctoral Guidance Committee. To François Crépeau, Vanessa Munro, and Gorik Ooms, no matter how many pages of preparatory reading I burdened you with, your unwavering enthusiasm was contagious and had me leave each meeting with more energy than before. This research would not have been possible without you, nor without the support of the asylum authorities where it was welcomed.

I do not underestimate the discomfort that comes with being the subject of critical research. I genuinely thank all asylum officials who took the time to participate in the interviews, as well as the First President of the CALL, Marc Oswald, the Commissioner General, Sophie Van Balberghe, and Deputy Commissioner General, Annick Goeminne, at the CGRS, and my liaison contacts at both authorities: Annick De Smet, Marie de Hemricourt, Valentine Audate, and Sylvie Decoodt. The self-reflection and willingness to advocate for change that you demonstrated when learning about the results were to be admired.

This equally goes for the other members of the Advisory Board that guided this research from beginning to end. Thank you for providing it with the practice-oriented and interdisciplinary foundation I always envisioned. My special thanks also go out to my (on- and off-line) colleagues at the WiRL

Network, CESSMIR, RLI Feminist Theory Working Group, HRC, and to Marleen Maes Torres Loredo for reading, offering a platform for, or otherwise supporting my work.

Talking about the indispensable pillars supporting this research, I cannot fail to mention NANSEN NGO, where the fieldwork and interviews with applicants took place. Julie, Alice, and Valérie, thank you for grounding me and the research in practice. You generously welcomed an academic alien into the magical world of real-life impact. I sent you flowers after my last fieldwork day and I would have done so every day after if the FWO budget rules had allowed me to.

Next to you, I had the luxury of being surrounded by two more groups of wonderful colleagues. Thank you to the entire MigrLaw and ICRH team, you will forever prove anyone claiming a PhD is lonely wrong. I want to thank Birte, Trui, and Ruben for making office life – at a faculty where I have been hanging around for almost ten years – still feel so vibrant and new. Thank you Roos, Liselot, Maud, Sara, and Eva for reminding me to drink water, stand up, eat, and breathe fresh air during our writing retreats, and to be kind to ourselves when struggling. I would quite literally not have survived this journey without you. Thank you Leni for your rays of sunshine from the very first day of our shared PhD journey and every day thereafter, and Saar, Nele, Lisa, Ida, Frances, Jasmine, and Els for mental health talks, walks, and late night ice teas when most needed. Our research teams, that sometimes felt more like imposter syndrome self-help groups or activist collectives, have set the bar impossibly high for any future workplace I may enter.

Lastly, I owe this achievement to my friends and family. Thank you mom, for everything. My feminist and social justice aspirations are entirely intergenerational. I promise I'll finally make time to read *Le Deuxième Sexe* now that all this is over. You only half realise the inspiration you are and the love you deserve. Thank you, dad, for consistently believing in me from the very first days you taught me how to read and write, I'm sure this was the exact sort of output you had in mind at the time. *Dankjewel oma's en opa's, jullie alle vier, om me te steunen, ik beloof dit hoogdravend academisch gebazel voor jullie te vertalen (naar het Nederlands en vooral naar mensentaal).*

Thank you, Marie and Janne, for unconditional sisterhood, no matter the physical distance between us, and Lieselot, Lies, and Laura for unconditional (quasi) sisterhood, no matter whether we're blood-related, love-related, or both. Thank you, Jolien and Maud, for being my diary, my mirror, and my confirmation that one can never girlboss too close to the sun. Thank you Reinart and Dina for keeping me sane – I swear that oyster picking trip saved this PhD – and for making me feel seen since the very first day we entered the Blandijn's doors eleven years ago.

Thank you Jozefien for single-handedly reversing my metamorphosis into a shrimp by fixing my posture, feeding me countless dinners when all I could feed you was exhaustion, and for understanding who I am. It is impossible to do you justice here, but you feel everything I feel anyway, so there is no need. Last but impossibly least, thank you Brecht for showing me love in the most unexpected of ways and beauty in the smallest of things. As we have learnt, the latter is a vital skill when your entire life plays out in a Word document all of a sudden. Above all, thank you for making seem carrying me – at a time when that could be least expected of you – as easy as breathing.

It is hard to stay soft when researching topics like SGBV and forced migration. From my encounters throughout this PhD, I learnt that empathy is what remains when hope has evaporated. If there is any (r)evolution possible at all in this political climate, let it be one of care.

Lore Roels
Ghent, 28th of August 2025

www.ingramcontent.com/pod-product-compliance
Ingram Content Group UK Ltd.
Pitfield, Milton Keynes, MK11 3LW, UK
UKHW051905290926
8980IPUK00007B/924